A SUPPLY CHAIN LOGISTICS PROGRAM FOR WAREHOUSE MANAGEMENT

Series on Resource Management

A SUPPLY CHAIN LOGISTICS PROGRAM FOR WAREHOUSE MANAGEMENT

David E. Mulcahy ♦ Joachim Sydow

CRC Press
Taylor & Francis Group
Boca Raton London New York

CRC Press is an imprint of the
Taylor & Francis Group, an **informa** business

AN AUERBACH BOOK

Auerbach Publications
Taylor & Francis Group
6000 Broken Sound Parkway NW, Suite 300
Boca Raton, FL 33487-2742

© 2008 by Taylor & Francis Group, LLC
Auerbach is an imprint of Taylor & Francis Group, an Informa business

No claim to original U.S. Government works
Printed in the United States of America on acid-free paper
10 9 8 7 6 5 4 3 2 1

International Standard Book Number-13: 978-0-8493-0575-7 (Hardcover)

Library of Congress Cataloging-in-Publication Data

Mulcahy, David E.
    A supply chain logistics program for warehouse management / David E. Mulcahy and Joachim Sydow.
        p. cm.
    Includes index.
    ISBN-13: 978-0-8493-0575-7 (hardcover : alk. paper)
    ISBN-10: 0-8493-0575-6 (hardcover : alk. paper)
    1. Warehouses--Management. 2. Physical distribution of goods--Management. 3. Business logistics.
4. Materials handling. I. Sydow, Joachim. II. Title.

HF5485.M85 2008
658.7'85--dc22   2007039965

Visit the Taylor & Francis Web site at
http://www.taylorandfrancis.com

and the Auerbach Web site at
http://www.auerbach-publications.com

Contents

Chapter 4

Logistics Segment or Warehouse Operation Receiving Activity and Concepts with a WMS Program

Chapter 5

In-House Transport with a WMS Program

Chapter 6

Storage

Chapter 7

Chapter 8

Order Fulfillment

Chapter 9

Chapter 10

Picked SKU Quantity and Quality Check and Pack Activity 377

Chapter 11

Customer Order Package Manifest, Ship, Sort, and Load Activities 401

Chapter 12

Returns Process, Customer Return, and Vendor Rework Warehouse Activities

Chapter 13

Across-the-Dock, Prepack, Value-Added, Noncustomer Bonded Storage/Pick, Advance Customer Orders, and Inventory Control Activities

Preface

The objective for this book is to provide insights and tips for warehouse operation, distribution, logistics center, plant, IT, or WMS program professionals to make their storage or pick concept with a WMS program a less complex project, make their warehouse operation efficient and cost effective, and make their WMS program more responsive. The chapters focus on operation activities in a warehouse, distribution logistics center, or plant operation with a WMS program. Each chapter focuses on a particular warehouse operation activity to provide the reader with a quick and easy reference. The chapters cover warehouse operation with WMS program equipment applications, concepts, and practices that are considered for implementation, whether the warehouse operation is a large, medium, or small business. The book contains illustrations, forms, and tables that will assist in developing your warehouse operation with a WMS program to:

- reduce WMS identified SKU damage
- enhance WMS identified SKU flow
- increase employee productivity
- improve customer service
- reduce operating costs and improve profits
- maintain on-schedule customer-order deliveries
- assure asset protection

It is necessary to understand that the book's purpose is to help readers design, organize, and operate a warehouse operation with a WMS program project. Because the warehouse operation design and WMS program profession is constantly changing, the book may not include the latest changes in warehouse operation technologies, equipment applications, or WMS program technology.

It is also necessary to recognize that this book cannot cover all the available warehouse operation and WMS program equipment and technologies in the warehouse, distribution, logistics center, or plant operations field. The book does assist in training and obtaining practical experience, for which there is no substitute. To assist in this objective, lined illustrations and sketches are used to depict warehouse operation with a WMS program.

It is important for the reader to use the collection of data, concepts, and forms as a guide. Prior to the purchase and installation of your new warehouse operation with a WMS program, it is essential that you develop and project a correct, accurate, and adequate facility, WMS identified SKU inventory and number, WMS identified SKU transactions data, equipment layout, WMS identified SKU and customer-order flow, and design factors. Because these are the basis for your proposed warehouse operation with a WMS program, it is prudent for you to gather and review warehouse operation and WMS program vendor literature and to visit existing facilities that utilize the warehouse operation (position and vehicle) or equipment and WMS program application. These activities will permit you to become familiar with the operational characteristics of the warehouse operation concept, equipment application, or WMS program under consideration for implementation in your facility. The warehouse operation with a WMS program and performance specifications, physical design, and installation characteristics are subject to redesign, improvement, and modification, and are required to meet vendor and local governmental standards and specifications.

Each chapter in this book deals with key warehouse operation or activity aspects and issues of planning and managing a warehouse operation with a WMS program project. The book chapters are sequenced to mirror a vendor-delivered SKU as it becomes WMS identified and flows through the warehouse operation activities, and as a WMS identified SKU for a customer order and the order flows through the warehouse. Some issues are how your warehouse operation and equipment layout and WMS identified SKU and customer-order flow and location affects employee productivity; when to use the 80/20 rule and where to locate your power WMS identified SKUs; how to route your order pickers and organize their work for the best productivity; what is the best small item, GOH, master-carton/pallet warehouse operation with a WMS program; how to control the batch release; what is required for a good warehouse operation or WMS; how to WMS identify a storage/pick position and to WMS identify a SKU; what is the best in-house transport design for your warehouse operation; how to implement a WMS program in a manual or conventional warehouse operation, an automatic pick machine, or AS/RS crane storage operation; what is a warehouse operation and WMS program conference room pilot study; what is included in a warehouse operation with a WMS program business narrative; what are the important warehouse operation activities with a WMS program project and who are the members of your warehouse operation with a WMS program project; and how to plan, control, and complete a warehouse with a WMS program project.

Most logistics professionals have learned that a preplanned and organized warehouse operation with a WMS program project increases accurate and on-time deliveries, reduces costs, and improves profits. By getting and maintaining a warehouse operation with a WMS program project as outlined in this book, it improves your existing warehouse operation with future WMS program strategies.

The authors would like to express their thanks to all warehouse, distribution, logistics, plant and IS & T, or WMS program professionals with whom they have had an association at various companies, as fellow managers, as a client, as a speaker at seminars, and as publishers.

About the Authors

David E. Mulcahy was a project manager with the QVC Corporation International Group. He received his MBA from the University of Dallas, Texas. With the AMWAY Corporation, Mr. Mulcahy participated as a project manager for the design, building, installation, and start-up of order fulfillment operations in Japan, Korea, Taiwan, New Zealand, Australia, China, England, Italy, and Germany, which included pick-to-light concepts and wire-guided VNA storage vehicles with tall racks. He has been involved with remodeling operations in Spain, The Netherlands, Mexico, Canada, and the European Central Warehouse.

As a QVC project manager, he was involved with the remodel of the QVC Germany and Japan operations, and the WMS program written functional specifications for QVC Japan. For both QVC Germany and Japan, he was a key member in completing a warehouse operation design with Carton and Pallet AS/RS storage concept, GOH trolleyless transport concept, ship tilt tray sorter, pick to light concept, customer returns concept, and extensive conveyor network and WMS program.

Mr. Mulcahy has participated as a speaker at many conferences, has been a contributing author to many magazines, and is the author of Warehouse Management Handbook, Materials Handling Management, and Order Fulfillment and Across the Dock Operations Concepts, Designs and Operations Handbook.

In 1981 he designed a multilayer case selection concept that won a 1981 Materials Handling Institute award at the Material Handling Show.

Joachim Sydow has been Head of Technical Service at Henry Schein Dental Depot GmbH, the leading full-service distributor of dental consumables and equipment in Germany and Europe since 2002. He earned a graduate degree of engineering from University of Dresden and has more than 20 years of increasingly responsible experience in different fields of logistics. As head of logistics for the German pharmaceutical wholesaler ANZAG, he was responsible for time-critical distribution processes that required highly sophisticated warehouse operations and WMS systems. He was involved as senior industrial engineer with the remodel for the QVC Neuss Germany operations and a team member who participated in the WMS program written functional specification development, site selection, warehouse operation design with Carton and Pallet AS/RS storage concepts, GOH trolleyless transport concept, shipping tilt tray sorter with dual induction, pick to light concept, customer concept, and extensive conveyor network. For Henry Schein he is responsible for different projects in Europe, e.g., in Italy he led the project to install a RF-based WMS system. He has participated as a speaker at several conferences and has published several articles in European logistics magazines.

Chapter 1

Supply-Chain Logistics Segment or Warehouse Operation with WMS Program Considerations

Introduction

This introductory chapter has four goals: 1) to define the supply-chain logistics segment storage/pick concept with a Warehouse Management System (WMS) program; 2) to examine company vendor purchase orders, customer order information, and the physical SKU flows; 3) to outline the warehouse storage/pick concept and WMS program objectives; and 4) to identify the signals that indicate a warehouse requires a WMS program.

A warehouse with a WMS program is similar to all industry supply-chain groups, regardless of what is being processed: single small items, master cartons, or pallets. Most or all basic storage or pick/pack activities are performed at the warehouse:

1. Unloading, receiving, checking, and SKU identification;
2. WMS and company SKU identification, with associated SKU quantity and WMS scan; SKU identification and movement to a storage/pick area;
3. Storage activity, including deposit and withdrawal transactions and WMS SKU identification and storage/pick position identification scan transactions and information transfers;
4. SKU transport from a storage area to a packing or shipping dock area;
5. WMS SKU identification or symbology: receiving, storage, picking customer order SKUs; packing, scanning, weighing, preparation of manifests, and shipping preparation;
6. Warehouse customer order loading and shipping;
7. Handling returns, out-of-season SKUs, and customer transfers;
9. Maintenance, sanitation, and loss prevention;
9. Inbound and outbound delivery truck yard control;

1

10. Internal storage and pick locations reorganization (e.g., A, B, and C zones);
11. Handling SKUs with expiration dates and manufacturer lot numbers.

WMS programs can work in all kinds of warehouses. In a manually operated forklift truck storage/pick concept, an employee with a hand-held (or fixed-position) scanner scan or RF tag reader reads each SKU and storage location identification. Scanned transactions are sent to a computer to update SKUs and storage/pick location status. Some WMS programs work on a paper-based system. In that case, a program using paper, scanner, or reader transactions tracks the quantity to an identified position. In a storage/pick concept with a WMS program, each storage/pick position has a WMS identification and a SKU quantity. An identified customer order assures that the identified SKU is transferred on time to the correct location and, in due course, onto a delivery vehicle.

In an AS/RS crane storage warehouse, a WMS program performs the same functions as in a warehouse using a manual hand-held scanner barcode or RF tag-reader, except that the SKU identification is scanned by a fixed position fixed-beam scanner or RF tag reader, and a warehouse computer updates the identified location.

Control

When a company considers installing a WMS program in a warehouse, the design team determines who is responsible for SKU and customer order activities, tasks, and/or communications (e.g., company host, WMS program, or warehouse computer). Each SKU or customer order activity, task, or communication is related to an identified SKU, physical customer order, or specific information flow. The design team evaluates the warehouse control system's ability to modify extant warehouse activities, tasks, or communications, and decides where the responsibility should lie (e.g., the host computer, WMS program, or warehouse computer).

SKU and Customer Orders and Data Flows

In a WMS program using identified SKUs, transaction and information flows have patterns like water flowing through a large funnel. A funnel mouth accepts a large SKU volume, SKU mix, and information quantity. Over a predetermined time period, a wide SKU mix and various identified SKU quantities from vendors are delivered to the storage/pick facility.

Another important concept is customer order information flow for WMS-identified SKUs. These are the orders from WMS-identified customers that occur on a daily basis. The WMS-identified SKU is placed in a company inventory file along with the customer ordered SKUs. The time period for most storage/pick concepts to complete the order and delivery cycle is 24–48 hours. In some industries, such as pharmaceutical wholesale business, the customer order delivery cycle occurs three or four times per day, which means a cycle time of less than 24 hours. With high customer service standards, one can create special cut-off times to guarantee delivery within 24 hours (e.g., the latest customer order arrival time is 0400 p.m.).

As WMS-identified SKUs flow through the funnel, value-added activities are performed to ensure that orders are processed quickly and efficiently, and so maintains profitability. However, as the design team adds customer order numbers and order lines, increases customer order SKU quantity, and value-added activities handled by a storage/pick concept increases, the available time to perform value-added activities diminishes—this is small mouth of the funnel.

First Steps

When your company considers a WMS program for a warehouse, two key components are warehouse operation and WMS program. The first question is: What component warehouse or WMS program is most important? The answer is based on project type, cost, time, and other factors. There are two project types: remodel an existing warehouse or construct a new warehouse.

If the project is remodeling an existing warehouse, then the warehouse is an established operation in an existing building with activity stations, equipment layout, identified SKU and customer order travel paths, and employee activity procedures and practices. The warehouse has identified SKU storage/pick positions. Because the warehouse equipment is already in place, identified SKU and customer order travel paths and operational practices and procedures are unlikely to change, and there are no drawings required for governmental code approval, the design team will focus on 1) understanding the existing warehouse; 2) understanding the WMS program features; 3) understanding warehouse operations; and 4) determining what WMS program modifications or changes for implementation in your existing warehouse are needed. In some companies, designing a WMS program for an existing warehouse can be demanding and can create changes in an existing operation, such as when a WMS program needs to support SKUs with lot numbers. In that case, there will be a need to distinguish different SKUs lot numbers in a storage location with dividers to assure accurate and efficient picking strategies.

With the construction of a new warehouse, there is no existing building/warehouse equipment to be considered. The design team will have drawings that show how the facility will look, along with a description of operations to explain how vendor delivered WMS-identified SKUs and customer orders will flow through the facility, or how the warehouse will look and operate when using a WMS program.

As a new building and warehouse operation drawings are being finalized, written specifications and description of operations are drawn and developed and written (prior to RFQ transmittal to vendors for price and government for approval), WMS program features, description of operations are combined with a building and warehouse design parameters. Warehouse concept features and description of operations design parameters have an impact on a warehouse degree of mechanization or automation, activity locations, bar code/RF label use and location, control and size, scanner/reader location and type and WMS-identified SKU or customer order handling sequence, and how a WMS supported WMS-identified SKU or customer order transaction is reported to a WMS program.

Tie the Warehouse Operation and WMS Program Knot

Integrating a successful WMS program into a warehouse is like tying a knot. Your project design team leader and team members must understand the objective (the knot), how a knot will look, and how to move two strands to create the knot. When installing the WMS program in a warehouse project, the team members who tie the warehouse and WMS program knot are the warehouse/WMS integrator, warehouse equipment vendors, and WMS program team members. One strand is your warehouse team and host computer team; the other strand is the WMS program team. A completed knot is a company host computer and a warehouse with a WMS program that satisfies your company operational, cost per unit, and customer service standard objectives.

Pebble in a Pond

To design a warehouse with a WMS program, a warehouse concept with a WMS program and building design are based on specific design parameters:

1. Peak day vendor SKU delivery that includes pallets or master cartons;
2. Customer order number, lines per customer order, and associated SKUs per peak day;
3. Customer order cube and order/delivery cycle time, weight, and SKU mix;
4. Storage/pick position bar code or RF tag label location and required line of sight or a radio frequency tag within a transmission range; and
5. WMS program to completely understand WMS supported transaction locations and WMS-identified SKU and customer order flows.

If a change is made to one or several design parameters, a change has potential to affect each storage/pick WMS supported activity or WMS program. The activities are

1. Customer order process;
2. Vendor delivery truck control, receiving, and QA;
3. Transport;
4. Storage put-away and withdrawal;
5. Pick line or position setup and replenishment;
6. Customer order pick;
7. Batched customer order sort;
8. Customer order pack;
9. Customer order manifest, sort, and load;
10. Prepack and other value added activities;
11. Across-the dock, customer order returns and vendor re-work activities; and
12. Host computer, warehouse and WMS program integration.

Signals that a Warehouse Needs a WMS Program

As a warehouse business grows, business growth results from an increase in existing SKU inventory to meet seasonal demands, from new customers or from new SKUs. Business growth factors and variance from an actual SKU inventory compared to budgeted inventory are factors that create signals that a company has a requirement for a WMS program. Other signals are

1. Actual inventory balance or physical inventory balances have a substantial difference to the book inventory;
2. Demand for frequent, accurate, and quick SKU inventory cycle counts and inventory file updates;
3. Short customer orders due to "no stocks" or "stock outs;"
4. Customer back orders due to lost inventory;
5. Canceled customer orders or customer complaints;
6. Customer order numbers increase;

7. Small size customer orders increase;
8. SKU numbers or pick positions increase;
9. Vendor SKU deliveries and vendor number increase;
10. Inventory quantity and storage positions increase;
11. Assure proper SKU rotation;
12. Manufacturer lot identification accuracy;
13. Accurate and on-line receiving, storage, pick, replenishment, and manifest transactions;
14. Facility size, employee number, multiple shift operation, and mechanized or automated material handling equipment;
15. Decrease or to maintain your customer order/delivery cycle time with accurate orders that are delivered on time to a correct address; and
16. In summary, if your existing manual warehouse is overstretched.

Warehouse Storage/Pick Concept with a WMS Program Resources

To achieve a storage/pick concept with WMS program strategy objectives, your design team must efficiently use or allocate a warehouse and WMS program scarce resources. The resources are facility layout, warehouse storage/pick concept suppliers, employees or labor, site location, building that is owned or leased by the company, management team, company host, WMS program, and warehouse computer suppliers, SKU vendors, customers, consultants, and industry groups or associations.

Warehouse with a WMS Program Operational Objectives

A warehouse with a WMS program operational objective is to improve profits and customer service. To achieve the objective, a warehouse with a WMS program

1. Maximizes a facility, customer order ship carton, transport concept or vendor or customer delivery vehicle space utilization;
2. Maximizes a storage/pick concept utilization;
3. Maximizes employee utilization;
4. Reduces SKU handlings and assures an identified SKU is delivered to the correct location;
5. Assures WMS scan transaction information transfer, thus maintaining SKU accessibility and inventory tracking capability;
6. Assures a designed SKU rotation;
7. Minimizes company logistics operational expenses;
8. Protects a company assets; and
9. Assures satisfied customers.

Overview

The purpose of this book is to show the reader, when considering the implementation of a WMS program in a warehouse, the applications of a WMS program, as well as procedures, practices, tips, and insights. This will provide the design team with an opportunity to maximize a company profits 1) by reducing a warehouse storage/pick concept with a WMS program design, development, and installation time period and costs; 2) by reducing logistics operating costs; and 3) maximizing customer service with on-schedule and accurate deliveries.

Chapter 2

Understanding the Supply Chain Logistics Segment

Introduction

Warehouse components are arranged to provide cost-effective and efficient vendor SKU and customer-order flows. These components are 1) the warehouse facility; 2) the material handling equipment layout; 3) warehouse internal operations or activities (with management staff and employees); 4) vendor SKU and customer-order flows for small items, master cartons, or pallets; 5) company informational technology (IT), host, WMS, and warehouse computer systems, (for communications between company departments as well as between the company and vendors and customers); and (6) inventory control, basic warehouse management program, or WMS.

The design team's objective is to design, develop, and implement a WMS program in a cost-effective and efficient new (or remodeled) warehouse. To achieve this objective, the design team must understand your company's existing warehouse components (see above) and their interaction with a WMS program. The design team will 1) develop cost justification, 2) design a warehouse with a WMS program, 3) ensure that implementation occurs on time and within the established budget, and 4) review and audit the warehouse after the WMS program is implemented.

After a WMS program is implemented, the result will be a sphere with numerous connection lines and activity points. Between each WMS program transaction point and activity point are vendor WMS-identified SKU and customer-order flows (i.e., travel path and communication lines). In the interaction between a WMS program and a warehouse, the warehouse handles WMS-identified SKUs or customer orders between two WMS-identified positions/drop-points and the warehouse computer (or the employee that controls the SKU- or customer-order–handling equipment); and the WMS program tracks WMS-identified SKUs or customer orders through the inventory control or WMS-identified positions and has transactions sent to a WMS computer that handles data or information.

Warehouse Design Parameters and Operational Aspects

To design a new warehouse (or remodel an existing warehouse), the design team collects, evaluates, reviews, projects, and approves your present and proposed vendor-SKU and customer-order physical transaction volumes, SKU numbers and inventory characteristics, and other operational parameters for each warehouse activity (e.g., new or additional warehouse operations, handling manufacturer lot numbers, serial numbers, expiration dates, hazardous materials, and customer delivery companies or freight forwarders). Warehouse operational design parameters establish transactions for the completion of the vendor-SKU storage and physical-customer order and delivery cycle. These design parameters are

1. The average number of SKU and customer orders per day; the most frequent vendor SKU and customer orders per day; and the peak vendor SKU and customer orders per day;
2. The average SKU number per vendor delivery and customer order; the most frequent SKU number per vendor delivery and customer order; and the peak SKU number per vendor delivery and customer order;
3. The best equipment or technologies for a warehouse, based on vendor SKU and customer order volume;
4. The most frequent SKU number per vendor and delivery vehicle; the average SKU number per vendor and delivery vehicle; and the peak SKU number per vendor and delivery vehicle;
5. SKU specific inventory classification;
6. The present and proposed in-house SKU- and customer-order transport conveyor (or vehicle) travel speeds;
7. The present and proposed vendor SKU and customer-order shipping plan;
8. The down-load time for the IT customer-order host computer, and the time it takes to communicate with warehouse operations (or computer);
9. Customer order priority;
10. Customer service;
11. Profile of the warehouse storage and pick areas;
12. Proposed warehouse design, including vehicle aisle, rack layout, and facility for all required activities, simulations, and computer requirements;
13. Proposed warehouse receiving, in-house transport, storage, order fulfillment, manifest and shipping, and other operational concepts, with SKU and customer-order flow paths; plans should include block, plan view, and detailed view drawings showing all required operational activities.

The data collection and analysis ensures that the proposed warehouse is designed to handle vendor-SKU, customer-order, and WMS-program transactions. Moreover, the features ensure a cost-effective and effective warehouse.

Peak, Average, and Most Frequent SKU or Customer-Order Volumes

Monthly SKU or customer-order volumes are used to project warehouse volume. SKU and customer-order volumes are translated into warehouse- and WMS-program–supported transactions. Note that vendor SKU transactions are less common than customer-order transactions, but customer orders are more time sensitive. In a small-item warehouse, small items are received as loose SKUs (e.g., single pieces or less than master cartons) in master cartons (or master cartons on a pallet) to have the opportunity to have valued added activities and are shipped as loose single items. In a carton warehouse, a master carton (or a pallet of master cartons) is sent to customers as a single master carton or master cartons on a pallet (or as a replenishment of loose SKUs or single pieces on a pallet to a pick position). Finally, in a pallet warehouse, an SKU is received (and sent to customers) as a single pallet or is sent as a replenishment pallet to a master-carton or single-piece pick area.

Peak, average, and most frequent monthly SKU or customer-order volumes are used to project a warehouse's future transactions. Future SKU or customer-order volumes and transactions are based on present SKU or customer-order volumes handled during a specific time period (e.g., day, week, month, year) and anticipated growth. Future SKU or customer-order volumes are key factors when projecting labor and material handling equipment necessary for order processing, and to justify labor quantity, costs, savings, and other operational expenses associated with a WMS-program capital expenditure request.

Vendor-Delivered–SKU and Customer-Order Characteristics

After the design team decides upon an annual SKU- or customer-order volume, the team applies SKU or customer-order characteristics to each volume.
The company's receiving department will have the following vendor-delivered–SKU characteristics:

1. Purchase order number, per purchase order lines, SKUs, master carton SKUs, or pallet SKUs;
2. Receiving documents or tally sheet numbers;
3. SKU master carton or pallet, label numbers;
4. Special receiving dock time slots for vendor delivery.

The customer-order process (or control department) will have the following customer-order characteristics:

1. Customer-order numbers;
2. Customer-order type numbers for single line/single pieces, single line/multiple pieces, multiple lines/multiple pieces, SKU combination, express shipments, orders from foreign countries, and cash on delivery (COD) orders;
3. SKU or printed lines per customer order;
4. Pieces per line and customer order;
5. Shipping package type and size.

Projecting Vendor–SKU and Customer-Order Warehouse Transactions

In a warehouse, an employee or a computer-controlled machine completes each transaction. Each activity has standard or hybrid SKU or warehouse physical activity for a WMS-program–identified SKU (or customer order) and to determine each warehouse activity as a WMS-program scan or non-WMS transaction. A WMS-program transaction is sent to a WMS computer that accounts for a WMS-program–identified SKU or customer order. When the project team plans the warehouse with WMS-program activity transactions, each activity is included in a warehouse and WMS-program transaction projection.

SKU and Customer-Order Characteristics

Vendor delivered SKU activity is not as time critical as a customer-order completion activity, which is completed within 24 hours of credit approval. After the design team selects a design-year SKU and order volume, the team applies SKU and customer-order characteristics to each volume. The company's receiving department will have the following vendor delivered SKU characteristics:

1. Purchase order number, per purchase order lines, SKUs, small items, master cartons, or pallets;
2. Receiving documents and tally sheets per purchase order;
3. Master cartons/containers or pallet labels per purchase order.

Vendor-Delivered–SKU Inventory Projection Characteristics

Each SKU group has unique characteristics that determine the storage inventory SKU quantity. A vendor master carton or container inventory quantity with few SKUs is handled as an individual item. Each master carton is given an inventory identification and placed in an identified storage position. Each master carton quantity is then entered into the inventory files. If vendor master cartons or containers are placed on pallets, a storage identification is placed on the pallet, the pallet is placed in an identified storage position, and a pallet SKU quantity is entered into the inventory files.

With a small-item operation, a design-year piece/quantity inventory projection is divided by the piece number into vendor master cartons or containers. SKU inventory projection quantity options for vendor master cartons or containers use an average existing SKU quantity for each master carton or container or to obtain an existing SKU quantity range for each master carton and apply each SKU quantity range percent to the inventory projection.

With a master carton or container warehouse inventory number, a design-year SKU quantity projection is divided by the SKUs for each master carton or container and a master carton container number for each pallet.

Warehouse Operation Storage Position Utilization

A warehouse storage position utilization factor is the percentage of occupied pallets. During peak activity periods, the pallet-storage position factor allows for open pallets to handle vendor delivered and received SKUs.

WMS-Program–Identified Storage-Pallet Locations

To create a WMS-program–identified storage position for a full, high pallet and half, high pallet number, the design team counts the full high and half high pallets and determines the percentage for each pallet type. Full high pallet and half high pallet percentages are applied to the projected pallet inventory. The calculations determine the full high pallet and half high pallet-storage position numbers.

Master Cartons

To obtain a master carton quantity for each pallet, the design team completes a master carton count for each pallet in the warehouse and develops a percentage. Using this percentage, the projected inventory piece quantity is created for each pallet.

Pieces

To obtain a piece quantity for each master carton, your design team completes a SKU piece count for each master carton in a warehouse storage area and develops a percent range. Based on a SKU percent range for each inventory control identified master carton, a projected inventory SKU is projected based on actual SKUs for each master carton percentage.

SKU Life Cycle

The SKU life cycle traces sales over a specific time period. The time period encompasses the first day a SKU is available for sale, is promoted to customers, and majority of sales occur. The life cycle show the SKU's characteristics for each day of the time period.

In a warehouse there are limited storage/pick position numbers. One answer is to design the storage area or pick line with an "ABC approach" with two storage/pick zones. One zone is designated for fast moving SKUs, and one zone is designated for medium/slow moving SKUs. New (or promoted) SKUs are allocated to the "A" zone or the fast-moving zone. Old (or nonpromoted) inventory SKUs are allocated to the "B" and "C" zones or medium/slow-moving zone.

The promotion or life cycle described above is usually linked to TV marketing, catalog, or retail warehouse industries. In other industries, such as dental or pharmaceutical, SKUs are promoted and have a SKU life of two to three months.

To achieve high productivity in the storage area or pick line, storage area and pick line SKUs are allocated to the storage/pick positions. The allocation is based on sales volume and storage and pick area employee productivity rates.

The storage and pick zone numbers, SKU life cycle, and total inventory SKU numbers assist SKU storage area and pick line allocation. To achieve proper SKU hit concentration and density, new and promoted SKUs that been allocated to the "A" storage/pick zone and are plotted on a historical life cycle day number. When the life cycle chart shows a decline for a day number, the SKU is reallocated to the "B" or "C" zone.

Inventory-Control–Identified SKU Storage and Pick Positions

After a warehouse receives a vendor-delivered SKU and checks the vendor quantity against a company purchase order quantity, the SKU is transferred to a storage position and the quantity and position is entered into inventory. Each warehouse storage and pick position has a discreet identification, which is used when customer orders are sent to the warehouse by the host computer.

Projecting Inventory-Control–Identified Storage Position

To project a storage position, the design team must know the storage position number, type, and SKU number for each position. To project inventory volume and the associated storage position number housed in an operation, the projection methods are similar for small items, master cartons, or pallets.

Master Carton and Pallet-Storage Volume

To project the SKU inventory, pallet inventory volume is the SKU volume housed in a storage area, static volume stored in a floor stack, conventional forklift truck, or automatic/computer storage and retrieval system (AS/RS) crane rack, flow rack, hand stack, or standard shelf. A master carton or pallet-storage inventory number is divided into master carton or pallet height, pallet size, and special storage conditions. Master carton or pallet inventory volumes provides fiscal year end master carton or pallet volume; the average volume for a specific number of months; and the average master carton or pallet volume for a predetermined period with the emphasis on a predetermined month period. In most companies, the period is the last three months of the fiscal year.

Master Carton and Pallet Pick-Position Projections

A master carton or pallet warehouse position is the master carton's or pallet's SKU in a pick position. In a dense storage warehouse, the master carton or pallet position adjacent to the main aisle is the pick position. Based on your existing pick position number, your design team applies a SKU growth number or percent to obtain a SKU number in a design year or SKU growth number or percent and completes calculations to determine a design-year SKU number.

SKU Types: Pallet, Master Carton, and Small Items

Vendor-delivered SKU and customer-order pieces determine equipment type and layout. A warehouse can be set up to handle one SKU type or all SKU types.

Master Carton Warehouse

In a master carton warehouse, a vendor carton or vendor master carton has a SKU inventory and storage position identification, and is handled as individual master cartons or master cartons on a pallet. If a master carton does not have side wall strength, or product is not self-supporting or is not square, master cartons are stored in a container, a tier rack, or a stacking frame (to make stackable and uniform unit loads), or as individual master cartons that optimize the cubic (air) storage space. A container or stacking frame has fork openings and the tier rack is placed on a standard pallet.

A master carton warehouse, to have maximum inventory flexibility and accountability, will determine at the receiving dock how master cartons are handled. If a SKU has a low master carton quantity, the cartons are handled as individual SKUs. If a SKU has a high master carton quantity, the cartons are handled on a four-wheel carton, slip sheet, stacking frame, tier rack, or pallet. This will permit an employee-controlled or AS/RS crane to move the largest number of cartons each trip, thus providing the fewest handlings from receiving, through the storage/pick area, to the shipping dock, and onto the delivery truck.

It is important for the design team to know master carton or container dimensions, including length, width, height, and weight, as well as the smallest, the average, and the maximum size master carton. The size range that is developed can be used to determine storage/pick position, number of cartons for each pallet, and the conveyor travel path window.

Small-Item Warehouse

A small-item warehouse handles small items as single pieces in vendor master cartons, containers, or master cartons/containers on a pallet. Master carton or container dimensions determine the number of items stored on each pallet.

Pallet Warehouse

A pallet warehouse receives, stores, and ships SKUs on pallets. The vendor delivery tally sheet will show a suggested ti and hi or master carton quantity for each pallet. If a master carton ti is within a pallet (bottom support device) perimeter, the master carton hangs over the edge of the pallet (length or width). If a master carton ti overhangs a pallet, the master carton dimensions overhang becomes the storage pallet dimensions. The pallet's dimensions determine floor stack pallet position number in a storage area or pallet number wide in a rack bay between two rack upright posts. Rack dimensions along with clearances determine rack row and rack bay number that will fit between two building columns.

Pallet height determines the pallet number in the floor stack in the rack bay in the vertical stack. A pallet height is the distance between the bottom deck board and the highest master carton top. The vendor delivery tally will show a suggested ti and hi or master cartons for each pallet that will not exceed the pallet-storage position height.

Pallet weight is the entire pallet, securing material, and total master carton weight. The pallet weight determines pallet number for each floor stack, pallet or load beam level number for each rack bay and design, rack posts base plate thickness, foot print, design, and forklift truck wheel size. The forklift truck or AS/RS crane weight determines the floor thickness and rebar characteristics. The vendor delivery tally will show a suggested ti and hi or master cartons for each pallet that will not exceed the storage/pick position weight capacity.

Pallet Bottom Support Device

A pallet supports a wide SKU mix and is easily handled by forklift, AS/RS crane, or pallet trucks. The pallet's length, width, and fork entry opening (unit load bottom support device) determine what kind of rack may be used. In a facility that uses a forklift, the pallets hang over the load beams or extend into an aisle or flue space by two to three inches. The forklift's stack requirement determines the width of the aisle.

The fork entry opening is between the pallet's top deck board bottom and bottom deck board top. The entry opening determines a forklift truck or AS/RS crane set of fork/platen length.

Pallet-storage operations use a standard pallet, including captive pallets, throw-away pallets, or exchange pallets; a take-it or leave-it pallet; and a specially engineered or designed pallet.

Warehouse Operation Objective

A warehouse's purpose is to house SKU inventory; ensure that the host computer or IT department communicates between WMS-identified SKU scan transaction locations; ensure staff counts for delivered SKU quantity; ensure quantity and quality are correct; ensure the SKU is available in a storage or pick position; and ensure the customer order is delivered in the correct quantity and on time to the correct address at the budgeted cost for each unit.

To satisfy inventory availability and accuracy objective, a company with manual inventory control should consider implementing a WMS program in their warehouse, implement a WMS program in a remodeled warehouse, upgrade their existing WMS program, or design the new warehouse with a WMS program.

If the company does not have a WMS program, or is considering a WMS program for an existing operation, what are the signals that a warehouse requires a WMS program? A warehouse with a WMS program is designed to move and track inventory or service the customer at the lowest possible operational costs. A warehouse options are (1) store and hold or conventional or (2) across-the-dock warehouse operation. Each warehouse type has different SKU and customer order and information flows that are the bases for a future warehouse with a WMS program.

Conventional Warehouse: Store and Hold

A store-and-hold inventory or conventional warehouse has a warehouse receive SKUs or SKU quantity. Each SKU has a company SKU identification, is placed into an assigned SKU inventory file, and is physically placed into a warehouse facility identified storage position. For each customer order, a SKU quantity is withdrawn from a warehouse storage position and replenished to a pick position. After completing a customer order, the SKU inventory in the files is decreased by a moved SKU quantity, identified warehouse position status is updated in inventory files, and the picked SKU is sent to a delivery truck or to a customer address. The conventional warehouse is designed to ensure that SKUs meet the company's quality standards, that the correct identified SKU is transferred from the storage position to the correct pick position, in sufficient quantity, at the assigned time. Next, the warehouse operation ensures that the SKU is withdrawn from the pick position in the correct quantity, in correct condition, on schedule, with a packing list in a protected and labeled shipping container, properly manifested and delivered to a delivery location within the delivery cycle time. Finally, the manifest is scanned and entered into a company host computer files as a completed customer order.

Across-the-Dock Operation

In an across-the-dock warehouse SKU (or customer-order flow operation), the warehouse unloads and counts all SKUs from the vendor delivery vehicle. SKUs are customer-order single SKUs mixed in a master carton, GOH, master carton, pallet, or master carton mix on a pallet. SKUs are prelabeled or labeled on a receiving dock, are sorted by quantity and address, and immediately are either placed in an outbound staging area or loaded directly onto a customer delivery vehicle. With some small-item SKUs an across-the-dock operation completes the sorting or places a price ticket onto each SKU or repacks the SKUs prior to the sorting. SKUs are not entered into a warehouse inventory. An across-the-dock operation is designed to ensure that each SKU meets the company standards, is properly packaged and labeled with a discreet (or sort) identification, is unloaded at a proper time, is sorted or separated by identification, and that the total piece count matches the vendor delivery document and company purchase order. The delivery truck ensures that the order arrives at the delivery location at a specific time that satisfies customer demand at the lowest operating cost. After across-the-dock sorting, there may be a residual SKU quantity, which is identified and placed into a storage position. The SKU quantity and storage position have the same operational procedures as a conventional warehouse.

Information Flows

Warehouse information flow exists in three areas: externally, between the SKU vendor and the company, and between the customer and the company; and internally, between company departments.

The information flow from a company to a SKU vendor occurs via the purchase order issued to the vendor. After receipt of the purchase order, the vendor communicates with the receiving department and establishes a delivery time.

The information flow within a company begins when the purchase order information is sent from the merchandise department to a receiving department. The receiving department notifies a quality control (QA) department that a sample is ready for inspection. The receiving department confirms with the merchandising and finance departments that the purchase order is accurate and complete and that the vendor has completed the contract. The QA department sends information to the receiving and merchandising departments regarding SKU status (e.g., "OK," "rejected"). The storage department sends a SKU deposit to the inventory control department to reserve a storage position. The host computer sends customer orders to a warehouse computer; the warehouse computer sends pick instructions to the pick area printer or pick machine. The storage department sends replenishment to a pick position or transfer from a storage position to a pick position to inventory control department. The pick area sends completed pick transactions and inventory update to a WMS computer. The warehouse computer sends the packing slip to the check and pack station to use as an instruction. The ship scanner/reader reads and sends the identification at the manifest station to the warehouse computer and the delivery company. If necessary, the returns department sends approval to host computer to issue customer credit. The returns station sends information returned SKUs to inventory control. Return SKUs are deposited into a position and sent to a WMS computer for inventory update. Information flows between a customer and company occur when a quantity is sent to the host computer; when the company sends a delivery address and identification to a delivery company; and when, following the completion of an order, the delivery company notifies the company of a nondeliverable package or a customer notice of a customer order over, short, or damaged.

Warehouse Activities

A storage/order fulfillment operation has the following activities:

1. Prepick activities, including a) vendor SKU or delivery truckyard control; b) vendor delivery SKU unloading and palletizing; c) receiving and SKU quality and quantity checking; d) assuring a SKU discreet identification and assigned storage location for each SKU; e) to package some small items and flat wear, SKUs as individual SKUs and to label each SKU with a price ticket; f) internal transport activity; g) deposit and withdrawal in an inventory program of identified storage or pick positions and updating inventory files; and h) inventory control, such as a SKU inventory cycle counts;

2. Customer-order pick activities, including a) printing pick documents and labels, or, for paperless picking, the host or warehouse computer downloads the information to a warehouse computer that controls a pick to light RF or automatic pick machine; b) carton make-up, including the identification label and insertion of the packing list into the container/carton; c) releasing a SKU from an automatic pick position (by manual pick or computer); d) SKU replenishment; and e) trash removal;

3. Post-customer-order pick activities, including a) picked SKU sort to customer-order location; b) sorting SKU quality or quantity check; c) placing the packing slip into a shipping carton, filling container/carton voids, and with a WMS identified customer order associated with a permanent identified pick tote, tote zero scan is sent WMS computer to disconnect a customer order WMS identification to a permanent tote identification; d) sealing containers; e) scanning the shipping label and manifest, and updating the WMS and host computer SKU inventory and customer order files; f) loading and shipping; g) handling customer order returns, credits, and notifying the host computer of a returned SKU disposition, placing a returned SKU into a storage/pick location, and updating the WMS program inventory files; h) handling retail store returned out-of-season SKUs and SKU transfers to another retail store; and i) maintenance, sanitation, and loss-prevention activities.

An across-the-dock operation is a more streamlined warehouse. The activities are vendor delivery vehicle yard control; SKU quality control, count, identification labelling and sorting; and packing and loading onto a customer delivery truck.

Within an across-the-dock warehouse, other activities are 1) vendor SKU preparation; 2) downloading and printing labels; 3) unloading, receiving, and labelling SKUs; 4) quality control, counting, sorting, or separating by identification; 5) sorting, packing, and creating manifests; 6) sorting SKUs held in a shipping dock staging area or direct loading onto delivery trucks; 7) handling residual SKUs and customer order returns, retail store returned out-of-season SKUs, and SKU transfers to another retail store; 8) customer delivery; and 9) maintenance, sanitation, and loss prevention.

Inventory Control

A storage/hold warehouse inventory control activity ensures that SKUs are transferred from a receiving area to a storage area and from a storage position to a pick position in the correct quantity. Other inventory control objectives are 1) proper SKU inventory rotation; 2) accurate inventory counts; 3) assuring minimal "stock outs" or "out-of-stocks." ("Stock out" is when the pick position is depleted but an inventory file indicates an on-hand SKU inventory quantity. "Out of stock" is when the pick position is depleted and the inventory file has no on-hand inventory quantity.); 4) tracking SKU flow through the supply chain or each warehouse; and 5) verifying that each storage/pick transaction is completed and inventory files are updated.

SKU Storage and Pick-Position Locator

A warehouse SKU storage and pick locator is designed to facilitate and identify a storage or pick position. During a SKU storage area deposit transaction, a locator may be employee-directed: a forklift truck driver determines the storage or pick position. This approach features minimal cost, random SKU placement to a position, and a paper-based or RF transaction record. It does not optimize storage/pick transaction employee productivity and it is difficult to track SKUs. A second approach uses the warehouse computer to suggest a storage/pick position based on a storage philosophy. A forklift or an AS/RS crane completes the transaction.

SKU Location in a Storage Area

The concept of SKU warehouse storage location focuses on SKUs' physical position in a storage aisle. The location is determined by a storage position philosophy. This has guidelines based on whether the storage activity used a manual forklift truck or an AS/RS crane. An inventory program either permits an employee to determine the product transaction location or controls the storage strategy by suggesting or directing the transaction location.

Storage position philosophy includes:

1. SKUs' physical width, height, length, and weight. In a storage operation, heavy or short SKUs are located at floor level, tall and light SKUs are located in high positions.
2. SKU velocity, sales, or physical movement for a complete fiscal year. In a storage aisle, fast-moving SKUs are located at the aisle start, medium-moving SKUs are located in the middle of the aisle, and slow-moving SKUs are located at the end.
3. SKU value. High-value SKUs are placed in positions with limited or controlled access.
4. SKUs that have specific environmental storage conditions. For example, temperature-sensitive SKUs are located at a low position or in a separate storage area.
5. Hazardous classification. SKUs with such a classification are housed in a position that restricts an SKU flight or has a barrier or pit connected to a containment chamber that restricts flammable liquid run-off.

Inventory Locator: Philosophy and Principles

An inventory locator philosophy influences the arrangement of warehouse equipment and storage/pick activity locations (i.e., receiving, storage, pick and ship areas). The most important area is the SKU storage/pick area. In a storage/hold operation, storage/pick activities have a large floor area and have the greatest number of employees. Storage layout philosophies and principles are

1. SKU popularity or Pareto's Law (i.e., the "80/20 Rule");
2. ABC theory;
3. Unloading and loading ratio;
4. ABC theory with a family group;
5. Power (or fast moving) SKUs in a single pick area;
6. Family group, including SKU value, environmental issues, and hazardous SKUs;
7. SKU rotation;
8. Rack row and aisle direction;
9. Aisle length, width, and adequacy;

11. Building height;
12. Customer-order picked SKU order fulfillment and sort.

SKU and Customer-Order Flow through a Facility and Value-Added Activities

Vendor-delivered SKU or customer-order flow has an impact on the warehouse's process. A building's shape, size, number of floors, and the value-added activities also affect the pick line or area location, as well as the vendor-delivered SKU or customer-order flow pattern through a facility. The design team determines the most cost-effective and efficient flow pattern and value-added activities sequence. Vendor-delivered SKU or customer-order flow patterns are 1) for a single floor facility, a horizontal vendor-delivered SKU or customer-order flow pattern that are either (a) a straight (i.e., "one-way") vendor-delivered SKU flow or customer-order pattern or (b) a two-way pattern (i.e., "U" or "W"); (2) a vertical (i.e., up and down) flow pattern, which is used in a multi-floor facility.

Single and Multiple Floors

In metropolitan areas, available sites commercial prices are high but allow buildings to have a 30 to 40-foot clear ceiling above ground level. Building options are, first, a low-bay or ground-floor building. A low-bay or single-floor facility has value-added activities and employee support activities on the ground level floor. This design has the highest square footage for each pick position, low space utilization, and the longest travel distance and time locations. The alternative is a high-bay or multi-floor warehouse. This is good for small-item order fulfillment. Vertical transport equipment would be designed to locate slow moving, light weight/small cube SKUs. Value-added activities, pack areas, administrative support offices, storage area and high volume, heavy weight/high cube SKUs would be placed on an elevated floor. Receiving and shipping dock areas, fast moving and heavy weight/large cube SKUs, and pick and pack areas would be placed on the ground floor. (As an alternative, heavy/high cube SKUs could be located on the ground floor and pack stations placed on an elevated floor with direct flow to the manifest/shipping area.)

In a high-bay, multi-floor facility, the storage area, high-volume, and heavy/high cube SKUs are located on the ground floor. The office, administrative and employee support, low volume, light/small cube SKUs, and value-added activities are located on elevated floors. To assure maximum flexibility, elevated floors are designed to support dynamic and static forklift truck loads, one to three high-pallet storage racks, and automatic or other pick lines. The pack area options are either the ground floor or an elevated floor.

SKU STORAGE

SKU storage concept is a major factor in determining the building's area. A master carton, or pallet warehouse, can either use single master carton, or pallet storage, or dense storage. The preferred storage is determined by SKU number, storage units for each SKU, inventory requirements, and SKU rotation.

Single Deep Storage

Single deep storage has shelves or racks that are serviced by an employee, an employee-controlled forklift truck, or an AS/RS crane. If master cartons are a SKU, an employee, an employee-controlled high-rise order picker (HROS) vehicle, or AS/RS crane completes the transactions. If using an employee for storage transactions, master cartons are stacked one, two, or more high in a storage position. If a building has a 40- to 60-foot clear ceiling, a VNA lift truck is used; with a 60- to 80-foot ceiling, an AS/RS crane is used. Single deep storage provides maximum access to all SKUs, low storage density (i.e., fewer SKUs per square foot), FIFO, or first-in-first-out, SKU rotation, and requires a large facility.

Dense Storage

Dense storage means that there are two or more SKUs deep in each storage position and the storage position requires one or two aisles to complete storage transactions. In a low-bay building, dense storage layouts use floor stacks or stacking frames/containers/stack racks, two-deep racks, drive-in racks, drive-thru racks, mobile shelves or racks, gravity flow racks, or sort links. In an AS/RS storage operation, dense storage options are gravity or air-flow racks, car-in racks, and two-deep racks.

When compared to a single deep storage concept, dense storage layouts have few aisles, greater product per square foot, and wider SKU numbers; most layouts do not provide a FIFO. SKU rotation requires a smaller facility, and a WMS program with enhancements or dynamic features to track an SKU.

Aisle and Position Identification

In a warehouse, each master carton or pallet aisle has identified master-carton or pallet-storage positions that use alphabetical characters, numeric digits, or an alphabetical character and numeric digit mix with a bar-code/RF tag. In a warehouse with a WMS program that has floor stack, drive-in, drive-thru, pallet flow rack, or car-in rack storage layout, the format sequence is warehouse, warehouse aisle, bay within an aisle, and level within a bay. Dense storage layouts that use pallet storage have the same SKU for each storage lane. With a WA, NA, high-rise order picker (HROS), or VNA, a forklift truck or AS/RS, or a crane operation with a master-carton or pallet rack system, the identification information sequence is

1. The first component is an alphabetical character that identifies the warehouse.
2. The storage aisle is identified by an alphabetical character or digit. In a dynamic storage operation, there will be sufficient combinations of characters to identify all storage operations with 26 alphabetical characters and double character usage.
3. The rack bay is identified with numeric digits that progress arithmetically from the aisle entrance to the end of the aisle. Numbers are used in bay identification to the match pallet or rack bay numbers in a nominal building length.
4. The load beam or rack level within a rack bay is identified with an alphabetical character. In a WA, NA, HROS, VNA, AS/RS or tall rack operation, the 26 alphabetical characters will be sufficient to identify all pallet levels in a rack structure. Creating an identification of two

numbers separated by an alphabetical character will make it less likely that a forklift truck driver will become confused than with three consecutive numeric or digit components.

5. The master-carton or pallet position in a rack bay is a significant component in a forklift truck driver instruction format. At a SKU position in a bay, the forklift truck driver (or AS/RS crane) completes directed SKU tran ctions. The driver reads the SKU position that is assigned to a master carton or pallet position. The SKU position is identified with numbers and is easy to read on a digital display or paper document.

In a pallet-storage warehouse, to ensure accurate and on-time transactions, signs identify each aisle and pallet-storage position. Storage aisle identification options are:

- One-way vision placard that is placed flat against the end of the aisle, either upright or hanging from the ceiling. The aisle identification faces outward and allows a forklift truck driver to identify an aisle. One-way vision placard is also used to identify each AS/RS aisle on the AS/RS front wall.
- Two-way vision placard options are:
    - Two placards. Each upright frame placard extends outward from an upright post into a main traffic aisle. At a proper elevation a placard is easily recognized and will not be damaged.
    - Three placards. Two placards extend outward into a main traffic aisle and an additional placard is placed flat between two placards. With a two-way sign, each aisle number is easily recognized from a main traffic aisle. This approach is used in a forklift truck driver operation.
- A four-way aisle placard is a ceiling-hung placard with four sides. Each side has an aisle identification. Each aisle number is easily recognized from the main traffic aisle.

Master Carton and Pallet-Storage Position Identification

In a master-carton or pallet-storage warehouse, SKU position identification has a direct impact on the transaction productivity and accuracy of the forklift truck drivers. Storage position may be identified by a floor stack group that is hung from the ceiling, embedded in the floor, or attached to a upright post or by rack group.

Floor Stack Storage Pallet Position Identification

A master-carton, pallet-floor, or block-storage position identification uses a placard hung from the ceiling for storage lane position identification. Clearance between the placard and the forklift truck mast is a factor. If necessary, the position identification may be embedded in the floor, but identification durability in the floor is a factor. Another option is to erect a rack post between two floor stack lanes. As an employee or forklift truck driver faces the upright post, the left-hand master carton or pallet lane is on an upright post on the left side, and shows master-carton or pallet-storage identifications; the right-hand master carton/pallet lane is on an upright post on the right side, and has the master-carton/pallet-storage identification. An upright rack post maintains clearance between storage lanes.

Rack Identification

Storage SKU position identification is attached to a rack bay metal structural member, in the line of sight (so a hand-held scanner may be used). Rack identifications may be hand written on the position, use self-adhesive labels or tape, or preprinted self-adhesive labels (with individual characters, digits, or the complete identification with human/machine-readable symbologies).

Master-Carton and Pallet Warehouse Storage Vehicle

Master-carton, or pallet warehouse storage vehicle is a key factor in determining aisle width and the master-carton or pallet-position number (load beam levels) above the floor surface. Vehicle aisle width and maximum master-carton or pallet-position (load beam) elevation above the floor influences facility storage utilization, land and building/equipment costs, and annual operating costs. The vehicle allows the driver line-of sight to use a hand-held scanner line or to manually read the master-carton, or pallet identification and master-carton/pallet position identification to complete a bar-code scan/RF tag read transaction.

Master-Carton and Pallet-Storage Vehicles

Each vehicle group name is determined by a vehicle basic operating characteristic. Storage vehicle type groups are wide aisle (WA); narrow aisle (NA); very narrow aisle (VNA), including a high-rise order picker (HROS), car-in rack, and AS/RS vehicles; mobile-aisle (MA), or transfer or bridge car (T-car); and captive-aisle (CA).

Storage- or Pick-Aisle Characteristics

Storage-aisle philosophy options are

1. Aisle length. In a short aisle facility, the aisles are 20-feet long (small-item pick aisle) or 75-feet long (in a master-carton or pallet operation). In a WA or NA forklift operation, the rack row and aisles run in the short direction in the facility. The storage or pick area has turning aisles at each rack row and aisle end. The short aisle approach provides lower density and lower employee productivity, due to greater nonproductive aisle end turn numbers. In a long aisle facility, the aisles are 40-feet long (for small-item pick aisle) and 150-feet long (in a master-carton or pallet operation). In a WA, NA, or VNA forklift truck operation, rack rows and aisles flow in the long direction of a facility In a WA or NA storage vehicle design, there is a cross aisle in the middle of the rack rows or aisles to provide easy and quick transfer to another facility aisle. In a VNA, there are no cross aisles—there is a continuous aisle from start to end. A long-aisle warehouse provides greater density and fewer nonproductive employee turning aisles.
2. Aisle width. The storage aisle dimension is SKU to SKU plus six inches. A conventional warehouse aisle width provides sufficient width for two-way employee or vehicle traffic with 4- to 12-inch allowance between two SKUs or two vehicles.

Aisle or Rack Height

The aisle or rack height is determined by an employee's or forklift truck set of forks' reach height to complete a storage or pick transaction. In an employee pick concept, a nominal employee reach height is between 4 feet, 6 inches to 5 feet, 6 inches. A storage rack aisle height is determined by a storage rack height, forklift truck type, or AS/RS crane.

Picker and Forklift Truck Routing

The forklift truck routing pattern has a sequential or arithmetic progress through the storage/pick aisle with SKU storage or pick positions on both sides of the aisle. With a storage put-away or customer-order pick instruction, a routing pattern makes it easier for a forklift truck driver, AS/RS crane, or picker to locate the desired storage/pick position.

Forklift Truck and AS/RS Crane Routing Patterns

A fundamental rule for a successful storage warehouse is that a storage transaction instruction follows a pattern through each storage aisle. An instruction form directs a WA, NA, or VNA forklift truck driver or AS/RS crane to a computer-suggested or employee-determined storage position. In an employee-directed storage operation, a forklift truck driver selects a deposit storage location and, for a withdrawal transaction, the computer suggests a storage location. In an AS/RS storage design, the warehouse computer determines an identified storage position. To assure proper inventory tracking and storage-position control, the SKU storage position identification and the SKU identifications that were involved in the transaction are sent to the inventory control office to update the inventory file.

A sequential storage aisle number or routing pattern has a WA, NA, or VNA forklift truck driver or AS/RS crane enter an aisle, complete a storage transaction, and exit the same aisle. As the forklift truck driver or AS/RS crane travels through an aisle, the lowest storage position number is at the entrance from a main aisle and the storage position number numbers are progressive to highest number at the end of the aisle. This assures maximum forklift truck driver or AS/RS crane productivity. Storage aisle options are 1) storage position numbers that end with even digits, located on the right side of the aisle, with position numbers that end with odd digits and are located on the left side of the aisle; or 2) each aisle rack row or side has an aisle number and storage position numbers are progressive for the next storage position.

In a storage warehouse, a forklift truck or single cycle AS/RS crane storage transaction handles one pallet per trip. The aisle routing pattern will have the forklift truck or AS/RS crane enter an aisle from a main traffic aisle, complete the storage transaction, and travel (i.e., back out) to a main traffic aisle. A dual cycle AS/RS crane has ability to carry two pallets and to complete two pallet-storage transactions in one aisle or to complete dual commands for each aisle trip. Nevertheless, an AS/RS crane follows the same routing pattern.

Warehouse Operation Customer-Order Fulfillment and Sort

The SKU storage and pick philosophy has an employee or machine transfer SKUs from a pick position onto a load-carrying surface. A load-carrying surface transfers each SKU to an identified location.

Manual Order Fulfillment

Manual order fulfillment places all pick positions at 5 feet, 6 inches to 6 feet above the floor. The height permits a maximum of two pallets or four to five levels of hand-stacked master cartons in a decked rack or shelf levels. There is a wide aisle to allow employees to walk or ride a vehicle through the pick aisles. This design requires the most employees, thus increasing both the required functions and total area. Some manual warehouse pick options include 1) single pick designs, such as a four-wheeled cart, picking into a carton or tote onto a nonpowered conveyor surface, a mobile step stool, rolling ladder, or ladder attached to a cart or pick-position structural member, pallet truck, platform truck, two-wheel truck, or semi-live skid or cart; 2) batched pick designs, such as an aisle-end sort shelf, mobile shelf cart, tote on conveyor, or pick, transport, and sort to shelf, tote, or carton; 3) pick/pack or pick/pass (single pick designs) in which the employee picks into a captive tote or carton; and 4) sort to light.

Mechanized Order Fulfillment

A mechanized order fulfillment warehouse has a medium-sized facility. It uses a conveyor and permits elevated floor or mezzanine construction for additional pick levels. In a two- or three-pick elevated floor facility, pick position replenishment is performed by a WA, NA, or VNA forklift truck or conveyor and increases the area needed for building pick positions. Because SKUs are separated onto a mechanized or conveyor travel path or a manual (or non-conveyable) section, the facility has a medium-sized building and employee number. In mechanized pick designs, employees pick master cartons or loose small items into a tote or loose onto a conveyor path, from a S.I. Cartrac platform, a powered horizontal carousel basket, vertical powered carousel bin, or HROS pick truck, or VNA man-up forklift truck, pick car, and decombe elevating order pick vehicle.

Automatic Order Fulfillment

An automated order fulfillment warehouse has a small facility. Pick positions are narrow and long with multiple pick levels in a stack. Pick positions are replenished by a forklift truck or employee; pick positions release SKUs onto a conveyor or into a carton/tote. There are manual SKU pick positions for non-conveyable SKUs. Automated pick concepts are 1) small-item pick concepts that are an S.I. Itematic, Robo Pic, and an "A" or "H" frame; 2) master-carton concepts that are S.I. Ordermatic, carton AS/RS, and Vertique; and 3) pallet concepts that are a pallet AS/RS or Sort Link.

Order-Picker Routing Patterns

A picker routing pattern guides the picker through the pick aisle to pick positions. Each picker routing pattern follows a pick position and aisle layout. There are many picker routing patterns for an order fulfillment operation. There are advantages for the warehouse when a picker routing pattern matches SKU characteristics, through-put volume, and pick area layout. A picker routing pattern match helps obtain the best picker productivity, accurate picks, on-schedule activity, and on-budget activity. Picker walks to a pick position routing pattern can be 1) a nonsequential routing pattern group, or 2) sequential routing group that includes single side pattern, loop pattern, horse shoe (i.e., "U" pattern), (d) "Z" pattern, block pattern, and stitch pattern.

Nonsequential Routing Pattern

In a nonsequential pattern pickers determine their own pick path through a pick area aisle. Disadvantages are low employee productivity because an employee may walk the same path twice, employee fatigue from increased walking, and employees spend nonproductive time trying to locate a SKU pick position in a pick aisle. There are no advantages.

Sequential Routing Patterns

The fundamental characteristic of a sequential picker routing pattern is that there is an arithmetic progression to pick position numbers in each pick aisle. Thus, the lowest SKU pick position number (1 or 0) is at the entrance to a pick aisle and highest pick position number (99 to 100) is at an exit of a pick aisle. A picker starts at the first SKU pick position in a pick aisle and as a picker travels down the aisle to the end, the next required SKU pick position is as close as possible to the previous SKU pick position. Sequential picker routing patterns provide an efficient and productive picker routing group. Advantages are reduced employee nonproductive time (two or more trips down a pick aisle), reduced employee fatigue, minimized employee confusion, and increased employee productivity. The basic elements of a picker routing pattern and pick aisle conditions are

1. Pick position numbers that end with an even digit are located on the right side as a picker travels in an aisle; pick position numbers that end with an odd digit are located on the left side as a picker travels in a pick aisle;
2. It uses arithmetic progression through a pick aisle;
3. It keeps a picker in a pick aisle as long as possible;
4. It improves SKU hit concentration and density;
5. It starts pickers in the fast moving and high cube section;
6. Customer order SKU quantity cubed out; and
7. It keeps pick aisles clear, and helps maintain good housekeeping and well illuminated aisles.

Picker Aisle Travel

In an order fulfillment operation, to complete a customer order, a picker travels through a pick aisle to complete transactions. The first option is straight in and out picker travel through a pick aisle. For each pick instruction format, a picker travels in and out one pick aisle. During pick aisle travel, a picker completes all pick transactions. With a straight in and out approach, the lowest pick position number is at a pick aisle (001) entrance and progresses through a pick aisle to the highest pick position number at the pick aisle (001) end. After the transactions are completed, the picker turns the pick cart and walks back through aisle to the main aisle entrance. Leaving aisle 001, a picker walks to the adjacent aisle and enters pick aisle 002. During travel in pick aisle 002, a picker completes all pick transactions and repeats the process for aisle 003. The second approach is serpentine picker travel. During pick aisle 001 travel, the lowest pick positions are at the entrance to pick aisle 001. After all pick transactions are completed, a picker exits pick aisle 001 at the end or at the highest pick position number location and enters pick aisle 002 at the lowest pick position number location. Entering pick aisle 002, a picker walks and completes all pick transactions and enters a main aisle. From a main aisle, a picker enters aisle 003. With a serpentine approach, the lowest pick position number of each pick aisle starts at the aisle entrance and progresses to the highest pick position number at an exit. In a rectangularly shaped order pick area, each aisle entrance has an even number aisle entrance at a main aisle (front) and odd number aisle picker entrance from the rear aisle.

Horizontal Picker Routing Pattern

A horizontal picker routing pattern is used on a carton flow rack, decked rack, or shelf pick approach. A picker routing pattern has a single side picker routing pattern that directs a picker in a pick aisle or along a pick line to the SKU pick position and a horizontal picker routing pattern at an assigned flow rack bay that directs a picker activity across carton flow rack pick positions. A horizontal routing pattern starts as the picker enters a pick aisle along a carton flow rack bay front. As the picker enters the aisle, the first pick position is the upper first flow rack bay and ends at the lower last carton flow rack bay.

Picker Faces Carton Flow Rack Bay Pick Positions on an Aisle Right or Left Side

For each a pick aisle layout, a picker enters a pick aisle's right side (single or mirrored pick module) and faces the first pick zone. The carton flow rack bay pick positions are on a pick aisle's right side. With a right-aisle approach, as the picker proceeds in the pick aisle, at each carton flow rack bay and as a picker faces the pick positions, the first pick position is in a carton flow rack bay upper right-hand corner. At each pick position, the picker starts at a carton flow rack bay upper right corner, progresses horizontally across each carton flow rack bay level, and the last pick position in a carton flow rack bay is at the lower level right corner. With a left-side concept, a picker enters a pick aisle left side (single or mirrored pick module) and faces the first pick zone, the carton flow rack bay pick positions are on a pick aisle's left side. As the picker proceeds in the pick aisle, the first pick position is in a carton flow rack bay upper level left corner. Routing pattern design has the picker start in the upper left corner, work horizontally across each carton flow rack bay level, and end at the carton flow rack bay lower level left hand corner.

With a horizontal routing pattern, the first possible pick position is at a carton flow rack bay top corner at a pick aisle entrance and across the top pick level to a bay end. After all transactions on the carton flow rack bay top pick level, the picker proceeds to the next lower pick level left corner. At each carton flow rack pick bay, a horizontal picker routing pattern is repeated until customer-order or cube completion. As the picker proceeds to the next carton flow rack bay that has a pick transaction, the horizontal pick pattern is repeated at the appropriate level.

A horizontal picker routing pattern is preferred for a pick/pass warehouse that has carton flow rack bay pick positions. This permits a Golden Zone that is between a picker's knees and shoulders, and the arrangement in a pick bay assures good replenishment activity, makes it easy to add SKUs to the pick bay, and high picker productivity.

Order-Pick and Sort-Instruction Label

Pick and sort instructions (characters and digits) are human- and machine-readable symbologies that are important items on a label. With a label, small characters or instructions are difficult to read, thus reducing productivity and increasing errors. The preferred method is to have pick and sort instructions with equal emphasis with different style characters (or digits) with a different colored backgrounds or in a different location.

Picker Instruction

Options for picker instruction are:

1. A computer-controlled printer prints each pick position, SKU description, piece pick quantity, and order number onto a paper. As the picker arrives at a pick position, the picker checks that the document pick position matches the pick position number and removes a SKU quantity from the pick position into a carton or tote. This method is used in a single pick or a batched pick and sort.
2. A computer-controlled printer prints a self-adhesive label with each pick position, SKU description, and order number. As a picker arrives at a pick position, the picker makes sure that the label pick position matches the pick position number, removes the SKU, labels it, and transfers the picked and labeled SKU into a tote or onto a conveyor. Self-adhesive labels are used in batched pick and sort or pick, transport, and sort designs.
3. Paperless pick concept options are:
   a. Digital display: a manually controlled paperless pick design. A paperless pick design has a light display at the pick position. When the light is illuminated, it serves as a picker instruction. The pick-to-light method has customer orders sequenced by the warehouse computer. The picker starts at entrance to pick aisle or at the lowest number. For each identification, a warehouse computer activates assigned pick lights within each pick zone or aisle. Walking in a pick aisle to the first lighted pick position, a picker removes product from the position and presses a "pick complete button," that registers the pick. The warehouse computer then reduces the SKU quantity on the digital display by one. If another pick is required at the same pick position, a picker repeats the activity until the digital display indicates zero. Picked SKUs are placed with or without a label onto the vehicle load carrying surface or a powered conveyor. A picker walks in a pick zone to the next pick position. After all picks in a pick zone, a picker presses a pick zone light that activates pick zone pick lights for the next customer order.
   b. Computer-controlled paperless picking. In a RF device method, the computer downloads pick instructions to a hand-held or finger scanner. As the forklift truck driver rides or picker walks in the storage/pick aisle, the RF device's digital display indicates the storage/pick position. Arriving at a storage/pick position, the forklift truck driver or picker points the scanner/RF tag reader at the storage/pick position bar-code/RF tag. The digital display indicates that the SKU is on the forklift truck, withdrawal instructions, customer order, and required SKU pallet or pick quantity. A picker removes the assigned quantity from the pick position onto a vehicle load-carrying surface or powered conveyor. A computer-controlled paperless AS/RS crane or pick method is an automated pick system. A computer transmits a pick impulse to a SKU pick position device to pick/release one SKU from a pick position onto a conveyor. In some computer-controlled systems, the picker device is a moving flipper. In an AS/RS crane system, a computer directs an AS/RS crane to complete a pallet withdrawal transaction and place a pallet onto a P/D station.

4. A voice-directed pick instruction method uses a computer system and a picker microphone or earphones (headset). The pickers have on-line communication with the computer (using voice recognition and speech synthesis). Each picker talks to the computer via radio transmission through the microphone and receives verbal pick instructions from the computer through the head set. Arriving at a pick position, a picker receives the SKU quantity and removes the SKU quantity from the pick position onto a vehicle load-carrying surface or a powered conveyor.

Pick-Position Replenishment

There are three general options for single-item or carton replenishment:

1. Pallet replenishment. The entire pallet is transferred from a storage area to a pick position. Pallet replenishment replenishes approximately 50–75 cartons for each transaction, and best used for high-cube or fast- to medium-moving SKUs to a pallet pick position.
2. One- or two-layer pallet layer replenishment. One or two carton layers from a pallet are removed and transferred to a pick position. The pick position is a hand-stack rack position, case-flow rack position, or shelf position used for medium-moving SKUs. One to two master-carton layer replenishment is performed in a storage or pick area. If layer removal is performed in a storage area, master cartons are removed from a pallet and transferred onto a conveyor system or vehicle load-carrying surface for transport to a pick aisle. In a pick or replenishment aisle, master cartons are transferred into a pick position. If layer removal is performed in the pick area, a forklift truck removes a pallet from the storage position and transports it to a pick area. In the pick area, an employee transfers required master-carton layer(s) from the pallet to the pick position. After a replenishment transaction, a forklift truck transports the partially depleted pallet from the pick area to an assigned storage position.
3. A method for very slow moving SKUs or for single items involves less than a full pallet layer (that has one or more master-cartons). A picker picks slow-moving cartons from a pallet-storage position and transports the cartons to a pick area. In the pick area, an employee transfers master cartons into an assigned pick position.

Replenishment Timing

Single item (or carton fixed-pick–position) replenishment is performed the moment that a pick position becomes depleted, and with a SKU quantity that maximizes pick position space and employee transaction activity. To achieve this, the replenishment control options are:

1. Manually controlled replenishment. This relies upon employees to determine the time at which single items or cartons are transferred from a storage position to a pick position.
2. Computer-suggested or controlled replenishment. A computer or inventory control program suggests that an employee perform a SKU replenishment transaction. Replenishment is based on SKUs and inventory quantity in the pick position. There are two methods for directing an employee to complete a replenishment transaction. First, a paper document that lists all replenishment transactions is created for each shift. SKUs are listed by SKU or storage position numbers. The description, in a sequential order, is based on the anticipated time that a pick position will become depleted. The first column lists the storage position;

the second column is for employee marks, who withdraw a SKU from a storage position. The employee mark verifies that a SKU withdrawal transaction was completed on schedule. The third column lists the pick position, and the fourth column is for the employee mark to verify that a SKU replenishment transaction to a pick position was completed. The second approach uses a bar-code scanning/RF tag receiver. The tag is scanned by a hand-held RF device, and the information is transmitted the warehouse computer. The computer determined required replenishment activities and the sequence in which the activities will occur. In addition to a RF tag device, a bar-code/RF tag is on each SKU, storage position, and pick position. The bar-code scanning/RF tag device transmits replenishment information on line as a position update in the inventory files. A computer-controlled replenishment method is one of the advantages of a warehouse with a WMS program.

Deposit and Withdrawal Transaction Verification and Inventory Tracking

A very important order fulfillment operation activity is SKU deposit and withdrawal transaction verification. Replenishment transaction verification activity options are:

1. Manual memory. An employee remembers the storage and pick positions for a SKU replenishment transaction. An employee remembers the storage location, and when there is a demand to complete a SKU pick position replenishment, an employee remembers the SKU storage location and completes the transaction.
2. Manual handwritten method. A replenishment employee uses a printed form to record each replenishment transaction.
3. Manual bin file. Storage position cards that correspond to a storage position in a storage aisle are used. The cards are placed in sequential order in a cardholder. In a carton order-fulfillment operation, cardholders have a slot for each storage position or pick position in the rack bay. The cardholder is attached to a rack upright post. A card has a storage position number printed on top left side and has three columns. An employee who performs a replenishment transaction completes the columns. One column lists the SKU identification number involved in the transaction. Other columns are used to indicate deposit or withdrawal transactions. After the replenishment transaction is completed, an employee obtains a storage position card from the holder. On the card, an employee lists a SKU identification number and places a mark in the "in" or "out" column (reflecting a transaction). The completed card is returned to a cardholder for future reference.
4. Automatic (or bar-code scanning/RF tag reading) replenishment. Each transaction component (e.g., tote, carton, or pallet) has human/machine-readable symbology as part of a SKU, replenishment/pick position identification, and hand-held bar-code scanner/RF tag receiver. A replenishment transaction and SKU quantity is transmitted to the inventory computer, and a RF tag receiver accepts a RF tag signal. In a bar-code scanning/RF tag replenishment operation, each tote, carton, or pallet movement, or replenishment transaction activity, or move to a pick position, is bar-code scanned/RF tag read and the scan/read information is sent on-line or delayed to a WMS computer for inventory file update. To complete a replenishment transaction, an employee is directed to a storage position. At the storage position, the employee scans the storage position bar code or receives a signal from a RF tag, transfers a unit or product quantity, and moves to the pick area. In a pick area, the employee scans the SKU and pick position bar-code/RF tag and enters the SKU quantity. The transactions are communicated to the computer inventory file.

Pick and Order Fulfillment

Methods of warehouse sorting are:

1. Manual single item or carton order fulfillment. All pick positions are at 5 feet, 6 inches to 6 feet above the floor. A pallet-storage/pick warehouse uses a forklift truck to complete all storage transactions. A manual pick approach uses wide aisles because employees walk or ride a vehicle through facility pick aisles and because of the large number of employees needed.
2. Mechanized single item carton order fulfillment. This method uses a medium-sized facility. It utilizes a conveyor and permits an elevated floor, mezzanine construction for additional pick levels, and a medium-sized staff.
3. Automated single item carton or pallet order fulfillment. This approach uses a small facility. Pick positions are narrow and long, and there are multiple levels in the stack. It also has the small staff.

Customer-Order–Picked SKU Sorting

In a single item master-carton batched pick order fulfillment or an across-the-dock operation with SKUs (or customer orders), SKU or customer-order sorting is critical to accurate and on-time shipping. Sorting allows an order-fulfillment or across-the-dock operation to handle a high volume of orders and SKUs. In an order-fulfillment operation, sorting is the first post-customer–order pick activity. When a single item, or master-carton pick activity uses a batched pick mode, sorting separates each labeled single SKU, or master carton from a mix of customer orders and labeled SKUs. Sorting verifies that a SKU was withdrawn from a pick position and was transported to a pack area or directly onto a customer delivery truck.

In an across-the-dock operation, as mixed customer-order labeled SKUs, master cartons, or SKUs are unloaded from the vendor delivery truck and transported on a sort conveyor travel path. For each SKU sort or customer-order label, a scanner/reader on a sort conveyor reads each label and sends the data to a sort computer for sorting each SKU or master carton from the sort travel path into a sort holding area or direct load conveyor lane. SKU sorting requires a 1) human/machine or human-machine bar-code label or RF tag on each SKU exterior; 2) a sorter constant travel speed; 3) communication between a bar-code scanner/RF tag receiver to a sort computer, tracking device sort computer, and sort conveyor divert device; and 4) customer assigned divet lane with queue space.

To assure maximum good bar code/RF tag reads and diverts activity, SKUs or customer orders are singulated on a sort travel path to a customer assigned sort location. A sort location can be a bin, container, chute, or conveyor. A scanner reads the bar-code/RF tag, and sends the data to a computer that controls the sort. The computer activates a divert device to transfer the SKU or customer order from the travel path to a holding location, outbound staging area, or a delivery truck.

Pack Activity

A customer-order pack activity may be manual, mechanized, or an automated single-customer pick/pack operation; a batched customer-order pick, sort, transport, and pack operation; or a batched customer pick, transport, sort, and pack operation. Shipping options are a carton or a corrugated or chipboard box or a corrugated, treated, or plastic bag. Customer-order pack activity ensures that a picked, checked, and packed SKU is protected against damage or from being lost during delivery and that the delivery address and company return address are clearly listed on the package's exterior. The company's industry (e.g., direct customer contact or catalog; e-mail or direct marketing group; retail store or commercial customer group) determines how SKUs are handled at a pack station.

Customer-Order Pack Activity: Centralized and Decentralized

Pack activity and its relationship to order fulfillment can be described in five parts:

1. Selecting (and, if necessary, forming) shipping carton/tote and applying an address label the exterior;
2. Picked SKUs, company sales literature, and packing slip are placed in the shipping carton/tote;
3. A picked check is done;
4. Carton void spaces are filled; and
5. The shipping carton/tote is sealed.

Pack activities vary according to each pack station type, whether it is a manual, mechanized, or automated order fulfillment operation, and by carton/tote.

Decentralized Customer-Order Pack Activity

If an order fulfillment operation is a pick/pack into a shipping carton/tote operation, pack activity is decentralized. In this type of operation, packing is separated into different activities, and at different locations, on the pick line. After the computer-selected shipping carton/tote is formed and transferred onto the pick line, a shipping label is placed on the carton/tote by an employee or machine-label applicator. At the start station, an employee or insert machine places a packing slip into the carton/tote and the SKU is transferred directly into the shipping carton/tote. Checking is performed by an employee or by using the "check weight on the fly" method. After the carton/tote has been checked, an employee or machine places filler material in the shipping carton/tote void spaces. Finally, the shipping carton/tote is sealed with tape over top flaps or a plastic band around the carton/tote.

Centralized Packing

Packing is centralized in order fulfillment operations that pick/pack into captive totes or is a pick, sort, transfer, and pack operation (or if transfer occurs before sorting). At the central location, a pack station employee handles all functions from the packing slip to making up a computer-suggested shipping carton/tote. The employee completes the checking and transfers SKUs and packing slips into the carton/totes. The employee also adds filler to void spaces in the carton/tote, seals the carton/tote, and applies the shipping label.

Shipping Carton Manifest

Creating a shipping carton/bag manifest involves an employee and a bar-code scanner/RF tag reader to record each shipping carton, bag, or pallet identification. The identification is a human/machine-readable code on each shipping carton, bag, or pallet. For each delivery company, an identification list is sent (via paper copy, diskette, on-line, or delayed communication network) from the fulfillment facility to the delivery company office. A shipping carton, bag, or pallet manifest can be a hand-written or computer-printed list obtained from a hand-held or fixed position bar-code scanning/RF tag reading device. The warehouse computer transfers the packed parcel information (weight, parcel number, and routing information) to the delivery or freight forwarder company.

Package Load

Direct Fluid Load

In a storage/pick or across-the-dock direct load operation, cartons or bags travel from a sort travel path to a delivery truck. A carton shipping conveyor travel path has either a serpentine or straight-run gravity conveyor that runs from the sort conveyor to an extendible conveyor (e.g., powered belt, powered roller or skate wheel, nonpowered roller, skate wheel conveyor). The extendible conveyer extends into the delivery truck. Cartons are transferred from the extendible conveyor and placed on the delivery truck floor.

Shipping Carton Unitizing

In a facility that unitizes cartons, orders travel on a shipping lane conveyor. This has travel paths leading from the sort conveyor to a unitizing station. At the unitizing station, cartons to be transferred are placed onto a cart, slip-sheet, or pallet. After the cart, slip sheet, or pallet is unitized to a predetermined height, the filled cart, slip sheet, or pallet is identified with a code and transferred to an outbound staging area. The pallet is added to other pallets or is placed onto a delivery truck.

Return Process

The return process is an order fulfillment operation, in which returned packages and SKUs are taken through the returns process area to final disposition. Return process activities are:

1. Whenever possible, the delivery company presorts return packages by major SKU classification.
2. Delivery company vehicles with returns are staged in a truckyard or delivery company return packages (or BMCs) are unloaded onto a return conveyor or into a returns dock staging area. The delivery company separates high-value SKUs (identified as such on the original order). As returns arrive at the returns dock, the high-value returned SKUs are unloaded to a secured area.

3. Return packages may be opened
   a. At a separate open station; the return package is removed from a return BMC or conveyor and an employee opens the package, removes any filler material, and returns the package back to a conveyor travel path; or
   b. At an unload station; the return package is opened and transported on a conveyor to a returns process station.
4. Package filler material and empty returns may be transferred to a recycle or trash transport. If the return package is opened at a separate station, return items are placed into a return carton, which is sent to a returns process station.
5. Customer-order and SKU return verification and return credit is dealt with at a process station.
6. Trash may be handled at a separate open and filler material removal process station; after proper customer verification, the empty return carton is transferred to a trash transport.
7. For each SKU quality, SKUs are either transferred or presorted to an assigned disposition container or transferred as loose items onto a conveyor for later sorting to an assigned container.
8. For each a container, SKUs or mixed totes are transferred from a presorting area to an individual, temporary, nonsaleable holding position. SKUs are later transferred to saleable SKU inventory in a storage/pick position.

Warehouse Operation Drawings

The warehouse equipment layout (plan view) drawings have all dimensions and notes necessary to show a completed warehouse. The layout drawing shows all the material handing equipment and SKU or customer-order travel paths. An effective warehouse drawing will identify each functional area, each activity station has an identification, and warehouse equipment is identified with symbol or number.

Block Drawing

A block layout drawing is a schematic building representation that can be developed in a short time at a low cost. A block drawing shows possible building column locations, fire or load bearing walls, receiving and shipping dock areas, where and how each warehouse activity is located in a facility, but does not show any warehouse equipment. Each floor is identified as ground floor or elevated floor. If there are multiple elevated floors in the facility, each elevated floor is identified and shown in sequence adjacent to above the ground floor. This floor arrangement helps the design team to understand the relationship between the elevated floors, potential vertical in-house transport concept travel paths, and employee stairways. A block drawing permits lines drawn between activities or processes to ensure proper SKU or customer-order piece sequential flow. Additional lines represent communication lines between the various warehouse process or activity locations. The design team will list all storage/pick activities, SKU or customer-order flow paths that occur for vendor-delivered SKUs or customer orders, and data communication flow paths for vendor-delivered SKUs or customer orders. The team will write an initial description of operations and a flow chart for each activity. Directional arrows on flow charts show a flow direction, activity descriptions, description of operations, SKU classification change, and warehouse computer equipment.

Plan View

A plan view drawing is a two-dimensional view that shows the warehouse facility length and width from a CAD computer. A plan view drawing allows one to trace the SKU or customer-order flow and travel paths through the warehouse. It permits the design team to identify key activity stations and determine facility size and the necessary size for each warehouse activity station. It helps the design team understand warehouse activity, WMS-program interaction locations, and to look for offices and other key administrative areas.

Elevation View

An elevation view drawing is a two-dimensional plan drawn to scale that shows height and width or height and length. The drawing details the warehouse facility and provides a view for the clear distance (space) from the floor to building equipment and to the building's ceiling steel/mezzanine support members, and shows the interface between building items and forklift truck or conveyor.

Detail View

A detail-view drawing is drawn to scale, and shows each warehouse activity area, including all equipment and building items. From a detail drawing one will be able to understand the interrelationship between warehouse activities and space.

Warehouse Operation Review

During the design team's visit to the existing warehouse, the team develops an understanding for actual SKU and customer-order flows and supportive operational data and records. The design team observes each warehouse employee activity. During the warehouse visit (the existing warehouse or another company's facility), the design team obtains samples for each warehouse activity document, label, or procedure. Meeting with a warehouse manager, the design team obtains all facility or warehouse vendor drawings, block drawings, training manuals, operational manuals, job descriptions, and descriptions of operations.

Chapter 3

Warehouse Operation Interaction and Interface with a WMS Program

Introduction

A warehouse with a WMS program has three major interacting information components that direct warehouse SKU transactions and customer-order transactions. The components are 1) the host or company IT computer with a program to maintain and account for the total SKU quantities in the warehouse; 2) a computer that tracks the SKU quantity in each position and order entries and exits from the warehouse; and 3) warehouse control or computers that direct employees or equipment to move SKUs between positions or drop points, as well as completing pick transactions by moving SKUs from pick positions into containers or cartons. As a vendor-delivered SKU becomes a SKU, and then becomes an order, the SKU (and relevant information) flows through a warehouse (see Figure 3.1).

Host IT Computer

The host computer with an ERP program focuses on

- External communications: between the company and vendors and between the company and customers.
- Accounting for physical assets, including total inventory. As an order is received for a SKU, the host computer depletes the SKU inventory quantity by the amount specified in the order. The host computer activity assures customer-order SKU sales over a company SKU inventory quantity that accounts for "out of stock" and back orders.
- Company income, warehouse expenses, cost of goods sold, expenses, and refunds.

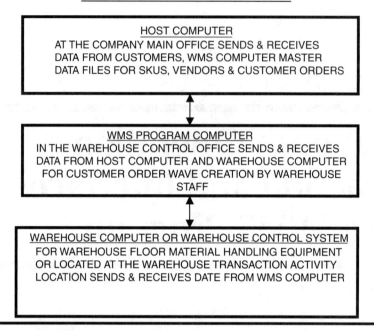

THREE COMPUTER COMPONENTS

Figure 3.1 Three Computer Components

- Order review and group order identifications. In some operations, the computer sends orders to the WMS computer for a warehouse staff member to create a customer order wave or work day customer order number, vendor delivery quantities, order withdrawals, and returns updates.
- Order cancellations. In most applications, the warehouse staff and computer creates order waves or work day orders as picks are completed. Order waves, and completed or manifested orders are then sent to the WMS computer. The computer updates the files and sends all completed and manifested orders to the host computer.

Overall, the host computer is the master in the system for all orders, vendor purchase orders, SKU master data, stock numbers, and other company data such as accounting.

WMS Program Computer

The WMS program computer receives processed order identifications and associated SKU quantities from the host computer. The WMS computer updates the vendor-delivered or order returns placed into a position. The quantity is received as individual entries or grouped order identifications and SKU quantities. With order identifications and SKU quantity, based on a warehouse wave creation, the WMS program allocates SKUs from storage/pick positions to complete orders.

The WMS computer receives from a warehouse computer:

- SKU pick and pack for orders or withdrawals from the inventory quantity in a storage/pick position;
- Order manifested (or registered) as loaded/shipped on a delivery truck;

- SKU inventory updates from the receiving or order returns departments. The computer also maintains SKU age, rotation, and manufacturer lot numbers;
- SKU quantity relocation or reorganization from one position to another;
- Receives transactions from the host computer on order cancellations or noncustomer-orders;
- Optionally, the computer receives orders and creates order waves and associated SKU quantities for a work day (wave planning may also be done with the WMS computer by warehouse staff;
- Receives information on 1) completion of SKU moves or other transactions, 2) returns, 3) inventory counts, 4) Q/A department that determines SKU inventory status (e.g., "stop sales," "not available for sale," "OK").

WMS Program Commands

Based on a warehouse order wave creation/work day customer orders and associated SKU inventory, the WMS program allocates SKU quantities and directs the warehouse to complete relevant move transactions. The transactions move SKUs 1) as a reorganization strategy, from one storage position or another; 2) from a storage position to a pick position (as part of the pick-line setup); and 3) from a pick position to a container/carton (as order pick activity).

Standard Operational Commands and Procedures

A standard operational command is designed for transactions or activities that involve SKUs or orders and that occur every work-day. An example is to zero pick (i.e., clean-up) a pick position with residual SKU quantity. A standard operational command for this will have an employee to zero scan a position and transfer SKU residual inventory quantity from the pick position to a storage position or another pick position. In a pick-position zero-scan transaction, an employee scans the depleted pick position and enters "0" as a SKU quantity. All scan transactions are sent to the WMS computer for inventory and position status update.

Priority or Special Commands

A priority (or special) command is designed for nonrepetitive warehouse transactions that involve SKUs or orders. A priority command is ranked above all standard or standard operational procedure (SOP) commands. It is used to complete a warehouse activity that does not occur every work day. A priority command is used to complete an activity that involves a SKU. For example, a priority command would be used to have a SKU inventory cycle count for a SKU inventory quantity or all positions for one SKU. All scan or count transactions are sent to the WMS computer for inventory and position status update.

Location of Order Computer Preparation Activities

The WMS program computer or host computer is used to complete various order preparation activities, including order allocation and wave creation. The design team can locate these activities in the host, if the host computer has sufficient capacity. Otherwise, these activities are handled by the WMS program computer.

Warehouse Operation Computer

The warehouse computer receives from the WMS program computer:

- Wave-planned orders, noncustomer-order identifications and the associated SKU quantity, and suggested SKU move transactions;
- SKU cycle count requests or adjustments due to damage;
- Suggested shipping bag/carton size;
- Order cancellations.

The warehouse computer sends to the WMS program:

- Completed SKU order and noncustomer-order withdrawal transactions;
- Vendor-delivered or order return SKU identification and quantity;
- Completed SKU move transactions;
- Completed order picked SKU transactions;
- Order cancellations;
- Order manifested or shipped list;
- SKU count and adjustment.

Warehouse Operation Interaction and Interface with a WMS Program

A warehouse with a WMS program has standardized warehouse operation tasks and activities that follow specific steps. The program affects vendor SKU receiving activity, and continues through warehouse order process activities: storage, pick-line setup and replenishment, order pick, picked SKU check, packing, manifest preparation, loading and shipping, returns, and SKU or position count activities.

In a conventional forklift truck or AS/RS crane store, pick-and-pack operation, or across-the-dock operation, a WMS program affects vendor and customer-order return SKUs and data flows through the warehouse.

A conventional store, hold, pick, and pack warehouse operation with a WMS program functional list includes (see Figures 3.2 and 3.3):

- Vendor-purchase–order and customer-order process;
- Vendor-delivered SKU and QA activity with SKU identification and inventory update;
- In-house transport to storage positions;
- Deposit a SKU into a storage position;
- Allocation and suggested SKU warehouse withdrawal from a storage position;
- In-house transport to a suggested drop point or location;
- SKU warehouse transfers to pick positions;
- Customer-order release to a pick area and customer-order identification;
- Order SKU transfer from a pick position to a carton or tote with a permanent warehouse or disposal identification;
- Order picked SKU check;
- Order pack into a customer shipping carton and SKU accounting;
- Order identification manifest;

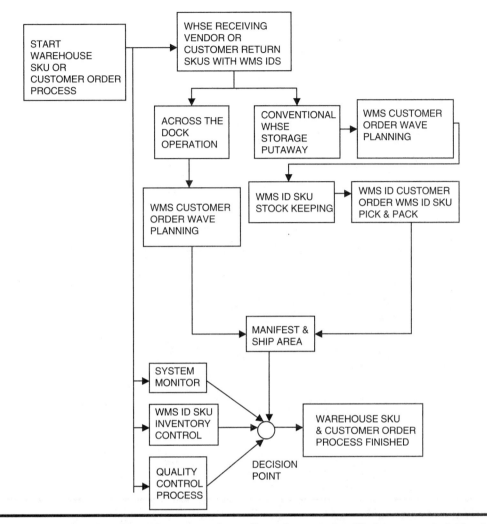

Figure 3.2 Conventional Warehouse Vendor Delivered WMS Identified SKU or WMS Identified Customer Order Flows

- Order loading and shipping;
- Order returns with return to stock and vendor SKUs;
- Prepack SKUs;
- Value-added SKUs;
- Inventory control;
- Nonorder pick activity;
- Advanced order sales;
- Import or custom tax, pay and duty draw back, foreign country vendor delivered SKUs placed in a bonded or free trade zone

An across-the-dock warehouse (see Figures 3.4 and 3.5) with a WMS program functional activity list has both similar and different activities. What is different from the above-described

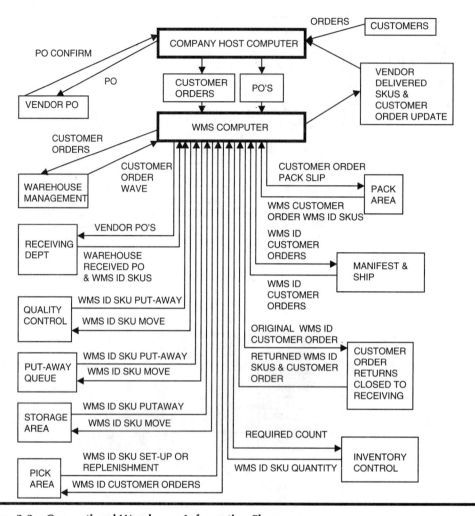

Figure 3.3   Conventional Warehouse Information Flow

activities is the direct in-house transport from the receiving to the shipping dock. An across-the-dock warehouse similar activities to match a customer order quantity by completing picks or sorts from a large master carton quantity into smaller customer-order quantities, to perform prepack or value-added activities, or to handle customer-order returns.

SKU Tracking File Location

The program file tracks each SKU as it flows from a receiving area, through a storage position, to a pick position, to a packing area, through a manifest area, and onto a delivery or freight forwarder truck. In a receiving area, a receiving employee attaches an identifier to each SKU (e.g., single SKU, master carton, or pallet). A SKU moves from a receiving area to a storage position and from the storage position to a pick position. As a SKU flows through a warehouse, an employee or machine scans/reads each SKU and position identification at each position. SKU and position identifications and SKU quantities are sent to the WMS computer or warehouse computer, which periodically sends SKUs and position scan transactions to the WMS computer. Factors that

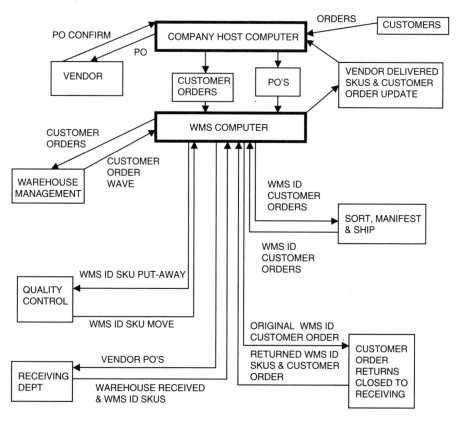

Figure 3.4 Across The Dock Warehouse WMS Identified SKU and Customer Order Flows

determine a file track or inventory file locations are interface capabilities, hardware capabilities, computer program, and software and IT department philosophy or strategy.

Customer-Order Process

Order flow through a warehouse is determined by the warehouse strategy. In an across-the-dock or order push warehouse, orders are preentered in the host computer or entered into the host computer by the purchasing or sales departments. In a conventional store, a hold, pick, and pack (see Figure 3.6) operation, or demand pull warehouse strategy, orders are sent from a company host computer to the WMS computer, which sends orders to a warehouse. With a pool of existing and new orders, the warehouse staff creates an order wave or a work-day order number and SKU quantity in the WMS computer. For customer order SKU allocations and suggested SKU move transactions sent to a warehouse, a completed customer order wave is released to the WMS computer. All noncustomer wave orders are held in the WMS computer noncustomer-order pool.

In a customer-order push or demand-pull warehouse, the host computer will have a specific time period in which it receives orders. A warehouse with a WMS program order entry has two options. First, to achieve on-time completion of the order/delivery cycle, the standard procedure is that all orders that are received prior to the stop time are sent to the WMS program. In a standard

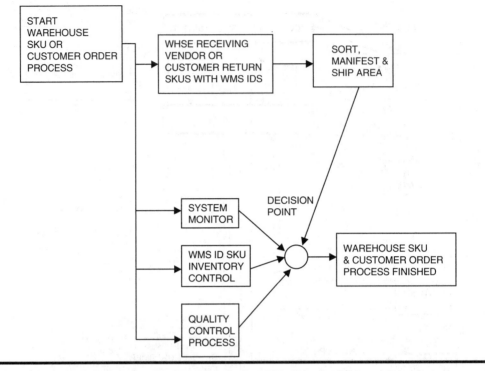

Figure 3.5 Across the Dock Information Flow

WMS program, a section has an order pool for a warehouse staff to complete a warehouse customer order wave plan and release a completed customer order to a WMS computer for WMS computer customer order wave process. Alternatively, if customer orders (or special orders) are received late or past a cut-off time, they may be added to existing orders, although this will incur additional labor and handling expenses.

Customer-Order Cancellation

In an order fulfillment warehouse, a customer-order cancellation feature permits a customer to cancel or modify (e.g., change the SKU quantity) an order. Cancellations made by 1) while the order is in the host computer; 2) as the order is scanned at a warehouse pack station; 3) as the order is scanned at the manifest station; or 4) at the warehouse's central or remote printer.

Canceling an Order in a Host Computer

When an order fulfillment warehouse cancels (or modifies) an order in the host computer, the order is removed from the computer (or an adjustment is made to the SKU quantity). The WMS computer does not receive an order identification and associated quantity, because the warehouse does not process or incur distribution expenses. Thus, it is preferred to cancel orders in the host computer.

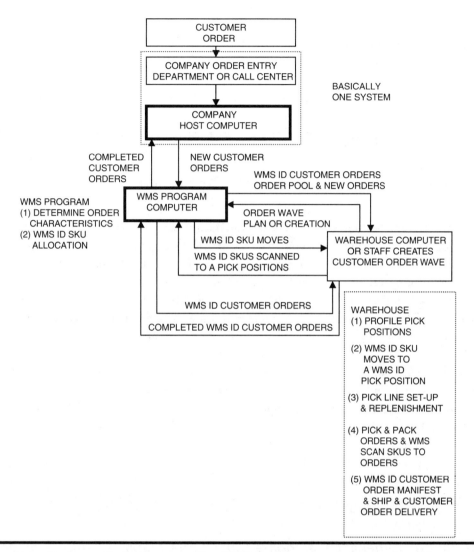

Figure 3.6   Customer Order Process with a WMS Program

Canceling an Order at a Warehouse Operation Pack Station

In a warehouse that has a single pick-and-pack or batched order fulfillment operation, the host computer sends all order identifications and SKUs to the WMS computer for wave creation or planning activity. Based on the wave plan, the program completes the SKU allocation and sends move requests to the warehouse computer. A warehouse sends a SKU quantity from a storage position to a pick position. With a fixed position approach, there will be residual SKU quantity in the pick position to satisfy a wave, so replenishment is not necessary. At the pick position, the picker completes the pick transaction and the completed order is sent to a pack station. If a warehouse cancels an order at a pack station, it means that the host computer received a cancellation. The host computer sends the cancellation to the WMS program, which holds the cancellation. The packer scans the completed order identification. The transaction is sent to the computer, which recognizes the cancellation. At the pack station, the program notifies the packer that an order has been canceled. The packer transfers the order and all documentation from the pack table to a problem station. In the problem area, the cancelled SKUs are handled in the same manner as returns that are "not available for sale." The employee or conveyor transfers customer SKUs from the problem station to a temporary hold position. At the hold position, an employee hand scans each SKU, enters a quantity, and scans a "return to stock position" identification. Scan transactions and SKU quantities are sent to the computer to update identification and return-to-stock position status. Canceling orders at the pack station avoids employee pack and supply expenses.

Canceling an Order at a Warehouse Manifest Station

It is a complex warehouse activity to handle canceled orders after packing and shipping is done. As noted above, the host computer sends all order identifications to the WMS program. Based on the order wave and SKUs, the computer allocates the SKUs and creates withdrawal transactions to setup and replenish the pick positions. In a single order pick line, pick/sort, or batched order fulfillment operation, the program sends all order identifications to a warehouse manifest computer. The manifest computer verifies that the order identification is within the download. A canceled order is sent from the host computer to the WMS computer, which, in turn, sends a cancellation identification to a warehouse manifest station computer. Because the WMS computer has allocated the SKU quantity in the inventory file and sent to the warehouse a SKU transfer/ move transaction from a storage position to a pick position, the warehouse transfers the SKU to a pick position and sends the picked SKUs to a packing station. At the packing station, the order is packed into a shipping carton and a shipping label is attached to the carton. The carton is sent from the packing area to the manifest reading station via the conveyor. At the reading station, the manifest computer noted that there is no order identification of the carton, and diverts the canceled order to the "do not ship" lane. The carton is taken to a problem station. The completed picked, packed, and labeled canceled order is treated in the same manner as a "return to stock" SKU. (See above.)

Canceling an Order at a Warehouse Operation Central or Remote Printer

When a canceled order is received by the host computer, the computer sends a cancellation identification to the WMS computer. If the process of cancelling an order has not begun, and if the packing slips and shipping labels have not yet been printed, the order is canceled from the WMS program. The cancellation process will leave a residual SKU at the pick position. The options dealing with this are 1) leave the SKU at the pick position—it becomes the pick position for a next order wave or work-day. The SKU is in an "available for sale" pick position and all future SKU setup activities will be made to it's specific pick position. Or 2) zero scan each vacate pick position identification that is sent to the WMS program and assure no SKU quantity in a pick position, for each pick position with a residual SKU(s) to complete a zero scan transaction and move the SKU(s) to another pick position. The SKU(s) new pick positions, and SKU quantity data, are sent to the WMS computer for inventory and position update. In this approach, the warehouse has a computer program to cancel customer order identifications in a printer that requires additional program expense and incurs SKU handling expenses.

Special Order Handling

Based on the order wave and SKUs, the WMS computer allocates SKUs and directs the warehouse computer (or employee) to move SKUs from storage positions to pick positions and pick activity. SKUs, pick positions, and SKU quantities are sent to the WMS computer for inventory and position update. Based on freight delivery company sort time or company dispatch time from the warehouse to the freight company terminal, the warehouse establishes time schedules to ensure that the order/delivery cycle is maintained per established customer service standards. For example, the time scale for a warehouse that operates from 6:00 a.m. to 8:00 p.m., the last order would be 4:00 p.m., the pick and manifest/load goes to the delivery or freight forwarder by 7:00 p.m., and delivery to the customer's delivery location takes place the next day or within 24 hours.

A special order is received and accepted by the company after the host computer has started to process on-time orders. After the host computer has started to process orders, it is difficult to insert a special order into the order/delivery process. When the host computer has processed the orders, the orders are sent to the WMS computer, which sends all orders to the warehouse computer for the creation of order wave plan. Based on the wave, the WMS computer allocates the SKU(s) and sends move transactions to the warehouse. After the SKU move or pick-line setup is complete (or for an order wave, a fixed pick position has been verified to have sufficient SKU quantity), the WMS computer releases orders to begin pick activity. The options for handling special orders are:

- In a company host computer or before WMS computer customer order pool transfer to a warehouse customer order wave creation;
- After a WMS program receives a completed customer order wave and a WMS computer has completed a SKU allocation and SKU move transactions sent to a warehouse, special orders are handled as a special order group that is added to a warehouse customer order wave. This requires the WMS program to accept another order in a customer order pool, add the SKUs to the existing customer order wave allocation and move transactions, or to have the warehouse staff create a separate order wave; or not allow special orders.

Special Orders Added between the Host Computer and the Warehouse Computer

To insert a special order between the host computer and the WMS computer means that a special order is included in the planned order wave or group. The host computer has a separate order identification number and associated SKU quantity; the WMS computer sends the special orders as a group with other orders to the warehouse to create the order wave. Based on the special order wave, the WMS computer SKU allocations ensure that SKUs and quantities are accurately allocated from storage positions to pick positions, the warehouse sets up a pick line and starts pick activity, and that there are no additional warehouse costs.

Some warehouses do not have order waves. After an order is checked by the host computer, it is processed, and sent to the WMS computer. The WMS computer verifies that there is sufficient SKU quantity in the pick position for the order and releases the order for the pick.

After the WMS Computer Process

After the WMS computer has sent all orders to the warehouse, the warehouse creates an order wave. Based on this order wave, the WMS computer allocates SKUs and directs the warehouse to move the SKUs from the storage position to the pick position. After the WMS computer receives verification, it releases orders to the warehouse, which begins the pick activity. If a special order is transferred from the host computer to the WMS program, it means that a WMS program sends a special order to a warehouse to create a customer order wave. This means that a special order has a separate customer order wave and WMS computer has another SKU allocation and move request that is sent to the warehouse. For a warehouse work day, it means two order waves that have a WMS program made two separate SKU allocations and sent the warehouse two separate SKU move transactions. For a warehouse, it means two separate SKU move/transfer transactions from a storage position to a pick position. The first SKU allocation is a large allocation for on-time orders; the second SKU allocation is a small allocation for special orders. Small SKU allocations mean higher cost per unit for warehouse operations and scans due to added computer time and because employees handle smaller SKU quantities for each replenishment.

No Special Orders

Not allowing special order means that orders arriving late are entered into the host computer and held till the next day for processing. This approach maintains regular cost per unit for processing and eliminates the need for special activities.

Noncustomer Order Handling

A noncustomer order is an order that does not originate with a normal business customer, but is a company request (e.g., return to vendor, charity, company store, or jobber) for a SKU withdrawal from a storage position. Prior to the withdrawal, the warehouse sends an order wave to the WMS computer. The WMS computer allocates a SKU and sends a move request to the warehouse. After the warehouse withdraws a SKU, the SKU is transferred to a special pack station. The SKU quantity is verified and matched to a company noncustomer-order request and an employee scans/reads the SKU. The scan/read activity and SKU quantity are sent to the WMS computer (which updates the inventory) and the SKU is prepared for shipment.

Storage and Customer-Order Transaction Communication

In a warehouse with a WMS program, to move or complete a WMS transaction and to accurately account for SKUs, SKU identification, position identification, and SKU quantity, scan transaction information is communicated from the warehouse activity location to the WMS computer. Scan information flow data includes the SKU and position. After completion and notification of a warehouse SKU move transaction, the WMS computer updates position status and SKU identification status and sends a SKU inventory update to the host computer. Scan transaction completion data flow can be 1) from one warehouse component to another component, which then communicates with the WMS computer; or 2) from the warehouse component directly to the WMS computer.

Warehouse Operation Communication: Component to Component

This type of warehouse communication involves two components: the component that completes SKU transactions and the component that receives SKUs. After the receiving component receives a SKU, it communicates a transaction completion to the WMS computer. The WMS computer updates SKU and position files. In this setup, the WMS program has less accountability, there will be some time delay for the WMS computer to receive and update files, the warehouse computer program might require modification and have some potential problems with inventory accuracy or control.

Warehouse Communication: Component to WMS Computer

In this communication design, one component communicates the SKU and position identification (or SKU transaction and quantity) to the WMS computer. The WMS computer is the brain of the warehouse, maintains inventory accounting, and completes inventory and position file updates. Characteristics of this design: simple tasks flow as set sequences for SKU transaction completions, with small SKU quantities for each warehouse transaction and communication, transactions are easy to complete, and communication between the warehouse and the WMS computer is direct and clear.

Vendor-SKU Delivery

The company's purchasing department sends a vendor purchase order from the host computer to the vendor, WMS computer, and warehouse receiving department. The important purchase order information includes the vendor's name, e-mail, fax and telephone numbers; SKU description, SKU and master-carton quantity and pallets; warehouse receiving department telephone, e-mail or fax numbers; purchasing department telephone, e-mail; and delivery date range.

SKU Quantity or Pack Key

The correct SKU quantity for each master carton, tote, or pallet is important for an accurately functioning warehouse. Some companies refer to a SKU pieces as a pack key. The WMS program tracks SKU quantities. At a receiving dock, order returns process station, or SKU entry station, the warehouse ensures that each SKU inventory count is accurate, is associated with an identification, and that the identification and count are entered into the WMS computer.

The design team will need to make certain that

1. Same SKU quantity for each master carton (or same master-carton quantity) is placed onto a given pallet (see Figure 3.7);
2. If there are different SKU quantities for master cartons, the warehouse can either place master cartons with the same SKU quantity on separate pallets, or the warehouse and WMS program can assign each master carton an identification (i.e., each master carton is handled as a separate SKU); and
3. If there are different SKU quantities for master cartons on given pallet, when an individual master carton is moved or transferred, an employee must locate a master carton with a SKU quantity that matches a move transaction, or the employee must transfer the first available

WAREHOUSE HANDLING UNIT	WMS ID SKU PACK KEY QUANTITY	NUMBER OF WMS IDS
SINGLE PIECE	ONE	ONE ON EACH SKU OR PIECE
SLEEVE WITH 6 PIECES	SIX	ONE ON EACH SKU OR PIECE
MASTER CARTON WITH 12 PIECES	TWELVE	ONE ON EACH SKU OR PIECE
(A) HANDLED AS A MASTER CARTON		ONE ON EACH MASTER CARTON
(B) HANDLED ON A PALLET OR SLIP SHEET		ONE ON A PALLET OR SLIP SHEET
PALLET OR SLIP SHEET WITH 50 MASTER CARTONS WITH 12 PIECES PER CARTON	SIX HUNDRED	ONE ON A PALLET OR SLIP SHEET

Figure 3.7　Pack Key and WMS Identified SKUs or Pieces

master carton that could have different master-carton SKU count. Since a WMS program suggests master carton move quantity that is based on a standard master carton SKU quantity. Master cartons with different SKU counts mean that a SKU master carton move transaction from a storage position to a pick position or pick transaction with different master carton SKU quantities has potential for a warehouse to incur SKU quantity over or short master carton pick or replenishment activity. The result is a potential problem: the WMS program may not be able to ensure that the SKU quantity for each position is correct.

SKN and SKU Identification

In a jewelry or flat-wear apparel warehouse, it is critical for the WMS program to properly identify each SKU quantity in the inventory. In receiving, storage, and pick activity, the program may have to deal with an SKN and/or SKU. An SKN factor is for flatwear and jewelry merchandise that has one style with many sizes and colors. There is one SKU for each style, size, and color. The design team needs to ensure that warehouse receiving separates each SKN into each SKU by style, size, and color as a SKU quantity in a storage/pick position.

SKU Identification Number

Each vendor-delivered SKU has an identification that uniquely identifies each SKU from the same and other vendor-delivered SKUs. The design team SKU identification number sequence options are

1. A random generated identification number. Each identification number is unique but identification labels are printed in a nonarithmetic (i.e., alpha-character) sequence. A random number table creates numbers that are printed onto each label. To create an identification number that included the date the SKU was received, the WMS program adds a date to the SKU identification inventory file (e.g., 10101, 21400, 67100);
2. Using the Julian date. Each SKU identification is printed with the Julian date or number (i.e., 1–365). As each label is printed, the next number is increased by one. WMS SKU identification number increase creates a unique SKU identification number (e.g., January 1, 2005 = 04001; January 31, 2004 = 04031); and

3. A numeric progression. Each identification number is printed as a group of digits (e.g., 0001, 0002, 0003).

Warehouse Receiving Dock Identification: Tally Sheet and Labels

A WMS tally sheet for each vendor delivery is printed for the receiving clerk. The printed tally sheet indicates all required information the receiving clerk must complete when processing a vendor delivery. After SKUs are unloaded onto the receiving dock, each SKU receives an identification label. In a pallet/master-carton warehouse, each pallet (and a predetermined master-carton quantity) receives an identification at the dock. In some companies, each master-carton quantity below a certain number receives an identification and associated SKU quantity. In a facility using a four-wheel cart design, each cart receives an identification. With an individual master-carton quantity (or single item), each master carton receives an identification. There are two options for designing identifcation label printing:

- Print on-demand. When the delivery truck arrives at the receiving dock, the clerk reviews the delivery driver's documents and enters a purchase order or advance shipping notice (ASN) into a tally sheet and label printer. The WMS program suggests a master carton ti and hi (palletize pattern). Based on the pattern or master-carton quantity, the printer prints a label number for each SKU. To minimize low receiving productivity due to a printer problem or print queue, there are at least two label or document printers; or

- Preprint. A receiving clerk refers to a receiving dock schedule for a work day's tally sheet and identification number. Based on the schedule, tally sheet, and identification number, clerk preprints a WMS tally sheet and identification label for each ASN or purchase order. Preprinted labels are placed with the preprinted tally sheet. When the delivery truck arrives at the dock, the receiving clerk already has the entire receiving document package ready. Preprinting tally sheets and identification labels improves receiving clerk productivity and ensures a constant SKU flow from the receiving area to the storage area.

Host Computer and WMS SKU Inventory Classifications

The host computer and WMS program keeps track of SKUs received from vendors or order returns. The classifications are "available for sale" or QA-approved/OK status, and "not available for sale," which can be QA hold, vendor recall, and stop sales.

Available for Sale

After vendor-delivered or order returns are approved QA "OK," SKUs are "available for sale"—in a pick position or ready for transfer to a pick line.

Not Available for Sale

In a warehouse with a WMS program, a SKU placed into a "not available for sale" status allows the receiving department (after receiving a vendor bulk SKU delivery) to clear the receiving dock and transfer each SKU to a storage position. Clearing the dock permits the receiving department to turn (complete a vendor truck receiving activity) receiving docks an increased number of times per day or to handle additional deliveries through an existing receiving dock. It also permits customer service staff to place RTV (return to vendor) SKUs in a pick position or RTS (return to stock) SKUs in a temporary hold position.

QA Hold

A receiving department constantly has SKUs being delivered from delivery vehicles into the receiving dock staging area. With a receiving clerk actual or detail count activity, SKUs are placed on the receiving dock or are sent to a detail receiving area. During detail counting, a QA sample SKU quantity is transferred from the receiving area to a holding area or position. The QA department is notified that a sample is in a holding position, but the work-load frequently delays the actual inspection. To ensure constant turn-around at the receiving docks, the WMS program designates all non-QA department inspected SKUs in a storage position as non "QA hold." (This also maintains company SKU quality standards by preventing poor quality SKU becoming available for sale.) It means that each delivered SKU receives an identification and is ready for transfer to a storage position. After the QA department inspects and approves a SKU sample, the department sends a confirming message to a receiving department. The receiving department notifies the WMS program that the SKU has been QA approved/OK and is "available for sale."

Vendor Recall

In a vendor recall, a vendor or government agency advises a company to stop selling delivered, received, and QA-department–approved SKUs and to have the SKUs returned to a vendor. The host computer and WMS program place the SKUs on "not available for sale" status. To ensure that vendor-delivered SKUs are in a warehouse storage area, the WMS program reviews the delivery records, manufacturer's lot numbers, and SKUs in storage/pick positions. If there are SKUs in positions, the WMS computer places all SKUs on "not available for sale" status. The SKU is withdrawn (as a noncustomer-order) and transferred to the shipping dock for vendor delivery.

Stop Sales

If a company receives customer complaints concerning a specific SKU, the purchasing department will have the host computer (via the WMS computer) place the SKU in "stop sale" status. The SKU is picked (as a noncustomer-order) and transferred to the dock for vendor delivery.

Order and SKU Quantity Preparation

Customer order preparation focuses on order SKU process activities. After the host computer receives and collects orders, the host computer or WMS computer processes orders according to company policies:

- Single-line/single-piece orders
- Single-line/multiple-SKU orders

- Multi-line and single- or multiple-SKU orders
- Combi-order with two SKUs each from a different pick section
- Multi-line order with multiple SKUs from one pick section
- Batched or grouped orders that have mixed customer-ordered SKUs picked as a group and per a sort concept are separated to a customer order position
- Shipping carton size and customer order age/date received by host computer, express mail, delivery zone, or other company factors

After the host computer groups orders, the customer orders and SKU quantities are sent (see Figure 3.8) to the WMS computer, which, in turn, sends this information to the warehouse order pool for wave creation. Wave creation establishes how many orders can be completed within a work day or within different periods of a day. Based on the wave, the WMS computer allocates a SKU in a storage position to complete an order. Once this occurs, the SKU will not be allocated to another order wave group. The wave groups are the warehouse area, SKU or SKU type, warehouse pick zone, date received for FIFO rotation, manufacturer lot number, priority customer, express shipper, carrier or delivery company, postal zip code, order shipping-carton size, and order type (e.g., single-line/single SKU, single-line/multiple SKUs, multi-line with single or multiple SKUs, combi multiple SKU group, COD [cash on delivery], credit, or cash).

After a SKU has been transferred to a pick position, it is scanned with its associated quantity and pick position and the scan transaction is sent to the WMS computer. At that point, the computer releases the order. Each completed order is transported (conveyor or vehicle) to a manifest scanner/reader. The manifest scanner sends the order identification to the WMS computer and the delivery company. (As an alternative, the delivery company may complete a separate order identification at the shipping dock, load conveyor, or freight company terminal.) Orders are then loaded onto a delivery company (or freight forwarder) truck for delivery. When the order arrives at the delivery location, the delivery company sends the warehouse or WMS computer a message that delivery is complete. This confirmation is then forwarded to the host computer.

Host Computer Order Acceptance

The host computer receives (or accepts) all orders. The design team and company management (see Figure 3.9) will have determined at what point each day the host computer will "cut off" orders and forward received orders to the WMS computer. (The "cut off" will allow sufficient time to complete all process activities and for the warehouse staff to complete an order wave plan.) Orders are processed on "first-in, first-out" basis. Using SKU and master-carton spatial data, the host or WMS computer determines the necessary customer shipping-carton size (or, in the case of a large order, several cartons); each customer carton is given an order identification.

WMS Computer Order Pool

In a warehouse using a WMS program, the host computer receives orders, verifies that the specified SKU is available for sale, and performs necessary activities, and forwards the orders to the WMS computer. In the WMS computer, new customer orders from the host computer and existing customer orders make up an order pool. Still in the WMS computer, a customer order pool is sent to a warehouse staff for a warehouse order wave creation plan (customer order quantity that is planned for warehouse order pick activity completion within a work day). Based on a warehouse

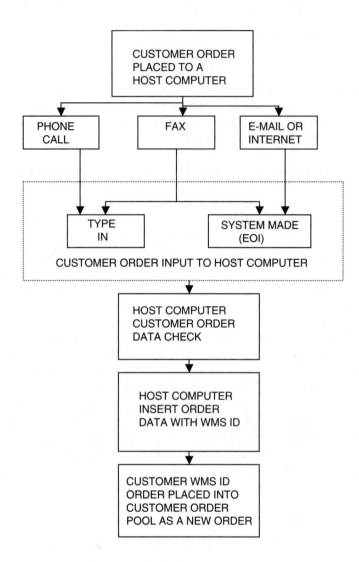

Figure 3.8 Customer Order Flow from Host Computer to WMS Identified Customer Order Pool

order wave, a WMS computer allocates order wave SKU quantity for an order wave pick activity and sends SKU move transaction messages to the warehouse.

After the warehouse staff creates an order wave in the WMS computer, a WMS computer with a customer order wave or planned to work orders depletes the customer order wave orders from the order pool. If a warehouse order wave has an order quantity less than the WMS computer order pool quantity, the WMS computer has an existing customer order pool quantity that is available for a warehouse next work day/order wave. If a warehouse created order wave quantity is equal to the WMS computer order pool quantity, the WMS computer has a zero customer order pool quantity for a warehouse next work day/order wave.

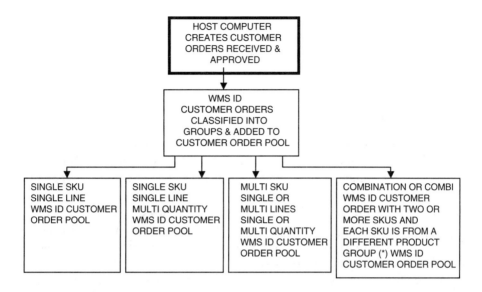

Figure 3.9   Customer Order Classification

Order-Wave Creation

Each warehouse establishes an allocation priority as part of the order wave. To make an order wave for a warehouse pick design, based on an order number, customer order SKU quantity and warehouse budgeted employee productivity rates, a warehouse wave planner adds each customer order wave component to the base until a total customer order wave customer order number and customer order SKU quantity equal to an employee number and budgeted employee productivity. If the number of orders and the quantities ordered exceed the warehouse employee budgeted time and productivity, the pick design can carry over the order base to the next work day or order wave.

Examples of order wave components are:

- Customer order age or date host computer received the order
- Express orders
- Orders for special or promotion SKUs
- Single-line single SKU orders
- Single-line multiple SKU orders
- Multi-line mutli-piece
- SKU group combination
- Special handling
- By shipper

- Distinguish between different countries your operation has to deliver through different customs and pick-up for different country deliver
- Other company criteria

Order-Wave Planning

An order wave is the maximum number of orders out of a given order pool that a warehouse can effectively and efficiently handle within a given time period. It is based on predetermined operational parameters (e.g., employee productivity, existing customer order carry-over and company carry-over procedures, customer order age, express customer order, customer order carton size, or zip code). For example, the time periods are the predetermined work-day hours. The number of orders waves per work-day may have a minimum of one or be defined by other parameters. Some warehouses are designed to receive orders every two hours or at specific time slots, which are then sent to warehouse staff to create an order wave.

After the warehouse staff creates an order wave in the WMS computer, the computer allocates SKUs transactions from storage positions to pick positions. After the computer is notified that SKUs have been scanned at a position, the computer releases the order wave to the pick area. Warehouse order wave plan options are:

- Warehouse area
- SKU or SKU type
- Warehouse pick zone
- Date received for FIFO rotation
- Manufacturer lot number
- Priority customer
- Express shipper
- Carrier or delivery company
- Postal zip code
- Shipping-carton size
- Order type (e.g., single-line/single SKU, single-line/multiple SKUs, multi-line with single or multiple SKUs, combi or multiple SKU group, COD, or credit or cash).

Order-Wave Characteristics

An order wave may be fixed or continuous, as determined by the design team.

Continuous Order Wave Flow

A continuous customer order wave is basically a nonstop order wave in which the WMS computer provides orders on a continuous flow to the warehouse. In a warehouse using a continuous flow design does not allow for an opportunity to profile, clean up, or reorganize pick positions. A continuous flow approach has customer order Wave 1 or Work Day 1 in a pick zone "C" SKU movers are adjacent to customer order Wave 2 or Day 2 "A" SKU movers. This SKU arrangement creates lower picker productivity due to increased walk distance between two picks. To assure "A" SKU movers are in adjacent pick positions you pick clean pick positions with a residual "C" moving SKU inventory. This approach requires minimal labor to reorganize a pick line, and additional time to profile a pick line.

Fixed Order Wave Flow

In a fixed order wave flow, the WMS computer groups orders with predetermined customer order numbers. An order wave number is based on order wave parameters (e.g., employee productivity, customer order age). In a fixed flow design, the warehouse is expected to complete all orders (or order waves) within a predetermined time period as well as pick-line clean-up or reorganization.

Order Wave: Ensuring Optimal Warehouse Performance

One of the objectives of an order fulfillment warehouse with a WMS program is to provide accurate customer service within an order/delivery cycle time period and at the company's desired cost per unit. The five steps for achieving this objectives are:

1. Complete order wave size activity, which determines the number of orders per wave;
2. Determine the number of orders per wave and what customer order types are included in an order wave;
3. SKU handling;
4. Order processing (i.e., pick, pack, manifest, and ship orders); and
5. Cleaning and/or reorganization of pick positions.

Order Numbers and Totes

In a warehouse with a WMS program using a warehouse tote as an order tote, a picker transfers picked SKUs from a pick position into the tote. The tote is moved to the check/pack station. The objectives of using a tote are:

- It provides a secure in-house container that ensures that picked SKUs arrive at the next warehouse activity station;
- It provides an exterior surface that permits bar-code scanner or RF tag reader to receive a signal from the tote identification;
- It is designed with features that permit an employee (or machine) to handle an empty or full tote and transfer picked SKUs between a tote and employee (or machine) pick position or work station.

A warehouse tote is manufactured from hardened plastic, corrugated plastic, or corrugated cardboard. The tote's exterior dimensions match the warehouse's pick/pack transport design; the interior dimensions are designed to hold SKUs. As a tote enters the warehouse pick design, the tote's identification travels past a bar-code/RF tag reader, which sends the identification to the warehouse computer. The warehouse computer associates the tote identification with one or more orders. This association permits the warehouse to complete order pick, check, weigh, and pack transactions. The design team may create a design with one order per tote or multiple orders. (If the warehouse uses totes as order delivery containers, one customer order per tote is preferred.)

CUSTOMER ORDER PICK CARTON OR TOTE	CUSTOMER ORDER VESSEL PICK CARTON OR TOTE WMS OR WAREHOUSE IDENTIFICATION	WMS ID CUSTOMER ORDERS PER CARTON/TOTE
CARTON/TOTE ID = AB100 WMS ID CUSTOMER ORDER = CC900 WITH 2 WMS ID SKUS OR 2 PIECES	ONE CUSTOMER ORDER PICK CARTON OR TOTE WMS OR WAREHOUSE IDENTIFICATION AB100	ONE WMS ID CUSTOMER ORDER CC900 WITH 2 WMS ID SKUS OR 2 PIECES

CARTON/TOTE ID = AB100
 	
WMS ID CUSTOMER ORDERS
CC901 WITH 3 WMS ID SKUS
  AND 5 PIECES
CC902 WITH 3 WMS ID SKUS
  AND 5 PIECES
CC903 WITH 3 WMS ID SKUS
  AND 5 PIECES
	ONE CUSTOMER ORDER PICK CARTON OR TOTE WMS OR WAREHOUSE IDENTIFICATION AB100	THREE WMS ID CUSTOMER ORDERS CC901 WITH 1 WMS ID SKU WITH 3 PIECES, CC902 WITH 2 WMS ID SKUS WITH 6 PIECES AND CC903 WITH 3 WMS ID SKUS WITH 9 PIECES

Figure 3.10   Customer Order Number per Tote or Carton

Multiple Orders per Tote

As a tote enters a warehouse pick line, a bar-code scanner/RF tag reader sends the tote identification to the warehouse computer. The computer associates two or more orders with the tote. As the tote moves through a pick design, the picker (or pick machine) is instructed to pick (or release) an order for two or more SKUs from a pick position into the tote. This approach features

- Fewer pick tote numbers on a warehouse pick or in-house transport design;
- Order pick instructions are for two or more or multiple SKU orders;
- Increased manual picker pick errors;
- A larger pack station;
- At a pack station, for a packer to complete a quantity picked SKU check activity with a pre-printed or printed on-demand customer order packing slip or a PC (personal computer) to flip or show multiple customer order packing slips has
- Potential pack errors;
- A more complex WMS program or warehouse computer program is necessary to group multiple orders in one tote and to ensure accurate packing slip presentation.

One Order per Tote

In this design, the tote enters the pick line and a bar-code scanner/RF tag reader sends the tote identification to a warehouse computer. The warehouse computer associates one customer order with the tote. As the tote moves through the pick design, the picker (or pick machine) is directed to pick (or release) a SKU from a pick position into the tote. This approach features:

- More totes on the in-house transport. With a high-volume operation, this could require a second pick line or shift;
- Faster conveyor speeds or a second warehouse shift;
- Simple pick instructions;
- Fewer manual picker errors;
- Simple pack station activity and a smaller pack table;
- It uses a SKU picked quantity pick check activity;
- Fewer pack errors;
- Less complex computer program.

Order Identification Sequence

After a warehouse with a WMS program design team has determined that each customer order uses either a host or WMS computer customer order identification or associate a host or WMS computer customer order identification to a warehouse customer order identification, the design team next customer order identification option is to determine customer order identification sequence. Customer order identification sequence either use a host or WMS computer customer order identification or warehouse operation customer order identification.

The purposes of customer order are to 1) permit the host computer customer order identification to uniquely or discreetly identify one customer order from other customer orders that allows customer order recorded and tracked in a company; 2) to associate a customer order identification with customer order SKUs or pieces; 3) to ensure that SKUs are picked and assembled to comply with a customer order; and 4) to have a simple customer order identification pick and check activities that has each customer order identified tote/carton progressively move past pick positions.

Customer order identification sequence options are

1. A random generated number that has a host or WMS computer program refer to a random number file. A random number file is created by a computer and each number printed onto a customer order identification label is discreet. A discreet number is required to uniquely identify each customer order identification in an order fulfillment operation. A random number generated four customer order identification (e.g., 101010, 239499, 728549, 066837);

2. A random number generated customer order identification approach has a large number quantity, requires a separate computer program, customer order identification requires an alpha characters or numeric digits that uniquely identifies each customer order and difficult to have customer order identifications that have an arithmetic or orderly progression. To provide a customer order identification with a Julian date and random generated number, each customer order identification required front digits are random generated numbers that are printed as a customer order identification number. As required by a host or WMS computer program customer order identification digit number, zeros are added or printed onto a label face. Each customer order identification is a generated number (e.g., January 10, 2006 with four customer order identifications = 1106010, 0206010, 2306010, 4006010);

3. A Julian date with a random number generated customer order identification approach has a large number quantity, requires a separate computer program, customer order identification requires numeric digits that uniquely identifies each customer order and customer order identifications that have an arithmetic or orderly progression Julian date and lowest number uses a Julian date and number arithmetic sequence. If required to create a number for each year, two additional digits are used to identify the year (e.g., for January 10, 2006,

the first customer order identification = 06010; the second customer order identification = 06011). To provide a customer order identification, as each customer order identification is printed, the next customer order identification number is increased by one. As required by a host or WMS computer program customer order identification digit number, zeros are added or printed onto the label face. Each customer order identification is a generated number (e.g., for January 10, 2006 with four customer order identifications = 06010, 06011, 06012, 06013). A Julian date with a random number generated customer order identification approach has a large number quantity, requires a separate computer program, customer order identification requires numeric digits that uniquely identifies each customer order and customer order identifications that have an arithmetic or orderly progression;

4. Arithmetic progression from lowest number that is sequenced by a lowest number has a host or WMS computer program that prints each customer order identification number from a lowest number to a highest number. With sufficient digit or number positions, the first customer order identification number starts with "1" and each customer order identification number is increased by one. With this customer order identification print sequence, each number printed onto a customer order identification label is discreet. Discreet numbers uniquely identify each customer order in an order fulfillment design (e.g., 000001, 000002, 000003, 000004). An arithmetic number progression from a lowest numbered customer order identification approach has a unlimited number quantity, separate computer program, customer order identification uses alpha characters or numeric digits that uniquely identifies each customer order and customer order identifications that have an arithmetic progression.

In-House Transport

The SKU's identification is a signal to the in-house transport that the SKU is ready to be moved to a storage position. The in-house transport (manual or automatic) moves the SKU from the receiving dock to a drop point/location or storage position. With automatic transport, bar-code scanners/RF tag readers along the transport path update the computer as the SKU travels to the drop point/location or storage position.

Depositing an Identification SKU into a Position

When a SKU is on the in-house transport carrier surface, an employee, employee controlled fork-lift or AS/RS crane travels to a vacate storage position. Again, each inbound SKU travels past a bar-code scanner/RF tag reader that updates the SKU's movement. All inbound SKUs travel past a size and weight station to verify that each SKU's physical characteristics match design parameters.

In an employee directed SKU put-away/deposit design, an employee randomly selects a storage position. A forklift truck driver scans the SKU identification and storage position. Scan transactions are sent to the WMS computer, which updates the inventory. In a warehouse using an AS/RS crane or computer-directed storage deposit design, the storage strategy determines the storage position, the AS/RS crane design communicates the completion of a storage transaction; the WMS computer updates inventory files regarding the SKU and it's position.

SKU Storage Transaction Files: Entry and Storage

As a warehouse employee, employee-controlled forklift truck, or an AS/RS crane completes a pallet, master carton or single SKU put-away transaction, the SKU and storage/pick position identifications are scanned (with a quantity) and sent to the computer. The SKU quantity and position status is updated in WMS inventory files. In WMS inventory files and especially for a dated SKU that requires a FIFO rotation, with a vendor delivery and customer order returns for one SKU, a WMS program tracks an oldest SKU as next SKU picked for a customer order. The file entry options (by SKU) are:

- With a lowest identification number as an oldest SKU transaction completed and entered into the WMS inventory storage files. The WMS computer uses a SKU identification label number to determine the oldest SKU. The lowest SKU number is identified as the oldest SKU in the inventory files.To have an effective SKU age in the inventory files, the SKU identification uses (a) Julian date with a progressive SKU identification number, (b) progressive SKU identification number, or (c) random SKU identification number, but a date is entered with an identification number into the inventory files;
- A SKU identification number is created when SKU is unloaded/received from a vendor delivery truck. A receiving clerk places an identification label onto each SKU. An employee-controlled forklift truck completes the deposit transaction by placing the SKU into a storage position and scanning the identification and storage position. The scans and SKU quantity are sent to the WMS computer, which updates the SKU storage position status in the inventory files;
- By a SKU put-away transaction sequence as the first SKU transaction completed and entered into the inventory files as the oldest SKU. The forklift truck driver scans a SKU identification, places the SKU into a storage position, and then scans the storage position. The scan transactions and SKU quantities are sent to the WMS computer. The computer updates the SKU storage position status in the inventory files.

Storage Area Reorganization Strategies

For a warehouse designed to use a forklift truck or AS/RS with cartons or pallets, with a one- or two-shift order fulfillment operation, and advanced order SKU demand knowledge (i.e., host computer transfer SKU demand), there are several possible SKU reorganization strategies. Warehouse reorganization occurs off-shift. The WMS computer directs the forklift trucks or AS/RS cranes to move a SKU from one storage position to another. (Scans and SKU quantities are updated in WMS computer files.) The design team SKU reorganization strategy is focused on high-volume. During low volume time periods, there is an opportunity to reorganize obsolete ("C" or "D") SKUs or noncustomer-order related SKUs. In a reorganization strategy, priority warehouse positions are located at a storage aisle first position to a position that is three-quarters from the first position or aisle front.

The reorganization strategy for high-volume SKUs is built around a put-away strategy to have SKUs remain in existing storage positions. In this strategy, the warehouse forklift truck or AS/RS crane completes a deposit transaction to the storage position. During an off-shift, the SKU remains in the initial storage position. Upon receipt of an order, the computer directs the warehouse to move the SKU to another storage position. The SKU identification and new storage position are sent to the computer for update. This approach means quicker travel time from the storage position to the P/D station.

For high-volume SKUs in a warehouse where only one aisle has a high SKU quantity, the reorganization strategy option is to spread SKUs to other aisles during off shifts. The first step is to make the initial SKU deposit transaction to a vacant storage position. The host computer and management team will have estimated (or has exact) SKU sales volume (this occurs during a nonproductive shift). Based on projected sales data, the WMS computer and warehouse reviews SKUs storage positions in each aisle. If there is a high number of SKU transactions in one aisle, the WMS computer directs the warehouse move SKU transactions to aisles with fewer transactions. A SKU relocation or move transaction to an aisle, the WMS and warehouse computers ensure that anticipated AS/RS crane SKU withdrawal transactions for customer orders per aisle are within an AS/RS crane design transaction number.

The option is for high-volume SKUs in warehouses with preplanned vacant storage positions in aisle front storage positions. To move high-volume SKUs from an initial deposit aisle (middle or rear) position to an aisle vacant front storage position, there are three steps.

1. During a regular put-away activity, the WMS computer keeps the front two or three storage positions in each aisle vacant.
2. The WMS computer directs the employees to deposit high-volume SKUs to vacant storage positions.
3. During a nonproductive shift, the WMS computer has estimated sales volume for high-volume SKUs. Based on the projected sales data, the WMS computer sends a message to a warehouse to direct each aisle AS/RS crane of forklift truck to complete SKU move or relocation transaction.

Each SKU move transaction moves an order wave (or next work day high-volume SKU) from an initial storage position to vacant front two or three storage positions. When compared to other reorganization strategies, this approach decreases a forklift truck or AS/RS crane travel time and increases the number of AS/RS crane storage transactions.

For "C" or "D" SKUs or noncustomer-order related SKUs with preplanned vacant storage positions from a rear aisle to a three-quarter aisle, the reorganization design has three steps.

1. During a regular put-away activity, a WMS program and warehouse computer in each aisle keeps an aisle last three-quarter positions vacant.
2. The WMS computer directs "C" or "D" SKUs or noncustomer-order related SKUs to be deposited in vacant storage positions.
3. On a nonproductive shift, the WMS computer has estimated "C" or "D" moving SKUs or noncustomer-order related SKUs. Based on the projected sales data, the WMS computer sends a message to the warehouse to direct each aisle AS/RS crane of forklift truck to complete the move or relocation transaction.

Each transaction moves "C" or "D" SKUs or noncustomer-order related SKUs from an initial storage position to an aisle last three-quarter vacant positions. Having 'A' moving SKUs in an aisle front positions, decreases forklift truck or AS/RS crane travel time and increases the number of storage transactions.

SKU Rotation

SKU rotation is dictated by the SKU life cycle. The purchase department and the vendor indicate the SKUs that require a specific rotation. There are two SKU rotation options. First, there is a FIFO rotation. In a SKU FIFO (First-In, First-Out) rotation design, a SKU that is received first in the warehouse is withdrawn first from the inventory or storage position. A FIFO rotation indicates that a SKU has a predetermined life (or time limit) before it spoils. After a specific date and if a SKU is not withdrawn from a storage position for orders, the SKU is placed in a "not available for sale" status. As each SKU is received into a warehouse, it is given a date entered that is entered into the inventory. As the computer receives orders for a SKU, the computer directs that the oldest SKU is withdrawn first.

Second, there is a LIFO (Last In, First Out) SKU rotation. A SKU that is received last is withdrawn first from inventory or a storage position. A LIFO SKU does not have a specific shelf life and does not require a WMS computer to track the age of the SKUs.

Manufacturer Lot Numbers

A SKU manufacturer lot number is dictated by SKU type and the company's desire to track specific SKUs. The purchasing department and vendor ensure that each SKU has a manufacturer lot number. As a SKU is received at a facility and receives an identification, a manufacturer lot number is entered as part of the identification. If there is manufacturer recall or "stop sell" notice for a SKU, the computer lot number ensures accurate access to a SKU that potentially requires additional positions. If the warehouse needs to register a customer who has received a lot or serial number, it is a complex process that requires a complex computer program

SKU-Identification Sequence in the Inventory Files

After a receiving clerk attaches an identification to a SKU, a clerk scans the SKU identification, enters a quantity into the computer inventory files, and sends the data to the computer. The computer files associate the SKU with a quantity and tracks the identifier and quantity as it flows through the storage/pick design. With a SKU that has a shelf life or has a FIFO, lot, or serial number rotation, the data ensures proper rotation and the computer ensures that the forklift truck or AS/RS crane has access to an assigned SKU. The withdrawal sequence options are by:

1. Oldest SKU as a first identification label scanned at the receiving dock.
2. Lowest SKU identification number.
3. Julian date and lowest identification number.

SKU Storage Characteristics

SKU physical characteristics determine environmental SKU storage characteristics. Physical storage characteristics include pallet, master carton, single pieces in a tote or container, temperature sensitive, high value, toxic, edible, hazardous, and flammable. The design team ensures that each SKU is assigned to its proper storage position within a warehouse storage area or aisle. To assist in a proper SKU movement from the receiving dock to the proper storage area, each storage area is included in the WMS SKU identification.

SKU Put-Away/Deposit Strategies or Philosophies

The warehouse's put-away or deposit strategy, storage philosophy, or principle for positions are factors that determine transaction equipment and storage positions in the warehouse. The warehouse storage area is an important area in a facility. It occupies the largest area (square feet) and contains the highest inventory value. SKU deposit strategy or storage philosophy options are

SKU popularity or Pareto's Law (The 80/20 rule)
ABC theory
unload-and-load ratio
round-robin
family group or kit
pallet, carton, or GOH height
temperature sensitive
security
toxic and nonedible
flammable
power in one aisle
power to the front
SKU inventory digit number
SKU rotation

SKU Popularity—Pareto's Law (The 80/20 Rule)

A warehouse storage design based on a SKU popularity has a SKU allocation to a storage position derived from Pareto's Law (after Vifredo Pareto, an Italian economist, 1848–1923). This law states that 80% of the wealth is held by 20% of the people. In the storage/pick industry, 80% of the volume shipped to customers is derived from 20% of the SKUs. Many studies have indicated that another 10% of the volume shipped to customers results from another 30% of the SKUs and that an additional 5% of the volume shipped to customers can be attributed to 55% of the SKUs. In recent studies, the results show that 95% of the volume shipped to customers is obtained from 55% of the SKUs. This is referred to as "Pareto's Law revisited."

ABC Theory

When a warehouse professional refers to the three zones of Pareto's Law, this refers to the ABC theory. The ABC theory states that "A" storage/pick zone positions have fast-moving SKUs deposited to aisle storage/pick positions. These SKUs are few in number and have a large inventory quantity per SKU. "B" storage/pick zone positions have medium-moving SKUs deposited to aisle storage/pick positions. These SKUs are medium in number and have a medium inventory quantity per SKU. "C" storage/pick zone positions have slow-moving SKUs deposited to aisle storage/pick positions. "C" SKUs are large in number and have a small inventory quantity per SKU.

An ABC theory increases SKU hit concentration (the SKU number that appears on an order group) and density (the number of SKUs per customer order line per aisle) and minimizes the travel time necessary for storage transaction, which is particularly useful for warehouses using AS/RS storage, employee controlled forklift truck, or manual designs.

If a warehouse has receiving and shipping docks on the front side of the facility, and SKU storage position allocation is based on a ABC theory, "A" SKUs are allocated to storage/pick positions that are at the facility front; "B" SKUs are located in an aisle middle storage positions; and "C" SKUs are located in an aisle rear storage positions. If the warehouse receiving and shipping docks are located on opposite sides of a facility, fast-moving SKUs are located according to an unload and load ratio.

Unload and Load Ratio

An unload and load ratio compares the number of trips an unload/storage employee and storage/load employee require to handle a vendor SKU truck. When an employee's unload/storage trip number equals an employee's storage/load trip number, SKUs are allocated to positions near shipping docks or any position in an aisle. When an employee's unload/storage trip number is greater that an employee's storage/loading trip number, SKUs are allocated to positions near the receiving dock. This feature reduces employees' total travel distance.

Round-Robin

A round-robin allocation attempts to spread a SKU quantity evenly over all warehouse storage aisles. With a round-robin, each AS/RS crane or forklift truck handles the same number of fast-moving SKUs. A round-robin works best in an AS/RS storage operation, but with an employee conventional forklift truck or operation, it reduces SKU hit concentration and density per aisle.

Family Group or Kit

A family group or kit allocation is dictated by a company's requirement that SKUs are allocated to a storage position with SKUs that have the same inventory classification or components to a manufacturer's final SKU. Thus, SKUs are assigned by the WMS or warehouse computer to specific storage/pick positions in a zone or aisle. This approach requires that the warehouse storage area be designed to handle SKUs with similar dimensions, weights, or final SKU components in a retail store aisle; normal, refrigerated, or freezer storage conditions; high security, separation of toxic from nontoxic, separation of edible from nonedible, and flammable materials: and that non-stackable SKUs are stacked on a special storage or a different pallet size.

Pallet or Master Carton Height

The design team SKU pallet height options are either a one-pallet or master-carton height that has all storage positions set at the same height; or two-pallet or master-carton heights that has both short and tall storage positions. A pallet or master-carton height design is based on the pallet or master-carton height as it enters the warehouse storage area. A two-pallet or master-carton height design is designed to handle short pallets or master cartons that result from a purchase order quantity that has less than full pallets or master cartons returned from a warehouse. In an AS/RS facility, having short pallets or master cartons openings on lower levels improves structural strength. After storage rack elevations are installed in the warehouse storage area with fire-sprinklers, it is difficult to change the elevation of a pallet or master-carton storage position. This is especially true in an AS/RS crane operation. During an order pick transaction, half-high pallet or master-carton short positions are created; at maximum storage position utilization, a half pallet or master-carton short position number provides maximum storage space utilization. This means that all high-pallet or master-carton short positions have tall pallets or master cartons and not half-high pallets or master cartons.

A tall pallet/master carton has greatest number of SKU per pallet with the allowable maximum master-carton layers (i.e., that will not crush bottom-layer cartons). A short pallet has fewest number of SKU on a pallet/master cartons per position. When compared to a short-pallet/master-carton position, the tall-pallet/master-carton option means fewer transactions or trips; the maximum number of SKU on a forklift truck; fewer dock positions; fewer handlings; reduced potential for SKU, equipment, or building damage; and maximum position flexibility. It also increases the need to secure SKUs on a pallet. A two-position design requires the WMS program to flag a SKU for allocation to a specific position.

Temperature Sensitive

In a warehouse that does not have a temperature-controlled storage area, temperature-sensitive SKUs are allocated by the WMS program to lower storage levels. In a conventional storage design with tall racks, the highest storage positions are the warmest and the floor level positions are cooler.

Security

In a warehouse with tall-rack storage design and high-value SKUs, most restrictive storage positions are at the top level of the racks. To easily and quickly access rack positions, employees use a forklift truck, which reduces the possibilities of unauthorized access to the positions. If a warehouse does not have a high-bay storage section, one can use special cages for which only approved employees have keys, or there can be cameras focused on the entrance.

Toxic and Nonedible

In a warehouse that handles toxic and nontoxic or edible and nonedible SKUs, toxic or hazardous SKUs require a separate storage area. Many local codes require that toxic SKUs be stored in a storage area with a containment chamber and a holding tank to contain any accidental run-off. If a warehouse handles both edible and nonedible SKUs, many local codes require that nonedible SKUs have a separate storage area and that nonedible SKUs are not stored above edible SKUs. This requires the WMS program to flag a SKU for allocation to a specific position.

Flammable

In a warehouse that handles flammable SKUs, flammable SKUs require a separate storage area. Many local codes require that flammable SKUs be stored in a warehouse storage area with additional fire-sprinkler protection and barriers to prevent the uncontrolled movement of flammable SKUs. This requires the WMS program to flag a SKU for allocation to a specific position.

Golden Highway (Power in One Aisle)

The Golden Highway (or power in one aisle) is a warehouse storage/pick design in which high-volume SKUs are located in a single aisle. During pick activity, a Golden Highway design improves a picker SKU hit concentration and density.

Power to the Front

Power in the front is similar to ABC theory. In this design, high-volume SKUs are placed in aisle front storage positions, with two or three front storage positions left vacant; high-volume SKU initial placement is in the middle or rear storage position. On an off-shift the WMS program directs a forklift truck or AS/RS crane to relocate SKUs from a middle or rear storage position to a vacant aisle front storage position.

SKU Inventory Digit Number

In a warehouse using SKU inventory digit numbers, SKUs are allocated to storage aisles by the last digit (or last two digits) of the inventory number (e.g., all SKUs that have an inventory last digit of "1" are placed in aisle 1; all SKUs that have an inventory last digit of "2" are placed in aisle 2). If the warehouse receives orders with a large SKU number, SKUs with the same final digit may be allocated to several aisles. Finally, there is a vacant position number between the last two digits, which can be used for SKU expansion and warehouse position flexibility. Overall, use of SKU inventory digit numbers improves employee productivity in returns processing.

Storage Design Vehicles

A warehouse storage design vehicle has two activities: completing warehouse storage transactions to storage/pick positions and lining up scanners (e.g., facing the scanner [i.e., line-of-sight], RT tag readers) to record SKU and storage position identification. Determining what kind of vehicle should be used will be based on:

■ warehouse storage position design
■ WMS program
■ SKU classification (e.g., pallet, stacking frame, container or pallet cage; master carton; or single items)

SKU Storage Put-Away or Withdrawal Transaction Type

A SKU put-away or withdrawal storage transaction (i.e., a SKU deposit to a storage position or pick from a storage position) is done by a manually controlled forklift truck or an AS/RS crane.

Automated Storage Transaction

In a warehouse using an AS/RS crane, the WMS computer directs the crane to the selected storage position. At the storage position, the transaction is completed and the computer received updated information concerning the SKU and its storage position. One option has the WMS computer suggest a position for the SKU and the warehouse computer updates the WMS computer when the transaction is complete.

Manual Storage Transaction

In a warehouse using manually (or employee) controlled forklift truck, transaction may be manually directed. In this type of transaction, a warehouse employee or lift truck driver determines a vacant storage position. At an employee-selected storage position, the employee completes the physical transfer of the SKU, as well as scanning the SKU identification and storage position, which are sent to the WMS computer. A potential problem with this approach is that the a deposit may not follow the established storage philosophy. Thus, although a manually directed approach functions well in many warehouses, computer-suggested position is preferable in warehouses using a WMS program.

Separate Identification Label for Each SKU or Group

Each SKU classification has unique storage/pick characteristics with separate storage/pick positions within a warehouse. To facilitate a SKU class movement to the proper storage/pick area—and as a check—a unique component (e.g., digit, numeric, alpha character) in each identification label functions as a SKU classification identifier. Examples of classification identifiers are:

Pallet SKU identified by (a) random-number (e.g., 101010PLT, 239499PLT, 728549PLT, 068397PLT), (b) lowest number (e.g., 000001PLT, 000002PLT, 000003PLT, 000004PLT); (c) Julian date with the lowest number (e.g., 0104010 LT, 0204010PLT, 0304010PLT, 0404010PLT); and (d) Julian date with a random number (e.g., 1104010PLT, 0204010PLT, 2304010PLT, 4004010PLT);

Master-carton SKU identified by (a) random-number (e.g., 101010MC, 239499 MC, 728549MC, 068397MC); (b) lowest number (e.g., 000001MC, 000002MC, 000003MC, 000004MC); (c) Julian date with the lowest number (e.g., 0104010MC, 0204010MC, 0304010MC, 0404010MC); and (d) Julian date with a random number (e.g., 1104010MC, 0204010MC, 2304010MC, 4004010MC);

GOH-SKU identified by (a) random-number identification (e.g., 101010GOH, 239499GOH, 728549GOH, 068397GOH); (b) lowest number (e.g., 000001GOH, 000002GOH, 000003GOH, 000004GOH); (c) Julian date with the lowest number (e.g., 0104010GOH, 0204010GOH, 0304010GOH, 0404010GOH); and (d) Julian date with a random number (e.g., 1104010GOH, 0204010GOH, 2304010GOH, 4004010GOH);

Small-item SKU (e.g., jewelry) identified by (a) random number (e.g., 101010JW, 239499JW, 728549JW, 068397JW); (b) lowest number (e.g., 000001JW, 000002JW, 000003JW, 000004JW); (b) Julian date with the lowest number (e.g., 0104010JW, 0204010JW, 0304010JW, 0404010JW); and (c) Julian date with a random number (e.g., 1104010JW, 0204010JW, 2304010JW, 4004010JW);

Cold-temperature SKU identified by (a) random number (e.g., 101010CT, 239499CT, 728549CT, 068397CT); (b) lowest number (e.g., 000001CT, 000002CT, 000003CT, 000004CT); (c) Julian date with the lowest number (e.g., 0104010CT, 0204010CT, 0304010CT, 0404010CT); and (d) Julian date with a random number (e.g., 1104010CT, 0204010CT, 2304010CT, 4004010CT);

Hot-temperature SKU identified by (a) random number (e.g., 101010HT, 239499HT, 728549HT, 068397HT); (b) lowest number (e.g., 000001HT, 000002HT, 000003HT, 000004HT); (c) Julian date with the lowest number (e.g., 0104010HT, 0204010HT, 0304010HT, 0404010HT); and (d) Julian date with a random number (e.g., 1104010HT, 0204010HT, 2304010HT, 4004010HT).

WMS SKU Identification Sequenced in the WMS Program Files

After a receiving clerk attaches an identification to a SKU, the clerk scans the identification and enters the associated quantities into the WMS computer files. The WMS computer associates a SKU and quantities with a WMS identifier and tracks the identifier and SKU quantities as they flow through the warehouse. This becomes particularly important during an employee-directed identification withdrawal from a storage position. SKU withdrawals may be completed using the following options:

- oldest identification label or first WMS label scanned
- sequenced by lowest identification number
- by Julian date and lowest WMS label number

Picked by Identification or Total SKUs

In a single-item or master-carton warehouse (with a floor stack storage design and a WMS program) that uses a conventional forklift truck, as the pallet/carton identification is scanned, an employee enters the associated SKU quantity on a hand-held scanner. The WMS program associates the SKU quantity with the SKU identification. As the identification is scanned and transferred to a storage/pick position and scan transactions are sent to the WMS computer, the WMS program associates the identification with the SKU located in a storage/pick position. As ordered SKUs are transferred from the host computer to the WMS computer, the WMS program allocates the order quantity to an assigned SKU. When the order quantity equals a SKU quantity, the WMS program allocates a SKU quantity to an order pick. The allocation process is completed for each order quantity that equals a full or partial SKU. In a dynamic warehouse, the WMS computer allocated order quantity could equal one full pallet, one full master carton, and one SKU. To ensure accurate SKU counts or inventory, a warehouse has a less than master carton or individual SKU section for less than a full master-carton or individual SKU quantity pick transaction.

SKU Identification Options

A WMS program requires that each SKU have an identification or symbology that discreetly identifies one SKU from another SKU (see Figure 3.11). The options are:

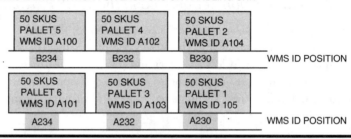

Figure 3.11 SKUs or Handling Units Per WMS Identified Position

1. The "one for each" approach, in which each pallet/master carton receives a discreet identification, and is associated with a specific SKU quantity. As the WMS program completes the order SKU allocation process, the program allocates an order for each SKU (pallet/master carton) identification quantity. For each pallet/master-carton SKU quantity, a WMS program prints or creates a warehouse storage/pick WMS move transaction for each SKU quantity. During warehouse forklift truck withdrawal, at a warehouse storage position a forklift truck driver matches a storage position and SKU identification to a warehouse storage position identification and SKU identification. Using this approach will create better forklift driver productivity because employees spend only a minimal amount of time counting master cartons.

2. The "one for all" approach, in which an entire pallet or group of master-cartons has a single identification associated with a SKU. During the withdrawal process for orders, a forklift driver will need to calculate the pallet/master-carton piece quantity and the actual pallet/master-carton number to match the transaction quantity. This approach has low forklift driver productivity, more potential errors, and limited position flexibility.

Identification or SKU Number for Each Storage/Pick Position

When designing a warehouse, the objectives are to optimize storage/pick position space utilization, ensure good employee put-away and pick productivity, and ensure an accurate inventory. There are three ways one can use SKU identifications for each storage/pick position to achieve these objectives.

1. A single SKU for each position.
2. Multiple SKUs for each position.
3. Multiple SKUs for each position but no SKU separation.

One SKU for Each Storage/Pick Position

This approach is particularly appropriate for high-volume or high-values SKUs. Placing one SKU one storage/pick position requires that the warehouse have a large storage area (see Figure 3.12). The approach provides for simple storage and pick activity, is easy to count, allows for simple tracking of SKUs, and it is easy to keep an accurate inventory. Moreover, this approach involves simple storage and order pick transactions with minimal chance of error. For a SKU put-away transaction, an employee scans the SKU identification and storage/pick position and sends the transaction and SKU quantities to the WMS computer. To complete a warehouse pick transaction for a SKU, an employee scans the SKU and enters the picked quantity into a RF device for transfer to the WMS computer.

In the following example, a pick position level is an alpha character, the pick position is digits or numbers, there are four containers per level, and each container has four subcompartments.

In bay 01 with level A:

1. first container pick position is 01A01 has SKU 10001,
2. second container pick position is 01A02 has SKU 2002,
3. third container pick position is 01A03 has SKU 3004 and
4. fourth container pick position is 01A04 has SKU 5004.

In bay 01 with level B

1. first container pick position is 01B01 has SKU 9808,
2. second container pick position is 01B02 has SKU 6098,
3. third container pick position is 01B03 has SKU 7321 and
4. fourth container pick position is 01B04 has SKU 1873.

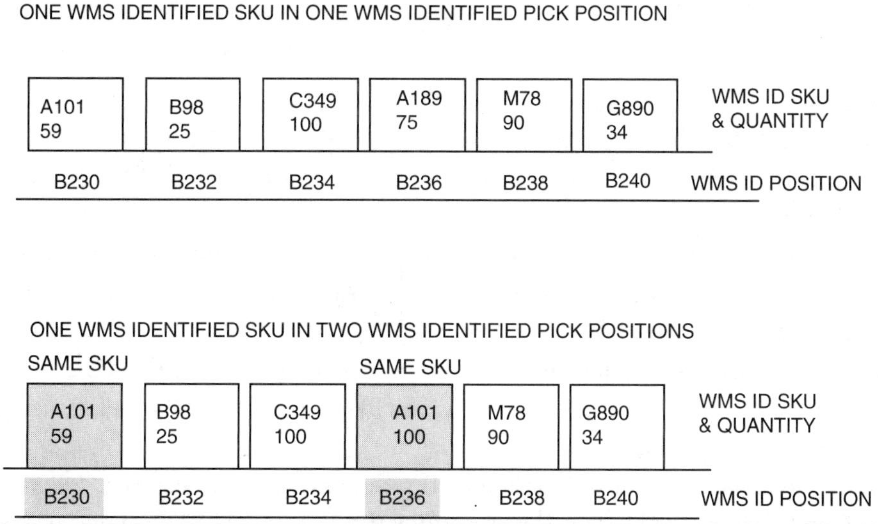

ONE WMS IDENTIFIED SKU IN ONE WMS IDENTIFIED PICK POSITION

A101 59	B98 25	C349 100	A189 75	M78 90	G890 34	WMS ID SKU & QUANTITY
B230	B232	B234	B236	B238	B240	WMS ID POSITION

ONE WMS IDENTIFIED SKU IN TWO WMS IDENTIFIED PICK POSITIONS

SAME SKU   SAME SKU

A101 59	B98 25	C349 100	A101 100	M78 90	G890 34	WMS ID SKU & QUANTITY
B230	B232	B234	B236	B238	B240	WMS ID POSITION

Figure 3.12   WMS Pick Positions for One WMS Identified SKU

Multiple SKUs for Each Location; Each SKU Location is a Separate Storage/Pick Position

If the design team elects to place multiple SKUs into a separate containers, each compartment becomes a storage/pick position. This requires that warehouse storage positions (or containers) have separators that divide the container into smaller compartments. Each compartment will have its own position identification.

Mixed SKUs in multi-compartment container features will be physically small and be low-value SKUs. This approach requires that the warehouse have a medium-size storage area. Put-aways are simple; order pick activity requires that an employee check for the correct SKU, which will mean slightly lower productivity, some additional count time, and added difficulty in tracking a SKU and maintaining an accurate inventory. The slightly lower employee productivity is offset by the consolidation of SKUs with low hit density and concentration, which permits the consolidation of SKUs with higher hit density and concentration in other pick areas, thus improving picker productivity.

In a put-away transaction, an employee scans the identification and storage/pick position, which are sent with the quantity to the WMS computer. To complete an order pick transaction, however, an employee scans a SKU, ensures that the SKU or SKU code number matches the order and enters the picked quantity into a RF device. In an efficient warehouse, the pick position identification appears on the front of the container, which faces the pick aisle, and each subcompartment identification also faces toward the front or the aisle. To simplify employee storage and pick activities, all subdivided containers should be grouped together in one warehouse pick zone or aisle. If the WMS program is designed with two digits for a pick position for each shelf level, a shelf pick position could potentially have 10 pick positions per level.

In the following example, the pick position level is an alpha character, the pick position is identified by numbers, there are four containers per level, and each container has four subcompartments.

In bay 01 with level A:

1. First container has four pick positions: 1) WMS pick position 01A01 has SKU 9080, 1090, and 2456; 2) WMS pick position 01A02 has SKU 7892, 2457, and 0973; 3) WMS pick position 01A03 has SKU 9876, 1789, and 9064; and 4) pick position 01A04 has SKU 1235, 5454, and 8889.
2. Second container has four pick positions: 1) pick position 01A05 has SKU 4563; 2) pick position 01A06 has SKU 9241; 3) pick position 01A07 has SKU 0045; and 4) pick position 01A08 has SKU 5690.
3. Third container has four pick positions: 1) pick position 01A09 has SKU 2704; 2) pick position 01A10 has SKU 8932; 3) pick position 01A11 has SKU 5689; and 4) pick position 01A12 has SKU 65643.
4. Fourth container has four pick positions: 1) pick position 01A13 has SKU 99990; 2) pick position 01A14 has SKU 1119; 3) pick position 01A15 has SKU 2232; and 4) pick position 01A16 has SKU 4445.

In bay 01 with level B:

1. First container has four pick positions: 1) pick position P01B01 has SKU 6667; 2) pick position 01B02 has SKU 7779; 3) pick position 01B03 has SKU 8880; and 4) pick position 01B04 has SKU 1121.
2. Second container has four pick positions: 1) pick position 01B05 has SKU 6767; 2) pick position 01B06 has SKU 0019; 3) pick position 01B07 has SKU 4587; and 4) pick position 01B08 has SKU 3567.
3. Third container has four pick positions: 1) pick position 01B09 has SKU 9432; 2) pick position 01B10 has SKU 2323; 3) pick position 01B11 has SKU 5656; and 4) pick position 01B12 has SKU 0505.
4. Fourth container has four pick positions: 1) pick position 01B13 has SKU 7732; 2) pick position 01B14 has SKU 2020; 3) pick position 01B15 has SKU 8989; and 4) pick position 01B16 has SKU 5555.

Mixed SKUs for One Storage/Pick Location; No SKU Separation

In a storage design in which mixed SKUs are placed into one storage/pick position with no position or interior container separation, a warehouse put-away employee places several SKUs into one storage/pick position and scans each SKU to one position. The scan information is sent to the WMS computer to update inventory files. This design requires a warehouse with a medium-sized area. It features simple SKU put-aways, but slow order pick activity. It is difficult to count SKU pieces, difficult to track SKUs, and has the potential for inaccurate inventory records.

Pick-to-Light, Sort-to-Light, or Automatic Pick Machine

In a warehouse using pick-to-light, sort-to-light, or automatic pick machine design with a WMS program, the WMS computer indicates warehouse orders and associated SKUs. A warehouse ensures SKUs are transferred or moved from a storage position to a pick position. A pick position can be a pallet flow lane, carton flow lane static shelf, mobile cart, sort-to-light, or automatic pick sleeve/lane position. With an automatic pick machine, SKU replenishment is made from a ready-reserve position to an automatic pick machine pick position. After a warehouse pick-line setup or replenishment, employee sends scan transactions and quantities to the WMS computer, the WMS computer transfers the order to an automatic pick machine computer, which picks or releases the order quantity.

To complete an order from a pick-to-light or sort-to-light position, the WMS computer sends SKU move transactions (based on the order wave) to the warehouse. After a SKU is scanned into a pick-to-light pick position or sort-to-light travel path, scan transactions and quantities are sent to the WMS computer to update inventory files. Orders and associated SKUs are then released to a warehouse. A warehouse tote identification is associated with an order identification. As the tote/carton travels past a pick-to-light position, the warehouse activates a pick-to-light display that indicates the order piece quantity. A picker presses the pick-to-light pick button or completes a pick transaction for one piece. A pressed button or break laser beam on a pick position front decreases the SKU pick quantity by one; the pick-to-light display screen is depleted by one. If the next pick transaction is for the same SKU, the pick-to-light display shows the pick quantity and the picker repeats the pick activity. If the next pick is for a different SKU, the pick-to-light display shows "pick completed" and a picker moves the tote/carton to the next active pick-to-light position.

With an automatic pick machine, the picked SKU is transferred from a pick position to a tote/carton or is placed between two cleats on a belt conveyor travel path. With a sort-to-light design, as the SKU arrives at a pick station, the display screen shows the total SKU quantity for pick station orders. A picker removes the total pick quantity from the tote/carton. For each SKU order, each order at the sort-to-light position is illuminated to show the pick quantity. The picker transfers the SKU into a container, and then presses the sort-to-light button. The procedures that follow are the same with the pick-to-light design.

There are two options for recording depleted SKUs: the inventory update can be done as part of a pick transaction, or a separate scan transaction can be done at the check/pack station.

Picked SKU Depleted by an Order Pick Transaction

A SKU depletion by pick transaction will send the pick transaction from a warehouse to the WMS computer. Each pick transaction reduces pick position SKU quantity by one SKU and is a one-step process. If an order has two-SKU pick quantity, the automatic pick machine releases one SKU quantity and releases another, and the WMS computer depletes one SKU per tranasction. A picker ensures that the pick transaction and pick button activity (or automatic pick machine impulse) is for one SKU. This approach features good communication between the warehouse and the WMS computer, accurate pick position replenishment, and accurate pick transactions for orders. The design means that a picker will not have over-, under-, or wrong picks, no additional scan station is necessary, or additional computer program cost.

Order SKU Depleted by a Separate Scan Transaction

A warehouse in which SKUs depleted by a separate scan transaction is using a two-step process for pick and scan transactions. At a pick position, a picker completes the pick transaction into a tote/carton. The tote/carton is transported to the check/pack station, where a checker or packer scans each picked SKU. Scan transactions are sent to the WMS computer to reduce the pick position SKU quantity by the amount of the order. This design features are clear communications between the warehouse check/pack station and the WMS computer. At a separate station, order checker or packer scans each SKU that is considered a picked SKU check activity. The features are: additional scanners/readers and floor area, an additional warehouse activity and additional scan transactions that are sent to the WMS computer.

SKU Withdrawal Activity

Based on a total SKU quantity of a customer order wave plan, the WMS computer allocates SKU quantities from storage positions and sends SKU move or transfer transaction to the warehouse pick. In a warehouse, each SKU quantity is physically transferred and scanned to pick positions for orders. SKU quantities are rounded up or down to a full master-carton or pallet SKU container. After a WMS program allocates SKU quantities, the WMS computer sends a SKU move transaction to a warehouse. A warehouse employee, employee controlled forklift truck or AS/RS crane completes a SKU withdrawal from a specific storage position.

Master Carton or Pallet AS/RS Crane Transfer or Delivery Locations

In a warehouse designed with an AS/RS crane, the crane (a computer-controlled forklift truck) takes picked SKU to a delivery (or out-feed) station. The delivery station ensures that withdrawn SKUs are transferred onto the warehouse travel path. Warehouses can also be designed with delivery stations at the end of each aisle or with multiple stations.

Delivery Station at an Aisle End

With a single delivery station at the end of an aisle, cartons/pallets travel on a conveyor travel path from the storage area to the pick area. SKUs are delivered to the pick area on a first-on, first-delivered basis that does not match order demand on a pick line. In this design—based on a random SKU discharge—there is the potential for high-volume SKUs mixed with low- or medium-volume SKUs.

Multiple Delivery Stations

With multiple delivery stations at the ends of aisles, cartons/pallets travel on multiple travel paths from the storage area to the pick area. A multi-level warehouse can have conveyor paths on each floor; a single-floor warehouse can use multiple-level or stacked travel paths. With multiple conveyor travel paths, the highest volume SKUs travel on one travel path whereas medium- or low-volume SKUs travel on other paths. With the design, there is a constant flow of high-volume SKUs that matches the order demand on pick lines.

SKU Position Priority

For a small-item warehouse to have a constant order flow, budgeted SKU pick position replenishment, picker productivity, and on-time customer service, SKUs need to flow on-time from storage positions to pick positions or pack stations. SKU position priority options are:

- SKU transfer for (a) all ordered SKUs from a storage area to a pick area or (b) a predetermined SKU quantity, based on a minimum and maximum pick position capacity, to transfer SKUs from a storage position to a pick position;
- WMS identification on each SKU position as (a) pick position, (b) ready-reserve position in a pick area, and (c) remote reserve position in a storage or pick area.

To complete orders, SKU transfer options

- All SKU pieces are transferred from a storage area to a pick area; or
- For a predetermined order quantity, based on minimum and maximum pick position capacity, to transfer specific SKU quantity from a storage area to a pick position or ready-reserve position (discussed above).

Pick Position

A pick position is the most critical position if the warehouse is to have on-time and accurate SKU pick completion and high picker productivity. Each pick position is located along the warehouse pick line and faces the pick aisle (or pick machine) and the take-away travel path. Each pick position is entered into the WMS computer files and includes length, width, and height of each position. To complete a pick line setup or replenishment transaction, an employee scans the SKU and pick position identification and enters the SKU quantity into a scanner. Scan transactions and SKU quantity are sent to the WMS computer. The WMS computer updates the SKU quantity and pick position status. A pick position holds a SKU quantity that is in a WMS inventory files and is a SKU quantity that is available for orders. The WMS computer allocates SKUs for orders. A SKU quantity in a pick position is a SKU quantity that is available for orders. In a standard shelf, hand stacked decked pallet rack, carousel bin, automatic machine pick sleeve, or lane or case flow rack lane, a pick position SKU quantity is a master carton or captive tote capacity that is allocated to a pick position. In a pallet warehouse operation, a SKU storage position is an order SKU pick position.

As SKUs are picked to complete orders, each completed pick transaction depletes a pick position quantity. From all picks, a WMS program creates SKU replenishment transaction for SKU quantity from a storage or ready-reserve position to a pick position.

Ready-Reserve Position

A ready-reserve pick position is used in manual, mechanized, or automatic master-carton or small-item pick warehouses. A ready-reserve position is located in a pick area that is behind, above, or below a pick position. Each ready-reserve position has an identification. Ready-reserve positions accept all SKU quantities (pick position setup or replenishment) that do not fit into a pick position. A ready-reserve position serves as a buffer storage location (i.e., between a storage area and a pick area), and it ensures the lowest necessary time to maintain minimum SKU quantity in a pick area. A ready-reserve position also compensates for a SKU/master-carton and position dimensional error or a master carton that does not fit into a pick position

After SKUs are transferred from a storage position to a pick area, a pick-line setup or replenishment employee scans and transfers a SKU quantity into a pick position. If there are extra SKUs, they are scanned and transferred to a ready-reserve position. Scan transactions and SKU quantity are sent to the WMS computer for inventory update.

During order pick activity, when pick position inventory drops below a predetermined SKU quantity, the WMS program suggests that a SKU quantity be transferred from a reserve position to a pick position.

In a warehouse using standard shelves, hand-stacked decked pallet racks, or carousel picks, ready-reserve positions are extra pick positions and are placed in difficult-to-reach or pick positions (e.g., top or bottom pick position levels). In a warehouse using a carton flow rack pick design, ready-reserve positions are placed on frame top members or below bottom level flow lanes. In a warehouse using standard shelves, hand-stacked decked pallet racks, carousel, or automatic pick design, ready-reserve positions are placed behind pick positions. Additional master-carton or pallet ready-reserve positions are parallel or perpendicular to the replenishment aisle.

Remote-Reserve Position

A remote-reserve position is a SKU storage position located adjacent to a pick area and houses a main or large SKU inventory quantity. Each remote reserve position has an identification. During replenishment transactions, SKUs are sent to storage or ready-reserve positions.

Pick-Line Profile Frequency

A pick-line profile allocates SKUs to pick positions. SKU rotation determines the pick-line profile frequency. Profile options are historical sales, or the daily sale or order wave.

Historical Sales Volume Pick-Line Profile

A warehouse using a historical sales volume pick-line profile will assign a SKU to a pick position based on past sales performance (plus other factors). This approach has the following features:

1. A SKU is allocated, assigned, or profiled to a pick position on a more permanent basis.
2. SKU is allocated for at least one week, month, or a company-selected duration in which the SKU remains in a pick position for a longer period.
3. Pick line SKUs in "A" moving pick positions are not rotated or fewer reorganizations to other moving pick positions
4. The WMS computer creates SKU replenishment or move transactions to a pick position more frequently that is at least two times per customer order wave.
5. It is easier to forecast picker productivity.

Day-by-Day Pick-Line Profile

A day-by-day pick-line profile is based on SKU demand for each work-day or order wave. For each work-day new SKUs are profiled, allocated, or assigned to a pick-line pick position. A profile could change by day, season, by the introduction of a new SKU, or by a new SKU generation. A day-by-day profile design features:

- The pick-line profile is changed each work-day, order wave, or more frequently;
- It is more difficult to forecast or develop a pick-line profile or allocate SKUs into a suggested pick position
- At the end of a work-day (or order wave) all pick positions are zero scanned and vacated for the next work-day (or order wave) SKUs. If there is a residual SKU quantity in a pick position, it is moved to another pick position;
- It is difficult to project picker productivity;
- Only allocated SKU quantities are sent to pick positions.

Pick-Line Slotting Activity

SKU slotting on a pick-line design has a direct impact on the number of SKUs picked per hour and the number of orders completed per pick line. In most pick-line designs, each sale or pick number determines the SKU's pick position on a pick line. Pick lines and pick areas may be designed with single or dual pick lines. The design team options are either one SKU slotted in one SKU pick position or one SKU slotted into two separate pick positions.

SKU Slotted on a Single Pick Line in a Single Pick Position

A design with one SKU slotted in one SKU pick position has a SKU with a high-order pick volume slotted (allocated or assigned) to a single pick position (i.e., "A" pick zone). The "A" zone is located at the front of the pick line. This ensures a constant order flow over a pick line and basically controls order flow or volume from the pick line to a pack station. Given that high-volume SKU orders will be transferred into an empty pick tote/carton, high picker productivity will result. As the tote/carton leaves the high-volume pick position, each succeeding order will have a lower pick volume, thus completed orders will have an even flow, orders will be completed at an increasing rate, and with slower moving SKUs and fewer orders, each pick zone pick position number increases.

If there are multiple SKUs per order with a high-volume SKU in most orders, the majority of the cartons/totes will receive a high-volume SKU. In this design, there is an open space between two totes/cartons—or there are fewer totes/cartons in a pick train—after the high-volume pick position.

In a warehouse using this design, the WMS computer or warehouse order assignment to a pick line is a basic program that does not require a special program. If there is concern about completing a large number of orders with a maximum pick rate of three to four seconds per pick transaction, the design team may consider dual pick lines. A dual pick-line design has two or more separated pick lines that has selected fast-moving SKUs or complete order wave SKUs.

A SKU Slotted on One Pick Line in Two Separate Pick Positions

If a warehouse slots one SKU on one pick line with two separate pick positions, two pick positions are assigned to a high-volume order SKU separated by other SKUs in other pick positions. In a single pick-line profile, a high-volume order SKU is allocated to two pick positions. As previously stated, one pick position is located in the front of an "A" zone; the second pick position is located in the rear of the "A" zone or in a "B" zone. Splitting the high-order SKU pick volume between two pick positions means fewer pick numbers for each pick position. The benefit of this approach is to "even out" the pick numbers for each position.

For a double-slotted SKU in two pick positions, the WMS or warehouse computer allocates the pick transaction to the first or second pick position as totes/cartons enter a pick line. If a high-volume SKU has a pick transaction at the first position, tote/carton picker in the "A" zone front completes the transaction as a tote/carton enters the zone. Next, after the "A" zone picker completes other transactions (or has no other SKU picks in the zone), the tote/carton is pushed onto the take-away conveyor travel path. If a high-volume SKU does not have a pick transaction in this first position, the tote/carton "A" zone picker completes other transactions and pushes a tote/carton to the "A" zone rear and completes a high-volume SKU pick transaction. The tote/carton is then pushed onto a take-away conveyor.

The design characteristics of a SKU double slot allocation to two pick positions are:

- SKU pick volume is more evenly spread between two pick positions
- If moving a high-volume SKU in two pick positions does not maintain the picker productivity rate, and totes/cartons move at the same or slower speed, there will be no picker hour savings and there will be a decrease in completed orders per hour
- If moving a high-volume SKU in two pick positions does maintain the picker productivity rate, and totes/cartons move at the same speed, there will be a savings in total picker hours and an increase in completed orders per hour
- It is difficult to maintain a SKU replenishment activity
- With one take-away conveyor travel path, it is difficult to achieve a high number of completed orders
- A more complex WMS or warehouse computer program is required to assure that both pickers have transactions
- It is possible to end up with two pick positions with a residual SKU quantity

Pick-Line or Pick-Area Layout and Profile Options

The objective of a pick-and-pass design is to have accurate and highly productive pickers and on-time order fulfillment activity. A warehouse will realize good picker productivity through the use of a pick-line profile or SKU allocation. The options for establishing a good pick-line profile involve having the WMS computer allocate days or order wave pick volume based on a download from the host computer or on historical sales volume.

With either option, an important factor is each SKU's physical characteristics. SKU pick line profile or allocation to a pick position is based on budgeted picker productivity for each zone. With each pick zone, higher moving SKUs are typically placed in pick positions that are referred to in ergonomic terms as a Golden Zone. In pallet and carton flow lane pick positions and mobile or fixed shelf pick positions, Golden zones are pick positions that are located approximately between a picker knees and shoulders. Other SKU profile or allocation factors are high cube and heavy weight SKUs are at a pick line front pick positions, "C" or "D" SKUs are at a pick line last pick positions, SKU life cycle in a pick area that determines a SKU (a) remains in a pick area, and (b) rotated each pick day/order wave and order release to a pick area. An example of pick-to-light or pick-and-pass pick line layout, pick positions are located or profiled 1) for fastest of the fast moving or "A" moving SKUs, pallet flow pick positions at a pick line start, 2) for other "A" moving SKUs, next carton flow lanes that have one or two pick positions per pick zone, 3) for "B" fast moving SKUs, standard size carton flow lanes with standard pick position number, and 4) for "B" slow moving SKUs last section with static shelf pick positions.

Two examples of pick-line layouts are:

- Using SKU volume and physical characteristics—a SKU will remain in a pick position for several order waves
- Using a pick train that has a customer order container group move on a conveyor past all pick positions, pick cell with limited SKU pick positions that has customer order container scanned/read on a conveyor and it has a pick for a cell SKU, the container is diverted to the pick cell a SKU is rotated from a pick-line pick position as soon as the SKU is set up or replenished to another pick position

SKU Remains in a Pick Position for One Order Wave or Release: Volume and Physical Characteristics

After the warehouse has made pick-line setups or replenishments to each pick position, slow-moving SKUs (or SKUs at the end of their life cycle) are placed at the last pick positions or at flow rack non-Golden Zone pick positions. After the warehouse has physically placed and scanned (or transferred) SKUs to pick positions and all scan transactions have been sent to the WMS computer, orders are released to the pick lines.

A pick design requires a setup or replenishment employee to physically transfer and scan a SKU to a pick position. Pickers are then allocated to a pick line, based on a budgeted picker productivity. In a pick-and-pass design in which a SKU remains in a pick position, SKU set up/or replenishment is made to a specific pick position. Based on the order wave, the WMS program allocates SKUs for move transactions to a pick position. After the WMS computer receives scan transaction updates, orders are released to the pick line. With a SKU that remains in a pick position, a SKU profile for a high-volume SKU is allocated to a pallet/carton flow lanes Golden Zone position. SKUs are allocated to each picker zone in a manner that equals (or equals as closely as possible) the budgeted picker productivity rate. Examples of a pick-line layouts:

- Pallet lane pick positions that have the highest volume SKUs are at the front of the pick line or in a pick zone;
- Slow-moving high cube and heavy weight SKUs are in multiple carton flow-rack pick positions;
- Standard-sized carton flow lanes with standard-sized cartons and medium- to fast-moving SKUs in a Golden Zone;
- Slow-moving SKUs are assigned to top/bottom level pick positions at the end of a pick line;
- Slowest of slow moving SKUs are assigned to fixed shelf pick positions

Pick Cell and Pick Zone

In a warehouse using pick cells or zones, SKUs are rotated from a pick line as soon as they are set up/replenished. SKUs that are allocated to a pick-line cell or zone are based on each SKU's historical or projected sales volume and physical characteristics. After a setup and replenishment employee scans a SKU to a pick position (with associated SKU quantity), the transfer is complete and is sent to the WMS computer. After the transaction is received by the WMS computer, orders are transferred to a pick line. SKU allocation or pick-line profile options are

- Allocating all SKUs by highest to lowest volume SKU in a descending sequence from the first to the last pick position
- Placing fast-moving SKUs at a pick cell's first position; slower moving SKUs are placed at a pick cell last position, or in flow-rack non-Golden Zone pick positions;
- At the end of a pick day or order wave, all SKUs with a residual inventory are moved from their existing pick position to another position in another pick area;
- After the allocation process and after move transactions are sent to the pick design, SKUs are transferred and scanned at a pick position. After the WMS computer receives the scan transactions, orders are transferred to a pick line.

In a pick design in which SKUs are rotated from a pick line and new SKUs are set up/replenished on a pick line, SKUs are allocated to a pick-line cell or zone that is based on each historical or projected sales volume and physical characteristics. At the end of a work-day or order wave, residual SKUs are rotated from one pick position to another. During pick-line setup and replenishment, high-volume SKUs are physically transferred and scanned to a pick position. After WMS computer receives the scan transactions, orders are transferred to a pick line. SKUs are allocated to pick lines from highest to lowest volume SKU or from first to last pick position. In an example of a pick-line layout, pick positions have

- Pallet lane pick positions have the highest volume SKUs
- Carton flow rack pick positions have fast- to medium-moving SKUs in a pick cell or zone in the Golden Zone; slow-moving SKUs are in bottom/top level positions of four-level pick positions
- Shelf pick positions have slowest of slow-moving SKUs

Master-Carton Round Up/Round Down for Pick-Line Setup/Replenishment

In this design, one pick position section is for fast moving SKUs and a second section is for slow to medium moving (shelf and carton flow rack) SKUs. For a fast-moving SKU section, a pick-line setup or replenishment transaction smallest quantity is one master carton. There are two WMS computer pick-line setup and replenishment options.

First, rounding up to a full master-carton piece quantity means that, based on the total SKU quantity, the WMS computer only sends full master cartons to a pick line. As each master carton leaves a storage area it has an identification, either the original identification it was given when received, or the identification it was given when the carton was transferred from a pallet. The master-carton identification is sent to the WMS computer. If an order quantity is less than a master-carton SKU quantity, there will be partially full master cartons in pick positions at the end of the work-day or order wave. For the next pick day or order wave pick, residual master-cartons either (a) remain in a pick position or (b) are relocated to another pick or slow-moving SKU area.

Second, rounding down to a full master-carton SKU quantity means that, based on the total SKU quantity, the WMS computer sends only full master cartons to a pick line. If there is pick area set up/replenishment for a partial master carton, the carton is sent to a slow-moving pick position. If the order piece quantity equals the master-carton quantity, there will be no master cartons or quantities in pick positions at the end of the work-day or order wave. For the next pick day or order wave, pick positions will be empty and available for new SKUs. During pick activity, if an order requires a SKU and a fast-moving pick position is depleted of that SKU, the WMS computer will direct a pick transaction to be picked from master-carton piece quantity in a slow-moving position in another pick area.

Combined Family Group and ABC

If the warehouse's pick design services a large number of orders or many orders from a large retail shop with same sales aisles layout as the warehouse, a combined family group with an ABC arrangement should be considered for a pick area layout. This design means that design aisles, pick cells, or pick zones mirror a retail store sales aisles. The advantages are that "A" SKUs are located at each aisle entrance; at the retail store, there is high productivity in restocking and easy control over stock.

Replenishment Employee Indicator

In a replenishment employee indicator design, each replenishment employee determines SKU pick position and quantity for replenishment. In a high-volume pick line with many SKUs, the pick line will have a replenishment employee(s) to look at each pick position. The replenishment employee completes round-trip replenishment transactions with a SKU quantity from a ready-reserve position. An employee completes a SKU identification and scan transaction for each replenishment transaction. Updated piece quantities are sent to the WMS computer. In this design, if a pick-to-light design does not communicate each pick transaction to the WMS computer, each SKU pick position status is determined by a replenishment employee. The disadvantages to this approach are

- Replenishment activity does not match a pick activity
- WMS does not suggest a replenishment activity

- Random SKU replenishment activity
- No priority and slow replenishment
- Employee-paced activity

The advantage is that there is no additional cost.

Replenishment Indicator: Hand-Held Scanner/Reader

In this design, a replenishment indicator is a hand-held scanner used by an employee as a picker completes a pick transaction. Prior to pick activity and if a SKU quantity exceeds the pick position capacity, the extra SKU quantity is scanned/read to a ready-reserve position. (SKU and ready-reserve position identifications and piece quantities are sent to the WMS computer.) The WMS computer depletes the SKU pick position quantity by the pick transaction quantity. As the SKU quantity is depleted in the files from the pick position, when the SKU quantity reaches a predetermined (or minimum) level at the pick position, the WMS computer sends a notice to a replenishment employee via the hand-held scanner/RF tag reader. The scanner/reader screen displays a pick position and SKU quantity for a replenishment transaction. This design features

- On-time replenishments
- Machine-paced replenishment activity
- Prioritized replenishment activity
- Added hand-held scanner cost
- Good warehouse and WMS computer communication

Flashing Light with a Scoreboard

In this design, prior to the pick—and if a SKU quantity exceeds the SKU pick position capacity—extra SKU quantity is scanned to a ready-reserve position. SKU and ready-reserve position identifications and piece quantities are sent to the WMS computer. After the pick transaction, confirmation of the pick transaction is sent to the computer. The computer depletes the SKU pick position quantity by the pick transaction quantity. As the WMS computer depletes the SKU quantity from the pick position, when the pick position SKU quantity drops to a predetermined or minimum level, the computer sends a notice to a replenishment area scoreboard with a flashing light. A scoreboard displays a pick position and SKU quantity for a replenishment transaction. Design features are

- On-time replenishments
- Machine-paced replenishment activity
- Prioritized replenishment activity
- Added scoreboard cost
- Good warehouse computer and WMS computer communication
- A good WMS computer program

Pick Position Allocation or Profile for Demand Pull SKUs or Inventory Flow

The objectives of a small-item pick design are to complete an order/delivery cycle in a minimum time and at lowest possible warehouse costs. These objectives translate into many order fulfillment operations. With a high number of orders, a large SKU mix, and an order mix that includes single-line orders, multi-line orders, and combi orders, as well as required host, WMS, and warehouse computer processing time, and SKU move transaction time, a company will need an early (or warm start for pick line and pack activity. A pick line warm start has SKUs in the pick positions and a pack activity warm start means that customer order containers are queued at pack stations.

The questions facing a warehouse manager is how to have early or warm start, and how to have all orders on an order wave completed in required standard time, because most catalog, e-mail, direct marketing, and television marketing warehouses have demand pull or based on actual customer order quantities inventory flow and dual pick lines with same SKU number in the same or different pick positions. A pick-line setup or SKU allocation to pick position may be done in two different ways:

1. SKU may be placed in a fixed pick position and SKU replenishment transactions are done from a storage area to a pick position
2. There can be a daily or periodic setup or allocation of SKUs to a pick-line position

Fixed Position Allocation

A fixed pick position allocation has a SKU allocated to a pick position. The allocation (or profile) is based on historical sales volume, projected sales volume, or another allocation philosophy. As orders deplete a pick position SKU quantity, the WMS program will direct the warehouse to complete a replenishment transaction. With the order pull inventory flow and a large number of SKUs, the pick line will be long and require a large area, and it will be difficult to achieve a high SKU hit density and concentration. The advantages are that the SKU will be in a pick position for early pick-and-pack activity or warm start-up; per customer order demand replenishments are made to a pick position and minimal pick-line setup time.

Order Wave, Daily, or Periodic Pick-Line Setup

If the business has a order wave or daily order demand pull, a limited number of SKUs, high order numbers, and a wide SKU mix for the pick activity, each day (or order wave) the pick line will be setup with new SKUs allocated to pick-line pick positions. The warehouse staff creates a order wave in the WMS computer and releases a order wave to the WMS computer. The WMS computer allocates SKUs and directs a warehouse to transfer a SKU from a storage position to a pick position. As a SKU is transferred to a pick position, an employee scans a WMS pick position identification and enters a quantity into a hand-held scanner. Scan transactions are sent to the WMS computer for order release to a pick line. To have the shortest time and travel distance for storage, transport, scans, and SKU transfer to a pick position, the options are to setup a pick line each day or to have dual pick lines and pre-setup one pick line for each day's orders or order waves.

Presetting Up a Pick Line Each Day or Customer Order Wave

To setup a pick line for each day's orders or order wave, the warehouse receives (from the WMS computer) each SKU quantity necessary to complete all orders; the warehouse staff prepares an order wave that is released to the WMS computer. Based on the order wave, the computer allocates SKUs and directs the warehouse to complete transactions that move SKUs from storage positions to a pick design. From the pick-line setup list, the storage and in-house transport design moves SKUs from a storage area to a replenishment aisle or side. At a pick-line replenishment side, an employee scans each SKU identification, pick position, and SKU quantity into a RF device. The RF device sends SKU and position scans and piece quantity to the WMS computer to update inventory files. If the transferred SKU quantity overflows a pick position capacity, each overflow SKU is scanned and transferred to a ready-reserve position. Scans are sent to the WMS computer to update inventory files. The orders are then released to the pick line.

With orders that have 500–700 SKUs per day, 100 full pallets, and 1,000–2,000 master cartons, a complete replenishment transaction has a nominal two-hour pick-line setup time. To have pick-and-pack area activity at 0900, pick-line setup starts at 0600–0700 and requires exact storage forklift truck drivers to assure all activities are completed on-time; in-house transport, scan and replenishment employees, and activities must be completed per the warehouse schedule.

Pick-Line Presetup for the Next Day or Order Wave

A presetup pick line for the next work-day orders (or order wave) means that the warehouse has two pick lines and that Pick Line 2 is setup on Day 1 for Day 2 orders (or Order Wave 2). To setup Pick Line 2 on Day 1, the warehouse anticipates Day 2 orders (or order wave) and SKUs. The estimate is based on projected sales SKUs from the purchase or sales department. One option is to base the projection on order entry or actual sales (from the IT department) at predetermined times and a SKU historical sales percentage for past customer order wave total SKU quantity. Based on estimated SKU sales, the warehouse estimates the quantities required to meet two- to four-hour pick-and-pack activities. Calculations are rounded-up to full pallets or master cartons. With a SKU full master carton or pallet, the warehouse is directed to move SKU quantities from a storage position to a pick position on Pick Line 2.

Prior to the end of the work day (or order wave completion), the warehouse withdraws a master carton and pallet from a storage position and moves a SKU to a pick line. In a pick-line replenishment area, an employee completes a scan and replenishment transaction to a pick position. A SKU identification, pick position, and SKU quantity are sent to the WMS computer and updated in the inventory files.

With SKU quantities in pick positions and in the WMS inventory files, on Day 1 (or Order Wave 1) Pick Line 2 has SKUs in a pick position. Based on the host computer orders and the warehouse staff's order wave plan, the WMS computer allocates SKUs for orders. The computer directs the warehouse to move SKUs in the warehouse to two pick locations. Design features are a warm (or on-time) warehouse pick line, and pack activity starts at 0600–0700. At 0600–0700 the warehouse creates additional SKU move transactions (from storage positions) to complete Day 2 orders (or Order Wave 2); during Day 2, an order wave (or all orders) are completed; during Day 2, Pick Line 1 is prepared for Day 3 orders (or Order Wave 3).

Dual Pick-Line Order Balance

Dual pick-line balance activity is an order wave creation or plan process used in a warehouse that has at least two pick lines or areas. Each pick line has the same SKU number. After the host computer transfers ordered SKU pieces to the WMS computer, the warehouse staff creates an order wave and releases the wave to the WMS computer. The order wave ensures that each pick line has sufficient SKU quantity and order number to achieve budgeted picker productivity rate and to maintain customer service standard. Other characteristics, such as priority orders, zip codes, and order ages, are in the order wave or order group plan process.

The options for pick-line balance time are:

■ An automatic or on-line pick-line balance design. This occurs as soon as possible after orders are received by the WMS computer. As orders are received, they are frequently transferred to an WMS computer to create an order wave. The order wave is released to the computer, and the warehouse staff makes sure that each order wave has SKU setup for each pick line. An on-line design requires a high-speed WMS computer, and the warehouse staff must create order waves and make sure that orders are randomly spread by SKU volume over two pick lines.

■ After the host computer order process close time. The host computer transfers all orders at one time to the WMS computer. After the WMS computer has received the day's orders, it adds existing orders (or an order pool and new orders) to the order wave plan creation. The warehouse staff plans order waves or creates SKU quantity and order numbers to be allocated between two pick lines. The order wave pick-line balancing may be done by (a) SKU quantity, (b) order number, (c) single SKU and multi-line SKU orders, or (d) shipping-carton size.

Order SKU Quantity Pick-Line Balance

In a SKU quantity pick-line balance design, the warehouse staff creates a daily order or order wave for a SKU quantity on a predetermined basis between two pick lines. If an order fulfillment operation for a work day has orders for 36,000 SKUs, a warehouse staff order wave plan for a dual pick-line balance has 18,000 SKUs allocated each pick line. The features are an evenly allocated order SKU quantity to each pick line, a simple order wave plan process, and randomly spread SKU quantities between two pick lines; SKU replenishment, however, is made to both pick lines and does not optimize replenishment, shipping-carton make-up, or pick activity.

Order Number Pick-Line Balance

In a warehouse using an order number pick-line balance design, the warehouse computer allocates a predetermined ddaily order number, divided between two pick lines. If the warehouse work day has 20,000 SKUs orders, the order wave plan will allocate 10,000 SKUs to each pick line. This design features

■ simple warehouse computer process
■ evenly allocated orders between two pick lines
■ randomly spread SKU and SKU quantity between two pick lines
■ SKU replenishments are made to both pick lines

This design does not optimize replenishment, carton make-up, or picker productivity, and with a SKU per order mix, SKU pick imbalance between two pick lines is a possibility.

Single SKU and Multi-Line SKUs on Two Pick Lines by SKU Quantity or Order Number Pick-Line Balance

When orders are released to the WMS computer, the warehouse staff separates orders for each pick line by multi-line and single-line order SKUs. For a predetermined SKU quantity, multi-line orders with the same two SKUs and single-line orders with the same SKUs are sent to Pick Line 1. Orders with different SKUs are sent to Pick Line 2. This approach features

- order waves for Pick Line 1 and Pick Line 2
- a more complex computer process
- concentrating customer SKUs to Pick Line 1 and other SKUs to Pick Line 2

The replenishment activity optimizes replenishment and picker productivity on Pick Line 1, but there will be lower productivity on Pick Line 2. Finally, there will be some degree of SKU or order imbalance between two pick lines.

Order Shipping-Carton Size Balance

This design has order wave plans for multi-line and single-line orders that have the same suggested shipping-carton size sent to Pick Line 1. For the next shipping-carton size (or sizes), order wave plans for multi-line and single-line orders are created for Pick Line 2. When the Pick Line 2 order number or SKU quantity matches Pick Line 1, the staff repeats the order wave plan process between two pick lines. This design features a more complex order wave creation process and random allocation of SKUs between Pick Line 1 and Pick Line 2. Because SKU replenishment is random between pick lines, it does not optimize replenishment or picker employee productivity. Finally, there will be some degree of SKU or order imbalance between two pick lines.

WMS Computer Order Release to a Pick Line

The WMS computer releases processed order identifications and associated SKUs to a pick design. After the WMS program receives a SKU transfer to a pick position with a SKU quantity from a warehouse, the computer sends order identifications and SKU quantities to a pick line, pick activity starts. The pick line attaches a warehouse identification to each order identification or uses a WMS order identification on a tote/carton. This permits a picker to complete a pick transaction. To assure good pick line set up/replenishment and picker productivity, the WMS order identification and associated SKU release to a pick line may be 1) random, 2) based on a pick-line profile, or 3) based on the movement of SKUs slotted to pick positions, with a highest volume SKU in the first position and lowest volume SKU in the last position.

Random Order Release to a Pick Line

In a random order release to a pick-line design, there is no pattern to how the WMS computer transfers orders to a pick line. For this design to have good productivity, it is necessary that each pick cell or zone is manned with pickers.

Order Release Based on a Pick Line Profile

In an order release design based on a pick-line profile, each SKU is physically transferred and scanned into a pick position. After the setup activity, the WMS computer releases all orders to a pick line. For this design to have good productivity, it is necessary that each pick cell or zone is manned with pickers.

Order Released as a SKU Slotted to a Pick Line

In this design the WMS computer releases orders to a pick line as a SKU is set up/replenished by an employee or machine, and the scan is entered into the computer. After a SKU is physically transferred and scanned to a pick position, the WMS computer releases orders for SKUs to the warehouse. After a SKU is slotted to a pick line, to have good picker productivity a pick line needs to have each SKU set up/replenished to a pick position.

Order Releases: High-to-Low SKU Movement

In a high-to-low SKU order release design, the pick line is set up/replenished with the highest volume SKU first, the next highest volume SKU second; this is repeated for the next high-volume SKU. As each SKU is physically transferred to a pick position and scanned, the WMS computer updates the files and releases orders to a warehouse pick line. In this design, several pickers are allocated to the first pick cells or zones, whereas other pickers are allocated to longer pick cells/zones with a larger SKU numbers. Finally, this design increases the number of completed orders.

WMS Computer Order Transfer to a Pick Line: Options

When SKUs are transferred from the storage area to the pick position, the warehouse has two options: total order allocation or specific SKU quantity.

In a total allocation design, the WMS program moves greatest SKU quantity that maintains a budgeted cost per unit, either to a pick position or a ready-reserve position (or both). The advantages of this approach are shorter development and implementation time; shorter process time, with a more realistic order release to a pick design, and faster pick-line setup or replenishment transactions.

In a specific SKU or order transfer design, the WMS computer allocates a specific SKU or the quantity for a specific order to a pick line, which is then scanned and moved to a pick position. To use this design involves a specially written program for the WMS computer. Thus, this design features higher WMS program cost, program development, and implementation time; longer order process time; potentially additional (or more frequent) pick-line move transactions (i.e., storage and transport activities); and pick position setup/replenishment transactions with a higher cost per unit.

Work-Day or Customer-Order Wave-End Pick-Position Management

At the end of a work-day or order wave, an employee completes a zero-scan transaction at each pick position that has been depleted of all SKUs. If a pick position has residual SKU quantity, the allocation options are

1. Move the SKU quantity from the pick position to another position. An employee then completes the zero-scan transaction.
2. Leave the SKU in the existing pick position, complete a scan transaction, and send the count to the WMS computer for inventory file update.

In warehouses that are designed with "A," "B," and "C" pick zones, it is necessary to ensure proper new SKU placement in an "A" zone. Thus, at the end of a work-day or order wave, the "A" pick zone is reorganized for new SKUs. The preparation options are:

- Multiple "A" pick zones
- Pick clean and zero scan each pick position and remaining SKUs are reorganized to other pick positions in another pick area
- Remaining SKUs stay in an existing "A" pick area

Multiple "A" Pick Zones

In a warehouse with multiple "A" pick zones, on Day 1 (or Order Wave 1) "A" SKUs are picked from Pick Zone 1A and Day 2 (or Order Wave 2) SKUs are set up in pick zone 2B. On Day 2, residual "A" SKUs are picked from Pick Zone 2B. SKUs can either remain in existing pick positions or are moved from the pick position in Pick Zone 1A to another position in the same zone or to a position in Pick Zone 2B. This design requires additional floor space, features additional pick equipment cost, SKU relocation labor, and the need for profiling the pick line to ensure good pick-line setup, replenishment, and productivity.

Pick Clean, Zero Scan, and Reorganizing SKUs in the Same Pick Area

In this design, remaining "A" SKUs are moved from the first position in the "A" zone to a lower pick position number. For Day 1 (or Order Wave 1), "A" SKUs are picked from pick zone's front position. At the end of Day 1, remaining "A" SKUs are reorganized and moved from the front pick position to other "A" zone front pick positions located at an end of zone "A." A pick zone reorganization steps are

1. Each pick position that is picked clean (i.e., all SKUs are picked from the position) is zero scanned into a WMS program. This ensures that a WMS inventory file does not have a SKU inventory in a pick position.
2. With a Day 2 (or Order Wave 2) pick-line profile, a SKU with remaining inventory SKU quantity in a pick position is moved from the pick position to another position.
3. Per the Day 2 pick-line profile, new "A" SKUs are moved to (or set up at) a suggested pick position.
4. If the Day 2 pick line does not have sufficient positions, remaining or new "A" SKUs with the lowest pick volumes are moved to another pick zone.

This design features minimal floor space (but some additional pick positions), minimal pick equipment cost and relocation labor (but some additional scan and move transactions), and requires a profile for good pick-line set up, replenishment, and pick productivity.

Adding New SKUs to a Pick Zone While Remaining SKUs Stay in a Pick Position

In a warehouse using this design, each Day 1 (or Order Wave 1) SKU with a residual inventory in a pick position remains in existing pick position and new SKUs are set up in vacant pick positions. A pick line is profiled around the SKUs in pick positions. If a Day 2 (or Order Wave 2) pick line does not have sufficient pick positions, remaining "A" SKUs with the lowest pick volume are moved to a pick position or set up in another pick zone. This design features minimal floor space (but some additional pick positions), and low pick equipment cost and SKU relocation labor (but some additional scan and move transactions). It is difficult to profile for good pick-line set up, replenishment, and pick productivity when using this design.

SKU Life Cycle: Impact on Daily Pick Line Setup

A SKU life cycle affects the pick-line profile or SKU allocation to a pick position, as well as pick-line setup and replenishment strategy (see Figure 3.13). After SKU promotion, the life cycle starts. As a day, week, or month number increases from the first "available for sale" day, orders for a

DAY OR MONTH NUMBER AFTER ADVERTISEMENT

	DAY OR MONTH 1	DAY OR MONTH 2	DAY OR MONTH 3	DAY OR MONTH 4	DAY OR MONTH 5	DAY OR MONTH 6	TOTAL
SKU VOLUME	84407	5976	2402	1311	978	798	95782
PERCENT	88%	6%	3%	1%	1%	1%	100%

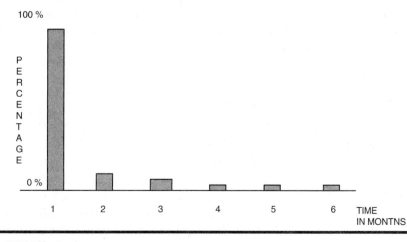

Figure 3.13   SKU Life Cycle

SKU decrease and pick-line setup quantities decreases. At the same time, pick setup SKU master-carton quantity increases, but master-carton/pallet quantities decrease and a single SKU master-carton quantities increase. In a pick-line operation that rotates SKUs each day (or order wave), a SKU has a five- to seven-day life cycle.

In a dynamic pick design, the daily pick-line setup options are:

1. The exact piece quantity for each SKU is delivered to a pick line for setup.
2. If a pick line has a ready-reserve location, an employee transfers a predetermined pallet/master-carton quantity to ready-reserve positions.

Transfer Exact Master-Carton/Pallet Quantity

In this design, the exact master-carton/pallet quantity for a SKU is moved to a pick position. After the master carton/pallet is transferred to a pick-line setup station, an employee transfers the exact quantity to the pick position. In a conventional forklift truck warehouse, a pallet is (a) delivered to the transfer station or pick line, and the SKU quantity is moved from the pick area's replenishment aisle to the pick position; or (b) an exact master-carton quantity is moved from a pallet to a replenishment vehicle. Master cartons are transported to a replenishment aisle and are transferred and scanned to a pick position. If the SKU quantity is in master cartons, the master cartons are transported to a replenishment area, and the master-carton identification is scanned to a pick position.

In a warehouse that uses VNA forklift trucks or AS/RS cranes, SKU replenishment occurs from a warehouse replenishment station. The forklift truck or crane delivers a pallet to a P/D station. At that point, the pick-line setup or replenishment options are:

■ The forklift truck delivers the pallet to a replenishment aisle. After the master cartons are moved from a pallet to a pick position, a partially depleted pallet is returned to a storage position. The master-carton quantity, pallet identification, and pick position involved in the move are sent to the WMS computer for inventory update.
■ A employee picks and labels each master carton from a pallet, and moves the master cartons onto a powered conveyor. A conveyor transports the labeled master cartons to a pick-line replenishment aisle and the master cartons are transferred to a pick position. Each master-carton identification, pick position, and pallet involved in the move are sent to the WMS computer for inventory update.

Transferring a Predetermined Master-Carton Quantity to Ready-Reserve Positions

In this design, after each pallet is transferred to a pick-line setup station, an employee transfers a predetermined master-carton quantity from a pallet to a pick position or ready-reserve position. During the transfer, the master-carton move (i.e., pallet and pick position and ready-reserve position) are sent to the WMS computer. In a conventional forklift truck warehouse, a pallet is delivered to a transfer station or pick line, and the master-carton move occurs from a pick area replenishment aisle or in a storage area. The exact master-carton quantity needed is transferred from the pallet to a replenishment vehicle. Master cartons are then transported to a replenishment aisle, transferred, and scanned to a pick position and ready-reserve position. The pallet, pick position, ready-reserve position, and master-carton piece quantity are sent to the WMS computer.

In a VNA forklift truck or AS/RS crane warehouse, replenishment occurs from a replenishment station. See "Transfer Exact Master-Carton/Pallet Quantity" for more information.

Warehouse Operation and WMS Program Transaction Key Components

As part of a warehouse and WMS program Business Narrative/Brief Description of Operation, the design team will review and decide upon the key components needed to complete a SKU transaction. These components are:

- Human/machine readable section with an identification bar-code/RF tag type;
- Identification RF tag/bar-code orientation as a ladder, picket fence, or hybrid on (a) storage or pick position, (b) on each SKU, or (c) on each order;
- Identification bar-code/RF tag location in a storage aisle for (a) man-down forklift truck that has a forklift truck driver remain on the floor level as the set of forks elevate or (b) man-up forklift truck that has a forklift truck driver move upward as the set of forks elevate. In an AS/RS storage design, giving each storage position an identification label is optional, but when there is an AS/RS storage transaction problem at a specific storage position, some identification is preferred;
- Identification RF tag/bar-code life expectancy, e.g., (a) permanent identification on a storage or pick position or (b) disposable identification on each SKU or order;
- A scanner/reader of some sort, e.g., (a) hand-held or employee held, (b) fixed-position or deivce does not move, (c) fixed-beam or one beam, (d) moving-beam or several beams over all directions and are focused on one area, or (e) waving-beam, a beam that moves between two directions that covers a greater area than a fixed beam scanner
- Scanner/reader transaction completion communication with the WMS computer, which can be (a) held in memory, (b) delayed or batched in a personal computer, or (c) on-line with RF device to the WMS computer;
- SKU label creation, which can be (a) printed on demand or (b) preprinted;
- Order delivery label and packing slip printing, which can be done (a) at central location, (b) at the pick-line entry, or (c) at a pack station;
- SKU or order number creation, which can be (a) random number generated, (b) Julian date, or (c) lowest number with a Julian date;
- Storage transaction file entry and storage sequence, which can be done (a) by SKU label number, with the lowest number as the first SKU transaction completed; or (b) by SKU transaction into a storage position;
- Order pick/pass design, which can be (a) captive tote with a permanent identification label, or (b) shipping carton/captive tote with a disposable identification label by random or same carton size.

Pick Locations

As we have discussed previously, in a single-item or master-carton warehouse, the pick-and-pack area is the heart of the warehouse. In a warehouse, SKUs are 1) placed into positions that employees can reach (preferred pick positions), or 2) placed into positions that can be reached by a forklift truck reachable positions (least preferred pick positions).

In a warehouse with a WMS program, pick position options are:

- All positions as pick positions;
- Separate storage and separate pick positions;
- Pick position type that is (a) fixed, (b) floating, or (c) random pick positions;
- Warehouse pick design that is (a) manual, (b) mechanized, or (c) automated;
- Pick position identification labels as (a) small, (b) large, (c) plain, (d) coated, and (e) human/ machine or machine readable;
- Order pick location type (a) regular or (b) fast pack.

Total Floating Pick Position

In a warehouse in which all SKU positions (both storage and pick positions) are pick positions, a SKU in a pick position is available for order completion and a picker may access all pick positions. A warehouse with this design is considered to have a total floating (or random) pick position design. As a SKU is transferred from a receiving area to a storage area, each SKU is placed onto a floor level or elevated storage rack position. The pick position is either in an employee-reachable (floor level) or forklift-truck–reachable (elevated rack level) position. The WMS program allocates a SKU that is in a position with a SKU available to complete a pick transaction. In order to complete all pick transactions, an employee with a pick cart or pallet truck will need to have access to floor or elevated pick positions. To complete an elevated pick transaction for one SKU, a picker will spend nonproductive time locating a forklift truck or ladder and completing the transaction from the elevated pick position. For the next picker (or next day pick activity for the same SKU), the WMS program allocates SKUs from an elevated pick position until pick activity has depleted the SKU quantity in the elevated position, or a forklift truck has completed a SKU move transaction from the elevated to the floor position. The features of this design are

1. Maximum position utilization
2. A forklift or HROS picker truck is required to complete an elevated pick position transaction
3. Low picker productivity
4. Low hit concentration and density
5. To complete an order a picker must travel past all pick positions
6. Replenishment transactions are not required

Separate Storage and Pick Positions

In a warehouse with separate storage and pick positions, as a SKU is transferred from a receiving area to a storage area or pick area, one SKU is placed into a pick position and another SKU is placed into storage position (see Figure 3.14). A warehouse with separate storage and pick positions means that a warehouse has a fixed SKU pick position (100A) and as customer orders deplete a pick position SKU quantity, a SKU replenishment activity moves a SKU quantity from a storage position to pick position (100a). The storage positions are located in a separate positions that have a forklift truck complete a SKU storage transaction and replenishment transaction to pick

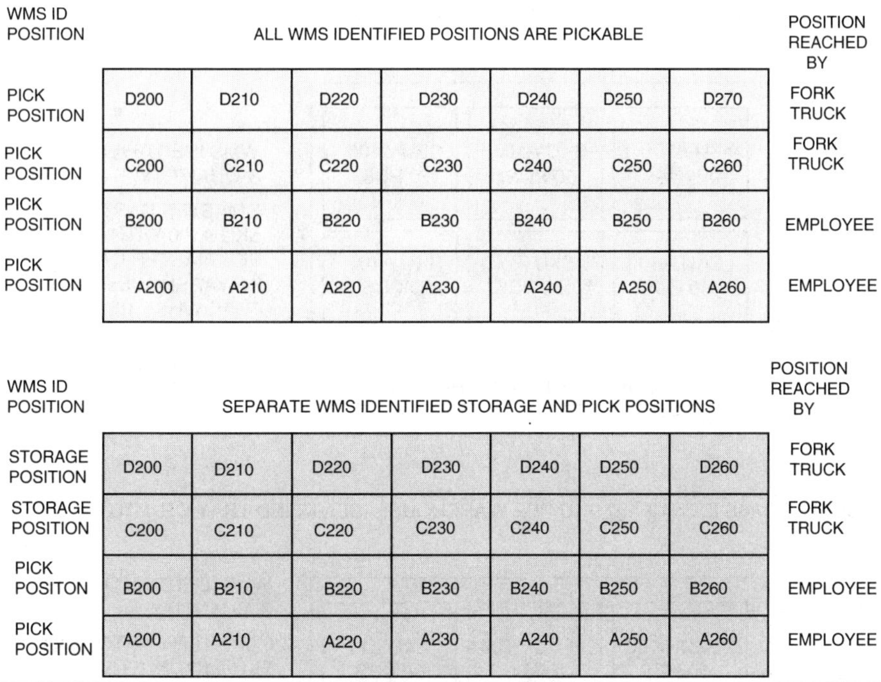

WMS ID POSITION	ALL WMS IDENTIFIED POSITIONS ARE PICKABLE							POSITION REACHED BY
PICK POSITION	D200	D210	D220	D230	D240	D250	D270	FORK TRUCK
PICK POSITION	C200	C210	C220	C230	C240	C250	C260	FORK TRUCK
PICK POSITION	B200	B210	B220	B230	B240	B250	B260	EMPLOYEE
PICK POSITION	A200	A210	A220	A230	A240	A250	A260	EMPLOYEE

WMS ID POSITION	SEPARATE WMS IDENTIFIED STORAGE AND PICK POSITIONS							POSITION REACHED BY
STORAGE POSITION	D200	D210	D220	D230	D240	D250	D260	FORK TRUCK
STORAGE POSITION	C200	C210	C220	C230	C240	C250	C260	FORK TRUCK
PICK POSITON	B200	B210	B220	B230	B240	B250	B260	EMPLOYEE
PICK POSITION	A200	A210	A220	A230	A240	A250	A260	EMPLOYEE

Figure 3.14   WMS Identified Storage and Pick Positions

position (100A). Pick positions are located in employee-reachable positions. As a pick position becomes depleted of a SKU quantity, the WMS program creates a replenishment transaction in which a SKU quantity is transferred from an elevated storage position to a fixed pick position. The design minimizes SKU replenishment transactions from a storage position to a vacant pick position, but requires two picker-reachable pick positions for a SKU. This design features good position utilization, does not require a man-up forklift truck to complete an elevated pick transaction, has good hit concentration and hit density, good picker pick productivity, good forklift truck productivity, and requires SKU replenishment transactions. To minimize "stock outs," a floating pick position design that has a SKU quantity placed into two pick positions (200A) and (420B) that are employee-reachable pick positions. After customer order pick transactions deplete SKU quantity in pick position (200A), the next customer order pick transaction occurs from pick position (420B). The design features are greater pick position number, lower hit concentration and density, lower pick productivity, fewer critical forklift truck replenishment transactions and lower pick position utilization.

SKU Number per Warehouse Operation AS/RS Carton Tray/Pallet

When a storage/pick warehouse with a WMS program has a master-carton or pallet AS/RS storage warehouse operation (see Figure 3.15), a warehouse has an identification that is attached to each master-carton or pallet SKU and each warehouse storage or storage/pick position has to have an identification. WMS information is entered into WMS inventory files. The design team objectives

ONE WMS IDENTIFIED SKU PER WAREHOUSE IDENTIFIED TRAY OR TOTE

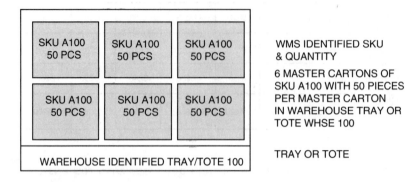

MULTIPLE WMS IDENTIFIED SKU PER WAREHOUSE IDENTIFIED TRAY OR TOTE

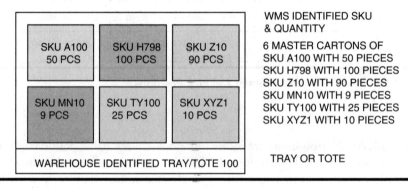

Figure 3.15 WMS Identified SKU per Warehouse Identified Tray or Tote

are to provide a design year storage position number, minimize costs, assure maximum employee productivity, and proper SKU rotation. To satisfy the above warehouse carton or pallet AS/RS design objectives, the design team carton or pallet AS/RS options are

- One SKU on one pallet/tray;
- Mixed carton SKUs on one pallet/tray;
- One SKU per pick position.

One SKU on One Pallet/Tray

In a design in which there is one SKU on one AS/RS pallet/carton tray, each storage position has one SKU. This design features a simple operation, high storage position utilization, minimal SKU transaction errors, and, if the warehouse uses a carton AS/RS crane, an opportunity to automate carton in-feed and pick transactions.

Mixed Master-Carton SKUs on a Pallet/Tray

In this design one pallet/tray has several SKUs in one pallet/tray storage position. When there is an order for one SKU from a tray/pallet with mixed SKUs, the WMS computer sends a message to the warehouse to direct an AS/RS crane (or forklift truck) to a storage position. The crane or forklift truck transfers a pallet/tray to a pick position. At the pick position—and after a tray/pallet is delivered to a pick position—a picker completes the transaction. This design improves SKU hit concentration or density, but with picker time to search and find a SKU among several other SKUs on a tray there is potential for low picker productivity. The design reduces the number of pallet/tray transactions, improves storage position utilization, and increases potential employee transaction errors. Mixed SKUs on a tray minimizes opportunities to automate in-feed and pick activities, and the WMS or warehouse computer program maintains tray vacancy to ensure high employee deposit activity.

One SKU Per One Storage/Pick Position

A warehouse's objectives are to optimize storage/pick position utilization, enhance good employee deposit and pick productivity, and assure proper SKU rotation. To satisfy these objectives, a SKU identification is assigned, and the SKU is deposited or placed into a storage/pick position. The design team options are 1) one SKU per one position; 2) mixed or multiple SKUs per a position with each SKU position in a separated position; and 3) mixed or multiple SKUs per a position with no separation.

Quality and Quantity Check

The WMS computer maintains SKU cube/dimensions and weight, shipping-carton internal dimensions and tare weight, and the percentage allowed for filler material. The computer projects each order's shipping-carton size and weight and SKU weight variance allowance. As per a manual or scale-picked SKU check design, each SKU quantity, description, and total weight (SKUs and shipping carton) is sent to a picked SKU check weight station that compares a customer order actual weight to a computer projected weight.

If the picked and checked SKU quantity and quality match the WMS computer projected quantity, weight, and description, the tote/carton travels from the check station to a pack station. If the picked quantity and quality check does not match, the shipping carton is sent to a problem station for corrective action.

In many warehouses, a picked SKU check is completed at a pack station. A packer reads (or uses a scanner/reader) each SKU code. The activities are used to check the picked SKU quality and quantity. In a scale check weight, the projected order weight, in comparison with the actual SKU and shipping-carton weight (with a predetermined weight variance) is used to verify order weight or quantity.

Order Packing Station

After orders are picked and checked, ordered SKUs are transferred into a shipping carton. With a pick/pass into a shipping-carton (or carton insert into a captive tote), ordered SKUs are transferred from a pick position into a shipping carton or a warehouse tote with a collapsed shipping carton inside a tote. After pick-and-sort activity, sorted SKUs are scanned/read and placed into the shipping carton.

High-volume or fast-moving single-line single SKU orders are bulk picked and delivered to a fast-pack or pick/pack station, at which pickers or robotic machines perform a customer order SKU pick-and-pack activity. A pick/pack activity includes SKU scan/read, WMS printed packing slip inserted into a shipping carton, shipping-carton seal and delivery label applied to a shipping carton or use a slapper envelop (clear plastic or window envelop with packing slip/sale literature) that is applied to a shipping-carton exterior.

If the pick or pick-and-sort activity does not deplete a SKU from a pick position, a pack employee completes a SKU scan transaction. Scan transaction is sent to the WMS computer that depletes a SKU from a pick position. A WMS packing slip and delivery label print location options are printed in a central location, remote a pick-line start station or remote at a pack station..]A selected print option is determined by a pick design and IT capabilities.

Shipping Carton Loading and Shipping

Shipping carton loading and shipping involves having an employee-controlled forklift or mechanical device that transfers a sorted and manifested carton from a staging area or dock onto a delivery truck. After the delivery truck is full, the package is sent from the warehouse to the freight company terminal for final delivery to the customer. If, during loading, the delivery truck becomes full and additional express or priority shipping cartons need to ship, an employee with a hand-held scanner/reader removes the order identification manifest and the loaded shipping cartons from a delivery truck. As shipping cartons are removed from the delivery truck, each order identification is scanned and sent to the WMS computer and is removed from the manifest list. The WMS computer sends each unloaded order identification to the host computer. Since the unloaded customer order identifications are not a manifest list, a WMS and host computer consider that an order identification is in a warehouse. If additional shipping cartons with manifests are loaded onto a delivery truck, an employee with hand-held scanner/reader completes the order identification scan, which sends each order identification to the WMS computer and delivery company. The WMS computer sends the order identifications to the host computer.

Prepack SKU Activity

In a warehouse, prepack activity occurs in a small item store-and-hold operation, when high single-line single-piece sales for a SKU are anticipated. An employee or robotic machine transfers SKUs into a shipping carton or bag. The shipping carton/bag is open and the SKUs remain in the WMS computer inventory. Because the SKU's physical characteristics do not change, the warehouse may reuse a WMS SKU identification and SKU quantity during a prepack activity; or remove an existing identification and use a new WMS SKU identification and quantity.

Value-Added SKUs

A warehouse value-added activity has an employee or robotic machine specifically modify a SKU physical appearance. A customer order has a request for a warehouse operation to modify a SKU. Examples are monogram or gift wrap.

Inventory Control

In a warehouse with a SKU inventory, the count is completed by an employee, based on physical SKU quantity in an individual SKU storage position/pick position or all SKU storage/pick positions.

A physical count of a SKU quantity is entered into the WMS computer as an entire SKU quantity in each storage or pick position or counts a SKU quantity in one position. In the host computer, this becomes the total SKU quantity "available for sale." Inventory count options are:

- Specific storage/pick position
- All storage/pick positions that contain a SKU
- Fiscal count of all SKUs and positions in a warehouse
- Specific count to verify a SKU count due to a quantity imbalance at a position or to account for damaged SKU(s)

Noncustomer Orders for SKUs

The host computer sends noncustomer-order requests for SKUs to the WMS program to complete a SKU move/transfer transaction for a noncustomer-order (a nonpaid demand for a SKU). Noncustomers orders include return to vendor, vendor recall, charity or donation, or employee award program. After the WMS program receives a noncustomer order, the WMS computer allocates a SKU inventory for transfer to a storage position. At that point, noncustomer orders are processed like customer orders.

Pick SKU Advance Customer Sales

A warehouse may offer a customer the opportunity to preorder a SKU or to have a late delivery date for a SKU. For a preorder, the vendor-delivered SKU is unloaded, received, and placed into a SKU position. The SKU position status is updated in the WMS and host computers.

As the host computer receives a preorder or late delivery, the computer identifies the order as an advance sale or as having late delivery status, and sends the order to the WMS computer. The WMS computer flags the order as a preorder or late delivery request. In the WMS computer, a SKU quantity is identified for a delivery date, and a SKU move transaction is created. The SKU quantity is transferred from the standard storage position to a special storage position. This special storage position is similar to a QA hold. The SKU in a special identified position is included in the host and WMS computers' inventory as "not available for sale" for new customer orders. This minimizes the possibility of sending the order to another customer. After the move to a suggested drop point, delivery location, or pick position, the warehouse notifies the WMS computer. The WMS computer adjusts the storage position and SKU quantity status in a pick position. After the pick transaction is completed, the WMS computer depletes the pick position SKU quantity and notifies the host computer that the SKU quantity is depleted and the order is complete.

Temperature, Hazardous, Toxic, and High-Value SKU Control

In a warehouse that handles a wide mix of SKUs, some SKUs require specific environmental or controlled storage/pick positions. As a purchasing department sends a purchase order to the host computer, the buyer indicates that the SKUs are being scheduled for a specific storage area. The host computer sends the purchase order to a WMS program; the WMS computer notices the storage characteristics and flags them. The WMS program transfers this information onto a tally sheet and the receiving documents.

After SKUs are received and unloaded onto a receiving dock, a receiving clerk attaches an identification to each SKU. A SKU identification and SKU quantities are entered into the WMS computer. In the WMS computer, a specific SKU number has a flag that identifies a SKU. As a SKU is moved from the receiving dock to a storage area, the WMS computer sends a message to the warehouse that a SKU move transaction should be conducted to a specific storage section (e.g., temperature controlled, hazardous, toxic, high value, edible, nonedible, flammable).

Customs, Bonded or Duty Free, and Duty Draw Back

A warehouse receives vendor-delivered SKUs from foreign countries, and a company is required to pay customs duty to the United States on these SKUs. In bonded warehouses, however, if SKUs from foreign vendors are unloaded, received, and stored in a specific bonded area, there is no customs duty payment due until the SKUs are removed from the bonded area and sold to customers.

When the purchase department communicates a vendor purchase order to the host computer, the buyer indicates that a foreign vendor is delivering SKUs, and that they are scheduled for storage in the warehouse's bonded section. The host computer sends a purchase order to the WMS computer. The WMS computer will note the bonded flag, and the computer will suggest a storage position in a specific storage area. When the WMS computer directs a printer to print a tally sheet, the receiving documents will indicate the requirement for storage in the bonded area.

After the SKUs are received, a receiving clerk attaches an identification to each SKU; the identification and the SKU quantities are entered into the WMS computer. The SKU is moved to a drop point for entry into the bonded section. After the SKU arrives at a storage position, the SKU and storage position are scanned/read and sent to the WMS computer. The WMS computer sends a message for the inventory files in the host computer.

As orders are received for a SKU in the bonded storage position, the WMS computer depletes the SKUs in the bonded section. The WMS computer sends a SKU quantity to the host computer, which issues payment to the U.S. Customs.

Order Returns

There are several steps to complete the return process. The process starts when return package is moved from a delivery truck onto the returns dock. From the returns dock, the package flows to a returns process and disposition station. At the station, employees scan the return label (accessing the order record) to verify that the return is valid. Once it has been verified that the SKU was ordered, a credit is authorized for the customer. Because each process station has access to orders, order options are held in the host computer. They can also be held in the WMS computer for a predetermined number of days. After a certain number of days, the records are sent to the host computer. This minimizes access to orders and reduces host computer transactions.

The next step is to dispose of returned SKUs. Each returned SKU becomes a company asset and requires an identification and transfer to a position. If each returned SKU has a WMS SKU identification or customer returns activity SKU disposition identification. If a returned SKU does not have a WMS identification, the computer will print an identification that includes a SKU identification and a SKU disposition identification.

As part of the returns process, each SKU is presorted into a separate container, e.g., return to stock (RTS), return to vendor (RTV), mixed RTS and RTV in one container, and destroy and dispose. Returned and processed SKUs are transferred to a pick or nonpick position. A pick position has RTS or "available for sale" SKUs and is scanned into a position. The SKU is then available for a pick transaction. A nonpick position has an RTV or "not available for sale" SKU: The SKU is placed in inventory for vendor return consolidation. Scan transactions and SKU quantities are sent to the WMS computer for inventory update.

Customer-Order Return-Label Delivery Address

If a warehouse has multiple SKU classifications in one facility and orders are for single-line and multi-line and combined SKU classifications, a return could have SKUs from several classifications or a single SKU from one classification. To improve the return process, the company has customers attach a preaddressed label to each packing slip. To improve the returns process and to provide security for high-value SKUs, preaddressed customer return labels may be handled in several ways. The first option is using one return address for all SKUs. With one address, a packing slip has a preprinted return address on each packing slip document. This reduces packing slip print time. Returns arrive at a single returns process dock. In a high-volume warehouse operation with returns from all SKU classifications, the advantages are:

- High-value SKUs are handled in a general return area (low security)
- Maximum space utilization
- High return unload and open productivity
- Fewer returns delivery locations

Second, the warehouse may use a separate return address for each SKU classification. If using this approach, packing slips can be prepared with a preprinted return address on each packing slip document.

Third, the customer order delivery company can use a separate return address label. The delivery company separates (or presorts) returns by SKU classification and delivers returns to a separate company address (returns dock) or in separate containers. In a high-volume warehouse with returns eparated by SKU classifications, the features are:

- High-value SKUs are handled in a separate returns area (high security)
- Good space utilization
- Good return unload and open productivity
- Additional returns delivery locations

Unique Order Shipping Label

In this design, a warehouse uses unique order shipping labels for two delivery companies and single or dual induction locations. One order delivery and induction station handles a specific SKU classification or carton size; the second delivery and induction station handles another specific SKU classification or carton size. A unique shipping label for each delivery company or SKU permits a shipping-carton or bag sort design flexibility. A ship sort design is designed with either a single induction and divert station section or a dual induction and two divert sections. This design allows a company to divert orders from a main sort conveyor to a divert lane for direct load into a delivery truck or delivery device (BMC). A sort or divert of packages permits the company to zone skip (i.e., bypassing the delivery company freight terminal that is close to the warehouse facility and is sent direct to a final delivery terminal that is closer to customer order delivery address). Zone skipping means lower freight charges for each package, faster package delivery, and improved customer service.

Across-the-Dock Warehouse Operation

An across-the-dock warehouse has a more streamlined order flow than a conventional warehouse. In an across-the-dock warehouse, each drop/ship location has its own identification. Vendor-delivered SKUs are unloaded, received, and updated in the WMS computer as they are received at the warehouse. Each SKU has an existing identification or the receiving department attaches an identification to the SKU. The receiving department verifies SKU quantity and quality. After receiving activity is completed, the same receiving procedures are used to verify the quantity. After quantity and quality has been verified, each SKU receives an identification. SKU identifications and quantities are entered into the WMS computer, which updates the inventory file.

A SKU move or transport transaction identifies a suggested drop point (or delivery location). At the drop-point, each identification is scanned. Scans are sent to the WMS computer, which depletes a SKU identification and quantity in the files. The computer increases SKU inventory that was placed onto a delivery truck. SKU identification and quantity are transferred to an order destination and updated in the WMS inventory files. In the host computer, the total inventory remains the quantity that was unloaded and received at the receiving dock. If a delivery truck is not parked at a WMS drop delivery/point shipping dock door, an across-the-dock pallet is placed and scanned/read at a shipping dock staging area for later loading with manifest activity on the delivery truck.

Warehouse Operation and SKU-Identification Symbology

Each identification label must have a human- and machine-readable section. A human-readable label has alpha characters or numeric digits printed in black on a white background; a machine-readable label has bars or symbology in black, blue, or gray on a white background. A black bar and white space between two black bars determine a code data. For maximum readability, there are quiet zones between the end of each bar code and the label edge. The length of the bar code is equal to the distance between the first and last bar codes. Bar-code labels may be printed on-site in an on-demand basis, or preprinted labels by a separate company. A bar code is read on a SKU, on a storage/pick position structural member, or on a carton/container travel path, and has sufficient width to contain WMS data. In a conventional warehouse with a WMS program, a

WMS order identification on a vendor-delivered SKU, fixed storage/pick position, or warehouse or container/carton identification may be read by an employee, a scanner, or an RF tag receiver. When the labels are designed, it is important to ensure that the alpha characters/numeric digits are easily understood by employees, as well as having a symbology that satisfies machine-reading parameters. The options are:

- 2 of 5 bar code
- Inter-leaven 2 of 5
- Code 3 of 9
- RF tag

Symbology Orientation

The symbology label orientation (black bars and white spaces) as an impact on the use of an employee hand-held scanner/RF tag reader activity or a fixed position bar-code scanner. Important bar-code label-ladder and picket-fence design features are:

- The identification label is printed with quiet zones between first and last black bar edge and paper label edge
- An oversquared or near-oversquared label has a black-bar length equal to the width of the total black bars and white spaces
- Each black bar is printed with sharp edges on a white background or RF tag transmits a signal that is received by a reciever

The bar-code label orientation design options are

1. A ladder orientation has one black bar and white space stacked on top of each other in a vertical direction or parallel to the floor surface. With the floor surface as "south," the black bars and white space run "east/west." With a bar code in a ladder orientation, the scanner light beam is vertical to the floor or conveyor. A storage/pick design that uses man-down forklift truck will use a narrow WMS label on a storage/pick position flat surface or on a SKU on a conveyor.
2. A picket fence orientation has black bar and white space bottoms that face or are perpendicular to the floor. With the floor surface as "south," the black bars and white space run "north/south." With a bar code in a picket fence orientation, the scanner light beam is horizontal to the floor or conveyor. A storage/pick design that uses a man-down forklift truck will use a wide label design on a storage/pick position flat surface or on a SKU on a conveyor.
3. A hybrid label face with ladder and picket fence symbology permits maximum flexibility in a warehouse that uses a manual forklift truck or AS/RS crane. An identification with a ladder and picket fence symbology means that the same symbology (black bars and white spaces) is printed in both orientations on one white surface. When an employee looks at a combination label, there are two bar symbologies or codes. One symbology is "north/south;" the second symbology is "east/west." With a hybrid label on a SKU, a fixed beam scanner will easily read a ladder label; a forklift truck driver with a hand-held scanner will easily read a picket fence label. The hybrid label ensures the maximum good readability with minimal scanner or label cost.

Vendor-Delivered SKU or Customer-Order Symbology Location

As a vendor-delivered SKU is unloaded and received, an identification label is placed on each SKU. The design team ensures that there is appropriate line-of-sight for a scanner (e.g., bar-code scanner, RF-tag reader) as a SKU moves over a travel path. In a conventional warehouse with storage/pick positions, the placement of the bar-code labels must allow an employee (using a hand-held scanner) to complete a storage/pick scan.

Vendor-Delivered SKU Label Design

After the design team has selected a SKU bar-code type and orientation (or RF tag), the label design options are:

- A label face has a white background with black bars printed on its surface
- the location on a SKU/carrier

The label background options are:

- Self-adhesive labels have a paper surface with a self-adhesive back. The self-adhesive surface has a protective cover that is removed (by an employee or machine) for attachment directly onto a SKU carrier or carton/container. The adhesive is tested to ensure the label remains on a pallet, container, or carton material; an employee can remove a disposable label from a SKU.
- Plain paper labels have the same characteristics as self-adhesive labels, except that the label is inserted into a pallet, container, or carton holder. A holder back is secured to a pallet, container, or carton.
- Chipboard labels have the same characteristics as the plain paper labels, except that chipboard is a more rigid material.

Symbology Label Face Direction

The symbology label face direction is the direction a label faces on a SKU as it travels on a conveyor or rests in a storage position. The choices are a single-face label or wrap-around label. Selection factors are SKU or order type, in-house transport, and storage/pick design.

Single Face Label

A single-face identification label has the symbology printed on a short label paper surface. The dimensions of this type of label permit an oversquared label to be printed on its surface, as well as permitting a picket-fence or ladder–bar-code orientation.

In a conventional forklift pallet/master-carton warehouse that uses single-face identification labels on pallets, master cartons, or single items in containers, the label faces one direction. As the labeled pallet, master carton, or container moves over a travel path (or sits in a storage position), a forklift truck will complete a scan/read and physical pallet, master-carton, or container storage transaction, and a scanner will be able to complete a scan.

Wrap-Around Label

A wrap-around identification label has one long bar code or two identical symbologies printed on long label paper. With picket-fence symbology, the identification is printed onto two sides of the label face. This means that each bar code faces one travel direction. With a bar-code ladder label, a wrap-around bar code is (same one long label that covers a label face or the same bar code is printed twice in different sections on a label face or surface). With a wrap-around identification label on a pallet, carton, or container, or a SKU moving over a travel path (or sitting in a storage position), the label faces the forward direction of travel and on a SKU's side. A wrap-around facing two directions of a compass direction permits the best maximum line-of-sight (for a hand-held or fixed-position scanner) or RF tag reader reception, as well as maximum flexibility to move pallets, cartons, or containers between storage/pick positions.

Master-Carton or Pallet Symbology Location

Symbology location is the label's physical location on a master carton, pallet carrier, or tray. Symbology location (along with the design factors) ensure that the label will have good line-of-sight/RF-tag reader reception on a travel path or in a storage/pick position.

Master-Carton Symbology Location

In a master-carton/container warehouse, master-carton identification location options are side, top, front, and bottom. The most frequent locations for a single-face WMS symbology or identification label are on a master carton's side, front, and top. There are several bar-code scanner line-of-sight considerations (e.g., depth of field, travel speed, gap between two bar codes, bar-code tilt, skew) when a carton with a single-face WMS top identification label is moving on a travel path, or is in a storage position. The single-face WMS top identification label option is used on a shipping conveyor travel design. When a wrap-around identification label is used in a warehouse that has carton-replenishment activity to carton flow-rack pick positions, the most common label locations are on a master carton's side and front. Placing the identification on the side and front permits bar-code scanner line-of-sight along a travel path from two directions. A side and front label location also permits bar-code and employee line-of-sight for a carton flow rack or shelf pick position. A single-face bar-code label on a master-carton bottom permits bar-code scanner line-of-sight from one direction. When an employee handles a carton, a bottom bar-code location makes it difficult for an employee to read a bar-code label.

Pallet Identification

In a pallet warehouse, the identification location options are on the pallet's side, front, or top.

Side Bar-Code Label

A side-pallet identification label location is known as a solid stringer or notched four-way entry side. A front identification label pallet location is known as a fork opening side. With an identification label side option, the single-face or wrap-around identification is placed on the stringer side, block side, or the layer of a master carton. A single-face identification label faces one direction, and requires scanner-device line-of-sight or RF-tag–reader reception. In a conventional forklift truck warehouse, as a pallet with a side identification label is placed into a storage/pick position, the pallet orientation has fork opening facing the forklift truck aisle; the WMS symbology is on a pallet side. In a conventional pallet storage warehouse, the side bar-code identification label requires double handling by the forklift truck, which lowers employee productivity. In an AS/RS warehouse, it is not a problem for an AS/RS crane to handle a side-labeled pallet due to a fixed-position scanner used to read the identification, but when a forklift truck completes a P/D station transfer, there will be a restriction on bar-code scanner line-of-sight/RF tag reader. The RF tag reader will receive the identifcation, but the employee's ability to read the identification will be restricted.

A wrap-around identification label on a pallet side means that one bar-code picket-fence label faces a side and one label faces front or one long bar-code label that has a ladder orientation on a label face. A two-bar–code label permits scanning from both the side and the front. With a conventional forklift truck or AS/RS warehouse, this feature minimizes line-of-sight problems on the travel path or in a storage/pick position.

Stringer or Block-Pallet Symbology or Label Location

A stringer pallet has three stringers (also known as bearer boards) that support the top and bottom deck boards. A pallet stringer side has a solid, flat, and smooth surface that permits an identification attachment (the label can also be attached to an exterior stringer's front). A block pallet has blocks on pallet corners; some pallets have a middle block. Each block permits an identification attachment (or, again, to an exterior stringer's front). A pallet identification uniquely identifies a pallet and permits a forklift truck driver or an AS/RS crane to complete a storage transaction, as well as allowing line-of-sight or RF tag reader reception. The design options are:

- With a single-face label, stringer or block side;
- With a wrap-around label, right stringer or block;
- With a wrap-around label, left stringer or block;
- With a single-face label, stringer or block, middle stringer or block;
- With a single-face label, master carton on bottom layer;
- With a wrap-around label, master carton on a bottom layer.

To assure good productivity when the forklift truck driver scans the labels, the identification is on the pallet fork's opening side.

When a pallet identification is placed onto a pallet's right stringer side or master carton's bottom layer, a wrap-around label face is used with a bar-code label facing two directions to ensure maximum scanner line-of-sight and good employee productivity. One label direction has an identification face on the fork's opening side or front, which permits the forklift truck driver's bar-code scanner (or RF tag reader) to make an identification. Bar-code scanners (or RF tag readers) are set along a conveyor path. When a single-face or wrap-around identification is on a pallet's right stringer front, an identification label may be read by both a conventional forklift truck and an AS/RS with in-feed and out-feed conveyors. A label on a pallet's right side and front (fork opening) permits right-handed forklift truck drivers to make an identification.

When a single-face identification is placed on a pallet's left stringer side (or a master carton's bottom layer), a wrap-around label faces only one direction and has limited scanner line-of-sight flexibility. A pallet bar-code label faces a fork's opening side. If the identification is on a pallet left side and front, a right-handed forklift truck driver, with some additional effort, will have scanner line-of-sight to make an identification. Placing a single face or wrap-around identification on a pallet's left stringer front will ensure line-of-sight for a conventional forklift truck, as well as meeting requirements for AS/RS with in-feed and out-feed conveyors. An identification on a pallet's right side and front will permit a forklift truck driver's scanner line-of-sight to make an identification.

When a single-face label is on a pallet's middle stringer front (or a master carton's bottom layer), the label's location ensures line-of-sight for a conventional forklift truck and meets the requirements of an AS/RS with in-feed and out-feed conveyors. An identification on a pallet's middle stringer front and face means that a right-handed forklift truck driver, with some additional effort, will have bar-code scanner line-of-sight (or RF tag reader reception) to make an identification.

Bar-code scanners/RF tag readers are set at an angle along a conveyor path to ensure line-of-sight for scanners and optimum reception for RF tag readers.

Warehouse Operation Bar-Code Identification on a Carton AS/RS Tray

With a carton AS/RS design that uses a tray to support master cartons in a storage location, a design team has the following options regarding the location of tray bar-code identification:

- With sufficient edges, the identification can be on the side, front, or rear
- With sufficient lip width or interior space, the identification can be on the top
- The identification can be on the bottom

An AS/RS tray travels on a conveyor between a storage position and a master-carton transfer station. At the transfer station, the conveyor is designed to ensure that a bar-code label faces an employee hand-held scanner or a fixed-position bar-code scanner/RF tag reader.

Machine-Readable Symbology: Life Expectancy

When machine-readable symbology is used in a warehouse, the design teams may opt for:

- Permanent symbology may be used to identify a storage/pick position, tote/carton, or storage device (e.g., pallet, tote, trolley, cart). To minimize damage to the black bar or white space, the surface is coated to last a long time. Alternatively, it is placed in a sleeve and is attached to a storage/pick position, the flat surface of structural member, or to a captive SKU or order carrier (e.g., stacking frame, pallet, cage). In a warehouse that has a reusable SKU carrier or pick container, a permanent identification is zero scanned by an employee. The scan is sent to the WMS computer, and the permanent symbology SKU quantity is updated to zero and is made available for another SKU or order.
- Disposable symbology is used on a vendor-delivered SKU or shipping container/carton. It is printed on plain paper or a self-adhesive label. After it has served its purpose, the label is removed from the SKU or carton and thrown in the trash.

Symbology: Scanner or Reader Options

A vendor-delivered SKU or pick activity is a WMS supported or non-WMS supported transaction. With a WMS supported transaction, a WMS program has an employee controlled or fixed position bar-code scanner/RF tag reader scans/reads a SKU, order or storage/pick position identification. In a warehouse with a WMS program, the design team symbology scan/read device options are

- Hhand-held scanner that is (a) contact or (b) noncontact scanner. In a dynamic warehouse, a contact scanner is not preferred due to low employee productivity and read rates
- Fixed position scanner with a laser light beam that is (a) fixed, (b) moving, and (c) waving

Noncontact Bar-Code Scanner/RF Tag Reader

When a SKU, order or storage/pick position is stationary, a scan transaction is completed by a noncontact hand-held scanner/reader device. A hand-held scanner/reader is controlled and operated by an employee. An employee directs a hand-held scanner light beam at a bar-code/RF tag, ensures that a scanner/reader obtains a good read, and per a storage/pick activity, an employee enters a piece quantity into a scanner/reader and sends a scan/read transaction to the WMS computer. To minimize hand-held scanner/reader damage, an employee has a scanner holster, scanner/reader is attached to a work table, or a forklift truck has a scanner/reader holder. The design team hand-held scanner/reader options are 1) small battery powered device that has battery replacement or battery recharging and is used for a forklift truck, picker or packer scan transaction and 2) wire connected to an electric outlet or forklift truck battery that has sufficient electric cord length to permit an employee to walk from a process station or forklift truck operator platform to scan/read a position or SKU.

Fixed Position Symbology Scanner or Reader

In a warehouse with SKUs or orders that move over a conveyor travel path, a warehouse with a WMS program uses a fixed position symbology scanner/reader device. With bar-code scanning/RF tag reading SKUs or orders on a moving travel path, important scan/read factors are 1) sybmology presentation. RF tag presentation factor is to assure that a RF tag transmission is received by a local reader. Bar-code presentation factors are (a) side identification that is used on a master carton, pallet, or container, (b) top identification on a master carton, pallet, or container, and (c) front identification that is used on a master carton, pallet, or container, 2) depth of field that is, as a SKU WMS bar code passes a scanner, the distance between a scanner is closest to and furthest from a SKU WMS bar-code or RF tag reader receives a signal, 3) travel speed that is a SKU WMS bar-code travel speed as it passes a bar-code scanner/RF tag reader, and 4) gap between two SKU WMS bar codes/RF tags that is an open space between two SKU WMS bar codes/RF tags.

Fixed position WMS bar-code scanner options are 1) fixed beam scanner that means a scanner light beam is thrown on a conveyor travel path location. A fixed beam scanner is used with a standard SKU WMS bar-code location, side scan operation and is low cost. With a fixed position scanner, a SKU WMS bar-code ladder orientation and a SKU WMS bar-code placement window on a SKU improves bar-code good read number, 2) waving beam bar-code scanner that means one scanner light beam is moving in (a) vertical direction between above a conveyor travel path or (b) in horizontal direction between two locations on a conveyor travel path. A waving beam bar-code scanner is used on a side scan operation with a fixed bar-code scanner location but some flexibility with a degree of tilt, 3) moving beam WMS bar-code scanner that means several elliptical shaped light beams are thrown on a conveyor travel path location. A moving beam bar-code scanner is used on a top or side scan operation, maximum SKU WMS bar-code tilt and skew and location and a higher cost, and 4) RF reader requires general area due to a RF receiver receiving a RF tag signal.

Symbology Scanner/Reader Location along a SKU Transport Design Travel Path

A powered carton, pallet, or in-house transport moves a SKU past a symbology scanner/reader located along the travel path. A RF tag symbology reader requires a RF tag transmission. A fixed position bar-code scanner emits a laser light beam onto a SKU travel path, which reads the symbology. The design team's bar-code scanner location options are:

1. Side location. A bar-code scanner that is side located along a travel path allows a short depth of field, more constant bar-code location on a SKU/order, and a less costly bar-code scanner device. A bar code on each pallet, carton, trolley neck, or order on a travel path creates a gap between two bar codes. This permits a fixed-position scanner to read codes. When a carton or pallet-side label is scanned with a hand-held scanner, there is line-of-sight to the bar code.

2. Top location. A bar-code scanner that is above a travel path allows a moderate depth of field, and restricted bar-code location on a pallet, master carton, or order. A bar code on each pallet, master carton, or order on a travel path creates an open space between two bar codes. An employee will have some difficulty completing a scan.

3. Front bar-code scanner location has a long depth field and the scanner light beam is angled onto a travel path. To scan a pallet or master-carton front label, the bar-code label travels past a constant location and the powered travel path creates a gap between two codes. A bar-code scanner has a higher cost.

4. Bottom bar-code scanner location. This has no application in a warehouse that sends pallets, master cartons or cartons to outside customers, or that are handled in other warehouse work stations. This is due to the difficulty to hand scan a bottom-attached label.

Symbology Location in a Storage/Pick Aisle

In a storage/pick aisle, a storage/pick position symbology location is determined by the warehouse's forklift truck type, storage design, and pick design. A label on a storage or pick position's structural member ensures that a forklift truck driver, replenishment employee, or scanner/reader (e.g., picker hand-held scanner/reader, RF tag reader) can make a position identification. In a conventional storage/pick design with a man-down operated wide aisle or narrow-aisle forklift truck, the identification is located on a storage/pick position load beam, upright post, or placard. In a narrow-aisle man-up forklift truck storage/pick design, the identification is located on a storage/pick position shelf or rack structural member.

Identification at a Pick Position

A design team ensures that each SKU pick position in standard shelf/rack design pick side has a discreet identification. In a gravity flow-rack with a pick aisle and replenishment aisle, each pick position has a SKU replenishment and pick-side identification. Both pick- and replenishment-position identifications ensure good scans/reads. During a SKU pick-line setup, replenishment to a pick position, or completion of a pick transaction, the pick-position identification is considered an employee instruction component. Each SKU pick position has specific design characteristics:

- In a warehouse using a standard pallet rack or shelf storage/pick design, the identification is located on a rack load beam/shelf lip or upright post. If a warehouse is using a floor stack pallet storage design, the pick-position identification may be embedded in the floor, be on a placard hung from the ceiling, or attached to an upright position that is between two floor stack lanes.
- In a warehouse using a small single-item pick design, the pick-position identification is a self-adhesive label attached to a pick side structural member, replenishment side structural member, or automatic pick machine replenishment sleeve or lane.

Symbology Scan/Read Transmittal to the WMS Computer

The data from a WMS supported transaction and completed scan/read transaction is transmitted from the scanner to the WMS computer. The design team reviews peak scanner/reader transactions, transmittals per hour, and computer hardware capability to determine an acceptable number of scan/read transactions/transmittals per minute. The design team's scanner/reader transaction transmittal options are:

- Scanner/reader holds scan/read transactions in memory and transmit at a later time
- Scanner/reader transmits the scan/read transactions to a PC (personal computer), which batches and transmits scan/read transactions at a predetermined time
- Scanner/reader transmits on-line to the WMS computer

With a hand-held scanner/reader, the options are an RF transmittal that has RF antennas and communication network connected to a PC WMS computer or an electric wire to a PC or WMS computer.

A fixed-position scanner/reader has a direct communication with a PC or WMS computer. The design team selects a scan/read transaction transmittal option based on the cost of the scanner/reader and communication network, value for transaction on-line, and number of scan/read transaction transmittals per minute.

Scanner/Reader Data Transfer

A key feature of a scanner/reader is the ability to transfer data to the WMS computer. This transfer may be done in the following ways:

- On-line (or real-time) transfer. In an on-line data transfer, the scanner/reader transfers data immediately to the WMS computer. To use on-line data communication, the WMS computer must be capable of receiving scan data along with other communications. Because the WMS computer must always be available to receive data, on-line data transfer requires large computer capacity (and, therefore, higher cost).

■ Delayed (or held in memory). A delayed data transfer scan/read identification transactions are either held in the scanner's memory or sent to a PC to be held in memory. At a predetermined time (or when the WMS computer is available to receive data), scan data are batched and sent to the WMS computer. This approach allows greater flexibility regarding receipt of scan data, and thus requires smaller computer capacity than on-line transfers (and lower cost).

Identification Scanner Transaction Accounting

Identification scanner transaction accounting is used by a pick, pack, check, or manifest employee to record a transaction, SKU, or order into a hand-held scanner. The employee may either physically press a button for each scan transaction (2–3 seconds per transaction), or the hand-held scanner can be set to a default mode in which it registers a transaction as an automatic entry every time the employee presses the "entry" button. The latter approach increases employee productivity by two to three seconds per transaction).

Using an Order Shipping Carton as a Pick Carton

If a pick/pass design uses a shipping carton as a pick-line carton, as orders are introduced to a pick line, each order has a shipping carton predetermined by a order piece cube. Shipping-cartons may enter a pick line in random size order or by order group in which the shipping cartons all have the same size.

Order Pick Cell or Pick Train

In a pick-to-light design, orders are sent to all pick-to-light pick positions or orders travel on a take-away conveyor and diverted from a take-away conveyor onto a separate pick-cell conveyor or entire pick line conveyor. In each design, the permanent identification or WMS order identification is sent to a pick-to-light pick zone. In a pick-to-light pick zone, each SKU pick position has a SKU on an order. Order identifications may reach pick-positions as a pick train on a conveyor or as an order diverted to a pick cell.

Order Pick Train

In a pick-to-light pick train design customer order presentation is involved in all pick positions. The design has all totes/cartons at a pick-line start station enter onto a zero pressure pick-line conveyor that moves totes/cartons past all pick zones and past all pick positions. A pick train option has pickers to pick pass totes/cartons over a nonpowered pick-line conveyor travel path for travel through all pick zones and past all pick positions. The components are:

■ Order identification bar-code scanner/RF tag reader

- A nonpowered pick-line travel path with crimp plate stops, or a zero-pressure conveyor with pop-up stops
- SKU pick-to-light pick positions with pick-zone indicators
- Powered take-away conveyor for completed orders

After a tote/shipping carton receives (or becomes associated with) an order identification, the identification is used by the pick-line computer to activate pick-to-light pick positions that have ordered SKUs. Along a main or in-feed conveyor, a scanner/reader associates the warehouse's permanent identification with a transferred WMS order identification, or the warehouse computer prints a disposable WMS order identification, which is attached to a tote/shipping carton. A tote/carton enters a pick line on a pick-line conveyor. A pick-line conveyor is a nonpowered or is a powered zero-pressure roller conveyor. A pick-line conveyor is a continuous conveyor that directs each carton/tote past all pick positions with a pick-to-light section. If a pick line is a nonpowered conveyor, the first picker pushes or passes; with a zero-pressure pick conveyor travel path, if a picker does not grab a tote/carton, powered rollers move the carton/tote train from one pick zone to another.

On a pick-line travel path, a tote/carton pick-train order identification sequence is maintained on a pick conveyor until all ordered SKU picks are completed for an order or are within a pick zone. After an order is completed within a pick zone, a picker pushes a completed tote/carton from a pick-line conveyor onto a take-away conveyor or pushes the tote/carton train member along a pick-line conveyor. A tote travels the entire pick line as an one-way travel path and all totes take the same path from start to end. At the start or end, an employee (or machine) adds packing slips, invoices, sales literature, delivery address labels, and other company information. It should be noted that if a tote/carton requires SKU picks from a slow-moving section (i.e., another pick area), each order identification may be scanned/read to a pick-line section at an entrance to each pick-line pick zone, or the picker maintains a completed order transfer and matches a tote/carton identification to the pick-to-light display screen. If there is no match, a pick-to-light vendor procedure is followed. A take-away conveyor gap plate is installed between pick and take-away conveyors for easy transfer from the pick-line conveyor to a take-away conveyor.

To maximize picker productivity, a pick line is separated into multiple pick zones. Each pick zone has a predetermined number of pick-positions. To ensure controlled tote/carton movement, as totes/cartons queue in a pick zone, the middle or end section of each pick-line pick-zone has a pop-up stop (a moveable crimped or flat-stop plate) that permits a picker-controlled movement of totes/cartons between two pick zones. A pop-up stop is controlled by the picker assigned to a pick zone. Each pop-up (or plate) stop is located in a pick zone that permits a picker maximum access to pick positions. If a pick zone has a high-to-low profile, a stop located in the middle of the zone is the preferred location: it minimizes a picker's walk to activated pick-to-light positions. If a pick zone has a low-to-high or random profile, a stop located at the end is the preferred location. If a picker in a pick zone does not maintain expected picker productivity, tote/carton movement is halted by the stop device. This design is used with pallets, carton flow racks parallel or perpendicular (with an aisle between sections) to a pick conveyor, or shelf sections parallel or perpendicular (with an aisle between sections) to a pick conveyor.

A scanner/reader is located at each pick zone entrance. As completed orders are pushed from a pick conveyor to a take-away conveyor, the carton/tote pick train is pick/passed or pushed from one zone to the next with a different carton/tote identification sequence. The scanner/reader at the zone entrance sends each carton/tote identification in a first-in–first-out sequence to a pick-line computer. A warehouse computer sequences orders in a pick-to-light design to match the tote/carton train sequence.

Flags (or indicators) are used along a pick-line conveyor to identify the zone start and end. This helps ensure good picker productivity. To help accurate SKU transfer from a pick position into a tote/carton, a picker uses a clip to identify the tote/carton that matches the order identification shown on the display screen. During high-volume pick or order days, in a pick zone with high SKU pick volume or tote/carton movement, pop-up stops are deactivated or crimp plate stops are removed and additional pickers are added to the zone. This helps minimize delays.

The order take-away conveyor is along-side the pick conveyor. The carton/tote take-away conveyor permits a picker to transfer a completed carton/tote from a pick train onto a high-speed conveyor for transport from one pick section to the next or to a pack area. With fewer cartons/totes in the pick train, a pick train is more easily pushed over a nonpowered pick conveyor and creates gaps between cartons/totes on a powered zero-pressure conveyor. With high-volume SKU picks for one pick zone, picker productivity determines the number of order completions. On a low-volume day, pick zones are expanded and orders are completed in less time.

Order Pick Cell

A pick-to-light pick cell design is a way of presenting cartons/totes to pick positions within a specific pick zone. In this design, all totes/cartons travel on a powered take-away or by-pass conveyor. Along a powered take-away conveyor, there are scanners/readers that control pick-cell divert devices. After a scanner/reader reads each tote/carton identification, the warehouse computer activates a divert to transfer the tote/carton onto a pick-cell conveyor. The components of a tote/carton pick cell are:

- Each pick cell has a scanner/reader
- A powered take-away conveyor with a divert for each pick cell
- A pick-line conveyor with a front-powered belt conveyor at the front and nonpowered or zero-pressure roller conveyor
- A pick-to-light SKU pick position with pick zone indicators

After a tote/carton receives a WMS order identification label or becomes associated with a WMS order identification, the computer transfers all order identifications to a label placed onto the carton/tote. The order identification is used by a pick-line computer to activate a pick-to-light SKU pick-position displays.

As the tote/carton leaves an identification station, order identifications are on a first-in–first-out sequence on a take-away or main conveyor. On the conveyor, each carton/tote is directed past a pick-cell scanner/reader. Each pick cell has a front-power conveyor to move cartons/totes from an in-feed pick-cell conveyor section on the conveyor. A pick cell divert and powered conveyor section permits continuous carton/tote transfer from the main conveyor onto a pick-cell conveyor.

If a WMS program or warehouse carton/tote requires a SKU from a pick-cell pick position, the carton/tote is diverted from a take-away conveyor onto a pick-cell conveyor. As the carton/tote travels on the conveyor travel, the scanner/reader sends a message to the pick computer, which activates the pick-cell pick-to-lights. Because each order identification is scanned/read and diverted into a pick cell, each carton/tote is sequenced on a first-in/first-out basis. On a pick-cell conveyor, the tote/carton sequence is maintained until all picks are completed or an order is completed and pushed onto a take-away conveyor. If a tote/carton has another SKU pick from another pick cell, the carton/tote travels on a take-away conveyor and the process is repeated at a different pick cell. If a carton/tote is a completed order, a take-away conveyor transports the tote/carton to a pack station.

If a pick-cell SKU profile has high-volume SKUs at the pick-cell entrance and low-volume SKUs at the pick-cell end, the majority picks will be in the pick-cell's first half. As a picker completes an order, a pick-to-light display indicates a complete order and the picker pushes the completed order from a pick conveyor onto a main/take-away conveyor. On the take-away conveyor, the tote/carton travels to the next pick-cell scanner/reader for transfer to another pick cell or a pack area.

Bar-Code or RF Tag Label Packing Slip

In a catalog, e-mail, or direct marketing warehouse, a packing slip is placed with SKUs in the shipping carton/container. Prior to a shipping carton/container leaving a warehouse, a delivery address label is placed on the sealed shipping-carton's exterior. In a pick/pass or in a batched order warehouse, each ordered batch of SKUs or shipping carton has a packing slip and delivery label. In a pallet operation, a packing slip accompanies the pallet to the customer location. The options for packing slips and delivery address labels are:

1. A design team can decided to have batched pick labels or packing slips and delivery labels centrally printed and distributed to a pick/pass line entry station. Packing slips and delivery labels are printed in the same sequence as the order sequence at an entry to a pick line. With a batched pick design, labels are printed in pick-position sequence. Batched pick labels are delivered to a picker dispatch station. With a pick-and-pass design, each packing slip and delivery label group is delivered to an assigned pick line that has received the WMS computer order transfer. As each pick/pass tote/shipping carton enters a pick line, it receives a packing slip/delivery label and identification that matches the order identification sequence. The design is used with a pick/pass design, minimizes a printer number and print request, increases packing slip/delivery label controls and distribution to a proper pick line.
2. Another option is to have packing slips and delivery labels centrally printed and distributed to each pack station. Packing slips and delivery labels are printed in the same group sorted to each pack station. Packing slips and delivery labels are sorted/separated into groups. The warehouse moves a SKU pick or inventory code to ensure that a specific SKU is diverted to the assigned sort/pack station. Each packing slip and delivery label group is delivered to the assigned pack station. This design minimizes the number of printers and print request but increases packing slip controls and distribution to a proper pack station. The design is used with a batched pick and sort design.
3. The third choice is have packing slips and delivery labels printed at each pick-line entry location or start station. Packing slips are printed in the same sequence for an order's entry to a pick line. This is especially useful for a disciplined pick line with a specific entry or sequence (e.g., shipping-carton size). This design downloads packing slips/delivery labels to various print locations. If there is a requirement for separate packing slips and delivery labels printers, there will be two printers at each pick-line entry. Each packing slip and delivery label is printed at the pick-line entry/start station and the pick-line transfer matches the packing slip. The design minimizes the number of printers and print requests.
4. Packing slips and delivery labels can be printed at each pack station. Each pack station receives a complete order in a tote/carton. After a pack station employee scans the order

identification, the printer at the pack station prints the packing slip and label. This design has the number of print requests and requires a printer at each pack station.

Captive-Tote/Shipping-Carton Identification at a Print or Pack Station

When a captive pick-tote or pick/shipping carton arrives at a print-and-pack station, each captive tote/shipping carton has a unique warehouse identification. At the pick-line entry, the warehouse identification is associated with a WMS order identification. As a tote/carton arrives at a pack station, it is scanned to register order completion. A pack station scan removes the association with a WMS order identification. The scan allows the permament identification to be associated or reused with another WMS order. If a warehouse container is released without a warehouse scan, the WMS computer considers that a container has two WMS orders. This situation creates problems on a pick line, including low productivity on a pick line and pack station, and potential pick/pack errors.

Chapter 4

Logistics Segment or Warehouse Operation Receiving Activity and Concepts with a WMS Program

Introduction

Receiving functions and dock areas are as important as storage and pick function areas. The receiving dock is where everything in a warehouse starts. To ensure that a warehouse has an efficient and cost-effective receiving dock, six elements are necessary:

- A vendor vehicle dock schedule program.
- A central office to control all receiving activities, including the printing of tally sheets and identification labels, and to ensure closure on orders and accurate communication with the WMS or host computer.
- An identification for each SKU, to ensure that physical data sent to the WMS computer is accurate.
- A project dock/door number and a method for bridging the dock edge and truck gap.
- A large receiving staging.
- A sufficient number of well-designed SKU travel paths from a receiving area to a storage area.

A warehouse receives and unloads SKUs from vendor delivery trucks, ocean-going containers, or rail cars. At a receiving operation, a vendor delivery vehicle is unloaded and received at the truck receiving dock; a rail car is unloaded at the rail car receiving area. Each master carton or pallet

SKU receives an WMS identification and is sent from a receiving dock to a storage position. From a receiving area, each SKU quantity is sent to a WMS computer or host computer for inventory update.

Receiving functions include assigning a delivery truck to a dock position (or temporary holding yard), assigning a rail car to a spur location, and sending each identification and purchase order to the WMS computer. Using a receiving dock permits a warehouse to handle a large number of vendor delivery trucks, ocean-going containers, and rail cars; to unload, sort, and stage a greater SKU volume and flow through a facility. A receiving activity ensures that each SKU has a company and WMS identification; QA (quality assurance) department is sent a sample quantity; and that a received inventory is entered into a WMS or host computer that completes the receiving activity or closes a company purchase order.

A WMS Program Starts at the Receiving Dock

The WMS program starts at the vendor delivery or receiving dock. After a receiving clerk unloads the SKU (see Figure 4.1), a receiving clerk bulk counts or verifies the vendor's count for each master carton and pallet and verifies that the quantity matches the company purchase order. The clerk completes a receiving document and company purchase order. After the clerk identifies each SKU with a WMS identification and registers each SKU, the quantity and identifications are entered into the WMS computer.

When a receiving clerk enters each identification and quantity into the WMS computer, each identification and quantity entry starts a WMS program. The clerk closes a company purchase order and the computer sends a piece quantity to the host computer. At that point, the SKU is listed as "available for sale" or in a QA hold inventory status. The vendor's responsibilities are to provide quality merchandise that follow the specifications in the company purchase order, in the exact quantity and master carton size/quality, and with company identification on each SKU and master carton exterior surface (in an appropriate location). Some vendors apply a WMS identification to each SKU. This improves SKU flow through a receiving operation and minimizes warehouse expenses, but slightly increases the cost of goods sold. If a vendor provides a SKU without an identification on the exterior surface, it decreases SKU flow time through a receiving operation and label cost becomes a warehouse distribution expense (not cost of goods). It is not preferred for a dynamic storage/pick concept with a WMS program.

Vendor Delivery Purchase Order and Advance Shipping Notice (ASN)

A key member of the design team is from the company purchasing or merchandising department. A company purchase order starts the process that includes SKU flow and information and data flow. A company purchase order is essentially a contract between the company and the vendor, which states that the vendor is to deliver a specified SKU quantity within a specified date range to the warehouse. To have an efficient warehouse with a WMS program, the warehouse is designed so that copies of vendor purchase orders to be sent from the company host computer to a vendor and receiving department as either a paper or e-mail document.

The receiving department communicates with vendors and ensures that a vendor creates an advance shipping notice (ASN). An ASN is based on the company purchase order details, and indicates the vendor name, and delivery date (at the warehouse receiving dock), SKU quantity, the

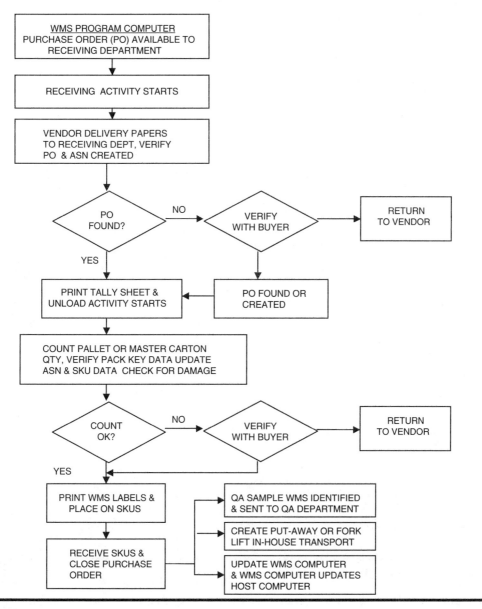

Figure 4.1   Receiving Process Overview

vendor's delivery company or dispatch telephone number, fax number, or e-mail address, and the purchase order number. An ASN is filed in the receiving dock PC (personal computer) or files and is critical to the receiving dock schedule program and in the unloading and receiving process.

Receiving Dock Schedule

A receiving dock schedule helps create an efficient receiving dock with high employee productivity, good dock utilization, low demurge charges, and smooth SKU flow from the dock to storage positions (see Figure 4.2). A receiving dock schedule program may be WMS supported or

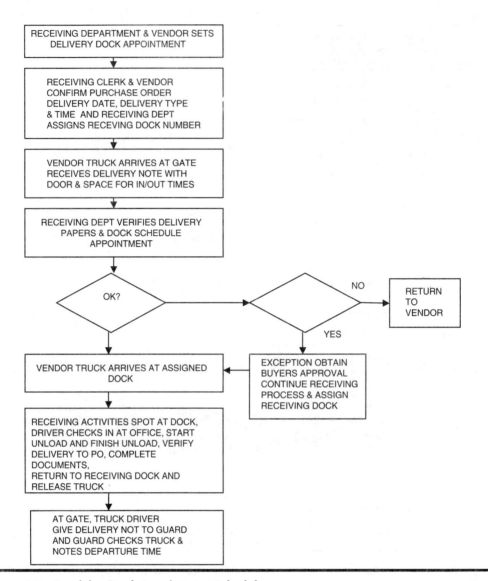

Figure 4.2 Receiving Dock Appointment Schedule

nonsupported. The dock schedule starts when the receiving department receives obtaining a purchase order or vendor ASN. After a receiving dock employee confirms the vendor name, SKU quantity, delivery company telephone number, fax number, and/or e-mail address, and company purchase order number, the clerk confirms delivery date and time.

The receiving dock schedule is a PC or paper spread sheet with a column or row for each day of the year. There is one column for each receiving dock location; each dock location is a discreet number. Each row is separated by intervals of 15, 30, 45, or 60 minutes, and has sufficient space to write or type important ASN information.

With a truck or ocean-going container ASN, a receiving company employee telephones or e-mails the vendor or delivery company, confirms the delivery date and time, SKU quantity, and load type. If the delivery date varies beyond a standard set by the merchandise department, the clerk obtains approval from the merchandise department. The clerk then assigns a receiving dock for the delivery vehicle. The clerk estimates total time needed to unload and sign delivery documents, and blocks out the required time for a specific dock location on the schedule. Late or early delivery truck arrivals are noted on the schedule sheet for future reference.

When a delivery truck arrives at the warehouse's entrance gate, a guard verifies the delivery on the receiving dock schedule, which shows the assigned receiving dock. After the guard notifies a receiving department clerk, a guard prepares a note with the arrival time and receiving dock number. The note is given to the delivery truck driver, who drives to the assigned receiving dock. When the delivery truck departs, the truck driver returns the note at a guard station. A guard indicates the delivery truck departure time on the receiving dock schedule.

Warehouse Receiving and Ship Dock Design

A warehouse with a WMS program is designed with separate receiving and ship docks. The design features are:

- A rectangular facility with dock doors with a short distance from the receiving dock area to warehouse storage
- Sufficient dock area warehouse equipment
- Truck dock guides and dock canopy
- Painted lines on a dock staging area floor or staging racks for controlled SKU staging
- Aisles in which all count and WMS SKU identification activities may be conducted
- Sufficient floor or ceiling strength to support imposed loads from the dock equipment, SKU staging, and transport
- Sufficient ceiling height for an elevated office

Given warehouse activity, receiving dock/doors may be located directly opposite each other opposite long sides, on corners on opposing long sides, or on corners on the same side.

If a warehouse handles master cartons or pallets, one of the objectives of the unloading/receiving department is to unload SKUs on schedule, verify that the SKU, master carton, or pallet quantity matches the company purchase order, and ensure each SKU has a company identification and each master carton (or single items in a master carton) or pallet SKU has a company-applied WMS identification.

If the quantities delivered by the vendor do not match the purchase order, the company receiving and purchasing departments make the necessary adjustments so that potential customer demand can be satisfied. If the company SKU identification is not present on each SKU, the purchasing department obtains approval from the merchandising department to have the vendor place the identification on each SKU. The receiving department ensures that each SKU tote, master carton, or pallet has a WMS identification in a proper location.

Receiving Dock Locations

The receiving dock's location directly affects SKU flow, in-house transport design, and employee productivity. The objective of a properly designed receiving dock location is to reduce the transport time between the receiving dock and a storage area. The receiving dock location is determined by the SKU storage position. Adding an additional receiving dock is a small cost compared to an increase in in-house transport expense, low employee productivity, poor SKU flow, late delivery, or the inability to unload critical SKUs on-time. Well-designed docks ensure sufficient truckyard space, easy delivery truck access to the truckyard, efficient truck movement within the truckyard, as well cost effective and efficient unloading, and accurate projections of deliveries unloading times.

Receiving docks may be designed in one of three ways:

- Combination dock concept—Receiving and shipping activities are performed in a single area; few dock positions are needed
- Separated receiving and shipping dock—Each activity is performed in a separate area, each with its own equipment, employees, and staff; this approach reduces in-house transport
- Scattered dock—This is a variation on the separated dock. Receiving docks are located along one building wall that is designated as the receiving dock area. Shipping docks are located along a wall.

Receiving, Checking, and QA Activities

As has been discussed previously, small items, master cartons and pallets flow through the warehouse from the delivery vehicle to the storage area, going through unloading, receiving, checking, and QA areas. This process has the following goals:

1. It ensures that the delivered and unloaded SKU quantity matches the purchase order quantity.
2. It verifies that the data on the delivery documents matches the purchase order.
3. It ensures that there is a standard SKU quantity for each master carton on each pallet.
4. It ensures that a company identification is on each SKU and that there is a WMS identification or license plate (bar code label or radio frequency [RF] tag) on each master carton or pallet. If a warehouse uses a permanent pallet or other storage device (e.g., stack frames, tier racks, pallet cage, cart), a WMS SKU support device is zero scanned to the WMS computer.
5. It ensures that each WMS identification and SKU quantity is transferred to WMS files.
6. It verifies that the quality of each SKU master carton/pallet matches company standards.
7. It ensures that the SKU quality and company shipping SKU master carton data includes length, width, height, and weight, and is entered into WMS data.
8. It ensures that SKU pallets/master cartons are transported from a receiving area to a storage area.
9. It ensures each SKU quantity and WMS master carton/pallet identification are communicated to the WMS computer and inventory file.
10. It ensures that any rejected small item, master carton, or pallet is communicated to the purchasing department for proper disposition. If the company is involved in a pallet exchange program, this process ensures proper or good quality pallets are transferred onto a delivery vehicle and signed for by the driver.
11. Finally, it ensures that a SKU sample number is identified with the company QA label and WMS identification and is sent to the QA department.

Projecting the Required Vendor Delivery Truck Dock Number

Vendor delivery truck dock numbers may be calculated manually, by manual simulation, or by computer simulation.

Delivery Truck Dock Design Factors

When designing a delivery truck dock, the design team must consider climate, weather conditions and prevailing winds, available land, security, delivery truck traffic flows and control, employee comfort, safety, cost, vehicle type, and delivery load type. The options for dock designs are

- A flush dock, which can be a cantilever dock or a vestibule dock
- An open dock, which can be an open dock or an open dock with sliding curtains or panels
- An enclosed dock, which can be a straight-in-entrance enclosed dock or a side-load or finger dock
- Unloading and loading in a truck yard
- A staggered or saw-tooth dock
- A pier dock

Unloading

Unloading at a receiving dock is the physical movement (manual, mechanical, or automated) of master cartons/pallets from a delivery truck onto the receiving dock.

Master Carton Unloading and WMS Identification

When unloading master cartons from a delivery truck, the options for WMS identification are:

- An employee applies a WMS identification to each master carton, which is transferred to a conveyor to a storage position.
- An employee may transfer master cartons onto a conveyor and an employee at a receiving dock places a WMS identification onto each master carton, which continues to travel to a storage position.
- An employee transfers master cartons onto a conveyor and an employee at a receiving dock places the master cartons onto a pallet. The pallet is transported to a storage position.

Dock Area Conveyor Merger to an In-House Transport Conveyor Travel Path

To connect the dock area to the rest of the warehouse, a stationary (or portable) conveyor is connected to the main conveyor in the warehouse. This connection may be design incline or decline section that is attached to extendible (or retractable) conveyor housing (or shell), or it may connect at each merge location on the main travel path.

Floor-Stacked Master Cartons

In this approach, master cartons are placed on the floor of the delivery vehicle. To unload master cartons from a delivery vehicle, employees lift and transfer master cartons onto a cart, platform truck, pallet, or conveyor. All unloaded pallets or SKUs will have a WMS identification placed on them. The disadvantages of this approach are:

■ Potential employee injuries
■ Low employee productivity
■ It requires the highest number of employees and dock locations
■ Long unloading times: unloading a delivery vehicle requires four to five hours; unloading a rail car requires five to six hours

The advantages of this design are that it has excellent delivery vehicle cube utilization and no extra weight on the delivery vehicle.

Prepalletized Master Cartons

If the vendor places purchase order master cartons onto a pallet or slip sheet, this approach is called using "prepalletized" master cartons that match the warehouse's design parameters (pallet length, width, height, and weight), has fork openings and bottom deck board features, and has sufficient space for the WMS identification. Palletized delivery improves receiving productivity and truck dock turn number or utilization.

In prepalletized delivery, the receiving department unloads and places a pallet in a receiving dock staging area. A receiving clerk verifies that the delivered quantity matches the purchase order, pallet quality matches a company standard, and confirms the SKU quantity for each master carton, and the number of master cartons per pallet. After the clerk places a WMS identification on a pallet, the identification and SKU quantity are sent to the WMS computer. The pallet is sent to a storage area.

If a pallet's physical dimensions do not match the company standards, the pallet is reworked, and the receiving department transfers a master carton quantity onto a company pallet.

If a pallet does not match a warehouse quality standards or does not match a warehouse pallet top deck, stringer or bottom deck board standards, the warehouse options are either to place a nonstandard (or poor quality pallet) on a standard pallet or create a double stack pallet, or to transfer master cartons from a prepalletized pallet onto a warehouse pallet. It should be noted that a double-stacked pallet height is an additional six to eight inches in height. Warehouse staff must verify that forklift trucks and transport vehicles can handle a double-stacked pallet.

In terms of pick activity, there are two concerns for double-stackeds pallets. First, the additional pick height. Second, when SKUs are depleted from a double-stacked pallet, a picker must handle two empty pallets. These factors result in nonproductive time and lower pick productivity, possible pick line congestion, and low completed customer orders.

If a warehouse uses an AS/RS crane, the physical dimensions and weight of double-stacked pallets must match the AS/RS design parameters. If double-stacked pallets are used, they will lower inbound handling pallet volume.

If master cartons have been restacked or transferred from a poor quality or nonstandard pallet onto a warehouse-approved pallet, the options are

- Manually repalletizing, in which an employee physically transfers master cartons from a nonstandard pallet onto a warehouse standard pallet.
- Using a forklift truck to repalletize, in which a forklift truck with a tall clamp device transfers an entire master carton onto a warehouse approved pallet. This approach assumes that the warehouse's master carton ti and hi ("ti" is the number of master cartons per pallet layer; "hi" is layer number high) permits using a clamp on a forklift truck to transfer a master carton layer to another pallet.
- Mechanical concepts: a pallet inverter, a pallet changer, or a pallet lifter. After a pallet is placed onto an inverter, an employee places a standard pallet on the top of a master carton and the inverter turns the pallet so that master cartons rest on the standard pallet, which receives a WMS identification. The poor quality pallet is removed and recycled. A pallet change is used when a poor quality pallet is sent to a warehouse storage area. A forklift places the poor quality pallet onto the changer. The changer machine clamps a master carton load and raises it to a height that permits a forklift or conveyor to remove the poor quality pallet. A standard pallet is placed under the master carton load and the changer lowers the load onto the pallet. Finally, a pallet lifter creates a double-stacked pallet. The lifter raises a poor pallet, a conveyor moves a standard pallet under the poor pallet and a pallet lift lowers the poor quality pallet onto the standard pallet.

Poor Pallet Changing and WMS Identification

If a SKU pallet has received a WMS identification, but the pallet does not meet warehouse standards, the warehouse changes the pallet for a warehouse-approved pallet. The identification may be removed from the old pallet and reapplied to the warehouse-approved pallet. (The warehouse's re-palletizing activity ensures that the SKU quantity transferred between two pallets matches the SKU quantity on the purchase order.) The alternative is to cancel the identification on the old pallet and to associate the SKU quantity with a new WMS identification. This approach minimizes errors and ensures an accurate inventory.

Pallets

A pallet is a master carton support device with top and bottom deck boards and support stringers or blocks. A pallet stringer's/block's surface dimension can accept a WMS identification, that a scanner will be able to read the identification. The pallet material ensures that a WMS identification remains on a pallet stinger end or block. To lift a pallet, a forklift/pallet truck with a set of forks are inserted into a pallet fork opening. This permits the truck to transport a pallet between a delivery vehicle and a receiving dock.

Receiving Dock Zero WMS Scan Transaction

If the warehouse uses permament identifications on captive SKU support devices (e.g., pallets, stacking frames, tier racks, pallet cages, carts, totes), prior to reuse, a receiving clerk completes a zero scan transaction on the support device identification. The transaction is sent from the clerk's scanner to the WMS computer, which updates the SKU quantity to zero. Thus, as a new SKU is transferred to a captive SKU support with a permament identification, it will not be mixed with another SKU quantity.

If a captive support device is not zero scanned, it is possible that a small SKU quantity could be attached to the support device. If a SKU is stacked on an unscanned support device, the WMS computer will have two SKUs on one support device. This creates inaccurate inventory, potential storage errors, and pick errors.

Slip Sheet Concept

If a warehouse uses slip sheets, prior to transfer onto a delivery vehicle, master cartons are unitized onto a corrugated, plastic, or fiberboard sheet with a lip. The lip extends forward from a unit load and permits a pallet truck or forklift truck with a slip sheet attachment to clamp onto the lip and lift the unit. After the unit is secured on the slip sheet attachment, the unit is transferred to a pallet in a receiving dock staging area. WMS identifications may be placed options on the pallet stringer end or block surface or on a master carton on the unit load's lowest layer.

Vendor Delivery Problems

During receiving activity, there is a potential for delivered SKUs to be damaged, overage, the wrong SKU, or be under the purchase order quantity. During receiving, any SKU damage, shortage, overage, or wrong SKU is verified and communicated to the purchasing department. In accordance with instructions from the purchasing department (e-mail, verbal, written), the receiving department makes adjustments to the delivery documents and ASN. As with other deliveries, the receiving department completes the receiving activity by placing a WMS identification on each SKU and sends a SKU identification and associated quantity to the WMS computer. SKUs are sent to a storage area; all rejected or return-to-vendor SKUs are returned to the delivery vehicle. All receiving documents are signed by a receiving clerk and the delivery driver.

Master Cartons Delivered as Individual Master Cartons/Pallets

The receiving department receives a wide SKU mix and piece quantity. Master cartons may be delivered as half or full pallets (see Figure 4.3). The quantity delivered has a direct impact on a forklift's or AS/RS crane's ability to complete storage transactions as well as storage space utilization. When designing the warehouse and WMS program, small quantity master cartons may be handled as individual master cartons, master cartons may be palletized onto half or full height pallets.

Small Master Carton Quantity

If a warehouse takes delivery of small master carton quantity, it is handled as individual master cartons. The receiving department confirms the purchase order/ASN master carton and SKU quantity. When it is ready for put-away, a receiving clerk places a WMS SKU identification on each master carton and scans the quantity. Each master carton is transported to a storage area, where each SKU is scanned and placed into a storage position. The WMS master carton identification, storage identification, and SKU quantity are sent to the WMS computer. If the warehouse

MASTER CARTONS ON A PALLET

MASTER
CARTON

PALLET

WMS IDENTIFICATION

SINGLE MASTER CARTON

MASTER
CARTON

WMS
IDENTIFICATION

PALLET TI = (3 x 4) 12
HI= 3
TOTAL MASTER CARTONS PER
WMS IDENTIFICATION = 36
50 PIECES PER MASTER CARTON
WMS IDENTIFIED SKU QUANTITY = 1800

TOTAL MASTER CARTONS PER WMS
IDENTIFICATION = 1
50 PIECES PER MASTER CARTON
WMS IDENTIFIED SKU QUANTITY = 50

MASTER CARTON COUNT ON A WMS IDENTIFIED PALLET

ON A PALLET MASTER CARTONS
WITH DIFFERENT SKU COUNT

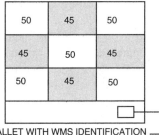

PALLET WITH WMS IDENTIFICATION

PALLET TI = (3 X 4) 12
HI = 3
TOTAL MASTER CARTONS
PER WMS IDENTIFICATION = 36

TOTAL SKU COUNT PER WMS IDENTIFICATION
MASTER CARTONS WITH 50 X 20 = 1000
MASTER CARTONS WITH 45 X 16 = 720
                                1720

ON A PALLET MASTER CARTONS
WITH SAME SKU COUNT

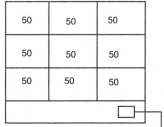

PALLET WITH WMS IDENTIFICATION

PALLET TI = (3 X 4) 12
HI = 3
TOTAL MASTER CARTONS
PER WMS IDENTIFICATION = 36

TOTAL SKU COUNT PER WMS IDENTIFICATION
MASTER CARTONS WITH 50 (3 X 12) = 1800

Figure 4.3   Pallet and Master Carton Receiving Quantity

is treating the SKU as a master carton in a single master carton storage position, there will be 100% space utilization. In a warehouse that uses an AS/RS crane, one carton on a three-carton tray means at least 33% utilization. If a warehouse is using both carton and pallet AS/RS storage, a small carton quantity on a pallet means high transaction activity and low storage position utilization.

Half and Full Pallets

Master cartons that are handled as a half or full pallets are placed on pallets by the receiving department. The pallet and the associated quantity is scanned and physically transferred to a

WMS computer. In an AS/RS crane warehouse, the pallet's height is determined when the pallet travels past a size/weigh station. If an AS/RS crane has a half-high pallet position, the warehouse computer directs an AS/RS crane to deposit a half-high pallet to a half-high pallet position. In a warehouse the uses a conventional employee-controlled forklift, the driver makes a visual determination for a pallet position. The use of half- or full-high pallet positions improves space utilization and storage vehicle transactions.

SKU Quantity for Each Master Carton/Tote/Pallet

In a storage or pick warehouse with a WMS program, the SKU quantity for each master carton, tote, or pallet is a key factor affecting whether a warehouse will function accurately as well as the WMS program's ability to track SKU quantities. It is at the receiving dock, customer returns process station, or other SKU entry where a warehouse ensures that the delivered SKU quantities are accurate, associated with a WMS identification, and that the identification and associated quantity are entered into the WMS computer. To achieve these goals, the design options are

- Having the same SKU quantity for each master carton that makes up one pallet
- If there are different SKU quantities in each master carton, a receiving clerk makes sure that master cartons with the same quantity are placed onto separate pallets, or each master carton receives a WMS identification. This means each master carton is handled as a separate SKU.
- If there are different SKU quantities in each master carton on a single pallet, and an individual master carton is transferred from a pallet, there is potential for piece "overs" or "shorts" when completing pick or replenishment transactions. This is because each master carton quantity is different, and the inventory potentially inaccurate.

Receiving Tally Sheet

In a manual receiving warehouse, each company purchase order or ASN has a printed tally sheet. A tally sheet is basically a road map for the receiving clerk, charting delivery receiving activity for each purchase order/ASN. A tally sheet is based on existing SKU, master carton, or WMS data provided by the vendor or merchandise department. It lists important delivery information,

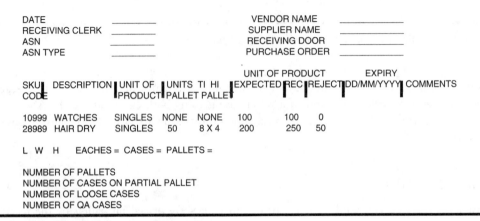

Figure 4.4   Receiving Talley Sheet

such as the vendor's name and e-mail address, fax and/or telephone number, the purchasing telephone number, SKU and piece quantity, master carton quantity, pallet number, pallet ti and hi, SKU inventory number and description, WMS identification number, and space for the receiving clerk's calculations.

Receiving Department Count Options

A receiving clerk may conduct counts in two ways:

- A manual count, in which the clerk may physically handle each SKU and quantity for each master carton or the clerk may determine SKU quantity or master carton ti and hi for each pallet and then calculate total SKU quantity.
- A mechanized count (i.e., "count on the fly"), in which the warehouse has a count station with a scanner/reader and a mechanized counter/register to count/read each master carton or pallet SKU WMS identification as the SKU travels on a conveyor. A receiving clerk enters each SKU count prior to placing the SKU on the travel path. For maximum efficiency, there should be a gap between adjacent SKU/WMS identifications. As a SKU travels over a scale, a computer compares the actual weight to the projected carton weight. A predetermined variance is allowed.

Accurate receiving activity ensures that a proper SKU sample is identified with a QA label and WMS identification and is sent from the receiving department to the QA department. The QA department may check all the pieces (if the SKU is from a new vendor or a vendor with past delivery problems), or may use random selection: checking 7–10% of randomly selected merchandise pieces. QA sample criteria is based on the vendor's past performance, merchandise value, purchase order quantity, and other company policies. To maintain an efficient and cost effective SKU flow between receiving and QA, all QA samples are whole master cartons. If one or several SKUs have a different SKU count, these SKUs are considered for a QA sample.

Receiving Options

In a high-volume warehouse that operates with single-shift receiving activity at the end of the work day, with large deliveries from vendors, there are two options for receiving.

First, all receiving activity can be handled by a receiving department, which unloads, receives, and place WMS identification each SKU in a single day (this may require overtime). SKUs can be sent to a storage position on the same day, or held on a receiving dock and transferred to a storage position the next day. It should be noted that SKUs at this point are "not available for sale" because they have not been inspected and approved by the QA department. After inspection and approval, the QA department notifies the WMS computer that the SKU has been approved or "available for sale." A WMS computer changes each SKU WMS identification from "not available for" to "available for sale." When the receiving activity is complete, the receiving department closes the purchase order/ASN and updates the WMS computer.

Second, the receiving department can conduct partial receiving. The delivery vehicle is held at a receiving dock and the receiving department keeps the purchase order/ASN open until all activities are completed.

QA Rejected Vendor SKU Delivery

Normal receiving activity is completed prior to QA department SKU inspection and approval/rejection. When a receiving department and QA department imbalance occurs to clear a receiving dock staging area, maintain a constant vendor delivered WMS identification SKU flow and transport from a receiving area to a storage position.

Receiving Dock Hold/Clear Options

In a high-volume warehouse with a large number of SKUs, all received SKUs are QA-approved before a SKU is made "available for sale." The receiving dock has a fixed receiving dock door number and SKU staging lane number. To ensure that receiving activity complies with the receiving dock schedule, the receiving department has two options.

1. If, after unloading and receiving a vendor delivery and creating a WMS identification for each SKU, the QA department has not inspected or approved a SKU, the receiving department holds the SKUs in a staging area. After QA approval, a receiving clerk scans the SKU WMS identification and enters the quantity into the WMS computer and releases SKUs for transport to a storage area. The features of this design are the need for large receiving queue dock area, the potential for receiving shut down and off-schedule vendor deliveries, and the creation of transport surges to a storage area.
2. If, after unloading and receiving a vendor delivery and creating a WMS identification for each SKU, the QA department has not inspected or approved a SKU, the WMS places each SKU on "not available for sale" status, which permits the receiving department to release SKUs for transport to a storage area. SKUs are transported from a receiving dock area, which opens up a receiving dock door and staging lane for another delivery. In a storage area, each SKU is scanned and physically placed into a storage position. WMS SKU and storage position identifications and SKU quantity are sent to the WMS computer. The computer updates SKU and storage position status. After QA approval, the QA department and receiving clerk notifies the WMS computer to change each SKU in a storage position status from "not available for sale" to "available for sale." The features of this design are that only a small receiving queue dock area is needed, it improves door availability and maintains a receiving dock schedule and scheduled vendor deliveries, and it reduces transport surges to a storage area.

Not Available for Sale

If the receiving department releases SKUs to the in-house transport, but the QA department has not completed their inspection, noninspected SKUs are placed in a QA hold inventory status ("not available for sale") until the inspection is completed.

Available for Sale

After the QA department inspects and approves the delivered SKUs, the department notifies the receiving and merchandising departments to change the SKUs' status from "not available for sale" to "available for sale."

SKU Quantity for Each SKU Master Carton/Pallet

In a warehouse with a WMS program, a SKU quantity per SKU master carton and pallet is a most important factor that determines an accurate functioning warehouse and WMS program ability to track and account for a SKU quantity. At a receiving dock, SKU entry into a warehouse with a WMS program, a warehouse ensures that each SKU count is accurate, associated with a WMS identification and both WMS identification with associated quantity are entered into a WMS computer.

In a warehouse with a WMS program, a design team criteria is (1) same SKU quantity for each master carton a pallet, (2) if there are different SKU quantity per master cartons, (a) master cartons with same quantity are placed onto separate pallets or (b) a warehouse has each master carton receive a WMS identification, and (3) if there is different SKU quantity per master cartons on one pallet, when an individual master carton are WMS moved or transferred from a pallet, with different master carton counts, there is potential for a warehouse to incur piece overs or shorts to complete a WMS suggested warehouse pick or replenishment transaction.

Warehouse Operation Company Purchase Order Close Activity

After a receiving clerk completes receiving activity, a tally sheet is returned to the receiving office. The clerk returns with WMS SKU identification labels and places a label on each SKU. In the receiving office, a clerk confirms that the delivered SKUs and quantity match the purchase order. The clerk then closes the purchase order and sends the information to the WMS computer for inventory update. The WMS computer updates the host computer.

Vendor Delivery with SKN and SKU Receiving Activities

A small-item warehouse will receive deliveries with a wide variety of SKUs and SKNs. A wide SKU or stock keeping unit variety (one style with several colors and sizes, shoe musical or many sizes, and jewelry rings in various sizes) and SKN or stock keeping number, adds to the complexity of receiving activity when verifying that the vendor SKU and SKU quantity matches the purchase order/ASN quantity. The receiving department has two options:

1. Bulk receiving, in which the receiving department unloads the delivered SKUs (or total pieces). Small SKUs are counted and compared to the purchase order/ASN piece quantity. If the count matches, the delivery driver is released and the SKU quantity is entered into the WMS computer. A receiving clerk places a WMS identification on each SKU; the SKUs are released for in-house transport to a detail area.
2. Detail receiving, in which a receiving clerk separates SKN or bulk SKUs quantity by each SKU (size and color) (see Figure 4.5). A detail receiving can operate as a single receiving operation, with bulk and detail receiving occuring simultaneously; as second activity that occurs after the completion of bulk receiving; bulk and detail receiving occurs after a bulk received SKU quantity is separated on a receiving dock, during which time a receiving clerk completes the detail receiving count for each SKU. To verify the vendor total piece and SKU delivery accuracy, each SKU count is compared to the purchase order/ASN SKU quantity. If the counts match, the bulk received SKU count remains in the WMS computer. If there is a variance between the delivery SKU count, the purchase order/ASN count, and an actual count, detail received SKU counts are entered into a WMS computer. After a receiving

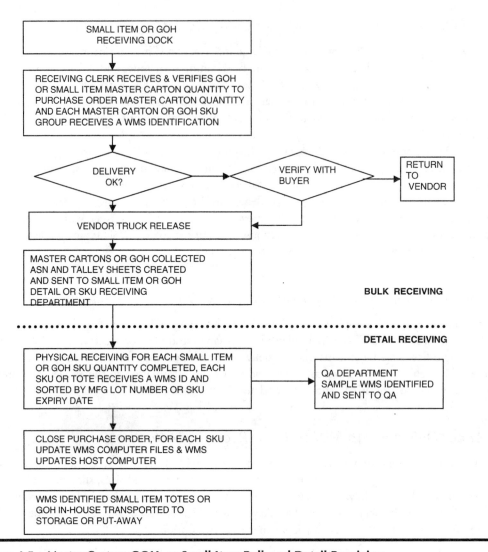

Figure 4.5 Master Carton, GOH, or Small Item Bulk and Detail Receiving

clerk completes detail receiving, each SKU receives a WMS identification and is sent to a storage area. The approach requires a large receiving queue dock area, there is the potential for receiving activity shut down and off-schedule vendor deliveries, and it creates in-house transport surges to the storage area.

Detail Receiving

A second receiving activity occurs after a SKU bulk quantity is received in a dock area. To verify delivery accuracy, the entire delivery is sent from a receiving dock to a detail receiving area. In this area each SKU count is compared to the purchase order/ASN quantity. If there is no variance, the bulk count remains in the WMS computer. If there is a variance, the counts made at the detail area are entered into the computer. After a receiving clerk completes a detail receiving activity, each SKU receives a WMS identification and is sent to a storage area.

Vendor Delivered SKUs for Warehouse Customer Orders and Activities

A warehouse receives vendor SKUs that are "available for sale" for customer orders, "not available for sale and for QA inspection. To maintain a receiving dock schedule and ensure a constant SKU flow from a receiving area to a storage area, the receiving process ensures that delivered SKUs are unloaded and received (i.e., matched against a company purchase order/ASN). To achieve these objectives in a cost effective and efficient manner, the receiving department must provide a signal to that a SKU is released for transport.

A receiving department's release options are

- Verbal, in which receiving clerks and transport employees are required to accurately communicate in-house transport instructions for a specific SKU. This method has the potential for errors due to unclear instructions or mistaken SKU selection.
- Non-WMS identification (or special tag SKU) has a receiving clerk apply a special tag to a SKU. This can be a special label, which identifies a suggested storage position and serves as a signal that a SKU is released for transport, or a WMS label with a special label. If a WMS label is used for an activity, a unit of product is "not available for sale" or is placed in a special inventory class.
- WMS identification. A receiving clerk places a WMS identification onto each SKU listed as "available for sale." The identification serves to attach a SKU quantity to a WMS identification, track a SKU through a warehouse, and signal for the start of transport activity. This identification may be read by employees, scanners, or tag readers.
- QA tag. In a warehouse with a QA department, a QA sample is sent from a receiving department to a QA department. To maintain a constant QA flow and to maintain simple transport instructions, each QA sample receives either a WMS identification, which ensures accounting and tracking as a SKU moves through the warehouse operation, or a special colored QA tag, which serves as a transport signal to identify a SKU destination.

Large Master Carton and Repacking

Some deliveries will have pieces in a SKU or master carton with physical dimensions that exceed storage or pick position dimensions. If a vendor's master carton size exceeds a warehouse's standard master carton size, the receiving department receives a SKU quantity and each master carton receives a WMS identification. A WMS identification and SKU quantity are entered into the WMS computer as "not available for sale" and the master cartons are moved to a repacking area, where an employee moves a master carton onto a repacking table. At the repacking table, the employee cancels the WMS identification. The SKU quantity is transferred into a standard size carton, which receives a WMS identification, and the identification and SKU quantity are entered into the WMS computer. A SKU is sent to a storage or pick position and is available for sale.

Vendor Reworking

If a delivered SKU package does not match company standards and, per a QA inspection, is not approved for sale, a receiving clerk, the purchasing department, and the vendor authorizes reworking the SKU quantity. Reworking a SKU is either performed at a warehouse by receiving department or vendor employees or sent off site. A SKU entered as "not available for sale" may or may not be removed from inventory, depending on company policy.

After a SKU is transferred to a reworking area, the WMS identification is removed, disposed of, and removed from the WMS computer. After reworking, a vendor SKU is sent to the receiving department with a new company purchase order/ASN.

Quality Assurance Activity

Sample SKUs from each vendor are sent from the receiving dock to the QA department (see Figure 4.6). The QA department verifies that the sample matches the purchase order's specifications. The QA department ensures that inspected samples are placed in a transfer station with a WMS identification for transport to a storage position (and the WMS inventory file is updated).

QA SKU Sample Quantity

A QA sample quantity is a random sample that is removed from a vendor delivery. After a receiving clerk has selected the sample master cartons or SKUs, the clerk places a WMS identification onto the sample quantity. The clerk scans the WMS identification and sample into a QA department storage position. WMS computer notifies the QA department that the sample is available.

QA Sample SKU Disposal

After the QA department completes the quality control test, SKUs that do not meet a company quality standards are disposed of (in the trash), the rejected SKU quantity is documented and deducted from the quantity sent to the QA department.

QA Sample SKU Transfer to a Position

QA pieces that meet company quality standards receive a WMS identification, are scanned to a holding position, and the SKU quantity is entered into the WMS computer files. The SKUs are held in a position for pick-up, transfer to a storage/pick position, and are available for sale.

Master Carton and SKU Physical Data

In a high-volume, high-technology, and computer-controlled storage/pick warehouse operation, the company host, WMS, or warehouse computer uses a cube or volumetric program to determine the number of SKUs per order. A small-item warehouse with multi-line or several SKUs per customer order that is cubed to a shipping carton has greatest requirement for SKU and master carton dimensional data. Computer projections are based on each SKU's physical dimensions and weight. For a warehouse to obtain SKU physical dimensions and weight, the warehouse may use the vendor, the purchase department, or the receiving department. Given that a receiving department has limited time and space to complete SKU and master carton measurements, it is difficult to complete spatial data collection. On the other hand, the QA department has the time and space to collect the spatial data.

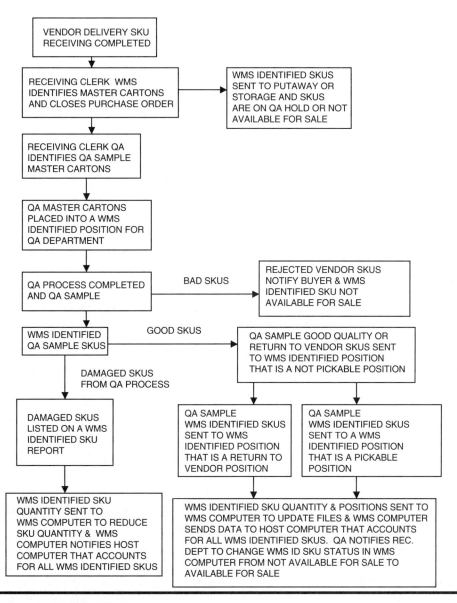

Figure 4.6 QA Sample Flow

A factor that ensures an efficient, cost-effective, accurate, and on-time warehouse is making sure that a SKU pick quantity matches an order pick tote/carton or the sort/pack station capacity. The options are to use manually projected SKU pick quantity or a computer projected pick quantity. In a dynamic warehouse, a computer-projected quantity is the preferred option. For a pick-and-pack warehouse, a computer determines the order SKU cube pick quantity that fits into an order pick tote/carton. The pick quantity factors are the order carton's internal dimensions, actual SKUs cube and weight, the company's desired shipping carton utilization rate, and the delivery company's standard carton weight.

Calculate Your Customer Order Pick Tote or Pick/Ship Carton Size

SKU spatial information includes each SKU actual length, width, height, and weight as it is transferred from a pick position or pack table into a customer order ship carton. It is noted that a SKU cube data is not the best criteria to determine a customer order small item pick tote or pick/ship carton. An example is an umbrella. An umbrella dimensions are 24 inches length, 2 inches wide, and 2 inches in height, which has 96 cubic inches. Based on the SKU cube data, a carton size could be 6 inches long by 4 inches wide by 4 inches high. But a 24-inch umbrella will not fit into a 6-inch long carton.

In a pick warehouse, accurate SKU spatial information for a shipping carton means less nonproductive picker and packer time, reduced SKU damage, computer selection of the best size of shipping carton and less filler material. The features are realized due to the fact that for each order a computer allocates a sufficient SKU quantity (length, width, and height) to maximize the utilization of a shipping carton.

Vendor Method

In a vendor spatial collection method, the warehouse must rely on the purchasing department to notify each vendor that the warehouse requires SKU data. After the warehouse receives this data, weight and dimension information for each SKU is entered into the WMS computer; this data becomes the basis for determining each customer order cube. The disadvantages to this method are

- loose SKU
- the information does not reflect a picked SKU's shape
- potential errors
- the data does not change as the SKU moves through the warehouse
- there is no management control

The advantage to the method is that there is no data collection expense or investment.

Manual Method

In the manual cube data collection method, the warehouse assigns an employee to data collection activity. The employee measures and weighs each SKU, and enters this information and the company SKU identification number on a document. Each SKU's weight and dimensions is entered into the computer files.

Cube Platform

A manual cube platform is a three-dimensional platform. A cube platform has a bottom surface and two sides that all intersect at one point. The bottom surface and each side has a set of colored lines. Each colored set of lines represents a ship carton. After an employee places a new SKU onto a platform, the colored lines that contain the SKU show the shipping carton size appropriate for the SKU. The disadvantages to this approach are that is time consuming, has labor expense, and potential errors. The advantages are accurate SKU spatial information.

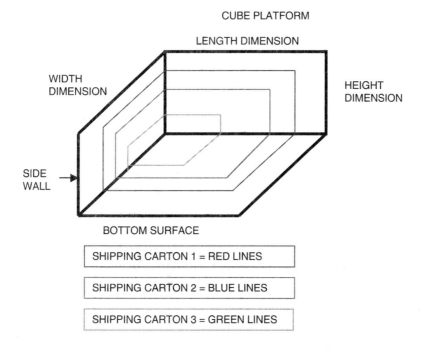

SHIPPING CARTON 1 = RED LINES

SHIPPING CARTON 2 = BLUE LINES

SHIPPING CARTON 3 = GREEN LINES

SIZE AND WEIGH MACHINE

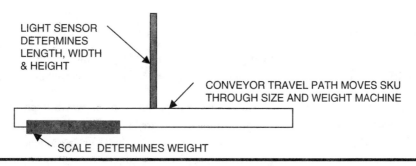

Figure 4.7   Cube Platform and Machine

Mechanized Method

In a mechanized spatial and weight collection method, an employee uses a scale and a cube device to weigh and measure SKUs. To determine a SKU's spatial information, each SKU is sent through a cube device. As the SKU passes through the device, it cubes a SKU to 0.04 inch and determines a SKU weight within 0.01 pound. This information is sent to (or manually entered into) a computer. SKU spatial information includes a SKU length, width, and height. The disadvantages to this method are the monetary investment (in the equipment) and the required employee time. The advantages are that it cubes all SKUs, it is quick and easy to do, the device is mobile, it provides accurate on-line data, and may be used on new SKUs.

Master Carton and SKU Length, Width, Height, and Weight Information

In a small-item warehouse, vendor master carton dimensional (i.e., length, width, height, weight) data is used for pick line setup and replenishment to ensure that a master carton fits into a pick position and with a carton flow lane the master carton number per pick position or lane. In a gravity flow-rack pick design, the length of the master carton determines the number of master cartons per flow lane. With a manual/carton AS/RS crane setup or replenishment, accurate carton flow lane ensures minimal carton handling and good utilization.

SKU Master Carton/Pallet SKU and WMS Identification

A SKU master carton/pallet with a company SKU and WMS discreet identification is a key component in efficient and cost-effective receiving. After a receiving clerk has completed all unloading and receiving activities, the clerk attaches a WMS discreet identification to each SKU master carton/pallet. A company SKU discreet identification is a human/machine readable code that is placed on each SKU exterior surface, and is readable at each supply chain logistics strategy segment: vendor, company facility, customer location. The identification identifies one SKU from other SKUs in the inventory. During customer order pick and return processing activities, a company SKU discreet identification is important for efficient and cost-effective flow.

Receiving Department WMS Identification Label Print Time

During receiving activity, a receiving clerk attaches a WMS identification to each unloaded and received SKU master carton/pallet. There are two options for creating the identification.

1. Using pre-printed labels has the receiving department print WMS identification labels for an entire week or month. The pre-printed labels are based on a tally sheet master carton/pallet and the WMS program's print label sequence. A label print sequence can be random, number generated, or progressive number. After a label is printed in the receiving department, the labels are available in a receiving office as a roll, sheet, or stack placed in a file or envelope with a vendor tally sheet or ASN document. This approach eliminates any delays in printing labels; minimum printer number in the receiving department; requires label storage space in a receiving office; requires the use of a label print sequence; and minimizes unloading and count delays.
2. In the print-on-demand approach, receiving department prints labels quantity for each vendor delivery or for an entire work day. The quantity is obtained from a tally sheet or ASN. Using a label print sequence, a receiving clerk prints labels for each vendor delivery truck. Labels may be kept at a guard station or in a file or envelope with a tally sheet or ASN document.

Master Carton or Pallet WMS SKU Identification

In a storage warehouse, each master carton or pallet has a SKU WMS identification. At the receiving dock, the identification is attached to each pallet stringer, block, or bottom layer master carton. The location must allow for the use of a hand-held or fixed-position scanner. The options are:

- Ladder
- Picket fence
- Hybrid
- RF tag that can face one direction or wrap around a master carton, pallet stringer, or block
- The label can be attached to a pallet component or bottom layer master carton, pallet stringer, or block with tape, staples, self-adhesive labels, a sleeve, or a pallet indentation

A bar code's relevant characteristics are it's height, length, and quiet zone.

Permanent Identification

A permanent identification means that the identification associated with a fixed asset does not change. In a warehouse, each SKU storage position has a permanent identification. A permanent identification is listed in the WMS computer files. Other assets with permanent identifications are warehouse order pick totes, stacking frames, portable racks, automatic guided vehicles, carts, and load carrying surfaces. After a SKU or order quantity is removed from a pick tote, pallet, master carton, or stack frame, an employee zero scans the permanent identification. The zero scan permits a permanently identified device to be used for another SKU or customer order.

Warehouse Permanent Identification Attachment

If a warehouse elects to use a permanent warehouse identification attachment, the warehouse identification becomes a permanent component of the handling device (i.e., stack frame, pallet, tote). The options for attachment are

- A transparent sleeve is glued to the handling device and permits a warehouse paper/chipboard identification to be inserted.
- An indentation on a handling device permits the identification to be glued to the device.

Disposable WMS Identification

A disposable WMS identification is associated with an asset with a limited life. A pallet, master carton, or shipping carton has a disposable WMS identification. After all master cartons have been removed from a pallet, the WMS pallet identification has served its purpose and is discarded.

Self-Adhesive Label

A self-adhesive label is widely used in warehouse design for disposable master carton/pallet WMS identification and permanent storage/pick position identification. A label's white face provides a surface on which to print label that can be read by machine, scanners, tag readers, and human beings. The self-adhesive surface is a positive method to secure the identification to a pallet block, stringer, or master carton. After master cartons are depleted from a pallet, the master carton/pallet identification is removed from the pallet or empty master carton and discarded.

Nonadhesive Labels

A nonadhesive label is printed on white paper or thin cardboard. A printed WMS label is slipped into an insert secured to a master carton's top or pallet stringer/block. The sleeve/insert has a self-adhesive back and a transparent front and can be read by employees, scanners, and tag readers. After master cartons are depleted from a pallet, the pallet identification is removed from the insert/sleeve and discarded; the sleeve/insert remains on the pallet.

Radio Frequency (RF)

A design that uses RF tag identifications on master cartons/pallets has a WMS identification tag (symbology) attached to each master carton/pallet SKU. On each forklift (or as a fixed position device along a conveyor) is a receiver (antenna). An RF tag has a transponder that transmits a radio signal. The radio signal is produced from an antenna grate circuit located inside the WMS identification tag. Each tag has a unique transmission that discreetly identifies a unit of product. The forklift or fixed position receiver picks up the signal from a tag, and a reader decodes and validates a signal for transmission to a computer, which identifies a SKU storage position or SKU.

Ladder Identification Orientation

A WMS identification ladder orientation on a SKU storage position has a bar code with white spaces and black bars that resemble steps on a ladder. When a person looks at a ladder WMS identification, the black bars and white spaces are vertical and the quiet zones are at the bottom and top. In a warehouse that uses forklifts, to minimize the number of times a forklift driver needs to turn a hand-held scanner to read a WMS identification, the scanner has a vertical light beam. In an AS/RS warehouse, a fixed position scanner is easily turned to read a pallet ladder WMS identification. If a WMS identification is wrapped around a pallet stringer/block or master carton, a ladder WMS identification has the same bar code printed on both sides of a wrap-around label.

Picket Fence Identification Orientation

A WMS identification with a picket fence orientation has a bar code with white spaces and black bars that resemble slats in a fence. When a person looks at a picket-fence WMS identification, the black bars and white spaces are horizontal and quiet zones are at the right and left. In a warehouse that uses a forklift, a forklift driver with a hand-held scanner reads the WMS identification. In an AS/RS operation, a fixed position scanner on a conveyor reads a ladder SKU WMS identification.

If the WMS identification is wrapped around a pallet stringer/block or master carton, a picket-fence WMS identification has one long bar code printed on a wraparound label face.

Ladder and Picket Fence/Hybrid Bar Code Identification

A hybrid WMS identification has a ladder and picket-fence bar code combination on a SKU master carton/pallet. A hybrid WMS label permits maximum flexibility in a warehouse that uses a manual forklift or an AS/RS crane. A WMS identification with a ladder and picket-fence bar codes means that the same bar code is printed in both orientations on one label. When a person looks at a combination WMS identification label, there are two bar codes. One bar code is in a north/south compass direction and a second bar code is in an east/west compass direction. With a hybrid SKU WMS label, a fixed beam scanner can easily read the ladder label and a forklift driver with a hand held scanner can easily read the picket-fence label. A hybrid WMS label ensures a maximum number of good reads with minimal bar code scanner or label cost.

Identification that Faces One Direction

A WMS identification that faces one direction has a SKU WMS identification face in the direction of travel. The direction of travel means that the SKU must be placed in a specific orientation (e.g., pallet fork opening) in the lead. In this design, one identification is attached to a pallet stringer/block or master carton in a position that ensures it can be read by hand-held or fixed-position scanners.

Identifications Wrapped around a Pallet Stringer/Block or Master Carton

An identification that is "wrapped around" has a bar code label that faces two travel directions. The label can be printed with two bar codes or one long bar code, and is attached to a pallet exterior stringer/block or master carton. Thus, the SKU WMS identification faces a pallet fork opening and an exterior stringer or a master carton on a pallet's two exterior sides, and can be read by hand-held or fixed-position scanners.

Pallet Stringer/Block Identification Location

In a warehouse with stringer/block pallets, there are two basic approaches for the location of the SKU identification.

- The identification may be placed on right exterior block/stringer. This is the preferred approach. This provides readability for fixed-position and hand-held scanners. In a WA, NA, or VNA forklift warehouse, scan transactions may be completed quickly and easily. Each pallet identification is located in a consistent pallet location and above the floor. This is an advantage because most employees are right handed and most forklift platforms and steering devices are designed for a right-handed employee.
- The identification may be placed on the left exterior block/stringer. A WMS identification in this location also provides readability for fixed-position and hand-held scanners. In a manual WA, NA, or VNA forklift truck warehouse, however, there will be lower employee

productivity because having the identification on the left exterior stringer/block requires additional employee effort and time to complete a scan transaction: because most employees are right handed, employees must transfer a hand-held scanner; forklift platform and steering devices are designed for a right-handed employee; and potential damage from a hand-held scanner being dropped.

Middle Exterior Stringer/Block

A WMS identification may be attached to a pallet middle exterior stringer/block. A middle exterior stringer/block WMS identification location provides fixed position scanner line of sight and a forklift truck driver with a hand-held scanner does not have bar code label line of sight. In a WA, NA, or VNA forklift warehouse, the forklift mast components block WMS identification on a pallet. A pallet identification on a middle exterior stringer/block is not the best pallet identification location. It is difficult to design a fixed scanner to read a pallet WMS identification in this location.

Pallet or Bottom Layer Master Carton

A WMS identification attached to a pallet's bottom left or right master carton provides readability for fixed-position and hand-held scanners. In a WA, NA, or VNA forklift warehouse, employee productivity would be the same as in a warehouse using WMS pallet identification on a block or stringer. However, there would be low picker productivity due to the need to ensure that a master carton is the last carton on a pallet. With the pallet identification on a bottom layer master carton, it is difficult to have each pallet identification in a constant pallet location and above the floor.

Pallet or Master Carton WMS Identification Attachment Options

There are four methods for securing a WMS identification to a pallet stringer, block, or master carton.

1. Tape. To secure a WMS identification onto a pallet or master carton, an employee places clear transparent tape with sufficient length to cover a WMS identification quiet zone and pallet stringer/block or master carton. The tape is tested to ensure that a scanner can read the identification through transparent tape. Disadvantages of this method are additional employee activity, additional expense, tape adhering to a pallet or master carton, and difficulty for a scanner to read through clear tape. The advantages are that this method has no waste paper and does not require glue, the label is easy to remove, there will be no damage to the identification label, and tape interfaces with all pallet materials.

2. Staples. This method is used to secure a WMS identification to a wood pallet stringer, block, or master carton (it cannot be used with plastic or metal pallets). An employee holds the label against the pallet stringer/block or master carton front/side and places staples into the label's quiet zones. Tests are conducted on a wood pallet stringer/block or master carton to ensure that the staples entered the wood pallet or master carton, and that it will remain attached to the SKU. Disadvantages are the need for additional employee activity and expense, staples left in the label, potential WMS identification damage, it cannot be used on metal storage/pick positions, plastic or metal pallets, and the staples are difficult to remove. Advantages are that this method is secure, there is no waste paper, and it does not require glue.

3. Self-adhesive label. In this method, the computer-controlled printer prints each human/machine-readable identification onto a label's white front. The label's self-adhesive back is removed and is placed onto a carton or pallet.
4. Plastic sleeve. The sleeve is inserted or secured to a tote, stack frame, or pallet. After a computer-controlled printer prints each human/machine-readable WMS identification onto a paper or chipboard front, each printed label is inserted into a sleeve or insert.

Single Item Receiving Sequence of Operations

In a single-item warehouse, a receiving department separates each SKU's delivered quantity by style, color, or size. This ensures that ticket and SKU identification activities are cost effective and efficient and that each storage master carton or tote receives a WMS identification.

Master Carton Open Activity

After master cartons are unloaded from a delivery truck, inspected, and approved, each vendor identified SKU master carton receives a WMS identification and flows to a storage area; all non-identified SKUs flow through a SKU identification process or master cartons with a large quantity are placed onto a pallet. Each master carton/pallet SKU quantity is entered into the WMS computer.

Master cartons with no SKU identification are placed in assigned open lanes. If there is no space available on a lane, extra master cartons are placed into temporary storage positions (e.g., floor-stacked pallets, stacking frames or portable racks, storage racks, or carton conveyor lanes directly behind a lane). When a lane or work station becomes available, master cartons are transferred from the temporary storage position to an assigned vacant lane or work station.

SKU Identification and WMS Identification Options

Prior to a SKU arrival at a storage area, each nonidentified SKU receives a SKU identification. After receiving an identification, the options for master carton WMS identification are:

- The old WMS identification remains on the master carton. This approach requires an employee to ensure that a master carton SKU quantity is the same as the SKU quantity associated with the WMS identification.
- The old master carton WMS identification is removed, disposed of, and each master carton receives a new WMS identification. The identification is scanned and sent to the WMS computer, along with the SKU quantity. The receiving department's company SKU identification activity is considered vendor rework and, depending on the agreement between the vendor and the purchasing department, is charged to the vendor or purchasing department.

Master Carton/Pallet Receiving Dock Staging Area

A master carton/pallet receiving dock has queue floor space, racks, or a conveyor. The staging area is based on master carton/pallet type and volume, planned flow, and transport design. In a receiving activity, master cartons/pallets are transferred from a vendor delivery truck and staged and permits a receiving clerk to detailed receive in a receiving staging area. A staging area ensures that the master carton/pallet receives SKU and WMS identifications, is QA tagged (and a sample is sent to the QA department), and the master carton/pallet is transported to a storage location. When designing a receiving dock area with a WMS program, floor space considerations are

- SKU conveyable and nonconveyable peak quantity
- Potential delivery truck no-show
- Potential failure (mechanical or power) of the conveyor or scanner
- Queue area **to hold pallets** due to insufficient employees to handle a delivery truck unload or in-house transport volume

If a receiving dock activity is designed for unloading, counting, labeling, and put-away, vender delivered SKUs are unloaded, counted, the quantity entered into the WMS computer, and released for transport to a storage area. This design has a low requirement for a dock staging area. If receiving dock activity flow is designed to hold SKUs for a period of time, the receiving dock operation has a high requirement for a large dock staging area (or a dock staging area with temporary SKU storage positions).

When designing a receiving dock staging area, the factors are

- The number of vendor master cartons/pallets quantity
- The ability to utilize storage racks, portable stack racks/frames, standard racks, push-back racks, or gravity-flow racks
- Employee/vendor delivery truck availability
- The in-house transport's ability to handle a given volume

Floor Stack or Block Staging Designs

A floor stack or block staging design places pallets directly onto the receiving dock floor. There are two lanes located directly behind a dock door aisle with the capacity to hold pallet quantities from two delivery vehicles. Each pallet lane is a maximum of 6 to 10 pallets deep per lane. A pallet lane length is designed with pallet fork openings facing a main traffic or take-away aisle and to provide space for a receiving clerk to inspect pallet wood, master carton ti and hi, SKU condition, and to apply WMS identifications to pallets. In a staging lane, the space between two pallets is 30 to 36 inches.

Pallets are stacked one or two high. The height is determined by space between the floor and ceiling, the master carton's side wall strength (to support stacked load weight), and receiving activity to attach a WMS identification to each pallet and count the master carton or SKU quantity. If a warehouse has a very tall pallet stack (i.e., above an employee reach), a forklift lowers a pallet for a receiving clerk to complete receiving activity and to place an identification on the pallet. Lane width is designed to handle pallet width. Each receiving door has two lanes outlined in white lines six inches wide. White lines are painted between the two long lanes to ensure proper forklift pallet placement. With a pallet opening facing a main traffic aisle and after a WMS identification is placed onto a pallet, the WMS identification serves as a signal for a forklift truck driver to move a pallet from a receiving area to an in-house transport concept.

Stack Frames, Pallet Cages, Portable Racks

A pallet cage, tier rack, or pallet stack frame is used when a master carton is crushable, extends beyond pallet edges, or is not self-supporting. The method is used to make a stackable and uniform unit load. These devices are stackable and are handled in the same method as floor stack pallets. A permanent or disposable WMS label is attached to each stack frame, pallet cage, or tier rack.

Standard Pallet Racks

A standard pallet rack receiving staging design has single rack row or back-to-back standard pallet rack rows.

Rack rows start a sufficient distance from a dock leveler for a forklift to be able to turn and extend to a main traffic aisle. Each pallet has a pallet stringer/block that faces a forklift aisle and has sufficient space for a receiving clerk to attach a WMS identification to each pallet. Dock doors are eight to nine feet wide, with three to four feet between dock doors. With a single 44-inch deep pallet rack for a four-foot long pallet, a rack row is located between the two dock doors. One rack row side faces an aisle between a dock door and the main traffic aisle. One rack row elevated pallet positions on the nonforklift truck transaction side has safety netting to prevent potential accidents and all racks overhead are tied to each other. Rack row layout is repeated for each dock door.

With a back-to-back rack row design, single deep rack rows are against a wall and in the middle with aisles are back-to-back rack rows. Back-to-back rack rows have the same distance between a dock leveler and rack row start and the rack row ends at the main traffic aisle. Back-to-back rack row and aisle width design does not permit an aisle from a dock leveler to a main traffic aisle and a dock leveler aisle width is important.

With a counterbalance dock forklift, a right angle stacking aisle must have at least 9 to 10 feet between two rack faces. Pallet positions are floor level high and elevated on a load beam pair. Elevated pallet positions are two or three levels high. Each floor level and elevated load beam pair holds one, two, or three wide pallets. With all pallets on the floor or load beams, this design handles both stackable and nonstackable SKUs.

The options are to either have two high pallets set on the floor, with rack levels that are one pallet load high, or to have one pallet on the floor, one pallet on an elevated level, and a height of two on the highest load beam level. Rack installation design must be approved by the rack vendor. Rack post protectors are placed on aisle transaction side posts, dock leveler, and main traffic upright frame to reduce forklift truck damage.

For floor level pallets, a receiving clerk performs a detail count and places a WMS identification on each SKU, enters the quantity, and sends the information to the inventory files. Pallets on elevated positions are transferred to the floor for a receiving clerk to complete detail receiving, pallet WMS identification attachment, and WMS inventory update transactions.

Push-Back Racks

A staging design using push-back racks is a stand-alone or back-to-back rack design with one aisle that permits a forklift to complete pallet transactions. A push-back pallet rack design has the same structural components and design characteristics as a pallet gravity flow rack, albeit with some exceptions. This design can be three to four pallets deep and three to four pallets high. The pallet weight and height determines the slope and pitch to flow rack lanes. A push-back rack is designed as a single rack row installed along a building wall with an aisle for a forklift to perform all transactions or as back-to-back rack rows.

A push-back rack design can use a standard conveyor push-back rack. It does not require brakes but has end stops on both flow lane ends. Or the design can use a telescoping push-back rack. This has three pallet carriages that ride on a set of tracks. The carriage travels into an interior pallet position when not in use (i.e., without a pallet) to nest over an empty carriage adjacent to an aisle.

For all interior and elevated pallets, a forklift places a pallet on the floor so that a receiving clerk may complete detail receiving, WMS pallet identification attachment, and WMS pallet scan transactions.

Gravity-Flow Racks

A gravity-flow (or flow-through) rack design uses a single or stand-alone rack design with one aisle for pallet in-feed, and another aisle for pallet out-feed. A pallet gravity-flow rack design has upright frames, upright posts, braces, brakes, end stops, and skate wheel or roller conveyors for individual pallet flow lanes. In a warehouse that uses a forklift, pallet flow lanes are three or four levels high and three to eight pallet lanes deep. Pallet weight and height determines the slope and flow rack lane pitch. The pallet unit height/length ratio is 3:1. If pallets exceed this ratio, there is the potential for uneven flow through or hang-ups in a flow lane. In most pallet flow-rack systems, a pallet is placed onto a captive (or slave) pallet to ensure smooth flow through a lane. In some flow-rack designs, conveyor rollers have flanged wheels that act as guides for the pallet as it flows through a rack. To prevent rack damage, lane entry guides, upright post protectors, forklift stops, and sufficient forklift turning aisle widths are at entry and exit positions.

After a forklift unloads a pallet from a delivery truck, a receiving clerk verifies the SKU identification and quantity. A receiving clerk places a WMS identification on a pallet side that does not face the forklift, and the forklift transfers the pallet into a pallet flow lane. The clerk enters the WMS identification and SKU quantity into the WMS files. With the WMS identification on a pallet lead end in a flow lane, it ensures that the discharge end has the WMS pallet identification facing the withdrawal aisle. After a forklift truck in aisle "A" (or receiving dock aisle) places a pallet onto the gravity conveyor lane, gravity and the pallet's weight on rollers allow the pallet to flow toward the flow-lane exit. As the pallet moves through the exit, the WMS identification faces the forklift's driver. The pallet is removed by a forklift in aisle "B" or storage area aisle from the lane exit end. This permits the next pallet in the lane with a WMS identification in proper orientation to move forward to a withdrawal position. In a long pallet flow lane concept to reduce line pressure and SKU damage, pallet brakes and a pallet separator at the exit position are installed in a flow lane. After a pallet is moved from the flow lane, the WMS identification on the pallet faces the forklift driver and is ready for transport to a storage area. This design indexes pallets from a deposit (entry) position to a withdrawal position that allows each flow lane to accommodate one SKU per lane. This means that a three-high gravity flow-lane staging design has one SKU in all three lanes or three different SKUs with one SKU per lane.

Chapter 5

In-House Transport with a WMS Program

Introduction

Warehouse transport moves a SKU or an order via a vehicle (employee- or computer-controlled) or load carrying surface over a variable or fixed travel path. Possible travel paths:

- Moving a SKU from a receiving dock to a storage or put-away area, to an AS/RS in-feed station, to an across-the-dock ship location/drop location, or to a pick area
- Moving a SKU from a storage or put-away position or an AS/RS out-feed station through and from a pick area to an order packing area through a manifest station and onto a staging area or delivery vehicle.

Warehouse transport is not a WMS supported transaction, but is a warehouse system transaction. The design team develops TO and FROM locations to ensure accurate and timely SKU WMS identification at warehouse SKU pick-up (FROM) or delivery (TO) locations/drop points (see Figure 5.1).

In-House Transport: Objectives

The objectives of a transport design are:

1. To ensure that SKUs are transferred on time from a receiving dock, storage delivery station, or pick-up point/station. In a properly designed transport, as the SKU travels on a conveyor, the identification on the SKU can be read/scanned by fixed-position readers/scanners.
2. That, after the SKU has been scanned/read, it is moved to the drop/delivery station.
3. That, after the SKU reaches the delivery station, the in-house transport will transfer the SKU to a AS/RS crane in-feed station, a storage position, a shipping or pick location. In each case, the SKU is read/scanned, the scan transaction is completed, and updated information is sent to the WMS computer.

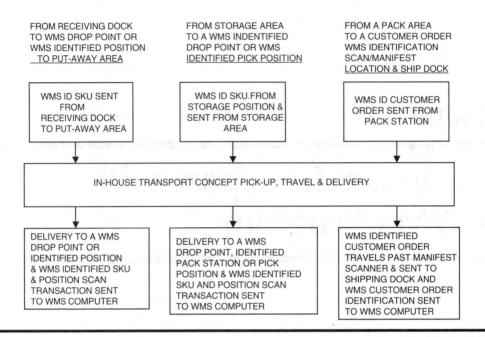

Figure 5.1 In-House Transport Flows

4. That, at an order fulfillment warehouse, each tote/carton will be moved past a scanner/ reader, past pick positions, and to a packing area. After a completed order is sealed and has a delivery label attached to the carton/bag, the in-house transport moves the carton/bag past a manifest scanner/reader and onto a dock staging area or into a delivery vehicle.

In-House Transport Design Parameters

To ensure on-time and accurate SKU delivery, a warehouse moves a SKU from a receiving dock, pick-up location, or order packing station, and scans a SKU or order. A SKU or order scan identifies a suggested SKU or order delivery/drop point. The travel path can be employee- or computer-controlled, variable or fixed, one way or closed-loop 2-way path. As a SKU or order arrives at a delivery location or drop point, the in-house transport discharges or drops the SKU or order at its drop point or location. After a SKU or order is dropped, a SKU or order identification and the drop point are scanned by an employee. The scan transactions are sent to the WMS computer.

Warehouse In-House Transport

Travel path options are:

■ a fixed travel path, which human- or power-driven carrying surfaces or containers move over a predetermined travel path between two locations. A human-powered design uses a cart or carton on an unpowered conveyor; powered designs use an electric motor, fuel power, air or vacuum pressure to move SKUs and order.

■ a variable travel path, in which human-powered carrying surfaces or containers move over a human-determined travel path between two locations. Transport designs may have two, three, four, or six wheels that allow a carrier or vessel to move with minimal friction or physical effort and maximum SKU or order carrying capacity.

■ a one-way or single command transport transaction has a transport carrier or vessel move with a SKU or order over a travel path from a dispatch station to a drop point and return empty to a dispatch station.

■ a two-way command transport transaction has a transport carrier or vessel move with a SKU or customer order over a travel path back and forth between dispatch stations.

■ a single carrier transport, in which a carrier's load carrying surface dimensions and structural strength is designed for one SKU or order.

■ a dual carrier transport, in which a carrier's load carrying surface dimensions and structural strength is designed for two SKUs or orders.

■ an automatic SKU or order transfer, in which the carrier or vessel and dispatch/delivery stations are designed to mechanically transfer a SKU or order between a carrier/load carrying surface and the dispatch/delivery station.

■ an assisted SKU or order transfer, in which the carrier or container at a dispatch/delivery station has forklift or other mechanical device transfer a SKU or order between the carrier/load carrying surface and the dispatch/delivery station.

Other important factors in designing in-house transport are:

■ The physical characteristics of the SKU or order and WMS identification. For every transport component, a SKU or order's length, width, height, weight, and bottom support members and WMS identification are factors affecting efficient and cost-effective transport.

■ SKU or order volume (or number). The SKU or order volume can be a surge or continuous and is determined by the dispatch and delivery station queue and travel path configuration. The delivery and dispatch station number and location and travel path configuration (straight travel, curve and curve type number, and elevation changes) determines container or carrier travel speed and number.

■ The dispatch and delivery station SKU or order queue. To ensure a continuous SKU or order flow, SKU or order availability, and a balance between warehouse activities (receiving, storage, picking, packing, and shipping), and a carrier or container at each pick-up (dispatch) or delivery (drop) location, a warehouse uses a staging area or lane. A pick-up/delivery station staging area or lane provides a queue that permits transfers between the transport system and delivery/pick-up stations.

■ Warehouse safety features, including "E" stop devices, which automatically stop driverless vehicles when they leave the travel path; UPS back-up electric power; and sufficient clearance between transport vehicle travel paths for two-way traffic.

Other factors that determine a horizontal or vertical transport design include which must be considered a warehouse type, SKU/order package characteristics, travel distance, multiple floors, an elevation change, elevated floor thickness, run-out space, and drop point number.

Using Identification Servers to Generate Pick-Up Signals

All vendor delivered SKUs are unloaded and staged on a receiving dock. In a conventional warehouse that uses forklifts or AS/RS cranes, after a receiving clerk completes a receiving update by entering each WMS identification and SKU quantity into the WMS computer, the clerk applies a WMS identification to each SKU, and identification is read/scanned at the pick-up and delivery station (P/D), and a message is sent to the computer indicating that the SKU is ready for pick up. The warehouse transport moves the SKU from the receiving dock or delivery station to the drop point.

In an order fulfillment warehouse, after an order is placed into a shipping carton/bag/tote, the carton/bag/tote is sealed and an order delivery label is placed on the carton/bag/tote. The completed order is transferred to the warehouse transport to be moved from the packing area to a manifest area. At a manifest station, the order identification is read/scanned, and the carton/bag continues to the delivery/drop point at a dock staging area or delivery truck. Meanwhile, the order identification is sent to a warehouse computer or WMS computer to update the order status.

In-House Transport: Receiving to Storage, Pick Position, or Across-the-Dock Drop Point

In a pallet storage warehouse with employee-controlled forklifts, a SKU move transaction ends at a storage position.

In a warehouse that uses master cartons or loose small items, a SKU in-house move transaction ends at a storage position, a pick position, or an across-the-dock drop point.

In a warehouse that uses AS/RS cranes, a SKU in-house move transaction ends at an AS/RS crane in-feed station position, and the move may involve a transport vehicle, pallet truck, forklift, pallet conveyor, STV, mono-rail, or shuttle car.

In an across-the-dock warehouse, a SKU move transaction ends at a dock location.

Drop Point (Delivery Location)

A transport design working with a WMS program ensures that a SKU leaves the receiving dock or storage location on schedule and arrives at the correct drop point on schedule. It also ensures that orders are transported to pick positions, through packing areas, and to manifest stations. A drop point/delivery location can be a storage position, AS/RS crane in-feed station, or an across-the-dock shipping or pick location.

Transport Interface/Interaction with a WMS Program

A transport design interfaces and interacts with a WMS program (as described in the previous section) but is not a WMS-supported process. Nevertheless, the transport has a close relationship to a WMS program. Thus, the types of interactions the design team take into consideration are:

- A SKU move transaction, in which a receiving dock forklift truck moves a SKU onto a conveyor or moves the SKU to a WMS-suggested drop point or storage position.
- A cancellation transaction, in which the WMS program permits an employee to cancel a SKU move. If the in-house transport has not moved a SKU, the cancellation feature

minimizes the number of move transactions and associated WMS communications. If the in-house transport has already moved the SKU, the cancellation feature has the in-house transport return the SKU to a receiving dock or start point.

■ If an order does not have a move transaction, it travels over the in-house transport through the required order processing stations. During this travel, scanners/readers bar code updates the order location in the warehouse computer, which in turn updates the WMS computer.

Identified Drop/Delivery Point

To complete a SKU transport move or transfer transaction, a WMS computer communicates a suggested SKU drop/delivery point to the in-house transport. The transport picks up, moves, and drops a SKU at the suggested delivery/drop point. To ensure an efficient, cost-effective, and on-time SKU transport, each drop point, storage/pick position, or work-station is entered in the WMS program. If you do not complete this drop point activity, a warehouse with a WMS program will never work—that makes it a must.

At a drop point or storage/pick position, the transport completes the SKU move to a drop point/position. The SKU and drop point identifications are sent to the WMS computer to update the files.

To ensure that the WMS program and in-house transport has a clear, precise, and understandable road map for each in-house transaction, the design team must identify each drop/delivery point, transaction point, storage and pick aisle, and divert location on the warehouse plan's view drawing.

A drawing of the warehouse's storage and pick elevation is used to show each storage/pick position level. A spread sheet is used to identify each storage or pick aisle position. On the spread sheet, each aisle has two columns. One column is for left-side aisle positions and starts with a lowest storage/pick position or the lowest position number at the aisle entrance. It progresses to each level and progresses down the aisle and ends at an aisle end or with highest WMS identification. The second column is for the other aisle or right side.

To and From Warehouse Points/Locations

To complete a vendor SKU delivery or order transaction, the in-house transport moves the SKU or order from a pick-up point to delivery point. In a warehouse with a WMS program, to develop an effective and cost-efficient operation with accurate and on-time transactions, a design team will list each SKU or order to/from locations in a warehouse.

On one or several drawings (one per activity), the SKU or order to/from locations are

1. From a warehouse receiving area to a put-away or storage position, QA department position, pick position, warehouse detail receiving department, rework or repack station, staging area, or delivery truck.
2. From a detail receiving area to a storage position, QA department position, or pick position.
3. From a storage position to another storage position, a pick position, shipping dock (for customer orders), special packing station or return-to-vendor assembly area (for noncustomer orders), QA department position, rework or repacking station, or order problem station.
4. From a rework or repacking station to a receiving department (as non-SKUs).

5. From a QA department to a storage position or disposal area (for damaged SKUs with a WMS identification).
6. From a pick position to a packing station, storage position, another pick position, order problem station, or order sort position.
7. From a sort position to a packing station.
8. From an order problem station to a packing station or manifest station.
9. From a packing station to manifest station or order problem station storage.
10. From a manifest station to a delivery dock or order cancel station.
11. From a cancel order station to a storage position.
12. From a customer return process station to return-to-stock or return-to-vendor position or disposal area for damaged SKUs (with WMS identification).
13. From a warehouse delivery truck to an off-load or temporary hold position.

Warehouse Master Carton/Pallet Storage Vehicle Transfer (Delivery Location Options)

As previously noted, an AS/RS crane is a computer-controlled forklift truck with out-feed or delivery (D) stations at the end of aisles. An out-feed or D station ensures that a withdrawn SKU is transferred from a storage position to a delivery station conveyor. At a delivery or D station conveyor travel path end, a powered conveyor, AGV, monorail, or forklift path is designed to pick up a SKU—this is the start of the transport travel path. The design team's options for out-feed, delivery, or D stations are:

- In single-level warehouse, the delivery or D station conveyor is a single travel path from an AS/RS aisle to a SKU transfer point. A one level AS/RS warehouse with multiple aisle end delivery stations is considered a standard AS/RS crane P/D station concept. On a floor level, a P/D station has a flush or sawtooth/staggered configuration. At the SKU pick-up/delivery transfer station end, a transport conveyor, AGV, monorail, or powered forklift picks up a SKU and transfers it to an assigned delivery/drop point. This option maintains a constant SKU quantity delivery to a pick position, work station, or delivery staging point.
- In a multiple-level warehouse, for an elevated floor an AS/RS crane has at least one or two elevated SKU delivery or D stations location. The end of each elevated and floor-level delivery station intersects with a powered conveyor, monorail, or powered forklift. In this design, SKUs are transferred to an assigned delivery or D station. Other D stations are on elevated floors, on the ground-floor level, or in an adjacent area through an AS/RS rack position side that reduces the SKU transport travel path distance and time.

In-House Transport: Space Requirements

To have SKUs transported on schedule to assigned drop points with minimal SKU damage (to the SKU, the order, of the equipment), a transport travel path must have adequate aisle dimensions between SKU or order travel paths. In addition, all SKU or order transfer and transport activities must be performed by trained employees, or by computer-controlled transfer and transport equipment.

A receiving or dock area will have a sufficient number of aisles (and the aisles will have sufficient width) for a transport vehicle or employee to transfer a SKU onto a powered travel path or a manual/mechanized SKU travel path or load-carrying surface. In a receiving or dock staging area, and between the receiving dock area and each drop/delivery point, the transport travel path aisle must be wide enough for two-way transport vehicle traffic. Finally, the design team must ensure that SKU/order WMS identification has the correct orientation on the travel path for scanning/ reading at each SKU/order transfer station.

At each drop/delivery point there must be a sufficient number of aisles (with sufficient widths for right turns) for a delivery vehicle to complete a SKU/order transfer to an AS/RS storage area in-feed station, a storage position, or a shipping delivery point/work station.

In-House Transport: Horizontal and Vertical Designs

A SKU can be transported from one warehouse position to another via a horizontal or vertical transport design. Horizontal transport designs move SKUs or orders between drop points across or overhead on one warehouse floor. Vertical transport designs move SKUs or orders between drop points on different warehouse elevations. Vertical transport designs are separated into incline and decline transport groups. Each horizontal or vertical transport group has four separate transport designs that are designed to handle a specific SKU or order type. The SKU types are small items, master cartons, and pallet transport groups; the order types are bags, totes, cartons, or pallets.

There are six manual or mechanized transport designs that can be used for an in-house transport:

- Powered or nonpowered above-floor horizontal transport
- Overhead powered or nonpowered horizontal transport
- In-floor powered or nonpowered horizontal transport
- Powered or nonpowered above-floor vertical transport
- Overhead powered or nonpowered vertical transport
- In-floor powered or nonpowered vertical transport

Chapter 6

Storage

Introduction

In a warehouse with a WMS program, the storage actitivtes begin with receipt of a SKU small item, master carton, or pallet. The item, master caron, or pallet is transported to a storage position. The SKU and storage scan transactions, position status, and SKU quantity, are sent to the WMS computer. The WMS computer update is the first step in tracking SKU flow, storage position occupancy in a warehouse, and SKUs available for pick transactions.

Storage Design With a WMS Program: Objectives and Components

When a storage plan is designed in conjunction with a WMS program, the design team will consider the factors that determine a warehouse's ability to satisfy the objectives of controlling operational cost, earning a profit, and satisfying and increasing customers. In addition to vendor SKU and customer order flow considerations, major design considerations are facility design, activities needed to complete a storage transaction, WMS computer interface with a warehouse computer, storage location philosophy and practices, whether or not the warehouse uses an AS/RS crane, carton handling, SKU WMS identification, SKU storage position type and identification, storage aisles, vehicles and vehicle routing patterns, SKU deposit activity, and transaction communication.

Storage Put-Away: Functional Description

After a WMS identification is placed onto a master carton or pallet, the master carton/pallet is ready for a move transaction (see Figure 6.1). In a conventional warehouse, a move transaction involves moving a SKU from a receiving dock to a storage position (suggested by the WMS computer or selected by a forklift truck driver). In a computer-controlled or AS/RS storage operation, each master carton, pallet, tray, or tote receives a profile check. A profile check confirms that the SKU dimensions and weight are within design parameters. If a SKU's dimensions and weight are within design parameters, the SKU continues to travel to the storage position. If the SKU's dimensions are not within design parameters, it is sent to a rework station, where corrective action is taken and the SKU is reintroduced to the AS/RS in-feed station. Finally, an additional check is done to ensure that the SKU secure method to a pallet allows a scanner bar-code line-of-sight and/or permits a RF tag to function properly.

In an across-the dock operation, a move transaction moves SKUs from the receiving dock to a drop position on the shipping dock. After a manually controlled forklift truck, AGV, or in-house transport vehicle arrives at the storage position or drop point, an employee completes the SKU and position/drop point scan transactions or a warehouse computer notifies the WMS computer of the transaction completion, which updates the SKU and position/location files.

Conventional Warehouse Storage Put-Away Exception Handling

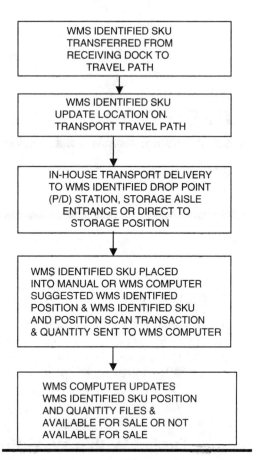

Figure 6.1   SKU Storage Area Flow/Putaway

As an employee completes a SKU put-away transaction, there is a potential that a problem will prevent completion of the transaction. In the development phase of the WMS program, a design team reviews exception handling occurrences and develops procedures to permit a SKU to be handled in an operation. Examples of potential exceptions are:

1. The SKU needs to be put in a different storage area. An employee travels with a SKU to the preferred storage area and completes a put-away transaction.
2. The put-away position is occupied. With an employee-directed or computer-directed put-away strategy, an employee selects another position, completes the put-away and scan transactions, and notifies the inventory control department of the situation. For a SKU in a position, the inventory control department completes a SKU cycle count. Following the cycle count, the WMS program updates the SKU and position files.
3. A broken pallet. If a forklift truck driver notices a broken pallet during put-away activity, the driver takes the broken pallet to a pallet exchange station. At the exchange station, the WMS identification is removed from a pallet, canceled in the WMS program, and thrown in the trash (or a whole pallet is thrown in the trash). An employee or mechanical pallet exchange device transfers the SKU quantity from the broken pallet onto a good pallet. Another WMS identification is placed onto a pallet and an employee enters the SKU quantity associated with the WMS identification. An employee completes the put-away transaction with a

new pallet. If a WMS identification is transferred from a broken pallet to a new pallet, an employee completes WMS identification and SKU quantity transfer transactions. Regardless of the option, an employee verifies that the SKU transfer quantity is accurate.

4. The SKU does not fit into a position. With an employee-directed put-away strategy, an employee locates another position and completes the put-away and WMS scan transactions. With a computer-directed put-away strategy, a forklift driver travels to another position and completes the put-away and WMS scan transactions.

5. The scanned bar-code or RF tag does not appear on a PC or hand-held display screen for a forklift truck driver put-away signal or put-away instruction. The forklift driver returns with the SKU to the receiving dock. At the dock, a receiving clerk cancels the WMS identification, places a new identification on the SKU and updates the WMS program.

6. An empty position is not available. With a manually directed put-away strategy, a forklift driver travels through all the aisles and determines that all aisles are full. The driver returns with the SKU to the receiving dock. At the dock, the management assigns the SKU to a vacant position in another section or in a remote warehouse facility. The warehouse team reviews the situation and takes corrective action, such as inventorying the entire warehouse to identify vacant pallet positions, moving "D" SKUs to another warehouse location, or creating and consolidating half-high pallets in half-high pallet positions.

Master Carton/Pallet AS/RS Storage Operation Exception Handling

In addition to the exception handling situation that occurs in a conventional storage warehouse, an AS/RS storage operation may experience other situations. The situations are:

1. An unknown SKU. An AS/RS conveyor sends the SKU to a rework station. At the rework station, an employee gives the SKU a WMS idenfication and ensures that the SKU and associated quantity is entered into the WMS program. The SKU is then reintroduced to the AS/RS conveyor.

2. The SKU's physical characteristics do not match the AS/RS design parameters. The situation is detected by an AS/RS check or profile station, which directs the "out-of-spec" SKU to a rework station. At the rework station, the SKU characteristics and problem is communicated through a PC or display screen to ensure that an employee understands the situation. If master cartons or SKU quantity is moved from a pallet to another pallet, an employee ensures that the old pallet SKU quantity, the new pallet SKU identification, and the associated quantity is sent to the WMS program. If individual master cartons are removed from a pallet and have individual WMS identifications, WMS move transactions are sent to the WMS program and individual master carton WMS identifications and associated SKU quantities are sent to the WMS program. After the program update, all SKUs are transferred to the pallet/master carton AS/RS in-feed system.

3. An aisle or crane breakdown. If an AS/RS aisle or crane breaks down, the AS/RS control room supervisor notifies the WMS program and warehouse management team. Warehouse management and WMS program teams ensure that all new SKU put-away transactions are assigned to another aisle; existing SKU withdrawal transactions are changed from the breakdown aisle to another aisle.

Carton, Tray, or Tote AS/RS Operation Exception Handling

In addition to the exception handling that can occur in conventional and AS/RS warehouses, a master carton, tray, or tote AS/RS storage operation can have additional situations. The situations are:

1. An unknown tray or tote. After an AS/RS conveyor system realizes that a tray/tote does not have a warehouse identification, the system sends the tray/tote to a rework station. At the rework station, an employee places a warehouse identification onto the tray/tote and reintroduces the tray/tote to the AS/RS system. If there is a SKU on the tray/tote, the employee scans the SKU and associated quantity. Also, a rework employee or inventory control employee completes a cycle count for each SKU on an unknown tray/tote. Cycle counts are entered into the WMS program.

2. The tote/tray is full. If the warehouse is designed to handle mixed SKUs, and a full tote/tray is sent to an in-feed/transfer station, an employee cannot add another SKU to an identified tote/tray at a transfer station. A transfer station employee sends a full tote/tray and sends the tote/tray status to a rework station. At the station, a rework station or inventory control employee completes a status update in the WMS and warehouse program. A cycle count is completed and entered into a WMS program for each SKU on a tote/tray.

SKU Operational Activities and Design Parameters

Design parameters for a SKU storage are:

- SKU dimensions that include length, width, height, and weight, and bar-code scanner line-of-sight/RF-tag transmission reception.
- SKU master carton overhang of a pallet/master carton bottom support (or side-wall bow or deflection) beyond design parameters.
- SKU tote, master carton, pallet description.
- SKU shape and master carton ti and hi on a pallet.
- Average, most frequent, and peak SKU receiving and customer order shipping volumes.
- Average, most frequent, and peak SKU inventory volumes.
- Unique storage environmental conditions.

If a warehouse's SKU inventory does not have uniform design features, then it handles pallets and stacking frames; SKUs with like design characteristics are placed in one storage area, whereas unique SKUs are placed in a separate storage area equipped with storage positions and forklift trucks. To ensure efficient and accurate SKU storage, rack and aisle layout is arranged in a facility, schedule the equipment and employees, establish procedures and practices, a warehouse should implement a WMS program, and organize vendor deliveries to handle projected SKU or customer order volumes.

A storage design with WMS program activities is:

1. Activities that precede storage activities: unloading, receiving, checking, securing SKU and QA sample; SKU and WMS identification and inventory control; SKU transport to storage area; and SKU deposit to a storage position and WMS computer update.

2. SKU put-away activities.

3. SKU withdrawal from storage position and WMS computer update.
4. Post-storage activities: SKU transport to a drop point, pick area, customer order shipping staging area, or delivery truck; and inventory control.

SKU Characteristics

SKU groups are a master carton, small items in totes, or pallets. The physical characteristics of each dictate separate storage designs.

Master Carton/Small Items in a Tote/Master Carton as a SKU

A master carton is a square or rectangular container made of cardboard. A master carton may support itself in a storage position, be placed on a tray, or stacked on a pallet. A tote/container is made of plastic, usually treated and/or corrugated. A master carton or tote/container side wall will have sufficient space for a WMS identification attachment.

Pallet as a SKU

Pallet height is a key factor in determining the number in a floor stack or a rack bay (in a vertical stack). Pallet height is the overall height between the bottom deck board and the highest master carton top. During SKU receiving activity, the vendor tally sheet shows a suggested ti and hi (i.e., number of master cartons per pallet that will not exceed pallet storage position height). Pallet weight includes the weight of a pallet, secure material, and total master carton weight. An employee attaches a WMS identification to a pallet stringer/block or bottom layer master carton, and ensures line-of-sight to a bar-code scanner/RF tag.

SKU in a Storage Area

The design of SKU storage area locations focus on positions in a warehouse storage aisle. A position in a storage aisle is determined by the warehouse's storage position philosophy. A storage position philosophy is determined by:

1. Height, width, length, and weight. For example, heavy-weight and short-height SKUs are located at a rack structure's lowest rack or floor positions;
2. SKU velocity, sales, or customer order demand. Fast-moving SKUs are located at an aisle's start, medium SKUs are located in an aisle's middle, and slow-moving SKUs are located at an aisle's end;
3. SKU value. High-value SKUs are allocated to positions with limited or controlled access;
4. SKUs that require specific environmental storage conditions, such as temperature-sensitive SKUs, are located at the lowest storage position or in a separate storage area;
5. SKUs classified hazardous. Most local codes require that hazardous SKUs be housed in a storage position that restricts SKU flight or has a barrier or pit connected to a containment chamber that restricts a flammable liquid run-off;

6. SKU dimensions. When a warehouse has pallets, master cartons, or storage devices with one or more dimensions or types, specific storage areas or aisles are allocated to a specific SKU dimension or storage device.

Rack Rows and Vehicle Aisle Design Parameters

When designing a warehouse with a manually operated forklift truck or AS/RS crane storage area, a storage position in a rack row or aisle is determined by:

1. A forklift truck or AS/RS crane's ability to complete a storage position transaction;
2. The type of vehicle or travel path used to move SKUs over a transport path;
3. The average and peak SKU storage inventory and number of SKUs;
4. The number and frequency of vendor deliveries and customer orders, as well as the vendor and delivery truck capacities;
5. SKU physical characteristics.

SKU Storage Location Philosophies and Principles

A storage layout philosophy influences storage equipment layout and storage activity locations (i.e., receiving, storage, pick, and shipping areas). The most important areas are SKU storage/pick areas. A storage design with a conventional or VNA forklift truck has a large floor area and requires the greatest number of employees; an AS/RS tall-rack facility requires few employees but operates at a high cost.

Storage layout philosophies are

1. SKU popularity or Pareto's Law (i.e., The 80/20 Rule);
2. ABC theory;
3. The unload/load ratio;
4. Power, fast moving, or Golden Highway SKUs in one storage area;
5. A family group that includes SKU value, temperature control, and hazardous SKU;
6. A family group with ABC theory;
7. FIFO or LIFO SKU rotation with lot number identification;
8. Rack row and aisle direction;
9. Aisle length and width;
10. Building height.

SKU Popularity, Pareto's Law (The 80/20 Rule)

When a storage design has a layout that is based on SKU popularity, it is based on Pareto's Law. In the context of warehouse storage, the Law indicates that 85% of the volume shipped to customers is derived from 15% of the SKUs. Many studies have indicated that an additional 10% of volume shipped comes from another 30% of SKUs, and that an additional 5% of the volume comes from 55% of the SKUs. Recent studies show that 95% of the volume shipped comes from 55% of SKUs and is referred to as "Pareto's Law revised."

ABC Theory

When a warehouse storage professional refers to the three zones of Pareto's Law, she or he is referring to ABC theory. The ABC theory states that the "A" pick zone is allocated to fast-moving SKUs, which are few in number but have a large inventory. The "B" pick zone is allocated to medium-moving SKUs, which are medium in numbers and have a medium inventory. The "C" pick zone is allocated to slow-moving SKUs, which are large in numbers but have a small inventory quantity. Using ABC Theory, the WMS program suggests a storage positions in these zones. If the receiving and shipping docks are located on the front side of the facility and the storage/pick location is based on ABC theory, fast-moving SKUs are located at the facility's front. If the receiving and shipping docks are located on opposite sides of the facility, fast-moving SKUs are located by the unload and load ratio.

Unload and Load Ratio

An unload and load ratio compares the number of trips needed for employees to handle a vendor delivery. When the number of employee unload trips equals the number of employee load trips, storage/pick positions are located near shipping docks or at any location in rack row. When unload employee trips are more numerous than load employee trips, storage/pick positions are located near receiving docks, which reduces employee total travel distance.

Power/Fast-Moving SKUs in One Storage Area or Golden Highway

This philosophy locates all power (i.e., fast-moving) SKUs in predetermined storage/pick positions. Storage/pick positions are adjacent to one another and are referred to as a "Golden Highway." The philosophy has all promotional, seasonal, special-sale, and fast-moving SKUs in one zone. This arrangement increases a picker's hit concentration (number of hits per pick aisle) and hit density (number of hits per SKU). A high hit concentration and hit density means high forklift truck driver productivity due to a short travel distance between two storage positions—these are keys to accurate, efficient, and on-time warehouse storage. Because a WMS program has the promotional, seasonal, or special-sale SKUs in its files, the program ensures accurate storage strategy.

Family Group

Family group philosophy is dictated by a company requirement that SKUs are located in a storage aisle with other SKUs with same inventory classification. This philosophy is designed to accommodate SKUs that

- Have similar dimensions, weight, and SKU components;
- Are located in the same aisle in a retail store;
- Require normal, refrigerated, or freezer conditions;
- Require high security;
- Form toxic or nontoxic materials;
- Include edible or nonedible substances;
- Are made from flammable or nonflammable materials;
- Are stackable or nonstackable; are crushable or noncrushable.

SKU Size

A storage layout philosophy based on a SKU height is determined by company specifications and vendors' ability to pack SKUs at a predetermined height. In a tall storage-rack warehouse, tall storage positions are the highest positions that compensate for forklift truck and AS/RS crane clearance; short positions are located at the low SKUs, which increase a rack structural strength. If a forklift truck or AS/RS operation has partially depleted (short) SKUs allocated to a storage area, a design with separate short height positions improves warehouse storage utilization. Two storage height philosophies are tall and short SKU.

Tall SKU

A tall pallet maximizes the number of master cartons that can be placed on a pallet (the maximum number on a tall pallet is that number that can be layered without crushing the master cartons on the bottom layer). The use of tall pallets means fewer storage vehicle transactions and trips, fewer dock positions (because of the higher number of master cartons on the vendor delivery trucks), fewer WMS transactions, and less potential damage to SKUs, equipment, and building due to fewer handlings. Using tall pallets does necessitate securing master cartons on the pallets and making sure that tall positions have maximum position flexibility.

Short SKU

This design means that each pallet will have the smallest number of master cartons, and therefore less potential for crushed master cartons. Using short pallets means more transactions and trips, increased WMS transactions, equipment and building damage due to increased handlings, minimum position flexibility, increased storage position number, increased rack cost (due to a higher number of rack members), and lower cube utilization. If the warehouse has a large short pallet number with all tall pallet positions than to add short pallet positions in a rack bay, it requires additional load beams, giving assurance that the rack upright frames have the capacity. The remodel improves space utilization.

Manufacturer Lot Number

In a storage design, the ability to track a specific SKU manufacturer lot or production run is similar to FIFO rotation. A manufacturer lot or production run is attached to the SKU WMS identification during receiving activity. The WMS program tracks the manufacturer run number. If the warehouse uses a lot number SKU identification design, different LOTs must be stored separately to ensure good accurate picks. This feature is difficult for a WMS program and lowers a storage/pick activity productivity. With a standard WMS program to assure LOT control, at a pack or shipping dock station, your pack or shipping activity ensures a LOT number registration to a customer order.

SKU Rotation

SKU rotation philosophy is dictated by SKU life cycle and the requirement for a specific SKU for a customer order. SKU rotation philosophy options are

1. FIFO rotation, in which the SKU that is received first is shipped out first. This indicates that a SKU has a predetermined life (time limit) before it spoils. After a specific date, a SKU is not withdrawn from inventory for customer orders. A SKU storage layout that is designed to have SKUs with a FIFO rotation requires access to all storage positions in a storage area and ensures that the oldest SKU is withdrawn first from a storage position. During the receiving process, the WMS program has this information entered into its files and the program ensures accurate storage strategy and suggests a storage position. The storage design ensures access to each SKU for proper rotation.

2. LIFO rotation, in which the SKU that is received last is shipped out first. This SKU type does not have specific shelf life. If a manufacturer's lot number is required by the WMS program in the receiving process, this information will have been entered into the program files, and the WMS program suggests storage positions that allow access to each SKU. This design does not provide access to the oldest SKU, but it does allow a carton/pallet storage layout that uses dense storage positions that reduce necessary space in the facility.

Storage Area Reorganization Strategies

In a warehouse that uses carton/pallet AS/RS storage design with a one- or two-shift operation, and advanced SKU demand knowledge (host computer transfer customer order SKU quantity to your WMS computer), there are several SKU or high-volume SKU reorganization strategies. The reorganization occurs off-shift: The WMS computer directs an AS/RS crane to move a SKU from one storage position to another. The reorganization strategy options are:

1. The SKU remains in a warehouse existing storage position, as per the warehouse's put-away strategy;
2. If only one aisle has a large SKU quantity, the SKUs can be spread to vacant storage positions in other storage design aisles;
3. If there are preplanned vacant storage positions in each aisle front, the AS/RS crane relocates SKUs from rear storage positions to the vacant storage positions in the aisle front.

Put-Away Strategy with "A" SKUs Remaining in an Existing Position

Following the warehouse's put-away strategy, the AS/RS crane deposits a SKU to a storage position. During an off-shift, the SKU remains in the initial storage position. When a customer order demand is received, the WMS computer directs an AS/RS crane to withdraw the SKU from the original storage position. To complete a high-volume SKU withdrawal transaction, an AS/RS crane travels to a storage position, takes a SKU on-board, travels to the pick-up-and-delivery station (P/D station) (at the end of the aisle), transfers the SKU, and a warehouse mobile vehicle transfers the SKU to a pick position.

Spreading "A" SKUs to the Other Aisles

Spreading high-volume SKUs to other aisles during an off-shift involves using an AS/RS crane (or employee) to move SKUs from one storage aisle to another. This reorganization strategy has two steps. The first step is depositing the SKU in a vacant storage position in a WMS or warehouse computer-directed aisle. Based on projected sales data and warehouse customer order wave plan, the WMS program allocates SKUs for customer orders, and reviews SKUs in storage positions in each aisle (the review may also be performed by the warehouse computer). If a high number of SKU transactions is projected in the first storage aisle, during a nonproductive shift, a WMS or warehouse computer directs an AS/RS crane (or employee) to evenly spread SKUs withdrawal transactions among all the storage aisles. SKU move transactions ensure that the anticipated AS/RS crane withdrawal transactions for customer orders per storage aisle are within an AS/RS crane design transaction number.

Moving High-Volume SKUs to Vacant Storage Positions

To move high-volume SKUs from an aisle's initial (middle or rear) storage position to an aisle vacant front storage position has three steps. During regular put-away activity, the WMS program and warehouse will keep two to three front aisle storage positions vacant. Second, the WMS program and warehouse computer relocates the high-volume SKUs to the vacant storage positions. During a nonproductive shift, the WMS program estimates high-volume SKU sales volume. Based on projected sales data (or customer order wave plan), the WMS computer sends a message to the warehouse to direct the AS/RS crane in each aisle to complete SKU move or relocation transactions. Each transaction involves moving a SKU from an initial storage position to a vacant front storage position. Compared to other reorganization strategies, using front vacant storage positions increases the number of AS/RS crane storage transactions.

WMS SKU Identification Sequence in WMS Files

After a receiving clerk attaches a WMS identification to a SKU, a clerk scans the identification and enters a SKU quantity into the WMS inventory files, and sends the data to a WMS computer. The WMS associates a SKU with a specific quantity and tracks the identification (and quantity) as it flows through the storage/pick design. With a SKU that has a shelf life—or if a FIFO rotation is used to ensure proper rotation—the WMS program directs a forklift or AS/RS crane to withdraw the SKU from a storage position. The withdrawal sequence options are:

■ By oldest SKU as the first label scanned;
■ By lowest SKU identification number;
■ By Julian date and lowest identification number.

Oldest SKU as the First Label Scanned

A design in which the oldest SKU is the first identification scanned is the first WMS SKU identification scanned on the receiving dock—and therefore is the oldest SKU in the inventory files.

Lowest WMS SKU Identification Number

A lowest WMS SKU identification number for vendor delivered SKU quantity is the SKU with a lowest WMS identification number and is considered the oldest WMS identification SKU in inventory.

Master Carton Transfer to a Master Carton Storage Design

A master carton replenishment, transfer, or move to master carton storage involves scanning and moving master cartons to a storage position. A storage design will have a predetermined quantity transferred to storage positions. A master carton quantity ensures fast and accurate master carton or SKU quantities can be transferred from a storage position to setup a pick position. After a master carton quantity is moved and scanned/read to a pick position, WMS scan transactions and SKU quantity are sent to the WMS computer for inventory update. For scanned SKUs in pick positions, the WMS computer releases customer orders to a pick process.

A dynamic pick design has multiple pick zones with pick positions. Each SKU has a life cycle. Each pick zone is setup for a SKU life cycle. One pick zone is setup for fast or "A" SKUs. Second/third pick zones are setup for medium or "B," "C," and "D" SKUs. Allocating SKUs to separate pick zones improves picker and replenishment employee productivity.

Each SKU has a life cycle. A life cycle means after a SKU is promoted or advertised to customers, the first several pick line work days experience high customer order numbers. As days go by, customer order numbers decline. When compared to the first day sales, customer orders during days 7 to 10 will be low.

A master carton replenishment, transfer, or move from a large carton quantity (from a pallet or receiving area) to a master carton storage area involves the following factors:

1. Pick design time requirement or when to complete a move transaction to a master carton storage area. Move transaction time options are (a) precustomer order pick activity or after a receiving activity, (b) during a customer order pick activity, or (c) post-customer order pick activity or as a separate pick activity;
2. Master carton transfer/move quantity options are (a) fixed master carton quantity or number, (b) fixed master carton quantity based on a percentage of received SKU quantity, and (c) variable percentage based on a SKU life cycle or percentage of a SKU's sales.

When to Complete a Master Carton Transfer/Move Transaction

In a master carton warehouse with a WMS program, customer orders or a customer order wave plan creates a demand for a WMS program to allocate and transfer/move master cartons from a large master carton quantity in storage to a small master carton quantity in a storage position. The objectives of this transaction are

- To provide master carton storage positions;
- To ensure a fast and accurate transfer that ensures on-time and accurate customer order pick transactions;
- To create a storage design that will complete the maximum number of pallet transactions.

Warehouse and master carton flow pattern objectives and operations review provide knowledge for a transaction activity sequence and available time to complete a transaction activity. They also maintain the warehouse objectives of ensuring maximum customer order number completion with accurate and on-time pick transactions. The extant warehouse review helps to determine a master carton transfer to a pick position strategy. Master carton transfer transaction time options are:

- Precustomer order pick or post receiving activity;
- During customer order pick activity;
- Post-customer order pick or separate master carton pick activity.

Precustomer Order Pick or Post-Warehouse Receiving Activity

In a precustomer order pick or post-receiving activity, a receiving clerk WMS identifies each master carton, and the transfer transaction sends a master carton quantity to a master carton storage area. Each master carton is placed into a storage position, and the WMS computer files are updated.

On a receiving department tally sheet, the WMS computer prints the master carton quantity required for transfer to the storage position. During vendor delivery or SKU unloading, a receiving clerk ensures that the suggested master carton quantity is placed onto a separate pallet. A pallet receives a unique human readable symbology and colored identification, which indicates that a pallet's master cartons are ready for transfer to a storage design. A WMS identification is placed on each master carton, and a receiving clerk completes the move transaction for each master carton. After a carton is physically moved and scanned, scan transactions or AS/RS transactions and the SKU quantity are sent to the WMS computer for inventory update. After the update, a master carton is ready and available for allocation to match a customer order wave plan. This design features are

- In a warehouse activity sequence, a master carton transfer transaction occurs within the maximum available time with minimal time restrictions.
- Ensures master cartons are in storage positions and updated in the WMS computer;
- Master carton transfer performed concurrently with a receiving clerk QA sample size or transfer activity;
- Permits a pallet storage design to focus on other transactions;
- Complete future master carton replenishment transfer transactions, based on a master carton transfer option;
- WMS program suggests master carton transfer quantity;
- Large master carton quantity is ready for replenishment to a pick line.

During Customer Order Pick Activity

If a master carton transfer occurs during pick activity, the WMS computer allocates a pallet to a master carton pick station. The master allocation quantity includes a storage master carton quantity. At a pick station, a picker completes pick position replenishment transactions and warehouse master carton transfer transactions. As master cartons are removed from a pallet, each master carton receives a WMS identification and is transported from a pallet pick area to a storage position. WMS scan transactions (or AS/RS crane transactions) and SKU quantities are sent to the WMS computer for inventory update. The master carton is now available for allocation to a customer order wave plan. The design features are:

- The master carton is transferred to a storage/pick position;
- Master carton transfer activity occurs with a pick line setup activity;
- The WMS program combines customer order allocation with master carton allocation;

■ Combined master carton pick activity increases a pick line's setup time, and increases the number of pallet transactions.

Post-Order Pick Activity or Separate Master Carton Pick Activity

Based on a customer order wave for a pick line design or master carton pick transactions, the WMS computer allocates master cartons from a pallet. The WMS computer also suggests a master carton quantity for transfer/move from a pallet to a storage area. To minimize the number of pallet transactions, the WMS allocation program attempts to combine all allocations onto one pallet that is then transferred to a pick station. At the pick station, as per the WMS computer allocation quantity, each master carton is transferred from a pallet, a WMS identification is placed on each master carton, and the master cartons are transported to a pick line or a storage position.

In a dynamic warehouse, and after a picker or machine has completed all pick line master carton pick transactions from a pallet, master cartons are transferred from a pick station to a pallet special master carton pick station. At the special master carton pick station, master cartons are picked and transferred to a master carton pick and storage area. A special pallet pick station design ensures that pick line master carton pick transactions are completed for the maximum number of SKUs and pallets. WMS scan transactions (or AS/RS crane transactions) and SKU quantities are sent to the WMS computer for inventory update. At that point, a master carton is available for allocation to a customer order wave plan. The design features are:

■ Master cartons transferred to a storage/pick position;
■ Master carton transfer activity occurs with pick line setup activity;
■ The WMS program combines WMS customer order master carton allocation with warehouse master carton allocation;
■ The combined master carton pick activity increases pick line setup time, but using a special storage master carton pick station minimizes the negative impact on master carton pick activity, and increases the number of pallet transactions.

What Master Carton Quantity to Transfer to Storage

If the warehouse is designed for separate master carton or pallet storage, the WMS computer must determine what master carton quantity is to be transferred from receiving to a storage position. As noted above, SKU life cycle, master carton quantity in storage positions, and the SKU quantity per master carton varies and affects the number of master cartons in a storage area.

At the beginning of a SKU life cycle or for two to four days a SKU is promoted for sale, customer orders for the SKU are high and probability for a SKU master carton transfer quantity is high from a pallet or master carton storage area to a pick line. In most warehouses with pallet and master carton storage areas, potential for full or half-pallet transaction quantity from a pallet storage area is greater than the master carton quantity in a master carton storage area; therefore, for a SKU first to four days after a promotion, a SKU is withdrawn from a pallet storage area. After two to four days following a SKU promotion, customer orders for a SKU are low. With fewer customer orders for a SKU and a matching master carton quantity in a master carton storage area, the probability for a master carton quantity transfer to a pick line is from a master carton storage area rather from a pallet storage design.

To maintain an accurate SKU inventory and ensure high employee productivity, SKU transfers use unopened master cartons. The feature has a WMS program to round-up or round down each SKU transfer quantity to a full and non-open master carton

The options for transfer quantities are:

■ A fixed master carton quantity;
■ A fixed master carton quantity based on a percentage of the received SKU quantity;
■ A variable percentage using full master cartons based on a SKU's life cycle or a percentage of a SKU's sales.

Fixed Master Carton Quantity

In this approach, the WMS computer suggests a predetermined master carton quantity for transfer to a storage area. As a warehouse receives SKUs at a receiving dock or pallets at a master carton pick station, the WMS computer indicates on a vendor delivery tally sheet (or pick station display screen) the number of master cartons to be transferred to a storage area. As a master carton leaves a receiving dock or pick station, each master carton receives a WMS identification.

During a SKU's life cycle, the WMS program allocates a pallet to complete customer orders. To maintain a fixed master carton number, the WMS computer reviews the master carton quantity in storage. If the inventory is below a predetermined quantity, the computer adds master cartons to a pallet allocated for customer orders. A warehouse sends the pallet to a pick station. The features are that it is easy to calculate and fewer master cartons for a small size SKU.

Fixed SKU Quantity as a Percentage of Total Inventory

In this approach, the SKU quantity assigned to storage by the WMS computer is based on a percentage of the total inventory. The percentage is determined by SKU classification, sales history, or company policy. Given that a SKU life cycle begins with a large SKU quantity, the master carton quantity in storage will be high. As noted previously, the WMS computer allocates a quantity for pick line replenishment from a pallet storage position, but on occasion a pick line replenishment is made from master carton storage. When a SKU life cycle ends, the quantity in storage will be low. With past master carton transfer quantities for a carton storage area to maintain a percent total SKU inventory from previous master carton transfer activities, master carton quantity in a storage area could be greater than an actual percent quantity. Additional master cartons will remain in storage because it provides the best storage space utilization and is readily available for customer orders. The features of this approach are that is more difficult to calculate quantities, it requires additional time to calculate (or the computer program must be modified to handle the additional calculations), and the number of master cartons will not match sales.

Variable SKU Quantity Based on SKU Life Cycle

In this design, the SKU quantity sent to storage by the WMS computer is a percentage of the total inventory. Again, the percentage is determined by SKU classification, sales history, or company policy. As a SKU's sales go through a life cycle, the WMS computer maintains the SKU quantity in storage by adding a master carton to a customer order allocation. A pallet is sent to a pick station, which transfers the suggested quantity to storage. In this design, quantities are again difficult to calculate, it requires additional time to calculate (or the computer program must be modified to handled the additional calculations), but the number of master cartons will match sales.

Identification Locations

In a warehouse, a vendor-delivered SKU receives a WMS identification as the SKU is unloaded, received, and entered into inventory by the receiving department. Returned SKUs receive a WMS identification as a customer order returns process employee enters the SKU into a WMS return to stock, return to vendor, or WMS identified SKU classification. Each SKU has unique physical characteristics, and warehouses are designed to handle particular types of SKUs. The use of master cartons (that include small items in totes) or pallets require that a SKU's WMS identification matches a SKU type.

SKU Identification Types

In a warehouse with a WMS program, each SKU receives a WMS identification prior to leaving a receiving area. For a master carton or pallet, the options are a bar-code label or RF tag.

Pallet Side Bar-Code/RF-Tag Label Location

A side pallet bar-code or RF-tag label location is the pallet solid stringer or notched four-way entry side. A pallet's forklift truck opening is the pallet front. With this option, a single-face or wrap-around label is placed onto the pallet stringer side, block side, or bottom layer of a master carton. A pallet single-face identification label faces one direction and can be read by a bar-code scanner or is within RF-tag receiver reception. In a forklift truck warehouse, when a pallet with a side label is placed into a storage position, the fork opening faces the forklift truck aisle. As a result, the label is on a pallet side and cannot be read/scanned by the forklift truck driver. In a conventional pallet warehouse, the forklift truck driver must use a double handle on the pallet to scan the identification, which lowers employee productivity. In an AS/RS warehouse, an AS/RS crane will have no difficulty handling a side-labeled pallet because the fixed position scanner (on the AS/RS crane) is designed to read a pallet label. The transaction between the AS/RS crane and pallet position is communicated between the AS/RS computer and the WMS computer. With a pallet-side identification, as a forklift truck completes a pick-up/delivery station transfer transaction, the bar-code scanner will have a line-of-sight restriction but not a RF-tag receiver reception.

If a wrap-around label is placed on the pallet's side, either one picket fence label faces a side and one label faces the front or one long label wraps around the pallet. Two-bar–code/RF-tag label faces permit scanning from the pallet's side and front. Using a wrap-around label minimizes scanner line-of-sight problems; and there will be no RF-tag receiver reception problems on a travel path or in a storage position.

Stringer or Block Pallet Front Bar-Code/RF-Tag Label Locations

A stringer pallet has two or three stringers that support the pallet's top and bottom deck boards. A pallet's stringer side or front has a solid, flat, and smooth surface that permits a WMS identification attachment. A block pallet has blocks on each pallet corner; some pallets have a middle block. Each block has a solid, flat, and smooth surface that permits an attachment. A pallet identification uniquely identifies a pallet and permits a forklift or an AS/RS crane to complete a storage transaction. The pallet bar-code label location options are:

- With a single-face label on the stringer or block side;
- With a wrap-around label on the right stringer/block;
- With a wrap-around label on the left stringer/block;
- With a single-face label on the stringer/block, middle stringer, or block;
- With a single-face label on a master carton's bottom layer;
- With a wrap-around label on a master carton's bottom layer.

To ensure good forklift truck driver productivity, on a pallet that is used in a conventional forklift truck or in an AS/RS crane warehouse, a single-face identification is on a fork opening side or stringer front.

When an identification is placed on a pallet's right stringer side or the bottom layer of a master carton, a wrap-around label ensures maximum scanner line-of-sight and good employee productivity. One label direction has an identification on the fork opening side. An identification on a pallet's right side and front ensures direct forklift truck driver scanner line-of-sight. Scanners and readers are set along a conveyor travel path to ensure the label can be scanned or read.

Placing a single-face or wrap-around identification on a pallet's right stringer front ensures line-of-sight for a conventional forklift truck and meets AS/RS with in-feed and out-feed conveyors and identification requirements. An identification on a pallet's right side and facing a front (fork opening) ensures a (right-handed) forklift truck driver can successfully scan or read the label. Scanners and readers are set at an angle along the conveyor travel path to ensure successful scanning or reading or labels.

When a single-face identification is placed onto a pallet's left stringer side or a master carton's bottom layer, the label faces one direction and has limited scanner line-of-sight flexibility. If the identification is placed on a pallet's left side, with some additional effort a direct a right-handed forklift truck driver will be able to achieve scanner line-of-sight. Scanners and readers are set along the conveyor travel path to ensure successful scanning or reading of labels.

When a single-face or wrap-around label is placed on a pallet's left stringer front, the location will have adequate line-of-sight for a conventional forklift truck, and meets AS/RS identification requirements. Placing an identification on a pallet's right side and front permits direct forklift truck driver scanner line-of-sight. Scanners and readers are set at an angle along the conveyor travel path to ensure successful scanning or reading of labels.

A single-face label, placed on a pallet's middle stringer front or a master carton's bottom layer, ensures line-of-sight for a conventional forklift truck and meets AS/RS identification requirements. If the identification is placed on a pallet's middle stringer front, with some additional effort, right-handed forklift truck drivers will have line-of-sight to the label. Scanners and readers are set at an angle along the conveyor travel path to ensure successful scanning or reading of labels.

Bar-Code/RF-Tag Label Identification on a Carton Tray

When a carton AS/RS warehouse with a WMS program uses a tray to support a master carton or master cartons in a storage position, the options for locating tray bar-code/RF-tag identification are:

- With sufficient tray edge height, the side, front, and rear;
- With sufficient tray lip width or interior space, on the top;
- The bottom.

A carton AS/RS tray with a single-face label travels on a conveyor travel path between an AS/RS storage position and a carton transfer station. At a tray/carton transfer station, the conveyor travel path will have been designed to ensure that a label faces an employee hand-held scanner, fixed-position bar-code scanner, or RF-tag receiver.

SKU Storage Position Types and WMS Identification Locations

Each SKU storage position must have a WMS identification. A storage position identification location permits a scanner/reader to complete SKU and WMS scan transactions. Each SKU type has a storage position that is designed specifically to handle that type.

Small Items in Totes/Master-Carton Storage Positions

To have maximum inventory flexibility and accountability, each tote with small items or master carton has a WMS SKU identification.. Options for storing small items are

- Containers stacked on a floor or attached to a cart;
- A standard pallet rack;
- Hand stacked containers on decked pallet rack;
- Versa shelving;
- Standard shelves, including open type, closed type, wire meshed, wide span shelving, and drawer;
- Powered carousel;
- Carton AS/RS crane.

Pallet Storage Position WMS Identification

Each pallet storage position has a WMS identification. As a pallet deposit is completed to a storage position, scan transactions are sent to the WMS computer or the AS/RS crane computer sends a message to the WMS computer.

A pallet storage design objectives are:

- A pallet or bottom support device to support the SKU, permit a forklift truck or AS/RS crane to complete a storage transaction, and allow a WMS identification attachment to a secure location that permits scanner line-of-sight or RF-tag receiver reception;

■ A floor stack or rack position structural support members to support a SKU, permits a fork-lift truck or AS/RS crane to complete storage transactions, and allows a WMS identification location with line-of-sight to a forklift truck driver or RF-tag receiver.

Pallet Materials

Pallets are manufactured from a wide variety of materials. Factors that determine a pallet material for a warehouse are master carton characteristics length, width, height, weight, and total weight and ti and hi a pallet; allowable pallet deflection or bowing; combined SKU and pallet weight acceptable to a storage position and forklift truck or AS/RS crane design; warehouse storage and safety considerations, such as spark-free, noncorrosive, freezer, or high humidity environments; pallet purchase plan, pallet exchange program, or a captive pallet; pallet material as permitted by local codes; if the material permits a WMS pallet identification attachment to a stringer or block; and operational factors. Prior to a pallet purchase, a warehouse company should complete WMS identification attachment and secure tests. Pallet materials are:

■ Wood (e.g.,hardwood, medium hardwood, soft hardwood, and softwood);
■ Plastic;
■ Corrugated material;
■ Pressboard or fiberboard;
■ Rubber;
■ Metal and metal clad.

Block Pallet

A block pallet is a four-way pallet with equally spaced blocks along its length and width. Deck boards are attached to blocks; a block provides good WMS pallet identification location, and allows a front-face or wrap-around WMS identification label. In a drive-in or drive-through rack or AS/RS crane carrier with a platen, a pallet bottom deck boards spans a pallet storage position two arms or rails. If a block pallet is used in the storage area, prior to implementation in a storage area, a block pallet is tested in a storage position. The pallet material determines the identification attachment method, which includes self-adhesive glued, sleeve insert, staple, or tape. If a block material does not accept one of the attachment methods during label attachment tests, the identification may be attached to a master carton on a pallet bottom layer.

Stringer Pallet

A stringer pallet has two exterior stringers and one interior stringer for top and bottom deck board attachment. Small-width stringer pallets have two exterior stringers. Exterior stringers either are solid or have two notches in a stringer side. Notches are additional set of fork entry openings, are 5 to 5½ inches high, and permit a forklift truck chisel forks to handle a pallet from all four sides. A pallet stringer provides a good location for permament or disposable identification, and can take a front face or wrap-around identification label. The pallet material determines the attachment method. If a stringer does not accept one of the aforementioned attachment methods, one option is to have the identification attached to a master carton on a pallet's bottom layer.

Pallet Identification Types and Attachment Designs

Pallet identification types and attachment designs are warehouse components that uniquely identify a SKU. In a warehouse with a WMS program, each SKU receives an identification at a receiving dock, and a receiving clerk ensures that the identification is securely attached. For more about pallet identification types and attachment designs, please see Chapter 4.

Storage Designs

Pallet storage can be single deep master carton or pallet storage and dense storage. Storage design is determined by the number of SKUs, SKU inventory requirements, and required SKU rotation. When a warehouse facility is designed, storage design is a major factor in determining a building's square feet.

Single Deep Storage Designs

Single deep storage features SKU floor stack or pallet rack storage positions that are serviced by an employee, an employee controlled forklift truck, or AS/RS crane. If a warehouse building has at least a 40- to 60-foot high clear ceiling, a VNA lift truck is used; with a 60- to 80-foot high clear ceiling an AS/RS crane is used. A single deep storage design provides maximum access to all SKUs, low storage density (i.e., fewer SKUs per square foot), FIFO SKU rotation, a large square-foot facility, uses a basic WMS program, and is easy to complete specific SKU deposit and withdrawal transactions.

Dense Storage Designs

Dense storage design means that there are two or more pallets deep per storage position, and that one or two aisles are needed to complete pallet storage transactions. In a low bay building, dense storage designs are floor stack, two-deep racks, drive-in racks, stacking frames/containers/stack racks, drive-through racks, mobile shelves or racks, gravity flow racks, or sort links. In an AS/RS storage design, dense storage options are gravity or air flow racks, car-in or mole racks, or two deep racks. Dense storage designs have few storage vehicle aisles, greater SKUs per square foot, few SKUs a smaller square-foot facility, some do not provide a FIFO SKU rotation, and it is difficult to complete a specific SKU withdrawal transaction (although the problems can be minimized with WMS program modifications).

Pallet Storage Designs

In a pallet storage design with a WMS program, each storage position has a WMS identification that is entered into the WMS computer; forklift trucks or AS/RS cranes are used to complete SKU storage and scan transactions. Pallet storage designs are:

■ Floor stack or block designs that are either 90- or 45-degree angles;
■ Tier racks, stack frames, pallet cages, or containers;
■ Double deep/two deep racks;

- Standard pallet racks that include two pallets on a floor;
- Bridge an aisle;
- Drive-in racks;
- Drive-through racks;
- Gravity/air flow racks;
- Push back racks;
- Mobile or sliding racks;
- Cantilever racks;
- High-rise or AS/RS racks;
- Mole, car-in, or sort-link racks.

Floor Stack or Block Storage Designs

In a pallet floor stack or block storage design, a pallet is placed directly on the floor or another pallet (see Figure 6.2). A floor-stacked design is a dense storage design that provides a maximum of 6 to 10 pallets deep per storage design lane. A storage lane can be a single lane or back-to-back storage lanes. Due to pallets leaning and forklift truck placement variance on the floor and on another pallet, longer or deeper storage lanes reduce manually controlled forklift truck's ability to complete storage transactions with good employee productivity. To utilize air space, additional pallets are stacked on other pallets to a maximum of three to four pallets in height. To ensure good forklift truck productivity and minimal SKU damage, three to five inches of open space is allowed between two storage lanes. To ensure accurate pallet placement in a floor stack lane, open space is painted with white or yellow paint to guide the forklift truck driver. If a slip sheet on a pallet is used in a floor stack design and a slip sheet lip remains on a unit load, at least six inches is allowed between two storage lanes. The floor stack practice has master cartons that are capable to support a stacked weight and that a master carton (SKU) at an aisle position is the same SKU for an entire floor stack storage lane. Floor stack storage design when full, provides the highest storage density with lowest cost but poor pallet accessibility. A 60% utilization factor is used to determine a pallet storage position number and is used due to honeycombing (vacant pallet positions in a vertical stack) and vacant pallet positions in a storage lane depth. This is due to normal forklift truck storage transaction activity. In a floor stack design, to make a pallet transaction, a forklift truck enters a storage lane from aisle "A," travels to a pallet position, completes a transaction, and backs out from the same aisle. When a floor stack storage area is designed, the number of pallets per storage lane is varied to bury building columns in or between storage lanes. The design has a LIFO SKU, handles a high through-put volume, and interfaces with wide-aisle or narrow-aisle forklift trucks.

Floor stack options are

- A 90-degree stack design with a pallet fork opening; the pallet identification faces a main aisle;
- A 45-degree floor stack design allows a minimum right-angle forklift truck turning aisle, one-way forklift truck traffic, and fewer pallet openings per aisle.

To track a pallet in a floor stacked storage location, as a pallet is placed into a storage position, a forklift truck driver hand scans the pallet identification and storage position identification.

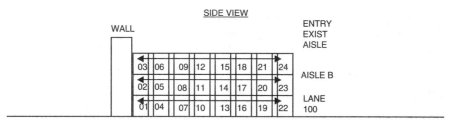

PLAN VIEW

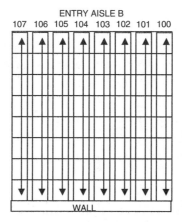

FLOOR STACK DEPOSIT AND WITHDRAWAL TRANSACTION SEQUENCE

DEPOSIT TRANSACTION				WITHDRAWAL TRANSACTION		
PALLET DEPOSIT SEQENCE	PALLET WMS ID #	WMS ID STORAGE POSITION	SCANNED WMS ID POSITION	PALLET WITHDRAWAL SEQENCE	PALLET WMS ID #	WMS ID STORAGE POSITION
FIRST	120789	101F	101F	FIRST	7832	101A
SECOND	398500	101E	101E	SECOND	69301	101B
THIRD	45714	101D	101D	THIRD	9472	101C
FOURTH	9472	101C	101C	FOURTH	45714	101D
FIFTH	69301	101B	101B	FIFTH	398500	101E
SIXTH	7832	101A	101A	SIXTH	120789	101F

Figure 6.2   Suggested Identification Arrangement for Floor Storage

Scans are sent on-line or delayed to update inventory files. In a floor stack design, WMS program considerations are:

- How to ensure that a floor stack storage lane has proper identification;
- To complete a WMS identified pallet withdrawal transaction, WMS identified pallets in a floor stack storage lane do not have the same sequence as that suggested by a WMS program.

WMS identified pallet deposit and actual pallet sequence in a floor stack lane has the first WMS identified pallet that is a pallet on the floor level and in a floor stack deepest pallet position from a main aisle. In a floor stack lane, the last pallet is the highest pallet on the floor stack adjacent to an aisle. In a standard WMS program, when the program suggests the withdrawal of a pallet from a floor stack lane, the pallet that is adjacent to a main aisle is the first pallet accessed by the forklift truck driver. The driver scans the first pallet's identification but it is not the corresponding pallet identification suggested by a WMS program.

To comply with a WMS program and floor stack storage design, the floor stack pallet position identification options are to have storage pallet lane position and identifications that are:

- Ceiling hung above each lane, which limits the floor stack height;
- Embedded in the floor in the front of the middle of each lane;
- Attached to an upright post between two floor stack lanes, which corresponds with the open space between two lanes.

To ensure that each pallet identification and storage location identification is scanned by a forklift truck driver, and to ensure that forklift trucks have access to computer-suggested SKUs, the options are

- Pallet identification substitution;
- Floor stack lane pallet directory;
- Hybrid dense SKU storage program.

Floor Stack Design Transaction Substitution with a Pallet

A WMS pallet identification substitution design is based on the criteria that a) all pallets in a master carton or pallet floor stack lane are for one SKU and b) there is a pallet storage position identification that identifies each floor stack storage lane. After a received SKU is placed and scanned in a storage lane, scan transactions and SKU quantity are sent to the WMS program. To complete move or customer order pick transactions, the program instructs a forklift truck driver to withdraw a specific pallet from a floor stack lane. In a floor stack design with a WMS program, when a forklift truck driver arrives at an assigned floor stack lane, the driver completes the pallet scan transaction (with a hand-held scanner) by scanning the pallet identification that faces a main aisle. With a full floor stack storage lane, the first pallet available to a forklift truck driver is the top pallet in a pallet floor stack adjacent to a main aisle. After the driver scans the top pallet's identification, if top pallet is not the first pallet identification that was entered into a pallet floor stack lane, the scanner display indicates the pallet is unacceptable.

With a pallet identification substitution approach, the WMS program permits a forklift truck driver to enter an actual/accessible pallet identification adjacent to a main aisle or has been withdrawn from a bottom pallet on the deepest floor stack position. The suggested pallet identification is retained in a inventory file and the actual withdrawn pallet identification adjusted in the inventory file. Pallet identification substitution design features are:

- It does not maintain WMS integrity;
- It requires additional forklift truck driver WMS training;
- It requires WMS program enhancement;
- It does not maintain WMS program SKU security.

Floor Stack Design with a Pallet Identification Location Directory

A floor stack design and pallet identification location directory is used in a warehouse with a LIFO SKU rotation or no SKU rotation requirement. A pallet floor stack position with a WMS program and pallet identification location directory has two floor anchor upright frames located between two floor stack lanes. With one upright post for each floor stack lane, pallet storage position identification options are a) onto an upright post face or b) onto a placard attached to an upright post.

An upright post adjacent to a main aisle and post flat surface with WMS identified positions face a main aisle. On a main aisle upright post for a three-deep and three-high pallet floor stack design, there are nine pallet position identifications. With a four-deep and three-high pallet floor stack design, there are 12 pallet position identifications.

In a floor stack and pallet identification location directory design, as a forklift truck driver completes a first WMS identified pallet deposit to a bottom and deepest floor stack lane pallet position, a forklift truck driver scan transactions are a) read a WMS pallet identification or b) for the first pallet deposit transaction, on an upright post or placard, read the pallet position identification associated with pallet storage position A109, which is placed on the deepest pallet position and scan placard position A101 identification. A second pallet identification deposit transaction has a forklift truck driver place a pallet on a rear middle and deepest pallet top and to scan the pallet identification and, on a upright post or placard, the pallet storage position associated with WMS pallet position A102.

Pallet storage position identifications are numerically sequenced, either from highest (oldest) to lowest (newest), or from lowest to highest. If a forklift truck driver scans a previously scanned pallet position, the WMS program will not accept the scan. The program will send a message to the scanner instructing the driver to scan/read the next lower identification pallet position label. If the pallets are sequenced from highest to lowest, to complete a withdrawal, the WMS program and floor directory design indicates that a WMS identified pallet for a withdrawal transaction is a WMS identified pallet on the floor pallet stack that is adjacent to a main aisle. If the pallets are sequenced from lowest to highest, to complete a pallet withdrawal transaction, a floor stack and pallet identification location directory design indicates that a WMS identified pallet for a withdrawal transaction is a WMS identified pallet on the floor stack that is adjacent to a main aisle.

A floor stack and pallet identification location directory design features are SKU identification integrity and security, the need for additional operator training, it can be used in a floor stack storage design, and it requires minimal WMS program upgrade.

Portable Containers, Tier Racks, Pallet Cage, and Stack Frames

A dense storage design uses portable containers, tier racks, pallet cages, or stack frames. When vendor delivered master cartons that are placed in a floor stack storage design are crushable or are not square, a container, tier rack, or stack frame storage design optimizes cube storage space by making uniform unit loads. All of these devices have fork openings; a tier rack is placed on a standard pallet. It is common practice to have one SKU per pallet storage lane and stack. In a storage design with a WMS program, a pallet identification is attached (permanently or temporarily) with a sleeve, tape, or adhesive label to a container, stacking frame, or tier rack structural member. In a storage lane, each SKU identification faces a main aisle; forklift truck practices and scan transactions are the same as those in warehouse using a floor stack storage design with a WMS program.

Standard Pallet Racks

A standard pallet rack design has one, two, or three pallets in a rack opening, level, or bay (see Figure 6.3). The number of pallets per rack bay is determined by the pallet width and load-beam length. Pallets in the first vertical bay are placed on the floor; pallets in other vertical rack bays are placed on a pair of load beams. In a WA/NA forklift truck operation, there is a three- to six-inch clearance between a pallet and an upright pallet, between two pallets, and between top and load beams. If a straddle or NA forklift truck is used with a 40-inch pallet on the floor, at least 5 inches is allowed between the pallet and the rack upright post or between pallets. In a VNA forklift truck storage design, both options are considered for a rack and forklift truck design. A rack bay has two vertical upright frames; each rack bay above the floor has two load beam support pallets and are attached to upright frames. To provide good stability, there should be a minimum of one pair of load beams on the first level and a second pair on an upright frame top. Many conventional rack installations are three or four pallet bays high. In a warehouse with a tall building, rack bays are at least 4 or 6 levels high; a warehouse that uses AS/RS crane rack bays are 10 or more pallets high.

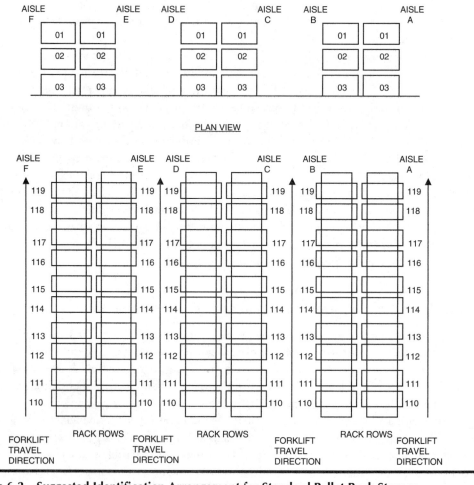

Figure 6.3   Suggested Identification Arrangement for Standard Pallet Rack Storage

In a standard pallet rack warehouse with a WMS program, pallet storage identifications locations are with a WA, NA, or VNA man-up forklift truck on a load beam that supports a pallet position. The identifications are a) on a load beam, which ensures forklift truck driver line-of-sight; and b) on a upright post, for load-beam levels above a forklift truck driver's line-of-sight. As a storage lift truck driver faces a rack bay, pallet position identifications are stacked on a load beam under rack pallet right side or upright frame with hand-held scanner line-of-sight.

Pallet Placement in a Rack Position

If the pallets are 48 inches long by 40 inches wide, pallet placement is directed by the warehouse and affects label placement. There are three purposes of pallet identification and rack position:

1. Track a pallet in a storage position.
2. Track a pallet in a pick position.
3. Ensure good forklift truck productivity and maximum space utilization.

In a manual or mechanized pallet storage design, pallet placement in a manual storage/pick position also has an impact on a pallet label type and location. Pallet placement options are a 48-inch dimension into a rack or a 40-inch dimension into a rack.

Two High Pallets on the Floor Level

If the pallet storage design has a large number of pallets for one SKU, two high pallet stacks of the same SKU on a floor is an option. If the warehouse is using a standard storage design with drive-in/drive-through rack design, and two high pallets on the floor, a two high pallet stack is set on the floor and rack bays are designed for one pallet. Upright frames and posts are manufactured with additional strength for increased vertical height on the bottom level. (The rack vendor will need to approve the design.) Rack post protectors are placed on each upright frame post aisle side to reduce forklift truck damage. In a two pallet high stack in a bottom rack position with a WA/NA forklift truck operation, pallet position identifications are placed on an upright frame and additional labels are placed an upright post. The labels face an aisle to minimize any problems forklift truck drivers might have scanning/reading the labels, and colored labels and direction arrows are used. As a driver faces a rack bay, the left-hand pallet position to an upright post left side has a pallet storage identification and a right hand pallet position to a upright post right side has the pallet storage identification. With an upright post between two storage lanes and pallets on each side, labels are adjacent to each other. It should be noted that this arrangement could cause incorrect scans, or make it impossible to use a hand-held scanner.

To track a pallet deposit to a pallet position and to ensure withdrawal of a pallet identification from a pallet position, a warehouse using two high pallet storage with a WMS program uses pallet identification substitution or directory location program.

Double-Deep or Two-Deep Racks

A two-deep or double-deep pallet rack design is a dense storage design with a two-deep NA forklift truck design. With few exceptions, two-deep pallet rack components and design characteristics are similar for a standard pallet rack design. A rack upright frame is determined by pallet weight and desired flexibility (for reusing upright frames at another location). Two-deep rack options are:

- Long frame with four load beams and two upright frames;
- Standard upright frame with four standard load beams and four upright frames.

Two-Deep Rack Characteristics

In a two-deep pallet rack design, the first pallet deposit is made to an interior pallet storage position; the second deposit is made to an aisle or exterior pallet storage position (see Figure 6.4). The first pallet withdrawal transaction is made from an aisle or exterior pallet position; the second withdrawal is made from the interior pallet position. The features are for interior pallet transaction additional time required to extend a set of forks in the storage postion, provides a LIFO SKU rotation and ability to handle a medium volume. With four pallets per rack bay, a two-deep

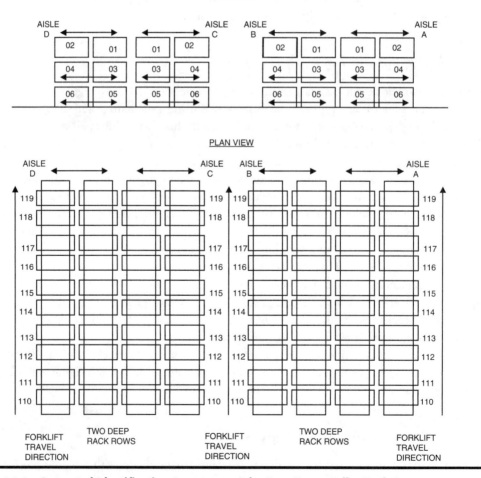

Figure 6.4 Suggested Identification Arrangement for Two-Deep–Pallet Rack Storage

rack design provides medium position density and fair pallet accessibility. Two-deep rack design options are:

- Up-and-over (i.e., raised above the floor). In an up-and-over design, the bottom rack opening is raised above the floor. An open space permits forklift truck straddles to pass under bottom load beams and to turn in a narrow aisle. An aisle allows easy pallet transactions at any rack level because the straddles are not required to straddle a floor-level pallet. This design handles pallets with narrow widths or pallet widths that exceed the distance between forklift truck straddles. The design has a narrower rack opening but increases rack cost, and requires additional rack upright post height and building height.
- Bottom pallets set on the floor. In this design, all pallets in elevated rack positions are directly aligned with the floor pallet. This reduces forklift truck driver productivity because additional time is required to line up the forklift truck straddles between the floor-level pallets.

A two-deep pallet storage design is a dense storage design that stores the same SKU in interior and exterior positions. To ensure proper identification, labels are placed on load beams or upright posts. To complete pallet storage position identification and pallet identification scans, a forklift truck driver may use the substitute method or floor stack design and pallet identification location directory design.

Bridge Racks or Bridge across the Aisle

A standard pallet rack design is designed for a pallet operation and interface with WA or NA forklift truck aisles and standard pallet racks (see Figure 6.5). A standard pallet rack bridge over an aisle increases pallet positions within a facility and has same rack design and operational characteristics as a standard pallet rack design. Load beams with front to rear members (cross) span a forklift truck aisle and are connected to rack rows' end upright frames, which forms a bridge across an aisle. For

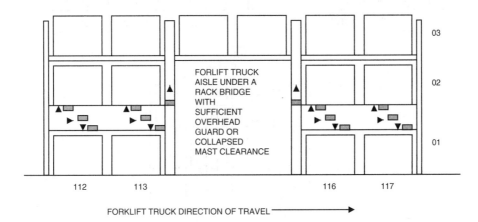

Figure 6.5   Identification With Bridge an Aisle

each rack bay over an aisle, a bridge across an aisle provides one or two additional pallet openings. An important consideration is to allow sufficient space for a collapsed forklift truck mast. To minimize forklift truck driver problems, colored border identification labels and direction arrows are used. Pallet position scan transactions are similar to standard pallet rack scan transactions and use a standard WMS program. As a forklift truck driver faces a bridge rack bay, the left hand position is on a bridge left upright frame/post and the right hand position is on a bridge right upright post.

Drive-In Racks

A drive in-rack storage design is for non-self-supporting master cartons on a pallet. A drive-in rack has pallet rack storage lanes and is a dense pallet storage design. Drive-in rack storage lane pallet positions are used for a single SKU. Rack components are upright frames, upright posts, support arms, guide rails, support rails, and side, top, and back bracing. A drive-in rack bottom lane has bottom pallets (one SKU) set on the floor and elevated storage lane pallets (same SKU) set on rack structural members. Each pallet position level has two support arms and rails. Support arms are attached to each upright post. A drive rack lane is 2 to 10 pallets positions deep and 3 to 4 pallets high. A drive-in rack layout provides medium to good storage density but poor pallet accessibility; SKU rotation is LIFO. A drive-in rack is designed with either a single row or back-to-back rows. Drive-in rack design allows distance between a rack second level storage lane/structural members and floor to have height that permits a WA or NA forklift truck overhead guard/collapsed mast and as required straddles to enter and exit a floor-level storage lane. A second rack design

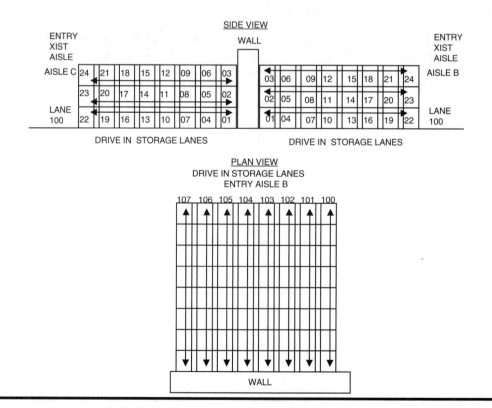

Figure 6.6 Suggested Identification Arrangement for Drive-In Rack Storage

parameter is that a forklift truck mast is able to travel through the open distance between a rack lane two pallet support rails.

Drive-in rack storage lanes are best designed between two building columns. The number of pallets in a warehouse is varied to be able to place building columns within the flue space that is between back-to-back drive-in rack rows All warehouses using a drive-in rack design require fire sprinklers, a forklift truck mast, and overhead and straddle clearances. Most drive-in rack designs are designed with pallet fork opening sides facing an aisle. To complete a pallet transaction in a drive-in rack storage design, a forklift truck enters a floor-level storage lane from aisle "A," completes the transaction and backs out into the same aisle "A." Due to this operational characteristic, a drive-in rack design handles a medium volume and has a LIFO SKU rotation.

In a warehouse that uses drive-in rack storage with a WMS program, pallet position identifications are placed on upright posts and have same identification design as floor stack and pallet identification location directory designs. The design also permits a forklift truck driver to use pallet identification substitution. As the truck driver faces a rack bay, the right hand upright frame has a pallet position identification for a pallet on an upright frame left side.

Drive-Through or Through-Racks

A drive-through or through-rack design is a dense storage design that handles non-self-supporting master cartons on a pallet. In this design, drive-through racks and storage lanes are used for a single SKU. Drive-through racks have same rack components and design characteristics as a drive-

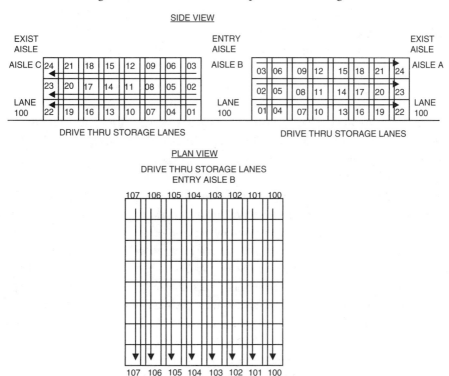

Figure 6.7 Suggested Identification Arrangement for Drive-Through Rack Storage

in rack design, and a 66% utilization factor. One difference is that drive-through racks use top bracing rather than back bracing. Thus, drive-through racks are designed as stand-alone rack rows with forklift truck aisles on both sides. There are no back-to-back rows designs. Drive-through racks handle a medium volume and SKU rotation is LIFO or FIFO. With a LIFO SKU rotation, the warehouse and WMS program features are the same as a drive-in rack.

With a FIFO SKU rotation, a forklift truck enters a drive-through rack lane from aisle "A," completes a pallet storage transaction to an elevated lane and drives-through the rack lane into aisle "B." After all elevated pallet storage lanes are full, a floor-level lane is handled as a drive-in rack lane. An alternative procedure in a FIFO SKU rotation is to exit a storage lane by driving without a SKU through a drive-through storage lane and to exit into aisle "B." To retrieve a pallet, a forklift truck enters a rack lane from aisle "B," retrieves a SKU, and backs out from a drive-through storage lane into aisle "B." Drive-through racks have medium storage density and poor pallet accessibility. In a warehouse using a drive-through rack design with a WMS program, pallet position identifications are placed on upright posts. Because a WMS program suggests a SKU for withdrawal, from the withdrawal aisle a forklift truck driver must use a pallet identification substitution method. The drive-through pallet withdrawal transaction creates nonproductive forklift truck driver time because the driver must walk to a pallet front to scan/read the label.

Mobile/Sliding Racks

A mobile or sliding rack design is similar to a standard rack design, except that a) it is a dense storage design, b) it has fewer forklift truck aisles and rack rows, and c) those aisles and rack rows move to create forklift truck storage transaction aisles. Mobile racks are standard single deep-pallet rack rows or back-to-back rack rows on moveable bases. A mobile rack design has end two single deep rack rows as fixed rack rows that do not move and the interior rack rows as mobile rack rows that move to create a transaction aisle. All rack rows are placed in an arrangement that is 90 degrees or perpendicular to the main traffic aisle. A mobile rack is designed with nominal six back-to-back moveable rows and one forklift truck aisle. At each end is a single deep rack section or row. Mobile racks are four to five pallets high to one pallet deep. If sprinklers are required in the racks, this can be added by the rack vendor.

For access to a pallet position, a mobile rack moves to a side and creates a WA/NA forklift truck storage transaction aisle between two rack rows. A forklift truck enters an aisle, performs the required transaction, and exists into a main traffic aisle. After completion of the transaction, mobile rack sections are moved to create a new aisle between two different rack rows. Sensing devices on moveable rack base bottom section sense an object or employee in the mobile rack section travel path—if there is an object, then the rack section stops. This feature prevents equipment damage and employee injuries. With one access aisle, mobile racks provide high pallet position density and good accessibility. A mobile rack design has an 85% utilization factor and handles low to medium volume due to slow rack movement. A WMS program and batched customer order transactions for each row will improve forklift truck transaction productivity. In a warehouse using a mobile rack design with a WMS program to ensure WA/NA forklift truck line-of-sight, pallet position identifications and pallet identifications have the same arrangements and scan procedures as standard pallet racks.

Gravity/Air-Flow Racks

A gravity (i.e., "flow-through," "air-flow") rack design is a stand-alone rack design that uses aisle "A" for pallet in-feed and aisle "B" for out-feed. Each flow lane is allocated to one SKU. Thus, in a four-level pallet gravity rack, the options are:

■ One SKU per each pallet flow lane. The means that a three-high flow rack design has one SKU per flow-rack lane or three different SKUs, one SKU in all pallet flow lanes in a stack.

A gravity flow rack design has upright frames, upright posts, braces, brakes, end stops, and skate wheel or roller conveyors that make up the individual pallet flow storage lanes. In a WA/NA conventional forklift truck warehouse, pallet flow lanes are three or four levels high. In a VNA forklift truck or AS/RS crane warehouse, pallet lanes are designed five to eight pallet lanes high. Pallet weight and height determines the slope and pitch of the pallet flow rack lanes. The pallet height and length ratio is 3:1. If pallets exceed this ratio, there is a potential for uneven pallet flow through or hang-ups in a flow lane. A gravity flow design is designed with 3 to 20 pallets per lane. In most flow rack designs, a pallet is placed on a slave pallet to ensure smooth flow through a storage lane. In some designs, conveyor rollers have flanged wheels that act as guides for pallet flow through the rack. To prevent rack damage, lane entry guides, upright post protectors, forklift truck stops, and sufficient turning aisle widths are designed for entry and exit positions.

A flow rack design uses a WA/NA forklift truck for access to the deposit side. After a forklift truck in aisle "A" places a pallet onto a conveyor, gravity/air and the pallet's weight move the pallet through the flow lane to the end of the lane. SKUs are removed by forklift trucks in aisle "B" from the end of the lane, and the next pallet in the lane flows index to a withdrawal position. In a long pallet flow rack design, pallet brakes and a SKU separator (at an exit position) are installed in a flow lane to reduce line pressure and SKU damage. A warehouse pallet flow design that indexes pallet movement from a deposit position to a withdrawal position allows each flow lane to accommodate one SKU per storage lane. The feature permits flow racks with two aisles, high storage density, and fair pallet accessibility. In a gravity flow design with a WMS program, as a pallet is transferred to the flow lane a forklift driver has line-of-sight to a pallet WMS identification. Flow rack pallet position identifications are placed on upright posts and have the same pallet position identification arrangement as the floor stack. Because the WMS program suggests SKUs for withdrawal, forklift truck drivers must use the pallet identification substitution method for withdrawals. Unfortunately, the gravity rack pallet withdrawal transaction will cause nonproductive forklift truck driver time: To obtain pallet identification, the driver must walk to the front of the pallet.

Push-Back Racks

A push-back rack design is a stand-alone rack design with a single aisle. A push-back pallet rack design has the same components and design characteristics as a gravity flow rack, albeit with some exceptions. A push-back rack design is designed as a single rack row that is installed along a building wall, in a location that allows for an aisle (for a forklift truck to perform entry and withdrawal transactions) or as back-to-back rack rows. A push-back design will be three to four pallets deep and three to four pallets high with one SKU per lane or three to four different SKUs per push-back rack bay. To complete a deposit, a forklift truck places a pallet against an existing pallet in a push-back position. When an existing pallet is sufficiently pushed back into the storage lane, it creates a required new pallet space. To withdraw a pallet, a WA/NA forklift truck raises a pallet two to three inches above a push-back conveyor and backs out a pallet from the lane. As the pallet is removed, gravity moves the next pallet into a lane exit or aisle position. The design permits 66% lane utilization and a LIFO SKU rotation. A push-back rack provides good storage density, fair accessibility, handles a low to a medium volume, and each lane handles one SKU. A push-back rack design has two options:

- A standard conveyor push-back rack design. This approach does not require brakes but requires end stops on both ends of flow lanes.
- A telescoping push-back rack design This design feature has three carriages that ride on a set of tracks. After forklift truck places a pallet on a carriage, a forklift truck pushes the carriage forward that has a carriage travel on the tracks into an interior pallet position. With no pallet on a carriage, by gravity force a deepest empty carriage moves forward and nests over a carriage that is adjacent to an aisle

In this design, pallet position identifications are placed upright posts and has the same identification arrangement as a gravity-flow rack design and pallet identification location directory design. It also permits a forklift truck driver to use a pallet identification substitution design. Because the WMS program suggests SKUs for withdrawal, a forklift truck driver has to use a pallet identification substitution method for withdrawals. The push-back rack pallet withdrawal transaction permits line-of-sight for pallet identification.

Cantilever Racks

A cantilever rack design is designed to handle long pallets with SKUs, such as pipe. A cantilever rack is designed as a single-arm row or double-arm rows. Arms extend outward from an upright post and create pallet positions. Cantilever pallet positions are serviced by a WA or NA forklift truck. Cantilever racks permit a FIFO SKU rotation, excellent storage density, SKU accessibility, and 85% position utilization. A cantilever rack design ensures WA/NA forklift truck line-of-sight for pallet position identifications. Reading the identifications uses the same procedure as standard pallet racks.

AS/RS High-Rise Racks

A carton/pallet AS/RS high-rise rack facility has very tall rack rows and an AS/RS crane aisle between two rows. Rack and aisle design uses a site's vertical air space rather than a horizontal footprint. A high-rise rack design is designed in conventional building or in a rack-supported structure, which has rack upright frames and posts for support and attachment members for in-rack sprinklers, walls, and roof. AS/RS designs require a dead level or F75/F100 level floor and a vehicle guidance system. Prior to rack installation it is a good practice to use a laser beam to ensure that the floor is level to the company's specifications. The structure is designed for snow, seismic and wind forces, fire protection (e.g., walls, barriers, and sprinklers) and AS/RS crane mast clearance at the top of the racks. In an AS/RS high-rise facility, all cartons/pallets pass through a size and weight station and a scanner to verify that pallet dimensions and weight conform to system design standards and have readable pallet identifications. Pallet transactions are controlled by the warehouse computer, which communicates with the WMS computer and updates files. Thus,

AS/RS rack positions do not have physical rack position identifications. High-rise rack facilities are designed with single-deep racks, two-deep racks, and flow racks. Each AS/RS pallet position is entered into both warehouse operation and WMS program files and physical pallet position is an option.

AS/RS High-Rise Pallet Rack Bay or Openings

An AS/RS single deep pallet rack bay or opening may be a standard pallet rack bay with two or three pallets per set or load-beam pair, or a four-arm pallet bay with four-load arms and two pallet rails that support one pallet per opening. The four-arm rack bay has a captive or slave pallet, and an AS/RS crane with a set of platens that go under a pallet to complete a storage transaction. The first rack level is approximately 17 to 24 inches above the floor; an additional 3 to 6-inch clearance at each level is included for the platens between the pallet top and the next pallet position level's support arms. As a pallet travels to an AS/RS crane storage area, scanners/readers along the travel path read each pallet identification. In an AS/RS storage area, the warehouse and WMS computers assign a pallet to a storage position. After an AS/RS crane places a pallet into a storage position, the warehouse computer sends the transaction to the WMS computer to update the inventory files.

Car-In Rack or Mole

A car-in rack or mole design uses upright frames, posts, car rails, pallet support rails, car-in rack vehicle, slave pallets, and aisle travel vehicle. The design includes space between pallets and rack members or storage lane for fire sprinklers and a car with pallet travel in a storage lane. A car-in rack design is three to eight pallet levels high and has 10 to 20 pallet positions per lane. Each lane has one SKU. From an aisle P/D station, an AS/RS crane carries a car-in rack vehicle between rack rows to the lane for storage transactions. As a pallet travels to an AS/RS car-in rack or mole storage area, scanners/readers along the travel path read each pallet identification; in an AS/RS storage area, the warehouse computer or WMS computer assigns a pallet to a storage position. After an AS/RS crane/car-in rack or mole places the pallet into a storage position, the warehouse computer sends a message to the WMS computer to update the inventory files.

One-Aisle Car-In Rack Design

In one-aisle car-in rack design, a car-in rack vehicle leaves the AS/RS crane from aisle "A," enters a storage lane, arrives at an assigned pallet storage position, performs a pallet deposit transaction, and exits the storage lane back on to aisle "A." The arrangement provides a LIFO SKU rotation and 66% position utilization. One-aisle car-in rack design provides high pallet density, excellent security, but poor pallet accessibility. To ensure pallet identification tracking, the WMS program has a pallet identification substitution enhancement.

Two-Aisle Car-In Rack Design

A two-aisle car-in rack design uses two AS/RS cranes and two car-in rack vehicles. In a two-aisle design, from the inbound aisle "A," all pallet deposits are made by aisle "A" vehicle with its car-in rack vehicle. From the outbound aisle "B," all pallet picks are completed by the aisle "B" AS/RS crane with its car-in rack vehicle. A two-aisle car-in rack design provides FIFO SKU, excellent security, high pallet density, but poor pallet accessibility. If pallets in a storage lane are indexed forward by a car-in rack vehicle toward a pallet withdrawal aisle, a two-aisle car-in rack design has an 85–90% position utilization. In a two-aisle design, pallets are withdrawn in the same sequence as they were entered in the WMS file; pallet identifications are not oriented for forklift truck pick-up and identification scan transactions. To ensure that pallet identifications have the correct orientation, a conveyor has a turntable to turn a pallet to the correct direction for forklift truck line-of-sight.

Sort-Link Design

A sort-link design is an automatic or computer-controlled pallet storage design. The components are captive/slave carrier and travel path, a rail-guided horizontal four-wheel pallet carrier or cart and travel path, multiple storage level facility, vertical cart carrier, dense cart storage lanes, and computer controls. A sort link carrier/slave carrier is manufactured from a hardened and coated steel frame and is designed to handle a pallet. Under each metal frame corner is a flanged wheel. Flanged wheels move a carrier in two travel directions. Travel directions are between a pallet carrier and a storage or discharge lane. To improve the ability to move carriers, a carrier's lead end has a special coupler and hook. When one carrier hook is engaged to another carrier's coupler, the motor-driven parent device can move up to four carriers between two locations. The hooking device engages/disengages a carrier each storage transaction. A carrier moves over a dual rail guide path that interfaces with a carrier flanged wheels. The guide path ensures that carriers are in a straight line. The guide rail travel path is a straight travel path that runs the length of an entire storage facility. Depending on the facility's design and storage lane configuration, there may be one or several guide paths to serve one level. Four-wheel devices are motor driven to travel over the rail guide path, to take onboard an inbound carrier at pick-up locations, and to complete deposit or pick-up transactions in storage areas.

The warehouse computer ensures smooth and regular pallet carrier movement through a facility, and makes sure that pallets are assigned to a proper storage area. Computer inventory files track the inventory. As a pallet travels to a sort-link storage area, scanners/readers along the travel path read each identification and relay the information to the warehouse computer. After a sort-link carrier places a pallet into a storage position, the warehouse computer sends a message to the WMS computer, which updates the inventory files. A sort-link design is capable of rearranging pallets in a storage lane for pallet withdrawals.

Storage Position WMS Position Format

Information on a storage position uniquely identifies a design position. Each SKU storage position is entered into the WMS program. Storage position information is printed on a self-adhesive label. The label face has alpha characters and numeric digits with a bar-code label/RF tag. A human/machine readable format has alpha characters and numeric digits, a SKU description, and a bar-code label/RF tag. With the bar-code label/RF-tag application, SKU transactions (with a hand-held bar-code scanner/RF-tag wave receiver) can be sent to the WMS computer on line or in a delayed information transfer. The disadvantages are label expense, the need for wide or large labels, and the cost of scan equipment and computer program. The advantages are that this approach detects transaction errors, has accurate data transfer, and minimizes employee reading.

Storage Position Identification

During a SKU storage transaction, a storage position identification is an employee instruction component that identifies a WMS computer suggested position. Each SKU identification storage position type has specific design characteristics. If a warehouse is using a standard pallet storage rack and storage vehicle type design, the rack load beam and pick design determine the storage position identification, which needs to be to a load beam or upright post. With a flow rack design, an identification is attached to a rack structural member located on a gravity flow rack's charge and discharge ends. With a floor stack pallet design, the identification may be embedded in the floor (or taped to the floor) in a floor lane center (after a scan test); it may be a placard hung from the ceiling; or it may be attached to an upright post between two floor stack lanes. A disadvantage to attaching the identification to an upright post is the potential for damage to the identification or upright post during transactions.

Pallet Storage Position Identification Locations

In a storage design using standard racks and a forklift truck, each pallet storage position has a storage position identification. The options are determined by:

- Forklift truck type: man-up or man-down
- Load-beam aisle front surface: flat or indented
- Upright post
- Load-beam location

Pallet Position Identification Location in a Storage Aisle

In a storage aisle, the position bar-code label location is determined by the type of forklift truck type and storage position used to complete storage transactions. A label may be located on a shelf or rack structural member. In either case, the forklift truck driver must have line-of-sight to the label so that a hand-held scanner may be used.

Man-Up VNA Forklift Truck Warehouse

With a man-up VNA forklift truck at the P/D station, an operator completes a pallet scan transaction at each storage level. With a good WMS scan, a forklift truck travels in an aisle to a computer-assigned or employee-directed storage position. During aisle travel, an operator platform and a set of forks rise to the storage position. Each position has an identification on a rack load beam or upright post. At the proper elevation, the driver completes the transaction, the pallet identification, and storage position scan. Because a forklift truck has the capability to elevate a driver, the position identification is attached to a load beam; the hand-held scanner will have clear line-of-sight to a pallet position and pallet storage position identification.

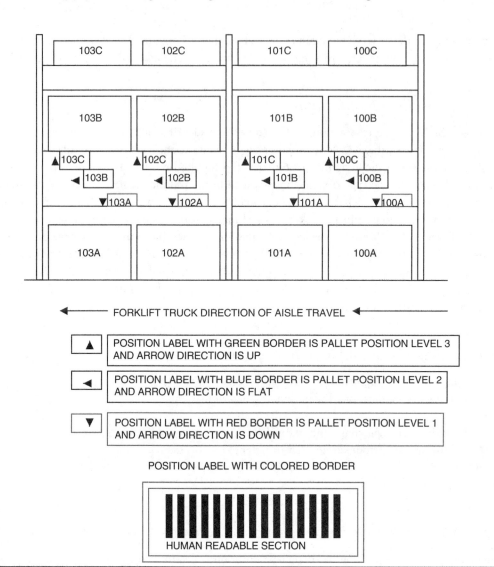

Figure 6.8 Direction Arrows and Color-Coded Labels on a Load Beam

Man-Down Forklift Truck Warehouse

With a man-down WA, NA, or VNA forklift truck design, an operator completes pallet scan transactions at a receiving dock or P/D station. Given a good scan, a forklift truck travels in an aisle to a computer-assigned or driver-directed storage position. A VNA forklift truck picks up a SKU at an aisle-end P/D station, the truck operator platform remains at ground level, and the driver scans the pallet identification. The forklift truck's set of forks rise with the pallet to an assigned or employee-selected vacant pallet storage position. At the storage position elevation, the truck driver completes the storage transaction (see Figure 6.9). While the forklift truck driver is at ground level, a storage position identification is attached to a low-level upright frame post location or load beam that permits a forklift truck driver line-of-sight for scanning position identifications. On a load beam or upright post, pallet storage position identifications are sequenced in the same sequence as the load-beam levels. To ensure an accurate pallet identification relationship to an

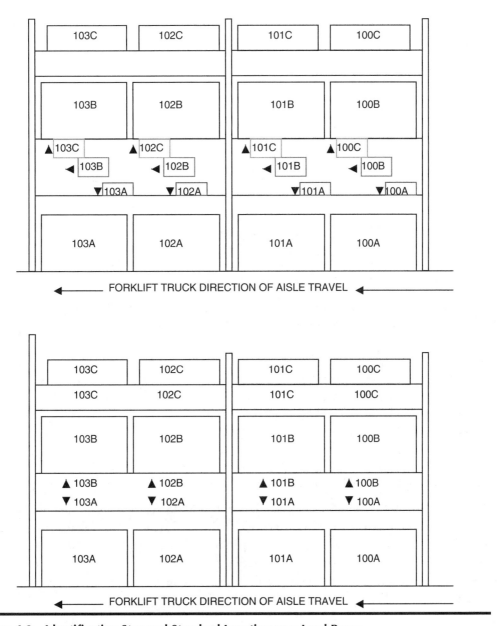

Figure 6.9   Identification Step and Standard Location on a Load Beam

elevated load-beam level, each level is identified numerically (e.g., 1, 2, 3, 4, 5, or 6) with direction arrows and a colored-coded label. A direction arrow points down for a floor-level pallet position, there is no arrow for the first load-beam pallet position, and an arrow points up for an elevated pallet position. If using a colored label design, each load-beam level has a light colored label (e.g., yellow, white, pink, orange, light blue, or light green). Selected label colors are tested in a storage area aisle with a scanner/reader to ensure good reads from a scanner or the forklift truck driver's operator platform. After completing a deposit transaction, the driver hand scans the corresponding position identification.

Load-Beam Face Storage Position Identification

The space for a pallet storage position identification on a rack load beam is five to six inches high. In a VNA man-up forklift truck operation with a bottom pallet level on load beams, this will be sufficient space for the identification attachment for clear line-of-sight. If the bottom level has a line-of-sight problem, a bottom position identification is placed on the next load-beam level. If a load-beam level has two position identifications, the first (i.e., lowest) position identification is placed on the lowest load-beam face, and top (i.e., highest) position identification is placed on the top load-beam face for easy forklift truck recognition. As identifications are placed onto a load beam, each label is arranged in a step pattern (i.e., each bar-code identification is on a different elevation above the floor), which minimizes the chance of a scanner reading two bar codes that could create a "no read" or an incorrect code. Additional istructions for forklift truck drivers instructions are color-coded labels (see above), and direction arrows placed before or after a label.

Rack Flat Load-Beam Identification

In a warehouse using forklift trucks and a WMS program, with one pallet storage position identification per load beam, a standard pallet storage position identification label may be attached to the flat front (see Figure 6.10). If the warehouse uses two pallet storage positions, identifications for each load beam are on a flat front load beam. A standard load-beam front is 5 to 6 inches high that may permit two storage position labels arranged one above the other. When two labels are attached to one load beam, direction arrows before or after a label bar code or a color coded label face are used to make sure the forklift truck driver understands the relationship between the labels and the relevant storage position.

Rack Indented Load-Beam Identification

If a WA, NA, or VNA forklift truck operation with a WMS program application uses two pallet storage position identifications for each indented front load beam, this design has a smaller flat front (3 to 4 inches) than a rack flat load beam. A three- or four-inch flat front does not provide sufficient space for two labels and with a man-down forklift truck operation will have potential scanner line-of-sight problems when attempting to complete scan transactions at elevated positions.

Upright Post Pallet Position Identification

In an operation in which identification labels are attached to upright posts, the guidelines are (see Figure 6.11):

1. To have each left- and right-hand pallet position location on a consistent upright post location. As identifications are placed on a middle upright post, labels should be arranged in a step pattern. A step pattern has a bar-code/RF-tag identification for different load-beam elevations above the floor. During scanning, a step pattern minimizes the chance that a hand-held scanner could read an incorrect bar code or result in a "no read."

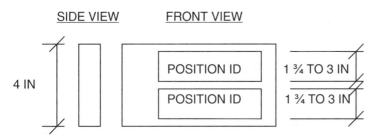

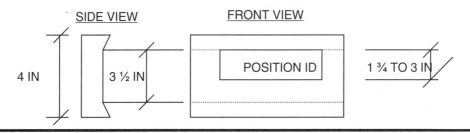

Figure 6.10   Flat and Indented Load Beam

2. Directional arrows are used before or after an identification to identify a pallet storage position. Color coded labels and storage position direction arrows minimize forklift truck problems.

Load-Beam Pallet and Position Identification

In a forklift truck design in which storage position identification labels are placed on pallet storage position load beams, the preferred location is one a forklift truck driver faces to complete a pallet storage transaction. With two pallets per bay, a storage position on the right side has an identification on a load-beam's right side under a pallet. With a pallet identification on a pallet right hand stringer or block, a forklift truck driver will have clear line-of-sight to both pallet identification and storage position identification. In a WA, NA, or VNA forklift truck design, position identification and pallet identification locations increase forklift truck driver productivity because most a) forklift truck driver platforms have access on the truck's right side, and b) most forklift truck drivers are right handed and hold a hand-held scanner/reader in their right hands to complete pallet and storage identifications scan transactions. Scan activity does not require a forklift truck driver to transfer a hand-held scanner/reader between hands and minimizes scanner damage (i.e., less chance of being dropped from a forklift truck) and decreases the time needed to scan both identifications.

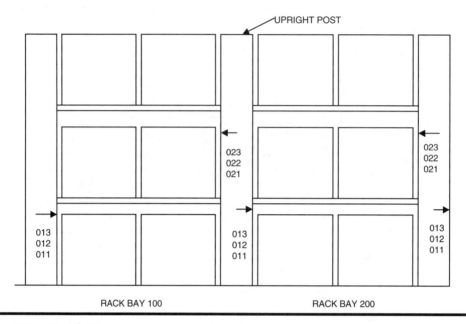

Figure 6.11 Upright Post

Computer-Controlled Storage Retrieval or AS/RS Crane

An AS/RS crane has an aisle that is a nominally three to six inches wider than a pallet. An AS/RS is an automated crane designed with one or two masts to complete pallet transactions at 40- to 80-foot high rack positions. An AS/RS crane has a dead-level floor, middle rail travel/guidance, first storage level 34 inches above the floor, clearance at the ceiling for a mast and ceiling, and an attached DC system. All AS/RS cranes have a 15- to 20-foot run out to perform pallet transactions at end rack positions. Run-out length is determined by vehicle length. A crane operating area has minimal utilities; tall racks support the roof and walls. In an AS/RS crane operation with a WMS program, a pallet position identification is not required because an actual AS/RS crane is computer controlled and a crane computer sends a storage transaction completion message to the WMS computer. To ensure that an assigned pallet has arrived at the assigned aisle, each pallet on an AS/RS conveyor or shuttle car in-feed and out-feed system has a pallet identification and clear line-of-sight for fixed-position scanners/readers. As a good practice—and because employee-controlled forklift-truck activities require a pallet identification scan transaction—a pallet identification is attached to each pallet.

Sort Link, Mole, or Car-in-Rack Design

A sort-link, mole, or car-in-rack design has dense (i.e., multiple deep) pallet storage positions and a mobile cart or car. A DC electric-powered mobile cart or car transport pallets travel over a fixed travel path between a storage area and a pallet pick and delivery station. In a warehouse using this design with WMS program, a pallet position identification is required (because of scanner/reader tracking as a cart travels on a travel path) and is updated in the warehouse.

Automatic Stacking Guide Vehicle

An automatic stacking guided vehicle (AGV) is a counterbalanced (i.e., straddle) vehicle. It is powered by rechargeable electric batteries. An AGV has three to four wheels (at least one of which is for steering), a fixed mast, a set of load carrying forks, a manual or remote-controlled on-board control device, a wire guidance system, and runs on a very flat floor. Pallet transaction aisle width is 10 to 12 feet wide for a counterbalanced truck, but less for a straddle truck. Due to floor-stacked pallet instability, the majority of AGVs stack pallets one high on the floor. In this design, the AGV or system updates the WMS computer when a pallet is placed into a pallet storage location.

Computer-Controlled Pallet AS/RS Crane Considerations

To have an efficient and cost effective AS/RS pallet storage design, AS/RS crane factors are:

- A pallet handling device is an AS/RS crane component that carries one or two pallets between a P/D station and the storage position and completes a storage transaction. AS/RS pallet handling options are a) having an AS/RS crane insert a set of forks into the pallet fork opening and complete the transaction to a rack position. The features of this approach are minimal vertical clearance in a pallet position, exact tolerances, a design that must be approved by a seismic engineer, lower pallet position cost (with two to three pallets per bay), and maximum pallet number per aisle; and b) a set of platens that interfaces with a rack opening that has two rails, two support arms and sufficient top and bottom pallet position clearance for a platen to complete a pallet transaction. This option has a higher cost per pallet position because there is only one pallet per bay, with an increase in upright number per aisle, there are fewer pallet openings per aisle but tolerances are not as tight. Again, the design must be approved by a seismic engineer.
- Pallet handling capacity options are a) single shuttle or carrier, which will have the capacity to handle one pallet per aisle trip. The feature has less run-out space, less weight, and lower overall productivity; or b) dual carriers or shuttles, which have the capacity to handle two pallets per trip into an aisle. An AS/RS crane is designed with a carriage area to take two pallets on board. This approach means additional run-out space and crane weight, and 20 to 25% productivity increase due to fewer crane trips to an end of aisle pallet transfer station. There is no 100% productivity increase because of additional starts and stops and slower travel speeds in an aisle.
- AS/RS crane commands, which refer to the warehouse computer commands that direct an AS/RS crane to complete storage transactions. AS/RS crane command options are a) single command mode, in which the computer directs an AS/RS crane to make one down-aisle trip. During the aisle trip, the crane completes one pallet storage transaction. Using the single command mode, an AS/RS crane completes 18 to 24 transactions per hour. A single command mode does not require inbound or outbound pallet transaction balance; or b) dual command mode, in which the computer directs the AS/RS crane to complete a pallet deposit transaction after entering an aisle, and complete a pallet withdrawal transaction when exiting the aisle. This represents two pallet transactions per trip; the AS/RS crane will complete 22 to 26 dual commands per hour. A dual command mode does not double a single command productivity rate because additional aisle travel time and set of fork activity time to complete a storage transaction. Dual command mode requires a balance between inbound and outbound transactions and the use of aisle end P/D stations.

Pallet P/D Stations

An aisle end P/D station is designed as a static or dynamic pallet station and is a temporary holding pallet position for a pallet. The pallet is transferred between a VNA forklift truck or AS/RS crane storage area and an in-house transport vehicle. In the pallet storage industry, many companies have increased their storage space utilization and forklift truck productivity by implementing a VNA forklift truck or AS/RS crane storage design. In these storage designs, a VNA forklift truck or AS/RS crane performs a storage transaction to tall rack positions, operates within a very narrow aisle, and performs the maximum number of pallet transactions per hour. VNA trucks and some AS/RS cranes are mobile aisle vehicles. A typical pallet storage operation's inbound activity is skewed to the early morning hours, whereas outbound activity is skewed to the late morning or afternoon, which creates an imbalance in projected pallet storage and customer order pick transactions in an 8 hour day. To obtain the desired pallet storage/pick transaction balance and return on investment, VNA forklift truck and AS/RS crane designs have pallet P/D stations at each storage aisle end.

P/D stations are pallet positions located at each aisle end. A P/D station

- provides a temporary inbound and outbound queue for pallets assigned for deposit or transport to another warehouse operation location;
- gives a VNA forklift truck or AS/RS crane direct and unobstructed access from an aisle to pallet fork openings;
- ensures that pallet fork openings and pallet identifications are in correct orientation for pickup or delivery by a VNA forklift truck or transport vehicle.

A P/D station improves forklift truck or AS/RS crane productivity; decreases SKU, rack and forklift truck, or AS/RS crane damage; reduces transaction errors; and ensures clear line-of-sight for pallet identification.

P/D Stations: Designs

An aisle end P/D station may be designed as static or dynamic design. Static P/D stations are staggered or flush to a main traffic aisle. P/D station options are:

1. Static type, which includes floor, structural stand, or standard pallet rack;
2. Dynamic types are four-wheel carts, on-board transfer car, gravity-powered conveyor, powered roller conveyor, and powered shuttle car.

VNA Aisle Middle P/D Station

In some VNA forklift truck operations, an in-house transport pallet truck places a pallet in the middle of a VNA forklift truck aisle. After an in-house transport pallet truck picks up a pallet in a receiving area, the pallet identification faces a pallet truck driver. As the driver enters a VNA aisle, the identification faces the driver and, if a VNA forklift truck is in an aisle, the driver will not have pallet identification line-of-sight. Thus, a VNA aisle middle P/D station is not preferred for a VNA forklift truck operation due to the fact that a VNA forklift truck driver will need to perform additional transactions for pallet identification line-of-sight.

Captive Aisle Vehicle

With a captive aisle VNA forklift truck or AS/RS crane design, there are multiple VNA forklift trucks or AS/RS cranes in a pallet storage aisle. One truck/crane remains in one storage aisle and performs all pallet storage transactions at its maximum transaction activity rate (i.e., the storage area computer spreads daily pallet storage transactions as evenly as possible over VNA forklift trucks or AS/RS cranes aisles).

Mobile Aisle Vehicle

Mobile pallet storage vehicle major groups are

- wide aisle or WA forklift trucks;
- narrow aisle or VN forklift trucks;
- very narrow aisle or VNA forklift trucks;
- AS/RS crane with a transfer (T-car) car.

Mobile Aisle Forklift Truck

With a mobile aisle forklift truck design, a WA, NA, or VNA forklift truck has access to any storage aisle from a main traffic aisle. To move between storage aisles, a WA/NA forklift truck design has turning aisles at the end of aisles; for a long rack row, a middle cross aisle is designed in a rack row. For a VNA forklift truck design, the options are turning aisles at the ends of aisles, or a single turning aisle at the front of the aisle and a rear aisle that permits access to the last pallet position and the employee emergency exit.

With a mobile aisle design, the storage area computer distributes the storage transactions based on an arrangement to maintain forklift truck productivity standards and service and receiving and shipping area requirements. A mobile aisle forklift truck is powered by a rechargeable battery, has three or four wheels, is manually controlled. A VNA forklift truck uses wire or rail guidance in a storage aisle.

AS/RS Crane T-Car/Bridge Car

Most AS/RS cranes are restricted to a single storage area aisle. With a proper storage area design, a T-car (transfer car), computer controls, and sufficient time, a captive aisle AS/RS crane may be transferred by a transfer or bridge car between aisles. The T-car, which is computer controlled and DC-electric powered, has both the mobility and capacity to transfer an AS/RS crane. A T-car receives an AS/RS crane in its cradle or bridge, travels in a T-car aisle (a rail-guided travel path), and aligns itself for AS/RS crane discharge into another aisle. A T-car aisle width is 25 to 40 feet wide (depending on the crane length); a T-car aisle located at the rear or at non-P/D station in the facility.

If the warehouse uses a sequential aisle number or routing pattern, the WA, NA, or VNA forklift truck driver or AS/RS crane enters an aisle, completes a pallet storage transaction, and exits from the same aisle. As a forklift truck or AS/RS crane travels through a storage aisle, the lowest storage position number is at an aisle entrance and increase progressively to the end of the aisle. To ensure maximum forklift truck driver or AS/RS crane productivity, sequential aisle number patterns should have an arithmetic progression through an aisle. Options:

■ Pallet position numbers that end with an even digit can be located on the right side of the aisle, numbers that end with an odd digit can be on the left side
■ Each aisle rack row or side has an aisle number and position numbers are progressive to the next pallet position, e.g., a right side rack row has 100 and a left side rack row has 200

It is important to keep warehouse aisles clear and well illuminated, and to maintain good housekeeping.

In most designs, a forklift truck or AS/RS crane handles one pallet per trip in storage transactions. Some AS/RS cranes have the ability to carry two pallets and to complete dual pallet storage transactions in one aisle.

Forklift Truck Routing Pattern

A forklift truck routing pattern is a sequence for positions in an aisle, that provides instructions for a forklift truck driver. Position numbers guide a driver through an aisle to a position. The objective of a forklift truck routing pattern is to minimize nonproductive travel time between two positions. To achieve maximum driver productivity, a routing pattern is implemented in conjunction with good warehouse operation practices. The practices are:

1. The 80/20 Rule, the Golden Highway family group principle, and profile SKUs to positions for your budgeted productivity.
2. Using the Golden Zone.
3. Clear and properly illuminated aisles.
4. Understandable and clear pick instructions.
5. Clear and understandable aisle and position identifications.

Forklift Truck Driver Aisle Travel

In a warehouse operation, to complete a dual cycle storage transaction, there are two basic approaches for forklift truck driver travel in an aisle to complete a pallet transaction.

1. Straight in-and-out through an aisle for each storage transaction. During aisle travel, a picker completes all storage transactions. With a straight in-and-out design, each aisle's lowest position number starts at the main aisle end into an aisle (001) and arithmetically progresses to the highest position number at an aisle end. After completing all storage transactions, a driver turns the pick cart and travels back through aisle 001 to the main aisle entrance. Leaving aisle 001, the forklift truck driver travels in the main aisle to adjacent aisle (002) and enters. The driver completes a storage transaction and repeats an aisle 002 travel, exit, and aisle 003 entrance procedures. The disadvantages to this approach are a) double travels in each aisle, b) low productivity due to traveling past positions that do not have SKU transactions or where the driver has already completed storage transactions, (c) aisle width to permit a forklift truck turned in an aisle, and (d) the potential for two forklift trucks traveling in different travel directions in one aisle. The advantage is that the operation does not have carton pick activities on low rack positions.

2. Serpentine through aisles design. The driver travels in the first aisle (001). During pick aisle 001 travel, the lowest positions are an entrance to pick aisle 001. After all storage transactions, a forklift truck driver exits pick aisle 001 at the end (i.e., the highest position number location) and enters aisle 002 at the lowest position number location. The driver completes a storage transaction and enters the main aisle. From the main aisle, the driver enters aisle 003. With a serpentine design, each aisle lowest position number starts at an aisle entrance and arithmetically progresses to the highest position number at the exit. In a rectangularly shaped facility with a main aisle and rear aisle, each aisle has an even number entrance at the main aisle (front) and odd number entrance at the rear aisle. The advantages of the serpentine approach are a) one trip through each aisle, b) improved operation productivity when used with a carton pick activity on lower rack positions, c) minimal aisle width, and (d) low probability of two drivers in one pick aisle.

Pallet Deposit Activity

Pallet deposit activity involves placing a pallet into a computer-assigned or operator-directed storage position. Either the forklift truck driver scans both pallet and storage position identifications or an AS/RS crane tracks the pallet and position identification. Scans are sent (on-line or delayed) to the WMS computer for computer file update. An accurate and on-schedule pallet deposit to a storage position ensures that the right SKU is in the proper place, in the proper quantity, in correct condition, and at correct time. Accurate and on-time SKU deposit activity and communication to a WMS computer ensures inventory update and on-time pick activity.

Computer-Assigned Pallet Storage Position

A warehouse with a WMS inventory program that assigns pallets to storage positions is called a directed or assigned pallet storage transaction. In this design, to complete a deposit storage transaction, a forklift truck driver scans the pallet identification and a RF hand-held scanner indicates the assigned pallet storage position. After the driver arrives at the pallet position, the driver places the pallet into the storage position and scans the storage position identification. Pallet and pallet storage position scans are sent (on-line or delayed) to the WMS computer for inventory update. To complete a directed pallet withdrawal transaction, a driver reads scanner/reader, which indicates the assigned position for the withdrawal transaction. The driver travels to a storage position, scans the pallet at the storage position and the storage position identification. Scans are sent to a WMS computer, which updates the inventory files.

Operator-Directed Pallet Storage Position

In this design, to complete a deposit storage transaction, a forklift truck driver scans a pallet identification and a hand-held scanner/reader's visual display indicates a pallet is ready for deposit. After the driver arrives at a driver-selected storage position, the driver places a pallet into a position and scans the pallet and storage position identifications. Scan transactions are sent on-line (or delayed) to the WMS computer for SKU and position inventory file update. To complete a WMS- or warehouse-computer–directed withdrawal transaction, a driver reads a scanner's display. The scanner indicates a position for a pallet withdrawal transaction. The driver travels to WMS computer's assigned location. At the storage position, the driver scans pallet and pallet storage position identifications. Scan transactions are sent to the WMS computer inventory file update.

SKU deposit activity involves completing a SKU scan and physical transaction to a storage position. This activity is similar for all SKU types.

Pallet Storage Design Transaction Verification

A pallet warehouse with a WMS inventory program activity is to have a forklift truck driver verify a storage transaction completion. A storage transaction completion verification ensures that a pallet has been:

1. Deposited between an assigned or employee selected pallet storage position;
2. At the correct time, a pallet is withdrawn from a pallet storage position and moved to another storage position;
3. Scan transaction for a pallet position and pallet identification are sent and updated in the WMS inventory file.

SKU storage transaction verification completion designs are:

1. Manual hand-written method. A forklift truck driver uses a printed document to record each SKU storage transaction. The document has four columns separated into two groups with two columns each. Two columns ("deposits") are used to list all SKU deposit transactions. Two columns ("withdrawals") are to list all withdrawal transactions. After a forklift truck driver completes a transaction, the driver lists the position and SKU identifications that were involved in the transaction. At the end of the shift, activity documents are sent to an office. An office clerk performs an inventory update. This approach is not considered for a warehouse with a WMS program. The disadvantages are that it only handles a low volume, requires a clerk effort, adds to a forklift truck driver work, and creates transposition errors. The advantages are low cost, it can be used in a two-shift operation, and can be used in a large facility.
2. Automatic or bar-code scan/RF-tag read method. To verify a pallet storage transaction, a forklift truck driver uses a hand-held scanner/reader to scan a pallet and storage position. Pallet or storage position labels are human/machine readable and discreet. After a label is attached to a pallet, a scanner/reader with line-of-sight reads pallet and pallet position labels at each position. Scan transactions are held in memory or, with a RF device, sent on-line (or delayed) to the WMS computer for inventory update.

In a warehouse with a WMS inventory program that directs all SKU transactions, prior to picking up a pallet, a driver scans a pallet label and, according to a storage transaction instructions, travels to a WMS-assigned or employee-selected position. Arriving at the assigned pallet position, the pallet is placed into the position. The position and pallet identifications are scanned/read by the driver. Scan/read information is sent on-line (or delayed) to the WMS computer. In an employee-directed warehouse with scanning/reading, a driver scans a pallet, picks up a pallet, and selects a storage aisle. In the aisle, the driver selects and scans a position and a pallet, and places the pallet into the position. In an AS/RS crane warehouse operation, as a pallet travels over a travel path, fixed position scanners/readers read each pallet. The pallet information and warehouse tracking devices update a pallet location on a travel path to a warehouse/AS/RS crane computer. After an AS/RS crane completes a deposit transaction, the AS/RS crane computer sends SKU and position information to the WMS computer. The disadvantages are cost, employee training, position and identifications, and management control and discipline. The advantages are accurate information, on-line or delayed information transfer, and high employee productivity.

Chapter 7

Replenishment

Introduction

SKU replenishment transaction activity ensures that the correct SKU quantity is transferred from a storage position to a correct pick position, which allows a picker to complete a pick transaction. To complete a replenishment transaction, the majority of replenishment activity time involves two activities:

1. SKU withdrawal from a storage position. In a typical conventional forklift or AS/RS storage design, a SKU withdrawal takes two to three minutes. This is based on the travel distance between a P/D station to a storage position and to the P/D station (for a forklift truck or AS/RS crane).
2. Transport activity time, which ranges from two to four minutes. Transport time is based on the travel distance between the storage area, the SKU queue at P/D stations, and drop points, the travel path design, and SKU volume.

SKU Replenishment to Warehouse Pick Design

Pick position setup or replenishment activity occurs in a manual, mechanized, or automatic pick design (see Figure 7.1). In an order fulfillment warehouse with a small-item or master-carton fixed pick-position operation, a SKU replenishment quantity is transferred from a storage position to a pick position. In a pallet operation, a storage position is a SKU pick position. SKU setup or replenishment activity to a pick position is based on an order wave or employee suggestion in which the WMS computer allocates a SKU quantity from a storage position to a fixed pick position. After a SKU quantity is placed into a pick position, an employee or machine communicates the quantity, the SKU identification, and the pick position to the WMS computer. After the computer receives the scan transactions and quantity, the computer releases customer orders to a pick activity.

To ensure the reader's understanding of pick-position setup and replenishment activity, we present a detailed comparison of pick-position setup and replenishment activity. Pick-position setup activity occurs for a new SKU when it is placed in a pick position or pick line. Replenishment

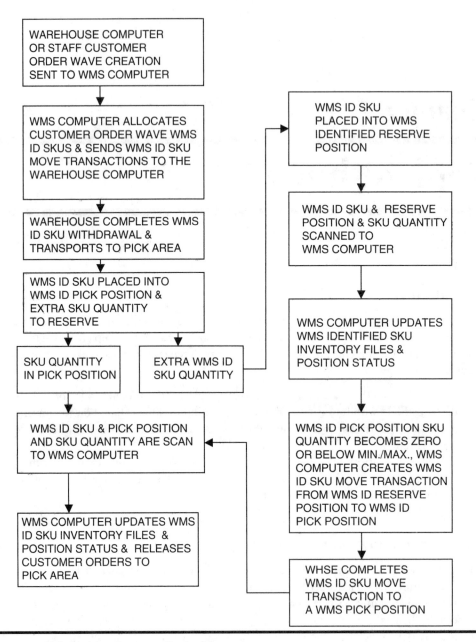

Figure 7.1   Pick-Position Setup or Replenishment

activity is a reoccuring activity for an existing SKU in a pick position or pick line and ensures that there is sufficient SKU quantity for the customer order wave or batched customer orders.

If a warehouse uses a floating pick-position design, when a pick position becomes depleted during customer order pick activity and the WMS computer allocates customer order picks to another pick position with the same SKU (i.e., floating slot), this is considered pick-position replenishment activity.

In a warehouse with a WMS program, pick-line setup or replenishment to a pick position is a major step in the customer order fulfillment process. The WMS program suggests a SKU quantity be moved from a storage position to a pick position, fast-pack station, or ready-reserve position. After the warehouse completes a transfer to a pick position, the warehouse computer communicates the SKU, quantity, and pick position to the WMS computer. The WMS computer updates the quantity and pick-position status in the program files and releases customer orders for a SKU quantity in a pick position. Pick-line setup or replenishment activity is an important warehouse activity, and helps ensure on-time and accurate customer order completion and accurate SKU accounting in the warehouse, WMS computer, and host company inventory files.

Pick-Position Setup and Replenishment Activity: Functional Description

In a manual small-item or master-carton warehouse with the WMS program, a pick-position setup or replenishment activity is a computer-directed activity. After a customer order wave is created, the WMS computer provides the warehouse with the SKU quantity and storage positions. A manually controlled forklift truck or AS/RS crane travels to the storage position and withdraws a SKU. The SKU is transported from the storage position to a pick area. In the pick area, an employee or AS/RS crane completes the SKU physical and scan transactions to a pick position. The pick-position scan transaction and SKU quantity are sent to the WMS computer, which releases customer orders to a pick area.

Manual or AS/RS Crane Pick-Position Setup and Replenishment Exception Handling

In a manual or AS/RS small-item or master-carton order fulfillment operation, pick-position setup and replenishment activity has potential problems. A design team will list potential pick-position setup and replenishment exception handling or problems and develop resolutions. Some potential problems:

1. Unknown WMS identification. In a storage area, a warehouse employee or AS/RS crane searches for a SKU, but it is not located in the storage files. The warehouse computer or the WMS program allocates another SKU to complete the transaction. Both the warehouse and WMS program team research the situation (including cycle counts) to make sure that the SKU is physically in a storage area.
2. The storage position is physically blocked, a blocked aisle or a broken or down crane. An employee or AS/RS crane sends the WMS computer a message that the withdrawal transaction cannot be completed. To complete a pick-position setup and replenishment, the WMS program substitutes another SKU in another storage position. To ensure no future pick-position setup or replenishment delays, the program places the SKU and position on hold and has the warehouse complete a SKU count. The count is updated in the WMS program.
3. The WMS identification is not in correct position. A forklift truck or AS/RS crane withdraws an incorrect SKU and it is delivered to a control/check station. At the control/check station, the WMS program directs a forklift truck or AS/RS crane to withdraw another SKU from another storage position to complete the customer order wave plan. At a control/check station, an employee verifies with the WMS program the SKU and quantity and redirects a forklift truck or AS/RS crane to complete the SKU put-away transaction. After the put-away transaction is completed, the warehouse or inventory control department completes a SKU count. The count is entered into the WMS program to update storage positions.

4. During a master-carton removal from a pallet, it is discovered that the pallet's WMS identification has nonreadable bar-code or RF tag problem. A forklift truck or AS/RS crane withdraws a SKU and sends it to a transfer station for a pick-line setup or replenishment. At the transfer station, a transfer employee cannot obtain a good read with a scanner/reader. A transfer station employee has the SKU transported to a control/check station. A control/check station employee with a SKU description obtains a list of SKU identifications and quantities. The control/check station verifies that the SKU matches the SKU listed in the WMS program and removes the existing WMS identification from the pallet, disposes of the old identification, and removes the identification from the WMS program. A control/check station places a new identification on a pallet. The pallet identification and SKU quantity are entered into the WMS program. The SKU is transported from the check/control station to a master-carton transfer station. At the transfer station, the pick-line setup or replenishment is completed and transactions are updated in the WMS program.

5. An unknown warehouse tote/tray/pallet identification (or no identification). The tote/tray/pallet, suggested for withdrawal by the WMS program, cannot be located. After the warehouse notifies the WMS program, the program suggests another tote/tray/pallet to complete the customer order wave plan. After the transaction is completed, both warehouse and WMS program team members research and correct the problem.

6. A device is not in the correct tray or pallet location. After a tray/tote/pallet arrives at a transfer/withdrawal station and the identification is in an incorrect (nonreadable) location, an employee sends the device to a control/check station. At a control/check station, an employee removes and cancels the old identification and places a new identification on the tray/tote/pallet. An employee scans the SKU and new identification and sends the scans and quantity to the WMS computer for update. A properly identified device is sent to a transfer/withdrawal station to complete the transaction.

7. A master-carton, transferred from a pallet to another pallet, cart, or conveyor, does not have an identification or the identification is damaged. The warehouse conveyor diverts the master carton to a no-read station. At a no-read station, an employee enters the SKU code and has a local printer print an identification. The identification is applied to the master carton. The SKU quantities and identification are scanned and sent to the WMS program. The SKU count is completed and entered into the WMS computer. If the warehouse uses a pallet/cart transport design and preprinted labels, there will extra labels at a transfer station. An employee locates an unlabeled master carton and applies an identification to the master carton.

8. A short pick from a pallet/tray/tote. A master-carton picker or conveyor system verifies as many picks as possible—there is a possibility that the pallet/tray/tote has a master carton with an incorrect quantity or a damaged master carton. When an employee becomes aware of the problem, the WMS program requests another pallet for delivery to a transfer station. When the second pallet arrives at the transfer station, an employee completes a master-carton pick. A cycle count is completed for all SKUs in storage, at pick positions, and at transfer stations. Counts are sent and updated in the WMS computer.

9. In a warehouse using an AS/RS crane, an empty pallet is sent to a stacker crane but has a master carton on its surface. As the pallet travels on a conveyor, the master carton is detected by laser beams/sensors/detectors and the conveyor diverts the pallet to a check/clear station. At the station, an employee completes an identification scan and master-carton quantity entry transactions to update the WMS computer. The pallet with the master carton is sent to a storage position. A SKU count is completed and entered into the WMS program.

10. A picker scans the wrong SKU from a tote/tray/pallet with mixed SKUs. If an employee scans a wrong SKU, the WMS program PC or hand-held scanner screen shows the error and directs the employee to make another (correct) pick.

11. A SKU master carton quantity does not physically fit into a pick position at a pick and replenishment area. If the warehouse is using a pallet/master-carton design, after all master-carton transfer activities are completed, and the pick position is filled, the pallet with remaining master cartons is placed into a ready-reserve position. A replenishment employee scans the pallet and ready-reserve position's identifications, and sends the scan to the WMS computer. If the warehouse is using a design in which individual master cartons are transferred from a conveyor or cart, master cartons that do not physically fit into a pick position are transferred to a ready-reserve position and scan transactions are sent to the WMS computer. The warehouse team confirms that the master carton dimension data in warehouse and WMS computers are accurate.

12. A SKU is damaged during a replenishment activity. In a warehouse designed for pallets with a WMW program, and following company procedures, the options for handling a damaged SKU are: a) a customer order picker sends the container with the damaged SKU to a check/control station; or b) the SKU is handled by a replenishment employee. To ensure quality SKUs in a pick position, a replenishment employee scans the damaged SKU and then moves it to a special reserve position (i.e., a temporary hold position). After the WMS computer receives the scan transaction, the computer places the SKU on hold and designates it "not available for sale." The warehouse team sends a noncustomer order request to the WMS computer for an additional SKU quantity. The WMS computer allocates the SKU quantity and the warehouse completes the replenishment transaction.

13. The SKU in an "A" slot is not classified as an "A" SKU. To resolve this situation, a pick-line setup or replenishment employee completes a SKU move transaction from one pick position to another. The move transactions are sent to the WMS computer to update the SKU pick position and quantity.

14. A master carton does not fit into a pick position. A replenishment employee's options are a) complete the SKU move transaction from a large master carton to a carton/tote. The new master carton identification and SKU quantity are sent to the WMS computer to update pick-position SKU quantity. The large master identification is deleted from the WMS computer; b) in a pick area with various-sized pick positions, a replenishment employee selects another pick position and completes the replenishment transaction. The design team ensures that master carton dimension in warehouse and WMS computers are accurate.

Fixed/Variable Pick Positions

Small-item or master-carton SKU pick-position options are:

■ A fixed pick-position means that there is a SKU customer order wave permanently allocated to a pick position in a pick area, on a pick line, or in automatic pick machine computer files. During the SKU receiving process or during a pick-line setup activity, the WMS program or warehouse computer has a predetermined SKU quantity allocated to a pick position. Other quantities of the same SKU are allocated to storage positions, or a pick-line setup employee scans a quantity to a pick position. After a picked SKU quantity (for a customer order) depletes the quantity in a pick position, the WMS program creates a SKU replenishment transaction to move a quantity from a storage or pick-area ready-reserve position to a pick position. This approach maintains pick-line profile productivity, ensures top picker productivity, allows family grouping, requires less floor space, minimizes potential replenishment errors, minimizes potential stock-outs, and ensures on-time and accurate pick-position replenishment.

■ A variable (or random or floating) pick position means that a SKU quantity is temporarily allocated to a pick position in a pick area, on a pick line, or in an automatic pick machine computer file. After the receiving process, during which each SKU receives an identification, the WMS program allocates SKU quantities to several pick positions in a pick area and no SKU quantity is allocated to a storage position. For customer order pick activity, the WMS program allocates SKUs to a pick area and a pick-line setup employee scans each SKU, each pick position, and the SKU quantity. The data are sent to the WMS computer. In a pick area, a SKU remains in each pick position until first pick-position quantity is depleted by customer orders. When the SKU quantity in a pick position is depleted, the warehouse computer assigns next the customer order pick to another pick position with a SKU quantity. In this approach, it is difficult to maintain a pick-line profile, there is increased walking distance (which means lower picker productivity), and additional pick positions and floor space are required. However, this approach minimizes replenishment activity, labor, and errors.

Warehouse Interface and Interaction with the WMS program

A conventional store, hold, pick and pack warehouse with the WMS program, pick-line setup and replenishment, and SKU information list includes:

■ Vendor purchase order and customer order process;
■ Vendor-delivered SKU and QA activity with SKU identification and WMS computer and host computer inventory update and purchase order closure;
■ Transport to a storage position;
■ Deposit a SKU into a storage position with transaction data sent to the WMS computer;
■ WMS program suggests SKU withdrawal from a storage position;
■ Transport to a suggested drop point;
■ Warehouse staff completion of a customer order wave plan with release to the WMS computer for SKU allocation:
■ SKU transfer to a pick position; at the end of customer order wave, the WMS computer zero scans each pick position, and moves residual SKU to another pick area; transaction data sent to the WMS computer;
■ Customer order release to a pick area and customer order identification with the WMS customer order identification;
■ Customer order SKU transfer from a pick position to a customer order carton/tote with a permanent or disposable identification; pick transaction completion sent to the WMS computer;
■ WMS computer zero scans captive pick tote.

SKU pick-position setup or replenishment activity objectives are to ensure:

1. sufficient SKU inventory in a pick position; and
2. prior to a withdrawal from a pick position for a customer order, the correct SKU quantity is transferred from a storage position or ready-reserve position to a pick position. In other words, the pick-position replenishment activity objective is to minimize the occurrence of "no stock" or "out of stock" (stock out) conditions at a pick position on a pick line, in a pick aisle, or at an automatic pick station.

"No Stock" Condition

A "no stock" condition occurs when the SKU physical inventory is physically in a pick position but the WMS computer inventory file does not reflect SKU inventory in the pick position. When this situation occurs with a customer order, the WMS computer does not release customer orders to print a customer order pick transaction instruction for a picker or pick machine. In an order fulfillment warehouse, this situation falls below the company standard for customer order service, and it creates an inventory control problem that requires a SKU count and allocation to another pick position.

"Out of Stock" or "Stock Out" Condition

A "stock out" or "out of stock" condition occurs when a SKU inventory file shows inventory in a pick position when there is none. A "stock out" or "out of stock" condition creates nonproductive picker/pick machine activity because the picker/pick device traveled to a pick position but could not complete the pick transaction.

SKU replenishment activity is completed prior to inventory depletion in a pick position. Pick-position replenishment design factors are:

- The pick-position philosophy is determined by the pick activity.
- SKU replenishment is from a storage location located in a storage position or ready-reserve position. In other words, a convenient location of the SKU reserve quantity ensures a quick and accurate transfer to a pick position.
- The pick-position SKU capacity or type determines the best replenishment quantity.
- SKU replenishment timing, i.e., when to replenish a pick position.
- SKU replenishment transport method.
- SKU replenishment verification. After the WMS computer updates the inventory files, the computer releases customer orders.

Zero Scan a Depleted Pick Position

A pick design in which a SKU in a pick position is changed or rotated each work day requires a pick-line profile change for the customer order wave. For each customer order wave, a SKU profile is developed for a pick line.

After a replenishment employee physically transfers and scans a SKU to a pick position, the scan is sent to the WMS computer. The computer releases customer orders for that SKU and a picker completes the pick activity. At the end of the pick day, the warehouse performs a pick-position zero scan, which is sent to the WMS computer. A zero-scan confirms that a pick position is vacated and ready to accept the next SKU replenishment.

If the WMS program sends only full (round-down) master cartons to a high-volume SKU pick line, a pick line will have a few SKUs remaining in pick positions at the end of a customer order wave. Pick-line preparation for new SKUs includes a zero scan for each pick position.

If the WMS program sends only full (round-up) master cartons to a pick line, at the of the warehouse work day or customer order wave end, a pick line may have SKUs with residual inventory in pick positions. Pick-line preparation for new SKUs includes moving SKU quantity from one pick position to another. On a main pick line, an employee zero scans each pick position and moves each SKU identification (partial or full master carton) from a pick line to another pick position. At the new pick position, the SKU, position, and quantity are sent to the WMS computer, which updates the inventory files.

Pick-position preparation options are:

1. Accept a pick-position's SKU status as zero. If the WMS program accepts that all SKUs have been picked for customer orders from pick positions, pick-line setup for the next customer order wave is a simple task. After the warehouse transfers and scans SKUs to a pick position, at the end of the customer order wave the WMS computer recognizes that all pick positions are picked clean (no SKU quantity). If there is a warehouse miss pick (picked wrong SKU) or over-stock situation, the WMS computer would not recognize that there is old SKU quantity in a pick position. After pick-line setup for a customer order wave, there would be another SKU replenished to a pick position. Two SKUs in one pick position can cause customer order pick errors.
2. Zero scan each pick position. A zero scan of a depleted pick position occurs after all customer orders are completed and at the end of a customer order wave. An employee scans each pick position. Pick-position zero scans are sent to the WMS computer, which updates a SKU quantity as zero in each pick position, and confirms that each pick position has a SKU zero quantity and is ready to have a new SKU physically transferred and scanned. After a new SKU is scanned into a pick position and sent to the WMS computer for inventory update, the computer releases customer orders to a pick line.

Customer Order-Wave Carry-Over

In an order fulfillment warehouse with the WMS program, there is the potential for customer order wave carry-over (see Figure 7.2). Each work-day has at least one customer order wave. In the WMS computer, after the warehouse staff completes a customer order wave plan, the staff releases a customer order wave to the WMS computer to allocate SKUs for customer orders. In accordance with a pick-aisle/line profile, SKUs are physically transferred from storage positions and scanned to pick positions. Customer order carry-overs are orders in a customer order wave that are not completed within a work day or customer order wave (day 1). A customer order carry-over results from uncontrollable situations, such as:

1. A host, WMS, or warehouse computer problem;
2. Electrical, mechanical, or pick line problems;
3. Employee illness;
4. Unexpected occurrences.

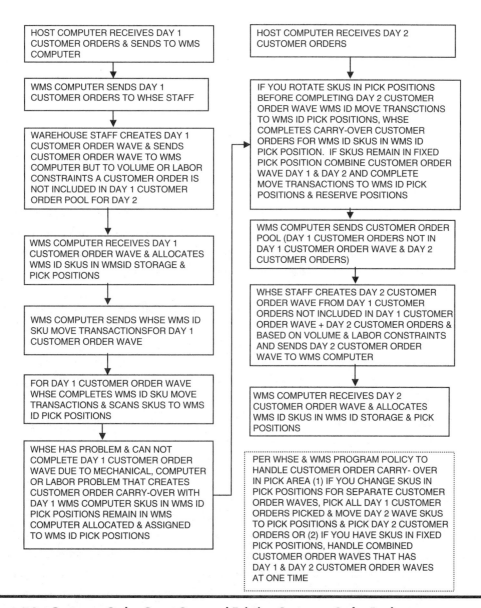

Figure 7.2 Customer Order Carry-Over and Existing Customer Order Pool

SKUs Rotated to Pick Positions

If a warehouse rotates SKUs on the pick line, carry-over customer orders must be completed within the next work day (day 1) and prior to the next customer order wave plan (day 2). A customer order carry-over means that the customer order wave 1 pick line was not able to pick or complete all customer orders; the customer order wave 2 pick line must complete all day 1 or customer order wave 1 customer orders before starting to pick customer order wave 2 customer orders.

SKUs Remain in Pick Positions

If the SKUs remain on the pick line, carry-over customer orders are completed within the next work day (day 2) and the next day customer order wave plan (day 2) is completed with SKUs in the same pick positions. The WMS program releases customer orders to a pick line and the relevant SKU to the same pick position.

If an order fulfillment warehouse has customer order carry-over, customer order pick philosophies and designs will have an impact on the WMS program. Customer order carry-over options are:

1. A SKU transferred to a fixed pick position that has each customer order wave and SKU transferred from a storage position to the same pick position. With a repetitive SKU pick aisle/line setup to a same pick position, customer order carry-over has minimal problems for a pick activity and WMS program due to the fact that the carry-over customer orders SKUs and the next customer order wave for customer orders SKUs are allocated to same pick positions.

2. A SKU transferred to a different pick position. Each customer order wave has a SKU transferred from a storage position to a different pick position. Each customer order wave and SKU has a different profiled pick position that is based on a SKU customer order demand or other criteria. A SKU customer order demand determines a SKU profile. A pick aisle/line profile has SKUs arranged in a pick-position sequence to obtain the highest picker productivity.

3. A dual pick line concept has two similar pick lines with equal pick position numbers and position types. For customer order wave 1, SKUs are moved and scanned to pick-line pick positions. Some customer orders for wave 1 are carry-over customer orders. If customer order wave 1 had pick positions on pick line 1. On day 2 for customer order wave 1, a warehouse continues to pick customer orders from pick line 1 and customer order wave 2 transfer SKUs to a pick line 2. All SKUs and SKU replenishments to pick positions are scanned and the quantities are sent to the WMS computer. The computer updates inventory and releases customer orders for day 2 or customer order wave 2 to pick line 2. After customer order wave 1 has completed all carry-over customer orders and pick-position zero scan transactions are sent to the WMS computer for inventory update, customer order wave 2 SKUs are setup in pick-line 1 pick positions. After the WMS computer is updated, the computer releases customer orders (customer order wave 2) customer orders to pick line 1.

SKU Setup in a Warehouse with Multiple Pick Zones

With multiple pick zones, the WMS program directs the warehouse to transfer SKUs to an assigned pick zone according to the customer order wave plan. A SKU withdrawal and pick-line setup has a SKU scanned to a pick position. The pick position and SKU identifications and quantity are sent to a WMS computer that allows the WMS computer to release customer orders to a pick concept. The SKU withdrawal options are:

1. Total SKU quantity for all customer orders. The WMS computer directs the warehouse to withdraw a SKU quantity from storage positions to match the total customer order demand. SKUs are delivered to a discharge or drop point by a fork-life truck or AS/RS crane. At the drop point, an employee allocates the proper SKU quantity to each pick zone. If a warehouse has a depalletize station, an employee removes and identifies each master carton. Each labeled master carton is transferred to each pick zone. The number of master cartons transferred is sent to the WMS computer to update the inventory files. The method features a) the largest SKU quantity per warehouse transaction, b) few warehouse transactions, c) a greater SKU quantity on each pick zone travel path, d) high transfer employee productivity, e) less potential SKU damage, f) all customer orders for one SKU are released at one time, and g) ready-reserve positions in a pick area.

2. The exact SKU quantity for each pick zone. The WMS computer directs the warehouse to withdraw a SKU number that matches each pick zone customer order or customer order wave SKU demand. An exact quantity of SKUs are delivered to each pick zone drop point with a fork-lift truck or AS/RS crane. At a depalletize station each pick zone replenishment SKU quantity is a SKU move transaction: A warehouse employee completes the withdrawal transaction and delivery to a depalletize station or drop point. At a depalletize station, an employee removes master cartons and applies an identification label to each master carton. The labeled master carton is transported from the station to an assigned pick zone. The number of master cartons transferred is a move transaction that is sent to the WMS computer to update inventory files. Features of this method are a) the SKU quantity for each warehouse transaction that varies, b) increased number of warehouse transactions, c) fewer SKUs on each pick-zone travel path, d) slightly lower transfer employee productivity, e) increased potential SKU damage, and f) exact SKU quantity for each pick zone means fewer ready-reserve positions.

Pick Design Impact on SKU Replenishment Activity

A small-item pick area layout design has an impact on a pick-position replenishment activity. The basic designs are:

1. A manual picker walks or rides to a pick-position concept
2. A mechanized or stock/pick position moves to a picker concept
3. Automatic or computer controlled pick concept.

Manual Pick Concepts

A manual picker walks or rides in an aisle with pick positions on one or both sides. The options are:

1. Shelves or decked-rack pick-position rows with a pick and replenishment aisle between two rows;
2. Carton flow-rack rows with pick and replenishment aisles;
3. A shelf and flow-rack combination.

Shelf/Decked-rack/Carousel Pick Designs

SKU replenishment transaction to shelf, decked-rack or carousel pick position with

a nominal 3 to 8 SKUs per bay. Sku number is determined by a SKU cube, pick-position cube and
employee reach height. Features are:

1. Separate SKU storage aisles;
2. Limited ready-reserve positions in a pick aisle;
3. C and D SKUs;
4. A replenishment employee transports a SKU quantity from a storage position to a pick position.

For maximum employee replenishment productivity, SKU replenishment transactions are separated by each pick aisle. With this criteria, the aisle floor level (i.e., replenishment employee reachable positions) have SKUs for pick aisle 1. This ensures that SKUs are withdrawn from a storage position and replenishment transactions in storage aisle 1 are for pick positions in pick aisle 1. The SKU separation design features more efficient and cost-effective replenishment employee activity, few pick position replenishment errors, few employees, few congested storage and pick aisles, a large number of SKUs, and low quantity per SKU.

Gravity Flow-Rack Pick Design

The features of a SKU replenishment to carton gravity flow-rack pick positions are:

1. For high-moving SKUs, an employee transports a SKU quantity from a storage position to a replenishment aisle. It would be helpful if a reserve position is close to a flow-rack position. The preferred flow-rack reserve position is above or on the other side of a replenishment aisle.
2. For medium- to slow-moving SKUs, an employee transports a SKU quantity to a replenishment aisle and places directly into a pick positions. Extra SKUs are placed into temporary ready-reserve positions.

For maximum replenishment employee productivity, a SKU replenishment quantity is separated by pick zones or sequential carton flow-rack bays with 10 to 30 SKUs per flow-rack bay. The number of SKUs per bay is based on master carton width and height. For maximum replenishment employee productivity, SKUs that are allocated to pick zone 1 are allocated to a storage aisle 1; SKU storage allocation mirrors a pick-zone sequence. The feature ensures that SKUs are withdrawn from a storage area for a pick-zone or flow-rack bay sequence.

Replenishment to an Automatic Pick Concept

The features of replenishment transactions with an automatic pick machine are:

1. Medium- to fast-moving SKUs with small to medium cube. SKUs pick positions are dense, with many pick positions per ln ft and is determined by SKU physical characteristics.
2. Each replenishment lane holds one or two master cartons with a nominal 12 SKUs per master carton.
3. The ready-reserve location is opposite a replenishment lane charge end and aisle.
4. During down time, ready-reserve replenishment positions are pick positions.

5. SKU replenishment is a computer-controlled activity. To assist with replenishment timing, there are visual controls to signal a pick-lane replenishment: a blocked photo eye in a pick position lane that activates a flashing light, and mark on a replenishment sleeve or lane.

A consideration in automatic pick-position replenishment is to have ready-reserve positions located directly behind the pick machine replenishment side. A replenishment aisle is between an automatic pick machine and ready-reserve positions, and has sufficient width to permit an employee to perform all replenishment transactions, to setup a temporary pick transport conveyor, and to complete all pick transactions. An automatic pick machine ready-reserve design is a carton flow-rack that is either perpendicular or parallel to an automatic pick machine replenishment aisle. The parallel arrangement is preferred, because it minimizes employee travel and replenishment positions face the replenishment lanes.

When an automatic pick-position number exceeds the replenishment position number, a carton flow-rack design is perpendicular to a replenishment aisle. This design provides the greatest number of replenishment pick-positions per aisle but slightly decreases employee productivity because of the increased walking distance (from the carton flow-rack aisle to the replenishment aisle). A SKU replenishment sequence along ready-reserve carton flow-rack positions has the same sequence as a pick machine SKU sequence. The options for a ready-reserve shelf, decked rack, or pallet rack row and aisle are parallel, perpendicular to a pick area, short aisle, and long aisle. In some high-tech warehouses, replenishment is done automatically from a temporary storage position to the pick position. In many just-in-time replenishment warehouses, such as pharmaceutical wholesale operations, with an automatic pick machine, master cartons are sent from a receiving area on a conveyor to a pick area.

SKU Allocation in a Pick Area Affects Replenishment Activity

SKU allocation to a pick position on a pick line/aisle has an impact on replenishment activity. A basic storage/replenishment/pick-location principle is to keep a travel distance for storage, replenishment, or pick employees as short as possible between two travel transaction positions. In a single item replenishment design, travel distances are between a SKU reserve position and pick position and between one pick position and the next. The practice increases dual cycle transactions and improves hit density and concentration. The feature reduces nonproductive time and improves replenishment and picker productivity. SKU allocation to pick-position options are:

1. ABC or Pareto's Law;
2. Family group;
3. Power SKUs in one pick area.

On a pick line, each pick zone is allocated a SKU number that provides budgeted picker productivity rate.

SKU Allocation to a Warehouse Pick Design

If SKUs are allocated to a pick position by SKU volume, the options are high-volume SKUs and low-volume SKUs. Each SKU is separated into a group that is based on historical or estimated sales volume or SKUs with similar volume characteristics are grouped together in one pick zone. With high-pick volume SKU allocation method, SKU number with a high pick volume is allocated to a pick zone that matches your budgeted picker productivity rate. A high-volume method minimizes picker queue in a pick aisle or zone and increases completed customer order number. With a low-pick volume SKU allocation method, SKUs with a low pick/sales volume are allocated to one pick zone. This approach minimizes a picker travel distance between two customer low-volume SKU picks.

SKU High to Low Pick-Position Profile

A high to low SKU volume replenishment method is used for an order fulfillment warehouse to group high-pick volume SKUs in a pick area. A pick area that has pick positions follows an 80/20 SKU approach, increases the potential to complete customer orders with two hours (or within a company customer order standard).

Pick-Position Profile Designs

Pick aisles with shelves or carton flow-rack pick-line profile or setup designs can be:

- Continuous flow-rack pick line or shelves with a random SKU allocation or profile along a pick line/aisle
- Continuous carton flow-rack pick line or shelves with specific flow-rack lanes or shelves that are allocated or profiled for high demand SKUs
- A pick area with three modules that are separated into three sections

Carton flow-rack pick line/aisle shelves has a predetermined flow-rack bay, channel, lane, or shelf number to provide pick positions for a design year SKU number. As previously stated, high-demand SKUs have a three- to seven-day life cycle, which is separated into "A" (high demand), "B" (medium to high demand), and "C" (low to medium demand). In some industries, such as pharmaceuticals, a SKU life cycle may last months.

Pick-Line SKU Slot Activity to a Pick Position

A pick line/aisle SKU slotting to a pick position on a pick line/aisle has a direct impact on picker productivity and the number of completed customer orders per pick line/aisle. In a pick line, each SKU sale or customer order pick number determines its pick position on a pick line/aisle. A pick line is designed with single or dual lines. A design team SKU pick-line slot to a pick-position options are one SKU slotted in one pick position or into two separate pick positions.

A Single SKU Assigned to a Single Pick Line/Aisle and a Single Pick Position

In this design, one fast-moving SKU is assigned to one pick line or aisle, and one high-volume SKU is assigned to one pick position. In a single pick-line profile, a high-volume SKU is assigned to a pick line/pick aisle "A" pick zone. This pick zone is located at the front pick positions of the pick line/aisle. A picker will have a high pick rate, which will ensure a constant customer order flow over a pick line or through a pick aisle.

As a customer order tote/carton leaves a high-volume pick position, each progressive SKU customer order pick volume is lower and, allowing for picker productivity rate, the customer order flow should remain even. The number of completed customer orders will increase and the number of pick zone pick-positions will increase. If there are multiple SKUs per customer order with a high-volume SKU in most orders, the majority of customer order cartons/totes that receive a high-volume SKU are picked into the majority of cartons/totes. All completed customer orders are pushed from a pick line or aisle onto a conveyor or into full carts. This approach means potential open space between two customer order totes/cartons, fewer customer order identified totes/cartons in a pick train, or multiple pickers in an aisle. With one pick position for each SKU, replenishment to a pick position is made to a single pick position, which means simple replenishment activity. With a single pick position, the WMS or warehouse computer assignment of a SKU to a pick line/aisle requires no special program.

A Single SKU Assigned to a Single Pick Line/ Aisle but to Two Separate Positions

Two pick positions assigned to a high-volume SKU are separated by other SKUs in other pick positions. In a single pick line/aisle profile, a high-volume SKU is allocated to two pick positions. One pick position is in a pick line/aisle "A" pick zone. One pick position is located in the "A" zone front and the second pick position is located in the "A" zone rear or "B" zone front. With the high-volume SKU split between two pick positions, there are fewer SKU picks for each pick position than for one pick position, which evens out the number of picks for each position.

For a SKU assigned to two pick positions, as totes/cartons enter a pick line or aisle, the WMS or warehouse computer assigns pick transactions to the first or second pick position on a predetermined basis. If a high-volume SKU has a pick transaction at the first pick position, as a tote/carton or pick cart enters pick zone "A," a picker completes the pick transaction. Next, the "A" zone picker completes other pick transactions. If there are no other picks in the pick zone, the tote/carton is pushed onto a conveyor, across a pick conveyor, or into a cart to travel to the next pick zone. If a high-volume SKU does not have a pick transaction at the first pick position, as a tote/carton or pick cart enters pick zone "A," a picker completes other pick transactions and pushes the tote/carton or pick cart to the "A" pick zone rear and completes a high-volume SKU pick transaction. This means that the picker pushed a tote/carton or pick cart travel past several SKU pick positions without completing a pick transaction. At the "A" pick zone rear and after completion of all customer order picks, a completed customer order tote/carton is pushed on the pick conveyor or transferred onto a cart for transport to the next warehouse pick zone.

Features of this approach:

- It more evenly spreads the SKU pick volume between two pick positions;
- Moving a high-volume SKU into two pick positions does not maintain picker productivity rate, and totes/cartons or pick carts move at the same or slower travel speed, there is a no picker hour savings, and there will be a decrease in completed customer orders per hour;
- If moving a high-volume SKU into two pick positions does maintain the picker productivity rate and the totes/cartons or pick carts move at the same travel speed, there will be total picker hour savings and an increase in completed customer orders per hour.

If a pick aisle is designed with a shelf or decked-rack pick position, the aisle is between the shelf or decked-rack pick positions. The shelf or decked-rack pick position separation options are:

1. one section with specific shelf/decked-rack rows and aisles; or
2. multiple shelf/decked-rack rows and aisles.

The aisle width allows multiple carts to travel in an aisle. As a picker or replenishment employee completes an aisle activity, an employee follows the picker or replenishment routing pattern through all the pick aisles, past all the pick positions, to complete a single customer order pick, a batched customer order pick, or replenishment activity.

SKU Assigned to a Pick Position

In this approach, a pick line/aisle has sequentially profiled pick positions, and each SKU has been assigned to a pick position by the WMS computer. After assignment to pick position is completed and updated in the WMS computer, the computer releases the SKUs for move transactions. The warehouse transfers and scans all SKUs to pick positions, after which the WMS computer releases customer orders, and customer order fulfillment activity starts. There are two options for SKU profiling to a pick position: preassignment and real-time assignment.

Preassignment Time Approach

This approach means that after the WMS computer has allocated customer order SKUs, a warehouse employee profiles each SKU to a pick position. Several hours prior to a scan and transfer/move to a pick position (based on a pick-line profile strategy), a warehouse employee profiled each SKU to a pick line or aisle pick position. To have the WMS computer release all customer orders, all customer order SKUs are moved and scanned to a pick position. All scan transactions and SKU quantities are sent to the WMS computer for file update and customer order release.

Real-Time Assignment Time

In this approach, after the WMS computer allocates customer order SKUs, as the warehouse moves a SKU from a storage position to a pick area, a warehouse employee profiles or assigns each SKU to a pick position. As a SKU arrives in a pick area, the SKU is moved and scanned to a pick position. A pick-line profile is not based on a preplanned strategy to optimize picker productivity. To have the WMS computer release all customer orders, all customer order SKUs are moved and scanned to a pick position. This approach is difficult to plan and control.

High-Volume SKU Profile to a Pick Position

A batch of customer orders or a customer order wave with a large number of picks for a few SKUs means that a few SKUs are required to complete a large customer order (or large number of orders). During pick activity, SKU replenishment and pick transaction numbers are at their height. The pick position options for high-volume SKUs are:

1. A pick line with one pick position or slot per SKU. In this approach, each SKU is assigned or profiled to one pick position. For example: A SKU placed into pick position 100A and an additional SKU per pick position means that the pick line/aisle has a high pick concentration and density. Completed pick transactions deplete the inventory in pick position 100A. Based on a quantity per SKU, the WMS program creates a replenishment transaction from a storage position to pick position 100A. This approach features are high picker productivity, some potential for SKU and equipment damage, pick area ready-reserve positions, and the number of maximum SKUs per pick line/aisle.

2. A floating pick position. In this approach, a high-volume SKU is profiled to several pick line/ aisle pick positions. As a pick line setup employee completes a floating pick position setup transaction, a SKU is scanned and transferred to two pick positions, which are adjacent to each other. The SKU inventory is scanned and moved to pick position 100A; additional SKU inventory is scanned and transferred to pick position 100B. When pick transactions deplete the SKU inventory in pick position 100A to zero, the WMS computer transfers the next pick transaction to pick position 100B. A floating pick position features good productivity; requires the WMS program to allocate SKU to adjacent pick positions and to transfer pick transactions from one pick position to another; a minimal number of pick positions; and less than the maximum number of SKUs per pick line/aisle.

3. A round robin slot approach. As a pick line/aisle setup employee completes double-slotted SKU pick line/aisle setup transactions, a SKU is scanned and moved into two or more non-adjacent pick positions, for example, pick position 500B. When completed pick transactions have depleted all SKU inventory from pick position 100A, the WMS computer transfers the next pick transaction to pick position 500B. This means that a customer order with a pick transaction from pick position 500B passes pick position 100A. This approach features good picker productivity; requires the WMS program to allocate a SKU into two pick positions on a pick line; pick transactions are transferred to the first pick transaction from one pick position (100A) and second pick transaction to another pick position (500B); in a pick area extra pick positions; and a pick line/aisle travel path that permits totes/cartons or pick carts to pass pick position 100A and to have a pick transaction completed from pick position 500B.

Pick-Line/Pick-Aisle Pick Position Profile Frequency

A pick line/aisle profile allocates SKUs to pick positions. The warehouse's procedures, business model, and SKU rotation determine a pick-line/aisle profile frequency. A warehouse pick-line/aisle profile options are historical SKU sales volume and SKU daily sale volume.

Historical SKU Sales Volume Pick-Line/Pick-Aisle Profile

With a warehouse historical SKU sales volume pick line/aisle profile, the warehouse or WMS computer uses each SKU sale volume (plus other criteria) to assign a SKU to a pick position. Using this approach, SKUs are allocated, assigned, or profiled to pick positions:

- Permanently;
- For one week or longer;
- Pick-line SKUs are changed less frequently or there are fewer reorganization activities;

- The WMS computer creates replenishment transactions to a pick position more frequently;
- Tt is easier to project productivity.

Day-by-Day Customer Order Wave Pick-Line/Aisle Profile

Day-by-day SKU pick-line/aisle profile is based on the SKU demand for each day. For each work day or customer order wave, new SKUs (with associated sales volume) are profiled to a pick line. A pick profile is the basis for SKU allocation. The features of this approach are:

- the pick-line/aisle profile is changed each customer order wave or more frequently, if necessary;
- it is more difficult to forecast or develop a pick-line/aisle profile;
- at the end of a customer order wave all pick positions are zero scanned and vacated for a new customer order wave's SKUs;
- it is difficult to project picker productivity;
- only an allocated SKU quantity is sent to a pick position.

SKU Profile for a Dual Pick Line

Second Pick Line for Partially Completed Customer Orders

In a two pick-line design, there is a high potential for customer orders to have several high-volume SKUs that exceed one picker's budgeted productivity and creates a need for a second pick line. High-volume SKUs are 5 to 20 SKUs per order. With two or three SKUs per customer order, customer order picks represent approximately 20% of the completed customer orders. It is understood for maximum picker productivity and constant completed customer order flow from a pick area to a packing area that the high-volume SKUs are profiled on one pick line in one pick zone. In a pick zone, SKUs are assigned to adjacent pick positions. With a dual pick-line approach, high-volume SKUs profile options are to allocate SKUs:

- That complete customer orders profiled on pick line 1 and
- Evenly profiled between two pick lines.

SKUs that Complete Customer Orders: Profiled on a Single Pick Line/Aisle

In this approach, high-volume SKUs profiled to pick line/aisle 1 and high-volume and medium/low volume SKUs are profiled to pick line/aisle 2. The warehouse staff creates a customer order wave in which the WMS computer directs the transfer of a high-volume SKU quantity to one pick line/aisle to complete customer orders. SKU master cartons or pallets are transferred to the pick area for scanning and replenishment to a pick position. After the scan transactions and quantity are sent to the WMS computer, the computer updates the files and releases customer orders. As customer orders for high-volume SKUs are completed, the orders are transferred to a take-away conveyor or a pick cart (which is pushed from a pick area), and transported to the packing area. After all customer orders are completed, pick line 1 has no additional customer orders in a customer order wave and is ready for clean-up or reorganization.

The other pick line/aisle pickers continue to complete pick transactions for SKUs for the remaining 80% of customer orders. SKUs are combined with high-volume and medium- and low-volume SKUs. Completed customer orders are sent on a separate take-away conveyor from the pick area to a packing area. For example, high-volume SKUs are A = 4,754 SKUs, B = 35,953 SKUs, C = 2,622 SKUs, D = 2,466 SKUs, and E = 1,985 SKUs. Twenty percent of the customer orders are completed with the five high-volume SKUs and 80% of customer orders are completed with a combination of five high-volume and medium/low volume SKUs.

With high-volume SKUs that complete a customer order approach, a pick line SKU allocation has 20% for "A" = 951 SKUs, "B" = 719 SKUs, "C" = 288 SKUs, "D" = 271 SKUs, and "E" = 218. With two SKUs per customer order and "A" having 951 SKUs, there are 951 customer orders traveling on a pick conveyor or as pick containers on pick line/aisle pick carts. At 900 picked SKUs per hour pick rate, a picker takes 1.1 hours to pick SKU "A." The SKU number is determined by your company industry.

If customer orders are completed with mixed SKUs, a pick line/aisle SKU allocation has 80% for "A" = 3,803 SKUs, "B" = 2,874 SKUs, "C" = 2,334 SKUs, "D" = 2,195 SKUs, and "E" = 21,767 SKUs. With two SKUs per customer order, and if SKU "A" has 3,803 SKUs, then 3,803 customer orders travel on a conveyor as pick containers on pick line or pick carts in a pick aisle. At 900 picked SKUs per hour, a picker takes 4.2 hours to pick SKU "A." This approach will feature:

- SKU allocation imbalance between two pick lines
- Pick volume imbalance between two pick lines or two pick aisle sections
- Warehouse, customer order carton, or tote imbalance between two pick lines

SKUs Evenly Profiled Between Two Pick Lines/Aisles

In this approach, high-volume and medium/low volume SKUs are profiled to two pick lines/aisles that complete customer orders. In most catalog and telemarketing warehouses a high-volume SKU is five SKUs per order.

With an one pick-line/aisle approach, a warehouse creates a customer order wave that has the WMS computer allocate a SKU quantity to complete customer orders. SKU master cartons/pallets are transferred to a pick concept for scan and replenishment to pick positions. After the scan and SKU quantity are sent to the WMS computer, the computer updates files and releases customer orders. On each pick line, as customer orders for high-volume and medium/low volume SKUs are completed on a pick train or pick cell, completed customer orders are transferred to a take-away conveyor or full pick carts are pushed to holding area. A completed customer order take-away conveyor transports completed customer orders or full pick carts direct from a pick area to a pack area. After all customer orders completed, both pick line/aisles will have no additional customer orders in the customer order wave and are ready for a pick position reorganization.

The other pick line/aisle completes pick transactions for SKUs for the other 80% of the SKUs. Customers orders are combined with high-volume and medium/low volume SKUs. Completed customer orders are sent on a take-away conveyor or full pick carts from a pick area to a packing area. For example, high-volume SKUs are "A" = 4,754 SKUs, "B" = 3,583 SKUs, "C" = 2,622 SKUs, "D" = 2,466 SKUs, and "E" = 1,985 SKUs. With SKUs evenly split between two pick lines, both pick lines have a SKU allocation that has 50% for "A" = 2,377 SKUs, "B" = 1,797 SKUs, "C" = 1,311 SKUs, "D" = 1,233 SKUs, and "E" = 983 SKUs. With two SKUs per customer order, if "A" has 2,377 SKUs, 2,377 cartons/totes travel on a conveyor as pick containers on pick line. At 900 picked SKUs per hour, a picker takes 2.6 hours to pick SKU "A." The features of this approach are:

- SKU allocation balance between two pick lines/aisles
- Pick volume balance between two pick lines or aisles
- Carton/tote balance between two pick lines/aisles

Fast-Pack Station Setup and Replenishment SKUs

A high-volume single-line single or multiple SKU(s) customer orders are completed at a fast-pack station. A SKU is delivered to a fast-pack station, and an employee picks/packs a customer order. With a fast-pack approach, the setup or replenishment options are:

1. SKU quantity by master carton or pallet; and
2. Flow options, which can be direct flow and forklift truck.

Master Carton SKU

Each master carton has a SKU identification. When a master carton is placed onto conveyor, it is transported from a storage area to a pick line or fast-pack station. At each pick line or fast-pack station, a sensing device that controls a divert device directs the master cartons to the conveyor replenishment travel path or to a packing station. At a packing station, an employee scans a master carton's label and prints a packing slip or shipping label for each SKU in the master carton. To complete a pick line replenishment activity, master carton and pick position identifications are scanned and the scan data with SKU quantity are sent to the WMS computer, which updates the SKU and pick position status. The features of this approach are:

1. The main conveyor travel path and divert controls, replenishment conveyor travel path and cost.
2. Some master carton double handling.
3. Use of full master cartons with medium- to low-volume SKUs.
4. High fast-pack employee productivity with packing slips/labels at a packing station.
5. Accurate pick line setup or replenishment to a pick position.

Pallet SKU

Pallet replenishment to a pick position or fast-pack station involves having a AS/RS crane or manually controlled forklift truck withdraw a pallet from a storage position. A pallet is delivered to a pick position or to a fast-pack station's set-down point. At the set-down or drop location, SKU and drop location identifications are scanned and sent to the WMS computer for file update. After a fast-pack employee scans a pallet, a pack employee transfers master cartons onto a packing table or picker to complete a customer order. At a fast-pack station, preprinted packing slips/delivery labels are available to a packer or a packing station printer prints labels. The features of this approach are:

- Fast-pack station pallet set-down spot
- Delivery packing slips or labels printed at a packing station
- Forklift truck or conveyor travel path
- It is used for high-volume SKUs

- High picker and packer productivity
- Lower conveyor cost

Pallet SKU Replenishment

A warehouse with direct pallet flow has in a storage area an AS/RS crane or forklift truck place a SKU onto a pallet conveyor or transport travel path. A conveyor travel path or in-house transport travel path is a short travel path from a storage area to a pick area or fast-pack station. At a pick or fast-pack station, a packer transfers a master carton from a pallet onto a packing table; at a pick station a master carton is transferred to a pick position. An AS/RS crane computer communicates directly with the WMS computer or forklift truck driver hand scans the pallet, fast-pack station identification, and SKU quantity, all of which is sent to the WMS computer for inventory update. The computer releases customer orders.

The WMS program projects the number of pallets and has an AS/RS crane or manually controlled forklift truck transfer the pallets to a pick area. An option with an AS/RS crane is to have pallet transport bypass the standard front-end P/D station and use a separate delivery station and conveyor that has direct travel to a pick line or packing station. A conveyor provides a pallet queue and moves pallets from the AS/RS to a fast-pack station or pick position replenishment. Because a pallet conveyor ends at a pallet pick position or packing station, after the transportation delivers a pallet to a fast-pack station, fast-pack instruction or pick position activation options are:

1. Fast-pack station options: a) an employee scans the pallet identification and a local printer prints packing slips and delivery labels, or b) preprinted packing slips and delivery labels are delivered with the pallet to a fast-pack station. With either option, a packing employee depletes the pallet SKU quantity by a packing slip and scan transactions are sent to the WMS computer. An empty pallet is removed from the fast-pack station. For another SKU, the WMS program creates another pallet transfer transaction, which is sent to the warehouse.
2. A pallet replenishment to a pick-line pallet pick position has each master carton receive an identification that depletes a pallet SKU quantity and allows the WMS program to track a master carton and account for the SKU quantity on a pallet. Options are a) in a pick aisle, a picker or master carton open employee prepares each master carton for a pick transaction, b) from the pallet flow lane, a pallet flows to a replenishment aisle and an employee scans and moves or a master carton from a pallet to a master carton pick conveyor, c) in a forklift replenishment aisle, an employee moves master cartons from a pallet to another pallet on a pallet flow lane. Pallet and flow-lane identifications are scanned and sent to the WMS computer for update, and d) in a forklift truck replenishment aisle, a replenishment employee moves master carton direct to a pick conveyor. Pallet and pick position identifications are scanned and sent to the WMS computer for update.

Master Carton Preparation for a Pallet Pick Position

In a pick line approach that has a pick line setup on a daily basis, pick line setup and replenishment timing is critical for customer order release from the WMS computer to a pick line. In this approach, an entire pick line's SKUs are reprofiled and moved to a pick line for customer order wave SKUs.

To achieve a pick line setup for each customer order SKU, warehouse activities are:

1. Zero scan each SKU pick position and move existing SKUs from one pick position to another.
2. Move each required SKU from a storage position to a warehouse/WMS computer-profiled pick position. At each pick position, SKU, SKU quantities, and pick position identifications are scanned and sent to the WMS computer. The computer updates pick position and storage position status and releases customer orders.
3. In a pick position, for high picker productivity, each SKU master carton has a cut top or cut top with an open front. With the above-mentioned event sequence for a SKU, a SKU is scanned to a pick position and each master carton presentation is ready for pick activity.

With a pick to light pick position, master carton presentation activity options are: in a pick aisle, at a pick position, or at master carton open station, between a pallet flow lane and pick position. An example, with 12 SKUs per master carton, and 30 master cartons per pallet, employee time to open a master carton is 45 seconds.

Opening Master Cartons in the Pick Aisle or at a Pick Position

A picker or an associate employee opens each master carton in a pick position. With a pallet pick position, this means that there is at least one open master carton on a pallet. In a high-volume pick concept with 800+ SKU picks per hour and 12 SKUs per master carton, for a picker to maintain a 800-SKU pick rate, a picker must open a master carton every minute (800/60 = 13 seconds). With 45 seconds to open a master carton, a picker will not maintain budgeted picker productivity rate. This means low picker productivity, pick line congestion, recirculation, or pick line shut down.

If an associate employee is assigned to open master cartons, a picker has the opportunity to reach the budgeted picker productivity rate. Picker productivity rate is achieved because the second employee opens a master carton, which permits a picker to obtain a high picker productivity rate. Per a WMS computer customer order download to a pick line computer and pick line profile, there is the potential for an open employee not to have an opened master carton or to be at the same pick position with a picker. When there is a second employee and picker at the same pick position, the situation creates the same low picker productivity rate mentioned above, plus an hourly employee expense that increases the cost for each picked SKU.

Opening a Master Carton Between a Pallet Flow-Lane and a Pick Position

Prior to pick activity, a pallet WMS Identification is scanned to a pick position. The scan transaction is sent to a WMS computer and the WMS computer releases customer orders to a pick line concept. SKU scan transaction options are:

1. A forklift truck driver or open employee scans pallet and pick position identifications, which are sent to the WMS computer. Using a scan transaction approach means a) there is potential for customer orders on a pick line with no open master cartons in a pick position, and b) fewer scan transactions.
2. For each master carton that is transferred from a pallet, an open employee completes a move transaction with a scan transaction from a pallet to a pick position. This approach means that a) a SKU is in a pick position before customer order release, and b) more frequent and additional SKU and pick position scan transactions are sent to the WMS computer.

During pick activity, an open employee removes a master carton from a pallet, opens it, and transfers the opened master carton onto a pick position conveyor. Until customer orders have depleted the SKU quantity, the open activity is repeated for each SKU on a pick line to maintain each pick position with full and opened master cartons. An open employee walks in an open aisle to complete open activity for other SKUs on a pick line. With 12 SKUs per master carton, an open rate of one master carton opened every 45 seconds, and a pick rate (800/60 = 13 minute) a picker will reach the budgeted productivity rate and ensure a constant completed order flow.

Forklift Replenishment Aisle Transfer: Master Cartons Direct to a Conveyor

After a forklift truck deposits a pallet in a replenishment aisle and an open employee opens each master carton, then scans or transfers each opened master carton from a pallet into a SKU pick position. A pallet scan to a pick position is completed prior to pick activity, the pallet is scanned to a pick position (the WMS computer has already released customer orders to the pick line). During pick activity, an open employee removes master cartons from a pallet, opens and transfers master cartons onto a pick position conveyor and scans a pick position identification. Until customer orders have depleted the SKU quantity, open activity is repeated for each SKU on a pick line to maintain each pick position with full and opened master cartons. An open employee and pallet remains in a replenishment aisle to complete open activity for SKU. With 12 SKUs per master carton, an open rate of one master carton opened every 45 seconds, and a SKU pick rate of 13 picks per minute, a picker will match the budgeted productivity rate and ensure a constant completed customer order flow.

To ensure that released customer orders match an open master carton in a pick position, the options for scanning are:

1. As a pallet is deposited in a replenishment aisle. The potential is that customer orders will be released but no opened master cartons will be in a pick position.
2. With a pallet in a replenishment aisle, an open employee scans the pallet identification. This increases the probability that an opened master carton will be in a SKU pick position. The problem of not having open master cartons or SKU quantity at a pick positon is minimized with increased management pick-line control and supervision. An open employee is assigned to handle replenishment activity for a limited number of pick zones.
3. Have an open employee scan or move a master carton from a pallet to a pick position before the WMS computer releases customer orders to a pick line.

Pallet Flow Lane End at a Replenishment Aisle for Transfer to a Conveyor

In this method, forklift trucks deposit pallet in a replenishment aisle and an open employee opens each master carton. After opening a master carton, the employee transfers the opened master carton onto a pallet on a pallet flow lane. The move transaction—from an old pallet to a new pallet—is sent to the WMS program for update. Prior to pick activity, the new pallet is scanned to a pick position to which the WMS computer has released customer orders. During pick activity, an open employee removes master cartons from a pallet, opens a master carton, and transfers an opened master carton onto a pallet on a pallet flow lane. All repalletized full pallets are pushed with opened master cartons forward on a pallet conveyor. At the pallet conveyor end, a pallet is located for access by a picker. Until customer orders have depleted a SKU quantity, an open employee continues to remove master cartons from a pallet, opens the cartons, and transfers opened master cartons onto a pallet on the conveyor, and completes the scan. Until customer orders have depleted SKU quantity, open activity is repeated for each SKU on a pick line to maintain each pick position pallet with opened master cartons. With 12 SKUs per master carton, an open rate at a master carton opened every 45 seconds, and a SKU pick rate of 13 picks per minute means that picker will make the budgeted picker productivity rate and ensures a constant completed customer flow.

To ensure that the WMS computer releases customer orders that match an open carton in a pick position, the scan options are:

1. As a pallet is deposited in the replenishment aisle. There is potential to have a customer order released but no opened master cartons in a pick position.
2. With a pallet in a replenishment aisle, an open employee scans the pallet identification. This scan location increases the probability that an opened master carton is in a SKU pick position. The potential problem of not having an open master carton or SKU in a pick is minimized with increased management pick line control and supervision by assigning an open employee to handle a replenishment activity for limited number of pick zones.

Pallet Fast-Pack Station and Pick-Line Replenishment

Fast-pack station pallet replenishment features are:

- Conveyor travel path costs
- Packing slips/delivery labels are printed at a fast-pack station, or a central/remote location, and delivered to a fast-pack station
- Constant replenishment to a pick position
- Minimal pallet/master carton handling
- Fast-pack stations handles a high SKU volume
- High employee productivity
- Easy SKU change
- Pallet/master carton queue for on-time replenishment to a pick position/packing station

Pallet Forklift Truck Replenishment

This replenishment method uses an AS/RS crane to place a pallet on an AS/RS pallet conveyor, which leads to a P/D station. At the station end, a forklift truck picks-up the pallet, scans it and the drop-point/station identifications, and moves the pallet to a pick position or drop-point/fast-pack station. At a fast-pack station, an employee scans the pallet identification and a local printer prints packing slips/delivery labels (or preprinted packing slips/delivery labels are sent to the fast-pack station). After the employee depletes the pallet's SKU quantity, the empty pallet is removed from the fast-pack station. The WMS program sends another pallet transfer transaction and the warehouse moves a pallet from a storage position to a drop-point/fast-pack station.

In a warehouse that uses forklift trucks, a forklift truck withdraws a pallet from a position in a storage area and transports a SKU to a pick position or drop-point/fast-pack station. At a pick-position replenishment position, a forklift truck driver scans the pallet and pick-position idenfications and sends scans data, including SKU quantity, to the WMS computer. After the WMS computer updates inventory files, the computer releases customer orders to a pick line.

At a fast-pack station, a fast-packer scans a pallet identification, fast-pack station identification, and sends scan transactions, again with SKU quantity, to the WMS computer. After the WMS computer file update, the computer has a local printer to print packing slips/delivery labels (or preprinted packing slips/delivery labels are delivered to the packing station).

Forklift truck replenishment features are:

- It transports a pallet to a fast-pack station or to a pick position
- Packing slips/delivery labels are printed at a fast-pack station or printed by a central/remote printer and delivered to a packing station
- The approach requires additional forklift pallet and master carton handling
- It handles a high SKU volume
- High packer and picker productivity
- For on-time replenishment, it is necessary to provide a SKU queue at a fast-pack or a pick-area ready-reserve position

Customer Order Wave End Pick-Position Reorganization

With multiple pick lines/aisles, you rotate SKUs in pick positions at a customer order wave end to assure pick position preparation for the next customer order wave, and each pick position is picked clean or customer orders have depleted all SKUs and each pick position is zero WMS scanned. An employee performs a zero scan at a pick position, and the data is sent to the WMS computer. If there is a SKU quantity in a pick position, an employee moves the SKU quantity from the pick position to another pick position. After completion of the move transaction, an employee completes another pick position zero scan. From your main pick line pick position, as a moved/relocated SKU arrives in another pick area, an employee WMS scans a SKU and pick position WMS identifications and sends SKU and pick position WMS identifications with SKU quantity to the WMS computer that updates a SKU and pick position status.

In high-volume pick areas, use an ABC layout. A pick area has a high-volume ("A") SKU pick zone and a combined or separate pick zone for medium-volume ("B") SKUs and low-volume ("C") SKUs. To ensure proper new SKU placement into the "A" zone, at an end of a work day/customer order wave 1, the "A" pick zone is reorganized for next day or customer order wave 2 SKUs. High-volume end of day/customer order wave 1 "A" pick zone preparation options are multiple "A" pick zones, a single "A" pick zone, and having the remaining SKUs stay in existing pick positions.

Multiple "A" SKU Pick Zones

A multiple "A" pick-zone design has a pick line designed with two "A" SKU pick zones. On Day 1 customer order wave 1, "A" SKUs are picked from pick zone 1A, and next day/customer order wave 2 SKUs are setup in pick zone 2A. The remaining SKU quantity in zone "A" customer order wave 1 pick positions are transferred to pick zone "B" (i.e., medium moving SKU section). If a particular SKU that has been transferred to zone "B" is customer order wave 2 for fast-moving SKUs, a SKU quantity is transferred from the zone "B" pick position to a pick position in the customer order wave 2 "A" pick zone. Multiple "A" pick zone features additional floor area; additional pick equipment; SKU relocation labor; profiles for quick and good pick line setup, replenishment employees, and high picker productivity; and constant completed customer order flow.

Single "A" SKU Pick Zone

In a design using a single "A" SKU pick zone, all "A" SKUs are picked from one pick zone. The "A" pick zone is separated into "A," "B," and "C" pick zones. With one pick zone at customer-order wave 1 end, remaining "A" SKUs in "A" pick zone that are not part of customer-order wave 2 "A" are reorganized from the "A" pick zone to the "B" or "C" pick zone pick positions. Pick zone reorganization steps are:

1. Each pick position that is picked clean (i.e., all SKUs are picked from a pick position) is zero scanned into the WMS program. This ensures that the WMS inventory does not have SKU inventory in the WMS computer pick position file.
2. With customer-order wave 2 pick line profile, each SKU with remaining inventory is moved from the pick position to another pick position.
3. Following the customer-order wave 2 pick line/aisle profile, new "A" SKUs are setup and scanned to a suggested pick position; scan transactions are sent to the WMS computer for the file update.
4. If the customer-order wave 2 pick line/aisle SKU assignment does not have sufficient pick positions, extra "A" SKUs or new SKUs with the lowest customer order volume are profiled or moved to another pick zone and scanned to a new pick position. The scan is sent to the WMS computer for the file update.

Features are:

■ Minimal required floor space, but some additional pick positions will be needed
■ Minimal pick equipment cost
■ Minimal SKU relocation labor, but there will be some additional scan and move transactions
■ Profile for good pick line/aisle setup required, high setup and picker productivity

"A" SKUs Remain in Positions and Add New "A" SKUs

Each SKU for customer order wave 1 that has a residual inventory in a pick position remains in an existing pick position and new SKUs for customer order wave 2 are setup in vacant pick positions. For customer order wave 2, pick-line/aisle positions are profiled around existing SKUs in pick positions. If a pick line does not have sufficient vacant pick positions for customer order wave 2 SKUs, existing SKUs from customer order wave 1 with the lowest customer order pick volume are moved and set up in another pick zone pick position for customer order wave 2 "A" SKUs. Features are minimal required floor space, but some additional pick positions; minimal pick equipment cost; minimal SKU relocation labor, but some additional scan and move transactions; and profiles for good pick-line setup, replenishment, and picker productivity.

Pick-Line/Aisle Pick Position Clean-Up Strategy

An approach using a SKU rotation or zero scan permits a pick design to physically scan/move another SKU to a vacant pick-line/aisle pick position. Clean pick options are:

1. Activate all pick lights or zero scan all pick positions;
2. Activate specific pick lights or zero scan the position with a SKU quantity.

With a paper pick design, the WMS computer creates a pick position and an employee completes zero scan transactions for each listed pick position.

Activate All Pick Lights/Paper-Pick Zero Scan

In this action, the warehouse computer activates all pick-line pick lights and pick-to-light displays to show if a SKU quantity remains in a pick position. This is performed after each customer-order wave completion. With a paper-pick concept, the WMS computer creates a pick position and an employee completes a zero scan for each listed pick position. As a pick employee walks a pick line/aisle, the employee zero scans each pick position and sends the transaction to the WMS computer to update inventory files. After a pick position scan is sent to the WMS computer, an employee presses a pick-to-light–complete button or marks a paper document. If a pick position has a SKU quantity, an employee transfers a partial full master carton or SKU quantity to a tote on a take-away conveyor or cart, and sends the move transaction to the WMS computer. A SKU quantity is transferred from pick line/aisle A to another pick area pick position/storage position. The scan transaction and SKU relocation ensures that each pick-line pick position is vacant and has zero quantity or is ready for the next day or customer-order wave pick-position setup with a new SKU. With a manual paper pick approach, an employee zero scans each pick position to achieve a picked clean pick line/aisle. After the zero scan, the WMS computer has a vacant pick position. These approaches: ensure that all pick positions are vacant, requires employee activity, requires time, and requires customer-order wave end planned activity.

Activate Specific Pick-Line Lights or Zero Scan a Pick Position

This is a pick-line clean-up strategy. Each pick position that has a SKU quantity has a warehouse computer activate an associated pick light to show that a SKU quantity remains in the pick position. This approach is considered a specific and planned activity that is performed after each customer-order wave completion or during customer-order pick activity. As a pick employee walks a pick line/aisle, at each pick position with a SKU quantity, an employee zero scans the pick position and sends the scan to the WMS computer for update to the inventory files. The employee then presses a pick to light complete button or marks a paper document. If a pick position has a SKU quantity, an employee transfers a partial full master carton or SKU quantity onto a take-away conveyor or into a tote, and transmits the completed move transaction to the WMS computer. The SKU quantity is transferred from a pick line to another pick area pick position or storage position. The scan and relocation ensures that each pick-line/aisle pick position is vacant and is ready for the next customer-order wave pick position setup.

Features are:

- It ensures that only specific pick positions are vacant
- It is an employee activity
- It can occur during a pick activity. A clean out pick transaction is not a pick transaction that can create a pick-line slow down, customer-order congestion or recirculation.
- It is a planned pick-line activity at a customer-order wave completion or during a customer pick activity
- It requires additional employee training

Pick-Line/Aisle Clean-Up Tray Released from a Storage Area for Travel to a Pick Area

If a pick design requires a clean-up activity with master cartons transferred from pick positions onto a warehouse tray, a pick-line/aisle clean-up activity assures that a warehouse identified empty tray or tote quantity is at a pick-line/aisle. An empty tote/tray quantity ensures productive clean-up employee transfer activity and the activity is completed in a short time. Empty tray or tote supply options are a) to have the warehouse computer release trays/totes from a storage area to a pick area, or b) to have an empty tray/tote supply in a pick area.

Pick-Line Clean-Up Transport Device

A pick-line/aisle SKU rotation or zero scan permits the warehouse to scan and move a new SKU to a pick-line/aisle vacant pick position. The transport device may be tray/tote, a carton on a conveyor, or four-wheel cart.

Pick-Position Clean-Up Location

A pick-line/aisle has pick positions that are sequentially profiled with SKUs profiled to each. If the warehouse policy does not allow customer-order carry-over, a SKU is moved from a pick-line pick position to another pick area or storage area position. In a pick-line pick-position clean-up activity an employee removes a SKU from a pick-line/aisle pick position and places the SKU on a transport. As a pick position is cleaned up, an employee zero scans each pick position and each scan is sent to the WMS computer for file update. The second step is each SKU inventory quantity is scanned to another pick position or a storage position. Again, scans and SKU quantity are sent to the WMS computer for file update. SKU scan location options are at pick-line/aisle pick position or at a new pick or storage position.

Pick-Line/Aisle SKU Pick Position

In a pick-position pick-line/aisle clean-up strategy, each pick position is zero scanned to the WMS computer, or the SKU is moved to another pick position. An employee completes all clean-up activities at a pick-line/aisle pick position. In addition to the SKU transfer to transport, the employee completes a SKU inventory, updates scan, pick-position zero scan, which are sent to the WMS computer for file update. As the employee transfers a SKU from a pick position to a transport, the employee's scanner or pick-to-light display shows the WMS computer inventory quantity. An employee verifies the SKU count or enters the actual SKU count into a scanner. The scanner sends the actual SKU count to the WMS computer for file update.

New SKU Scanned at a Pick/Storage Position

A pick-line/aisle clean-up strategy at a new pick position has each SKU scanned to a new storage/pick position. An employee transfers a SKU from a pick position onto a transport. It moves the SKU from the pick area to another pick position or to a storage position. At the new pick area position, an employee's hand-held scanner indicates the SKU inventory quantity and the employee counts the actual SKU quantity. The SKU count is either verified or the actual SKU count is entered into the scanner. The scanner sends the count to the WMS computer for update, and the SKU is scanned and transferred to a pick/storage position. Scan transactions are sent to the WMS computer file for update.

Pick-Position Replenishment Capacity

SKU capacity is a factor in replenishment. Pick-position capacity factors are:

1. The minimum pick-position quantity needed to satisfy a customer-order quantity.
2. SKU physical characteristics, i.e., length, width, height, weight, fragility.
3. SKU classification, e.g., flammable, edible, toxic, or hazardous.
4. Pick-position physical space or cube, i.e., the internal dimensions between pick-position structural members.
5. The existing SKU quantity in a position and pick design.

A pick position is designed to hold a SKU quantity that satisfies a predetermined customer order, customer-order wave, or pick quantity. A pick-position type determines small-item or master-carton pick-position capacity. In a pick design, the pick-position design capacity is designed to accept one vendor master-carton SKU quantity plus an additional SKU quantity. The additional SKU quantity is determined by management and is either safety stock or extra SKU quantity in a pick position. The pick-position type capacities are:

1. with small items, the smallest pick-position capacity are drawer, small bin, tote, or box that is placed into a shelf, carton AS/RS, carousel position, peg board, or automatic pick machine
2. medium pick-position capacity is standard shelves, one deep-decked pallet racks, full horizontal carousel basket, and S. I. Cartrac
3. large small-item SKU pick-position capacity is carton flow rack or push back flow rack, slide or chute, two-deep decked-racks/wide span shelves, standard decked cantilever racks, and pallets or stacking frames
4. with a master-carton operation, small master-carton quantity is in a hand-stack position, S.I. Ordermatic, or manual carton gravity flow rack
5. Vertique tower or in a pallet position
6. in a pallet position in any operation, pallet quantity is one pallet or a number of pallets in a dense storage concept

SKU Replenishment Quantity

A reserve position physically holds a SKU replenishment quantity. In a warehouse, to ensure excellent SKU inventory control and minimal SKU damage, the SKU quantity is one vendor master carton or pallet.

Pick-position replenishment quantity factors determine SKU replenishment quantity. Options are: An employee. An employee option is not preferred option.

A WMS or computer projection method is preferred for a pick design because a replenishment activity is computer printed or RF-device or terminal directed. The WMS program suggests a SKU replenishment priority, a SKU quantity, and a storage position that corresponds to a pick activity or SKU volume (that matches customer orders/customer-order wave), and a SKU replenishment quantity that matches a pick-position capacity. After a SKU replenishment, SKU and pick-position identifications and SKU quantities are sent to the WMS computer for inventory update and customer-order release.

SKU Replenishment Quantities

SKU replenishment quantity objectives are to ensure that there is excellent space utilization in a pick position, SKU rotation, and sufficient SKU quantity for customer-order waves. To satisfy these objectives, a SKU inventory control program determines the replenishment quantity that is transferred from a storage position to a pick position. The most important factor is SKU rotation and profile frequency. Other factors are:

1. The quantity in a storage position
2. Beginning SKUs in a pick position
3. Replenishment transactions/deductions for picked SKUs in the WMS program update
4. Predetermined SKU capacity for a pick position
5. Predetermined safety stock, i.e., extra SKUs in a pick position
6. Historical/expected customer-order demand
7. Ready-reserve position number and capacity

SKU replenishment quantities to a fixed pick position may produce minimum quantity, maximum quantity, capacity quantity, quantity needed to match customer-order wave SKUs, or pick-clean quantity.

SKU Minimum Quantity

A minimum SKU replenishment quantity is the safety stock quantity in a permanent pick position or a pick design that has few pick-line profile changes. When a pick-position SKU inventory quantity reaches the minimum quantity and all picked SKU transactions are completed for a work day or customer-order wave, the WMS computer creates a minimum quantity for replenishment. The minimum replenishment SKU quantity is one reserve master carton, and is considered a low-priority SKU replenishment transaction because there is sufficient SKU inventory in a pick position for a next warehouse customer-order wave.

SKU Maximum Quantity

Maximum SKU replenishment quantity is based on the pick position quantity that ensures excellent pick position utilization with the fewest replenishment trips and is used with either the permanent pick position design or a pick design with few pick-line profile changes. Maximum pick position quantity holds a minimum inventory quantity plus one master carton. Note that this maximum SKU quantity is greater than one master carton because of a pick position capacity. Maximum replenishment quantity has a medium priority because the pick position inventory level has sufficient SKU to satisfy most of the next customer-order wave.

SKU Capacity Quantity

Capacity SKU replenishment quantity is the maximum SKU number that fits into a pick position. The situation is created when a pick position's SKU quantity reaches zero or an "out-of-stock" condition. The SKU quantity required for a pick position includes the pick position's capacity. Capacity replenishment to a pick position receives the highest priority because a pick position SKU quantity cannot satisfy customer orders or customer-order wave.

SKU Pick-Clean Quantity

A pick-clean SKU replenishment quantity is made to a pick position that serves as a pick position for a next customer-order wave SKU quantity or a pick design that uses a pick-line profile for each customer-order wave. The pick-clean SKU replenishment quantity is the exact SKU quantity that, based on customer orders, is required for a pick wave. As pickers complete SKU pick transactions, the SKU quantity is reduced by pick transactions. After picking the last wave or SKU quantity, the pick position SKU quantity will be zero. To ensure a vacant pick position, an employee completes a zero scan, which is sent to the WMS computer for position update. This approach ensures there is only one SKU in a position for a next customer-order wave. If there is a residual SKU quantity in a pick position, a replenishment employee completes a SKU move and zero scan, which relocates the residual SKU quantity to another pick position. With a pick-clean SKU replenishment, pick positions are replenished with a different SKU and quantity for another customer-order wave or next-day customer orders. A pick-clean activity allows an employee for next day/customer-order wave to profile an empty pick line, which increases hit concentration/hit density and enhances setup and picker productivity.

Pick-Line Setup and Replenishment Considerations

In a small-item pick design, a host computer receives customer-order SKU quantities and customer-order numbers from the WMS computer. After a warehouse establishes a customer-order wave, the WMS program allocates SKU quantity to be withdrawn from a storage position and transferred to a pick position. A SKU allocation program sends the total SKU withdrawal transactions to a customer-order wave. The storage and transport design handles SKU transfers as a pick-line setup or transaction. SKUs are transported from a storage area to a pick area. In a pick area, an employee places SKUs into pick positions. When a pick position is full, an employee ensures that allocated SKUs are withdrawn from a storage position and each SKU is placed into a pick position in a pick area. If a SKU is physically placed and scanned into a pick-area pick position, additional SKU quantity is placed into a ready-reserve position. As a picker completes customer orders, the pick activity depletes the SKU in a pick position. The WMS program then sends a SKU move transaction to move a SKU from a ready-reserve position to the pick position. The pick-line/pick aisle replenishment options are:

■ SKU setup or replenishment quantity that are all SKUs, capacity, or minimum or maximum
■ Setup or replenishment transports are two-wheel hand truck or four-wheel cart, powered forklift truck, nonpowered/powered pallet truck, or powered or nonpowered conveyor

■ Replenishment ready-reserve locations can be remote, directly behind each pick position, directly behind a pick position in a middle aisle, directly behind a pick position in a middle aisle off-set to one side, or above or below a pick position

Replenishment Master-Carton Label Printing

In a pick design with the WMS program and pick-line replenishment activity that uses less than a pallet or master-carton, each master-carton picked from a pallet requires an identification. Each master-carton is tracked by the WMS computer as it flows through the warehouse through identification updates from scanners/readers. At a pick station, an employee ensures there are sufficient identification labels available for a master-carton pick activity. To assist a picker with a master-carton label activity and help ensure an accurate pick transaction, a nonpowered roller or flat/solid surface is provided between a pallet and take-away conveyor. The label printing options are pre-printed labels or on-demand printed labels.

Preprinted Labels

The WMS computer-controlled printer prints the identification labels. At a central or remote print station, the WMS computer controls the label print sequence. After labels are printed (roll or sheet), they are placed in a master-carton pick location. At a master-carton pick station, following instructions for a customer-order wave or replenishment pick transaction displayed on a hand-held scan/read device or PC display screen, a picker removes an identification label from a preprinted label roll/sheet, removes a master carton from a pallet, and scans the move transaction. The scan data is sent to the WMS computer for update. To verify a picker has completed an accurate master-carton pick, a scanner/reader on a take-away conveyor reads each master-carton identification. The identification is sent to the WMS computer, which compares the actual master-carton quantity to suggested quantity. The comparison is performed periodically, and when the number does not match, the WMS computer suggests a count for SKU that was involved in the master-carton pick replenishment transaction.

Labels Printed on Demand

In this design, a master-carton pick station becomes a remote WMS identification label station. The WMS computer controls the label print sequence according to the label identification format. At a master-carton pick station, a hand-held or fixed position scanner/reader scans/reads a pallet identification and the printer prints labels for the suggested master-carton pick replenishment quantity. After the labels are printed (roll or sheet), a printed identification is printed on demand for a master-carton picker. At a master-carton pick station, a picker takes a label from a printed label roll/sheet, removes a master carton from a pallet, completes a master-carton or pallet scan. Scan data is sent to the WMS computer for update. To verify a picker has completed accurate master-carton pick, a scanner/reader on a take-away conveyor reads each master-carton identification. Each master-carton identification is sent to the WMS computer, which compares the actual quantity to the suggested master-carton pick quantity. The comparison is performed periodically, and when the number does not match, the WMS computer suggests a cycle count for SKU.

How to Control a Pick Position Replenishment

Each SKU pick position has a SKU replenishment activity. The replenishment activity has an employee or machine transfer a SKU quantity to a pick position. SKU replenishment concerns are when to send full pallets or partial pallets, how many full pallets to send, in a pick line how to handle overstock pallets. SKU pallet replenishment quantity considerations are:

- Send full or partial pallets;
- Send full pallets first and partial pallets second;
- Send pallets to match a pick approach and ready-reserve position capacity.

Sending Full or Partial Pallets

If pick positions have high-volume SKUs, the WMS computer allocates SKUs to complete customer orders. Pick-line pallet pick positions are two or four pallets deep with ready-reserve positions. All full and partial pallets are sent to a pick area. For replenishment activity, multiple SKUs with a large number of pallets are sent to a pick area. In the pick area, forklift truck drivers transfer pallets to a suggested pick position. After the first pallet is scanned and transferred to a pick position, the scan is sent to the WMS computer for updating, and the computer releases customer orders. Pallets in excess of the pick position number are placed in ready-reserve positions and, again, are scanned and the data is sent to the WMS computer for file update. This approach features:

- A large ready-reserve position number
- Additional forklift truck transactions
- Full and partial pallets randomly placed into pick positions

Sending Full Pallets, Followed by Partial Pallets

After the WMS computer has allocated SKUs to a pick line, the computer communicates with the warehouse computer for pallets required to complete customer-order wave. An AS/RS crane/forklift truck starts by bringing only full pallets to a pick line. In a pick area, a forklift truck driver scans a pallet to a pick position, and scans the position. If an allocated pallet quantity exceeds the pick position's capacity, additional full pallets are scanned and transferred to ready-reserve positions. (As always, scan data and SKU quantities are sent to the WMS computer for file update.) As a pallet is transferred from a ready-reserve position to pick area, the warehouse computer transfers a full pallet from a storage area to a pick area. In the pick area, the full pallet is scanned and placed into a ready-reserve position. After all full pallets are transferred to a pick area, partial pallets are transferred to a pick area. This approach features:

- Full pallets, with largest SKU quantity, are transferred to a pick area first
- Partial pallets, with smallest SKU quantity, are transferred to a pick area later
- Greater customer-order completion during pick activities, with the highest SKU quantity and the least handling of empty pallets
- Pick area ready-reserve positions are required

Sending Pallets to Match Pick Position Capacity

This approach differs from the preceding one in that after full pallets have been transferred to pick positions, as pallets are depleted by pick transactions, the warehouse computer transfers a full pallet from a storage area to the pick area. In the pick area, a full pallet is scanned and placed into a pick position. This approach features:

- Frequent pallet transfers in pick areas
- Onto time and accurate pallet replenishment transactions to a pick position, partial pallets with smallest SKU quantity are later transferred to a pick area
- No ready-reserve positions are needed

Withdrawing Partial and Full Pallets

If your warehouse has a non-FIFO partial and full pallet SKU quantity and completes a pick-line/aisle replenishment activity with a SKU quantity that equals or exceeds a full pallet quantity, the SKU allocation sequence options are either to first withdraw the partial pallet, then the full pallet or to first withdraw the full pallet and withdraw the second pallet as required.

Withdrawing a Partial Pallet First and a Full Pallet Second

With this option, to complete a move transaction a conventional or VNA forklift or AS/RS crane withdraws both a partial and a full pallet from a storage position. The two pallets are delivered to a transfer station or replenishment aisle, depending on the pick area design. In a standard WMS program, the SKU allocation sequence is based on the pallet received date: the oldest SKU is allocate first, regarding of whether the pallet is partial or full. In most warehouses, partial pallet is the most frequent occurrence. When a partial pallet arrives first at a transfer station, an employee completes a SKU move and either transfers master cartons to another pallet or places a label on each master carton for transfer to warehouse transport; or transfers the partial pallet to a temporary hold position. When a full pallet arrives at a transfer station, an employee either completes a SKU move and transfers master cartons from a full pallet to a temporary hold position or onto a partial pallet; or transfers each master carton to the in-house transport. This option features:

- The standard WMS program, with minimal computer calculations;
- FIFO SKU rotation;
- Partial pallets are withdrawn first;
- Two forklift or AS/RS crane withdrawal transactions;
- Two pallets on in-house transport;
- A transfer employee handles the greatest master-carton quantity;
- A transfer employees handles empty pallets;
- To return a partial pallet to a storage area requires additional transport activity and a forklift truck or AS/RS crane transaction

Withdrawing a Full Pallet; Withdrawing a Partial Pallet as Required

In this option, the WMS program determines the SKUs that require a full pallet quantity and matches the needed full pallet quantity to SKU pallet. In response to the needs of a customer-order wave, a full pallet is allocated and is withdrawn from a storage area. If a customer-order wave requires a partial pallet quantity, the WMS program allocates an existing partial pallet. The partial pallet is a last pallet withdrawn from a storage area and sent to a transfer station. At a transfer station or replenishment position, the full pallet is handled as described above. This approach features:

- A dynamic WMS program;
- Additional WMS computer processing time;
- Accurate pallet master-carton quantity;
- Only one forklift truck or AS/RS crane withdrawal transaction;
- Only one pallet on in-house transport;
- A replenishment employee handles a minimal number of empty pallets;
- There is no return pallet transport activity;
- There is no return pallet forklift truck or AS/RS crane put-away transaction

Master-Carton Robot Pick/Replenishment Activity

If your warehouse uses a pallet storage area and a master-carton conveyor network to supply master cartons to a pick line, robot pick activity should be considered by the design team. A robot pick design has the WMS program separate SKUs that require only a master-carton quantity from a pallet. Based on the customer-order wave SKU allocation, robot pick activity has the WMS program transfer SKU customer-order wave master-carton quantities and each SKU pallet ti and hi pattern to the warehouse robot machine computer. A forklift truck or AS/RS crane delivers partial or full pallets to a robot pick station in-feed conveyor. After a pallet is placed on a conveyor, a fixed position scanner/reader sends the pallet identification to the warehouse computer. Pallet travel on a conveyor is "first-on, first-off" basis and the SKU sequence is entered into the robot computer. When customer-order wave master-carton quantity and pallet ti and hi data is entered, a robot pick machine is ready to complete pick/replenishment activity. As a pallet arrives at a robot pick station, the pallet is stopped and a robot pick machine transfers a master-carton quantity from the pallet onto a carton conveyor. Each pick activity is sent to the warehouse computer as a complete pick transaction, and the SKU pallet quantity is reduced by one master carton. As a master carton travels on a conveyor, each master carton has a preapplied (or receives) an identification bar-code/ RF tag. Each master carton travels past a scanner/reader to ensure that the pick quantity matches the customer-order wave quantity. As a master carton is transferred to a pick position, scan transactions are updated in the WMS computer. The option features:

- Few employees;
- Exact SKU quantity;
- Machine-paced activity;
- With sufficient queue, pick can be performed 24/7;
- It handles a high number of SKUs;
- It handles a high volume of orders;
- It can be located on a mezzanine or elevated area

- It requires additional material handling equipment;
- It handles conveyable cartons;
- It requires accurate pallet ti and hi data;
- It requires some WMS program modifications;
- It requires additional WMS computer processing time

Pick-Position Replenishment Indicator

In a warehouse using ready-reserve positions and a WMS program, SKU transfer/replenishment to partially or completely depleted pick positions is a critical activity. Timely and accurate replenishment of a pick position ensures high picker and replenishment productivity, regular customer-order flow, and minimal "stock outs." In a dynamic pick design with ready-reserve racks and a WMS program, a timely and clearly understood replenishment notice/instruction is important for timely and accurate pick-position replenishment. The objective of a pick-position replenishment indicator is to identify a pick position that requires replenishment. The options for designing replenishment instructions are:

1. Visually determined replenishment
2. An employee hand-held scanner
3. A flashing light with scoreboard station

Replenishment Indicator: Employee

In this option, replenishment employees determine the pick position and SKU quantity for replenishment activity. In a high-volume pick line with many SKUs, a pick-line/aisle design requires a replenishment employee to look at each pick position. After determining a pick position's status, a replenishment employee determines SKU replenishment status and quantity. The replenishment employee completes the round-trip replenishment transaction, from pick-position replenishment side to a ready-reserve position and back to the pick position. For each replenishment transaction, an employee completes SKU and pick-position identification scan transactions and SKU quantity, which are sent to the WMS computer for update. The disadvantages to this approach are:

- SKU replenishment activity does not match pick activity
- The WMS program does not suggest SKU replenishment activity
- There is random SKU replenishment activity
- There may be slow SKU replenishment
- Employee-paced replenishment
- No priority SKU replenishment

The advantage is that this approach has no cost.

Replenishment Indicator: Hand-Held Scanner

In this option, prior to a pick activity, a SKU is setup in a pick position. If the setup quantity exceeds the pick position's capacity, additional SKU quantity is scanned and transferred to a ready-reserve position. SKU and ready-reserve position identifications and quantity are sent to the WMS computer for update. After the pick transaction, the pick-to-light design sends a pick transaction to the WMS computer. The computer depletes the pick position's SKU quantity from the position. When a predetermined or minimum SKU quantity is reached in a pick position, the WMS computer sends a notice to a replenishment employee's hand-held scanner. The scanner screen displays a pick position and SKU quantity and ready-reserve position for SKU replenishment. This approach features:

- On-time pick position replenishments
- Machine-paced replenishment activity
- Good replenishment employee productivity
- Replenishment activity transactions match withdrawal activity
- Hand-held scanner cost
- Good warehouse and WMS computer communication
- Use of the WMS computer program
- accurate and on-time SKU replenishments

Replenishment Indicator: Flashing Light with a Scoreboard

In this option, prior to pick activity, if SKU setup quantity exceeds a pick position's capacity, an additional SKU quantity is scanned and transferred to a ready-reserve position. After a customer order pick transaction, the pick-to-light design sends a SKU pick transaction to the WMS computer. The computer depletes the pick position quantity. At a predetermined or minimum SKU quantity, the WMS computer sends a notice to a replenishment area scoreboard. A flashing light on the score board displays the pick position, the ready-reserve position, and SKU quantity for a replenishment transaction. An employee or printer prints the replenishment data. Features of this option are:

- Timely pick-position replenishments
- Machine-paced replenishment activity
- Prioritized SKU replenishment activity that matches pick activity
- The additional cost of the scoreboard
- Warehouse and WMS computer communication
- WMS computer program
- Employee to write with pencil/paper

Pick Position Identification Replenishment Location

This option permits a replenishment employee to complete a SKU transfer from the in-house transport to a pick position. After the completion of a replenishment activity, to communicate the transaction, an employee scans the SKU and pick position identifications and sends the scan data to the WMS computer (or the warehouse AS/RS crane computer sends a message to the WMS computer), the computer updates the SKU identification and pick position status, and releases customer orders to a pick line/pick aisle.

Replenishment: Conveyor Considerations

In a pick design with the WMS program, SKUs are profiled to specific pick positions or a specific pick zone. Pick positions are serviced by a conveyor with divert devices that transfer master cartons from a main conveyor onto a pick-zone replenishment conveyor. A replenishment conveyor ensures that a master carton arrives at a pick position's replenishment side with a master-carton identification facing a replenishment employee. An employee or AS/RS crane then completes the replenishment transaction, following which master-carton and pick position identifications and SKU quantities are sent to the WMS computer, which, in turn, releases customer orders. Replenishment conveyor options are:

1. A short conveyor travel path
2. A long conveyor travel path
3. A powered queue conveyor
4. A nonpowered conveyor
5. From a main conveyor divert location to a replenishment zone, master carton forward travel direction is from high-pick volume SKU zone first pick position
6. From a main conveyor divert location to a replenishment zone, master carton reverse travel direction is toward a high-pick volume SKU zone first pick position

Replenishment: Order Fulfillment Considerations

Each pick design for an order fulfillment operation has unique pick position replenishment characteristics, pick position identified locations, and pick employee or machine activities. Pick position replenishment designs may be manual, mechanized, or automatic.

Manual/Carton AS/RS Crane Replenishment to a Pick Position

In this option, an employee with a hand-held scanner/reader or carton AS/RS crane complete a SKU replenishment and scan transaction to a manual pick position. A paper replenishment document is a back-up system. Manual pick position classifications are:

1. Standard employee replenishment transaction to a position with a separate replenishment and pick aisles and positions
2. Employee transaction to a pick and replenishment position that is the same location
3. AS/RS crane replenishment transactions to a pick position that has separate replenishment and pick aisles and positions

Pick Position with the Same Replenishment Position

A pick position with the same replenishment and pick position means that the replenishment and pick positions face one aisle.

Pick Position with Separate Replenishment Position

If a pick position has different replenishment and pick positions, SKU replenishment activities are made from a separate replenishment aisle whereas picks are made from a pick aisle. An employee, employee-controlled forklift truck, or carton AS/RS crane travels to a pick position to complete a replenishment transaction, whereas a picker or forklift truck travels to a pick position in a pick aisle to complete a pick transaction. With an AS/RS crane replenishment design, an AS/RS crane completes a pallet/carton/tote transfer to a pick position and sends a message to the WMS computer.

Replenishment to a Mechanized Pick Design

In this option, an employee uses a hand-held bar scanner/reader to complete a replenishment transaction and scan to a mechanized pick position. In mechanized pick designs, replenishment locations can be the same as the pick position, or it can use separate replenishment and pick positions. Pick designs can be powered small-item horizontal or vertical carousels, or an S.I. Cartrac. The separate position designs can be a Decombi, pick car, or loose SKU or master-carton pick to conveyor belt.

Replenishment to an Automatic Pick Design

In this approach, an employee with a hand-held scanner/reader completes, or an AS/RS crane completes a SKU replenishment to a pick position. A hand-held scanner/reader or warehouse AS/RS crane computer sends a transaction message to the WMS computer. After a replenishment is made to a pick position, and updated in the WMS computer, the WMS computer releases customer orders to an automatic pick machine. Automatic pick machine designs can be S. I. Itematic, Robo pic, "A" or "H" frame, and carton/pallet AS/RS crane.

Withdrawal and Delivery to Pick Position

After customer orders and associated SKU quantities are processed by the warehouse computer, the computer transfers customer-order data to the WMS computer. The WMS computer transfers customer orders and associated SKU volumes to the section in which the warehouse staff creates customer-order waves. The WMS program then creates or allocates master-carton, small items in totes, or pallet SKUs to complete the customer-order wave SKU quantity. Each SKU quantity is downloaded to a forklift truck or AS/RS cranes as move transactions, and each SKU is withdrawn from a storage position and transferred to a pick position or fast-pack station/drop point. The withdrawal and delivery options can be in a predetermined or random sequence.

Predetermined SKU Release

In a predetermined SKU withdrawal and delivery, an employee, forklift truck, or AS/RS crane withdraws SKU in accordance with the WMS program allocation. The strategy is to allocate a SKU for the first pick-line/aisle pick position, the second allocation is a SKU for a pick-line/aisle pick position. The strategy is repeated and completed for each SKU in a customer-order wave.

In a forklift-truck warehouse, after a truck completes a withdrawal transaction from a storage position, an employee or forklift truck travels from the storage area to a pick area. In a pick area, an employee or forklift truck driver transfers and scans the SKU to a pick position.

In warehouse designed with an AS/RS crane, a crane completes a withdrawal transaction from a storage position, which is communicated from the crane computer to the WMS computer. The crane discharges the SKU onto a powered transport on a "first arrive, first delivered" approach. Prior to the SKU's travel on a main conveyor, transport vehicle, or mobile forklift truck travel path, the WMS program releases a pick-area profile sequence to the warehouse computer. The computer controls the transport and pick-area divert device ensures that the SKU matches a predetermined SKU release sequence. As SKUs travel on the in-house transport, each WMS identification travels past a scanner/reader, and onto a recirculation travel path or pick line/aisle. The transport scanner/reader scans/reads the SKU identification and activates a divert device to transfer the SKU to a pick-line/aisle area. The identification transfer sequence ensures that SKUs are matched to a pick-line/aisle profile or pick position.

When a SKU arrives at a pick-line/aisle transfer station, an employee or forklift truck driver with a scanner/reader scans and transfers the SKU to an assigned pick position. After the first SKU is transferred to a pick line/aisle, an employee, forklift truck, or AS/RS crane transfers a second SKU into a second pick position. The scan transaction and SKU quantity are sent to the WMS computer for inventory file update and customer-order release. If a pick line/aisle is profiled by customer-order SKU volume, as a first SKU is placed on a pick line/aisle, pick position and SKU identification are scanned and SKU quantity are sent to a WMS computer for a pick line/aisle early setup to handle customer-order wave.

Random Identification Release Sequence

In a random transfer to a pick line/aisle, a forklift truck or AS/RS crane place SKU master cartons/pallets onto in-house transport on a "first arrive, first delivered." As a SKU travels on in-house transport, each identification travels past a scanner/reader. Depending on travel path status, a SKU is directed to recirculate or diverted onto a pick-line/aisle divert spur. A transport scanner/reader reads the identification and the warehouse computer activates a divert device to transfer the SKU from a main travel path onto a pick-line/aisle spur on a "first arrive, first diverted" approach. A SKU divert/transfer sequence does not match a pick-line profile or setup.

When a SKU arrives a pick-line/aisle transfer station, an employee or forklift truck driver with a hand-held scanner/reader ensures that the SKU is transferred to a pick position. After the first SKU is transferred to a pick-line/aisle position, an employee, forklift truck, or AS/RS crane transfers a second SKU into a pick position. Again, a pick-line/aisle setup does not match a pick-line/aisle profile.

Pick Position Allocation/Profile for a Demand-Pull Inventory Flow

The objectives of a small-item pick warehouse are to complete a customer-order delivery cycle in minimum time and at the lowest possible cost. Warehouse pick objectives translate that into completing customer-order delivery cycles within 24 to 48 hours from receipt of the order. With a high number of customer orders, a large SKU and customer-order mix, and required host computer, WMS program, and warehouse computer processing time, it is necessary to have a warm pick/pack activity start and increase the rate. The question facing a warehouse manager is how to have a warm start-up of pick/pack activity and have customer orders completed in standard customer service time. Most catalog, e-mail, direct marketing, and television marketing company pick designs have a demand-pull inventory flow and dual pick lines/aisles with SKU numbers profiled in same or different pick positions. A pick-line/aisle SKU allocation to a position options are:

- SKU in a fixed pick position and complete SKU replenishment transactions from a storage area to a pick position
- Daily or periodic setup or allocated SKU to a pick position

SKU Allocation to a Fixed Position

A SKU profile to a pick position is based on historical sales volume, estimated sales, or customer-order allocation philosophy. As completed customer orders deplete a pick position's SKU quantity, the WMS program directs the warehouse to complete a replenishment transaction from a storage position to a fixed SKU pick position. With high-demand or customer-order pull inventory flow and large SKU number, a pick line is long or has a large area for good replenishment and picker productivity. A pick-line profile by SKU movement or budgeted picker rate ensures high SKU hit density and concentration. The advantages to this approach are:

1. It is easy to implement.
2. SKUs are in a pick position for pick/pack activity warm start-up.
3. Requires a replenishment activity.
4. Minimal setup time.

SKU Allocation by Daily/Periodic Pick-Line/Aisle Setup

If the business has a daily customer-order demand pull, limited number of SKUs, high customer-order number, and wide SKU mix, each day the pick positions are setup with new SKUs. After the warehouse computer transfers customer-order information to the WMS computer, and it creates a customer-order wave, the computer allocates SKUs and transfers SKU information to the warehouse computer. The warehouse computer directs a forklift truck or AS/RS crane to transfer SKUs from a storage position to a pick position. As the SKU is transferred to a pick position, an employee scans the SKU and pick-position identifications and enters the SKU quantity into a hand-held scanner/reader. To have shortest time and travel distance from a storage area, the employee transfers the SKU into a pick position. The design options are a setup pick line/aisle each customer-order wave or customer orders, or a setup pick line for the next-day customer orders.

SKU Allocation or Pick-Line/Aisle Setup Each Day

In this method, the SKU pick-line/aisle setup for each customer-order wave receives a SKU quantity required for a customer-order wave. The warehouse computer receives each SKU quantity for each customer-order wave. From the pick-line/aisle setup list, the in-house transport moves SKUs to a pick-line/aisle replenishment aisle. On the replenishment side of the aisle, an employee scans/reads each SKU and pick-position identification and associated SKU quantity, and sends the data to the WMS computer. If a SKU quantity is greater than a pick position's capacity, each overflow SKU is scanned and transferred to a ready-reserve position. All scans are sent to the

WMS computer to update inventory files, and the computer releases customer orders. During pick activity, the WMS computer creates SKU move transaction from a ready-reserve position to a pick position.

In a typical pick design, customer orders have 500-700 SKUs per day, 100 full pallets, and 1,000-2,000 master cartons. To maintain a customer-service standard, pick-position replenishment transactions are completed within a two-hour pick-line/aisle setup time. To achieve active pick/pack activity within two hours, a warehouse pick-line setup activity starts two to three hours before the pick-line/aisle start hour with forklift truck drivers, transport, AS/RS crane, master-carton replenishment employee number, and activities are completed on schedule.

SKU Allocation or Pick-Line/Aisle Setup for the Next Day

A SKU pick-line/aisle setup for a customer-order wave has two pick lines/aisles. In other words, pick-line/aisle 1 is setup for customer-order wave 1 and pick-line/aisle 2 customer-order wave 2. To setup a pick-line/aisle 2 on day 1, a pick design anticipates customer-order wave 2 and SKUs. The estimate is based either on projected sales of each SKU (from the sales department) or on actual sales at predetermined times and historical percentage for sales (from customer-order or the IT department). Based on estimated SKU sales on a pick line, to assure maximum completed customer orders, a pick line/aisle profile employee estimates each SKU quantity that is required to meet a pick concept the first two to four hours of a pick/pack activity. The calculations are rounded-up to full pallets or master cartons. With a warehouse project customer-order wave for SKUs, the WMS computer directs the warehouse to move a SKU quantity from a storage position to a pick position on pick line/aisle 2.

Prior to the end of a customer-order wave, the warehouse withdraws master cartons and pallets from storage positions and moves SKUs via in-house transport to a pick line/aisle. In a pick-line/aisle replenishment area, a replenishment employee completes a SKU scan and replenishment transfer to a pick position. In WMS inventory status files, SKUs quantities in pick positions means that a SKU has been allocated to complete a customer-order wave.

With SKUs quantities in pick positions and WMS inventory files, customer-order wave 1 is being completed on pick line/aisle 1 and pick line/aisle 2 has vacant pick positions. Prior to customer-order wave 2, the warehouse computer completes a SKU move transaction from a storage position to a pick position in pick line/aisle 2. As the WMS computer determines the necessary SKU quantity for customer orders, the WMS computer sends a SKU quantity to a warehouse computer. From the total SKU quantity, the WMS computer accounts for the SKU quantity in a pick position and the remaining SKU needed to complete customer orders is allocated from storage positions. Prior to a pick-line start-up, the warehouse computer transfers SKUs from a storage position to a pick position or ready-reserve position. SKU, storage position identifications, and SKU quantity are sent to the WMS computer. The WMS computer updates SKU, pick position, and quantity and releases customer orders to a pick line/aisle. This approach features are:

- Warm pick/pack activity start
- The WMS computer allocates and creates additional move transactions for SKUs required to complete customer-order wave 2
- During day 2, all customer orders are completed
- During day 2, pick line/aisle 1 is prepared for customer-order wave 3

Pick-Line/Pick Aisle Setup or Replenishment Master-Carton Piece Quantity

In a pick design with a high-volume and paperless pick line/aisle with another pick area for slow moving SKUs, the WMS program allocates SKUs for a customer-order wave and the warehouse computer moves SKUs from a storage position to a pick position. The options for SKU allocation to a high-volume paperless pick-line are:

1. round up to a full master carton
2. round down to a full master carton

Round Up to Full Master Cartons

After the warehouse computer sends the customer-order SKU volume to the WMS computer, if the WMS computer rounds up to a full master carton, the computer allocates customer-order SKUs as full master cartons from a storage position to a pick area. For each SKU, the WMS computer rounds-up all customer-order SKUs to a full master carton. For example, if a master carton holds 24 SKUs and the customer-order SKU quantity is 20, the WMS program allocates one full master carton from a storage position or as a master carton from a pallet. Each master carton SKU is scanned and transferred to a pick position. At the end of a customer-order wave (all customer orders 20 SKUs are picked), there is residual SKU quantity (4) in a paperless pick position. The options for dealing with residual quantity in a customer-order wave 2 pick position are to remain in an existing pick position or transfer the residual quantity from a high-volume pick position to a slow moving pick position.

The features of this option are:

■ Additional picks in a high-volume pick area that has higher picker productivity
■ Fewer customer order picks in a slow-moving pick area that has lower picker productivity
■ One master-carton transfer from a storage area to a pick area
■ Residual inventory in a paperless pick area that has the potential for low-pick volume or additional move transactions to a low-volume pick concept

Round Down to a Full Master Carton

After the warehouse computer sends the customer order SKU volume to the WMS computer, if the computer rounds down to a full master-carton, the computer allocates customer-order SKUs from a storage position to a pick area. For each SKU, the WMS computer rounds down all customer order SKUs to a full master carton. For example, if a master carton holds 24 SKUs and customer order SKU quantity is 44, the WMS program allocates two complete master cartons from a pallet in a storage position and each master carton receives a WMS identification. The replenishment employee completes the necessary SKU move transactions that are sent to the WMS computer. One master carton is transported to high-volume pick line/aisle, scanned, and transferred to a pick position. The second master carton is sent to slow-moving pick position. At the end of a customer order wave, (all 44 SKUs are picked), there is a SKU quantity of 0 in a pick position. A residual SKU quantity remains in a slow-moving pick position for the next customer order wave.

This approach has the following features:

- 24 picks in a high-volume or paperless pick area that has a higher picker productivity
- 20 picks in a slow-moving pick area that has lower picker productivity
- Master-carton transfer from a storage area to a high-volume pick area and slow-moving pick area
- Residual inventory in a slow-moving pick area
- WMS program processing time to allocate two master cartons
- Additional warehouse controls to ensure proper master-carton transfer to an assigned pick area

SKU Replenishment Timing Methods

The objectives of pick-position replenishment activity are:

1. Best performed at the moment that a pick position becomes depleted.
2. Replenished with a SKU quantity that maximizes pick-position space and optimizes transport trips between a storage area and the pick position.
3. Before a customer order arrives at a pick position.

To achieve these objectives, all SKU pick-position replenishment transactions are made by the WMS computer, which determines the SKU quantity, which is based on the customer order.

The next major replenishment activity is to determine an appropriate time for a pick-position replenishment transaction to occur. SKU replenishment transaction control or time options can be manually controlled or computer controlled.

Manually Controlled Replenishment Timing

A manually controlled replenishment transaction design relies upon an employee to determine the time at which a SKU quantity should be moved from a storage position to a pick position. This approach is based upon employee experience and is not sequenced with pick activities. The replenishment transaction is made to a partially depleted pick position in which a replenishment employee wastes time transferring the remaining SKU to a pick position. The disadvantages of this approach are no employee activity control, low employee productivity, poor pick position utilization, and no coordination with a pick activity. The advantages are low cost and no need for employee training.

Computer-Controlled Replenishment Timing

With computer-controlled replenishment, the WMS computer directs (via paper document or RF terminal) an employee to perform a replenishment transaction between a storage or ready-reserve position and pick position. The factors are customer order SKU quantity and SKU quantity in a pick position. The options are:

1. A replenishment paper document lists all replenishment transactions that are to occur during an employee shift by priority. On the document, SKUs are listed in sequential customer order based on the anticipated time that a pick position will become depleted. SKUs are identified by SKU number and description. The first column lists a SKU storage position; the second column is for a replenishment employee mark. An employee mark indicates and verifies that a storage location, withdrawal transaction portion, and placement at a drop point was completed on schedule. The third column lists a pick position; the fourth column is for a replenishment employee mark to verify replenishment to a pick position. The paper document is not preferred for use in a dynamic pick design.

2. In a design using an RF device or terminal, an employee completes a replenishment transaction to each pick position with a hand-held, wrist, or finger scanner/reader. The scanner/reader scans/reads pick position bar-code/RF tag, and an RF device or terminal display screen shows SKU replenishment quantity and storage position. After each replenishment transaction, an employee scans/reads a pick position and SKU identification bar-code labels/RF tags. The scanning/reading verifies the completion of a replenishment transaction, and the verification is sent to the WMS computer for inventory update. Advantages are accurate activity records, excellent employee productivity, reduction in lost inventory, improved space utilization, and on-line/delayed transaction transmission.

Warehouse Ready-Reserve Design Considerations

A critical aspect of replenishment activity is the short time period in which the SKU is made ready and prepared for transfer into a pick position. A small-item pick area's design characteristics are:

- It handles a large number of SKUs with different physical characteristics and replenishments, which range from a single SKU to many SKUs.
- It covers a large area with many aisles and pick positions, occurs simultaneously with pick transactions, and, in some warehouses, it occurs in a pick aisle with pickers in an aisle or replenishment aisle.
- It is a dynamic activity performed by several employees.

To optimize pick position replenishment functions, a pick design includes ready-reserve positions adjacent or behind the pick position. Ready-reserve rack rows and aisles are arranged parallel or perpendicular to a pick area; the ready-reserve aisle may be short or long in length. To ensure accurate and timely replenishment, the pick area design should alllow sufficient aisle space to perform replenishments. If a pick area has been designed for extremely fast moving SKUs, ready-reserve positions are placed in the pick area's replenishment aisle.

To minimize replenishment problems, a pick area is designed to ensure that the correct SKU replenishment quantities are transferred at the correct time. The purpose of ready-reserve position is to provide a position between storage and pick positions. Because storage and transport has already been completed, the ready-reserve position greatly enchances the likelihood of fast, accurate, and timely replenishment to a pick position. Ready-reserve designs are:

- Shelves or decked racks with a pallet or forklift truck
- Shelves or decked racks with HROS vehicle
- Multiple carousels

- Carton AS/RS crane
- Pallet AS/RS crane with a container handling device

Common characteristics of replenishment designs are:

- The WMS computer that determines replenishment SKU, associated quantity and withdrawal from a storage position.
- The transport design ensures timely and accurate SKU delivery from a storage area to a pick area and from a replenishment position to a pick position.
- The use of identifications on both replenishment and pick positions.

Ready-Reserve Locations in a Replenishment Aisle

In a high-volume pick design, ready-reserve position in a replenishment aisle is an important design factor. A ready-reserve position provides a temporary holding position for SKU inventory quantity that did not fit into a pick position. A ready-reserve rack position ensures unobstructed access to extra inventory, permits warehouse and WMS computer inventory tracking, and easy and quick SKU transfer to a pick position. Ready-reserve position's factors are:

- Reserve position can be a pallet or master carton hand-stack position type
- SKU number and associated inventory quantity
- Building or free-standing mezzanine column locations
- Storage vehicle and transport equipment type

Ready-reserve rack position's options are pallet or decked-rack position for hand-stack master cartons/totes. Ready-reserve rack layout options are:

- Back-to-back rack rows in a replenishment aisle middle
- Single-rack row in a replenishment aisle middle
- Single-rack row offset in a replenishment aisle
- Wire meshed decks on flow-rack top

Carton AS/RS

A carton AS/RS design has a computer-controlled captive aisle stacker crane that travels between two shelves or flow-rack pick position rows or between a pick position row and a ready-reserve position row. In each shelf or position is a tote/carton/tray that contains a SKU. Shelf positions are ready-reserve positions. Following the WMS computer allocation (or transfer to the AS/RS warehouse computer), an AS/RS stacker crane is directed to complete a SKU withdrawal transaction. After a stacker crane receives a withdrawal transaction, it travels to an assigned aisle position and takes a master carton on board. An AS/RS crane end of aisle delivery and transfer options are

- With an AS/RS captive storage aisle crane. After a withdrawn SKU is placed onto an outbound P/D station, an AS/RS crane with dual cycle command activities from an inbound P/D station takes on board an in-bound master carton and travels direct to a storage position.

From a P/D station a SKU is delivered by a conveyor or four-wheel cart to a replenishment aisle and into a pick position.

■ Captive replenishment aisle AS/RS crane. An AS/RS crane receives a master carton from a storage position and transfers a master carton from a AS/RS crane into a pick position or completes a replenishment transaction. With ready-reserve positions on an AS/RS crane aisle's other side, master-carton replenishment from a ready-reserve position is completed with minimal time. The features are fast and accurate replenishment, good quality non-open master cartons with bottoms for travel over a conveyor, safety screen travel aisles, and some AS/RS crane carriers require open master cartons on a tray or in a tote.

Carton Flow-Rack Pick Positions Replenishment with a Carton AS/RS Crane

In a dynamic pick design that uses a pick-to-light approach with carton flow rack as a pick position, timely and accurate replenishment to a pick position affects a warehouse's ability to provide prompt and accurate customer-order picks at low handling cost. The carton flow-rack pick option has (see Figure 7.3):

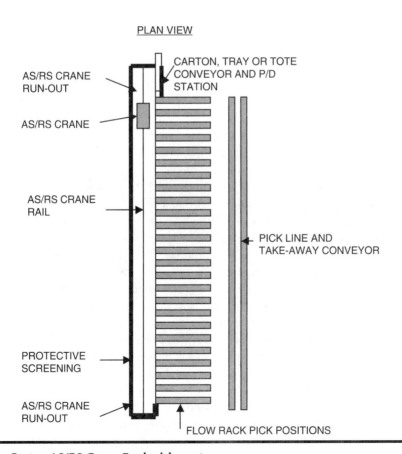

Figure 7.3   Carton AS/RS Crane Replenishment

■ Carton flow-rack bays with tote/carton flow lanes. Carton flow lanes are pick positions that face a pick aisle. After a carton/tote is placed into a carton flow-rack replenishment side, the carton/tote moves over a conveyor by gravity force to a flow-rack pick side.
■ Two aisles as part of a flow-rack pick design. In a pick aisle, a picker transfers SKUs from a pick position into a customer-order carton/tote and replenishment aisle. In the replenishment aisle, cartons/totes are transferred from a storage position to a pick position.

If the warehouse uses a WMS program and the facility is designed with an AS/RS crane aisle between carton flow-rack replenishment side and storage positions, or has two carton flow-rack replenishment sides, one option is to have an AS/RS crane perform all carton replenishment transactions. This option has:

■ An area for vendor master carton open activity. After the master open activity, SKUs remain in a master carton or SKUs are transferred from a master carton into a captive tote. The option is determined by the AS/RS crane type, its ability to handle open master cartons and master carton quality.
■ Tote conveyor travel path design
■ Empty master-carton or trash-conveyor travel path design
■ Crane P/D station
■ A single stacker crane aisle behind a carton flow-rack row and storage positions or a stacker crane between two carton flow-rack replenishment sides
■ In a pick area, an empty tote return conveyor system that uses the tote as a pick container

After the WMS computer allocates customer-order wave SKUs for a carton flow-rack pick position, the WMS computer sends SKU move transactions to the storage area computer. Master cartons are withdrawn and transported from a storage area to a SKU transfer area/master-carton open station. As each SKU bar-code is scanned/read, the transfer quantity is indicated at a work station. As an empty captive tote arrives at a work station, an employee moves a SKU quantity into a tote. All empty poor quality vendor master cartons are transferred to a trash transport. Residual SKU quantity is returned to a storage area in totes, which are transferred into a tote for storage. At a work station, a tote WMS identification is tied to a SKU. Full totes are placed on a conveyor, travel past a scanner/reader, to an assigned crane P/D station. Depending on warehouse storage area design, additional tote storage positions may be above carton flow racks.

After a tote/master carton arrives at the appropriate P/D station, each warehouse tote/master carton travels past a scanner/reader to an AS/RS crane pick-up station. The scanner/reader sends carton/tote information to the warehouse computer that controls AS/RS crane activities. At a P/D station, an AS/RS crane picks up a carton/tote and travels to a replenishment position. At the replenishment position, the crane transfers the tote/carton onto a carton flow lane. The tote/master carton flows over a conveyor from the flow-rack replenishment side to a pick side.

During a pick activity, as a tote/carton becomes depleted, a picker transfers the empty tote/carton to an empty tote conveyor or staging location, or an empty vendor master carton is transferred onto an in-house transport to a start/first pick position for the next customer order or onto a trash conveyor. The conveyor moves the empty tote from a pick aisle to an open station. If a vendor or master carton is used in the pick design, an empty vendor carton is transferred from a pick position to a start/first pick position for the next customer order. If cartons are not reused, they are placed onto the trash transport.

With an AS/RS crane replenishment approach, a carton flow-lane SKU quantity is picked clean. If there are SKUs or warehouse totes in carton flow-rack pick positions, the master cartons/totes are sent from a pick area to a storage area. This approach features:

- Few replenishment employees
- Small replenishment aisles
- Replenishment activity controlled by the WMS computer
- Minimal hang-ups in carton flow lanes with plastic totes or high quality cartons
- Master carton open area
- Each tote has a human/bar/RF tag symbology
- Trash consolidation area
- The AS/RS crane handles open cartons
- There is additional cost
- Increased storage space utilization
- Improved accuracy and on-time replenishment
- Reduced employee injury and equipment and SKU damage
- Improved security
- Operates 24/7

AS/RS Crane with a Multi-Carton/Tote-Handling Device

This design uses a warehouse-computer–controlled AS/RS crane with a carrier that handles up to six totes, two storage position rows, a P/D SKU transfer station, and a tote conveyor. After an AS/RS computer receives replenishment commands from the WMS computer, the warehouse computer directs an AS/RS crane to travel to a storage position. At the storage position, the crane carrier takes a tote/carton on board. An AS/RS crane with a multiple carrier device and multiple transactions per aisle travels to each position and picks up an additional tote/carton. With a full carrier (or the completion of the tote/carton withdrawal transaction), the crane travels to a P/D station. At the P/D station, the crane carrier transfers all totes/cartons onto a conveyor and picks up in-bound totes/cartons.

A multi-tote/carton AS/RS crane features are few employees, capital investment, increased storage space utilization, use of a standard tote, good quality carton/tray, improved accuracy and on-time replenishment, reduced employee injury and equipment and SKU damage, improved security, carton/tote uses a human/bar-code/RF tag symbology, good quality master carton, a metal or hardened plastic tote/tray, a properly designed conveyor, and it operates 24/7.

Pallet VNA Forklift Truck or AS/RS Crane Replenishment to a Pick Position

To have a VNA forklift truck or AS/RS crane complete pallet replenishment transactions to a pick position, the storage and pick areas have a unique design. The design options are:

1. Along a storage area side, a VNA forklift truck or AS/RS crane has its own aisle between two rack rows. One rack row has employee pick positions and other elevated positions. In the rack row have protective netting above the human pick aisle. Each pick position has one side facing a human master-carton pick aisle, and the other side faccing the forklift or AS/RS crane aisle. Each pick position has specially designed pallet transfer doors for pallet placement into a pick position. The transfer door options are a) bi-parting doors that are pushed open by a pallet and protect side entry to a pallet position. If a position has no pallet, bi-parting doors are closed to create a barrier at a pallet position.
2. Along a storage area front, the AS/RS crane has a powered conveyor or transport vehicle that transfers pallets to pallet flow lanes (see Figures 7.4 and 7.5).

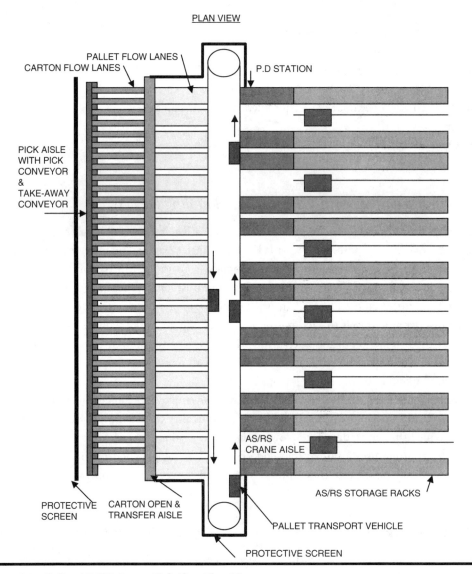

Figure 7.4   Pallet AR/RS Crane Pick Line Plan View

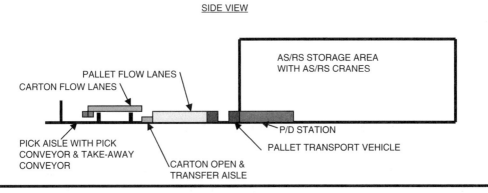

SIDE VIEW

Figure 7.5 Pallet AR/RS Crane Pick Line Side View

Along a storage area front side are pick positions that are replenished by a VNA forklift truck and AS/RS crane. A warehouse computer directs an employee-controlled forklift truck or warehouse-computer–controlled crane to withdraw a pallet from a storage position and move the pallet to a suggested pick position. A pick position is a two-deep pallet flow lane. Each pick position has two identical WMS identifications. One identification faces the forklift truck aisle; the second identification faces the human pick aisle.

With the VNA forklift truck design, a VNA forklift truck driver places a pallet in a pick position. As the truck's forks moves the pallet into a position, the driver activates a power safety door to open—or has a pallet move against bi-parting doors—to allow the pallet to be transferred to the pick position. The driver scans both WMS identifications. The scan transactions are sent to the WMS computer for pallet and pick-position update, and the WMS computer releases customer orders.

With an AS/RS crane design, a pallet moves over a pallet travel path to an assigned aisle. With the pallet on-board, the crane moves to a computer-assigned pick position. At the pick position, the warehouse computer activates a power safety door to open—or has a pallet move against bi-parting doors—to allow the pallet to be transferred to the pick position. The crane updates the WMS computer to update SKU and position files, and the WMS computer releases customer orders.

In a storage area front, which is either on the ground level or an elevated level, there are pallet flow lanes between a powered pallet conveyor or transport vehicle travel path and a human pick aisle. After an AS/RS crane transfers a pallet onto the conveyor travel path or computer-controlled transport vehicle, the pallet is transferred to a pallet flow lane. With a powered conveyor design, each pallet flow lane has a scanner/reader that sends a pallet identification to the WMS computer. With a computer-controlled transport vehicle, the computer sends a pallet update to the WMS computer. With either design, at a pallet flow lane charge end the warehouse computer opens a power safety door—or has a pallet move against bi-parting doors—to allow a pallet to be transferred to a pick position. Again, following the update, the WMS computer releases customer orders.

VNA forklift truck and AS/RS crane replenishments are designed for high-volume master-carton SKUs. Because all designs have a two-deep pallet pick position, each picked master carton receives a WMS identification and the master carton travels past a scanner/reader that sends a scan transaction to the WMS computer, which updates the pick-position master-carton pick quantity. When a pallet is depleted to a specific quantity, the WMS computer sends a move transaction to the warehouse computer, which directs a VNA forklift truck or AS/RS crane to repeat the replenishment transaction. The features are:

- High cost
- Accurate and timely replenishments
- Minimal or no labor
- With an AS/RS crane, a pick line is set up prior to pick activity
- Improved inventory control

SKU Replenishment Transaction Verification

SKU replenishment transaction verification ensures that the correct SKU quantity was transferred at a correct time from a storage position to an assigned pick position. Pick position replenishment transaction verification options are a) delayed update, b) on-line update, c) manual documentation, and d) automatic transfer.

Replenishment Transaction: Delayed Update

A delayed SKU replenishment transaction verification update has an employee complete a pick-position replenishment scan prior to the WMS computer update. All pick-position replenishment transactions and physical inventory relocations are completed and the WMS computer inventory file entry is made at a later time. Delayed replenishment transaction verification is used in a facility with a problem with on-line data transfer from remote RF devices, or the WMS computer has difficulty receiving/accepting multiple data transfers. In this design, a replenishment transaction is recorded in the warehouse computer or is marked on a document. The disadvantage is that a second transaction must be scheduled for an inventory quantity that has been reduced by a previous transaction. The advantage is that it minimizes the host computer investment and on-line communication network cost.

Replenishment Transaction: On-Line Update

An on-line update verification SKU file inventory adjustments are used when:

1. A storage position SKU quantity is depleted. The depletion/withdrawal is entered in the WMS inventory file as a SKU that has been transferred from a storage position.
2. A SKU is transferred from a warehouse transport to a pick position. During the transfer the SKU quantity is in a nonpick location. The design has an efficient, on-time, and accurate transport, SKU transfer to a pick position, and accurate and fast communication from the warehouse activity location (by a hand-held RF device) to the WMS computer. The design ensures on-time customer service and minimizes stock outs. The disadvantages are that the host computer has a large capacity and handles a large number of transactions and communication network costs. The advantages are accurate and on-time transactions and fewer update errors.

Automatic or RF SKU Replenishment Device Transfer

Automatic SKU replenishment transaction verification uses a bar-code scanning/RF tag reading and RF device communication device. The components are:

1. A replenishment transaction format that is a human/machine-readable label on each carton/warehouse tote and on each storage/pick position.
2. A hand-held, wrist, or finger bar-code scanning/RF tag reading device with a visual display terminal and a memory capacity in a scanner/reader device with RF communication network. An RF-data transfer design uses a transmission terminal with an antenna attached to a vehicle or to an employee and a storage/pick area with several receiving devices and a communication network attached to the WMS computer.

The considerations for installing such a design are:

1. The RF device must be attached to a forklift truck or employee.
2. What is the power source for a RF device and does the warehouse have spare batteries and RF devices?
3. Using an RF wave in a geographic area frequently requires government approval for a band or wave.
4. How many RF receivers will be needed? And at what locations?
5. The WMS computer will handle all transactions.
6. What are the installation costs for the facility? What are the ceiling and metal rack heights? Will these items affect the performance?
7. What are SKU replenishment storage, pick position, manifest, or other transactions per minute?

SKU Replenishment/Pick Position Identification

In a warehouse with a WMS program, the method that is used to identify a replenishment position and pick position has a direct impact on replenishment and picker transaction productivity and accuracy. A pick and replenishment position has a discreet identification that appears on a SKU pick-position charge and discharge structural support members. A hand-held scanner/reader easily reads a pick-position identification.

Replenishment or Pick-Position Identifications

A pick and replenishment position identification options:

1. Human-readable alpha characters and numeric digits may be used in any storage or pick concept. This is the basic method. In a dynamic pick design, a human-readable pick-position design is not preferred.
2. Human-readable alpha characters and numeric digits with a bar-code label/RF tag label is used to identify a pick and replenishment position in a fixed pick-position facility with a RD device. The pick-position identification design is referred to as a human/machine readable symbology. With a WMS identification on each position, each pick-position identification transaction and quantity scan is read by and entered into an RF device for a replenishment transaction. With the activity each SKU pick or replenishment transaction is scanned and transferred direct to a WMS computer inventory files. The disadvantages are label expense, wider or large label, and the cost of the scanning equipment and a computer program. The advantages are that it detects transaction errors, on-line and accurate data transfer and minimizes employee reading requirements.

Pick/Replenishment Position Human-/Machine-Readable Identification Methods

Pick or replenishment position human-/machine-readable identification methods are:

1. Machine-printed human- and machine-readable self-adhesive paper label, placed onto a structural member.
2. Machine-printed human- and machine-readable cardboard or paper label in a holder.
3. A placard hung from the ceiling or embedded in the floor.

Preprinted Self-Adhesive Label

A human/machine readable self-adhesive label is attached (by an employee) to a pick-position structure. Each pick-position replenishment transaction has an employee scan a pick-position identification and each SKU identification. Scan transactions are transferred to the WMS computer to update the inventory and position files. The disadvantages to this approach are additional label expense, possible damage, and employees placing labels onto SKU pick positions. The advantages are uniform label placement and label printing, having the labels read by a scanner/reader, and being able to use the labels as part of the WMS program.

Preprinted Human/Machine-Readable Cardboard/Paper Label in a Plastic Holder

A preprinted human/machine-readable cardboard/paper label is inserted into a plastic label holder. The holder is attached to a pick-position structure. An employee secures the holder onto the pick-position structure. After the holder is secured by self-adhesive tape or a magnet, an employee inserts the preprinted label into the plastic holder. In the WMS program, each replenishment and pick position has a WMS identification. For each pick, a replenishment transaction employee scans the pick-position identification and SKU or master carton identification. Scan transactions are transferred to the WMS computer to update inventory and pick-position files. When a plastic holder is used to hold a pick-position identification, a hand-held scanner/reader signal must obtain a good read through the holder. With a pick transaction, a picker with a RF device scans the SKU identification and enters the SKU pick quantity into a RF device. Again, scan transactions are sent to the WMS computer to update SKU inventory and pick-position status. Disadvantages are a) additional label and holder expense, b) some holders can blur a pick-position identification, and c) potential damage to a holder. Advantages are a) uniform label placement and label print, b) read by a scanner/reader device, and c) it can be used with the WMS program.

Pick-Position Identification Location on a Replenishment/Pick Position

In a pick design with the WMS program, the replenishment or pick-position identification location provides line-of-sight for an employee or forklift truck driver to read a human-readable code and to complete a machine-readable symbology scan transaction. The replenishment or pick-position identification location is determined by SKU type, pick-position type, pick-position structural member, identification size, and the type of scanner/reader. In a warehouse with an WMS program, a SKU replenishment transaction to a pick position has an employee, forklift truck, or

AS/RS crane transfer a SKU to an employee-reachable or machine pick position and to send transaction verification to the WMS computer.

SKU Characteristics and Pick-Position Type

In a pick concept, SKU type determines a pick position. SKU and pick-position options are pallet, loose or contained small items, and master cartons.

In a pallet warehouse, a SKU replenishment transaction is not required because a pallet storage position is a pick position. Because each employee-controlled forklift truck has a different operational feature and identification location, for additional identification replenishment location information please see Chapter 6. In a warehouse with an AS/RS crane, the AS/RS crane computer communicates each SKU and position to the WMS computer.

In a conventional warehouse with master cartons or small items in containers, a SKU replenishment transaction is required from a pallet/master carton storage position to a pick position. Master carton and containerized small-items pick position and replenishment positions are: a) with a combined position for replenishment and pick transactions, and b) with separate positions, one for SKU replenishment and one for pick transactions. To ensure accurate SKU replenishment to a pick position, SKU replenishment and pick position identifications are located in a pick/replenishment position center. Pick position designs that have a combined replenishment and pick position are standard shelves, decked pallet racks, a powered carousel and S.I. Cartrac, and a standard pallet in a conventional or AS/RS warehouse. A gravity flow rack is a pick position design with separate replenishment and pick positions and the same identifications. With multiple pick positions in each flow-rack bay, a pick-position identification is in the flow rack, slide or pushback, or drive-in lane center position.

In an automatic small-item and master carton automatic pick, SKU replenishment is made to an automatic pick machine pick position at the rear or top side. To ensure accurate SKU replenishment to a pick position, replenishment and pick position identifications are located in a position center.

SKU Put-Away, Withdrawal Transaction Verification, and Tracking Concepts

An important warehouse activity is SKU deposit and withdrawal transaction verification. A SKU put-away transaction is a SKU that is transferred from a receiving dock to a storage position. A SKU withdrawal, setup, or replenishment transaction transfers a SKU quantity from a storage location to a pick position at the correct time.

Bar-Code Scanning/RF Tag Reading

Using bar-code scanning/RF tag reading for replenishment verification means that a human/machine readable identification, bar-code/RF tag label (human/machine readable) format is placed on each SKU, as well as each storage or pick position. Employees use a hand-held bar-code scanner/RF reader that holds or transmits a replenishment transaction verification and SKU quantity to the WMS computer. Each SKU move, replenishment transaction, or activity is scanned/read and the information is sent on-line (or delayed) to the WMS computer for inventory and position update. Design considerations are:

1. Total warehouse scan/read devices and transaction number
2. Data transmission distance and clean lines
3. WMS and host computer capability to handle on-line transactions and other activity transactions
4. Scanner/reader device that is finger, wrist, or cord held
5. RF communications performed within a building
6. Does the government permit a RF communication wave use in a facility area?

The disadvantages to this design are cost, employee training, management control, and the possible need for temporary data holding capacity to handle all transactions. The advantages are that it handles a high volume, accurate transfer, accurate transaction record, permits on-line transaction transfer, and high employee productivity.

SKU Replenishment Transactions

A SKU replenishment activity occurs in a warehouse with a fixed pick-position method and ensures that the correct SKU quantity is in the correct pick position for a picker to complete a pick transaction. With any SKU replenishment concept, a replenishment employee with a bar-code/RF tag scanner/reader scans/reads:

1. In a storage area, storage position, and SKU identification;
2. In a pick area, pick position identification and SKU quantity;
3. Scan/read transaction data is transferred to WMS inventory files.

SKU Allocation to the Warehouse Pick Area

A basic pick position principle is to keep a picker and replenishment employee travel distance as short as possible between two transaction positions. SKU allocation to pick position approaches are no method, the ABC method, and the family group method.

No Method

With a no-concept design, SKUs are randomly assigned to pick positions within a pick area or pick aisle. With the method, a pick position has fast-moving SKUs separated by several slow-moving SKU pick positions; therefore, a replenishment employee increases the walk or ride time and distance to complete a two separate SKU replenishment or customer order pick transactions. Disadvantages are replenishment and picker productivity is low; it mixes SKUs from different groups in one area and does not maximize space. Advantages are easy to implement and do not require management control and discipline.

ABC Method

In the ABC method, pick positions in pick aisle are separated into three major zones that are zone "A," zone "B," and zone "C." Each zone is subdivided into micro zones: "A," "B," and "C" zones. Each zone is restricted to SKUs that have a specific annual movement. "A" zone pick positions are restricted to fast-moving SKUs. Pick positions within "B" zone are for medium-moving SKUs.

"C" zone pick positions are for slow-moving SKUs. Eighty percent of a SKU's movement (based on Pareto's Law) is from zone "A." The ABC concept improves a pick aisle SKU hit density and concentration. Disadvantages are management control and discipline, mixing SKUs from different family groups in one aisle, and accurate projections for SKU movement. Advantages are good employee productivity and that it handles a high volume.

Family Group

In the family group, SKUs with similar characteristics are assigned to pick positions within a pick aisle, zone, or area. A warehouse team determines the characteristics. Disadvantages are the increased requirement for management control and discipline, additional positions for new SKUs, the mix of fast and slow moving SKUs in one pick aisle or zone, and lower replenishment and picker productivity.

Replenishment of One Master Carton Layer of a Pallet

Pallet-layer master-carton replenishment involves one or two master-carton layers from a pallet which are removed and transferred from a reserve position to a pick position. The pick position is a hand stack rack position, carton flow rack, or shelf position.

If a master-carton layer removal activity is performed in a storage area, master cartons are moved from a pallet, conveyor, or vehicle load carrying surface for transport to a pick aisle. If a master-carton quantity is placed onto an in-house transport device, each master carton receives an identification that ensures accurate and faster replenishment transactions.

In a pick aisle or in a replenishment aisle, master cartons are moved from a pallet to a pick position. With the less-than-a-pallet replenishment approach, an employee with a RF device scans a pallet and pick position identification, and enters the master-carton quantity that was transferred to a pick position. The data is sent to the WMS files. The disadvantages are transfer equipment cost and required floor area, the SKU is handled twice, and an increase vehicle traffic in facility aisles. Advantages are that it minimizes the number of pallet moves, reduces potential SKU and equipment damage, has FIFO SKU rotation, and handles slow to medium SKUs.

If a master-carton layer removal is performed in a pick area, an employee removes a pallet from a storage area and transports it to a pick area. From a pallet, an employee moves a master carton number (layers) from a pallet to a pick position. After a SKU replenishment transaction, an employee removes a partially depleted pallet from a pick area and returns the pallet to the storage position. With less-than-a-pallet replenishment, an employee with a RF device scans the pallet and pick position identification, and enters the SKU quantity that was transferred to the pick position. The data is sent to the WMS files. Disadvantages are pallet double handling, increased potential SKU and equipment damage, and an increased number of forklift truck or pallet truck trips. Advantages are large inventory quantity transferred to a pick position, and the approach minimizes employee physical effort to bend and reach for master cartons.

Replenishment of Less than a Layer of a Pallet

The less-than-a-pallet-layer replenishment method is used for very slow moving SKUs. The method's operational characteristics are that an employee picks master cartons from a pallet in a storage area, places an identification on each master carton, and completes a master-carton move transaction from a pallet to a transport concept. The transport concept moves master cartons (SKUs) from a storage area to a pick position. With the less-than-a-pallet-layer replenishment concept, an employee with a RF device scans the pallet identification, pick position identification, enters the master-carton SKU quantity that was transferred to a pick position, and sends the data to the WMS files. Disadvantages and advantages are similar to the previous replenishment method except that SKU movement travels one way from a storage area to a pick area.

Master Carton Presentation in a Pick Position

Master carton presentation in a shelf, decked rack, or carton flow-rack pick position allows a picker to complete a customer order pick transaction with minimal nonproductive tasks and time. To satisfy the objective, a master carton is ready for a pick transaction with a full or half-open front and all filler material removed from the interior.

A master carton with all SKUs ready for removal from a master carton means that a SKU replenishment employee has:

1. Cut and removed master carton top flaps. Master carton preparation practice is preferred for master cartons that are allocated to pick level 1—the lowest pick level plus all master cartons allocated to the Golden Zone pick levels. When an empty carton is placed on a trash conveyor travel path, having the flaps removed minimizes jams, or, when it is manually folded into a cart, it means less work and a higher trash carton handling volume.
2. Master carton front side has a square cut, smiley face, or "V" cut pick front. The practice is used for all master cartons on the highest pick level or Golden Zone pick level and when a carton is not recycled in a warehouse but thrown in the trash.
3. If an empty or depleted master carton is used in packing activity, carton flaps are opened and secured to a carton sides by rubber bands or clips.

In a pick area, an empty or depleted master carton is transferred from a pick position to a pick-line start station or packing station. At the station, rubber bands and clips are removed from the carton and carton is introduced to a pick line or used at a packing station. Rubber bands or clips are returned to a carton gravity flow-rack replenishment side or to a shelf or decked-rack front.

Removal of carton filler material is done by a replenishment employee. The filler material is thrown in the trash. When master carton replenishment and carton preparation for a pick position practices are used on a small-item pick line, a picker performs pick transactions with direct and easy access to a master carton SKUs.

Pick-Position Master Carton or Bin Replenishment

One key to an accurate and on-time pick is to ensure that picker productivity meets the budgeted productivity rate. Most small-item pick professionals feel that a master carton or bin box in a pick position ensures a picker can quickly transfer a SKU from a pick position to a carton/tote. The preferred bin presentation in a pick position is to have a master carton open on the top and cut or open in the front. A pick-position bin front options are:

1. An open-face front pick position bin has a precut or modified (cut by a replenishment employee) standard bin box or vendor master carton. It has two side walls and a rear wall with an open top, open front, and solid bottom. If a box design has tape to provide strength and rigidity, tape secures the bottom flaps or specially designed inserts are secured in precut holes. An open bin box arrangement provides a bin with an open face for easy and unobstructed SKU transfer from a pick position to a customer order container. If a bin or carton with an open front does not have space, the pick-position deck member has sufficient support and a front surface for a pick-position identification. Most SKUs placed into an open-face bin box have characteristics that prevent SKUs from falling from a pick-position bin. An open-face bin box is used in a shelf, decked-rack, or carton gravity flow-rack pick-position design.
2. A pick-position bin box with a half- or quarter-high front barrier is precut or cut by a replenishment employee. A standard bin box or a vendor box has two side walls, a rear wall, and an open top, an open or closed top, a closed and solid bottom, and a half- or quarter-high open front. To provide strength and rigidity to a bin, tape secures the bottom flaps or specially designed inserts are secured in precut holes. To create a half- or quarter-high open bin front to a vendor carton, many small-item pick warehouses have a replenishment employee cut a square, smiley face, or "V" in a bin or carton front. With the cut section removed from a carton front, the carton or bin half- or quarter-high front barrier restrains SKUs that have a tendency to slide from a pick position, increases bin rigidity and stability, provides a location for pick-position identification, increases SKU quantity in a pick position, and open space for quick SKU transfer from a pick position to a customer order container. Other considerations are that with a low SKU inventory in a bin box with a front barrier, the front barrier makes it difficult to remove a SKU, and during an employee cutting, there is some potential for SKU damage or employee injury. Safety gloves minimize employee injuries. A pick-position bin box with a half or quarter-high front barrier is used in a shelf, decked rack, or carton gravity flow-rack pick-position design.

Chapter 8

Order Fulfillment

Introduction

A customer-order pick activity is a warehouse activity that completes a customer order. An order fulfillment customer-order pick activity has an employee or machine complete SKU pick transactions from a pick position as a (1) single customer order into a WMS or warehouse identified customer-order tote, or an open space between two belt conveyor cleats; or (2) as batched customer order pre-labeled SKUs picked and transferred *en masse* onto a belt conveyor or into totes or bulk, or picked *en masse* SKUs that are labeled for transport to a customer-order final sort and pick activity.

After a host computer has processed a customer order, the computer transfers customer orders and required SKUs to the WMS computer. The warehouse staff completes a customer-order wave and releases it to the WMS computer. To achieve budgeted employee productivity and cost per unit, the customer-order number in the order wave is based on warehouse criteria (e.g., employee productivity, age, priority delivery). If the warehouse desires to process only one or a few customer orders on an order wave, there is the potential for higher operational cost per customer order. Based on a customer-order wave plan, a WMS computer completes a customer-order SKU allocation and directs your warehouse move request to move a SKU from a storage position to a pick position. A warehouse completes a SKU move transaction and notifies the WMS computer. After a WMS computer receives a SKU identification and quantity transfer notification, the computer releases customer orders. During pick/pack activity, the warehouse verifies the pick transaction and notifies the WMS computer, which updates the pick position and inventory quantity and sends a quantity depletion to the host computer.

A customer-order pick transaction has a customer-ordered SKU quantity that is employee transferred or automatic pick machine released from a pick position into a customer-order carton/tote/belt conveyor travel path. To ensure accurate SKU quantity and pick position status, an employee scans/reads a SKU identification that is sent to a WMS computer warehouse and a computer-controlled machine releases a SKU and sends a SKU release message to a WMS computer that completes a customer order pick transaction. Each customer order SKU pick transaction and SKU quantity is sent from a warehouse computer to the WMS computer that updates a SKU inventory, pick-position status and with an automatic pick machine to attach a SKU to a customer order.

Customer-Order Pick Activity: Functional Description

In a customer-order pick activity, an employee or machine transfers a SKU quantity from a pick position into customer-order tote, bag, carton, or cart (see Figure 8.1). To ensure all customer-order SKUs are picked from a pick position, an employee, tote, carton or cart has capability to travel past all pick positions. The pick design will have the capability for employee/machine verification of pick transaction completion. For accurate pick activity, picked SKUs are placed into a warehouse or customer-order container, or each SKU has customer-order or SKU identification.

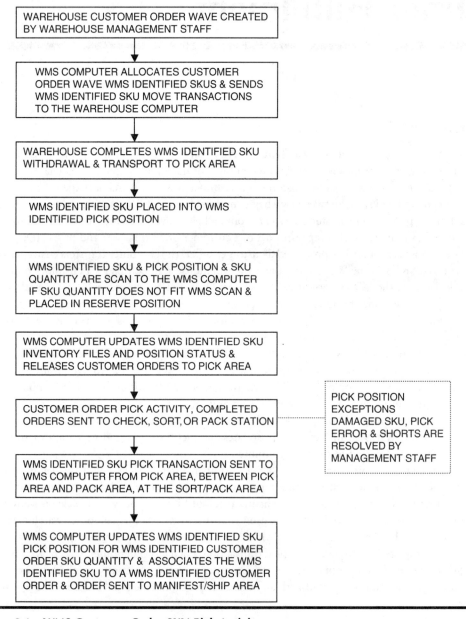

Figure 8.1   WMS Customer Order SKU Pick Activity

Customer-Order Pick Activity: Exception Handling

In a manual, mechanized, or automatic pick design, there can be problems in customer order pick activity. The design team will list potential problems or exceptions and develop resolutions. Some exception situations are:

1. To ensure that a customer-order identification exists, an employee requests to replace a WMS customer-order identification with another identification. The old identification is removed from the RF pick instruction device or container and placed onto a document. The identification is placed onto a pick instruction device or container. If the identification is new, the identification is deleted from a WMS computer. The employee test scans the new identification and is reintroduced to a pick design.

2. With a tote/carton pick design, a customer-order cancel message is sent to a pick-to-light or sort-to-light station. After a canceled customer order identification on a pick carton/tote, an identification scanner/reader sends a message to a warehouse computer that triggers a customer order cancel message to a pick light station; a customer-order tote/carton is removed from the pick line and sent to a check/control station. At a check/control station, an employee verifies that the message is correct and transfers SKUs from a customer-order carton/tote to a pick position. Pick position and SKU identifications and SKU quantity are sent to the WMS computer to update files.

3. With manual and paper bulk-pick/label-pick activity, lost pick instruction sheet or labels or a damaged sheet or label. If a picker loses a sheet/label, a picker with the remaining pick instruction sheets/labels goes to a supervisor station. A supervisor takes action to recreate the pick instruction sheet/label. With a bulk-pick paper document, the supervisor has the warehouse computer print a replacement. With a damaged SKU or customer-order pick label, a supervisor enters a cancel message for each damaged label, places the damaged labels on a control sheet, and the computer prints new labels. With lost labels, the customer-order or SKU code is identified and the conveyor scanner/reader system or check/packing station is updated to have a check activity complete a 100% check for batch picks.

4. With a paper pick document to verify a pick transaction. Each picker is directed to place a circle or check mark adjacent to a SKU human-readable code. At a pick control station, a picker passes the completed pick document to a supervisor who verifies the completed transactions.

5. With a pick/pass, sort/pick into a container, automatic pick, or pick-and-sort design with multiple customer orders on a cart/conveyor, a picker transfers SKUs into the wrong tote/carton. A pick error will not be detected until a completed tote/carton arrives at a check/packing station. For resolution, the order is handled as a problem order.

6. A pick-to-light, sort-to-light, or automatic pick machine breakdown. The warehouse notifies the WMS computer of the breakdown. The computer sets the broken pick positions on "nonallocate" or "hold" (i.e., a pick position is not accepting customer orders). The WMS and warehouse computers direct future orders to active pick modules and associated SKU replenishments are directed to other pick modules. In accordance with warehouse procedure (and estimated breakdown time length), SKUs are moved from the broken pick section to an active pick position. A WMS transaction has the same procedure as a pick-line setup or replenishment. For partial or total completed orders on a conveyor, the warehouse computer and conveyor diverts order to a check station or a specific pack station. At a check/packing

station, with a customer order pack slip/invoice paper document or PC display screen each completed customer order is checked for short picks.

7. A short pick occurs and a SKU is not transferred from a pick position into a customer-order container. A picker is not aware of the short pick, and a customer-order carton/tote or loose SKUs travels from a pick area to a check/packing station on a conveyor. At the check/packing station, a checker/packer recognizes the short pick and resolves the situation.

8. A pick-damaged SKU. When a picker identifies a damaged SKU, the options are a) complete a short pick with an undamaged SKU, place the damaged SKU into a special container located below a conveyor or on a cart, notify the inventory control department to complete a SKU count, and complete an additional SKU move from a storage position to a pick position, b) place the damaged SKU into a special bag or place a tag on a damaged SKU and transfer the damaged SKU into a customer-order tote/carton. At a check/packing station, a checker/packer moves the entire customer order (i.e., SKUs, packing slip, carton/tote) to a problem-order station. At the station, a supervisor notifies the inventory control department to complete a SKU count and complete an additional SKU move from a storage position to a pick position, or c) place the damaged SKU into a customer-order container or an automatic pick machine releases the damaged SKU onto a conveyor. The problem is resolved when a manual checker/packer detects the damaged SKU, the order is sent to a problem-order station, and the previously mentioned resolution activities are completed.

9. A master carton/tote has an undetected short piece count. The SKU quantity will not be detected until the customer-order wave is completed and the last order arrives at a pick position. Resolution options are a) with an exact inventory in a pick position, the last customer order has a short pick and is sent to a problem-order station and the previous mentioned resolution activities are completed, or b) in a round-up master-carton setup design, at a customer-order wave end when all customer orders are completed. During a pick-line reorganization, as a SKU is moved from one pick position to another, the transferred SKU quantity is verified and entered into the WMS computer. The pick position SKU quantity will not match the WMS computer quantity. To ensure an accurate SKU inventory, a cycle count is requested, and the count is updated in the WMS computer.

10. A customer order does not fit into a carton/tote. During pick/pass, pick-to-light, or sort-to-light activity, a picker realizes that an additional SKU will not fit into a carton/tote. A picker presses full-carton/tote button and pushes the full customer-order carton/tote onto a take-away conveyor. The warehouse computer sends a message to the WMS computer, which creates another customer-order pick instruction for another carton/tote. Per a warehouse conveyor and computer system, a customer-order warehouse or WMS identification on each pick carton or tote is sent to a check station. At the check station, with a customer order pack slip/invoice paper document or PC display screen, a checker ensures that the customer order is complete and sends it on to a packing station.

11. Carton/tote picks are required from several different pick areas. Pick instructions and the in-house transport moves the carton/tote to all required pick areas.

12. A sort-to-light, pick-to-light, automatic pick machine carousel, or conveyor breakdown. To correct this situation, the resolution is determined by the pick-area design, the customer-order pick instructions, or in-house transport design. If the pick area has multiple pick modules, the warehouse computer and conveyor diverts customer orders to a check station or a specific pack station. At a check/packing station, with a customer order pack slip/invoice paper document or PC display screen, each customer order is checked for short picks. If there is only one pick module, the warehouse computer and conveyor sends all partially

picked orders to a check station. At a check/packing station, with a customer order pack slip/invoice paper document or PC display screen, each customer order is checked for short picks. To continue with the order pick activity, orders are paper picked and sent to a check/packing station. At a check/packing station, SKUs are depleted from inventory and orders are checked for accurate picks.

Pick Designs

The pick design and SKU type determines the scan transaction location in a customer-order pick activity. In accordance with the warehouse's customer-order service standard, a pick activity completes customer-order pick/packing/shipping transaction for a customer-order single-line single SKU, single-line multiple SKU, multiple-line multiple SKU customer orders, or multiple SKU from different SKU groups.

Pick designs are:

- Manual or mechanized pick designs that complete customer-order SKUs picks for manual pick, single customer orders with one or multiple lines, or batched customer orders that are picked, sorted, scanned, and packed
- Manual designs for customer orders that are bulked with prelabeled SKUs, or customer-labeled SKUs sent to manual or mechanized powered sort designs
- Automatic designs that complete single-line customer order for SKUs

Customer-order pick activities are:

1. Based on a customer-order wave, WMS program SKU allocation for a customer-order pick activity
2. SKU transfer from a storage position to a pick position
3. Hand-held scanner/reader transaction and SKU quantity transferred to a pick position and sent to the WMS computer
4. WMS computer customer-order release
5. Warehouse customer-order identification that is associated to a customer-order identification
6. Pick instruction that directs a manual picker/automatic pick machine to transfer a SKU from a pick positiion into tote/carton or location on a belt conveyor
7. All completed customer orders are sent to a check, pack, or seal station

Manual Pick Designs

A manual pick design provides an accurate, cost-effective, timely, and efficient service for present and future customers at a reasonable profit. Key factors to a manual warehouse are operation cost and customer service standard for on-time and accurate deliveries. Manual pick design factors that influence customer service are:

- The pick philosophy that controls pick-line, pick-aisle, or automatic pick-machine activities.
- The pick methodology used to complete customer orders and replenishment.

Pick Multiple SKUs for Customer Orders

A manual small-item pick design picks multiple SKUs for customer orders. Multiple pick options are single customer orders (as single, bulk, or *en masse*) or to batched or grouped customer orders.

Single Customer Orders

If a small-item pick design picks multi-line or multiple SKUs for customer orders as single customer orders, one picker will pick all customer-order SKUs. In a single customer-order pick philosophy, the picker options are:

1. Pick one customer order per trip
2. Per trip, pick multiple customer-order small SKUs and sort customer order SKUs into a container compartment that Is assigned to a customer order
3. Pick each SKU *en masse* for a customer-order group and sort each SKU into a separate customer-order carton/tote or sent to a sort and assembly position

Customer-order pick philosophy features are:

■ Low picker productivity
■ Low packer productivity
■ Pick cart/tote cost
■ Less than optimum completed customer-order flow from pick area to packing area
■ Increased pickers per aisle with wider warehouse pick aisles
■ No sort labor
■ Minimal WMS computer program modifications
■ Any customer-order pick instruction format, such as a) paper printed document or label or b) paperless pick options that are pick-to-light, voice directed, RF device, or automatic pick machine instructions

Another single customer-order pick philosophy has one picker with a four-wheel shelf cart pick multiple customer-order SKUs onto one shelf or into a multiple-compartment tote. In accordance with the warehouse operation, customer-order number, and SKUs per customer order, a shelf may have several totes or a tote may have smaller compartments. Each shelf, shelf section, tote, or tote compartment has a customer-order identification. With a single customer-order pick design, a picker uses a customer-order pick-and-sort SKU instruction format, which can be a paper document, self-adhesive labels, pick-/sort-to-light, or RF device. When a shelf, shelf section, tote, or tote compartment is full, or all assigned customer orders completed, a tote/cart is sent from a pick area to a packing station. The features are:

■ Good picker and packer productivity
■ Few pick totes/carts
■ WMS or warehouse computer program assigns a customer order to a shelf/tote section and on each shelf/tote section a human-/machine-readable customer-order discreet identification
■ Queue at a pack station
■ Few pick cart trips in a pick aisle
■ No sort labor
■ Any customer-order pick instruction format

The last manual single customer-order pick philosophy has a picker with a four-wheel shelf cart to pick *en masse* each SKU for a customer-order group into a batched customer-order tote. A cart load carrying surface, each tote/rail has capacity to hold *en masse* SKUs for a customer-order group. Customer-order picked SKUs are sorted into each customer-order tote per a customer-order pick instruction format. A customer-order human-/machine-readable discreet identification is attached to the front of each tote; the pick instruction matches the customer-order sort identification. Ordered and picked SKUs are scanned to a packing slip/invoice in a pick area, at a separate scan station, or at a packing station, depending on the warehouse operation. The scan tranaction and SKU quanty are sent to the WMS computer for update.

Manual pick concepts are:

- Nonpowered approaches, which use a) a two-wheel hand truck, a four-wheel shelf cart, or platform cart, b) small items into a tote on a conveyor, c) nonpowered trolley with a basket, or master cartons/pallet with a hand pallet truck
- Powered concepts, which use a) powered tow cart, b) powered tugger with a cart train, c) powered pallet truck, forklift truck, high rise order picker truck, decombe, pick car, or d) small items in totes/cartons on a powered conveyor

Batched/Grouped Customer Orders

A multiple batched or grouped small-item or master-carton pick/sort/pack or master-carton pick-and-sort philosophy has the WMS or warehouse computer group mixed SKUs into batches. With a batched philosophy, one or several pickers are used to pick several SKUs. Each picker a) completes customer-order picks and places prelabeled or customer-order labeled SKUs as mixed picked SKUs into a tote or master carton, and then onto a conveyor, or b) picks prelabeled SKUs or labels each customer order picked SKU *en masse* into a tote, cart, or directly onto a conveyor for transport from the pick area to a sort area. To account for ordered and picked SKUs, the SKUs are scanned to a packing slip or invoice in a pick area, at a separate scan station. or at a packing station, depending on the warehouse operation. The scan transaction and SKU quantity are sent to a WMS computer for update.

The features of this approach are:

- Few picker aisle trips
- Constant picked flow to packing stations
- Low pick cart/tote cost
- Each SKU has a human-/machine-readable discreet code
- Sufficient table top surface is required at a packing table
- The sort area requires additional sort and pack employee time
- The approach handles high customer order number and SKUs per customer order

Customer Order Number per Tote

In a pick/pass design, customer order number (picked into) per tote is determined by the design team. The design team customer order number per tote can be one or multiple customer order(s) per tote.

One Customer Order per Tote

In the approach of one customer order per tote, the WMS or warehouse computer assigns one customer order to a pick line. At the pick-line entrance, an employee attaches a WMS identification to the tote warehouse identification. As a tote with one customer order travels over a pick line and arrives at a pack station, pick/pack activities are for one customer order. It is easier to complete pick transactions because the pick transaction is for one customer order, but it increases the number of totes needed to complete a customer order wave. With a tote, packer activities are simple because a single zero scan breaks the WMS identification to a warehouse tote identification and allows the tote to be used for another customer order. However, there is an increase in the number of zero-scan transactions needed to complete a customer order wave.

With one customer order per tote, the WMS or warehouse computer groups one customer order to a warehouse tote cube. With one customer order per carton/tote and based per customer ordered SKUs cube, a warehouse computer cubes or allocates SKUs to fill one a customer order carton/tote and the customer order overflow or additional SKUs are cubed or allocated to another customer order carton/tote. The feature is simple calculation that requires less time. At a pack station, and after a tote identification scan transaction, a pack station PC displays single-order SKUs or a printer prints an order pick slip or invoice and a packer transfers SKUs from a tote to shipping carton.

Multiple Customer Orders per Tote

Multiple customer orders per one tote has the WMS or warehouse computer to assign, bundle, or group multiple customer orders and SKUs into a single tote. As the WMS computer receives customer orders, the orders are cubed to match a warehouse tote cube. The WMS or warehouse computer allocates with small size SKUs, a few SKUs per customer order, or a fixed customer order number per tote. With mixed size SKUs and mixed SKUs per customer order, orders or SKUs are accumulated in a tote until the accumulated orders total cube matches a warehouse tote. In other words, the order number per tote ranges from two to five or six. The order number is determined either by cube data or is a predetermined number established by the operations or IT department.

With a bundled or grouped customer orders approach, as a tote moves over a pick line, at each pick position a picker has the potential for higher picker productivity due to the fact that each pick transaction has probability to have multiple SKU numbers per pick transaction. As SKU hit concentration and hit density increase, picker productivity may increase as well. When a tote with multiple customer orders arrives at a pack station, a packer completes a tote identification scan transaction. With multiple customer orders per tote, the station warehouse computer activates a printer to print each customer order packing slip/invoice and delivery label or displays a customer order pack slip/invoice on a PC screen. The features are in the pack area and increased equipment, additional packer activities, and additional IT/computer transactions or message. Equipment increase features are:

- A larger pack table surface to hold multiple customer orders and associated SKU number/cube
- After a warehouse tote identification scan completion that is sent to a warehouse computer, to have a warehouse computer controlled printer print the customer order packing slips/ invoice slips and delivery labels or display the customer order packing slips/invoices on a

PC screen. The paper document or PC screen customer order packing slips/invoices allows a packer/checker to associate/sort each SKU to a customer order packing slip/invoice SKUs.

Multiple customer-order SKUs in a single tote require a packer to complete a final sort activity and to make sure that the SKUs do not become mixed on a table. For a WMS or warehouse computer to complete customer order cube calculations increases computer processing time and at a pack station to have a warehouse computer display on a PC screen design to properly display each customer order packing slip/invoice on a pack station PC display screen. This approach requires that accurate SKU and carton/tote dimensions are stored in the WMS or warehouse computer. Also, as previously stated, a packer completes a warehouse tote identification zero transaction.

Bulk-Picked Small Single Item per Single Customer Order Means a Pick/Pack Activity

When a small-item pick design has high customer-order pick volume for a single or a pair of SKUs for a large customer-order number, the warehouse establishes a pick/pack activity. This activity that has one or two more steps than a normal customer-order pick activity. With typical pick/pack activity, there is a slight decrease in an individual picker's productivity because one picker picks, packs, scans a SKU to a customer order, and seals a carton. But for high-volume SKUs, a pick/pack activity dramatically improves total pick productivity:

- The repetitive activity by-passes regular pick activity and pack station
- Customer-order SKUs are picked *en masse* and transferred to a specific pick/pack station
- *En masse* premade ship cartons are delivered to a pick/pack station

Small Single-Item Pick/Pack Design

Small-item pick/pack activity can improve customer service, lower costs, and increase customer-order handling volume. Opportunities are determined by SKU volume, SKU physical and packing characteristics, customer-order number and SKUs per customer order, and pack stations that have access to an in-house transport conveyor. To justify pick/pack activity, a single SKU or a SKU pair must have a high sales volume. A high sale volume permits SKUs to be picked in large quantities and delivered *en masse* to a separate pick/pack area/line. An *en masse* SKU pick activity improves the total pick-area productivity. SKU characteristics are:

- A SKU cube whose length, width, height, and weight, and exterior packaging allows it to be placed inside a carton or shipped as a ready-to-ship vendor carton
- A SKU that is sufficiently fragile to require top and bottom filler inside a carton. If the SKU requires void space filler material in a shipping carton, a pick/pack line has separate top and bottom fill stations. If a SKU is in a vendor ready-to-ship carton, a pick/pack line has a combined label application and packing slip insert station
- If a pick/pack line handles a large single SKU or pair of SKUs for customer orders, a pick/pack line layout has both customer order pick and completed customer order take-away conveyor travel paths. Pick/pack line options are reviewed later.

Pick/pack line activity stations are carton make-up and introduction station, bottom fill, SKU pick or scan, packing slip/invoice insert, top fill, carton seal and label, and scan manifest station. Pick/pack line layouts are:

- For regular SKUs, a complete pick/pack line
- For vendor ready-to-ship cartons, a pick/pack (label) line with a) individual customer-order label or b) slapper label

Complete Pick/Pass Line

A pick/pass activity station number is determined by:

- A pre- or post-scan of a SKU to a customer order
- Customer-order package fill requirements
- How the packing slip and sales literature are inserted into/attached to a customer-order shipping carton
- How the shipping or address label is placed onto a shipping carton's exterior surface
- The SKU size and associated shipping carton

The options for a pick/pass line customer-order ship carton are:

- Place a SKU into a preformed bag, formed bag, chipboard box, or corrugated box
- Use a vendor ready-to-ship carton. Each shipping bag or carton type affects the pick/pack line design and operation

Mechanized Stock/Pick Position Transferred to an Employee Pick Design

Mechanized SKU or pick-position travel to a pick station group concept has each SKU or pick position that is moved to a manual customer-order pick station (see Figure 8.2). At a manual pick station, a pick employee transfers a SKU from a position as:

- Small-item loose labeled or coded *en masse* SKUs into a tote
- Small-item SKU into a tote section or shelf
- Loose labeled or precoded small-item or master-carton SKUs picked *en masse* directly onto a powered belt conveyor

A mechanized SKU to an employee pick design transfers a pick position to a pick station. Depending on the mechanized pick method, a picker removes a SKU from a pick position, labels the SKU or picks a coded SKU, presses a pick-to-light button, and marks a paper document or RF device to verify a pick transaction. The pick-position transfer is repeated until all SKUs are picked and transferred to in-house transport. Depending on the pick design, ordered and picked SKUs are scanned to a packing slip or invoice in a pick area, at a separate scan station, or at a pack station. The scan tranaction and SKU quantity are sent to the WMS computer for update.

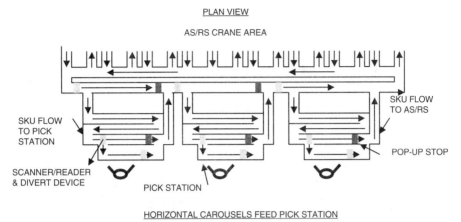

PLAN VIEW

AS/RS CRANE AREA

SKU FLOW TO AS/RS

SKU FLOW TO PICK STATION

POP-UP STOP

SCANNER/READER & DIVERT DEVICE

PICK STATION

HORIZONTAL CAROUSELS FEED PICK STATION

PLAN VIEW

THREE CAROUSEL HORSE SHOE DESIGN

FOUR CAROUSEL HORSE SHOE DESIGN

CAROUSEL 2

CAROUSEL 3

CAROUSEL 2

CAROUSEL 3

CAROUSEL 1

CAROUSEL 1

PICKER

PICKER

CUSTOMER ORDERS

CUSTOMER ORDERS

TAKE-AWAY CONVEYOR

TRIANGLE CAROUSEL DESIGN

CAROUSEL 2

CAROUSEL 3

CAROUSEL 1

PICKER

CUSTOMER ORDERS

CAROUSEL 4

TAKE-AWAY CONVEYOR

Figure 8.2   Mechanized Small Item Pick Conceptss

Mechanized Stock/Pick Position Transferred to an Employee Pick

Designs in which a mechanized SKU or pick position is transferred to an employee customer-order pick station:

- Small-item carousel concept group: horizontal carousel or vertical carousel
- Carton AS/RS or stacker crane warehouse group that includes pick tunnel
- S.I. Cartrac design: mini-load or pallet type with shelves

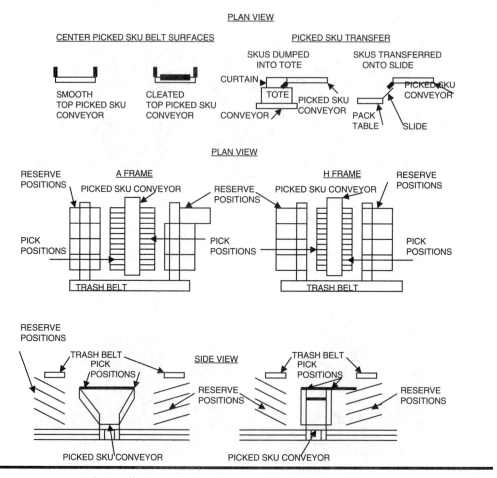

Figure 8.3   Automatic Small Item Pick Concepts

Automatic SKU Pick Group

In an automatic pick group, small-item, master-carton, or pallet SKUs are automatically (i.e., warehouse computer controlled) released from a machine pick position. Picked loose SKUs are released:

1. On to a conveyor for transport to pack stations, master cartons, or pallets
2. Into the open space between two cleats on a conveyor for transport and transfer into a tote/carton
3. Into a discreet carton/tote or master cartons/pallets withdrawn for transport to a next pick station and thence to a pack station

Ordered and picked SKUs are scanned to a packing slip/invoice in a pick area, at a separate scan station, or at a pack station. The scan tranaction and SKU quantity are sent to the WMS computer for update.

Customer Order Pick Designs

Small-item pick designs are:

- Single customer orders completed by a single picker
- Single customer orders completed by several pickers
- Batched customer orders completed by a single or multiple pickers

Single Customer Order and Single Order Picker/Pick Machine

A single customer order completed by a single picker is used in manual pick, pick/pack, or an automatic pick-machine operation. With this philosophy, to complete a customer order a single picker or automatic pick machine completes all SKU pick transactions. Picked SKUs are transferred from pick positions to a carton/tote or into an open space between two cleats on a belt conveyor. Depending on layout of the pick positions in a pick line/area, one picker travels all the pick aisles or the entire pick area to complete the pick transactions. Ordered and picked SKUs are scanned to a packing slip or invoice in a pick area, at a separate scan station, or at a pack station. The scan tranaction and SKU quantity are sent to the WMS computer for update. The disadvantages with a manual picker concept are:

- Low employee productivity, because of greater travel distances
- It handles a low customer order volume and small customer order size or cube
- It requires the greatest number of pickers
- It means longer customer order and delivery cycle time
- The automatic pick-machine means high capital cost

The advantages are that it maintains customer order integrity selection process, it is easy to identify and control problem pickers, and the automatic pick-machine provides accurate picks.

Single Customer Order with Multiple-Order Pickers/Pick Machines

A pick philosophy in which customer orders are completed with manual multiple pickers or automatic pick machines are used in a pick/pack pick design. A single customer order with multiple pickers or automatic pick machines has several pickers or automatic pick machines perform all pick transactions. Design options are:

- Manual pick/pack activity or an automatic pick design with customer-order picked SKUs transferred from a pick position into a warehouse or WMS tote
- Transport concept moves a tote/carton past all customer-order pick positions and per a customer order allows an employee or automatic pick machine to transfer picked SKUs directly into a tote/carton or onto open space on a belt conveyor travel path

Pick designs in which one customer order is picked by multiple manual pickers or an automatic pick machine are:

- With paper pick instructions on a manual pick line/aisle, in which a manual picker picks and transfers SKUs directly into a discreetly identified carton/tote
- With pick-to-light, voice directed or RF device instructions on a pick line/aisle, in which a manual picker picks and transfers SKUs directly into a discreetly identified carton/tote
- With paper or pick-to-light instructions with a cell pick line or pick-area layout for specific SKUs, in which a manual picker picks and transfers SKUs directly into a discreetly identified carton

A design in which a single customer order is handled by multiple pickers, a manual pick line, or automatic pick machine features:

- Discreet identification on each carton/tote
- A carton/tote transport that links all pick positions together, i.e., a transport that moves a discreetly identified carton/tote past all manual or mechanized pick positions or automatic pick machine discharge locations
- Pick instructions that include discreet identification, SKU quantity, and pick position identification
- Ordered and picked SKUs are scanned to a packing slip or invoice in a pick area, at a separate scan station, or at a pack station. The scan tranaction and SKU quantity are sent to the WMS computer for update.

The advantages of this approach are:

- Increased picker productivity due to shorter travel distances
- Shorter customer-order delivery cycle time
- The ability to handle a greater customer order number
- Customer orders with fewer SKUs per order and customer orders with several SKUs
- Medium number of pickers
- Management controls
- A well-designed pick area with a carton/tote in-house transport

The disadvantage is that it is difficult to identify problem pickers.

Multiple Customer Orders with Multiple Pickers/Automatic Pick Machines

When multiple customer orders are handled by multiple pickers, this pick philosophy is known as "batched customer orders with multiple pickers." In this approach, the WMS computer groups several SKUs together. SKUs are grouped by pick position; for all customer orders, each SKU is accompanied by a printed pick instruction or the pick design uses a precoded SKU. After a multiple (grouped/batched) customer orders SKU is picked and transferred from a pick position into a picker hand/apron, tote or onto a belt conveyor, the picked SKUs are considered picked/mixed customer ordered SKUs. Mixed customer-order SKUs are sorted by customer order a) in a pick area, with a paper document sort instruction that directs a picker to transfer a picked SKU into an assigned sort location, carton/tote; or b) self-adhesive label or SKU instruction, sent from a pick area as a mixed customer order picked SKU group to a customer ordered and picked SKU sort area. In a sort area, an employee or machine sorts each picked SKU to each identified sort location.

A high-volume batched pick operation has separate pick and sort area activities. The picker instruction format can be a self-adhesive label or a precoded SKU with a paper document or RF device. Each pick label or precoded SKU label has a human-/machine-readable symbology. A label is printed for each SKU, and as a picker completes a transaction, a customer-order label is placed onto the SKU's exterior. If the pick design has pre-SKUs, it does not require another label, but SKUs are transferred from a pick position directly into a tote/carton or other transport device. With a batched customer-order pick design, a picker travels through pick aisles. At a pick position, a picker transfers a SKU or handles a prelabeled SKU from a pick position, labels the SKU, and places the picked and labeled SKU into a tote or loose onto a conveyor, which moves the SKU to a sort area.

In a sort area, a human-/machine-readable discreet label on each SKU serves as a sort instruction for employees or is read by scanner/reader. The sort instruction permits an employee or mechanical device to sort mixed/batched SKUs by each identification into a sort location. A sort activity completes the pick, transport, and sort activity. As usual, ordered and picked SKUs are scanned to a packing slip or invoice in a pick area, at a separate scan station, or at a pack station. The scan transaction and SKU quantity are sent to the WMS computer for update.

Multiple Customer Orders with Single-Order Picker

In a small-item or flat-wear pick philosophy for slow-moving SKUs, a picker uses a printed label, a precoded SKU and a paper document, or an RF device for pick-and-sort instructions. Pick-and-sort activity has a picker pick and sort a picked SKU into a tote. A picker pick-and-sort approach has a picker perform pick and sort activities in a pick aisle or aisle end. To account for ordered and picked SKUs, SKUs are scanned to a packing slip/invoice in a pick area, at a separate scan station, or at a pack station. The scan tranaction and SKU quantity are sent to the WMS computer for update.

Customer Order Picked SKU Sort

The batched customer order philosophy concerns how to sort mixed and batched picked SKUs to an assigned customer order sort location. The options are:

- Manual approaches: picker pick-and-sort, and pick, transport, and sort
- Mechanized sorting (Chapter 9)

Customer-Order Pick-and-Sort Instruction

A pick philosophy in which multiple customer orders use multiple pickers involves a pick-and-sort instruction format. With unlabeled SKUs, the batched customer-order pick-and-sort instruction format is a self-adhesive label SKU instruction method. A pick employee places a customer order or SKU identification on the surface each picked non-SKU. In a prelabeled SKU and a sort philosophy, a picked SKU does not require a picker to place a label on it. In a prelabel or print-and-label pick philosophy, each SKU or customer-order identification is a human-/machine-readable code.

Pick-and-sort instruction format options are a paper document, an RF device, or paperless pick (voice directed or pick/sort-to-light) designs in which each SKU has a code that discreetly identifies it for a sort instruction. If the picked SKU sort design is mechanized with computer support and each SKU has a WMS identification, batched customer-order SKUs or precoded SKUs are picked with any customer-order pick instruction. This is because the mechanized and computer supported sort philosophy is designed to sort by discreet human-/machine-readable code.

Picked SKU In-House Transport

A second factor in multiple customer orders with multiple picker philosophy is in-house transport concept. The sort area location affects picked SKU in-house transport concept. The transport concept moves picked and sorted SKUs—as individual sorted or completed customer orders—through an entire pick area and from a pick area to a pack area. In a pack area, each completed customer order is packed into a shipping carton. Ordered and picked SKUs are scanned to a packing slip or invoice in a pick area, at a separate scan station, or at a pack station. The scan transaction and SKU quantity are sent to the WMS computer for updating.

Picked SKU Scan Locations

A picked SKU scan transaction location is completed in a pick area, between the pick/pack area or in a pack area. To complete a pick activity, the picked SKU quantity is scanned and sent to the WMS computer. The computer depletes the total SKU quantity by the scan transaction quantity and ensures that the customer order is complete and updates the pick position SKU quantity. With RF symbology and RF receiver, the read location is not a fixed location. Scan location options are determined by:

1. Customer-order type, such as (a) single-line single customer order that has one SKU per customer order, (b) single-line multiple SKU customer order that has one or more same SKUs, (c) multi-lines or multiple SKUs customer order that have two or more different SKUs from the same SKU group, and (d) multi-line from different product groups customer orders that has two or more SKUs
2. SKU type, such as (a) small item, (b) master carton, and (c) pallet
3. Pick design, such as (a) manual single customer order, single bulk pick, single customer order, and multi-line batched pick-and-sort, single-order pick/pass, (b) mechanized single customer order, single bulk pick, and multi-line batched pick/sort, and (c) automated single
4. Pick instruction format that are (a) paper document, (b) self-adhesive label or prelabeled SKU, (c) voice directed, (d) RF device, (e) pick-to-light, (f) sort-to-light, and (g) computer controlled or automatic
5. Customer-order pick container with a warehouse or WMS premanent/disposable identification

The previous pick design parameters provide numerous options. Scan location options are:

- Hand-held scan in a pick area
- Hand-held or fixed position scan in the sort and assembly area (a station between the pick and pack areas)
- Hand-held or fixed position scan at a pack station
- Pick-to-light or sort-to-light communicates a pick transaction
- Automatic pick machine computer communicates a pick transaction

If the pick philosophy uses a permanent warehouse identification on a captive pick tote, as the pick tote enters a pick line a scanner/reader reads the identification and sends the data to the warehouse computer. The warehouse computer associates a customer order with the permanent identification. After the completion of the pick transaction, an employee scans/reads a zero scan on the tote identification at a pack station and communicates the zero scan transaction to the WMS computer. The WMS computer removes the customer-order identification association from the tote identification and an employee completes the pack activity.

If a pick philosophy uses a warehouse or WMS disposable identification on a captive tote or pick/ship carton container, as the pick tote/carton enters a pick line, the customer-order identification is used on the pick line. At a pack station an employee completes the pack activity after completion of the pick transaction. No zero scan activity is required because the WMS disposable identification is not reused.

Hand-Held Scan SKU and Customer-Order Identifications Locations

SKU and customer-order bar code or RF tag identifications have the following options:

- Hand-held sca SKU and customer-order identifications in a pick area
- Hand-held or fixed-position scan for SKUs and customer-order identifications in a sort-and-assembly area located between a pick/pack area
- Hand-held/fixed-position scan for SKUs and customer-order identifications at a pack station
- Pick-to-light or sort-to-light communicates a SKU and pick transaction
- Automatic pick machine computer communicates a SKU and customer-order pick transaction

Pick Instruction

The host computer downloads customer orders and SKUs to the WMS computer. The WMS computer sends customer orders and associated SKUs to the warehouse computer. The warehouse computer creates a customer-order wave, and sends the customer-order wave plan to the WMS computer, which completes the SKU allocation process (for moving a SKU from a storage position to a pick position). When the WMS computer is updated that a SKU has been moved to a pick position, customer orders are released. The warehouse computer prepares a pick instruction for each ordered SKU that includes SKU quantity, human-/machine-readable WMS identified pick position. Pick instruction options are:

- Paper pick instructions, which are used in a manual pick philosophy, that are machine-printed paper documents or self-adhesive labels
- Paperless pick instructions, which include voice directed, RF device, pick-to-light, sort-to-light, and computer controlled/automatic pick machine

In most pick philosophies, a paperless pick requires a replenishment design that uses a paper or RF instruction. Picker instruction format differences and similarities are:

1. Format options are a) for paper includes paper document and self-adhesive label and (b) paperless formats that are voice directed, RF device, warehouse computer-controlled AS/RS crane or pick machine, or pick-to-light digital display.
2. Presentation to a picker: Manual pick instruction has human-readable alpha characters or numeric digits, which is machine printed onto a paper document or self-adhesive label, or appeared on a digital display. All manual pick instruction formats involve having a picker read the pick instruction. A RF device or bar code scanner/RF tag reader format has a picker point a hand-held, wrist, or finger scanner/reader at a human-/machine-readable pick position symbology, and on a RF device read a customer order SKU pick instruction. In a voice communication pick instruction, an employee hears the pick instruction. With an automatic pick machine or AS/RS crane approach, the pick instruction is a warehouse computer impulse.
3. A paper document or self-adhesive label: The information content includes, in addition to the previous information, human- or human-/machine-readable discreet identification. With a voice-directed instruction, the pick instruction is a verbal customer-order identification. With a RF device, pick-to-light, or sort-to-light digital display instruction, the customer-order identification appears on a carton and on a display device and is read by a picker, a finger/wrist, or hand-held scanner/reader. With an automatic pick machine or AS/RS crane approach, the pick instruction is a warehouse computer impulse to release a SKU or pick a SKU.
4. Pick verification: To verify a completed pick transaction with a paper document, a) a picker marks a paper document, b) with a self-adhesive label instruction, a picker removes the WMS or customer-order label from the self-adhesive back and places the label onto a SKU, which is read by a scanner/reader, c) with a RF device, pick-to-light, or sort light digital display instruction, a picker presses a button or breaks a light beam, and a signal is sent to the warehouse computer, d) a voice-directed instruction has no pick transaction verification, and e) with an automatic pick machine or AS/RS crane, the pick completion is registered by the warehouse computer.

In all pick philosophies, a warehouse has a scan check/packing station that completes a SKU scan transaction to a customer order.

Manual picker pick instruction format similarities are:

1. Presentation arrangement that are a) with a paper document or self-adhesive label pick and voice-directed instruction formats, with the SKU pick position first and SKU quantity second, and SKU symbology third, b) with digital display pick instruction for pick-to-light or RF device, the display shows the customer-order identification, the pick position, and the customer-order SKU quantity, and c) with an automatic pick machine or AS/RS crane, the pick instruction is a warehouse computer impulse.
2. WMS identification SKU presentation format. The SKU presentation form is a pick position numerical sequence and quantity for a customer order. Presentation format options are a) random pick instruction presentation, which has SKUs in inventory allocated to any pick position on a pick line or in a pick aisle in a random arrangement. As pick instructions are presented to a picker, pick instructions are not in a sequential order. A random pick instruction sequence is not preferred, b) SKU number sequence presentation. With a pick instruction presentation and SKUs in inventory are allocated to pick positions by SKU number, a pick instruction format has a sequential presentation. A SKU number pick instruction sequence is not preferred for implementation, and c) pick position sequence presentation,

in which the first possible pick position is the first position on a pick line/aisle. The features are arithmetic progression along a pick line, through a pick aisle, or in an automatic pick machine, and is preferred in a pick philosophy.

Pick Aisle and Pick Position Identification

To ensure accurate and on-time customer-order pick transactions, pick-aisle and pick-position identification clearly identifies each pick aisle and pick position. Pick-aisle identification permits a picker to locate a pick aisle; pick-position identification permits a picker to match a pick-transaction instruction to the pick position that contains a customer-order SKU. A pick-aisle identification is a placard with alpha characters, numeric digits, or a combination of both. The placard is placed at a pick-aisle entrance and exit or on a pick line at the pick zone start and end. Aisle-identification methods are:

- One-way vision placard
- Two-way vision placard
- Two-way aisle placard

In a static pick philosophy (i.e., standard shelves, racks or rails, and moving pick designs) a human-/machine-readable symbology is placed at the front of each pick position. In a floor-rack pick philosophy, a human-/machine-readable pick-position identification is placed on each pick and replenishment side.

Pick-Position Method Features

In a manual pick design, the method that is used to identify a pick position affects pick and replenishment employee productivity and accuracy. Pick-position identification features are:

- It is clearly visible.
- It is easily understood.
- It is permanent.
- It matches the warehouse pick instruction format.
- It is the back-up pick position for paperless pick or automatic pick machine designs.

Pick-Position Identification Locations

In this pick philosophy, the pick-position identification is attached to a structural member. Pick-position identification locations are:

1. A Golden Zone pick-position identification is attached to pick-position structural member that is directly below or above a pick position to face outward (to provide employee line-of-sight)
2. An identification is placed on a pick-position deck or shelf edge and faces upward
3. Identifications on upper-level pick positions face outward with a slight tilt
4. A pick position with SKUs in a permanent tote or a barrier across the front with a WMS identification

Pick-Position Identification Size

At a manual or at an automatic pick machine pick/replenishment position, a human-/machine-readable pick/replenishment position identification identifies a position for an employee to complete a pick transaction or a replenishment employee to complete a replenishment transaction. Label options are:

1. Small alpha characters/numeric digits and machine-readable symbology have a label surface size that is less than ½-inch high. The features are a) a small human-/machine–readable symbology on a small label surface, b) slightly lower label print expense, c) it can be used on all pick-position types, and d) it is difficult to read or complete a scan from the middle of an aisle, which results in slightly lower replenishment and picker productivity.
2. Large alpha characters/numeric digits of a 1/2-Inch height and an 1-inch high bar code/RF tag or machine-readable symbology length have a label surface size that is at least 1 3/4 inch high. The features are a) a large human-/machine–readable symbology on a large label surface, b) slightly higher label print expense, c) it can be used on all pick-position types, and d) it is easy to read and complete a scan from the middle of an aisle, which results in slightly higher picker productivity.

Alpha Characters/Numeric Digits with Bar Code/RF Tag and SKU Description

The first step in identifying a pick position is to determine what alpha characters/numeric digits machine symbology is to appear on a pick position. Options are:

1. Human-readable alpha characters/numeric digits. This is not preferred for use in a warehouse with a WMS program.
2. Human-readable alpha characters or numeric digits with a bar code/RF tag, which is used in an employee paper or paperless pick philosophy. Human-/machine-readable symbology is preferred for use in a warehouse with a WMS program.

Pick-Position Identification Methods

In a manual pick design, the position identification method discreetly identifies a pick position from other pick positions. After a picker reads and matches the pick instruction position identification to a pick-position identification, a picker completes the SKU pick transaction. Pick-position identification methods are:

- Machine-printed self-adhesive labels
- Human-/machine-readable label in a plastic holder
- Placard hung from the ceiling
- Digital display, pick-to-light, or RF device

Machine Preprinted Self-Adhesive Label/Placard with/without a Machine-Readable Code

In a philosophy that uses preprinted self-adhesive labels or placards, a warehouse-controlled print machine prints a pick-position identification onto a self-adhesive label/placard. After removing the back, an employee places a self-adhesive label/placard on a pick-position structural member. Machine preprinted self-adhesive label group options are:

- Individual preprinted alpha character/numeric digit label
- Preprinted label/placard with the entire pick-position identification With a bar code scanning/RF tag reading and inventory replenishment or pick philosophy, a human-/machine–readable code is printed onto each label face. The label/placard is placed directly onto a pick-position structural member.

Other pick-position considerations are:

- Human-/machine–readable paper or chipboard position identification is placed into a plastic holder. The holder has a self-adhesive back that affixes it to a pick-position structural member and permits an employee/machine reader to read a human-/machine-readable symbology.
- Placard hung from a ceiling member or embedded in the floor. If embedded in the floor, test should be conducted to verify that scan/read transactions are good.
- Digital display for pick-to-light, sort-to-light, or RF device

Pick Instruction

A pick instruction indicates to a picker or pick machine the pick position, pick quantity, and (as required) the customer-order identification. With a manual pick approach, a pick instruction is a human-/machine–readable symbology for a customer-order, WMS SKU identifications, and human-readable customer-order SKU quantity. Manual pick instruction options are:

1. Paper, which includes a) paper document and b) self-adhesive labels printed horizontally across a self-adhesive label sheet or self-adhesive label roll
2. Paperless, which includes a) voice-directed or voice recognition , b) digital display for a pick-to-light, sort-to-light, or RF device. With an automatic pick approach, the pick instruction is computer impulse that identifies a SKU pick and pick quantity.

Digital Display for Pick-to-Light, Sort-to-Light, or RF-Device Pick Instructions

A paperless pick instruction format is used in a small-item warehouse with pallet or carton flow racks, static shelves, a mobile cart with shelves or flow racks, deck racks, or a carousel or multiple carousel pick stations (see Figure 8.4). There are many pick-to-light, sort-to-light, and RF device instruction models available for implementation in a warehouse. A pick-to-light, sort-to-light, or RF device vary in how they introduce a pick instruction to a warehouse pick zone or verify a pick transaction.

Each SKU is placed into a pick position. After a scanner/reader completes a carton/tote scan/read, the WMS computer associates a customer-order number to the warehouse customer-order identification. After a picker completes the pick transaction in a pick area, a pick-to-light, sort-to-light, or RF device sends a SKU deplete transaction to the WMS computer, or, at a separate scan or pack station, a scanner/reader sends the scan transaction to the WMS computer. The computer completes a SKU and customer-order update.

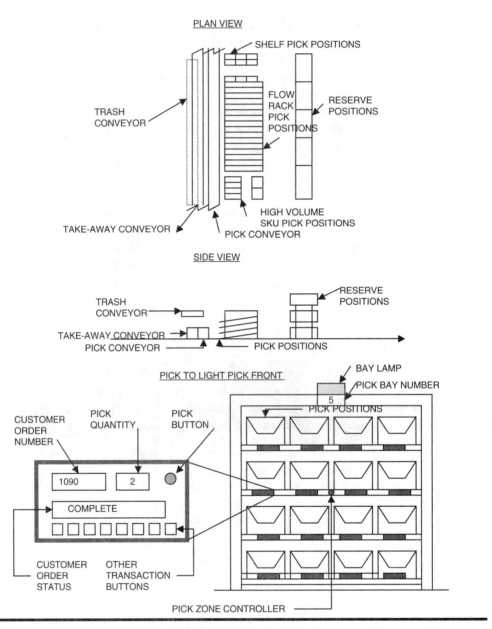

Figure 8.4   Pick to Light

Pick-to-light methods for pick instructions are:

1. In a sequence arrangement, a pick label on each carton/tote is introduced at the start of a warehouse pick line and an electronic transmission is made for each customer-order SKU or pick in an arithmetic progression. This is sent to all pick zones and pick lights on a pick line. In a pick area, the warehouse computer-controlled label print machine prints a customer-order identification number, which is attached to a carton/tote. (Alternatively, a customer-order identification is a WMS or a warehouse identification associated with a WMS customer-order identification.) A customer-order number is a unique number that is either

attached to a captive carton/tote or is used for one work day or customer-order wave. After a customer order completion in a pick zone, to pick another customer order pick transaction a picker presses the "next" button. For the next customer order, a warehouse pick computer activates a pick zone and on pick zone display to show the next customer order identification and on each pick light display to show the next customer-order SKU pick quantities. With a pick train concept, a completed carton/tote is pushed along a conveyor to the next pick zone and a new customer order carton/tote is introduced to the present pick zone. With a pick cell concept, after all customer-order picks in one pick cell, the completed customer order carton/tote is pushed forward from a pick conveyor onto a conveyor for travel on the main conveyor. Scanners/readers along the travel path relay the carton/tote identification to the warehouse computer to divert/transfer the carton/tote to another pick cell with a customer-order SKU.

2. At the entrance to each pick zone, a scanner/reader scans/reads a customer-order label. The scanner/reader sends a message to the warehouse computer to activate a pick zone/cell and all pick lights within a pick zone/cell. An activated pick light represents a pick instruction for a customer-order SKU or SKU quantity.

3. Follow the same procedure as in number 2 (above), except a magnetic strip on a card is read by a reader.

4. Other pick buttons include next, cancel, full carton/tote, or other company-required activity.

Pick-to-light, sort-to-light, or RF device instruction methods to verify a customer-order SKU pick transaction are:

1. The carton/tote enters a pick zone/cell and after a picker presses a pick-to-light system's "next" button, the warehouse computer activates a digital light display to show a customer-order identification. At a pick position, as a picker transfers a SKU from a pick position to a carton/tote, the picker presses a pick-position light for each picked SKU. The activity is performed at each illuminated pick-position light in a pick zone/cell for each customer order. When a picker has completed all picks in a pick zone/cell for a customer order, the pick transaction is completed when the picker presses the "next" button. The "next" button activates a new customer-order identification on a digital display and the pick-position lights in the pick zone/cell. Each pick transaction is sent to the warehouse computer. Pick transaction update options are a) at a pick position, by the warehouse computer, which sends a pick transaction to the WMS computer, or b) at a pack or next activity station that scans a SKU. The WMS computer updates the SKU and customer-order status.

2. A laser beam or other sensing device at each pick-position face. As a picker completes a SKU transfer from a pick position, the picker's hand or SKU breaks the light beam to register a SKU pick transaction, which reduces a pick-to-light quantity by one. The pick transfer activity is repeated until the pick-light display shows zero or is blank. Pick-transaction update options are a) at a pick position by the warehouse computer, which sends the pick transaction to the WMS computer, or b) at a pack or next activity station, which scans the SKU. The WMS computer updates SKU and customer-order status.

In a pick-to-light application that interfaces with a carton gravity flow rack, static shelves, or a mobile cart pick, preferred picker routing pattern is a horizontal pattern. The pattern starts as a picker enters a warehouse pick aisle or pick zone bay at each bay's upper first pick position and ends at each bay's lower last pick position.

SKU for a Customer Order

To have an effective and cost-efficient pick philosophy with a WMS program, each SKU small-item master carton or pallet requires a WMS SKU identification and customer-order identification to be scanned and sent to the WMS computer. The WMS SKU identification and customer-order identification WMS scan options are:

1. On a SKU, which means each SKU has a WMS identification and scanner/reader has a customer-order identification.
2. On a pick instruction, which means a paper document or paper label with WMS SKU and customer-order identifications.
3. On a packing slip that has WMS SKU and customer-order identifications.

The WMS SKU and customer-order scan identification option determines the pick philosophy and WMS scan location. Pick options are:

■ Pick
■ Pick-and-sort
■ Bulk pick-and-sort and assembly
■ Bulk pick, transport, and sort

Pick-Position Types

A pick position has a SKU quantity that is available for customer orders. In a warehouse using a WMS program, the pick-position options are all positions are pickable, or separate storage positions and pick positions.

All Positions are Pickable

All positions are pickable positions in a warehouse when all positions have SKUs. This approach is basically a floating pick-position philosophy. After customer orders deplete a SKU quantity in one pick position, the WMS computer directs a pick transaction to a pick position that contains an inventory quantity. In this pick philosophy, each SKU is transferred and scanned to pick positions that are employee and forklift-truck reachable. When all employee-reachable pick positions are depleted of inventory, and a next pick position is a forklift-reachable position, a forklift truck completes a replenishment transaction and relocates a SKU quantity from the forklift-reachable pick position to an employee-reachable position. If other pick transactions are required to complete a customer order, the forklift truck completes another replenishment and relocation from a pick position to an employee-reachable position. For the same customer-order wave, a note with a new pick position is placed onto an old pick position to direct other pickers to the new pick position. For the customer-order wave, a forklift driver scans the SKU to a new pick position and sends the scan transaction to the WMS computer. The WMS computer updates the inventory files.

Separate Storage and Pick Positions

A pick philosophy with separate storage and pick positions has pick positions that are employee reachable and storage positions that not employee reachable (i.e., are forklift truck reachable). In this philosophy all employee-reachable pick positions have SKUs that are available for sale and pickers have access to each SKU. Employee-reachable pick positions are considered fixed pick positions that receive replenishment from storage positions. Forklift-reachable storage positions are considered storage positions and the WMS computer allocates SKUs from these positions to fixed pick positions. As pick transactions deplete SKUs in a fixed pick position, the WMS computer directs a forklift truck driver to scan and move inventory from a storage position to a pick position. To ensure on-time SKU replenishment transactions, the preferred location for storage positions are above pick positions.

Small-Item Pick Position

The pick position contains sufficient SKU inventory to satisfy daily customer-order SKU volume (see Figure 8.5) and to ensure proper SKU rotation. Factors that determine a pick position are transport, customer-order SKU volume, seasonal affects, building design, maximum number of pick positions per aisle and Golden zone, SKU physical characteristics and allocation to a pick line, pick aisle or automatic pick machine, and economics.

Fixed or Variable Pick Positions

In a small-item or master-carton pick line/aisle design, pick-position arrangement options are:

1. Fixed pick position. In a pick area, on a pick line, or in automatic pick-machine warehouse computer files each SKU identification is permanently allocated to a pick position. Depending on the stored SKU volumes, a warehouse could have more than one storage position and more than one pick positon (e.g., two separate pick modules) with the same SKU. During the receiving process each SKU quantity is allocated to a pick position, and extra SKUs are allocated to storage positions. After customer orders deplete the inventory in a pick position, the WMS computer directs replenishment transactions from a storage position to a pick position. This approach maintains pick-line profile productivity, best picker productivity, SKU family grouping, requires less floor space, and maintains on-time and accurate pick-position replenishment, but there will be replenishment errors and stock-outs.

2. A variable, random, or floating pick position. A SKU is temporarily allocated to a pick position in a pick area, on a pick line, or in an automatic pick-machine warehouse computer file. After the receiving process, the WMS computer allocates SKU inventory to several free or open pick positions in a pick area; no inventory is allocated to a storage position. A SKU remains in each pick position until the first SKU pick-position quantity is depleted by customer orders. When SKU inventory in a pick position is depleted, the WMS computer assigns the next pick to another pick position with a SKU. In a variable pick-position application, the WMS computer floats a pick to the next pick position with a SKU quantity. This approach means that it will be difficult to maintain a pick-line profile; there will be increased walking distance, which will mean lower pick employee productivity; it requires additional pick positions and floor space; but the approach minimizes replenishment activity, labor, and errors.

IDENTIFICATION	SKU MOVEMENT RANGE	PICK POSITION
HIGH REACH	25% LEAST ACTIVE SKUS	LEVEL 5
GOLDEN ZONE	15% OF MODERATE ACTIVE SKUS	LEVEL 4
GOLDEN ZONE	20% OF MOST ACTIVE SKUS	LEVEL 3
GOLDEN ZONE	15% OF MODERATE ACTIVE SKUS	LEVEL 2
PIGEON HOLE	25% LEAST LEAST ACTIVE SKUS	LEVEL 1

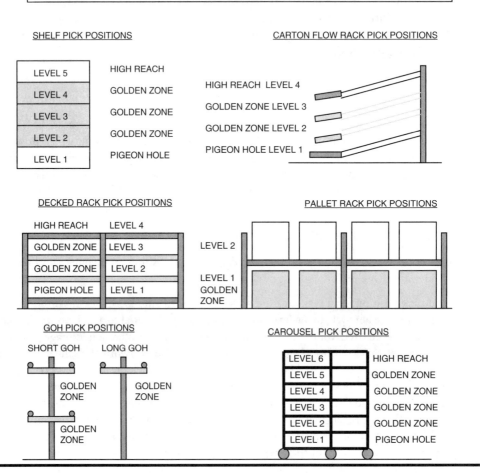

Figure 8.5   Golden Zone

Zone-Area Pick Design

A zone-area pick design separates a small-item or master-carton pick line/area into defined fixed/variable pick zones (see Figue 8.6). Each picker is responsible for customer-order picks in one pick zone. A fixed zone means that for each work day or customer-order wave a picker's pick zone is constant or has predetermined pick-position number. A variable pick zone means that for each customer-order wave a picker's pick zone or pick-position number changes. The options for pick zones are:

- One gravity pallet or carton rack bay
- Two or three gravity pallets or carton flow-rack bays
- Several static standard shelves and hand stacks on decked pallet rack bays

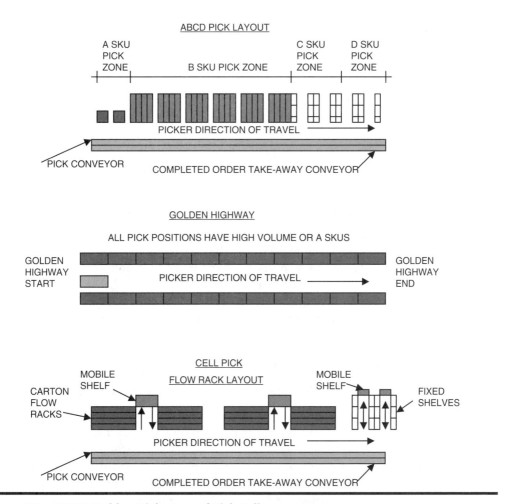

Figure 8.6   ABCD, Golden Highway, and Pick Cell

Golden Highway

In a pick philosophy in which power (i.e., fast moving) small-item, master-carton, or pallet SKUs located in a pick area/row/zone, fast-moving SKUs are located into one area, aisle pick positions, or Golden highway. In this philosophy, all promotional, seasonal, special-sale, and fast-moving SKUs are in one area or pick aisle. The pick area is located near pack stations or ship docks. This pick-position arrangement increases picker SKU hit concentration (hit number per aisle) and density (hit number per SKU), which, in turn, means high employee productivity due to the short distance between the active pick positions.

Pairs or Family Group Theory

A small-item pick-area layout philosophy is a pick-area layout that is dictated by the warehouse or local code requirements. In other words, SKUs are assigned to specific locations, zones, or aisles within a facility. In this philosophy, the pick area is designed to accommodate SKUs that compliment each other, have similar dimensions, are located in the same customer retail/plant aisle, require the same environmental conditions, require high security, contain toxic materials, or edible or nonedible, are hazardous, flammable or nonflammable, or are slow-moving SKUs.

Cell Pick Line Theory

Cell pick line theory is similar to a family group theory. Cell pick line theory is used in a small-item pick philosophy. There are separate groups within a SKU mix and number, such as each customer-order group with its own language or common language on SKUs. A pick area will have pick positions allocated for common SKUs that are available for all customer orders and separate cell pick positions (e.g., shelves or flow racks) allocated for unique SKUs for a customer-order group. A cell pick line layout has a) one series of shelves if a pick cart is used in the warehouse, or b) if pick shelves are used, the line has flow racks with a four-wheel cart, or zero- or low-pressure powered conveyor located along in each cell pick front. A cell pick line layout has pick modules for SKUs that are common for all customer orders. The pick layout uses standard equipment with gravity carton flow racks facing a pick conveyor or cart travel path, standard static shelf rows and aisles perpendicular to the pick conveyor, or a cart travel path at a static shelf aisle end with a standard shelf bay on casters (thus, the shelf on the pick-aisle end is mobile). A pick cell has standard gravity carton flow racks, standard static shelves, and a mobile standard shelf at the aisle end.

Family Group/Cell Group: Very Small SKU, Jewelry, Spare Parts

One type of SKU family group philosophy allocates each SKU group by a unique SKU description or by the last digit of the SKU inventory number. For example:

1. Family group approach has one aisle for gold watches or Ford spare parts, one aisle for other watches, one aisle for silver watches or GM spare parts, one aisle for gold bracelets or BMW spare parts, one aisle for silver bracelets or Toyota spare parts, one aisle for silver chains, one aisle for gold chains, one aisle for gold rings, one aisle for silver rings, one aisle for gold earrings, one aisle for silver earrings, and one aisle for other items
2. Using the last digit of the SKU inventory number has one aisle for number 1, one aisle 2, one aisle for 3, one aisle for 4, one aisle for 5, one aisle for 6, one aisle 7, one aisle for 8, one aisle for 9, and one aisle for 0.

The characteristics of allocating SKUs by unique description are:

■ The highest cube SKU group is located nearest to a pack area. With few vendor master cartons/totes per trip, the location minimizes receiving put-away and picker travel trips.
■ The smallest cube SKU group is located the greatest distance from the pack area. With the greatest number of vendor master cartons/totes per trip, the location minimizes receiving put-away and picker travel trips.
■ The SKU group assigned to the warehouse operation aisle is defined by the SKU physical description. Thus, employees will easily recognize a SKU assigned aisle.
■ With sales programs for one SKU group, each aisle has "A" movers that improve picker productivity.

SKU family group allocation to a pick aisle improves picker productivity by increasing SKU hit concentration and density and decreasing the number of picker trips between the pick area and a pack area. An improvement in customer returns processing activity results from the continuous customer-return flow from the processing station to a pick position. To achieve the objective, each customer-return process station has a tote for each SKU group. A returns processing station employee identifies a good quality SKU and quickly and accurately places the SKU in an appropriate container. At predetermined times (or when totes are full), the totes are transferred from the returns area to a pick area. The returns employee remains in one aisle and does not travel between aisles. SKUs may be returned to a pick position as mixed SKUs, or one SKU in a pick position.

SKU Rotation

SKU rotation philosophies for small-item, master-carton, or pallet SKUs are:

1. FIFO SKU rotation: The SKU that was received first in a warehouse is the SKU shipped first from operation. A FIFO pick-area philosophy indicates that a SKU has a predetermined life (i.e., limited shelf life) before it spoils. After a specific date, if the SKU is not withdrawn from a pick position, the SKU is no longer acceptable for a customer order. SKUs that have a FIFO SKU rotation have a one warehouse deep rack/shelf or gravity carton flow-rack pick position.
2. LIFO SKU rotation: The SKU that was received last at a warehouse has no specific rotation. LIFO pick-area philosophy indicates that a SKU does not have a predetermined shelf life and is allocated to a shelf, hand-stacked decked pallet rack, or pallet rack pick position.

SKU Location on a Pick Line/Aisle or in an Automatic Pick Machine

A SKUs physical location on a pick line/aisle or in an automatic pick machine is determined by whether the pick activity is manual, mechanized, or automatic. Pick-position guidelines are:

■ Heavy or high-cube SKUs are located at a pick line start; medium weight and medium cube SKUs are located in a pick line middle; light and small-cube SKUs are located at a pick line end
■ SKU velocity, sales, or physical movement for one fiscal year. Fast-moving SKUs are located at a pick line start; medium-moving SKUs are located in a pick line middle; slow-moving SKUs are located at a pick line end.
■ SKUs with crushable or fragile characteristics are located at a pick line end.
■ High-value SKUs are allocated to a warehouse computer-controlled pick machine, to a pick position that has limited or controlled access, or to a pick position with a security camera that is directed at a pick area.
■ SKU classified as hazardous are placed in a pick position that restricts SKUs flight and liquid run-off.
■ SKUs may be allocated to a pick line by family group or kit. In the kit philosophy SKUs with similar characteristics are located in sequential pick positions on a pick line or in a pick cell. Reasons for family group are a) the SKUs are located in a retail store aisle or b) SKUs are picked for a specific customer group, such as different languages on a SKU Spanish, French, or English and each language is considered a SKU.
■ Historical SKU movement to identify one or several SKUs with high movement per customer orders as candidates to be picked/packed off-line

- Pick-position elevation on a pick line (e.g., Golden Zone) are preferred manual pick positions for fast-moving, heavy, or high-cube SKUs. The bottom of Golden Zone is 15 to 20 inches above a floor surface; the top of a Golden Zone is 60 to 65 inches above the floor. Given average picker height and most SKU physical characteristics in a pick shelf, a Golden Zone is pick levels 2, 3, and 4. Prior to a pick line's final design, Golden Zone pick positions are finalized as design parameters.
- Pick-aisle factors are pick-position type; pick-position identification, which affects the picker and replenishment employee productivity and accuracy; and high-volume and low-volume SKUs.

Pick-Aisle/Line Profile

A pick-aisle/line profile is a method of allocating each SKU to a pick position on a pick line or in an aisle. When a pick aisle/line is separated into zones, and pickers are assigned to a pick zone, a proper pick-aisle/line profile and open master cartons are major steps to ensure that the warehouse realizes it's budgeted picker productivity. A pick-aisle/line profile uses a form or PC spread sheet and several facts:

1. Budgeted picker productivity rate, SKU historical/estimated movement and characteristics, pick-position type, and physical characteristics. A pick zone is one to two pallet or carton gravity flow-rack bays wide, which are parallel to one to four static shelf bays, and are perpendicular to a pick conveyor and pick-position identification.
2. Pick-aisle/line profile form is a PC spreadsheet (or paper profile form) completed by an employee. The spreadsheet shows each pallet or carton gravity flow-rack bay or static shelf bay pick position, estimated pick volume for each SKU or pick position, and for a each pick zone, a picker routing pattern or pick-position number sequence across a pallet or carton gravity flow-rack bay or shelf bay face pick position.
3. A pick-aisle/line profile spreadsheet allocates SKUs to pick positions within a pick zone for maximum picker productivity.
4. Shows each pallet, carton gravity flow rack, or shelf bay pick-position number.

Pick-Line, Pick-Aisle, Automatic Pick Machine Profile

An important pick-line/aisle or automatic pick machine design activty is a SKU profile (i.e., SKU allocation to a pick-line pick position). A SKU profile assigns each SKU to a pick position on a pick line, pick aisle, pick area, or in a pick machine. Without a SKU pick-aisle/line profile, the pick-aisle/line or automatic pick machine design has the potential for low picker productivity.

To assign a SKU to a pick-line/aisle or automatic pick-machine pick position, the factors that must be considered are the physical characteristics of each SKU, cube and weight, peak and average SKU movement, customer order container cube at a pack station, carton or vehicle load-carrying capacity, cube and load capacity per pick position, pick-position number per rack, shelf or gravity carton flow-rack bay, bin/automatic pick-machine side, pick-area layout and detail view drawings, anticipated customer-order SKUs per hour, pick rate per hour, and manual or PC with profile spread sheets.

After the above data has been collected and reviewed, SKUs are allocated to a pick position on a pick line, pick aisle, pick area or in a pick machine, on paper document or on a PC. SKU allocation to a pick position ensures there will be a pick position for each SKU and that each pick zone has sufficient daily customer order or customer-order wave SKU pick quantities to achieve the budgeted picker productivity rate.

Determining the Best Pick Position

A small-item pick-facility pick position is a discreet location for one SKU with a sufficient quantity to satisfy at least a customer-order wave. SKU inventory is allocated to a pick (forward or active) position, ready-reserve position, or remote storage position. With static shelves, racks or carousel, a ready-reserve position is adjacent, above, below, or behind a pick position. In other words, the SKU inventory is ready to replenish a pick position. With flow, push-back, two-deep, drive-in/drive-thru, or slide/chute, pick positions have the capacity to hold at least two master cartons or pallets. All master cartons and pallets are considered part of the pick-position inventory. A remote-reserve position is in a storage area; SKUs are transferred from a remote-reserve position to a ready-reserve position or pick position by the WMS compuer as necessary. Major factors that determine the best pick philosophy for small-item SKUs are:

- SKU type that are small items, master carton, or pallet
- Picker and replenishment employee height
- Pick-position type and capacity
- customer-order handling method, e.g., single or batched customer orders
- SKU rotation and inventory control method
- SKU demand or customer-order wave, SKU mix and sizes
- Building design
- SKU physical characteristics and classification
- IT host or WMS computer processing capability to cube and process customer orders

Other factors that influence pick-position selection are pick philosophy, risk management factors and seismic conditions, pick and replenishment procedures, and small-item pick into a captive tote, ship carton, or onto a belt conveyor.

Pick-Position Objectives

Pick-position objectives are:

- Satisfy a predetermined throughout or pick volume
- Ensure proper SKU rotation
- Provide best pick-position density per pick aisle
- Provide maximum positions per pick aisle
- Permit easy and quick SKU transfer to a replenishment transaction or from a pick position to a carton or small-item, master carton, or pallet transport
- Ensure lowest costs
- Provide pick-position identification
- Ensure pick-position identification line-of-sight

To satisfy pick-position objectives, pick-position methods for use in a warehouse are reviewed below.

Pick-Position Pick Philosophy Design Parameters

Prior to the selection, purchase, and implementation in a warehouse, the design parameters need to be clearly defined by the design team. Design factors are:

- Each SKU's average and peak sales volume, average and peak customer-order number, SKUs and lines per customer order, and customer-order and delivery cycle time
- SKU or small-item, master-carton/pallet, and pick-position dimensions, i.e., length, width, height, weight, and physical characteristics (e.g., loose, packaged, crushable, stackable, or ability to support additional SKU or fragile and classification).
- Building features, i.e., size of the pick-area (in square feet), including clearance height between a floor and ceiling joist bottom; building column spacing; building column size with building columns kept at a minimum; passageway, stairway, walls, or floor penetrations; floor surface and condition; and utilities availability and quantity.
- Average and peak on-hand inventory, replenishment method, inventory rotation requirements, and pick characteristics, e.g., singles or multi-packs
- Existing or proposed warehouse equipment, including fire protection, safety, and seismic requirements
- IT/host computer capability to process and download customer orders to the WMS computer
- Labor quantity and availability and reach height
- Other pick activities, e.g., carton make-up, packing, sealing, checking the manifest, and loading customer orders onto a delivery vehicle

Whenever possible, design parameters should be uniform. If design parameters are not uniform, SKUs with similar characteristics are grouped in one warehouse pick zone/area within a facility. For best results, the pick design is done in conjunction with good SKU allocation fundamentals, which dictate SKU location in a pick aisle or along a pick aisle/line. SKU allocation to pick-position considerations are:

- Single item or master-carton exterior package physical characteristics that allow a SKU stable in a position.
- Sleeve, inner pack, or multi-pack.
- Loose small SKU in a container or master carton. Each small-item SKU type has different characteristics that influence the pick-position selection. To assure minimal pick errors and good picker productivity, in a pick position small size SKUs have a consistent physical characteristic such as single items.

Small-Item Pick Positions for a Manual Pick Philosophy

Small-item pick-position designs handle SKUs that are stackable or nonstackable. Manual pick design options are:

1. Containers that are stacked on the floor
2. Standard pallet rack
3. Hand-stacked containers on decked pallet rack
4. Versa shelving
5. Standard shelves that are open, closed, wire mesh, mobile, round, or wide span

6. Carton flow racks that are mobile or stationary type, and can be straight, tiled, or slant back models
7. Push back flow rack
8. Slides or chutes
9. Peg board
10. Drawer
11. Kit

Nonstackable Small-Item/Flatwear Apparel SKUs

A nonstackable SKU has physical shape or exterior package characteristics that prevent stacking in a pick position. In a pick position, nonstackable SKUs are placed into a carton, bin, or container. In a carton, bin, or container, the maximum SKU inventory is allocated and retained in a pick position, which permits a picker to easily complete a pick transaction. With this approach, each bin remains in a pick position and SKUs are transferred and scanned to a bin. To ensure accurate inventory in a bin, after a bin SKU quantity is picked clean, or before a new SKU is placed into a bin, an employee completes a bin zero scan. All scan transactions and piece quantity are sent to the WMS computer to update inventory files and to release customer orders.

Small-Item Pick-Position Bin, Company/Vendor Master-Container Designs

A small-item pick-position bin or container is designed for placement in a small-item pick position used in a manual or mechanized pick philosophy. A vendor carton serves as a pick-position bin, which is made of preformed plastic, metal, wood, corrugated, or chipboard bin. Bin length, width, and height design factors are determined by:

- The SKU's physical characteristics
- Pick-position dimensions
- Desired inventory quantity in a pick position
- Whether the bin front has sufficient clearance or open space between side walls to complete a replenishment into a bin or pick transaction.
- If there is sufficient bin front surface that has proper width, height, and line-of-sight for a pick-position identification

Whenever possible, a pick-position identification is placed onto a pick-position structural support member or deck front lip. An option for the bin identification location is to have a WMS identification placed onto the bin front exterior wall. When the option is used in a pick design, bins or totes are captive to a pick shelf. Small-item pick concept bin considerations are:

- Outside dimensions, which determine the number of bins that can fit in a rack/shelf
- Internal dimensions, which determine the number of SKUs that can fit into a bin and still allow a picker to easily complete a pick transaction
- Stackable or nonstackable bins
- Dividers for a bin interior
- Permanent or removable bin front
- Structural support of a bin

- In-house transport design between two facility locations

With small bins that are 6.5 inches wide by 6 inches high, it is possible to place five bins on a 36-inch–wide shelf position. In a vertical stack, 12 pick-position levels high, a pick bay will have 60 pick positions in a 7-foot, 3-inch shelf bay.

Pick-Position Boxes

In a small-item pick philosophy, a pick-position bin, box, or container can be:

- Vendor carton
- Preformed corrugated plastic pick-position bins manufactured in standard sizes
- Preformed hardened plastic, metal, or wood bin, manufactured in standard sizes
- Preformed corrugated pick-position bin
- Preformed chipboard bin

Pick-position bin features that are:

1. Vendor carton is lowest cost but requires labor to open the top and front. A vendor carton is common in small-item pick philosophies that use gravity flow-rack or hand-stacked carton in a decked pallet rack, carousel, or shelf pick design.
2. Preformed corrugated plastic pick-position bin is used for flatwear SKUs and permits bins to be stacked on a shelf, carousel, or hand-stacked decked rack pick position.
3. Preformed hardened plastic, metal, or wood pick-position bins are used in a very small-item pick design.
4. Chipboard bin is a low-cost bin that is used for very small parts.
5. Corrugated bin is a medium-cost bin and is used for medium-sized parts.

Pick-Position Bin/Master-Carton Presentation

A key to an accurate and on-time pick philosophy is to ensure that picker productivity is at the budgeted productivity rate. A vendor master carton or bin box in a pick position ensures that employees will be able to easily and quickly transfer a SKU from a pick position to a container and for a hand-held scanner pick-position identification to have line-of-sight. Preferred vendor master carton or bin presentation in a pick position is to have a master carton open on the top or cut or open in the front. The options for having a pick-position bin front are:

1. An open-faced master carton is a precut or modified (cut by a replenishment employee) standard vendor box that has two side walls and a rear wall with an open top, open front, and solid bottom. An open master-carton arrangement does not destroy the master-carton WMS identification and provides a master carton with an open face for easy and unobstructed SKU transfer from a pick position to a container. A master carton with an open front has a pick-position deck member with sufficient structural support and front lip for a pick-position/bin identification. SKUs that are placed into an open-faced master carton have package characteristics to prevent a SKU from falling from the master carton. An open-faced bin box is used in a shelf or hand stack on a decked rack or gravity flow-rack pick-position philosophy.

2. A pick-position master carton with a half- or quarter-high front barrier is a precut or modi-fied (cut by a replenishment employee) standard vendor master carton that has two side walls, a rear wall, an open or closed top, closed and solid bottom, and a half- or quarter-high open front. This arrangement does not destroy the master-carton WMS identification. To provide strength and rigidity, tape secures bottom flaps or specially designed box inserts are secured in precut holes. To create a half- or quarter-high open bin front to a master carton, a replenishment employee cuts a square "smiley face" (or "V") in a bin or master-carton front. With the cut section removed from a master-carton front, features are a) a half- or quarter-high front barrier to retain SKUs that have a tendency to slide from a pick position. This situation is minimized by placing a cut cardboard in front, which creates a removable bar-rier; b) increased bin rigidity and stability; c) space for the SKU or WMS bin identification; d) increased SKU quantity in a pick position; e) open space for easy and quick SKU transfer from a pick position to a container; f) if there is low SKU inventory in a master carton with a front barrier, the barrier creates some difficulty when removing a SKU; and g) during the cutting activity, there is the potential for SKU damage. A pick-position master carton with a half- or quarter-high front barrier is used on a warehouse shelf, a hand stack on a decked rack, or carton gravity flow-rack pick-position philosophy.

Multiple SKU in a Single Tote/Box/Container

To consolidate pick-area space in a small-item pick philosophy, slow-moving or "C" or "D" SKU or obsolete SKUs can be consolidated into a single tote. A tote is placed into a pick position. The strategy improves slow-moving SKU hit concentration and density. The options for mixed SKU in a tote are:

1. Mixed SKUs are placed in a tote without separaters by a replenishment employee. Each SKU identifier and physical features separate one SKU from another. The philosophy has good tote utilization and increased number of SKUs per tote. To complete a pick transac-tion, a picker sorts SKUs and matches the identification and physical characteristics. With at least several mixed SKUs in a tote, it means lower pick productivity but higher put-away productivity.
2. Mixed SKUs are placed in a tote with separaters by a replenishment employee. Each sepa-rater has a WMS pick-position identification associated with a tote. During the transfer to a pick area, a replenishment employee transfers a SKU to a compartment inside a tote (pick position) and scans the WMS SKU and tote identifications. The scan transactions are sent to the WMS computer for file update and releases customer orders. This means that each SKU is separated by a separater and SKU and physical characteristics. With the philosophy, there is potential for lower tote utilization and fewer SKUs per tote. With an interior tote identification a picker has minimal sort and search time to match the SKU and physical characteristics to a complete customer order pick transaction. With physical SKU separation, mixed SKUs in a tote with separators means higher picker productivity. In a pick operation, mixed SKUs in a tote is used for very small-cube SKUs, SKUs with a small inventory quantity, RTV SKUs, an RTS SKU holding area, and obsolete SKUs.

Captive Tote to an Aisle or Shelf/Rack Bay

A captive tote is a tote with a permanent WMS identification to a aisle or bay. A tote is similar to a fixed pick position. In an aisle or bay, totes are arranged in a sequential/arithmetic progression. During a SKU transfer to a pick area, a replenishment employee transfers SKUs to a pick position and scans the SKU identification and the tote. The scan transactions are sent to a WMS computer to update files and release customer orders.

Floor Stack Pick

A floor stack philosophy is a basic pick philosophy with a large floor area. A floor stack pick philosophy has a low investment because employees stack vendor cartons/containers on the facility floor, on pallets, or on another material handling device. This approach uses SKU containers with sufficient rigidity and strength to be stacked and are noncrushable. As containers are stacked on a floor, to a stack height that does exceed an employees reach height and ensures line-of-sight to a WMS pick-position identification. A container stack options are:

1. One SKU per container container. This container philosophy is used for high-cube or high-volume SKUs. Additional containers are located in ready-reserve inventory positions.
2. One SKU per each container stack. This container philosophy provides maximum number of pick positions per aisle but the use of a bottom container creates a difficult location to complete a SKU replenishment or pick transaction.

Bins Clipped/Attached to a Support Member

A plastic bin design has a plastic bin designed to connect to a stationary or fixed support member with sufficient space for a pick-position identification. Support members are hooks or lips that extends outward and interfaces with a bin hook or lip; slots or holes that interface with a bin hook or lip and (2) on the wall sufficient clear space for a permanent pick position identification. Bin and support member components have sufficient structural strength to support a full bin or bin group. Most high-volume small-item pick operations do not use the floor stack or hook plastic bin pick-position design.

Standard Pallet Rack Pick Philosophy

In a standard pallet rack pick row, the first rack bay is considered a starter bay and has two upright frames and a pair of load beams for each elevated pick level. Each additional rack bay or add-on bay has one upright frame and a pair of load beams for each elevated pick level. A standard pallet rack is designed to handle high-cube, heavy, and very fast-moving SKUs; design options are:

1. Two 48- x 40-inch pallets in a rack bay with a pallet 48-inch dimension face a pick aisle. A rack bay design has a load beam with a 113-inch center line to center line dimension or between two rack mid post to mid post that provides four pick positions per rack bay a) 8-inch shorter picker reach into a rack bay, b) few pick-position number per pick-aisle, and c) for maximum flexibility and WMS identification line-of-sight, a wraparound label is used on a pallet stringer.

2. Two 48- x 40-inch pallets in a rack bay with a pallet 40-inch dimension face a pick aisle. A rack bay design has a load beam with 96-inch center line to center line dimension that provides a) four pick positions or faces per rack bay, b) 8-inch longer employee reach into a rack bay, c) increased pick-position number per aisle aisle, and d) single face WMS identification label is used on a pallet.

3. Three 40- x 32-inch pallets in a rack bay with a pallet 32-inch dimension face a pick aisle. A rack bay design has a load beam of 117-inch center line to center line that provides a) six pick positions per rack bay, b) 8-inch shorter employee reach into a rack bay, and c) medium pick position number per aisle.

4. Four 40- x 32-inch pallets in a rack bay with a pallet 40-inch face pick aisle. A rack bay design has a load beam of 156-inch center line to center line that provides a) eight pick positions or faces per rack bay, b) eight-inch shorter employee reach into a rack bay, c) greatest pick position number per pick-aisle with fewer upright frames, and d) a single-faced WMS identification is on a pallet.

A pick-position identification is placed on the pallet rack load beam surface that faces a pick aisle. With the first pallet pick position on the floor, the lower portion of the first load beam is the location for the floor pallet pick position; the upper portion of the first load beam is the location for a pick position. To provide two pick positions, the number sequence has "1" as the lowest or floor level pick position and "2" as the elevated pick position. Other pick-position identification options are:

■ Directional arrows at a pick position end to show a pick position.
■ Light-colored coded labels with one color for each level. The colored area is in a human-readable section or permits a scan/read transaction.
■ With a man-down forklift truck, identifications are attached to the upright posts for ready-reserve pallet positions above pick positions.

The disadvantages to this approach are low hit density and concentration, large floor area, few pick positions per aisle, and it is two pick levels high. The advantages are that it handles heavy weight, high-cube, and fast-moving SKUs with a large piece quantity in a pick position, minimizes replenishment activity, provides good SKU access, and reduces the number of ready-reserve positions.

Hand-Stacked Master-Cartons/Containers on Decked Pallet/Slotted Angle Rack Pick Philosophy

In pick philosophy in which master cartons, containers, or packaged small items are hand stacked on a decked standard pallet or slotted angle, rack bay has an upright frame and load beam components similar to a standard pallet rack. The exceptions are:

1. The design parameters have a lighter load that is supported by upright frames and load beams. With two cartons deep in hand stack rack pick position, the rack opening is nominally 8 feet, 3 inches long by 44 inches wide. A hand stack rack pick position with 16 master cartons, which are 1-foot wide by 1-foot long by 1-foot high and weigh 30 pounds per carton, means that a load beam pair rack opening carton load weight is 480 pounds. With a pallet rack bay deck material and safety factor, the estimated total load weight supported by a pair load beams is approximately 600 pounds.

2. The rack opening has deck material that covers the entire bay and provides a smooth, flat surface for small-item containers. To provide rigidity and ensure the deck supports a carton load, some applications have three to four cross members span the distance between two load beams.

The load beam's flat surface provides a surface for pick-position identification. One very important rack load beam design consideration is that load beams are designed for a hand stack application, not a pallet pick/storage position. If a pallet is placed onto lightweight load beams, the load beams will more than likely collapse, the load beams and SKU will be damaged, and there is the potential for employee injury.

In most warehouse operations, an elevated or second level load beam front has upper and lower pick-position WMS identifications. The factors that determine pick-position levels in a hand-stacked pallet rack vertical opening are:

- Bottom pick-position level elevation that is 6 inches above the floor on a pallet or a deck with underside support runners.
- The desire to have a bottom pick-position level supported by a pair of load beams or a pallet.
- Vertical open space between the top of a container and next load beam bottom, which permits a picker to complete a pick transaction or SKU transfer from a tote to a carton. If a container in a pick position has an open front, clearance is nominally 6 inches high. If a container front in a pick position is closed, the clearance is 9 to 12 inches.
- Load beam vertical height to support a load beam design load.
- Deck material vertical height and a deck design.
- Replenishment and pick employee height.

Hand Stack Options

Upright frame depth permits a pick design in which the warehouse can stack one or two cartons deep into a rack opening. The design options are:

1. Stack containers in a single rack row with pick aisles on both rack bay sides with a barrier on rack deck material to divide the deck surface depth into two sections. In section 1, WMS identifications face pick aisle "A"; in section 2, WMS identifications face pick aisle "B." Barrier options are a) angle metal with leg up and base leg secured to deck material, b) rope attached to two upright posts that spans a rack bay, c) metal or plastic pipe secured to deck material, or d) wood member secured to deck material. With cartons 21 inches deep on each barrier side (in a typical rack, which is 44 inches deep), the barrier width will be ½–1 inch. This ensures that a) cartons on each side are properly aligned in a pick position, b) if a replenishment/pick employee from aisle "A" pushes a carton into a rack bay that a carton on other side (aisle "B") will not fall into aisle "B," and c) it is easy to pick from a master carton. The option provides for the maximum number of pick positions in a rack bay with one or two cartons in a pick position.
2. Back-to-back rack rows or a single rack bay row with pick positions facing each pick aisle. The features are a) handles long SKUs and b) fewer pick positions.

Hand-Stacked Rack Bay Deck Material

A pallet rack opening deck design and material fits in a rack bay. A rack load beam design influences deck design and material. Load beam design options are step load, flat front, indented front, or box (or "H") structural load beam. A flat rack load beam front provides maximum surface for two pick-position WMS identifications attachment or one identification above the other identification. Pallet rack opening deck material has sufficient rigidity and structural strength to support a hand-stacked carton load weight and provides a smooth flat surface to easily move a carton across the deck. Deck material options are:

- Wire mesh that is flat or an inverted "V"
- Plywood or pressed board sheets
- Metal slats or sheets
- Gravity conveyors

A deck material design parameters are maximum load weight and carton length, width and height; load beam type and span between two load beams and upright frames; rack upright frame depth; and maximum allowable deflection.

Standard Shelves Pick Philosophy

A standard shelf pick-position philosophy is used for medium- to slow-moving SKUs, medium- to light-weight SKUs, and medium- to small-cube SKUs. With flexibility to easily add shelf level heights, shelves, shelf bays, handle a wide SKU variety, and have ready-reserve positions above pick positions, the shelf pick-position philosophy is common in small-item order fulfillment designs.

Shelf Pick-Position Designs

Standard shelf pick-position design options are:

1. A closed shelf bay design has a solid rear wall and two solid side panels with front open to the pick aisle. The open front allows SKU storage/pick transaction and scan transaction completion.
2. An open shelf pick-position bay has a no rear wall but each side has an X- or short-sway brace or a panel and, again, the front is open to the pick aisle for storage/pick and scan transactions.

With either design, an elevated shelf front lip with a 1-inch front is used for pick-position identification attachment. In accordance with the pick philosophy, a bottom shelf level WMS identification is placed on the lip front or shelf top facing upward, which provides an employee easy line-of-sight but must be protected to minimize damage.

Wire Mesh and Hardened Plastic Shelves

A wire mesh bay and a hardened plastic shelf bay are both similar and different to a standard shelf design. Similar in that the shelves have an open design and the shelf pick-position level has strands or slats in the deck surface. Strands create openings or slats in the deck surface that allow dust and

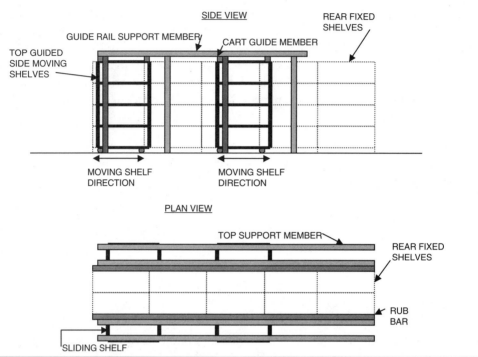

Figure 8.7 Sliding Racks Positions

dirt to fall to the floor and shelf fronts permit pick-position identification attachment with a self-adhesive label or label holder. The standard shelf major difference is a solid shelf.

Fixed-Track Mobile Shelf

This design uses a fixed-track mobile shelf bay (closed or open) or three- to four-wheel mobile shelf bay (see Figure 8.7). The design options:

1. The shelf is secured on moveable bases that travel over in-floor tracks. The shelves are moved (manually, mechanically, or by an electric motor) for access (and a pick aisle) between two shelf bays.
2. Each upright post top is attached to an overhead guide rail; each upright base has a caster and wheel. An employee moves shelf bays (manually or mechanically) to access a pick position. A shelf bay lip is the pick-position identification location.

A fixed-track mobile shelf pick-position has alternative designs, specifically:

1. A fixed overhead track mobile shelf has a one-deep open/closed shelf bay with a rectangular shelf. The long side is perpendicular to a main aisle. The mobile shelf bay travels perpendicularly to a main aisle front. When shelf bays are closed, bumpers on shelf base corners create an open space between each upright post so that an employee can reach an upright shelf and move a shelf.

2. A two-deep mobile shelf design has two shelf sections. The rear shelf section has fixed two shelf bays that face a pick aisle. The front shelf section is a mobile shelf bay that is manually moved along the front of the rear shelf bay. The mobile shelf bay faces the pick aisle. To access rear shelf pick positions, a picker moves the front mobile shelf to the appropriate location. A mobile shelf design can use in-floor tracks or an overhead fixed track for the front shelf's travel path. The shelf bay lip is the pick-position identification location.

3. An in-floor track mobile shelf design has a single shelf bay or back-to-back shelf bays set secured to a moveable platform. In most designs, one to two inches is allowed between each shelf bay. One bay per platform is used for a manual or mechanically moved shelf; two shelves per platform are used if the shelves are moved by an electric motor. To manually move a shelf bay, a picker pushes or pulls the shelf bay over the track. To mechanically move a shelf bay, a picker turns a wheel/handle, which moves the shelf over the track. To move a shelf bay with an electric motor, a picker controls the shelves from a control panel. A shelf bay lip is a pick-position identification location.

4. A four-wheel mobile shelf bay has one open, closed, or wire-mesh shelf or flow-rack bay. The shelf bay has rigid or swivel casters with a polyurthane covered wheels, which are placed either under each upright post or in the shelf bay's corners. The flow rack is three to four feet deep. Casters and wheels permit an employee to push or pull a shelf to a desired location on a pick line. The shelf bay lip is the pick-position identification location.

In a pick-area design in which the pick aisle is perpendicular to the conveyor, a four-wheel mobile shelf bay design with three- to four-fixed-shelf-bays wide and at the perpendicular pick aisle end. A perpendicular pick aisle is between two pick-position shelf rows, and is located at the end of the pick aisle. During pick activity, the mobile shelf bay is moved to the perpendicular pick aisle end with pick positions facing the pick aisle. In this position, the picker routing pattern directs a picker past the shelf bay's pick positions. To ensure easy movement of shelf bays, light SKUs are allocated to shelf bay pick positions, and swivel casters are preferred for the shelf bay. In a pick-aisle layout design, the perpendicular pick-aisle width is determined by the mobile pick shelf bay width that is normally three to four feet wide. In a manual small-item pick operation, a four-wheel mobile shelf is used to increase the number of pick positions for "D" SKUs.

Wide Span/Slotted Angle Shelves

A wide span shelf, slotted angle, or long span philosophy is a hybrid between standard open shelf and hand-stacked in a pallet rack designs. With a wide span concept, a pick position or deck span is between two upright posts, which is similar to a pallet rack load beam span. A wide span shelf load weight capacity is similar to standard shelf weight capacity. To ensure wide span shelving stability and rigidity, two load beams are attached to a upright post's top. A load beam front is a pick-position identification location.

Carton Flow-Rack Pick Design

A carton flow-rack pick-position design is used in a small-item pick philosophy to provide pick positions for fast- to medium-moving, high-cube, and heavy SKUs. SKUs are best allocated to carton flow rack because of the SKU presentation at a pick position and the additional cartons in a flow-rack lane. Carton flow racks are available in a variety of dimensions. The flow-rack face determines the flow-rack bay or the number of pick positions in a pick line/aisle. The flow-rack face presents a SKU pick position to a pick line/aisle and the pick-position identification. In a flow-rack design with a WMS program, the replenishment flow-rack side has a pick-position identification to allow replenishment scan transactions. For good picker productivity, the maximum number of pick positions are allocated to a flow-rack Golden Zone and other pick levels. The basic designs options are:

1. A straight back flow-rack design. The front and rear vertical post members are perpendicular to the floor. A perpendicular design has each pick-position level extend toward a pick or replenishment aisle at the same length. This means that the next highest pick-position level is directly above a lower pick position. The pick position in this design has a higher clearance between a carton and above pick-position member. To reduce this clearance to the minimum, a carton has a partially open front.
2. A layback carton flow-rack frame design has the front and rear vertical members at a 10% angle to the floor surface. The layback frame feature means that the lowest pick-position level extends outward or the furthest distance toward a pick aisle. The next highest pick level is set back by one or two inches from the lower pick level front. Viewed from the side, the layback feature resembles a stairway. The layback feature on the flow-rack replenishment side is straight back or angled. On an angled flow-rack replenishment side the highest pick level has the greatest extension into a replenishment aisle.
3. A layback carton flow-rack frame design with a tilt front presents a carton interior or SKUs at an angle. The SKU presentation feature enhances picker productivity and SKU transfer because it is easier to withdraw a SKU from a carton in a pick position.

Most flow-rack vendor pick level frames or shelf replenishment and pick side end members have sufficient space for a pick identification or pick-to-light module attachment on the pick level frame's pick side. Front and rear pick level frame members are 2½ inches high and full bay width. It is considered good pick practice to have a pick-position identification along with a pick-to-light module. This provides a paper pick for customer service during a pick-to-light problem or down time.

Tilt front flow-rack pick level frame configuration design options are:

1. Separate rollers or conveyor lanes that match the other pick level frame conveyor or roller lanes
2. A coated metal sheet tray or member that covers the entire front and is supported by a tilt front interior lip or edge. In most carton flow-rack small-item pick applications with normal employee reach, the maximum number of pick levels is five or four levels. Flow rack pick level design options are a) a straight front flow rack, b) a layback flow rack, and c) a layback with a tilt front flow rack.

Carton width, flow-rack bay width and pick-line profile are factors that determine the number of pick posistions per flow-rack bay and for each pick level. In terms of carton allocation, most designs allow one or two inches between two carton conveyor lanes/pick positions. In most pick-line profiles for a five-level flow-rack bay, the Golden Zone or middle pick levels are levels 2, 3, and 4. In a four-level flow-rack bay, the Golden Zone or middle pick levels are levels 2 and 3. SKU allocation to flow pick levels are as follows:

1. Golden Zone pick levels have fast-moving, medium-weight, medium-cube SKUs
2. The lowest pick levels have heavy, high-cube, slow-moving SKUs
3. The highest pick levels have light-weight, medium- to small-cube, slowest-moving SKUs

A pick-line profile or SKU allocation to a flow-rack bay zone matches SKU movement to budgeted picker productivity rate. One important feature of a flow-rack pick level with a horizontal picker routing pattern across a pick bay front is that very fast-moving SKUs are efficiently allocated to a single flow-rack pick level in a Golden Zone. This means that one pick position is the full width of the flow-rack frame. With a pick-line SKU profile, there is a large inventory in a pick position to minimize stock outs and ensure anticipated picker productivity. With a standard carton, most pick-line profile are four to five cartons/pick positions wide. With a small carton, most pick-line profiles are seven cartons/pick positions wide. A carton flow-rack pick bay has a pick-position range:

- A 5-high pick level and 5-wide pick level flow-rack bay has 25 pick positions
- A 4-high pick level and 5-high pick level flow-rack bay has 20 pick positions
- A 5-high pick level and 7-wide pick level flow-rack bay has 35 pick positions
- A 4-high pick level and 7-wide pick level flow-rack bay has 28 pick positions

SKU Pick-Position Flow-Rack Pick Designs Options

A high-volume small-item/flatwear apparel pick design in which there are frequent changes in the SKU mix requires a pick-line setup/profile. Pick-process instruction options are pick-to-paper-document, RF device, or pick-to-light. To ensure maximum picker productivity, accurate picks, and on-time customer orders, a flow-rack pick line has high-demand SKUs and medium- to low-demand SKUs in a pick position. Some professionals refer to high-demand SKUs as "power SKUs," which are promotional, seasonal, special sale, or daily promoted, and have a one- to three-day high-demand life cycle. Carton flow-rack line profile or setup philosophies are:

- Continuous flow-rack pick line with random SKU allocation/profile along the pick line
- Continuous carton flow-rack pick line with specific flow-rack lanes allocated/profiled for high-demand SKUs
- Pick area with three modules separated into three sections

A carton flow-rack pick line has predetermined flow-rack channels/lanes to provide pick positions for a pick concept design SKU number. As previously stated, high-demand SKUs have a life cycle of a certain length. A SKU life cycle is separated into first day ("A" or high-demand SKU), second day ("B" or medium- to high-demand SKU), and third day ("C" or low- to medium-demand SKU).

Continuous Flow-Rack Pick Line with Random SKU Profiles

In a flow-rack pick line with random SKU profiles, SKUs are profiled to any pick position on a pick line. The pick line has pallet flow and carton flow lanes. The SKU profiles to pick positions are completed randomly. This means that there is no specific SKU allocation to a pick position for a SKU life cycle or a specific day number that a SKU is available for sale. This in turn means that there will be a wide SKU mix along a pick line: "A" SKUs in a pick position; "B" and "C" SKUs in a pick position on both sides. The approach features:

- Increased picker travel distance and time between two pick positions

- Increased travel distance and time to complete a pick-line setup and pick-position replenishment transaction
- Increased travel time and distance to reorganize SKUs in accordance with SKU life cycles
- It is difficult to manage a picker zone to ensure budgeted or good picker productivity

Continuous Flow-Rack Pick Line with Specific SKU Profile

In a continuous flow-rack pick line with specific SKU profiles, SKUs are profiled to specific pick positions. A pick line has pallet flow and carton flow lanes. SKUs profiled to a pick position/picker zone are completed by SKU number, which provides projected pick SKUs to achieve budgeted picker productivity. If the SKU number profiled to a pick zone cannot achieve budgeted picker productivity, the profile achieves the highest possible picker productivity.

SKU profiles to pick positions are completed on a specific basis. This means that there is a specific SKU profile to a pick position for a SKU life cycle or there is a specific day number that a SKU is available for sale. With specific SKUs profiles, SKUs are separated into first day, in which high-demand or "A" SKUs are allocated to pallet flow lanes; second day, in which medium- to high-demand or "B" SKUs are allocated to a single-carton flow-rack lane or multiple-carton flow-rack lanes; and third day, in which low-demand or "C" SKUs are allocated to a single-carton flow-rack lane. The features of this approach are:

- A slight decrease in picker travel distance and time between two pick positions.
- A slight decrease in travel distance and time to complete a pick-line setup or pick position replenishment transaction.
- A slight decrease in travel time and distance to rotate a SKU to a proper pick position in accordance with the life cycle.
- It is easy to establish pick zones to ensure good picker productivity.

Carton/Tote In-Feed onto a Pick Line

In a pick/pass design, each carton/tote that enters a pick line has a WMS program or warehouse customer-order identification. The identification has a customer-order identification that faces a pick aisle. The identification attached to a carton/tote ensures a picker or scanner/reader line of sight and to ensure on a pick conveyor that a customer-order identification is in the same sequence (first-in first-out) as a customer-order identifications were entered into a pick-to-light computer program. As the carton/tote enters a pick zone, a picker matches the customer-order identification to the pick-position digital display.

WMS or warehouse carton/tote identification options are:

1. A disposable label. Customer order identification labels in the same numerical sequence as the WMS computer customer-order download sequence to a pick line warehouse computer are printed at a pick line entrance. At the pick-line start station, an employee/machine applies an identification label to each carton/tote side and makes sure that a picker has line-of-sight to the identification. If the warehouse processes a wide variety of cartons, a side label application machine is required.
2. A permanent label. Each label is preprinted and placed onto a tote, and the applier makes sure there is consistent height and line-of-sight for a scanner. As the tote enters a pick-line

conveyor, a scanner/reader reads the label and sends the scan data to a pick-line computer. The warehouse computer associates the WMS customer-order identification to the warehouse tote identification. The warehouse computer and the tote's travel sequence permit a picker to match the warehouse identification to the pick-to-light identification. To ensure employee line-of-sight to a warehouse customer-order identification, a pick tote may have labels on both exterior sides, labels on the tote lead and trail exterior ends, or labels on the interior sides.

The options for a carton/tote in-feed to a pick-line or start station are:

■ From a transport conveyor directly to a pick conveyor
■ Diverted from a transport or take-away conveyor to a pick conveyor

When we consider that a carton/tote travels directly from a transport conveyor to a pick conveyor, a pick conveyor design should have a single carton/tote start pick location. The features are:

■ There is sufficient container queue space prior to the first pick position or zone
■ The carton/tote transport travel path feeds directly to a pick-line conveyor
■ On a low or zero pressure pick conveyor, at a pick zone end fixed position flat stop device or an employee controls the carton/tote flow on a conveyor travel path
■ A carton/tote take-away conveyor starts at the first pick position

A pick area with multiple start locations design features are:

■ Prior to the first pick station/zone on a transport conveyor there is sufficient carton/tote queue with a scanner/reader and divert device to transfer a carton/tote from a transport conveyor onto a pick line conveyor
■ The carton/tote take-away conveyor starts at the first pick position

Pick Carton/Tote Travel on a Pick Line

A high-volume pick/pack or pick/pass carton/tote pick design uses flow-rack bays, a picker aisle, a carton/tote pick conveyor, and a container take-away conveyor (for completed and partial orders). There are several options for pick/pass pick-carton/tote movement over a pick module.

To divert a carton/tote onto a pick conveyor (a nonpowered or zero pressure roller conveyor) at a start station for travel through a pick line (or pick design) one pick zone has a "no zone skip." The "no zone skip" design has the first pick zone as each carton enters directly onto a pick conveyor from a transport conveyor. A "no zone skip" pick conveyor is continuous from first pick zone past all pick zones. In a pick design, cartons are transferred onto a pick conveyor to form a carton train. After a carton train is transferred to the pick conveyor, each carton passes each picker as it moves from one pick zone to the next. A carton train is in a sequence entered/read by a pick-line scanner/reader. Cartons are first-in first-out sequenced in a pick-line computer queue and appear on a pick-zone display light. If a carton/tote requires a pick from a pick position in a pick bay, a pick line computer triggers pick bay lamp. An activated pick bay lamp signals a picker that a pick transaction is required in the bay from one of the pick positions.

With a pick cell design, a tote/carton is diverted from a main conveyor to a pick cell. Along the main conveyor, scanners/readers send the customer-order identification to the warehouse computer, which activates a divert to a related pick cell. After all picks in a pick cell have been completed, a picker returns the tote/carton to a main travel path for travel to the next pick cell.

When a carton is completed in a pick zone, a pick-to-light digital display signals to a picker a completed pick message. When the pick-completed signal is given, a picker transfers (or pushes) the completed carton from the pick conveyor onto the take-away conveyor. If a carton is not completed in one pick zone, the pick-to-light digital display signals to a picker a next pick message. With a next pick message signal, a picker transfers or pushes a partially completed carton along a pick conveyor from one pick zone to the next. Each pick zone has one to three flow-rack bays. Each flow-rack bay has pick-zone controller with zone and bay lamps. The pick-to-light feature permits a flow-rack pick line to have variable pick zones or flow bays that can be expanded or shortened to match SKU volumes.

A carton train moves or is pushed along a pick conveyor from high-volume to low-volume pick zones. In a high-volume pick section, pick zones consist of one or two bays, and there are many cartons completed and pushed forward from the pick conveyor to the take-away conveyor. In low-volume pick zones, pick zones have two to four bays, and few cartons are completed.

The second option has two pick-line sections. The pick design has one major pick line at the front of a major pick section and at a second pick section in the rear. There is a carton/tote divert at the front zone for travel through the first and second pick lines. Or a carton/tote can pass the first divert device and divert at the second pick line or "one zone skip." A carton/tote flows through a pick/pass or pick/pack design, and has one or two divert locations or one zone skip. A one zone skip or two divert location design divides a pick-line section into two pick-line sections. The first pick line is at a pick line start; the second pick line follows the first pick-line section. On a carton/tote in-feed travel path, a scanner/reader reads each carton's symbology and diverts (or does not divert) the carton/tote onto pick-line section 1 that allows the carton/tote to travel to section 2. If a carton/tote has a pick from the first pick-line section 1, an in-house transport conveyor computer and divert device diverts the carton/tote to the first pick-line section conveyor. The carton/tote travels on a pick conveyor over the first pick-line section pick fronts, and at a pick zone end a picker pushes the carton/tote onto a take-away conveyor. As the carton/tote from the first pick-line section—or a carton/tote that by-passed the first pick-line section—passes a second pick-line WMS or warehouse symbology scanner/reader, the scanner/reader reads the label and determines if the carton/tote has picks from pick-line section 2. If the carton/tote has picks from a second pick-line section, the conveyor diverts the carton/tote onto pick-line section 2. The carton/tote handling is the same as the no divert or no zone skip design.

The third option has multiple pick zones along a pick line, one pick zone is at the pick-line front and other pick zones are along the pick-line middle for travel through each pick zone or a multiple-operation zone design. A multiple-zone carton flow through a pick/pass design is a long pick line separated into multiple zones. In a pick-line multiple separation, the first pick zone is at a pick-line section start, the second pick zone is a preassigned flow-rack bay number, and the third (or as many as required) pick zone has a flow-rack bay number. As a carton travels on an in-feed conveyor, a carton first travels past a scanner/reader that reads the symbology. If a carton has picks in the first pick zone, the conveyor diverts the carton into the first pick zone. A pick zone conveyor moves along only the first pick zone fronts. Upon completion in the first pick zone, the carton is pushed forward from the pick conveyor onto the take-away conveyor. A second symbology scanner/reader reads the carton. If the carton on the travel path has a pick from the next section, the conveyor diverts the carton onto a second pick zone pick conveyor line. If the carton on the travel path is not required at the next pick section, the carton is diverted to the appropriate pick line or zone.

This design features:

- The cost of two divert devices and symbology readers
- Less flexibility to have a variable pick zone length
- With a shorter pick line, a completed carton push-off, a multiple carton train is easy to push over a slow-moving SKU section
- Additional time to complete a pick-line profile, good picker productivity, and picker training

A Pick Line with 2/3 Pick Modules Separated into Three Sections

The 2/3 pick module with 2/3 sections design permits maximum flexibility in completing customer orders. With a customer-order wave with a large customer-order volume, 2/3 pick modules and 2/3 sections permit a pick design to activate all nine pick sections. With a customer-order wave with a medium number of customer orders, 2/3 pick modules and 2/3 sections permit a pick design to activate pick modules with 3/6 pick sections. A customer-order wave with a low number of customer orders, a three pick module and each module with three section concept permits a pick area design flexibility to activate or not to activate a pick module or section. The flexibility is to activate a) for a low to medium high volume customer order day, one pick module with its three pick sections; b) for a medium to high volume customer order day, two pick modules with the associated pick sections; c) for a very low volume customer order day, one pick module and one or two assocaited pick sections; and d) for a high volume customer order day, three pick modules and each pick module three pick sections. 2/3 pick modules that are separated into 2/3 sections is pick-line design in which SKUs are profiled to specific pick positions in each pick-line section. Each pick-line section has pallet flow lanes and carton flow lanes located along a pick line. SKU profiled to pick positions are completed on a specific basis. A specific profile means that there is a specific SKU profile to a pick position for a SKU life cycle or the day number that a SKU is available for sale. With a specific SKU profile to a pick line, most applications have a) first day ("A") SKUs profiled to a pallet flow lane, b) second day ("B") SKUs profiled to a single carton flow-rack lane or multiple carton flow-rack lanes, and c) third day ("C") SKUs profiled to a single carton flow-rack lane. The features are:

- Decreased picker travel distance and time between two pick positions.
- Decreased travel distance and time to complete a pick-line setup and replenishment transactions.
- There is required travel time and distance to rotate or remove SKUs to a proper pick position per the requirements of a SKU life cycle.
- It provides maximum management and pick-line flexibility and improves the ability to establish picker zones to ensure good picker productivity.

Mobile Flow Rack or Shelf Bay

An individual mobile shelf or carton flow-rack bay has the same structural components and capacity as a standard or carton flow-rack bay except for one feature. The unique feature is that a shelf or carton flow-rack bay has caster/wheels and is moved by an employee to a paper document pick line. A mobile shelf or carton flow rack with four structural posts design options are a) caster and wheel is securely attached to each post or b) four-wheel dolly that supports four structural posts.

Vendor Carton Presentation in a Pick Position

Vendor carton presentation in a pick position allows a picker to complete a pick transaction with minimal nonproductive tasks, which increases picker productivity. To achieve high picker productivity with a standard shelf, deck rack, or gravity flow-rack design, a carton should have:

■ SKUs ready for pick transaction completion
■ filler material removed from the carton interior

All SKUs ready for removal from a master carton means that a replenishment employee has:

1. Cut and removed carton top flaps. Master-carton preparation practice is preferred for cartons allocated to pick level 1 or the lowest pick level, as well as all cartons allocated to Golden Zone pick levels.
2. Made a square (or "V") cut front in the front of the carton. A "V" cut carton does not destroy the carton identification. The practice is used for cartons on the highest or Golden Zone pick level and when an empty carton is thrown into the trash.
3. Opened the carton flaps and secured them to a carton sides with rubber bands or clips if the empty carton is used in a pack activity. In a pick area, an empty carton is transferred from a pick position to a start or pack station. At a start or pack station, rubber bands or clips and the WMS carton identification are removed from the carton and the carton is introduced to a pick line or used at a pack station.

A gravity flow-rack pick-position is designed as a stand alone pick design in which pick positions face a pick aisle. In most small-item pick applications, flow-rack pick bays:

■ Are separated into pick zones. Each pick zone is profiled to ensure that SKUs profiled to a pick-zone's pick position match budgeted picker productivity rates.
■ Have 30 to 36-inch wide pick aisle between the flow-rack pick face and pick conveyor or vehicle travel path.
■ A replenishment aisle that has direct access to a flow-lane replenishment side and to ready-reserve positions.
■ After a predetermined pick bay number, in accordance with local codes and company practice, there is a cross aisle that provides employee entrance and exit from a pick line to a replenishment area or emergency exit.

Flow-bay rack pick-area design options are single pick line, dual or mirror pick line, two dual sets or mirror pick lines with separate take-away conveyors, and with a pick cell concept use short flow-rack lanes for unique SKUs.

Small-Item Pick of Fast-Moving SKUs from Pallet/Carton Flow Racks

Most small-item warehouses have very fast small items or fast-moving SKUs. SKUs are enclosed in master cartons and account for a large percentage of customer order pick volume. The pick-position options are:

1. A pallet pick position. A pallet for a SKU is placed onto a pick-line pick position. A pick-line design, a pallet is placed onto pallet flow lanes or is set on a floor. The pick area has a separate replenishment and pick aisle. After a replenishment employee scans a pallet and pick-position WMS identifications, WMS scan transactions and SKU quantity are sent to the WMS computer for inventory file update and customer order release. In a pallet pick position, if SKUs are presented to a picker in enclosed cartons, per the requirements of the order, a picker picks SKUs from a pallet. The picker cuts open a master carton, disposes of filler material and empty carton trash and transfers a SKU quantity from the carton to a container. One option has another employee cut open master cartons. To complete a pick from a pallet, a picker reaches across a 48- or 60-inch long pallet. When the pallet becomes empty, a picker must remove the empty pallet from the pick position, remove the WMS identification from the pallet, and transfer the empty pallet to an empty pallet holding area or pallet flow lane. The empty pallet flow lane design options are a) flat over a travel path or b) vertical or standing up over a travel path. When a pallet is placed on a pallet roller conveyor, a forklift truck completes a replenishment transaction on the conveyor. A nonpowered roller conveyor replenishment end is set at a slightly higher elevation than a roller conveyor pick end. This permits an employee to easily pull a pallet forward over the conveyor to a pick position. When the pallet is set on a floor, a pick position is one pallet deep. After SKU depletion from a pallet, an employee completes a timely empty pallet removal from a pallet position and a replenishment employee completes a pallet replenishment to a pick position. This design features lower picker productivity due to a) additional nonproductive picker activities, e.g., opening cartons, disposing of filler material, and moving cartons for access to SKUs, b) having a replenishment employee prepare a carton for a picker to complete pick transactions, c) removing an empty pallet from a pick line/aisle, and d) increased walk distance between two pick positions.

2. Master cartons transferred onto a flow-rack position. With fast-moving SKU placement on a pick line in flow-rack pick positions, a pick area will have a separate replenishment and pick aisle. From the replenishment aisle, a replenishment employee opens each master carton, transfers an opened master carton onto a flow-rack lane, and disposes of filler material and the empty carton top. In the pick aisle, a picker has easy access to SKUs in a master carton. If each master carton has a WMS identification, a replenishment employee scans the master carton and pick-position identifications. The scan transactions and SKU quantity are sent to the WMS computer for inventory update and customer order release. If a master carton is transferred from a pallet, a replenishment employee completes the move transaction from a pallet to a pick position. Again, scan transactions and SKU quantity are sent to the WMS computer for inventory update and customer order release. Depending on master-carton size and volume, SKUs are allocated to one or more master-carton flow lanes on the carton flow lane level. This means that a picker is more productive because a picker removes an empty carton from a pick position and throws the empty carton into the trash. A gravity flow-rack features are high picker productivity due to direct access to SKUs in a master carton and fewer nonproductive activities, separate replenishment aisle, and decreased walk distance between two pick positions.

Push Back Rack Philosophy

A push back pick philosophy is a unique or a modified flow-rack pick philosophy. If a pick facility floor space does not have sufficient floor space for a standard flow-rack replenishment aisle, a five- to eight-foot-deep flow rack is designed as push back rack. A push back flow rack is designed with an end stop at the back and at a flow-rack conveyor lane front. The pick-position identification is on the push back front. A push back pick philosophy is designed as a single row against a wall or as a back-to-back pick-position row.

Chute/Slide Pick Philosophy

A chute or slide pick-position has the same structural members (save one) as a standard pallet rack or shelving pick. With a slide rack or shelf pick position, each pick position has a solid deck and side guards to support loose SKUs. If SKUs are in a container or carton, a solid or wire mesh deck is a slide surface. With a wire mesh pick position, top wire strands are members that run from the front to rear that permit an employee to easily push a bin or carton into a pick position. All slide flow lanes have a pick-face end stop. A pick face has a pick-position identification on charge and discharge ends. A slide top surface is coated sheet metal, plastic, or coated wood that is sloped or pitched toward the pick aisle. To ensure container and loose SKU movement through a slide, the carton bottom exterior surface and slide surface has a low friction coefficient. With loose small items, the friction coefficient is minimal but a front barrier and high side guards retain SKUs in a pick position.

Cantilever Rack and Pegboard Pick Designs

Cantilever rack and pegboard pick designs are used for long SKUs that require a flat position and are not handled by one of the previously mentioned pick-position designs. With a solid deck or basket secured to arms, a pick position handles long SKUs. If SKUs are not stackable on a deck, a two- or three-sided container or open-ended basket holds SKUs in a pick position. Because cantilever rack arms support a solid deck or shelf, the deck, shelf front, or face has sufficient space for a pick-position identification or the position identification is attached to a solid deck front.

A pegboard design has pegs secured against a flat vertical surface and extends outward. A peg handles loose or packaged SKUs with a loop. A SKU loop is slipped over a peg and the SKU is retained in a pick position. The peg permits light-weight SKUs such as jewelry chains to hang flat in a pick position. The best location for an identification is directly above a peg.

Drawer Pick Design

A drawer pick design is used for pick positions for very small SKUs. A drawer pick design has a large fixed wall container with many small interior fixed wall drawers (i.e., containers). Each drawer has ability to move outward from the large wall container for pick transactions and to move back into the large container for storage. Another feature is that a drawer is separated into numerous smaller compartments and each compartment has sufficient surface for a pick-position identifier. A drawer pick design features are:

- Each drawer provides 15 to 20 pick positions with a maximum load capacity of 400 pounds
- the larger fixed wall container can house 8 to 10 drawer levels, which provides 120 pick positions per large container, which is a high number of pick positions in a small area

A drawer pick design is best for very small loose or packaged SKUs with a small SKU inventory on hand. A drawer pick design can have either a single row of drawers or back-to-back rows. The aisle width should be sufficient to extend each drawer into an aisle, and permit a second picker to pass while the drawer is open.

Drawer layout can place a drawer cabinet in a rack bay or a standard shelf bay.

Unique Small-Item Pick-position Considerations

Considerations for small-item SKUs in a pick position are:

- If SKUs are considered hazardous or combustible, they are allocated to a pick position that is protected with a wire meshed barrier, sheet metal enclosure, an enclosed area with a firewall, and have a containment chamber, pit, or pan.
- If SKUs have a high value, they are allocated to a pick position that has a lockable wire-mesh cage, enclosed cabinet, or area with controlled employee access.
- If SKUs are considered toxic, they are allocated to a pick position separate from other SKUs.

Pick Philosophies

Pick concepts provide an accurate, cost-effective, on-time, and efficient customer order service to present and future customers at a reasonable profit. Key factors to a pick concept are a) storage and pick operation cost and b) customer service standard of on-time and accurate deliveries. To achieve the objectives, pick transaction activities are important storage/pick concept activities in a warehouse operation.

Pick operation factors that influence an efficient, cost-effective, accurate, and on-time customer service are:

- A pick philosophy, which encompasses the company controls and practices for a pick line, pick aisle, or automatic pick machine activities.
- A pick methodology, which is used in a manual or mechanized pick design to complete customer orders or automatic replenishment transactions.
- A WMS program to ensure proper SKU and customer-order inventory tracking, control, and movement. When a pick design must pick multiple SKUs for a customer order, the pick options are single customer orders or batched or grouped customer orders.

Single Customer Orders

If a small SKU pick operation picks multi-line or multiple SKUs as single customer orders, there is one picker who picks one customer order. In this pick philosophy, pick options are:

- Pick one customer order per trip
- To pick multiple customer orders into a compartment in a separated container per trip
- For a customer order group pick *en masse* each SKU into a separate totes/cartons

A single picker with a four-wheel shelf cart picks multiple SKUs into a several compartments in a tote. Depending on the pick volume and SKU size, the tote is sudivided into smaller compartments. With a single-picker pick philosophy, a picker uses a pick-and-sort instruction format (e.g., paper pick document, paper self-adhesive labels, pick-to-light, or RF device). When the tote is full or all assigned customer orders are completed, the tote is sent from a pick area to a pack station. A scan of a SKU to the customer order is completed in a pick area or at a pack station. This approach features:

- Improved picker and packer productivity
- Fewer pick totes
- The warehouse computer program assigns customer orders to a tote section and a human-/machine-readable identification to each tote section
- A possible queue at a pack station
- Few pick cart trips in a pick aisle
- No sort labor
- Any pick instruction format

A picker with a four-wheel shelf cart picks SKUs for a group *en masse* and separates picked SKUs into a tote. Each tote has the capacity to hold an *en masse* picked SKU for a customer order. In accordance with the pick instruction, customer-order group SKUs are picked and sorted directly into each tote. For this option, a human-/machine-readable warehouse or WMS identification is attached to the front of each tote. Picker instructions should match each customer-order identification. When compared to a pick-and-sort into a separated tote, a pick-and-sort into an individual tote handles a larger number of SKUs or a cube with many pieces.

Single Customer Order and a Single Picker or Pick Machine

A single customer order completed by a single picker is used in a manual pick/pack or automatic pick-machine pick design. To complete a customer order one picker or an automatic pick machine picks the needed SKU quantity from a pick position. Picked SKUs are transferred from the pick position to a tote. Depending on the ordered SKUs and the pick-line layout, one picker travels all pick aisles or the entire pick area to complete all pick transactions. The WMS scan of SKU to a customer order is completed in the pick area or at a pack station.

Single Customer Order Picked Directly into a Customer-Order Carton

A design in which a single customer order completed by multiple pickers or automatic pick machines is used in a small-item pick/pack concept. A single customer order with multiple pickers, mechanized pick concepts, or automatic pick machines has several pickers or machines preform all pick transactions needed to complete a customer order. To ensure order completion, the design includes manual pick/pack activity (or mechanized or automatic pick designs) in which picked SKUs are transferred directly from a pick position into a tote and transported to a manual, mechanized, or automatic pick-position pick position. The SKU scan to the customer order is completed in a pick area or at a pack station.

A single customer order with multiple manual pickers, mechanized pick, or automatic pick machine designs are:

- Paper pick instructions on a pick line/aisle, in which a manual picker picks SKUs from pick positions directly into a carton
- Pick-to-light, voice directed or RF device pick instructions on a pick line, in which a manual picker picks SKUs from pick positions directly into a carton
- Paper or pick-to-light instructions, in which a cell pick line or pick-area layout for specific SKUs are picked from positions directly into a carton

Batched or Grouped Customer Orders

In a batched/grouped pick/sort/pack philosophy the WMS or warehouse computer groups several mixed SKUs into a single batch. With this philosophy, one or several pickers:

1. Picks and sorts SKUs into a tote
2. Picks prelabeled SKUs or labels each SKU *en masse* and transfers bulk picked and labeled SKUs in a tote or onto a belt conveyor for travel to a sort area. The SKU scan to a customer order is completed at a sort area or pack station.

The features are:

- Few picker aisle trips
- Constant customer-order flow to pack stations
- Low cart/tote cost
- Use of the computer program
- Each SKU has a human-/machine-readable identification
- It requires sufficient table surface at a pack table
- Requires a sort and pack employee activity
- High order volume

Multiple Customer Orders with Multiple Pickers with Precoded SKUs or Label Pick Activity

The philosophy of filling multiple customers with multiple pickers involves having the WMS or warehouse computer group ordered SKUs together. After the SKUs are grouped, each SKU is printed on a picker instruction. After the completion of pick activity, the picked and mixed SKUs are sorted:

1. In a pick area; a paper sort instruction directs an employee to transfer a SKU to an assigned sort location or carton; or
2. With a self-adhesive label for customer order, SKUs has a picker pick and label each SKU or with prelabeled SKUs pick. Picked SKUs are placed onto a transport concept and sent in bulk from a pick area as a mixed customer order picked SKUs to a sort area. A mixed

customer order picked and or a SKU group is sent in a tote or as loose *en masse* SKUs to a sort area. In the sort area, the SKUs are sorted to each customer-order location.

A high-volume batched customer order pick philosophy uses separate pick and sort areas. Picker instructions are on a self-adhesive label. A label is printed for each SKU and attached to the SKU's exterior (or each SKU is precoded). The picker travels through pick aisles. At an assigned pick position, the picker transfers a SKU from a pick position and RF scans the customer order, the SKU identification, or labels the SKU. The picker places the picked/labeled SKU into a tote or loose onto a belt conveyor.

After all pick transactions are completed, the picked and labeled SKUs are transported from a pick area to a sort area. In a sort area, the human-/machine-readable label on each SKU serves as a sort employee instruction or is read by a scanner/reader as a picked SKU sort instruction. The sort instruction permits the employee or mechanical device to sort mixed picked and labeled SKUs by each customer-order identification or by the SKU identification on the tote.

Multiple Customer Orders with a Single Picker

In a low-volume small-item warehouse for slow-moving SKUs in a high-volume warehouse, a paper document or RF device is the pick instruction format and a picker picks/sorts a picked SKU to a tote. The pick-and-sort approach has a picker perform pick/sort activities in a pick aisle. In the pick aisle, in accordance with the pick instructions, a picker removes a SKU from a pick position. The picked SKU is transferred from the pick position to a tote/cart section. The factors in this approach are:

■ The pick-area computer batches or groups ordered SKUs
■ Transport concept to move picked SKUs from a pick area to a sort area
■ In a pick, transport, and sort design, to assure proper balance between a pick area and sort area activities, in the pick area pickers have a batch customer order release concept
■ With a single picker approach, the picker completes the SKU pick-and-sort activity; with a multiple picker approach, to assure customer order transfer between pickers, a pick area has a good customer order transport concept.

SKU Pick-and-Sort Instruction

Multiple customer orders with multiple philosophy has a pick-and-sort instruction format. The most popular batched customer-order pick-and-sort instruction format is a self-adhesive customer-order label, or the SKU identification instruction method. With this latter method, each picked SKU receives a customer-order identification or has a WMS identification (precoded) on its surface. A SKU identification is a human-/machine-readable code. SKU pick-and-sort instruction format options are a paper document, an RF device, or paperless pick design with a SKU code used to identify a picked and sorted SKU sort instruction. If the design is mechanized with warehouse computer support and each SKU has a human-/machine-readable identification, SKUs are picked with any pick instruction. This is due to the fact that a mechanized design with computer support sorts by SKU identification. Manual and mechanized sort designs are reviewed in Chapter 9.

Large Tote or Self-Dumping Carton and Labeled SKU Transfer onto a Belt or Roller Conveyor

With a large tote or a self-dumping cart, a picker transfers each SKU *en masse* into a tote/cart cavity. SKUs are coded with self-adhesive pick labels, or are preidentified SKUs. When a tote/cart is full, it is pushed to discharge SKUs onto the in-house transport. The SKUs are dumped from the tote/cart onto a belt conveyor or into a tote that is transferred onto the conveyor. The conveyor moves the picked SKUs *en masse* or as a tote from a pick area to a sort/pack area. One option has a picker transfer picked SKUs (or each SKU with a code) in an apron and discharge picked SKUs directly onto a belt conveyor. Depending on the a pick-area layout, all pick belt conveyors merge onto a master belt conveyor. Picked SKUs *en masse* are transported from a pick area to a sort/pack area. In the sort area, an employee or mechanical sorter sorts mixed, self-adhesive, or SKUs with a code into an assigned sort location.

Batch Control Release

A pick-area batch release or how to control a picked SKU transfer to a transport. With a paper document pick instruction format, a picker picks and sorts a SKU directly into a tote section or a four-wheel cart section. A batch release control components are:

- A paper pick/sort document accompanies each tote/cart and each tote/cart is identified for each batch and customer order with the batch. At a pack station, the paper document is used to verify SKU pick-and-sort accuracy to the packing slip
- In a pick area, sufficient empty totes/carts to handle an out-of-balance situation between a pick/sort area and pack area activities
- Each tote/cart has sufficient visible space for a batch identification and each customer order location

In a multiple customer order and multiple picker design, each picker transfers SKUs that are labeled or coded and placed in a tote that is moved over a conveyor. In-house transport moves picked *en masse* SKUs from a pick area to a sort area. In the pick area, batch release or control ensures that pickers transfer the correct batch of picked SKUs on time onto the in-house transport. If a batched SKU group is not properly sequenced with the sort activity, there is great potential for sort errors or a decrease in sort productivity.

In a pick area and sort area design for a multiple customer orders with multiple pickers, guidelines to minimize an imbalance between a SKU pick and transfer activity and the picked and transported SKU's sort activity are:

- Determine a batched customer order number and SKU quantity or cube
- Each picked piece has clear pick-and-sort instructions
- In a pick area, have a device to indicate a proper batch
- In a pick area, have sufficient space to queue an out-of-balance occurrence and a predetermined pick tote/cart number
- Have multiple sort locations in a sort area for each sort station,
- In a tote transport design, identify a tote for each batch or color code totes for a batch and provide a queue in-feed conveyor

■ In a cart transport design, identify each cart for each batch or color code carts for a batch and provide a queue in-feed/out-feed cart travel path

Manual Sort Designs

Manual sort concepts are:

■ In a pick area with a paper document, RF device, or light pick/sort instruction, a picker picks and sorts SKUs from a pick position to a cart shelf or into separated tote
■ In a pick area with a paper document, RF device, or light pick/sort instruction, a picker picks and sorts SKUs from a pick position to a mixed customer-order picked tote or bin location
■ In a sort area with a label or SKU pick/sort instruction from a mixed SKUs tote, basket, or a cart, an employee sorts picked SKUs to a pigeon hole location
■ In a sort area with a label or picked SKU pick/sort instruction from a mixed tote, basket, cart, or belt conveyor, an employee sorts picked SKUs to a slide/chute location. Manual sort concepts are reviewed in Chapter 9.

Mechanical Sort Designs

Mechanical sort designs are flap sorter, gull wing, Bombay drop, SBIR or moving belt, nova sort, and tilt tray. Mechanical sort designs are reviewed in Chapter 9.

Automatic Pick Machine

A automatic pick machine design handles one customer order with computer-controlled pick device. To prevent picked SKUs of one order from mixing with picked SKUs from another order, a computer-controlled picker moves SKU from a pick position onto a belt conveyor section (between two cleats) or into a warehouse or customer-order tote/carton.

Pick-to-Light Position Options

In a dynamic small-item pick design, a pick-to-light or RF device pick philosophy is used on flow-rack and shelf pick positions. During a SKU profile, the basic pick-line profile criteria is:

■ All large-cube and fast- to medium-moving SKUs from groups "A" and "B" are profiled to pallet or multiple carton flow-rack pick positions.
■ All small-cube and medium- to slow-moving SKUs from groups "B" and "C" are profiled to pick-to-light shelf pick positions.
■ The remaining SKUs from "C" group are profiled to shelf non-pick-to-light pick positions or to a pick-to-light design with one light per shelf, carousel, or carton AS/RS. Each SKU is placed into a pick position. An option for "C" group is having SKUs paper batched picked by a SKU in customer-order number sequence (i.e., customer-order identifications) and placed onto a mobile cart or stationary shelf sort positions, completed by a sort-to-light pick design.

A pick-to-light approach is used in a pallet or carton flow-rack pick-position design that has one light for one SKU and with a shelf design in which there is one light for multiple SKUs. To ensure maximum picker productivity and minimum cost, a pick-to-light design has a pick-to-light and SKU allocation to pick-position options. A pick-to-light and SKU allocation to pick-position option is based on SKU movement and cube profile for a pick line. For optimum results, a pick line has a flow-rack and shelf pick-position combination.

Pick-to-Light from a Pallet Flow Lane or Pallet Rack

Pick-to-light from a pallet flow lane or pallet rack position is used to handle high-cube or high-volume SKUs with one pick light for one SKU (see Figure 8.8). To ensure line-of-sight and accessibility, a pick-to-light display is used for a pallet flow lane location and is located for picker line-of-sight

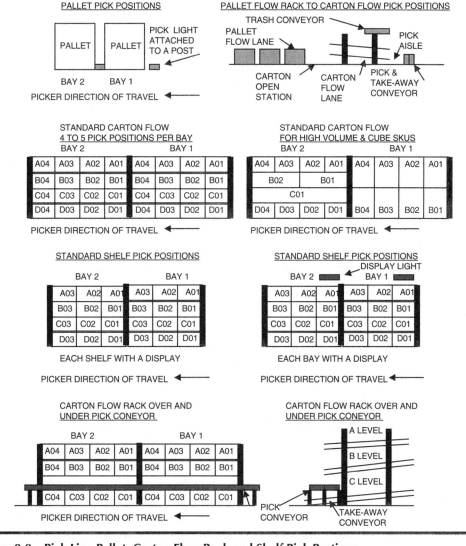

Figure 8.8 Pick Line Pallet, Carton Flow Rack and Shelf Pick Postions

but is adajcent, below, or above a pick position. A display is attached to a pick-position structrual member, above or across from a pick position (above a pick conveyor ensures an easy relationship to the pick position and reach for all employees). Options for pallet pick positions are:

- Pallet flow lane ends at a pick aisle; the picker open master cartons
- Pallet flow lane ends at a pick aisle; an employee other than the picker opens cartons
- Pallet flow lane ends at a replenishment aisle; a replenishment employee transfers open cartons onto carton flow racks

Pick-to-Light Carton Flow Rack

A pick-to-light concept and SKU prolife to carton flow-rack pick-position options are:

1. One SKU on one flow-rack level. This means that one fast moving SKU from "A" SKU group occupies the horizontal level of one entire flow-rack bay and has one pick-to-light pick position. An option for large-cube and fast-moving SKUs is to use a pallet flow rack. A pick-to-light position display shows the SKU pick quantity. SKUs are profiled to a Golden Zone. In a four-level flow-rack bay, these are levels 2 and 3. If the flow-rack design has flexibility with four or five pick lights on each horizontal level, with one SKU per level, one light is an active light and other light displays and replenishment bar codes/RF tags are covered with paper to minimize picker confusion.
2. One SKU on one flow-rack level with multiple flow lanes that are two pick positions wide. This means that one medium-moving SKU from "A" and "B" SKU groups has two or more flow lanes and one pick-to-light pick position. A pick-to-light position display shows the SKU pick quantity. If the flow-rack design has flexibility with four or five pick lights on each horizontal level, with one SKU per level, one light is an active light and other light displays and replenishment bar codes/RF tags are covered with paper to minimize picker confusion.
3. One SKU on one flow-rack lane on a flow-rack horizontal bay level. This means that one slow-moving SKU from "B" and "C" SKU groups has one flow lane and one pick-to-light position display that shows the SKU quantity.

   If there are many SKU allocations to a pick-to-light line, a carton flow-rack bay pick-to-lights design is flexible. Options are standard light arrangement with one light for each flow-rack lane. In a standard 4 to 5 level flow rack bay for high volume or 'A' moving SKUs, Golden Zone levels have one or two pick lights for the flow rack pick lanes and the bottom or top levels (non-Golden Zone levels) have one pick light per flow-rack pick lane that is usually 4 to 5 pick lights/lanes per level.

Pick-to-Light Standard Shelf Options

Pick-to-light design and SKU allocation to standard shelf pick-position options are:

- One SKU on one shelf level. This means that one slow-moving/large-cube SKU from "C" group occupies an entire shelf level and has one pick-to-light pick position. A pick-to-light position display shows a picker that a pick is required from the shelf and shows the SKU pick quantity. SKUs are profiled to a Golden Zone. In a five-level shelf, these are levels 2, 3, and 4.

■ Three SKUs for each shelf level. This means that each SKU from "C" group has three pick lights in a three-foot shelf width, with one SKU per pick-to-light pick position. A pick-to-light position display shows the SKU pick quantity.

■ One pick light per shelf horizontal level and there are three or more human-readable pick positions on each shelf level. These are small-cube and very slow-moving SKUs. This means that each shelf level has one pick-to-light for all pick positions on a shelf. When illuminated for a SKU a pick-to-light display shows the pick position and SKU pick quantity. When a bay lamp or pick zone lamp is illuminated, a picker reads a pick position and SKU pick quantity, completes a pick transaction, and presses a "pick complete" button. For a customer order, if there is another pick for a shelf level, a pick-to-light display shows the pick position and pick quantity. The features are a) cost with a range from $1750 to $2000 per pick position, b) it is paperless, c) employee needs to read a human-readable pick-position label and complete a pick transaction, d) training to assure pick-to-light button is pressed and SKU transferred to correct customer order carton/tote, e) potential pick errors, and f) high SKU hit density and concentration.

Where to Start Customer Orders in a Multiple Section Pick Design

A small-item pick design has a pick aisle or pick-line layout with fast-moving, heavy, and high-cube SKUs in pick area 1 and slow-moving, light-weight, and small-cube SKUs in pick area 2. If the warehouse is to obtain high picker productivity, a question for the pick-area manager is where to start a small-item picker? Using Pareto's Law, a manager knows that fast-moving SKUs (20% of SKUs) account for 80% of the pick volume and or medium- to slow-moving SKUs (80% of SKUs) account for 20% of the pick volume. On a small-item pick line or in a pick aisle, locations to start a picker are:

1. If the warehouse is using a small-item pick design, a picker starts in fast-moving, heavy, and high-cube SKU area, which results in a) improved pick-position replenishment, b) higher pick volume and constant completed order flow from a pick area to a check and pack station area, c) with slow-moving, light-weight, and small-cube SKUs at a pick line/aisle end, it is easier for a picker to top-off or place other SKUs into a carton, d) decreased carton handling, e) high picker productivity and SKU transfer to cartons because SKUs with high hit density and concentration—the heaviest and with the largest physical characteristics—are placed into a carton first. With a paper pick document, SKUs are the first order on the pick instruction document. Finally, if a pick design that handles each carton for a multiple carton order as a cubed-out carton and a pick line has a separate completed order take-away transport, the fast-moving, heavy, and high-cube SKU area is the preferred location to start a picker.

2. If small-item pickers start in a slow-moving, light-weight, and small-cube SKU area, the results are a) with a paper pick instruction document, it is more difficult to read because most picks or fast-moving SKUs are located at the bottom of the pick document, b) it is difficult to move a partially full carton or light-weight cartons along a conveyor, and c) increased nonproductive time to transfer large-cube, heavy, and fast-moving SKUs into a carton that has slow-moving, light-weight, and small-cube SKU in the bottom of the carton.

SKU Pick into a Captive Tote: Where to Start Customer Orders

If a warehouse uses a pick design with a captive tote, where to start the customer orders? Picked SKUs are transferred from a pick position into a captive tote and transferred into a shipping carton at a customer order pack station. A low-volume SKU pick design uses a computer-directed carousel, carton AS/RS, shelf pick-to-light, or sort-to-light pick design. A slow SKU pick section batches customer orders into predetermined groups.

Customer order start locations are:

1. A high-volume SKU pick zone. When customer orders are started in a high-volume SKU pick area, the features are a) both high- and low-volume locations have a packing slip transfer station; b) each location has empty tote introduction to the pick line; c) with a WMS customer-order download and batched customer-order design; a carousel or carton AS/RS are more effective if they have a queue area and totes or pick positions arrive just in time at a pick station. This means minimal nonproductive picker waiting time; d) from low-volume area, approximately 20% of the totes require introduction to a high-volume SKU pick zone. The design requires additional controls and conveyors; e) when partially completed totes arrive at the high-volume SKU pick area, there are some SKUs in a tote; f) the maximum number of customer orders are started and completed because of the use of two pick-start locations; and g) if a customer order has only SKUs from a low-volume SKU pick area, there is less transport.
2. A low-volume SKU pick zone. To have a picker transfer a picked SKU from a pick position into a tote is determined by the WMS computer, based on the SKU's cube and weight—and confirming that the cube and weight do not exceed a tote/ship carton's internal cube capacity. If SKUs exceed a tote/ship carton's internal cube capacity, the computer separates the SKUs into two pick totes.

SKU Pick into a Shipping Carton

In a pick design that uses a shipping carton on a pick line or in a pick activity, a picker transfers picked SKUs directly from pick positions into a shipping carton with a disposable warehouse or WMS identification. Features are:

Accurate update of each SKU exterior dimensions and weight and ship carton interior dimensions and weight

- Carton form machine or employee activity that makes-up a ship carton mix, applies tape to bottom flaps, and transfers a made-up carton onto a pick line
- With a wide carton mix, small size, and light-weight cartons on a powered conveyor increases conveyor controls and potential jam problems
- On a pick line, a wide carton mix slightly increases a picker difficulty to push a carton queue over a pick conveyor
- Identification on a carton side; the issues are a) it is difficult to use a mechanical label applicator, b) with a low height carton, on a pick line, it causes additional nonproductive picker time to see or scan/read the identification, and d) some small carton flaps do not have sufficient space for a customer order label
- Carton flaps extend upward a) carton travel window is designed for the tallest carton and b) increased picker pick SKU transfer height into a pick carton.

- If there are elevation changes over a pick-line conveyor, a wide carton SKU or mix creates transport problems
- If there is a curve in a pick-line conveyor layout, there is potential for jams with a wide carton mix
- If sales literature or a packing slip is required in a shipping carton, with a wide carton mix it is difficult to use mechanical insert equipment; the carton size requires an employee to fold items prior to inserting them into the carton
- If a cash on delivery, bank transfer, or hazardous label is required on a carton, a location is required on a conveyor for label attachment, as well as a location on a carton flap or surface for label placement.
- If a pick line has an activity that leaves a gap or open space between two cartons, the gap is pulled for the longest carton
- An identification label is placed on a carton side, or the identification is printed directly onto the carton
- It does not require empty totes to be returned to a pick area or pick-line start station
- Improves ship supply material inventory control and use

Handling Small Shipping Cartons on a Pick/Pass Line

WMS computer suggested carton options are:

- Pick into all ship carton sizes
- Pick into a captive tote and place small shipping carton into a tote and pack-out at a pack station
- Pick into a standard shipping carton and place small shipping carton into a shipping carton and pack-out at a pack station. A standard shipping carton is recycled through a pick line for another customer order.
- Pick into a standard shipping carton/tote with small shipping cartons at a pack station

Small Shipping Carton Picked in a Captive Tote/Standard Shipping Carton

When a pick design has a WMS computer suggested shipping carton inside a captive tote or standard shipping carton on a pick line, a pick function has an additional employee pick activity station. A carton make-up activity station has an employee or machine transfer an open empty carton into a tote/standard shipping carton or along a pick line to transfer a picked SKU direct from a pick position into a shipping carton. Option for very small or difficult to convey cartons are to place an open carton into a tote/standard shipping carton at a start station, from a pick position, at a pick-line end, or at a remote station.

SKU Mechanized Pick Design Group

In a mechanized pick group a picker rides a vehicle through pick aisles or walks in a pick aisle between two pick-position rows to a pick position. At an assigned pick position, a picker completes a pick SKU transaction. After paper document, paper self-adhesive label, pick-to-light pick, or RF device pick transaction completion, a picker repeats a pick SKU transaction until order completion or the tote becomes full. Mechanized pick groups are a picker a) rides on a powered vehicle through a pick aisle and picks loose SKUs. Picked loose SKUs are placed onto a vehicle carrying surface or into a tote for transport to a pack or sort station, b) walks or rides in a pick aisle and picked SKUs are transported in totes or loose *en masse* via a powered conveyor from a pick area to a pack or sort area.

Picker Walks or Rides and Picked SKUs are Transported by a Powered Belt Conveyor

A picker walks or rides in a pick aisle and the picked SKUs are transported from the pick aisle by a powered conveyor to a pack station or to a customer order sort/pack induction station. . As a picker walks or rides in a pick aisle, a picker is directed by paper document, paper label, RF device, or pick light pick instruction to a pick position. At the pick position, a picker completes a pick transaction by transferring a SKU from the pick position into a tote or placing loose SKUs onto a powered belt conveyor. With pick small-item SKUs into a tote concept and with a completed customer order or full tote, a picker transfers the tote from a pick conveyor onto a powered roller transport conveyor. With loose small-item SKUs on a powered belt conveyor or totes on a powered roller conveyor, conveyors transport picked SKUs from a pick area to a pack station or to a sort/pack station.

Picker Walks/Rides and SKUs Transported by Powered Conveyor Designs

Picker walks or rides in a pick aisle to a pick position and a picker transfers customer order picked SKUs into a tote or directly onto a conveyor travel for transport concepts are:

- Used in a batched customer-order methodology with multiple customer-order pickers who use a paper self-adhesive pick label instruction
- Large SKU number
- High SKU volume
- Large customer order number

Batched mechanized pick designs are:

- Pick loose SKUs *en masse* into a tote and transfer the tote onto a powered roller conveyor
- Pick loose SKUs *en masse* into an apron, bag, tote, or four-wheel self-dumping cart for loose SKU transfer directly onto a powered belt conveyor
- With a paper pick document, pick-to-light, or RF device pick instruction, a single customer order design with a) one picker/multiple pickers who pick/pack SKUs directly into a carton, or b) batched customer orders that have one picker who picks, sorts, and transports picked SKUs and sorts as completed orders to a pack station

Mechanized pick designs are a) pick into a tote, b) pick onto a belt conveyor; c) decombe; and d) pick car.

Mechanized Stock/Pick Position Transferred to the Picker

In a mechanized pick group, a stock or SKU pick position is transferred to a manual pick station. At the pick station, a picker transfers a SKU from a pick position a) as loose-labeled or coded *en masse* SKUs into a tote, b) into a tote customer order section or shelf, or c) as loose-labeled or coded SKUs *en masse* picked directly onto a powered belt conveyor.

Depending on the warehouse's pick methodology, a picker removes a SKU from a pick position, labels the SKU or coded SKU, presses a pick-to-light button, and marks a paper document or RF device to verify the pick. After the pick transaction, a mechanized stock to a picker device transfers a new SKU or pick position to the pick station. The pick-position transfer is repeated until all customer order SKUs are picked and transferred to in-house transport. The SKU is scanned to a customer order at a pick or pack station.

Mechanized Stock/Pick Position is Transferred to Picker: Options

The options for having a mechanized stock or pick position transferred to a pick station are:

■ Carousel group, that are either horizontal or vertical
■ Carton AS/RS group
■ Cartrac, that is either a carton AS/RS or pallet with shelves

Carousel

A carousel design has bins, baskets, or totes that are attached to a powered chain. A powered chain is an endless loop with necks, pendants, or open chain links that interfaces with a motor-driven sprocket wheel. As the sprocket turns, it moves the chain and basket back and forth over a travel path. The carousel movement is controlled by a control panel that receives its instructions from an operator or warehouse computer. Movement instructions rotate a carousel until a pick position is halted at a pick station. At the pick station, a picker completes a customer-order pick transaction by removing a SKU from a bin and placing the SKU into a tote. The tote (or a labeled or coded SKU) is placed on a take-away conveyor, and after a scan/RF device reads another customer order identification and the other customer order is at the pick station, a carousel computer advances a carosuel bin with a customer ordered SKU to the pick station.

SKU replenishment activities to a pick position are completed at a pick or replenishment station. If the pick and replenishment stations are at different locations (because, for example, of employee safety issues), the pick and replenishment interlock network will have been designed not to conduct pick and replenishment transactions at the same time. If there is no interlock, then replenishment transactions are completed on a different shift or during picker breaks. Carousel designs are either horizontal or vertical. The carousel design will determine the chain and bins' travel direction.

Horizontal Carousel

A horizontal carousel moves bins, baskets, or totes with SKUs across the horizontal travel path above the floor. Per a carousel design each SKU bin, basket, or tote travels past a replenishment station and past a pick station. A computer-controlled carousel design is capable of handling approximately 500 commands from six carousel units and has the capacity to handle a large customer order pick or SKU replenishment command number. A multi-carousel design permits a picker to pick from one carousel as the other carousel revolve SKU pick positions to a pick station. The multiple carousel movement means higher picker productivity due to minimal picker waiting time for an assigned pick position to arrive at a pick station.

Carousel Pick-Position Rotation

A horizontal carousel pick-position rotation past a pick station options are:

1. A one-way horizontal carousel in which all carousel bins/baskets rotate in a forward direction past pick stations. For example, carousel C, bin 10 is at a pick station and the next pick position is from bin 2, the carousel rotates bins forward until bin 2 arrives at the pick station. While the carousel basket is moving, there is nonproductive picker time because bins that do not have a pick position are traveling. With a multiple carousel design, nonproductive picker time is minimized because carousels A and B can be rotating bins while a picker is completing a pick transaction from carousel C.
2. A two-way bin rotation is controlled by a warehouse computer. In a two-way carousel design, the warehouse computer can rotate bins forward or backward past pick stations. This minimizes nonproductive picker time in which pickers wait for a bin to arrive at a pick station. For example, if carousel C, bin 10 is at a pick station and the next pick is from carousel C, bin 2, the carousel rotates bins forward or reverse from a pick station to bring the next required carousel bin to the pick station in the shortest travel time. Advantage is a reduction in a picker nonproductive waiting time. When a multiple carousel design interfaces with a single pick station, nonproductive picker time is probably reduced to zero: While a picker completes a pick transaction from carousel C, carousels A and B have completed a pick-position rotation and are at pick stations with SKUs.

Vertical Carousel

A vertical carousel moves trays or pans by chains over a closed loop vertical elliptical fixed travel path and are propelled by an electric powered motor and tooth sprockets. Vertical carousel options are:

- A pick position on one floor that completes pick and replenishment transactions
- Dual pick positions on both floors; each position completes both SKU replenishment and pick transactions. With a dual position design, a vertical carousel tray travel path is from the lower level pick station to the elevated level pick station. With dual pick positions, an interlock carousel computer program controls access to a pick station so that only one pick station has access to a vertical carousel tray and permits a picker to complete a pick or replenishment transaction at a pick station with minimal potential for injury. A vertical carousel travel path means that the entire travel path and trays are enclosed in a shroud. Depending on local code, the shroud is made from wire mesh, solid sheet metal, or fire resistant material and engulfs an entire vertical carousel travel path between two pick stations.

Carton AS/RS, Mini-Load, or Mini-Stacker

A design using a carton AS/RS, mini-load, or mini-stacker storage and retrieval bin has a single SKU in a tray/tote/carton or multiple SKUs in a smaller compartments within a large tray/tote. A carton AS/RS crane is a captive-aisle crane that travels to an aisle end in-put or out-put (P/D) station, takes a tray/carton/tote on board, travels down the aisle, and deposits the tray/tote/carton into a storage position. Depending upon the small-item design parameters, transactions, and facility design, a T-car can be used to transfer a carton AS/RS crane between two aisles. To withdraw a SKU, a carton AS/RS crane travels to a SKU position, withdraws a tote/tray/carton from the storage position, takes a tray/carton/tote on board, travels down aisle to an out-put (P/D) station, and places the tray/carton/tote onto a take-away conveyor. The tote/tray/carton is transported via a powered conveyor (or is placed onto in-house transport) for transport to a pack station.

Carton AS/RS crane control options are:

- A picker-controlled crane with a picker at an aisle end control station. A picker enters each stacker crane in-put/output SKU transaction into the controller, which directs each stacker crane vehicle to perform the transaction.
- The warehouse computer controls the carton AS/RS crane activities. A carton AS/RS crane provides savings from labor and on-time and accurate SKU transactions.

Carton AS/RS P/D and Pick Station Options

Carton AS/RS pick station design options:

1. A front-end pick station design has powered roller conveyors in a carton AS/RS crane aisle front (see Figure 8.9). The first conveyor moves items toward a carton AS/RS crane aisle and provides totes/trays/cartons to an input station; the second conveyor moves items away from a carton AS/RS crane aisle and is a tote/tray/carton output station; the third conveyor is a pick station that moves items from an output conveyor, over a pick station, and to an input conveyor; the fourth conveyor moves items across a carton AS/RS in-feed and out-feed front and ensures cartons/totes/trays are transferred to a P/D station conveyor.

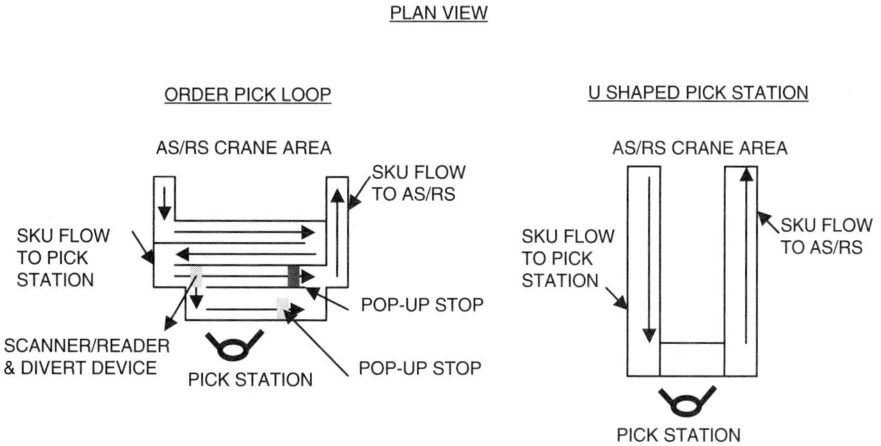

Figure 8.9   Carton AR/RS Pick Concepts

2. A front or rear pick station design has the same operational features, disadvantages, and advantages as a front-end carton AS/RS design except that both carton AS/RS crane aisle ends have a pick and in-feed powered conveyor network. The dual activity design allows the carton AS/RS to handle a higher volume and has additional cost.

3. A remote pick-station design has pick stations that are located in remote area from a carton AS/RS concept. A carton AS/RS has an in-feed and out-feed conveyor. A remote pick area has additional queue powered conveyor paths and divert devices due to the fact that it services large pick station number. A conveyor network is a tray/tote/carton travel path link between any pick station. An out-put conveyor allows a tray/carton/tote to be diverted at a pick station and queue prior to any pick station.

A carton AS/RS pick design uses:

- Paper document, self-adhesive labels, pick-to-light, or RF device pick instructions
- A pick philosophy that is: a) single customer order with a single picker, b) single customer order with multiple pickers, c) batched customer orders with a single picker who picks and sorts picked SKUs or, d) batched customer orders with multiple pickers who pick and label picked SKUs
- Pick methodolgy with mixed SKUs into a tote, SKUs into a separated tote/carton, and mixed SKUs onto a powered belt conveyor

Carton AS/RS Components

A carton AS/RS design components are:

- A stacker crane with a tray/carton/tote carrying surface and handling device
- A tray/carton/tote for loose small parts
- Tray/carton/tote storage positions along a stacker crane travel aisle sides
- A stacker crane operational or computer control station
- Tote/carton in-feed and out-feed stations
- Pick stations

A standard AS/RS stacker crane carrier options are:

- A single tray/carton/tote carrier. A single carrier handles one tray/carton/tote per trip in an aisle. A single carrier crane handles an estimated 50 to 70 trays/cartons/totes per hour.
- A multiple tray/carton/tote carrier. A multiple carrier stacker crane handles two or more trays/cartons/totes per trip. A multiple carrier stacker crane is capable of handling approximately 100 trays/cartons/totes per hour. A dual mast crane or modifed pallet crane carrier is capable of carrying multiple tray/carton/tote carrier devices a) one level with two side-by-side carriers that handle an estimated 100 trays/cartons/totes per hour, b) one level with three side-by-side trays/cartons/totes that handle an estimated 130 trays/cartons/totes per hour, c) two levels with two side by side carriers that handle an estimated 150 trays/cartons/totes per hour, d) two levels with three side-by-side carriers that handle an estimated 170 trays/cartons/totes per hour, e) three levels with two side-by-side carriers that handle an estimated 190 trays/cartons/totes per hour, and f) three levels with three side-by-side carriers that handle an estimated 180 trays/cartons/totes per hour.

Tray/Tote/Carton in a Warehouse Storage Position

Options for trays/totes/cartons in storage positions are:

- One-deep tray/tote/carton in a storage position. This design offers maximum flexibility, good storage position utilization, simple operation, and permits a selection from any carrier device type.
- Two-deep tray/tote/carton in a storage position. This design offers the ability to have one or two trays/totes/cartons and provides good storage density per aisle, has a special carrier, and low utilization per storage position.
- Multiple cartons per rack bay involves having a stacker crane carrier place a carton into a rack. Carton width establishes the carton type for a rack bay. Therefore, if a rack bay is 72 inches wide, and the carton is 17 inches wide, that means a rack bay has a four-carton capacity with 1-inch clearance on each side.

Tote Characteristics

Tote design parameters are:

- For crane carrier travel, a tote long dimension is perpendicular to the aisle with a tote short dimension facing the storage/pick positions. The tote short dimension position provides maximum positions per aisle
- From a rack storage or P/D delivery station, a tote short dimension faces a crane aisle and is the side that is handled by a stacker crane carrying and handling device.
- All small totes with a short height are at a rack stack base; all tall totes are at a rack stack top
- The tote interior can handle dividers or separators that make smaller compartments and permit a tote to handle multiple SKUs
- Maximum SKU quantity and weight
- Each small compartment within a tote has a discreet identification. Tote identification methods are a) machine-readable code (e.g., bar code, RF tag), b) alpha/numeric human-readable code, and c) human/machine code combination.

A tote's features provide:

- The maximum number of storage positions per aisle length and storage area
- Sturdy storage structure
- The ability to move on a powered conveyor
- Easy and quick access to a SKU at a pick station

Tray Characteristics

A stacker crane tray material options are metal, plastic, or wood. The preferred tray material meets a stacker crane design parameters and SKU characteristics. The tray design parameters are:

- A bottom surface that holds the maximum SKU/carton quantity and weight and ensures that a SKU is secured in a tray and that there is minimal bottom deflection
- Good storage area utilization
- To be compatible with a tray transport design and to be able to interface with a SKU/carton transfer design

Carton Characteristics

If a carton is used in an AS/RS concept, the carton material must meet the carton AS/RS crane design parameters. Carton design parameters are:

- A bottom surface that holds maximum SKU quantity and weight and ensures that SKUs are secured in a carton and that there is minimal bottom surface deflection
- Provides maximum storage area utilization
- Compatible with a carton transport design
- Permits WMS identification code attachment
- Allows access to all SKUs

Carton AS/RS Design as a Small-Item Pick Design

A carton AS/RS or stacker crane design as a pick design transfers a stock or pick position from storage area to a pick station. At a pick station, a picker or symbology reader reads a tray/tote/carton identification and matches a customer-order identification to a pick instruction (paper document, self-adhesive label, pick-to-light, or RF device). With a correct match, a picker completes a pick transaction and removes a SKU from a tray/tote/carton and transfers the SKU into a tote. After all picks from a tray/tote/carton are complete, the tray/tote/carton is released from the pick station onto a conveyor for transport to another pick station or to AS/RS crane in-feed station. After customer order completion or a full container, the tote/carton/tray is released from the pick area to a sort or pack station.

Carton AS/RS Crane with a Dynamic Conveyor Pick Front End

A carton AS/RS crane pick design with a dynamic conveyor pick front end has:

- Several computer-controlled stacker cranes with a single or multiple tray/tote/carton handling carrier
- A tray/tote/carton that holds a single SKU/multiple SKUs. Each tray/tote/carton has a discrete code.
- A conveyor front end that includes queue roller conveyors, pop-up stops, and right-angle transfers that service a pick station. Each pick station has a code scanner/RF tag reader.
- A pick-by-light or RF device pick instruction design at each pick position
- Several powered conveyors a) completed take-away conveyor, b) empty tray/tote/carton in-feed conveyor, and c) in-feed and out-feed tray/tote/carton conveyor to a AS/RS crane

After the warehouse computer completes a customer-order wave, the WMS computer allocates a SKU for a customer-order wave to a stacker crane pick-area computer, the stacker crane, following the customer-order sequence, retrieves a tray/tote/carton from a storage position. With a full stacker crane carrier device, a stacker crane deposits the tray/tote/carton onto an outbound conveyor that serves to transport trays/totes/cartons to a dynamic pick-area front end and the queue zone for a conveyor dynamic front end.

A conveyor dynamic pick-area front end has three or five powered queue conveyors, pop-up stops, and right-angle transfers. The first conveyor is a major conveyor from a stacker crane P/D station to a dynamic pick area. The queue conveyors with pop-up stops and right angle transfers that sequence trays/totes/cartons on their way to a pick station. The second conveyor is a pick conveyor that goes past each pick zone. Prior to each pick station, each tray/tote/carton code is read by a scanner/reader. At a pick station, a tray/tote/carton stops on a pick conveyor and the pick instruction (e.g., sort-by-light, self-adhesive label, RF device) shows the pick requirement. After the pick transaction, if a SKU has a pick at another pick station, the tray/tote/carton is sent to a queue conveyor and is held on the conveyor. If the SKU is required for another customer order at another pick station, the tray/tote/carton is sent to a conveyor for transport to another pick station. If a SKU is not required for a customer order on this order wave but is required for a customer order on another order wave, the tray/tote/carton is returned to the stacker crane in-feed conveyor.

With a single pick-statio design, as pick activity is completed at a pick station, tray/tote/carton conveyor queue travel path "A" releases a tray/tote/carton onto a pick-station conveyor. It ensures a constant tray/tote/carton flow from queue conveyor "A" to the queue conveyor that feeds a pick station. After all trays/totes/cartons have been transferred from queue conveyor "A," queue conveyor "B" releases totes to a pick-station conveyor. After all trays/totes/cartons are released to the pick station, queue conveyor C releases totes to a pick position.

After each queue conveyor releases trays/totes/cartons and a conveyor travel becomes empty, the design directs other trays/totes/cartons that contains a SKU required for a wave or the next order wave to vacant positions on a conveyor. With a multiple pick station design, the "1" (i.e., first pick-zone conveyor network) functions in the same manner as a single pick station design, except that a) the pick zone is capable of discharging trays/totes/cartons to pick station 2, b) conveyor transfer device and conveyor to have a tray/tote/carton that is not required at pick station 2 transferred to a transport conveyor to by-pass pick station 2 and have the tray/tote/carton return to a stacker crane in-feed station, c) it includes a conveyor for later tray/tote/carton transfer to pick station 2, and d) the queue conveyor sections serve the same functions as the queue conveyor that feeds pick position 1. The features are:

- The pick-to-light/sort-to-light or RF device design permits high picker accuracy and productivity
- Cost
- Few employees
- Having two or more pick stations per pick area permits one or more pickers for maximum picker productivity
- De-box area for SKU transfer to a stacker crane tray/tote/carton
- Needs only a small area

Carton AS/RS Crane Pick Tunnel

In AS/RS crane pick tunnel, design has:

- Several stacker cranes with single or a multiple tray/tote/carton handling carrier
- Bar-coded/RF tagged tray/tote/carton that holds one or multiple SKUs
- One-deep or two-deep tray/tote/carton storage positions
- With a bar-code/RF tag reader, pick-to-light, sort-to-light or RF device customer-order instruction design and pick stations
- In-feed empty tray/tote/carton travel path to each pick station, partial-order tray/tote/carton conveyor and completed order tray/tote/carton take-away conveyor. After customer orders are downloaded from the WMS computer to a stacker crane computer, the crane, depending on a) the customer order or b) a high to low SKU sequence, retrieves tray/totes/cartons from a storage area. With a full carrier, the crane deposits each tray/tote/carton at a pick position. Pick positions are between a crane aisle and a pick aisle. A stacker crane is captive to one aisle and services the aisles tray/tote/carton positions.

A picker aisle is between a pick position and customer-order locations. After a SKU or tray/tote/carton is placed into a pick position and a SKU is required for a customer order, the warehouse computer activates a customer-order location pick light, sort light, or RF device pick instruction. In accordance with activated pick lights or RF device, a picker transfers a SKU quantity from a pick position tray/tote/carton to a pick container. After all SKU picks for an order wave, an employee transfers partial or completed customer orders to a take-away conveyor. A take-away conveyor moves any partial orders to a next pick position in a different pick aisle and all completed orders are transported to a pack area. For the next order wave, if a SKU is required on an order wave, a SKU tray/tote/carton remains in a pick position. If a SKU is not required for the next order wave, the tray/tote/carton is sent to a stacker crane pick-up station. Features are:

- It reduces employee walk distance and reading
- A sort or pick-to-light or RF device pick instruction concept, which improves employee productivity and pick accuracy
- It enhances SKU inventory accuracy
- It requires an investment in stacker cranes, conveyors, pick positions, and computer controls
- It handles a wide SKU mix
- Minimal employee tray/tote/carton movement, it minimizes employee injuries and damage to equipment and SKUs
- High customer-order volume
- Optimizes space and cube utilization
- Separate area to de-box SKUs into a tray/tote/carton

Cartrac Pick Design

A cartrac pick design uses four-wheel carriers or carts with a load-carrying surface. As a rotating shaft revolves, it interfaces with the cart's underside and propels the cart forward over a fixed travel path. At a pick station, an employee transfers a SKU quantity from a cart onto a cart or pallet. After all picks have been completed, an employee travels to the next pick station and another cart with the SKU moves forward to a pick station. A cartrac pick design is available in both mini-load and pallet-load applications. Design parameters and operational characteristics are similar for both cartrac pick designs. A cartrac pick and WMS program requirements and features are similar to a horizontal carousel pick design.

Automatic Pick Machine SKU Pick Group

In a automatic pick design group, SKUs are automatically (warehouse computer-controlled) released from an automatic machine pick position. Picked SKUs are a) released onto a rough-top belt conveyor for transport to a pack station, b) released onto or between two cleats on a cleated rough-top belt conveyor for transport and transfer into a tote, or released into a discreet customer order carton/tote for transport to the next pick-area station and then to a pack station.

Automatic Pick Design Considerations

The design parameters for an automatic pick design are a) SKU length, width, height, weight, and exterior packaging; b) customer-order cube; and c) pick-line profile. Automatic pick design parameters are similar to manual pick-line design parameters, but there are restrictions for a) round or odd shaped, b) crushable or fragile, or very slow and very fast-moving SKUs.

SKU Allocation to an Automatic Pick Machine

SKU profile to a automatic pick machine is determined by a SKU's physical characteristics, velocity, and family group. Automatic pick machine pick activity progresses arithmetically from the first to the last pick position and begins at home base. Depending on design criteria and automatic pick machine vendor standards, home base is the pick position nearest a picked SKU transfer location or a take-away conveyor belt start. To complete customer order SKU pick transactions, an automatic pick machine with two sections that face one picked SKU gathering conveyor has the automatic pick machine computer SKU pick impulse pattern that is along an automatic pick machine one side and down the other side. An automatic pick machine has large-cube, heavy, and fast-moving SKUs located at the first pick position, and crushable, small-cube, light-weight, and slow-moving SKUs in the last pick position. Other automatic pick machine SKU profile features are:

■ Family group
■ Allocated as a) one SKU per pick sleeve/lane and b) fast-moving SKUs have multiple pick sleeves or lanes determined by the WMS and warehouse computer systems to handle a floating pick-position philosophy, lane capacity, and SKU movement
■ Verify and update a SKU pick-position replenishment and pick transaction

Automatic Pick Machine SKU Pick-Position Replenishment

An automatic pick machine replenishment is a pick sleeve, pick lane, or pick belt that holds a small inventory quantity. Because automatic pick machine rates are very high, and to minimize stockouts, on-time and accurate automatic pick machine pick-position replenishment is a must for a small-item pick operation. An automatic pick machine replenishment inventory locations are in a a) pick sleeve, lane, or belt, b) ready-reserve area, or c) remote-reserve area.

A pick sleeve, pick lane, or pick belt is an automatic pick machine pick position that holds an average of one or two master cartons, which is equivalent to 20 to 24 SKUs. To assist a replenishment employee in making on-time and accurate SKU transfer in a master-carton quantity to a pick position, a small-item pick design marks on a pick sleeve (with paint or tape) an appropriate location that holds a master-carton SKU quantity. During pick activity and when a mark becomes visible, a single replenishment employee performs a one master-carton replenishment transaction from a ready-reserve position to an automatic machine pick position.

A replenishment activity option is to have a photo-eye placed on a pick sleeve. When the photo-eye light beam is not broken by a SKU in a pick sleeve, the photo-eye sends a message to the warehouse computer to activate an alarm that signals that the pick machine pick position has a low SKU quantity and needs replenishment. For accurate SKU replenishment, a discreet identification human-/machine-readable code has been placed on the replenishment pick machine sleeve or pick-lane structural-support member. The objectives of an automatic pick machine ready-reserve inventory design are:

1. Inventory quantity is available for automatic pick machine replenishment
2. To provide pick positions for customer orders during an automatic pick machine mechanical or electrical down time

With 200 to 400 SKUs per automatic pick machine module, ready-reserve designs are carton flow-rack bays, decked standard pallet rack bays, decked wide-span rack bays, or standard shelves. Ready-reserve layout design options are having ready-reserve pick sides face a) the automatic pick machine replenishment side or b) the pick aisle between two flow racks. Replenishment employee transaction options are a) employee-controlled activity (previously reviewed) and b) computer-controlled activity. To ensure accurate and on-time SKU transfer from a remote-reserve area to a ready-reserve area, and for replenishment to an automatic pick machine pick sleeve, lane, or belt, an automatic pick machine uses computer-controlled replenishment instructions. SKU replenishment instructions can be paper documents or RF device instructions.

Customer-Order Entry or Automatic Pick Machine Activation

An automatic pick machine that handles a high customer-order SKU pick volume and large number of customer orders receives pick or release instructions from the warehouse computer. With these operational characteristics, the host computer sends pick requirements to the WMS computer. Based on the customer order wave, the WMS computer allocates SKU and directs an employee to move and scan SKUs to an automatic pick machine pick position. After the WMS computer receives scan transactions and SKU quantity, the computer releases customer orders to the automatic pick machine computer. The customer-order entry to an automatic pick machine options are:

1. Directly from the WMS computer to an automatic pick machine. This is not the preferred method because the WMS computer is busy with other functions and might not be capable of transferring a customer order.

2. The WMS computer downloads customer orders to the warehouse computer, which interfaces with an automatic pick machine. The feature means that all customer orders are readily available to an automatic pick machine.

An automatic pick activation method has a SKU for a customer order picked or released from a pick position on picked SKU transport. Automatic pick activation options are:

1. Customer-order sequence, which was downloaded from the WMS computer to the warehouse computer. The automatic pick machine starts the pick process and a partial carton/tote is sent from the automatic pick machine to another pick area or a customer order is completed by the automatic pick machine. The automatic pick machine picks SKUs into a tote/carton or onto an open section between two cleats on a belt conveyor.
2. Bar code/RF tag discreet identification on a carton/tote, which is transported in-house over a conveyor. Tote travel on a powered conveyor is on a "first-in, first-out" basis. The tote travels past a scanner/reader onto the automatic pick machine, and the bar coded/RF tag tote/carton sequence is maintained. A scanner/reader sends the customer-order identification to the warehouse computer. The warehouse computer activates the automatic pick machine to release SKUs from a pick position into a tote/carton or onto an open section between two cleats on a conveyor. Released SKUs from the automatic pick machine and customer-order container on the conveyor are in a "first in, first out" sequence..
3. An employee enters a customer-order identification into an automatic pick machine.

Automatic Pick Machines

Automatic pick designs are Itematic, Robo Pic, or "A" frame.

ITEMATIC Pick Machine

An Itematic is a stand-alone SKU pick machine. Each Itematic pick machine is a warehouse computer-controlled single customer-order pick method that handles a specific size, range, and number of SKUs. With an Itematic pick machine, individual SKUs are assigned to specific pick lanes. After a replenishment employee places a SKU into a pick lane on the Itematic machine back and is parallel to the floor, the Itematic is ready to pick SKUs for a customer order. During the pick process, a computer-controlled pick device that has a single customer order travels along the Itematic's pick side. As the Itematic arrives at a pick lane, the warehouse computer triggers a pick device to pick one SKU from the pick lane onto a take-away conveyor. The picked SKU travels on a rough-top conveyor from the Itematic pick machine a) onto a smooth-top belt conveyor or b) into a tote or shipping carton for transport to a pack station. At the pack station, the picked SKUs are transferred, collected, or packaged into a carton/tote. To maximize a pack station employee's productivity, a divert blade on a smooth belt conveyor is used to divert an individual picked SKU onto a specific section of a pack station slide. The Itematic is located on the ground floor or mezzanine level. Other design requirements are sufficient area for replenishment and ready-reserve positions that flow directly to an Itematic's replenishment side.

Robo Pick

A Robo Pick is an automatic pick design that is manually replenished and computer-controlled to pick single customer-order SKUs. A Robo Pick has a central tote belt conveyor with several SKU banks, item dispensers, or cleated rough-top pick belts. The conveyor ensures constant travel speed through a pick line and transports totes/cartons to the next pick area or to a pack station. As a tote/carton travels between two SKU pick belts rows, depending on the order the warehouse computer activates a SKU pick belt or item dispenser to index (i.e., move forward), which permits one SKU to be picked into a tote/carton or directly onto a central rough-top cleated belt conveyor. A SKU pick conveyor belt forward action automatically moves the picked SKU from a pick position past a sensor that transmits a signal to the warehouse computer, which verifies the pick transaction. All partial or full totes/cartons are transported to the next pick area or to a pack station and the order is prepared for delivery.

Manual replenishment to a SKU pick belt is made from the aisle by an employee. An employee places one SKU into an empty SKU belt lane or pick position. (The aisle is between a ready-reserve position and a pick position.) The Robo Pick handles loose or packaged SKUs that are medium to small cube, medium to light weight, and medium to slow-moving. The design provides a FIFO SKU rotation and a medium number of SKUs per pick line. A Robo pick handles a 54-batch batch and 20,000 pieces per hour.

"A" or "H" Frame

An "A" or 'H' frame automatic pick machine has pick sleeves arranged to release or pick SKUs onto a central gathering belt conveyor. An "A" frame is a computer-controlled machine that handles single customer-order SKUs. All customer orders are held in the warehouse computer and to satisfy a customer order delivery schedule, or as tote that passes a scanner/reader, the computer sends an impulse to the "A" frame to release SKUs. After the sleeve dispenser receives the pick impulse, the dispenser releases SKUs at a rate of 5 to 7 items per second onto a rough-top cleated belt take-away conveyor. At each SKU dispenser or sleeve bottom is a small forward rotating device with a small upward projection. As a forward rotating device revolves forward, the upward projection engages a SKU's rear side. The device moves the SKU from the pick sleeve onto a gathering rough-top belt conveyor. (Other "A" frame pick devices are wheels or plastic rubber bands.) After the SKU leaves the pick sleeve, the SKU slides over a short sheet metal slide with a curved discharge end onto a rough-top gathering conveyor belt. To ensure separation of picked SKUs on a gathering belt conveyor, an "A" frame gathering conveyor belt has cleats. Cleats project upward and are spaced every 12 to 18 inches, which restricts uncontrolled SKU movement over a travel path and minimizes the chance of mixing SKUs from two orders on the conveyor.

An "A" frame pick position or pick sleeve dispenser replenishment takes place during pick activity. A replenishment employee adjusts the pick sleeve holder from the pick sleeve dispenser, scans and moves SKUs from a ready-reserve position to the pick sleeve and replaces the sleeve holder onto the dispenser. SKU and pick sleeve WMS identification scans and SKU quantity are sent to the WMS computer. The computer updates inventory status and releases customer orders.

SKU Picked Transfer

After all customer order picked SKUs are on a gathering conveyor belt travel path, the SKUs arrive at a transfer station for transfer from a gathering conveyor belt onto a pack station. Activity options are:

1. Onto a slide. To ensure high employee transfer productivity, divert blades move SKUs from a smooth-top gathering conveyor belt travel path onto a slide section.
2. Waterfall or discharge onto a slide. A slide has a divert blade that directs picked SKUs to a specific section on a slide.
3. Waterfall or discharge into a captive customer order tote.
4. Waterfall or dump into a shipping carton.

When picked SKUs waterfall from a gathering belt conveyor into a captive tote/carton, and to ensure picked SKU transfer into a tote/carton, the options are:

1. The captive tote interior bottom surface is a vertically moveable surface supported by springs.
2. Coiled springs allow the bottom surface to adjust to the transferred SKU's quantity or weight.

- The tote/carton interior bottom surface is padded with a cushion.
- The transfer or waterfall location has a fabric or plastic shroud that extends downward and into a tote. A shroud inside a tote/carton serves as funnel to direct uncontrolled SKU transfer from a gathering conveyor belt into a tote/carton.

Carton/Tote Make-Up or Introduction to a Pick Design

In a small-item pick design, an important pick activity is carton/tote make-up and introduction to a pick line, pick vehicle, or pick aisle. In a batched customer-order pick design with a pick/sort and transport design or pick/transport and sort design, a shipping carton is introduced at a pack station. The objectives of carton make-up, introduction onto a pick line, pick aisle, pick vehicle, or automatic pick machine line are:

- Carton to retain picked SKUs
- Moves along a pick line, pick aisle, or automatic pick machine, and past all pick positions
- Move from a last pick position to the next pick line, pick-aisle activity, or to a pack area
- Ensure that a carton/tote receives and holds a customer-order identification that has line-of-sight to a picker or scanner/reader

If the pick container is a shipping carton, the carton moves from a pick conveyor onto a completed order take-away transport conveyor. To ensure a smooth travel for an empty carton over a pick conveyor and take-away conveyor, the warehouse computer releases a WMS computer suggested (specific) carton size to a pick-to-light pick area. A completed order take-away conveyor transports the pick carton over a completed order transport conveyor from a pick area to the next activity station.

The features of a customer-order shipping carton design for a SKU pick container are:

■ Carton material
■ How to make-up a carton
■ Where to make-up a carton
■ To seal a) one-piece carton bottom flaps or not seal bottom flaps, or b) with a two-piece carton to include a cover on the carton bottom or have a cover supply at a pack station
■ With a one-piece carton to have top flaps up or down
■ On some pick-line applications, to provide space on the carton surface for a shipping label
■ Carton type: new carton or reuse a vendor carton
■ With some cartons how to transfer and replenish cartons to a pack station
■ Carton sizes or number
■ Corrugated material and type
■ Carton color
■ Company return address and customer-order delivery address label location or label window printed on a carton surface

Carton Type

Cartons types are:

■ One-piece cartons with four side walls, four bottom flaps, and four top flaps
■ One-piece pop-out cartons with four side walls
■ Two-piece carton with four side walls, one integrated bottom surface, and a separate cover

Label Attachment to a Carton/Tote

Label attachment to a pick carton/tote side is a pick-line activity. On a manual, mechanized, or automatic pick line, customer-order label/identification code attachment activity identifies a pick/ship carton/tote from the other cartons/totes.

A customer-order identification code on a pick tote or shipping carton serves on another pick line as an employee or machine instruction to complete a task, which can be to a) direct a carton/tote to another pick zone, b) activate a customer-order check weight machine, or c) activate a manifest machine.

Label Activity in Batched or Single Order Pick into a Captive Tote

A customer-order identification is used in a pick-to-light design or in batched pick-and-sort SKUs into a captive tote design. With either design, the WMS or warehouse computer attaches a tote label to a customer-order number. A tote label identification appears as a pick instruction and an employee scans/reads a tote label at a pack station to identify picked SKUs and complete a customer order. The employee also zero scans the warehouse identification, which removes the WMS identification association to a warehouse identification from the WMS files.

Label Options

Customer-order label options are:

- A shipping carton with a nonreusable or disposal label.
- A captive tote with a permanent warehouse label. When a pick design uses a shipping carton on a pick line, a customer-order identification label is placed onto the shipping carton's exterior top flap or side at a pick-line start station. With the label in the proper location, the label's location satisfies all requirements for a labeled carton on a pick/pack or pick/pass line. In a pick-to-light design, a label permits a picker to compare the carton identification to the pick-to-light display screen number and line-of-sight for a scanner/reader.

Label characteristics are:

- a) Separate printers to print a label and packing slip; both printers have the same customer-order sequence. With this arrangement and carton travel on a pick line on a "first-in, first-out" basis, a label is placed onto a carton at a pick-line start station and the packing slip is placed into a carton, or b) one printer to print a combined packing slip and label. At a pick-line start station, an employee removes the label and places a label onto a carton and places a packing slip into a carton.
- Label back surface is self-adhesive
- Label contains all company information
- Label is not reusable
- A label is applied to a carton by employee or machine
- Used on a pick/pack or pick/pass line that does not have a pack station
- Employee or scanner/reader

When a pick design uses a unique permanent warehouse license plate or code on a captive tote, each plate or code is a tote component and is reusable. Each warehouse tote label orientation should be in the proper direction of travel and the degree of tilt and on the sides (two lead/trail ends or four interior and exterior side walls) should ensure line-of-sight for a scanner/reader or employee. After a tote passes a scanner/reader and the WMS computer attaches a tote identification to the customer-order identification, the tote identification becomes the customer-order identification as the tote travels over a pick/pack or pick/pass line. The interrelationship between a tote identification and the customer-order identification permits a permanent warehouse-labeled tote to satisfy pick-line requirements. After a pack employee packs a customer order, an employee zero scans the tote bar code/RF tag to complete a WMS customer-order identification and cancel the WMS customer-order identification attachment to the warehouse tote identification in the WMS program file.

To match a label with packing slip characteristics:

1. After scanning/reading a tote label, a packing slip is printed at a pick-line start station or a pack station
2. Warehouse computer system matches a permanent warehouse label with a WMS customer-order identification
3. Additional captive tote and permanent warehouse label cost

4. In a pick-to-light concept, with a pick-to-light problem, a permanent warehouse label with human-readable code on a carton permits a pick line to operate with paper pick instructions
5. Reusable label
6. Used on a pick/pack or pick/pass line that does have customer order pack station
7. Pick/pack employee training

Label Placement Technique

The factors of label placement on a carton exterior surface are:

1. Container size and material
2. Pick design
3. Label size and type label

In 1 (above), carton size ranges from a large to small cardboard carton to a jiffy paper or plastic bag. A carton material is cardboard, paper, or plastic. A second label placement factor is the pick design. In a manual or automatic pick design, a single customer-order carton moves on a conveyor through a pick area. Prior to a pick carton's arrival at the first pick-line station, a customer-order identification is required on a carton. A customer-order identification directs a picker or automatic pick machine pick activities. Actual label placement onto a pick carton is a manual or machine activity in which the label is placed onto a carton side or top flap to ensure proper employee, bar-code scanner/RF tag line-of-sight.

Manual Label Activity

Before a pick activity start-up, the WMS computer downloads all customer-order identifications and associated delivery information to the warehouse computer. The warehouse computer-controlled printer or printers prints all delivery labels. Manual label placement activity occurs at a pick-line start station. At the pick-line start station, label options are a) preprinted labels that match the customer-order sequence or b) labels printed on demand. With the preprinted label option, a pick-line start station employee has labels that are printed on sheets or in a roll. In proper sequence empty cartons arrive at the pick-line start station and an employee removes a label and places it onto a carton. In a manual preprinted label option, important factors are the removal of the label's self-adhesive back and label presentation to an employee for placement onto a pick carton. For a pick/pass pick line, preprinted labels on a roll is placed into a label dispenser, which a) ensures proper customer-order sequence, b) minimizes label handling problems, and c) reduces the problem of self-adhesive label back trash. In a batched pick-and-sort design, preprinted labels are placed in a stack at a pack station. To ensure good label separation, each label is printed onto a packing slip or sheet.

With a print-on-demand design, in a pick/pass design, as a customer order arrives at a pick-line start station, the WMS program has a label printer print a label. As a pick-line start employee removes a label from the print machine, the label's self-adhesive backing is removed and a label is placed onto a pick carton. In a batched customer-order pick-and-sort design, as a captive tote or first SKU arrives at a pack station, an employee scans the bar code/RF tag. The scanner/reader communicates customer-order information to the warehouse computer. Print options are a) the label printer prints a combined label and packing slip or b) there are two printers, one for customer-order labels and a second printer for packing slips. With a mechanical customer order pick-and-sort design, after mixed ordered and picked SKUs are presorted to a location with centrally preprinted and distributed packing slip, an employee completes the final sort activity.

Machine Label Activity

If the warehouse uses a machine to apply a self-adhesive customer-order label to a pick tote or shipping carton, the design factors are:

- Prior to a pick-line start station, a label application station is located on a conveyor travel path
- Label location on carton exterior
- Label type and size
- To secure a carton top and assure a scanner ability to read a top applied customer order delivery label, a label is applied to a carton top prior to a carton secure station or after a carton secure station
- Costs

Label Types

In the pick industry, label types are:

- A plain paper label that has glue or tape. It is used in a captive tote or batched pick design, which has a low volume and does not require scanning/reading.
- A printed label with a self-adhesive back, that is used in a batched pick concept with a customer-order pack station.

Label Location on a Shipping Carton

The first consideration is the label location on a shipping carton. With current machine label application technology, pick philosophy, and carton supply chain philosophies, label placement location options are the side and top.

Label Placement: Side

If the pick design is a pick/pack or pick/pass pick line that transfers SKUs directly from pick positions into a shipping carton, side label placement on a carton top flap is the preferred option. With a side label application machine, a label is applied to the side of a pick carton, which permits a picker to easily read the human-readable label, RF tag, or bar code. With a one-piece carton with four flaps up and two-piece carton, how a side label machine interfaces with the carton and applies a label is a major consideration. To have a label machine handle a wide range of carton heights, the options are to:

- Set the machine for the highest carton volume in your pick concept. Short cartons are placed inside a standard high pick carton with a peel-off label that assures each carton side label is set at a standard height above the a conveyor travel path. Each short carton is placed inside a standard high pick carton with a peel-off label. At a pack station, the short carton is removed and the order is packed into the short carton. The standard carton is reused on a pick line.

■ Set a machine to handle short cartons and have a picker lift each carton to match the customer-order number with the pick-to-light number. With this approach, the side label location does not interfere with the carton tape and does satisfy delivery company bar code scan requirements. In a design in which the machine applies a label to a carton side, the label is applied to a carton flap because of a supply chain top scan requirements. On a conveyor, the machine places a label onto a carton flap without a backstop device or at a label application location with a backstop behind the machine to ensure a rigid flap for label application. In a warehouse operation that has a customer order completed at a pack station, label placement onto a one- or two-piece carton is also completed at the pack station.

Label Placement: Top

Label placement on a carton top involves having an employee or machine place a customer-order delivery label onto the top surface of a shipping carton. With a top labeled carton, the design factors are:

■ Pick/pass four-flap carton and a label on a top flap. Operational characteristics are similar to side-labeled cartons but the concerns are a) space for a label on a carton top and b) sealing tape does not hinder scanner/reader.
■ When a pick design uses sealing tape that is colored or nontransparent to a human eye or a scanner/reader, the usable carton top flap surface is reduced by 0.5 to 1 inch. The tape width determines what the usable carton flap top surface is for a label.
■ With a customer order completed at a pack station, label placement onto a one- or two-piece carton is completed at a pack station and after secure tape is applied to a carton top. All supply chain segments conveyors have a top scanner/reader.

A warehouse that uses a top label design uses a four-flap carton and has a wide customer-order mix. Pick design characteristics are:

■ Wide carton size variety
■ Carton two top flaps have a small opening between two closed flap ends
■ Customer-order label that is placed on a carton exterior flap prior to a carton flap seal station

With a pick/pass design in which the label on the top flap carries pick instructions, for small cartons, pick instructions options are:

■ For short cartons, use a peel-off label on a standard carton and at a customer-order pack station, pack a customer order into a short carton and reuse the standard carton
■ Print a second customer-order label at a pack station
■ Ink jet spray a customer-order number on a carton side or flap for the pick activity and at a pack station to print a customer-order delivery label

Ink-Jet Spray Customer-Order Identification

With short cartons or cartons with a small flap, a computer-controlled ink spray has the capability to spray a customer-order number onto a carton flap or side. As a carton approaches an ink-jet spray station (on a rough-top belt conveyor to ensure controlled travel), the carton is aligned to a proper conveyor side. The warehouse computer has entered a customer-order identification number into the ink-jet spray device. The ink-jet spray pick device sprays the customer-order information onto a carton exterior surface or flap. To have sufficient time for ink to dry, a carton travels on a zero pressure conveyor to a pick-line start station. Prior to using an ink-jet design, spray tests should be conducted on a carton exterior surface to ensure that the required human and machine code clarity is present.

Sort or Put-to-Light Sort (Pick) Instruction

With a sort or put-to-light pick instruction, a sort-to-light design has each unique bulk or *en masse* picked SKU in a separate tote or tote section, and each SKU bar code/RF tag appears on a paper document or each SKU has bar code/RF tag (see Figure 8.10). A tote with unique bulked picked SKUs and associated bar code label/RF tag is delivered from a pick area to a sort station. At the sort station, a carton/tote has been assigned (scanned to) to a specific sort location. Each customer-order sort location has a sort or put-to-light display and a printed pack document is attached to each shipping carton or sort location. After a sort employee removes the paper document with a bar code labeled/RF tagged SKU from a pick tote, the employee hand scans/reads the SKU bar code/RF tag. The scanner/reader sends the bar code/RF tag information to the warehouse computer. The warehouse computer activates the appropriate sort or put-to-light display at each sort location. An activated sort or put-to-light display indicates a customer-order or sort locationa SKU. After the sort employee transfers a SKU quantity from bulk picked tote to a sort location, an employee presses a sort completion button on the sort or put-to-light display. This signals the warehouse computer sort activity completion for a particular customer-order SKU.

A sort-to-light display screen indicates if the sort employee is to repeat a SKU pick activity because the order was for two or more SKUs. When a sort-to-light is blank, or zero at the SKU pick position a customer ordered SKU pick transaction is complete. If a customer order requires a different SKU, a picker completes a SKU pick transaction. If a customer order is completed, the completed order is pushed pushed forward from a pick conveyor onto a completed customer order take-away conveyor.

Precoded SKUs

A precoded SKU is a SKU that has a human-/machine-readable code attached to it. A vendor or employee at a receiving dock ensures that each unit has a human-/machine-readable code attached.

SKUs Sorted to an Assembly Position

SKU transfer to a manual sort and assembly position options are:

1. A random, transfer transaction verified with a RF device
2. A predetermined SKU or SKU identification number scheme. At a separate scan station or at a pack station, picked SKUs and customer-order identifications are scanned and sent

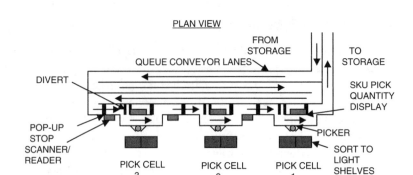

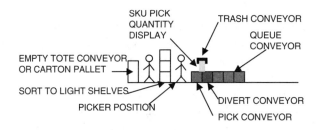

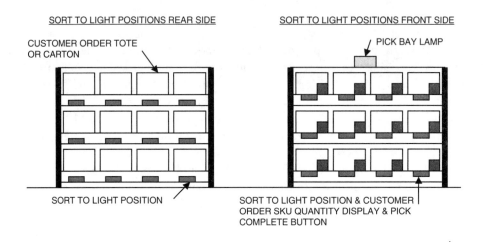

Figure 8.10 Sort to Light Concept

to the WMS computer for inventory and customer-order update. This approach features higher employee productivity, it minimizes employee confusion, no employee double-traveling (which means higher employee productivity), and it can be used for a wide SKU mix.

Random SKU Sort

In a random bulked picked SKU transferred to a manual sort and assembly position, an employee transfers a bulked picked SKU into a sort and assembly area discreet position. After all bulk picked

SKUs are transferred, an assembly employee is given a customer order or customer-order group to assemble. An employee with an assembly instruction format (packing slip or RF device) provides each SKU identification number or description and determines a SKU sort and assembly discreet position, walks to a SKU sort and assembly position, removes a SKU quantity from a discreet position and transfers the SKU to a shipping carton or captive tote. The activity is repeated for each SKU on an assembly instruction (i.e., packing slip) and for each customer order that was downloaded from a WMS computer to a sort and assembly area computer printer. At a separate scan station or pack station, picked SKUs and customer-order WMS identification are scanned and sent to the WMS computer for file updating. Because there is no customer-order assembly employee routing sequence, there is low assembly employee productivity, there can be employee confusion, there is employee double traveling in aisles (which means low employee productivity), and great walking distance between two pick locations.

Random SKU Transfer with RF Device Verification

Random bulked picked SKU transfer into a discreet SKU sort and assembly position with RF device verification concept has an employee determine a picked SKU sort and assembly position. After RF device verification each SKU transfer transaction and SKU quantity are sent to a WMS computer. The WMS computer updates a picked SKU sort and assembly position in the files. Each shelf, decked rack, or carton flow-rack position has a human-/machine-readable position identification that is easily recognized by an employee and is in the warehouse computer files. After the WMS computer updates the SKU inventory files, the computer releases customer orders.

After a customer-order bulk picked SKUs are transferred to sort and assembly positions, each SKUs position is updated in the WMS computer. After the WMS computer releases customer orders to the pick activity, customer order pick documents are printed and assembly employees are given pick instructions or packing slips. The packing slips list SKUs that were bulk picked and transferred to sort and assembly positions. An employee with an assembly instruction format (e.g., RF device, packing slip paper document) obtains a SKU identification number or description, scans/reads the bar code/RF tag on the packing slip, and reads the RF device display that shows the SKU sort and assembly position. The employee then walks to a sort/pick position, removes a SKU quantity, and transfers a SKU quantity to a shipping carton or captive container. The activity is repeated for each SKU on a customer-order assembly instruction or packing slip and for each customer order that was downloaded from the WMS computer to the sort and assembly area.

Transferring Picked SKUs by Identification Number

Customer-order bulked picked SKU transfer to a discreet sort and assembly position is determined by each SKU identification number. Each SKU Identification number is matched to a sort/assembly bay and position identification number. Within a sort/bay, each SKU identification number identifies a shelf or decked rack level. An aisle identification is not required because the sort/pick area has one or two aisles. The options for this approach are:

- SKU number's first digit is used to identify a bay and the last digit to identify a shelf/decked rack level. A sort and assembly philosophy is used when a SKU identification's first digits are 0 to 9.

- SKU number's first digit identifies a bay and the second digit identifies a shelf/deck rack level. A sort and assembly philosophy is used when the SKU identification's first digits are 0 to 9.
- SKU number's last digit identifies a bay and the next to last digit identifies a shelf or deck rack level.

Manual Sort and Assembly: Pick/Packing Slip Print Sequence

For a manual sort/pick design, the options for a pick/packing-slip print sequence options are:

1. A random customer-order pick/packing slip print sequence. This means that the print sequence is in any numerical sequence, and there is no concern with SKU allocation to sort/pick positions. This approach increases employee's walking distance from a central control desk to complete each customer order. Also, to pick a SKU, a picker double walks an aisle.

2. Customer-order WMS identification number sequence. This is essentially a random sequence, and the features are the same as those described above.

3. SKU number. This approach uses an arithmetic sequence. All SKUs that have SKU identification 1 as the first or last digit are printed in one packing-slip group. With packing slips grouped into numbers 0 to 9 and the first/last digit as a sort and assembly bay position, each packing-slip group is placed into a corresponding bay. As pickers assemble customer orders, the packing slips for the first SKU on each customer order will be in the same bay. This approach means increased productivity due to less walking for a picker to pick the first SKU in an order, as well as walking the same distance to pick the second SKU.

4. Sort and assembly bay location number print sequence. In a one-aisle concept, when packing slips are printed in the second digit SKU number arithemtic sequence for the bay/shelf, it groups packing slips into the second or next to last SKU number (0 to 9). Prior to the final SKU pick process, a pick/packing-slip print sequence permits packing slips to be distributed as a group to each bay, e.g., all customer orders with SKU 10095 are located in Bay 1 for first digit or Shelf 5 for last digit. During a final pick activity, having each packing-slip group in the appropriate bay improves picker productivity because the first SKU pick is at the bay with the packing slip. The features are customer order packing slips/invoices are in a sort/assembly bay for a customer order first pick transaction that improves employee productivity, minimal employee confusion, high picker productivity, it can be used for a wide SKU mix, it handles a low to medium volume, and it is low cost.

SKU Bulk Manual Sort and Customer-Order Assembly Location Design Options

A bulk or *en masse* pick of very small size SKU (e.g., jewelry, electronic parts), followed by a manual sort, has a low equipment cost but some cost in WMS and warehouse computer programs. Depending on customer orders, the WMS or warehouse computer prints a SKU bulk or *en masse* pick list. A picker bulk or *en masse* picks each SKU and transfers the bulk picked SKUs to a sort and assembly position. SKU sort and assembly positions are organized by the SKU number's last or first digit or RF device. After completion of all bulk pick-and-sort SKU transactions, a picker picks the SKUs from the sort/pick positions. Sort and assembly design options are:

■ A straight line sort and assembly position design has sort and assembly shelf or decked rack positions arranged in a straight line (0 to 9) (see Figure 8.11). The arrangement has the first sort and assembly position at the entrance to an aisle and the sort and assembly position numbers progressively increase to complete the required positions. With this arrangement, an employee starts at the first sort and assembly position and completes SKU withdrawal transactions. The approach features a potential increase in the walking distance and time between two sort and assembly positions, minimizes SKU hit density and concentration, and the aisle position number system has a progressive pattern.

■ A tunnel, "U," or horse-shoe–shaped sort and assembly position design has a sort and assembly shelf or rack positions as two rows with an aisle. The options for numbering are a) 0 to 4

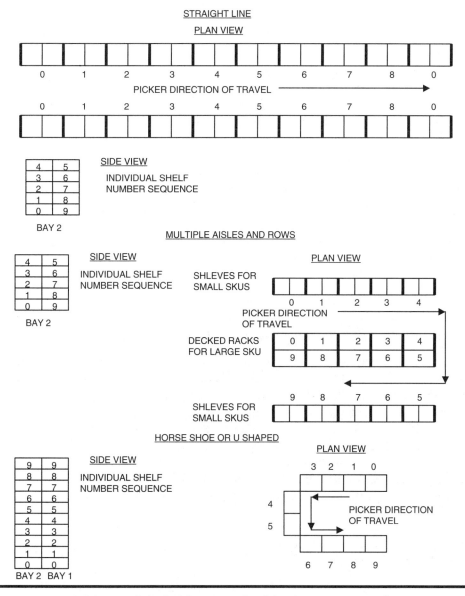

Figure 8.11   Manual Sort and Final Pick Layouts Straight Line U or Horse Shoe

on one side and 5 to 9 on the other side, or b) an employee routing pattern that uses a horse-shoe or "U" pattern (i.e., even numbers on an aisle right and odd numbers on an aisle left). A tunnel, "U," or horse-shoe–shaped sort and assembly arrangement has the first sort and assembly position at the aisle entrance and sort and assembly position numbers progressively increasing to complete the position. This approach features a potential decrease in walking distance and time between two sort and assembly positions, increases in SKU hit density and concentration, a number system with a progressive pattern, and ease of understanding.

How to Combine SKUs from Different Areas (Product Class)

If the pick operation has two separate pick designs or SKU pick areas (i.e., SKUs from different SKU classes) and a customer order has SKU picks from both areas, prior to a customer-order pack activity, multiple SKUs are:

1. Sent to a SKU manual or mechanized sort area.
2. Combined into a single tote/carton. To combine a customer order with multiple SKUs (from different classes) into one customer-order pick tote/carton, pickers from two separate pick areas place each picked SKU into a single carton/tote.

Options are:

1. SKUs can be transferred from a pick position directly into a carton/tote
2. In each pick area, pick by customer-order wave and send completed customer orders to a combined customer-order staging area. In the staging area, customer-orders are arranged by customer order number in positions that are sequenced in an arithmetic progression. To complete a customer order, as a customer order picked SKUs from the other pick section arrive in a combine customer order staging area, a picker travels to a customer order staging position and from the staging position transfers the SKUs into a customer order carton/tote

Customer-Order SKU Pick Directly into a Customer-Order Carton/Tote

For a customer order with SKUs from different pick zones or sections that arrive in another pick zone/section. In a customer order carton/tote from the other pick zone/section to pick SKUs directly into a customer-order carton/tote that is considered a pick/pack or pick/pass activity. In a pick/pass activity, each customer-order carton/tote is discreetly identified and travels past each pick zone and to the other pick design. The travel path can be a nonpowered conveyor, a powered conveyor, or a four-wheel cart. As the carton/tote arrives at a pick zone or in a new pick design, a picker receives the pick instructions (e.g., paper document with a carton/tote, RF device, or pick-to-light) and transfers the SKU quantity from the pick position into the carton/tote. In the next pick zone or design, a picker receives the pick instructions and completes all picks into the carton/tote.

Customer-Order Wave Pick to a Staging Location; SKU Sorted by Customer Number

For customer orders with SKUs from different pick zones, picked and labeled SKUs are staged at a position in each pick zone. Staged picked and labeled SKUs are arranged by customer-order identification in arithmetic sequence: the customer order with lowest number is at the shelf left-hand position and arithmetically increases to the shelf right hand position. To add shelf positions for staging, a lower shelf is used with the same sequence. A customer-order staging shelf position can be fixed shelves or a four-wheel cart with shelves; the staging position is adjacent to a customer-order travel path.

In the first pick zone, each customer-order carton/tote is identified with a human-/machine-readable identification that faces a pick area or staging area. As the carton/tote travels into a second pick zone, an employee reads the identification on a carton/tote and looks at the staging position. If the staging position has SKUs with the same identification label, the employee transfers SKUs from the staging position to a carton/tote. A carton/tote travel path is zero-pressure conveyor with a stop device or four-wheel cart. If a customer order is not cube for a carton/tote, an overflow carton/tote is added to the conveyor or, if a shelf transport vehicle is used, an overflow shelf is used to hold SKUs. If the picked SKUs are very small, a tote with separators is used on the transport to improve transfer productivity and minimize the number of cartons/totes on the travel path.

Warehouse design parameters are human-/machine-readable identifications on each carton/tote and a pick label on each picked SKU. The warehouse philosophy creates the customer-order waves and has the WMS computer move SKUs to pick positions. After the SKU pick, a picker transfers the picked SKUs to prepick zones and a staging area. In each zone, the transfer employees' activity is to control the transport stop/start controls and to stage each picked overflow SKU. The design features: wide SKU mix, it separates a pick area into zones, batched customer-order pick-wave space is designed to handle SKU volume and cube, employees needs to read labels, it handles a medium volume, requires medium number of employees, has good employee pick/sort productivity, is flexible enough to handle volume fluctuations, and higher warehouse operation or WMS computer cost, and requires a printer to print pick labels.

Paper Document for SKU Sort into a Carton/Tote

A customer-order wave pick, stage, and sort philosophy is a manual SKU sort design in which a transfer employee uses printed instructions to direct a SKU transfer from a combi customer-order staging location into a customer-order tote, carton, cart, or trolley compartment. The components are each customer-order container on a transport travel path, a printed document, customer-order identification on each tote, carton, cart, or trolley section, SKU transfer location, and completed customer-order take-away travel path.

A computer prints a document that lists, in an arithmetic sequence, each customer-order wave or batched customer-order identification. Each customer-order identification has the fewest possible digits and digits are clearly printed on the document.

Prior to ship carton/tote release, in each pick zone the required SKU quantity is transferred from pick positions to a combi customer-order transfer position. A combi customer-order picked transfer position is adjacent to the carton/tote travel path and permits an employee to easily transfer a picked SKU from a transfer location into a carton/tote. After the carton/tote is placed on the travel path, the carton/tote receives an identification. Each carton/tote identification faces a pick aisle or the transfer employee. The identification is large, bold, and clearly printed; the identification is either a self-adhesive label or is ink-jet sprayed onto the carton side. The identification corresponds to each identification on the printed document.

The identified carton/tote travels slowly on the travel path, permitting a transfer employee sufficient time to read and match the identification to the identification on the printed document.

With a match, the transfer employee transfers a SKU quantity from a staging position into the carton/tote. The SKU transfer activity is repeated for each customer-order number on the printed document.

A double-wide carton/tote order travel path can transport two customer orders, thus increasing customer-order volume. A double-wide conveyor is made up of a near-side conveyor in which cartons/totes start or end with a unique digit/alpha character (e.g., "1" or "A"), and a far-side conveyor in which cartons/totes start or end with "2" or "B." After a carton/tote travels through a pick zone, the in-house transport moves the carton/tote to the next pick/pass zone.

The features of this design are high volume, need for employee to read the document, excellent employee productivity, small building area, and minimal computer cost. It is best used for low-value or promotional SKUs.

The disadvantages are that it handles a small to medium number of customer orders, and few SKUs per order; to complete a pick transaction, requires a SKU sort/pick instruction; it requires management discipline and coordination between pick and sort zones; there are potential sort errors; it requires human-/machine-readable code; and there will be some SKU double handling. The advantages are low to medium cost; low impact on SKUs; it can be installed in a low-ceiling building; it permits batched customer-order pick activity; and it handles a wide SKU mix.

Chapter 9

Batched Picked SKU Sort

Introduction

A customer-order batched picked SKU sort design is the heart of a warehouse. The warehouse staff creates an order wave and releases the order wave to the WMS computer. The computer allocates SKUs for customer-order batch groups or order waves and sends move transactions to a storage and transport designs. The storage and transport design ensures that SKUs are transferred from a storage position to a pick position. After SKU transfer and bar-code scans to a pick position, the warehouse computer sends a message to the WMS computer. The WMS computer releases customer orders to a pick design. A pick design ensures that a picker/pick machine transfers a SKU from a position onto a transport design. A transport design moves picked SKUs from a pick area to the sort design. The sort design ensures that picked (e.g., precoded, prelabeled, or labeled) small items or master cartons are picked as a mixed and picked SKUs and are separated according to sort instruction and sent to a sort location.

Small-item or master-carton sort activity groups are:

- Picker sort designs
- Centralized manual sort designs
- Centralized mechanized sort designs

After a manual or mechanized SKU sort activity, a sort employee completes a) a SKU scan transaction, which is sent to the WMS computer. The computer depletes each SKU from the pick position inventory quantity and updates the SKU status, and b) scan transaction, which is sent to the WMS computer. The computer updates the customer-order status.

Small-Item and Master-Carton Sort Design

A multiple batched pick, transport, sort, and pack design with a WMS computer transfers customer orders to the warehouse computer. Based on warehouse guidelines and order wave per hour (or other unit of time), the warehouse staff creates an order wave that groups several (or mixed)

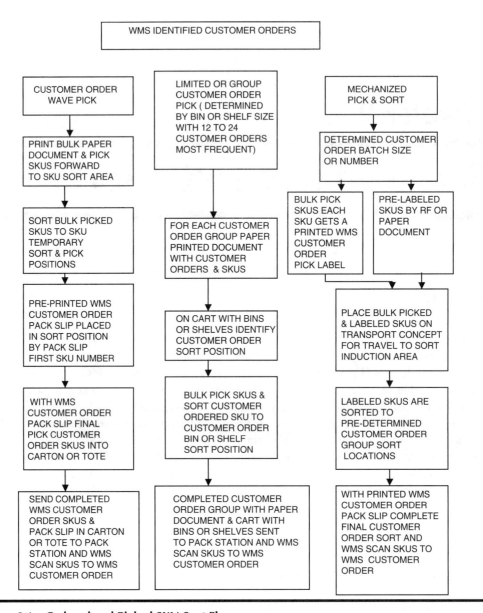

Figure 9.1   Ordered and Picked SKU Sort Flow

SKUs into several batches or groups. With a high customer-order operation, there are at least several customer-order batches or groups (see Figure 9.1). With a batched-pick philosophy, and after the completion of the order wave plan, the WMS computer prepares (with a batched customer order):

1. A printed sort label, which has a warehouse computer for each customer ordered SKU within a customer-order batch, order wave or group assigned to a customer order sort position. During pick activity, each picked SKU receives a SKU or customer-order identification, and is transported to the sort design and sorted to an assigned sort position.

2. If all SKUs have an identification label, a prelabeled SKU does not require a printed sort-design label. The WMS computer allocates each prelabeled SKU for a move to a pick position. Based on the order wave, the computer sends all customer orders to the warehouse computer, which assigns each to a sort position. During pick activity each prelabeled SKU piece is picked, transported, and sorted to an assigned sort position.

In a standard employee-controlled forklift truck pallet design, a pallet warehouse has a forklift truck handle one pallet per pick transaction, which is delivered to a shipping dock, pick line, or pack station drop point. In an AS/RS warehouse, one pallet is transferred to a drop point/delivery station and a forklift truck driver transfers a pallet to a shipping dock, pick line, or pack station drop point.

Small Items and Master Cartons with a WMS Program Requirement

For a small-item or master-carton sort design with a WMS program to be an effective, cost-efficient, accurate, and timely pick design, design factors are a) batched customer orders; b) pick-and-sort instructions; c) picked SKU transport design; d) sort design; and e) customer order and SKU identification scan location.

Batched/Grouped Customer Orders

After the WMS computer receives customer orders from the host computer, the WMS computer sends the existing customer-order pool and new customer orders (host computer received and transferred) to the warehouse staff. The warehouse staff develops order waves (or an order wave plan) based on new and existing (pool) orders. After the warehouse staff creates the order wave, it is released to the WMS computer, which allocates the order wave's SKUs. For an order wave SKU quantity, the WMS computer considers SKU inventory in a pick position and allocates an additional SKU quantity from storage positions, and directs the storage concept to complete a SKU move transation to a pick positon. After the scan and transfer to a pick position, the WMS computer receives an update from the warehouse. Upon receiving the update, the WMS computer releases batched/grouped customer orders to the pick design. A multiple batched/grouped pick/sort/pack philosophy has a computer group several customer ordered SKUs into a customer order batch/group. A batched pick philosophy uses one single or several pickers. Each picker a) completes SKU picks and places the mixed, picked SKUs into a tote, or b) picks or labels each SKU *en masse* into a tote, cart, load-carrying surface, or directly onto a belt conveyor for transport to the sort area. This approach features:

- Fewer picker aisle trips
- Constant picked SKU flow to pack stations
- Low pick cart and tote cost
- The use of the WMS and warehouse computer programs
- Each picked SKU has a human-/machine-readable customer-order identification
- Sufficient table top surface at a pack table
- A sort area with additional sort and pack employee time
- Handles high customer-order volume

Determing SKUs per Customer-Order Batch

With a batched/grouped customer-order pick design, a pick, transport, and sort design is designed according to the SKU quantity handled at each work station. The pick-and-sort design activity station that handles the lowest SKU volume establishes the employee productivity rate for the entire sort design. For a pick design with a sort activity, to determine a batch, order wave, or customer-order group, picked SKU options are picker driven or final-/sort-station driven.

Batched Pick and Sort Instruction

A pick philosophy involving multiple customer orders and multiple pickers uses a pick-and-sort instruction format. A batched pick-and-sort format uses a self-adhesive identification label or prelabeled SKUs. With a SKU pick-and-sort design, a picker places a customer-order identification on each picked and labeled SKU. With a prelabeled SKU pick-and-sort design, a picked SKU does not have a picker to label it. In batched pick-and-sort design, the SKU pick-and-sort instruction uses human-/machine-readable symbology. With manual SKU pick-and-sort designs, the pick-and-sort instruction is a human-/machine-readable code that is printed onto a paper document, label, or precoded SKU, and the customer-order and SKU identifications have a machine-readable symbology. A paper document or label indicates a discreet customer-order sort number.

With a manual centralized sort design, a small-item picked SKU sort activity has:

1. A human-/machine-readable label on each picked SKU (i.e., precoded SKU). Labeled SKUs are mixed in a tote, loose *en masse,* or on a nonpowered/powered vehicle/powered conveyor. Each picked SKU has a paper sort label attached to its exterior surface. If all SKUs have a WMS identification code, the code is the sort instruction.
2. Batched picked SKUs are separated by a human-/machine-readable SKU code. Each SKU is picked into a specific tote or into a specific compartment in a separated tote. With a SKU in one tote section approach, the sort instruction is a) human-/machine-readable paper document, or b) a bar-code label/RF tag that is scanned/read and used to activate a sort location or sort-to-light display.

With a mechanized centralized picked SKU sort design, small-item sort activity has a human-/machine-readable code on each label or a SKU code. A bar-code label/RF tag is attached to each SKU's exterior surface and is scanned/read in a sort area by a scanner/reader.

Paper Sort Document

A paper sort document is used in a pick aisle (or end of the pick aisle) in a pick design in which a document is printed for each customer-order batch. The document's first column shows each SKU pick position. Successive columns list alpha/numeric customer-order identifications. These identifications appear on sort locations. The first row of the document lists an alpha/numeric identification. The succeeding rows show pick positions for SKUs on a customer order in a batch. The paper document lists only those SKUs that are on a customer order and only those SKUs in a pick area. The SKU quantities are listed under each row.

To determine a batched picked SKU sort location, a picker or sort employee reads the SKU and pick position on a paper sort document. Depending on the SKU quantity that appears under each column, the employee locates the number of the sort cart/area bins and transfers the correct

SKU quantity to a sort location. The activity is repeated for each SKU on the sort document and for each tote or unique SKU. Scans of the completed picked/sorted customer-order are performed at a scan or pack station. A picker signs or marks each paper or row as part of a pick qualitiy check program.

Sort-to-Light/Put-to-Light Instruction

With sort-to-light or put-to-light instructions, the sort design has each unique bulk or *en masse* picked SKU in a separate tote or tote section; each SKU bar code/RF tag appears on a paper document (or each SKU has bar code/RF tag). A tote with bulk picked SKUs is delivered to a sort station. At the sort station, a customer-order carton/tote has been assigned (i.e., scanned to) to a specific sort location. Each sort location has a sort-to-light or put-to-light display and a paper pack document is attached to each shipping carton or sort location. After a sort employee removes the sort document from a pick tote, the employee scans the bar code/RF tag. The scanner/reader sends the bar-code/RF tag information to the warehouse computer. Depending on the ordered SKU, the warehouse computer activates an assigned sort-to-light or put-to-light display at each sort location. The activated display indicates a customer order or sort location that has picked SKUs. After a sort employee transfers the appropriate picked SKU number from a pick tote to a sort location, the employee presses the appropriate sort-completion button on the sort-to-light/put-to-light display. This signals the warehouse computer of a sort activity completion for a particular picked SKU. On a sort-to-light display screen, the screen instructs a sort employee to a) repeat the SKU pick activity (because customer order was for two or more SKUs), b) plank or zero (because a customer order has a different SKU), or c) transfer the completed order to a take-away conveyor.

Pick and Sort Label

A batched pick-and-sort design sort activity is completed by an employee or machine that reads/scans the human-/machine-readable symbology on each picked SKU. Sort instruction considerations are:

- Vendor prelabeled or vendor labeled SKU
- Nonlabeled SKU, which a picker labels with a SKU identification,
- SKU identification as a sort instruction
- A customer-order sort instruction

Machine-Printed Self-Adhesive Sort Label

A self-adhesive machine-printed label is a human-/machine-readable label created by the warehouse computer-controlled printer. The printer prints a label for each SKU in a customer-order batch. A label has alpha characters and numeric digits plus a bar code/RF tag that identifies a SKU pick position and a sort location. Information is printed in black ink onto self-adhesive label paper or stock white face. Important items for a batched pick label's face are:

- Pick position and SKU description
- Customer-order name and address

- Customer-order alpha/numeric identification or sort location
- Black bars with white spaces or a bar code/RF tag

In a pick area, the picker reads the pick position on the label face and travels to the pick position. At the pick position, the picker removes the back from the label and applies the label onto a picked SKU. Depending on the pick design, the picked and labeled SKU is placed into a tote or directly onto a conveyor belt for transport to a sort/pack area.

Precoded/Prelabeled SKUs

In a batched pick-and-sort design, a human-/machine-readable label is attached to each picked SKU. A precoded SKU is one onto which the vendor has placed a company WMS identification. The receiving dock or QA department employees ensure that each SKU has a human-/machine-readable code. A vendor delivers prelabeled SKUs per the company's specification in accordance with the purchase order. In a batched pick-and-sort design, depending on the pick instruction format, a picker removes the exact SKU quantity from a pick position and moves it to the in-house transport concept. At a sort station, an employee or scanner/reader scans/reads each precoded SKU, which identifies each picked SKU's sort location. The features are:

- Label cost is in the cost of goods
- Less warehouse print time and label expense
- Receiving and QA department verifies a vendor code
- Less picker work to carry pick labels
- A sort design uses a SKU number, depending on the label's specification

In a manual sort/pack design, after a tote with loose *en masse* picked SKUs or mixed picked SKUs arrives on a belt conveyor travel in a sort area, a sort employee picks-up a SKU, reads the sort identification and matches the SKU sort identification location to the sort location identification. With a SKU sort identification location and sort location match, a sort employee places a picked SKU into the appropriate sort location.

In a central mechanized sort design, picked and labeled loose *en masse* SKUs on a belt conveyor or picked and mixed SKUs in a tote arrive at a sort induction station. At the station, employee induction options are to place a) each picked/labeled SKU (with the label face up) onto sorter carrying surface or travel path, or b) picked SKU (with the label face up) onto an induction conveyor belt. Depending on the sort design, as an empty SKU sorter carrying surface arrives at a sorter induction station, an induction station conveyor belt advances the SKU forward for transfer onto an empty mechanized sorter carrying surface.

SKU Number or Customer-Order Identification Number as a Sort Instruction Identification

In a pick-and-sort design, batched pick-and-sort and scan-label format options are a) SKU identification number and b) customer-order identification number. A label format is used in a pick-and-sort scan, customer-order returns, and return-to-stock/vendor activities. A design with a SKU number label format option has a batched pick/sort label with a SKU on the front of the label. With a SKU label format, the vendor or company receiving department applies a label with human-/machine-readable symbology to each SKU. After pick-and-sort labels are printed, a picker completes a pick activity by removing the label back and applying a label to each SKU.

Pick Position and Pick Quantity Instruction

In a batched pick-and-sort design with a SKU and customer-order identification number format, the SKU pick label (or a separate pick instruction format) is the pick position instruction and SKU quantity instruction. The pick position instruction directs a picker to a SKU pick position. At the pick position (which may contain prelabeled or nonlabeled SKU), the picker transfers the picked SKU to a transport. With both prelabeled SKU and printed label SKU options, the pick position and pick SKU quantity instruction format options are:

- Paper printed document
- Paper self-adhesive label
- Voice directed
- Pick-to-light
- Sort-to-light
- RF device

Batch Pick Activity

A batched pick activity is a manual pick that has a picker travel with pick instructions and a transport device through pick aisles. When the picker arrives at a pick position, the pick activity is to transfer a SKU onto the transport device. With prelabeled SKUs, the pick activity is a transfer activity. With nonlabeled SKUs, the pick activity includes placing a label onto each SKU.

Batched Picked SKU Release

Batch customer-order release design controls picked SKUs' transfer to a transport concept. With a paper pick instruction, a picker picks and sorts SKUs into the section of a tote or four-wheel cart. Batch release control components are:

1. A paper pick/sort document accompanies each tote or cart; each tote or cart is identified for each batch. At a pack station, the document is used to verify an order's picked and sorted accuracy.
2. In a pick area, there are sufficient empty totes/carts to handle an out-of-balance situation between a pick/sort area and pack area activities.
3. Each tote/cart has sufficient space for a batch identification and each customer-order location.

If the design is for multiple customer orders and multiple pickers, each picker transfers mixed picked and self-adhesive labels or coded SKUs into a tote that is moved over a conveyor; or picked SKUs are transferred directly onto a belt conveyor. In-house transport concept moves a group of picked *en masse* mixed SKUs to a sort area. A batch release design ensures each picker transfers the correct batched, picked SKUs on-time onto a transport concept. If batched, picked, or coded SKUs are not properly sequenced with sort area activity, an unscheduled SKU release to a sort activity has the potential to create sort errors or decrease sort productivity and accuracy.

To reduce batch overlaps in a sort/pack area, the guidelines are:

1. Ensure that total picker productivity is equal to the warehouse's sort/pack station productivity.
2. Ensure that pick area provides sufficient queue space and totes to hold batch picked SKUs that are out-of-balance.
3. Ensure that the pick area uses a batch release design to instruct pickers about each batch's transfer time.
4. In a sort/pack area, ensure that each sort station has at least three sort locations.
5. In a pick area, the batch release designs are a) control clerk, b) clock and printed release time on a pick label, and c) score board.

Batched Picked SKU Transport Designs

A batched picked SKU transport design is a pick design that either moves batched picked SKUs from a pick-and-sort design consolidation area to a pack area, or is the physical link between a pick area and a centralized manual or mechanized sort/pack area. A manual pick-and-sort design has the in-house transport concept move a) batched picked SKUs in a four-wheel cart or trolley basket through pick area aisles with picked (but not sorted SKUs) to an on-board sort location or b) picked and separated SKUs for sort at a pick aisle end. A central manual or mechanized pick, transport, and sort/pack concept moves loose *en masse* SKUs from a pick area over a powered belt travel path, four-wheel cart, trolley basket, or in a conveyable tote over nonpowered/powered conveyor. From a pick area, batched picked SKUs are transported to a central manual or mechanized sort area.

Batched Picked SKU Conveyor/Vehicle

A pick conveyor/transport design is designed to move picked SKUs or loose *en masse* picked SKUs in totes on a nonpowered/powered cart/vehicle travel path, powered conveyor travel path, or belt conveyor from a pick position to a transport conveyor or vehicle travel path.

In-House Transport Conveyor/Vehicle Design

A transport conveyor or design ensures:

1. SKUs or picked loose *en masse* SKUs in totes, cart transport concept, or on a belt conveyor are moved from a pick area to a sort area
2. Sufficient queue conveyor travel path or transport vehicle queue lanes. In a pick area, a transport conveyor design has queue low pressure or zero pressure conveyor sections or open space for empty transport vehicles. At a sorter induction station a) loose *en masse* SKUs flow over a chute with sufficient length and queue against a stop. The loose SKU flow onto a chute that is from a powered in-feed belt conveyor travel path that is controlled by photo-eyes along a chute. When a photo-eye is blocked, a) it sends a message to a conveyor computer to stop the in-feed belt conveyor and b) SKUs in totes travel over low or zero pressure conveyor section and queue at the induction station. Tote flow to an induction station is controlled by photo-eyes along a tote powered travel path. When a photo-eye is blocked, it sends a message to a conveyor computer to stop the queue conveyor travel path, c) on a trolley travel path are

photo-eyes and when a photo-eye is blocked, it sends a message to a trolley computer to stop the trolley conveyor divert device, and d) a four-wheel cart or basket transport design has empty carton or basket in-feed and out-feed lanes at an induction area.

Picked SKU In-House Transport Designs

SKU transport activity objectives are to move batched, picked SKUs in a constant flow from a pick area to an assigned sort station, the in-house transport options are a) tote/carton past pick positions and to a next pick area activity, and b) picked loose batched SKUs from a pick area to sort/pack area.

Transporting Batched Totes or Loose SKUs from a Pick Area

All batch pick operations need to move loose SKUs and totes/cartons from a pick area to a sort/ pack area. In a pick design with a pick/sort and transport design, the next activity station is a quantity-quality-check and pack station. With a pick, transport, and sort design, the next pick activity is a sort and pack station. Transport is performed in a manual or mechanized design. Transport is the physical link between the pick area and the sort area and ensures that picked SKUs are delivered to a sort location on-time and with minimal damage.

Picked small-item transport design parameters are:

- Loose SKU or carton/tote characteristics that are length, width, height, weight, handles, and SKU fragile or crushable
- SKU volume and carton number
- Pick design, methodology, and philosophy
- Induction location has a tote tilted or level and sort method
- Travel distance and travel path configuration
- Time to complete an order and delivery cycle or batched orders/wave
- Order number and SKUs per customer order or per batched order group or wave

In a small-item pick operation with a transport design, a transport function is designed for picked SKUs as loose *en masse* SKUs or SKUs in a carton/tote. Loose *en masse* picked SKUs transport designs are:

- Employee carry
- Nonpowered four-wheel cart
- Slide or chute
- Powered vehicles
- Powered belt conveyor travel path
- Trolley basket or bag on a manual powered overhead trolley travel path
- Tele-car
- Pneumatic tube

Picked SKU Sort Designs

A batched picked SKU sort activity is the heart of a batched pick-and-sort design. It ensures that picked SKUs are separated from a mixed group of picked SKUs. Sort activity groups are:

- For small-item pick/sort designs, centra nanual sort designs, and central mechanized sort designs
- For cartons, central manual sort designs and central mechanized sort designs

Picked Sort Design Parameters

Each picked sort design group has both similar and different characteristics. The similar characteristics are that each sort design group has a method to determine a batched/grouped order quantity, a batched/grouped order release control design, a picked SKU transport design, and a mixed picked SKU separate/sort to an identified position. The unique characteristics are a SKU pick-and-sort instruction, a method to pick SKUs, and method to complete a picked SKU sort activity.

Picked SKU Sort Location

A picked SKU sort design has an employee or mechanized sort device sort an individual picked SKU from a picked SKU mix. A sort activity collects picked and labeled SKUs into a sort location. A sort location is a temporary holding location or conveyor lane for loose small SKUs or cartons until the batch sort process has been completed.

In a sort activity, sort location options are:

- for loose small SKUs, a sort side or window with a minimum of two or three openings, a solid bottom surface, two solid or mesh opening side walls, and a front opening that has a removable barrier. A barrier is solid full height, solid half height, solid with a wire mesh opening or clear plastic window, or opening permits SKUs to flow onto a pack table surface.
- for loose small SKUs, a sort window, structural support members, and a surface to support a shipping carton. In a sort location, carton options are a) carton with an open top with flaps down, b) carton with an open top face toward a sort window with flaps up, or c) open plastic container to face upward.

Ordered/Picked SKU Sort Location or SKU Holding Device

In manual or mechanized sort designs, *en masse* or picked and mixed batched SKUs or master cartons are sorted by customer order into a queue location that is a sort location. A small SKU sort location interior space is designed to hold a customer ordered SKU cube or quantity. If a picked small loose item sort location holds a customer order cube, the sort location is designed for an operation's customer order maximum or peak cube or SKU quantity.

Picked Small Items Held in a Sort Chute/Slide

A sort location has two solid or meshed side walls, solid bottom surface, a front opening barrier, and an optional solid top. After the completion of the sort activity, a sort/pack station employee performs a final sort. From the mixed sorted SKUs in a slide location, the final sort activity has the packer—according to the paper document (i.e., packing slip)—separate SKUs for each order. After the final sort, a packer transfers picked/sorted SKUs into a shipping carton.

In a centralized mechanized sort design, each sort location has one-sort window interface with a sort transfer device. A sort window is separated into three sort locations by a fixed-position solid divider or solid moveable flippers. With a chute and door at the discharge end, the design has an estimated sort location to hold a SKU cube volume of a third to a half of a sort-location cube. A step in a chute middle increases SKU capacity.

Picked SKUs Held in a Shipping Carton/Captive Tote

With this design, picked SKUs are transferred from the sort design into an assigned shipping carton or captive tote. The sort location has structural support members to provide sufficient rigidity and stability to hold picked/sorted SKUs and carton/captive tote weight and physical size. A sort location that has shipping carton or captive tote options are:

- The carton open side faces upward with flaps up, or two SKU carton with no flaps. A carton is designed to hold the maximum projected picked SKU cube, SKU number, and weight. Carton placement is used in manual sort-to-light sort designs and all mechanized sort designs. A sort and hold location has a high window to handle a carton with flaps up and a longer SKU drop from a discharge point into a carton; or if the carton open side faces upward with flaps down, it has the same design parameters and operational characteristics as a carton with flaps up except a shorter sort hold location window and picked SKU drop from a discharge point into a carton, which minimizes SKU damage.
- The captive tote design has the same design parameters and operational characteristics as a carton with flaps down.

Manual Batched SKU Pick-and-Sort Design

Manual pick-and-sort designs have a picker with a paper document, prelabeled SKUs or pick labels to pick-and-sort picked SKUs into a temporary customer order sort location. In a pick area, the temporary customer order sort location is a fixed shelf, tote, bin, or mobile shelf location. The various types of manual pick-and-sort designs have similarities and differences. The similiarties are that each design uses a printed document or paper label as the pick-and-sort instruction, the batched customer-order number is limited by the sort location number, SKUs with a cube that fits into a sort location, and each sort location has a human-/machine-readable identification that matches the identification on the pick/sort instruction. In a manual pick-and-sort application, any overflow picked SKUs at a sort location are placed into an overflow carton/tote and the carton/tote is in a separate location on a sort device. After sort activity completion—and depending on warehouse practice—picked and sorted SKUs are scanned at a sort station or at a pack station. The scan transactions are sent to the WMS computer to update the inventory files and customer-order status. Batched SKU pick-and-sort designs are:

- In a pick aisle or at a pick aisle end in order to use a four-wheel movable cart with shelves/bins.
- In a pick aisle end, multi-shelf location.

- In a pick aisle end to use a multi-shelf basket attached to an overhead trolley travel path.
- In a multiple compartment or customer order sort location in a tote that moves on a conveyor travel path.

Four-Wheel Cart with Multi-Shelves or Bins

In a design for a mobile four-wheel cart with multi-shelves or bins, the steps a pick-and-sort employee must follow in a pick are (see Figure 9.2):

1. Receive batched SKU pick-and-sort instruction document
2. Write the batch number onto a cart placard
3. Place each customer-order identification on each cart shelf or bin sort location
4. Verify that all written identifications match the customer-order identification on the pick instruction document.

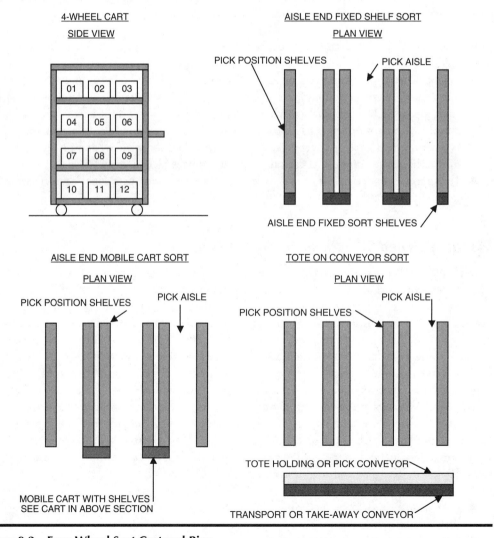

Figure 9.2   Four-Wheel Sort Cart and Bins

After the pick activity, the picker pushes a four-wheel cart into a pick aisle and walks to a first pick position that appears on the paper document. The picker removes the SKU quantity specified on the paper document from a pick position and transfers the quantity into four-wheel cart sort location. After completion of the pick-and-sort activity, a picker/sorter places a mark on a SKU pick/sort position number that is on a paper pick/sort document. The pick-and-sort activity is repeated for each SKU that appears on the pick-and-sort paper document.

When a pick-and-sort employee has completed all picks and sorts for batched customer orders, the paper document is placed onto a cart placard and the cart is pushed to the next warehouse operation pick zone or to a pack station area. A picker and sorter obtains the next batch order-wave document and prepares a new four-wheel cart for another SKU pick-and-sort activity. If self-adhesive labels are used in the design, the picker and sorter place the appropriate label onto a picked SKU and transfer the labeled SKU into a sort location. A prelabeled SKU does not require a WMS identification, but a sort design completes a sort transaction with the WMS identification. After completion of the sort activity, the picked and sorted SKUs are scanned at a sort or pack station. The scan transactions are sent to the WMS computer to update the inventory files and customer-order status.

Multi-Shelves/Bins at a Pick Aisle End

To ensure good employee productivity, the fixed multi-shelf or bins at a pick aisle end have two shelf sort locations on the sides. After a picker receives a pick-and-sort instruction document, the picker writes each batch number onto each shelf placard and writes the customer-order identification onto each shelf or bin sort location, and verifies that all written identifications match the customer-order identification on a pick/sort instruction document. The picker then walks to the first pick position that appears on the pick document. The picker removes the SKU quantity specified in the document, walks to the pick aisle end and transfers the SKU quantity to each shelf or bin sort location. After completing the pick-and-sort, a picker and a sorter mark a SKU pick/sort position number on a paper pick/sort document. The pick-and-sort activity is repeated for each SKU on the pick-and-sort document. Picked and sorted SKUs are scanned at a sort or pack station, and the scans are sent to the WMS computer to update files and customer-order status.

When the picker and sorter has completed all batched picks and sorts for batched customer orders, the paper document is placed onto a shelf placard. The picker and sorter obtains the next batch order-wave document and prepares a new four-wheel cart for another pick/sort activity. While a pick-and-sort employee is completing pick-and-sort transactions for the second batched group or wave, the master-sort employee transfers the picked and sorted SKUs from the temporary sort location (at the pick aisle end) to a master-sort transport device, along with the pick/sort document. In a check/pack area, the pick/sort document is used to verify the quantity and quality of the picked SKUs. If self-adhesive labels are used in the pick-and-sort design, a picker and sorter places the appropriate label onto a SKU and transfers the SKU to a sort location. After completion of the sort activity, picked and sorted SKUs are scanned at a sort or pack station, and the scans are sent to the WMS computer to update inventory files and customer-order status.

Overhead Trolley with a Multi-Shelf Basket

In a sort design that uses an overhead trolley with a multi-shelf basket, a picker/sorter receives a pick-and-sort instruction document and writes each batch number onto an overhead placard. The employee writes each customer-order identification onto a shelf location and verifies that the sort document and sort shelf locations match. The picker/sorter walks to the first pick position that appears on the document. The picker removes the appropriate quantity of SKU from a pick position and transfers the SKU quantity to various overhead trolley shelf basket cart sort locations. After completion of the pick/sort activity, the picker/sorter marks the document. The pick-and-sort activity is repeated for each SKU on the document. When the picker/sorter has completed all the picks/sorts, the document is placed onto a basket placard and an overhead trolley with a shelf basket is pushed to the next pick zone or to a pack station. The picker/sorter obtains the next document and prepares a new overhead trolley shelf basket for a new batch pick-and-sort activity. After completion of the sort activity, picked and sorted SKUs are scanned at a sort or pack station, and the scans are sent to the WMS computer to update inventory files and customer-order status.

Multi-Compartment Sort Tote on a Conveyor Travel Path

In a design that uses a multi-shelf or multi-compartment tote on a conveyor travel path, a picker receives a pick-and-sort instruction document. The picker writes the batch number onto a tote placard, and writes each customer-order identification onto each tote section. The picker verifies that each sort location matches the document's customer-order identification. The picker then walks to the first pick position that appears on the document. The picker removes the appropriate SKU from the pick position, walks to a tote on a conveyor, and sorts a SKU quantity to each customer-order container sort location. After completion of the pick/sort activity, the picker/sorter marks the document. The pick-and-sort activity is repeated for each SKU on the document. When a picker/sorter has completed all picks/sorts for the batched order, the document is placed on a tote placard and the tote is moved onto a take-away conveyor for transport to the next pick zone or to a pack station. A picker/sorter obtains the next batch or order-wave document and prepares a new multi-shelf or compartment tote for new pick/sort activity.

The manual paper pick/sort features are picker to read, small SKU volume or cube, with two to three SKUs per customer order, 16 to 20 customer orders per batch, four-wheel cart, trolley basket or conveyable tote, paper pick/sort document, low cost, handles slow moving, small cube SKUs, easy to implement and used with other manual pick concepts.

Centralized Manual Sort Designs

Centralized manual sort designs have batched, picked SKUs delivered to a centralized sort area as loose, *en masse,* batched picked SKUs in a tote or on a belt conveyor. The delivery designs are:

- Loose unique nonlabeled SKUs in a four-wheel cart cavity, trolley basket section, or conveyable tote
- Loose labeled and mixed SKUs in a four-wheel cart cavity, trolley basket section, or conveyable tote
- Labeled and mixed SKUs loose *en masse* on a belt conveyor

At a central sort station, a sorter handles each batched, picked SKU by removing the SKU from a transport device, reading the sort instructions, matching a picked SKU sort code to a sort location, and transferring a SKU to an assigned sort location. (The sort location is a temporary holding location, shipping carton, or captive tote.) If the sort design uses a four-wheel cart or overhead trolley basket to move SKUs from a pick area to a sort area and through a sort station, an efficient and productive sort area should have:

- A transport presort and a queue area for each sort location
- A travel path through a sort area
- A staging area for empty transport devices
- An early exit travel spur for empty transport devices

After completion of the sort activity completion, picked and sorted SKUs are scanned at a sort or pack station, and the scans are sent to the WMS computer to update inventory files and customer-order status.

Centralized Manual Sort with Paper Instruction Documents

Centralized manual sort that uses a four-wheel cart cavity, trolley basket section, or tote with a paper document instruction has the following functional areas:

1. In a pick area, a picker picks batched SKUs into one tote or a section in a tote. Other pick devices are a four-wheel cart or trolley basket with shelves or separate compartments. The picker places the batch customer-order number onto a tote, cart, or trolley basket section and walks or rides to a pick position. Per the pick document, the picker transfers all batched, picked SKUs into a tote or tote/cart/basket section, places the pick/sort document into the tote and transfers the tote/cart/trolley basket onto a travel path. To control a batch, each batch has a separate color or coded tote.
2. In sort area, a sort employee ensures that a) the sort location number has the proper customer-order identification and has a packing slip, or b) each sort location has a shipping carton or captive tote, proper customer-order identification, and a packing slip.

As totes/carts/baskets arrive in a sort area, a divert employee looks at the tote color and reads the batch number on the tote/cart/basket. The employee transfers the proper tote/cart/basket from the main sort conveyor onto an individual sort station conveyor queue. To ensure a proper sort, each sort station divert location has a batch number or color at a sort location. As totes/carts/baskets arrive at a sort station, a sort employee removes the pick/sort document from the tote/cart/basket and verifies that the batch number on the tote/cart/basket matches the sort station batch number. With a match, the sort employee removes a picked SKU from a tote and looks at the sort document for the first customer-order identification that has a SKU. If the sort document customer-order identification matches the sort location customer-order identification, the employee transfers the SKU quantity from the pick tote/cart/basket into a sort location. The employee repeats the activity for all SKUs in the tote/cart/basket and for each section. When a sort activity is completed for a batch, the sorter moves to the next sort station or transfers the completed totes/cartons onto a take-away transport concept. After all the picked/sorted SKUs for the batch have cleared the sort station, the station is ready to accept a new batch. After completion of the sort activity, picked and sorted SKUs are scanned at a sort or pack station, and the scans are sent to the WMS computer to update inventory files and customer-order status.

Centralized Manual Sort from a Tote/Cart/Trolley Basket with a Sort-to-Light Design

The features of a sort-/put-to-light centralized manual sort design are:

- Each batched SKU receives a bar-code label/RF tag, or is prelabeled and picked with a bar-code label/RF tag, or picked by a paper document into a separate carton/tote.
- The sort employee has a hand-held scanner that reads a bar code/RF tag. The scanner/reader transmits information to the warehouse computer.
- The warehouse computer activates all appropriate sort location sort-to-light displays that indicates a SKU pick/sort quantity on a customer order.
- Each sort-to-light location has a carton with a packing slip and sort-/put-to-light display module. Each sort-/put-to-light display module is connected to the warehouse computer and WMS computer by a communication wire or fiber optic.
- An in-feed SKU and completed carton/tote take-away conveyor.
- After completion of the sort activity, picked and sorted SKUs are scanned at a sort or pack station, and the scans are sent to the WMS computer to update inventory files and customer-order status.

Centralized Manual Sort from Tote/Cart/Trolley Basket/Belt Conveyor with a Label

In a centralized manual sort in which batched, mixed, and labeled SKUs are picked from a four-wheel cart cavity, trolley basket section, or tote, each transport device/belt conveyor surface contains batched, picked SKUs with a sort label instruction. The design parameters and operational characteristics are similar to a prelabel SKU pick activity except for one. The exception is that each SKU has a pick/sort label that is placed onto the SKU's exterior. The label has the sort identification printed on its face. During a sort activity, the sort label customer-order identification is matched to the sort location identification. A match is a signal for a sorter to transfer the SKU from a carton/tote into a sort location. Use of this approach improves a sorter and checker/packer productivity and accuracy. After completion of the sort activity, picked and sorted SKUs are scanned at a sort or pack station, and the scans are sent to the WMS computer to update inventory files and customer-order status.

Manual Small-Item Sort and Assembly Designs

The objective of a manual sort and assembly is to pick *en masse* individual SKUs for a customer-order group, to arrange bulk or *en masse* picked SKUs in sort and assembly locations, and, in accordance with the packing slip, pick document, or pick instruction, to final pick each SKU from a sort and assembly pick position into a captive tote or shipping carton. After activity completion—and warehouse practice—picked and sorted SKUs are scanned at a sort or pack station. The scan transactions are sent to the WMS computer to update inventory files and customer-order status.

Central Mechanized Small SKU Sort

To implement a central mechanized small SKU sort concep, the warehouse must provide a batched, picked SKU queue area prior to each sorter induction station and between a sort travel path and pack station. A mechanized sort design layout is in arithmetic progression from an induction station with sort locations on both sides of the travel path. Assigned sort locations have even numbers on the right aisle and odd numbers on the left. A central mechanized sort design functional areas are:

- A pick area, pick conveyor, or other pick in-house transport design
- A transport conveyor or design for picked SKU transport from a pick area to a sort area
- A sort induction station
- A sort travel path,
- A "no read" divert station and return conveyor travel path
- Customer-order assigned pack/sort locations
- A clean-out sort location
- A re-latch station, as required by the sort concept
- Control and electrical panels, air compressor, and minic display

Induction or In-Feed Station Conveyor

An induction or in-feed station conveyor is a location where each batched, picked, or prelabeled SKU identification is entered into a warehouse computer that controls a mechanical sorter to divert a customer order SKU from a sorter to a customer order sort location. At the induction station, each SKU is transferred from a conveyor or tote onto a sort travel path. An employee transfers each SKU onto a load-carrying platform or induction powered conveyor belt. An induction powered conveyor belt has at least four short belt conveyor sections that create a gap between adjacent SKUs and transfers each picked SKU onto a sort load-carrying surface or travel path. The difference between the two transfer designs is that a belt conveyor has a higher induction rate. An induction belt conveyor design ensures that as an empty surface or open space arrives at an induction station, the SKU is transferred forward onto the surface. This feature increases the load-carrying surface utilization and sort capacity.

Sort induction designs are:

- Manual induction with a key pad design
- Semi-automatic or hand-held scanner induction with a scanner/reader, in which each SKU has a human-/machine-readable code on its exterior
- Automatic or bar-code scanning/reading induction

In an automatic or scanning/reading induction design, each SKU has a bar-code label/RF tag attached to its exterior. In this design, each bar code/RF tag faces upward as a SKU travels onto a travel path. After an employee places a SKU onto a load-carrying surface or onto an induction powered conveyor belt, sort induction station options are:

- Single induction concept has one induction station that is located prior to the first sort location of a closed-loop travel path sort.

■ Dual induction concept is used on a rectangular or elliptically shaped and closed loop sorter travel path. An induction station is located prior to each sorter travel path straight section. The first induction station inducts SKUs for sorter straight travel path section/locations that are between the first and second induction stations and second induction station inducts SKUs for a sorter straight travel path section/locations that are between the second and first induction stations. A dual induction design has double components such as induction stations, scanners, photo-eyes, tracking devices, clean-out chutes, and "not read" stations.

When compared to the single induction design, the dual induction feature increases induction and sort productivity by an estimated 80%. The features are additional cost, human/machine-readable label that requires a larger label face than a machine readable label face, fewer induction errors, fewer employees, and it handles a high volume.

Sort Travel Path

With a sort design travel path, a load-carrying surface carries a SKU from an induction station, past a scanner/reader, to a sort station. Other travel path stations are "no read" stations, "did-not-sort" stations, clean-out stations, and re-latch stations (as required by the sort concept).

Carrying Surface Sort Techniques

A small-item carrying surface sort technique is a method for transferring a SKU from a load-carrying surface onto/into an assigned sort/divert location. A SKU carrying surface tips, slides, pushes, or drops a SKU from a travel path onto/into a sort location. Sort design stations follow an arithmetic progression from the induction station to the last sort station. The arithmetic progression begins with the first divert station past an induction station, which has the lowest number. Sort locations with odd-numbered last digits are located on the travel path left; sort locations with even-numbered last digits are located on the sort travel path right. Sort techniques are:

1. Active sorter characteristics are a) a powered induction station and sort conveyor travel path and b) a powered load-carrying surface that pushes or pulls a SKU from the carrying surface onto/into a sort location. Cross and moving belts and flap sorters are active sort designs.
2. Active-passive sorter characteristics are a) a manual induction station, b) a powered travel path, and c) a load-carrying surface that tips a SKU from a load-carrying surface into/onto a sort location. Tilt trays, gull wings, Nova sorters, platform sorters, brush sorters, and ring sorters are active-passive sort designs.
3. Passive sorter characteristics are a) a manual or powered induction station, b) a powered travel path, and c) a load-carrying surface that uses gravity to remove a SKU from the carrying surface into/onto a divert location. A Bombay drop design is an active-passive sort design.

A travel path runs from an induction station to all divert locations. Travel path designs are:

1. A straight-line travel path has a load-carrying travel path that runs in a straight line from an induction station to the last sort station. After the last sort station, the travel path ends, and the "did not sort" SKU travel path slopes to the floor. The empty load-carrying surface's return travel path to an induction station is beneath the sort travel path. Straight-line travel path designs are "L" shaped, horse-shoe shaped, and "U" shaped. A straight-line travel path

layout does not have an automatic reintroduction to an induction station for "did not sort" SKUs; all "did not sort" SKUs are dropped to the floor and are manually returned to an induction station or transferred and scanned to an assigned station. The disadvantages of this design are additional employees and low volume. The advantages are no dual induction and low investment.

2. An endless-loop travel path begins at an induction station's lead end and ends at an induction station's charge end. A travel path that starts and ends at the same location is an endless loop. The design options are "L" shaped layout, "U" shaped layout, "O" (i.e., elliptical layout), and rectangular layout. An endless loop travel path has "did not sort" SKUs continuing to travel on the carrying surface past the last divert station and onto an induction station. As a SKU travels on the path at an induction station, the customer-order identification is rescanned or reintroduced to the sort design. To ensure maximum carrying surface utilization and handling capacity, a warehouse computer has the ability to detect a repeated "did not sort" bar code. After a predetermined number of "reads" for a SKU identification, the computer diverts the SKU onto a clean-out chute or special divert station and the SKU is manually transferred to a pack station. The disadvantage is increased capital investment. The advantages are few employees, high volume, easy expansion, and it permits a dual induction design.

Central Mechanized Sort Designs

Centralized mechanical sort designs are tilt tray, flap sorter, Bombay drop, Nova sort, cross or moving belt, gull wing, ring sorter, brush sorter, and side tilting platform.

Tilt Tray

A tilt tray is a fixed travel powered by electric motor or linear drive. An electric motor turns a shaft that moves a tooth sprocket drive and drive train that propels a closed-loop chain. Each tilt tray is attached to the chain. A linear drive is new technology that uses an electric current sent through a bus channel. The tilt tray's aluminum foot extends downward into a channel opening. The electric current traveling through the channel drives the aluminum foot forward through a channel travel path. Each tilt tray is a load-carrying surface that carries a picked SKU. If a SKU is long, two trays are used. Depending on the computer, the tracking device, and the travel speed, a tray is tilted at an assigned sort station. Using the tray's tilt action, forward movement, and gravity, a small item is transferred from a tilt tray into/onto a sort location.

Flap Sorter

After the SKUs are transported to an induction station, a flap sorter moves a small item on a platform across a fixed travel path to the assigned sort station. A flap sorter travel path has many belt conveyor sections that are powered by an electric motor. At the sort station, the conveyor section or flap angles downward. The downward angle, gravity, and the forward momentum of the conveyor causes the SKU to fall into the sort station. After a predetermined number of seconds, the angled conveyor section returns to a level position, and the flap sorter transports another SKU to an assigned sort station. A flap sorter's components are:

- Fixed, short powered belt conveyor sections
- Flap or flexible short powered belt conveyor sections
- A SKU induction station
- A return belt conveyor section (i.e., "did not sort" station)
- Drive motors
- Drives and pulleys
- Sort stations
- Structural support members
- Warehouse computer and controls

BOMBAY Drop Design

A Bombay Drop sort design has platforms that are side mounted to an electric powered closed-loop chain; each platform is a SKU carrier. After a SKU is inducted onto a Bombay drop carrier, the warehouse computer, a tracking device, and constant travel speed ensures that the sort activity occurs at an assigned sort location. It is possible to design a Bombay drop as a dual induction system. Key Bombay drop sort design components are:

- SKU load carriers/bi-parting trays
- An electric drive motor
- Pulleys and sprockets
- Structural support members
- Frames
- Warehouse computer and controls

A Bombay drop is a SKU carrying surface/bi-parting tray. Each tray is designed to support a SKU with the largest cube characteristics and heaviest load weight per the Bombay drop design parameters.

NOVA Sort

A Nova sort is a modular tilt tray sort mechanism that has a closed-loop fixed travel path. A Nova sort has similar design parameters and operational characteristics as a tilt tray except that each Nova unit has its own drive train. A Nova sort design components are a three-to-four tilt-train train, a 500-pound load-carrying capacity, tilts to a travel path's left or right, a warehouse computer for each tray train, a fixed travel path with an electric bus bar, and on-board sensing devices to detect an employee in the travel path.

Cross or Moving Belt

A cross or moving belt sort design has individual belt conveyor carriers. Each carrier has a short platform that is motor driven and is on four wheels that travel over a closed loop. The closed loop goes past an induction station and each sort station. A bar-code label or SKU is placed onto a vacant carrier at an induction station. As the carrier with a SKU travels under a bar-code scanner, the scanner reads and sends the bar code/RF tag or SKU identification (i.e., sort location) to the warehouse computer. The computer, tracking device, and constant travel speed ensure that the conveyor moves forward and arrives at the assigned sort station. The sort station is on the left or right side of the travel path. Each sort location is designed with one, two, or three deep controllable chutes/flippers that open to accept diverted SKUs.

Moving Belt

The design options for a moving belt sort are:

- A vertical endless closed-look travel path that resembles the track on a tank. It has no "did not sort" SKU recirculation.
- A horizontal endless closed-loop travel path.

Moving belt sort designs have design parameters and operational features that are both similar to and different from tilt tray design. They are driven by an electric motor or extruded aluminum and electric driven belt platform, the travel path and platform size varies from five to eight inches, the closed-loop endless travel path directs short powered belt platforms past an induction station and each sort location, diverts a SKU to the right or left of a belt travel path, and handles a wide SKU mix. A single induction station has a nominal sort capacity and a powered moving divert platform.

GULL Wing

A gull wing sort design is an active-passive sort design in which many SKU carriers ride on a closed-loop travel path. The carrier has a bird or gull wing (i.e., a "V"-shaped carrier). A gull wing's operational features, disadvantages, and advantages are similar to a tilt tray. After a gull wing carrier arrives at an assigned sort location, a tipper is activated to move upward to tip the carrier to a side. The carrier's tipping action and gravity allows a SKU to slide from the carrier to an assigned sort/pack station.

Ring Sorter Design

A ring sorter design receives its name from the fact that the travel path is a circle or ring shape. After a SKU is inducted onto a ring sorter travel path, the SKU travels on a movable belt conveyor surface. Arriving at a SKU assigned divert location, the sorter computer activates a divert device for SKU transfer from a sorter belt travel path to an assigned customer order divert location. A ring sorter design has an induction travel path and overhead scanner/reader, powered belt sort lanes and dividers, sort designs and stations, structural support members, and sort platform and controls. The travel path has several short powered belt conveyor sections that ensure the SKU has a first-in first out sequence on a sorter travel path, and is moved forward to create a gap between two SKUs. With a proper gap space, a SKU travels over a belt conveyor that slopes downward and directs the SKU under an overhead scanner/reader (which reads the SKU bar code and sends the bar-code/RF tag data to a computer), and onto an open sort belt conveyor. The computer and the ring sorter's constant travel speed ensure that an assigned SKU is sorted from the conveyor onto a sort location.

Brush Sorter

A brush sorter is similar to a tilt tray sort. The similar features are SKU induction options and trays or carriers that travel over a fixed closed-loop travel path. The travel path directs a SKU under an overhead scanner/reader and past each sort location; gravity and a moving brush move the SKU from a tray carrier onto a sort location. To minimize employee injury from a sorter moving travel path, protective side guards extend downward from a sorter travel path to create a barrier to a sorter moving parts.

Tilting Platform Sorter

A tilting platform sorter has in-feed design, a sort platform that is activated by a sorter computer, and side-mounted tilt-table carrying trays. Each tray end is attached to an endless closed-loop chain, which is driven by an electric motor with tooth sprockets that interface with the chain, the tray leveler, and the discharge locations. After SKUs are singulated on an in-feed conveyor, they arrive at an in-feed station. At the in-feed station, each SKU is transferred to an empty tilting platform. The SKU then travels past a sensing/tracking device and arrives at an assigned sort location. At the sort location, the platform tilts forward, and the SKU slides onto the sort location. A tilting platform is used for a low- to medium-volume operation.

Label Attachment to a Shipping Carton or Captive Tote

Label Attachment to a Carton

When a WMS label or identification code is attached to a pick/sort carton, it is attached to the side that faces the pick aisle or pick position. In a manual, mechanized, or automatic pick design, the customer-order identification code/label identifies a pick/shipping carton from other cartons. During manual pick activity on a pick-to-light line that picks into a shipping carton, a picker or a scanner/reader matches the carton identification to the pick-to-light pick instruction. After the match, a picker transfers the SKU into a pick/ship carton. In the pick area, the identification code on a pick/shipping carton serves as a pick instruction to:

- Direct a carton to another pick zone or location
- Employee or automatic pick machine complete a pick transaction
- Activate a check weigh machine
- Scanned by a manifest scanner

Customer Label Activity in a Batched or Single Customer Order Picked into a Captive Tote

A captive tote with a permanent identification is used in a pick-to-light or in a batched pick, sort-into-a-tote operation. The WMS or warehouse computer associates a tote warehouse label to a customer-order number. On a pick line to assure maximum picker and scanner good label reads, each rectangle shaped tote has two, four, or up to six warehouse labels. Two labels are located on a tote exterior two long rectangle sides for picker or scanner line of sight, for picker line of sight two labels are located on a the tote interior two long rectangle side, and for picker line of sight a label is located on a tote exterior rectangle lead and trail ends or short sides. Label locations ensure a picker/packer and scanner line-of-sight to the warehouse/customer-order identification. A tote label functions as a pick instruction; at a pack station, a packer scans the tote label to have the computer identify SKUs and scan a completed customer order.

Customer-Order Label Considerations

Customer-order label design factors are a) label size and material, b) label placement on a carton, and c) how a label is placed on a carton. WMS label size factors are:

- Delivery address bar-code/RF tag width and height. An oversquared bar-code label with sufficient quiet zones provides the maximum number of good reads/scans at the fastest travel speeds with a bar code greatest degree of tilt on a sorter travel path to a top scanner light beam and widest depth of field between a short SKU on a sorter travel path and top scanner light beam source.
- Black ink and white paper.
- Available space on a carton exterior surface. In a pick/pack application, the label is placed on the carton flap or the side that faces a pick aisle. If the label placement is on a carton flap, carton tape or plastic band to seal a carton top flaps should not cover the customer-order identification.
- Human-readable information is easily recognized by pickers or line-of-sight for a bar-code scanner.
- With ink-jet spray, human-/machine-readable code quality from an ink-jet spray onto a carton's corrugated surface is easy to recognize and does not blend into the corrugated material.

Customer Order and Label Options

Pick tote or carton label options are:

1. Shipping carton/tote with a nonreusable label.
2. Captive tote with a warehouse permanent discreet identification.

When a pick operation uses a shipping carton as a pick carton, a customer-order identification label is placed on a shipping carton's exterior top flap or side at a pick line start station. With a customer-order label in the proper location, the label location satisfies the requirements for a labeled carton on a pick/pass line. In a pick-to-light design, the label permits a picker to compare the carton number to the pick-to-light display screen number and bar-code scanner line-of-sight. WMS label characteristics are:

- Label print options are a) separate printers to print labels and to print packing slips—both printers have the same print sequence. With this arrangement, and carton travel on a pick line is on a "first-in, first-out" basis, the label is placed onto a carton at a start station, and a packing slip is placed into a carton.
- One printer to print a combined packing slip and label. At a pick-line start station, an employee removes a label and places it onto a carton and places a packing slip into a carton.

- The WMS label back surface is self-adhesive.
- The WMS label contains all company information.
- The WMS label is not reusable.
- In the proper orientation, the WMS label is employee or machine applied to a carton.
- On a pick/pass line that does not have a pack station.

A pick operation that uses a permanent license plate has a code on a captive tote. Each license plate is a tote component and is reusable. The label orientation of each tote is in the proper direction of travel and degree of tilt on interior and exterior sides, and lead and trail ends to ensure line-of-sight for a picker or a bar-code scanner. After a labeled tote passes a bar-code scanner and the warehouse computer attaches the tote number to a customer-order number, the tote number becomes the customer-order identification as the tote travels over a pick/pass line. The relationship between the tote and the customer-order identification permits the tote to satisfy pick line requirements. After a packer packs SKUs into a carton, the packer zero scans the tote to complete the customer order and cancel the tote identification's attachment to the customer-order identification.

Packing slip characteristics are:

- After scanning/reading the tote label, the packing slip is printed at a pick line start or pack station.
- The warehouse computer system attaches the permanent label to a customer order.
- Additional captive tote and permanent label cost.
- In a pick-to-light concept when a pick-to-light problem occurs such as pick position lights do not function, a permanent label with human-/machine-readable code on a tote and human readable pick position identifications permits a pick line to operate with paper pick instructions.
- Reusable label.
- Pick/pass line that has a pack station.
- Picker and packer training.

Packing Slip Insert

When a pick operation has a packing slip accompany a carton/bag, a pick line or pack station employee places a packing slip into a shipping carton/bag. Packing slip placement options are:

1. At a pick line start station or first pick position. This means that preprinted or print-on-demand packing slips are sequenced according to the customer-order sequence on a pick line. During a pick activity, picked SKUs and filler material are placed onto a packing slip top. At the delivery location, picked/packed SKUs and filler material are removed from the carton to obtain the packing slip. This is potentially messy. If a start employee clips the packing slip to the pick carton side, an employee transfers the packing slip to the top of the SKU and filler material at a fill station or pack station.
2. After the last pick position and prior to a carton fill station. In this approach, preprinted or print-on-demand packing slips are arranged in customer-order sequence on a pick line. During a pick activity, picked SKUs are placed into a carton and, at the last pick station, a packing slip is inserted onto picked SKUs tops. After the last pick position or packing slip insert station, filler material is placed on the packing slip. At the delivery location, filler material is

removed from a carton to obtain a packing slip. The approach minimizes potentially messy conditions.

3. After a fill station. During a pick activity, picked SKUs are placed into a carton and filler material is placed onto picked SKUs. With the approach, a preprinted or printed-on-demand packing slip—in customer-order sequence—is inserted onto filler material top on a pick line and after a fill station. The approach minimizes potentially messy conditions, and ensures that a packing slip is retained in a carton.

In a pick/pass into a carton/tote operation, a customer-order slip is employee or machine attached or placed inside a carton/captive tote at a start station. If there is a pick-to-light failure, the packing slip serves as a pick document. In a batched pick/sort, transport, and pack, or pick/transport, sort, and pack operations, a packer places the packing slip into a carton.

In a high-volume ready-to-ship vendor-carton design, an envelope label or slapper label design is used in an operation. With this approach, a packing slip and sales literature is enclosed in a paper envelope with a plastic window or a clear plastic envelope. A clear plastic window or envelope permits an employee or scanner to read the delivery code. As the ready-to-ship carton passes an envelope application station, a machine or employee applies athe envelope to the carton side or top.

Packing Slip Printed Information

Packing slip insert activity has an employee or machine insert a specially printed packing slip inside a shipping carton. The packing slip is printed on-line or in advance of a carton arriving at the insert station. Each packing slip has a customer-order identification and information that matches picked SKUs. Order information includes customer name and identification, company name and address, all of which can be preprinted. The date, customer-order number, individual listing for each SKU on the customer order, along with SKU description and quantity, packing slip print, and transfer sequence matches the carton sequence on a pick line or picked SKU sort at a pack station.

Packing Slip Insert Options

In a pick operation, packing slip insert options are:

- A manual insert design, in which an employee reads the WMS number on a pick carton, matches the packing slip number to the WMS carton number and a) transfers a packing slip to inside a carton or b) clips a packing slip to the carton side flap or wall.
- A machine insert design, in which a scanner/reader reads the customer-order number on the carton, a mechanical device transfers, by air pressure or vacuum, a packing slip into the carton.

The factors that determine your pick operation packing slip insert options are:

- The pick operation type: a) pick/pass or b) pick, sort, and pack.
- The pick-line or pick-area layout factor at a pick-line start station, an employee or machine places a disposal customer-order WMS identification label onto each carton or a warehouse

captive tote identification is scanned, which associates a warehouse tote identification to a WMS identified customer order.

- Shipping carton sizes and volume.
- Pick design requirement to have a packing slip accompany a carton, which is determined by company policy, governmental codes, and delivery company.
- Packing slip page number and document characteristics that are a single page or a carbon copy.
- Available facility space.
- Costs and available labor.

Manual Packing Slip Insert

On a pick/pack line, manual packing slip insert options are:

- Pick-line start station activity, which is completed by a pick-line start-station employee.
- From a pick position, which is completed by a picker.
- At a pack station, which is completed by a packer.

Mechanized or Automatic Packing Slip Insert

A mechanized or automatic packing slip insert design group uses a mechanical device to insert a preprinted or print-on-demand packing slip into a carton. In this design, a carton with a customer-order identification passes a scanner/reader. The scanner/reader sends the customer-order identification data to a packing-slip print machine, which is controled by the warehouse computer. After the scan/read station, the carton travels on a conveyor on a "first-in, first-out" basis, and the warehouse computer ensures that the customer-order identification matches the customer-order identification download sequence. If the design uses a preprinted packing slip sequenced to match the downloaded customer-order identification numerical sequence, the insert machine removes a packing slip from a stack and inserts/releases the packing slip into a carton.

If the design uses a print-on-demand packing slip, the computer downloads all customer-order identifications (bar codes) in numerical sequence to the pick-label printer computer. After the customer-order identification is attached to a carton, the carton travels past a scanner/reader. The scanner/reader sends the customer-order identification to the insert machine computer, which controls the packing-slip printer. The data transfer activates the printer to print a packing slip from the customer-order identification file. The packing slip is inserted into a carton.

When mechanical packing slip print and insert options are compared,

1. Print-on-demand features are: handles an equal volume, has higher cost, and requires maximum queue conveyor length
2. Preprinted and insert design features are: label and packing slip sequence need to match, lower investment, less queue conveyor is needed, and the pack document must be tested to ensure that the automatic design device handles the warehouse pack format and size.

An automatic design is most effective on a pick/pass line with a pick-line start station; however, it is not effective in a pick, sort, and pack operation. It is most effective in a pick operation that permits SKUs to be placed onto a packing slip. The investment is higher, but no employee activity, queue conveyor, or floor area is needed.

Customer-Order and SKU Identification Scan Locations

To assure a picked SKU WMS identification is associated to a WMS identified customer order, WMS identified SKU and customer-order identification scan location options are:

1. A manual or voice-directed pick design, hand-held scan of picked SKUs, and customer-order identification in a pick area.
2. A manual or voice-directed pick design, hand-held scan of picked SKUs, and customer-order identification in a sort and assembly area.
3. A manual or voice-directed pick design, hand-held scan of picked SKUs, and WMS identification at a pack station.
4. A pick-to-light or sort-to-light pick design, after a picker presses a pick to or sort to light, a pick message is sent to the pick computer. The pick computer communicates a SKU pick transaction to the WMS computer that associates a WMS identified SKU to a WMS identified customer order or a pack station packer completes scan transaction for a WMS identified SKU and customer-order WMS identification that associates a SKU to a customer order.
5. An automatic pick machine design, after an automatic machine picks a SKU, the automatic pick machine computer communicates a WMS identified SKU pick transaction for a WMS identified customer-order to the WMS computer and or a pack station, a packer completes scan transaction for a WMS identified SKU and customer-order WMS identification that associates a SKU to a customer order.

If a pick design uses a warehouse permanent identification on a captive pick carton/tote, as the pick carton/tote enters a pick line a scanner/reader sends a warehouse identification to the warehouse computer, which associates the captive tote identification with a customer-order identification. After order completion, at a pack station a packer with a hand-held or fixed position scanner/reader completes a zero scan of the carton/tote identification and communicates the zero scan to the WMS computer. The WMS computer removes the customer-order identification associated with the warehouse identification on the captive tote and the packer completes a pack activity.

If a pick design uses a disposable customer-order identification on a captive/shipping pick carton/tote, as the disposable identified customer order pick carton/tote enters a pick line, a picker matches a customer order carton identification to a customer identification on a paper pick instruction or pick to light bay lamp that shows a customer order identification. After customer order completion, a packer completes the customer order pack activity with a disposable customer identification on a customer order ship carton/package.

Hand-Held/Fixed-Position SKU Scan and Customer-Order Identifications in a Pick Area

Hand-held/fixed position scan locations for picked SKUs with customer-order identifications are:

1. In a pick area. In a single pick or pick/pass operation with a WMS computer that scans the customer-order identification and picked SKUs in a pick design, a picker has a paper pick document with a customer-order identification for each SKU, and a hand-held scanner/reader. The pick instruction has human-/machine-readable symbologies for customer-order identification and each SKU, and has the SKUs arranged in pick position sequence. Three parts of a pick instruction are a) scanner/reader format with human readable symbology for each pick position and SKU, b) (for the picker) the customer-order identifications and each SKU in human-/machine-readable symbologies, and c) (in the pick position) each pick position and each SKU has a machine readable symbology. When arriving at a pick position, following the pick instructions from a hand-held scanner/reader, a picker transfers a SKU quantity from a pick position into a container. The picker scans/reads the customer-order identification and WMS SKU identification. Each scan transaction is for one SKU or the picker enters an exact SKU quantity. For each SKU, the picker repeats the physical pick and scan transaction. WMS scan transactions are sent to the WMS computer, which updates the SKU quantity and customer-order identification status. The WMS computer sends the SKU quantity and customer-order identification to the host computer to update its files. All completed customer orders are sent from the pick area to a pack area.

2. A hand-held/fixed position WMS scan of SKU and customer-order identifications in a sort and assembly area. In a bulk picked and sort and final assemble operation, bulked picked SKUs are picked and separated/sorted to sort and assembly positions. After bulk pick-and-sort transaction completion, the final pick activity has a picker use a packing slip and hand-held scanner/reader to complete the order. Depending on the pick instruction, the picker withdraws *en masse* SKUs for an order wave from pick positions. Bulk picked SKUs (in sequence—SKU first or last digit or RF scanned) are separated to sort and assembly positions. After completion of all bulk pick and separation to sort and assembly positions, a picker—following a packing slip, pick document, or hand-held scanner—completes the sort and assembly pick transactions for each SKU. WMS scan transaction options are a) the final picker uses a hand-held scanner/reader and a packing slip, in the sort and assembly aisle, and scans the WMS identification and SKUs, or b) the final picker uses a packing slip or pick document in the sort and assembly aisle and a completed customer order is transferred in a carton to a WMS scan station. At the scan station, an employee scans the WMS identification and SKUs. Each scan transaction is for a single SKU or the picker enters the exact SKU quantity. With a separate WMS scan station, to improve SKU scan activity and employee productivity, the scanner/reader is a fixed position scanner above a scan table that sends a scanner beam onto a table top or receives a RF-tag signal from a SKU. WMS scan transactions are sent to the WMS computer, which updates SKU quantity and customer-order identification. The WMS computer sends the SKU quantity and customer-order identification to the host computer to update its files. All completed customer orders are sent from the pick/scan area to a pack area.

3. A hand-held/fixed position scan of SKUs and customer-order identifications at a pack station design has a picker complete all SKU pick transactions. SKU pick activity is a pick/pass, pick-and-sort, or pick, transport, and sort at a pack station design. During a single or bulk-picked pick activity, a picker picks precoded SKUs or uses a customer-order label that is attached to each picked SKU. With a single customer order or pick/pass pick design, each completed shipping carton/tote is sent to a pack station. At the pack station, a packer completes a customer-order identification and SKU transaction, which are sent to the WMS computer. With a batched pick-and-sort in a pick area, a sort employee separates SKUs from

a mixed or batched picked group. A separated and completed order is placed into a shipping carton/tote and is sent to a pack area. At the pack station, a packer scans customer-order and SKU WMS identifications. Each WMS scan transaction is for a single picked SKU or the packer enters the exact picked SKU quantity. To improve a SKU scan activity and employee productivity, there is a fixed-position scanner above the pack table that sends a scanner beam onto a table top (or receives a RF-tag signal from a SKU). WMS scan transactions are sent to the WMS computer, which updates the SKU quantity and customer-order identification. The WMS computer sends the picked SKU quantity and customer-order identification to the host computer to update its files. All completed customer orders are sent to a manifest area.

4. A pick-to-light or sort-to-light design communicates a SKU and pick transaction. WMS scan transactions are completed prior to a pack station and are sent to a WMS computer that accounts for each SKU. The picked SKU scan options are a) a picker completes a SKU pick transaction and sends the completed order from a pick area to a pack station. At the pack station, a packer WMS scans customer-order and picked SKU WMS identifications. Each WMS scan transaction is for a single picked SKU or the packer enters the exact picked SKU quantity. To improve a SKU scan activity and employee productivity, a WMS scanner/reader is fixed above a pack table and sends a scanner beam onto a table top or receives a RF-tag signal from a SKU. WMS scan transactions are sent to the WMS computer, which updates the SKU quantity and customer-order identification. The WMS computer sends the SKU quantity and customer-order identifications to the host computer to update its files. All completed WMS customer orders are sent to a manifest area, or b) because a SKU was scanned to a pick position and a customer-order identification is associated with the warehouse permanent or WMS disposable identification, a pick-to-light or sort-to-light design communicates each SKU completed pick transaction to the WMS computer and the computer sends an update message to the host computer. All completed orders are sent to a pack area. At the pack station, with a customer-order identification on a carton, a packer scans the identification. To improve SKU scan activity and employee productivity, the scanner/reader is fixed above a pack table and sends a scanner beam onto a table top or receives a RF-tag signal from a SKU. The scan transaction is sent to the WMS computer, which updates the customer-order identification. The WMS computer sends the customer-order identification to the host computer, which updates its files. All completed customer orders are sent to a warehouse manifest area.

5. An automatic pick machine computer communicates a SKU pick transaction to the WMS computer, which sends an update message to the host computer. A carton arriving at a pack station has the same customer-order identification scan transactions as a pick-to-light design.

If a pick design uses a warehouse permanent identification on a captive pick carton/tote, as the pick carton/tote enters a pick line or automatic pick machine, a scanner/reader associates the warehouse identification with a customer-order identification. After completion of the pick transaction, at a pack station an employee with a hand-held/fixed position scanner/reader scans (or reads a zero scan) the captive carton/tote identification (or communicates a zero scan to the WMS computer). The WMS computer removes the customer-order identification associated with the captive tote identification and the packer completes the pack activity. If the pick design uses a WMS disposable identification on a captive or ship pick carton/tote, as the pick carton/tote enters a pick line or automatic pick machine, the pick design scans/reads each customer-order identification on the pick line. After completion of the pick transaction, a packer completes a pack activity.

Chapter 10

Picked SKU Quantity and Quality Check and Pack Activity

Introduction

In check and pack activities, picked or picked/sorted SKUs are handled and scanned. Depending on the warehouse design, picked SKU check and pack activities can be separate or combined activities.

Whether a warehouse handles small items, master cartons, or pallets, picked SKU check and pack activity occurs, to some degree, in all warehouses. In broad terms, a picked SKU check activity matches a small-item, master-carton, or pallet picked SKU quantity/description to a packing slip/invoice, and ensures that each picked SKU matches the warehouse's quality standards. Pack activity ranges from picked small items that are placed into a prepared sealed delivery container to master cartons or pallets that have been wrapped for protection, but each picked SKU is ready for delivery and has a delivery address label on a carton, tote, or pallet exterior.

Picked SKU Check Activity

A picked SKU quantity and quality check activity is designed for a manual, mechanized, or automated pick operation. In a pick activity, a picked SKU quantity and quality check (i.e., pick activity accuracy) ensures that the pick transaction for a SKU quantity matches the packing slip quantity and quality, or the picked SKU quantity and description matches the packing slip SKU quantity and description. At a check station, the SKU quantity, description, and weight is voice directed or appears on a digital display, label, or a paper document, which permits a checker or a machine to verify the picked SKU accuracy. It should be noted that an employee-based or RF-device check design verifies both the picked SKU quantity and quality check; a mechanical-scale–based check design verifies only the quantity.

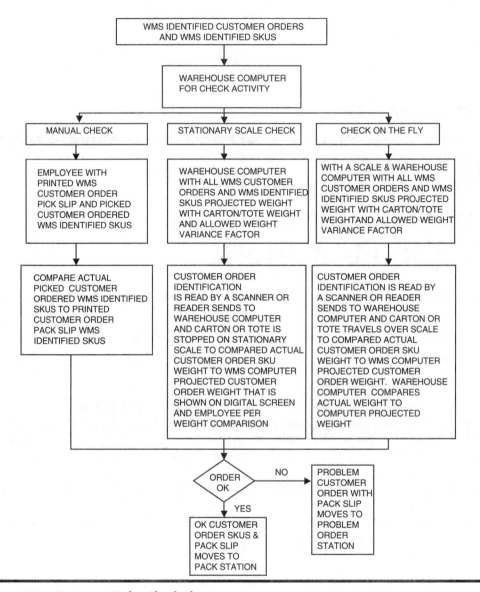

Figure 10.1   Customer-Order Check Flow

Reasons for a Customer-Order Check Activity

When a pick operation experiences customer complaints—e.g., customers have received shortages, overages, damaged, or incorrect SKUs at a delivery address—a pick operation implements a picked SKU check activity and station.

A problem occurs when an order is received at a delivery address and the picked, packed, and delivered SKU quantity and quality is different than the packing slip SKU quantity or description. Picked, packed and delivered SKU quantity problems are SKU shortage, SKU overage, SKU damage, and incorrect SKU.

A "SKU shortage" means that a customer received an order on-time but the delivered order quantity was less than the packing slip quantity.

A "SKU overage" means that a customer received more than the packing slip quantity. An overage means that an honest customer is dissatisfied with the warehouse pick operation because the customer had to take the time and expense of returning the extra quantity to the warehouse.

A "SKU damage" occurs when an order is received at a delivery address and the SKU is broken or not functioning. The customer is dissatisfied with the pick operation because the customer must take the time and expense to return a damaged SKU to the warehouse and because the customer did not receive a good quality SKU on-time.

An "incorrect SKU" occurs when an order is received at the delivery address but the deliverd SKU is not the SKU the customer ordered. The customer is dissatisfied with the pick operation because the customer must take time and expense to return the incorrect SKU to the pick operation and because the customer did not receive the correct SKU on-time.

SKU quantity and quality check objectives are to ensure that the picked SKUs a) match the SKU quantity and b) match the description and physical features on the packing slip.

Customer-Order Check Activity: Functional Description

In a customer-order check activity, all orders, specific orders, or a percentage orders go through a check or pack station. At a check/pack station, an employee or machine (i.e., scale and computer) verifies the pick accuracy to a packing slip or invoice. If a poor quality or quantity customer orders is discovered, a check employee corrects the order and send its a to a seal or pack station.

Customer-Order Check Activity: Exception Handling

With any pick design, there is the potential for a customer-order pick problem. When a problem order is detected, a check station employee corrects the order. The warehouse design team will list potential reasons and exception handling for an order that does not meet company quality and quantity standards. Depending on company procedure, a check employee lists problem orders, the associated reasons, and the picker who completed the pick transaction. Possible problems are:

1. Short- or overpick. A short- or overpick is a quantity problem. An order has a SKU quantity that does not match the packing slip or invoice. After a check employee determines the order status, a) for a short pick, the employee has determined that the SKU quantity is less than the packing slip or invoice quantity. To correct the situation, the employee creates a noncustomer-order pick request. The noncustomer-order pick transaction depletes storage/pick-position inventory and provides the employee with a SKU to complete an accurate order. With completion of the pick transaction, the position status is updated in the WMS computer. An inventory control employee completes a SKU cycle count, which updates the SKU inventory in the warehouse; b) for an overpick, a check employee has determined that the SKU quantity has more than the packing slip/invoice quantity. To correct the situation, the employee removes a SKU quantity and scans the SKU to a pick position. The SKU and position status are updated in the WMS computer, which makes the SKU available for an order. An inventory control employee completes a SKU cycle count, which updates the SKU inventory in the warehouse.

2. A damaged SKU. In this situation, a check employee detects a damaged SKU in a tote/carton. To complete an order, the employee obtains a replacement SKU (this is the same procedure as a short pick. To account for a damaged SKU, the employee places the damaged SKU

in a container and scans the SKU to a nonpickable position. The SKU is placed on hold in the WMS computer and is not available for sale.

3. Two cartons/totes. In this situation, a picker has pressed the "full tote" button, which sends a message to the warehouse conveyor system to divert the first and second cartons/totes to a check station. After the "full tote" button is pressed, the warehouse computer notifies the WMS computer that a second customer-order identification is required to complete the order. The WMS computer sends a customer-order identification to the warehouse computer; the warehouse computer has a second carton/tote enter the pick design. As the check station receives the first carton/tote, a PC or hand-held scanner display indicates that the carton/tote is the first of two orders. The employee transfers and scans the order to a temporary holding position. (The scan transaction is updated in the WMS computer.) As the second carton/tote arrives at the check station, the PC or hand-held display screen indicates the first tote/carton's holding position. The employee transfers the first tote/carton to a special pack station and goes to the temporary hold position. The first tote/carton is moved to a pack station and updated in the WMS computer. At the special pack station, a packer completes the customer-order check and pack activity.

4. The wrong SKU was picked. The situation is detected at a manual quality check station or pack station at which an employee completed a physical SKU check. After the wrong SKU is identified, a check/pack station employee completes several steps. These are a) the employee scans and places the incorrectly picked SKU into a pick or temporary hold position. The scan transaction is sent to the WMS computer to update SKU as available for orders, and b) the employee completes a SKU noncustomer-order pick transaction.

5. A specific customer-order check. If a warehouse desires a specific customer order to be manually checked for quality and quantity, a specific order is sent to a check station (via in-house transport), or, after scanning the customer-order identification, a message appears on a pack station display screen. The procedures for short pick, damaged SKU, overpick, and wrong pick are followed by a checker or packer.

6. The age of temporarily held orders. On a daily basis, the WMS computer lists held customer orders, which helps a warehouse maintain on-time and accurate order delivery.

7. No temporary hold positions are available for orders. When all check station temporary hold positions are full, the next order intended for a temporary hold area is placed on the floor in front of a position. The customer-order identification is scanned to the position and is updated in the WMS computer. In the WMS computer, the position is considered a position with mixed orders. During the retrieval process, an employee verifies the customer-order withdrawal with a scan, which is sent to the WMS computer.

8. A checker or packer, in some warehouse operations, completes a check for expiry date, manufacturer lot number, or manufacturer serial number. If a checker or packer discovers a problem with a SKU expiry date or manufacture lot number such as not readable, the checker or packer places the problem SKU and customer order pack slip/invoice onto a problem order shelf. Later corrective action is taken by a supervisor.

9. In post pack check activity, an employee verifies that the carton tape/tote band is correct, the carton is in good condition, the carton is not overpacked, and the delivery address label is in the correct location.

Customer-Order Pack Activity

Customer-order pack (i.e., fill and label) station activity occurs in any operation with a WMS program, whether it services a retail customer, catalog, e-mail, direct mail, or wholesale/commercial business customers. Pack station activity occurs in a small-item pick operation, whether it is a manual, mechanized, or automated; single pick/pack operation; batched pick, sort, transport, and pack operation; or batched pick, transport, sort, and pack operation. A master-carton/pallet manual, mechanized, or automated operation ensures that each master carton or pallet has a delivery label and protective wrap to secure picked master cartons on a pallet, cart, or slip sheet as required.

Small-item pick operation shipping options are a) carton, corrugated, chipboard boxes, or plastic totes and b) bags that are corrugated, treated, or plastic. A shipping carton or bag pack and master-carton or pallet pack activity ensures that picked, checked, and packed merchandise a) has its customer-order identification transferred to the delivery company, b) is protected against damage or from being lost during delivery, and c) has the delivery address and company facility return address clearly stated on the package, master-carton, or pallet exterior.

Customer-Order Pack Activity: Functional Description

In customer-order pack activity, picked SKUs are consolidated and placed into a shipping container. In a "pick into shipping carton" (i.e., fast-pack) design, a picker completes the SKU transfer into a shipping container but the filler material and seal are completed at a pack station. With a "pick into a captive tote/sort" design, the picked SKUs are transferred into a shipping container at a separate pack station. The pack activity ensures that the shipping container (e.g., bag, carton, tote, or pallet) has:

- A delivery label on an exterior correct location.
- A packing slip/invoice inside the container or on the container's exterior, attached in an envelope.
- Depending on warehouse procedure and supply chain characteristics, the packing slip/ invoice is printed a) on demand or preprinted, b) printed at a central, remote, or pick-line entry station, and c) inserted in the container at the pick-line entry, from a pick position, or at a pack station.
- Filler material added to the container's empty spaces.
- Sales literature added to the container's interior.
- Secure top and bottom surfaces, or the SKUs are secured to a pallet with seals, bands, string, tape, or plastic wrap.

Customer-Order Pack Activity: Exception Handling

In any pack activity, a packer has potential to have an exception/problem with picked SKUs, the suggested container, packing slip/invoice availability, or in-feed/out-feed transport. The design team reviews pack activity and develops a potential exception or problem list and associated resolutions. Some of these are:

1. A packer detects a short picked, overpicked, missed picked, wrong picked, or damaged picked SKU. a) Overpicked SKUs are tagged and placed into a problem-order station position. The

SKU is scanned to a pick position and the scan transaction is sent to the WMS computer. The computer updates the SKU in a pick position, and is made available for orders, and b) with a short, damaged, or wrong pick SKU, the packer places all picked SKUs, packing slips/invoices, and sales literature into a tote/carton. A tag is placed onto the carton/tote that indicates the problem (e.g., one tag/color for wrong pick, one for damaged SKU, one for short pick). If a damaged SKU has sharp edges or leaks, that SKU is placed into a plastic container or bag. A problem order carton/tote is scanned and transferred to a temporary hold position. The WMS computer updates the customer-order location. At a problem-order station, a supervisor reviews the problem order and resolves the problem. After resolution, the supervisor delivers the order to a pack station to complete the pack activity.

2. An order does not fit the warehouse's largest shipping carton, bag, or tote. A packer tags the order and transfers it, with the packing slip/invoice and sales literature, to a problem-order position. The scan transaction is sent to the WMS computer for customer-order location update. A supervisor removes the order from the cart for transport to a check or special pack station. At the station, an employee follows the WMS computer procedure to create new delivery labels and packing slips/invoices. The packing slip/invoice print procedure ensures that each packing slip/invoice matches the SKUs in each carton. Also, in accordance with the warehouse's shipping charge policy, the WMS computer ensures that the customer receives the correct shipping charge.

3. The order shipped without being scanned at a pack station. Because the customer-order identification is scanned/read at a manifest station, the manifest scan/read serves as a back-up system that confirms pack activity.

4. The wrong SKU mix in a shipping bag/carton, e.g., a heavy SKU with a fragile SKU. A packer places a problem tag onto the order and follows the procedure as stated in No. 2, above.

5. Reprint a packing slip/invoice or delivery label. Each packing slip/invoice and delivery label has unique identification that is registered in the warehouse or WMS computer. A customer-order packing slip/invoice or delivery label are re-printed. A re-printed statement is printed on a re-printed customer order packing slip/invoice/delivery label and the customer order WMS identification is entered into the WMS and manifest computers as a re-printed customer order packing slip/invoice or delivery label. The customer order reprinted documents are used in the pack and pack activities until a manifest scanner or reader verifies that a customer-order WMS identification as shipped from your warehouse. After a scan/read, the customer-order identification is accounted for in the warehouse and WMS computers, then it is dropped from the WMS identifications to be shipped. If a second customer-order identification travels past a scanner/reader, the warehouse computer will not have the customer-order identification listed to be shipped and will transfer the order to a "do not ship" lane for management review.

6. A canceled customer order. When a canceled order arrives at a check/pack station, the WMS computer will have already transferred the customer-order identification message to the warehouse computer. As the customer-order identification is scanned/read, the canceled order is transferred by in-house transport concept to problem-order station, or a "cancel" message appears on a PC screen. At the check/pack station, SKUs are scanned and placed into position and the SKUs, position, and quantities are sent to the WMS computer for inventory update. In the temporary hold position, the SKUs are available for orders.

7. Adding sales literature. To ensure that each carton/tote receives sales literature—and that repeat customers within a sale promotion period do not receive the sale literature a second

time—the WMS program receives list (from the host computer) of new orders that require sales literature. The WMS computer sends a message to the (warehouse) computer-controlled printer to print an insert instruction onto a packing slip/invoice or delivery label.

8. No zero scan transaction with a captive tote. A packer scans a tote (associated with an order) to have a packing slip/invoice and delivery label printed, or to have the packing slip appear on a PC screen. The packer also zero scans the tote to ensure that the customer-order identification is no longer associated with the tote's warehouse identification. If the packer does not complete the zero scan, future totes could have two customer orders. To ensure that a captive tote is zero scanned/read, all totes are zero scanned or read by a fixed position scanner/reader prior to pick area entry.

9. For dangerous SKUs or delivery to a foreign country, print proper and separate delivery documents and labels.

10. Correct manufacturer lot number/serial number. At a pack station, a packer enters the lot number/serial number and the customer-order identification into the warehouse computer for transfer to the WMS computer.

Customer-Order Check Designs

A warehouse customer-order check activity options are:

1. Manual check activity, which are a) SKU quality check, b) SKU quantity check, and c) SKU quality and quantity check. In a manual check design, an employee with a packing slip, paper document, or display on a screen completes an SKU check as outlined above.

2. Mechanized check activity, in which a digital scale indicates athe actual carton/tote weight and the WMS computer's estimated weight. On the scale display screen, an employee compares the WMS computer's projected SKU and carton/tote weight to the actual picked SKU and carton/tote weight.

3. Automatic check activity (i.e., "check on the fly"), in which the WMS computer downloads estimated weight data to the weight check computer and scale, which compares the SKU and carton/tote weight to the actual weight. Weight measurement is often a problem with SKUs such as an SKU with low weight or liquid- or powder-filled containers. Depending on the warehouse operation climate, a carton can have a different weight, i.e., a wet or humid area can add weight to a carton. The actual weight and computer weight tolerance (i.e., variance) is an important factor to establish in the warehouse weight check program.

Picked SKU Quantity and Quality Check Activity

Picked SKU check activity options are:

1. A quantity check activity verifies that the picked SKU quantity in a pick carton/tote matches the quantity that appears on a packing slip. Within a picked SKU quantity check group, the weight check design is basically a SKU quantity check that uses the estimated SKU and carton/tote weight and compares them to the actual weight.

2. A quality check activity verifies that a picked SKU quality, description, and physical features in a carton/tote matches the description on a packing slip and that the SKUs are in good condition.

For a pick design, picked SKU check activity design factors are:

■ customer-order volume, SKU value, and SKU mix
■ company check policy
■ the warehouse order fulfillment or delivery performance standard
■ order fulfillment operation type

Customer-Order Check Activity Location in a Customer-Order Flow

In a pick design, the options for a check station in an order flow are a) after SKU picked activity and before or during pack activity, or b) after pack activity and before manifest activity.

Check Activity before or During Pack Activity

SKU check activity before or during pack activity is the most common location approach for check station activity. A picked SKU check station, placed before or at a pack station, is used in a pick/pass, pick/pack, or pick/sort design. In a pick design, after all, SKUs are picked and assembled in a tote, a carton, or as a SKU group in a sort location; a checker completes a customer order picked and sorted SKU match to a SKU that is on a customer order packing slip/invoice. In a small-item operation, after a customer-order check activity, the order is sent to a pack or seal/label station; in a master-carton/pallet operation, the order is sent to a wrap/manifest station. The features are:

■ It is located near a pick area to correct problem customer orders.
■ It includes picked/sorted SKU check activity.
■ The activity can be manual or mechanized.
■ The past pick/pack activity past performance determines a customer-order check activity customer-order number and requirement to complete a SKU quantity check and a combined quality check or quantity check.
■ A pick check activity that is completed before a pack activity. It is a) a low checker productive activity because there is no opening a customer order package, removing filler material, possible customer order delivery label reprint, new shipping carton make-up, and another pack activity and b) completes a greater number of customer-order checks.
■ It does not include complete pack, carton seal, or label placement check.

Check after Pack Activity but before Manifest Activity

This approach is used in a pick design that requires, in addition to a picked, sorted SKU check, to verify packer quality. A packer quality check verifies that the SKUs are properly protected, package is properly sealed and labeled, and the package presentation meets company standards. With small items, after a customer-order check activity, the order is sent to a manifest station; in a master-carton/pallet operation, the order is sent to a wrap/manifest station. The features are:

■ It is located a distance from a pick area, which adds time and expense in correcting a problem order.
■ It includes a picked/sorted SKU check and packer package quality check.

- It is a manual activity.
- The past pick/pack activity performance determines the customer-order check activity, the number of customer orders checked, and requirement to complete a SKU quantity check and or a combined quality check or quantity check.
- When compared to a check activity before a pack activity, a post pack check activity, post pack check activity is a low checker productive activity due to opening a customer order package that creates potential trash, prints an additional customer order delivery label and requires carton make-up and repack activity, and only completes a minimum number of customer-order checks.
- A post pack check activity completes SKU pack, carton seal, or label placement check to assure that a customer order carton exterior appearance is per your company standards. Such as label in the correct location, tape sticks to a package sides, and no package exterior surface bulge due to excessive filler material.

Customer-Order Check Options

The objective of a small-item pick operation is to ensure that a carton/tote has an accurate picked SKU quantity and SKU quality. A master carton/pallet check activity objective is the same for a small item check activity, except that the check activity is for a picked master-carton or pallet quantity, and master carton quality of a pallet, slip sheet, or cart, and quality (how clean) of a delivery vehicle interior. An accurate order to a delivery address maintains the company customer service standard. To maintain the company customer service standard, the company has picked/packed SKUs checked for quantity and SKU quality before a pack/manifest station. A, master carton or pallet post pack station is before a manifest station and is a scan activity.

Manual Picked SKU Scan at the Pack Station

A single pick, pick/pack, pick/pass, or batched pick and sort operation has a packer scan each picked/picked and sorted SKUs and each customer-order identification, which serves two purposes. To scan each picked/picked and sorted SKU, a packer a) handles each SKU, which permits a packer to inspect each picked SKU (i.e., an SKU quality check), and b) scans each picked/picked and sorted SKU identification (i.e., a SKU quantity check).

Manual Picked SKU Check Options

Picked SKU check activity involves having an employee perform a random or 100% check of picked cartons/totes before they are transported to a pack/seal station (see Figure 10.2). Whether the check activity is random or 100% is determined by warehouse policy, the SKU value, or the number of past customer-order problems. The employee options are a) a total picked SKU count check that compares the picked SKU total quantity to a packing slip total quantity, or b) detail picked SKU check in which the check employee compares each picked SKU number to the packing slip SKU numbers.

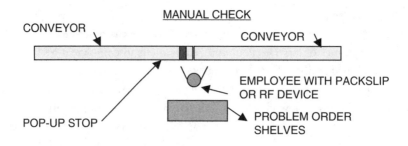

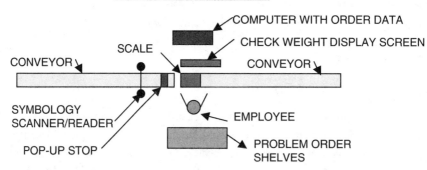

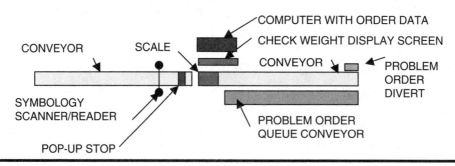

Figure 10.2   Manual Check and Weight Check

Mechanized Picked SKU Weight Check Design

A mechanized picked SKU weight check design has orders random or 100% picked checked before they are transported to a pack station. A random or 100% check procedure is determined by warehouse policy, order value, or the number of past order problems. With a picked SKU mechanized weight check design, the WMS computer estimates the shipping carton/tote weight for each order and the associated picked SKUs. The estimated order weight includes the weight of the suggested shipping carton/tote. In addition to accurate SKU and shipping carton/tote weights, an important weight check design characteristic is that a warehouse manager determines the allowable weight variance between the actual picked SKU and shipping carton/tote weight and the estimated weight. After the weight check process is completed, each order identification, the associated picked SKUs, and the suggested carton/tote weight are sent to the pick design computer. (The warehouse computer is in direct communication with the weight check scale.) A warehouse weight check design must have the following:

■ A separate conveyor or main travel path divert mechanism with a separate conveyor to ensure "first-in, first-out" order travel
■ Sensing devices
■ Order identification on each pick carton/tote
■ A fixed-position or hand-held scanner/reader
■ An in-line or conveyor travel path scale on the weight check conveyor with digital display, or a direct line to the weight check computer
■ A main conveyor travel path in-feed mechanism after a check station
■ Problem-order station with access to a pick area
■ Master file accuracy for shipping carton weight, dimensions, and cube capacity per master carton is important.

Mechanized weight check options are:

1. An employee design, in which an employee transfers a carton/tote from a conveyor onto a stationary scale. A visual display screen that shows the estimated total weight.
2. A carton/container design, in which the carton/container is momentarily stopped on a scale in the conveyor. An employee compares the suggested carton/tote total weight to the total weight displayed on a visual display screen.
3. A "check on the fly" design, in which a carton that is momentarily stopped on a scale on a conveyor that has a scale. The data is sent to the warehouse computer, which compares a picked SKU and suggested carton/tote scale weight to the total projected weight.

Order Check at a Pack Station or a Problem-Order Station

A pick operation in which a packer performs a check activity, which can be a SKU quantity check with a packing slip, a quality check, or both. If there are no problems, the order is packed, sealed, labeled, and sent to a manifest/shipping dock area. If there is a problem, the packer places the packing slip and picked SKUs into a shipping carton/tote, transfers the carton/tote to a problem-order station, and handles another order. Meanwhile, a pack-area supervisor resolves the order problem at the problem-order station, and a packer completes the order for transfer to a manifest/shipping dock area.

Accurate SKU and Tote/Carton Weight for a Computer Check Design

A WMS-computer-based mechanized or "check-on-fly" weight check handles a high customer-order volume, and makes sure that SKU and pick tote/carton data (i.e., physical characteristics plus weight) are accurate and updated in the computer files. During receiving or QA activity, SKU data is collected and sent to the WMS computer. Thus, SKU data is in the computer file prior to an SKU being available for sale in a storage/pick position.

The pick-line management team has a pick tote/carton design control. During the design of the pick-line, the design team enters each SKU, tote/carton weight, and internal specifications into the WMS files. As the company's SKU mix changes, new SKU and pick tote/carton weight and dimensional data are entered into the files. Many companies have consolidated warehouses and have not paid attention to the shipping carton and SKU dimensions. The situation creates poor operational results.

Customer-Order Check Considerations

The picked SKU check activity type is determined by the customer-order volume, SKU value, and SKU mix. Customer-order volume has an impact on the warehouse check activity. To complete a check activity, order check activity has space and adds time to "order and delivery" cycle time. With a small to medium volume, a manual or mechanized check design handles the volume. With a high-volume, a mechanized, or automatic check design handles the volume. High-value SKUs in customer orders require 100% checks.

SKU Weight Variance

A multi-line SKU order with a picked SKU mix has SKUs that are small cube, light weight, powered or liquid filled, and, in some cases, fabric. Customer orders with a wide SKU mix increase the difficulty to have cost-effective and efficient manual, mechanized, or automatic checks. With a wide range of SKU characteristics and an employee check design, it is a difficult for an employee to locate all small-size SKUs in a carton/tote or SKUs that have similar shapes and colors. With a mechanized or automatic check design, the SKU weight difference (between a small-size SKU, powder, or liquid SKU) the projected and actual/scale weights could potentially exceed the warehouse's acceptable weight variance.

The order-check requirement is established by the company's check and customer-service standards. The standards determine the order type and number that are sent through the check activity station. An order sent through a check station is based on the value, the customer history, and the company's past delivery performance. It is more difficult to select a specific order for a check activity with a manual pick and check design. With a mechanized or automatic pick design and picked SKU check design, the warehouse scanner/reader and computer identifies a predetermined order for check activity that is based on the computer's suggested customer order weight. If a pick operation's customer-delivery performance is acceptable, the check station will not perform a 100% check, but complete a random check. If a pick operation's customer-delivery performance is not acceptable, check station performs at least a random check. Based on the warehouse policy, a manual, mechanized, or automatic check is designed to handle the warehouse check requirements.

The type of pick operation is a design factor, and affects the need for check activity. A manual pick design has a greater potential for pick errors, and a greater need for check activity. A mechanized or automatic pick design has a lower possibility for pick errors, and less need for check activity. A pick design that uses paper has a high need for check activity, whereas a pick by RF, pick by voice, or a pick to/by light have a lower check activity requirement. In pick operations, a major error in pick activity is often based on errors created in receiving, put-away replenishment or picker activity.

Quality and Quantity Check Designs

A quality and quantity check design is based on the company's customer-service standard and past delivery performance. Check design options are: a) 100% do not check, b) random sample check, c) 100% check, d) specific customer check, and e) check by SKU or order value.

Pick Operation Type

Pick operation types are:

1. A batched-order design has picked and mixed small items flow from a pick area, through a manual or mechanized central sort area to a pack station. At the pack station, per the packing slip, the packer completes a final picked SKU sort and check, and packs the order in a carton.
2. Batched orders have several picked small items that are sorted by the picker into an assigned sort location. After completion of the pick activity, completed orders are placed in a four-wheel cart with shelves, large divided tote, or a divided trolley basket, which is moved to a pack area. In the pack area, a packer with a packing slip performs the check activity and packs the order in a carton.
3. Bulked picked small items are separated by SKU number to sort and assembly positions. A final picker with a packing slip or pick document completes a sort and pick activity from the sort and assembly positions. The sorted and picked SKUs are sent to a scan station; an employee packs the order or sends it to a pack station. A scan is a sorted and picked SKU check activity.
4. A single small-item pick/pass design has a picked SKU transferred from a pick position directly into a pick/shipping carton/tote. During pick activity, the packing slip is placed into the carton/tote and picked SKUs manually checked (i.e., "checked on the fly") for accuracy at a check station.
5. A single small-item automatic pick design has picked SKUs transferred from pick positions directly into a pick/shipping carton/tote or onto a divided conveyor. In this design, check activity options are a) a packing slip is placed into a carton/tote prior to a pick activity or b) with a printed packing slip, display screen, or on a warehouse scale, picked SKUs are checked for accuracy at a manual (i.e., "check on the fly") check station.
6. A manual master-carton or pallet pick design that uses paper documents has an order separated into different pick zones/areas. Pick accuracy is checked using a pick document, packing slip, or RF device.
7. A mechanized master-carton pick to conveyor design and a manual or mechanized central sort design that uses precoded SKUs or SKUs with a human-/machine-readable self-adhesive labels uses a scanner/reader to verify the pick, sort, unitize, or direct load accuracy.
8. A master-carton/tray/tote or pallet AS/RS crane or automatic carton pick design, uses a scanner/reader on precoded SKUs to verify pick accuracy.

With any batched picked, sorted, and packed design, the pick operation has all batched picked and mixed SKUs sorted by an employee or mechanical device. The sort design separates picked and mixed SKUs into:

1. Customer-order locations and pack stations. At a pack station, using a packing slip, a packer checks picked and sorted SKU accuracy. The packer makes the check visually or with a hand-held or fixed position scanner/reader. In either case, the SKU number is matched to the packing slip SKU number.
2. A sort location, which contains a predetermined number of orders. An employee or mechanical concept sorts picked SKUs from a large batched picked and mixed SKU quantity to a single sort location. The initial sort reduces a customer order number to a smaller predetermined number of orders and SKUs. From the presorted customer order picked and SKUs, at a sort station with a customer order pack slip/invoice, a sorter completes a final customer order pick that is a pick and sort activity. The final customer order pick and sort activity is also a check activity. The final customer order pick and sorted SKU check is completed to a customer order pack slip/invoice by a packer with her/his eyes or a hand-held or fixed position scanner/reader.

Single-Order Pick and Order Check Considerations

A single-order pick/pack design uses a picker or automatic pick machine, per a customer order, to pick SKUs from a pick position. The customer order picked SKUs are transferred directly into a WMS or warehouse pick/shipping carton/tote or between two cleats on a belt conveyor. A single customer order picked SKUs are transported to a manual, mechanical, or automatic check station.

Manual Order and Picked Check Designs

Manual picked SKU check designs are:

1. In accordance with the packing slip's detail line item, picked SKU check activity or picked SKU quality and quantity check activity
2. Picked SKU sum or total SKU check design, i.e., picked SKU quantity check design

Manual Detail Quality/Quantity Check

A manual detail quality/quantity check has a check employee perform a detailed check that the picked SKU in a carton matches the SKUs on the packing slip in quality and quantity. With a manual single-order check design, the packing slip has a SKU description and quantity that is easily understood by a check employee. With a scanner/reader design at a check station, the WMS computer downloads to a warehouse check computer, each customer order identification and associated SKU WMS identifications and SKU quantity.

With a batched pick, transport, and sort design, the final check activity is completed at a pack station. A packer transfers SKUs from a sort location into a carton/tote with a packing slip that is considered a check activity. In the pick area a picker completes a sort into a customer order sort location. With a picked SKU sort activity, each picker completes a customer order precheck. A second or final check activity is completed either at the pack station by a packer or at a scan station by a scan/read employee. The packer or scan/read employee a) verifies that a picked and sorted SKU quantity and quality matches the packing slip description and quantity or b) conducts the check with a hand-held or fixed position scanner/reader and has a PC or visual display screen display a packing slip. The PC design has the WMS computer transfer all orders on an order wave to the warehouse computer, check potential errors, but takes additional time to complete the check activity.

In a pick, transport, and sort batched design, the picked and mixed SKU quantity for each sort location is an estimated 50 pieces for 15 to 20 orders. For a picked SKU, each SKU has a human-/machine-readable identification that can be read by an employee or hand-held/fixed position scanner/reader.

A manual quality/quantity check design is used in a batched pick operation that has a pick or SKU label.

In a single-order or batched-order design, a manual quantity/quality check design is used to check a problem order.

An effective and cost efficient check activity:

■ Uses a packing slip with clear and bold print
■ Each SKU code is human/machine readable
■ Has SKU descriptions and quantity that are clearly visible and understandable
■ Has sufficient check station space or an off-line conveyor with adequate light fixtures
■ Picked SKU check activity is performed on either a random or 100% criteria
■ Has easy access to the problem-order station and the pick area, which permits resolution of problem orders
■ Has easy access to the main conveyor for final checked order return to transport for travel to a pack station

Total SKU Count: Manual Check

A pick design that uses has a total SKU count in an order check is a type of picked SKU quantity check. The features of this design:

■ The warehouse or WMS computer cube for each ordered SKU. The cube determines the SKU quantity per pick/shipping carton.
■ The pick design ensures that a packing slip is clipped or inserted into a carton/tote.
■ A packer physically counts each SKU quantity in a carton at a check or pack station.
■ An order check/pack station employee matches the actual picked SKU quantity in a carton/tote or on pack station table to the packing slip SKU total quantity.

The total SKU count is used in a check activity in any pick operation that uses a SKU label as a pick or pick/sort label. At a check station, each packing slip has the SKU quantity printed in bold print and in a location that is easily recognized by a check employee. When your pick and pack activity has a computer cube program to determine a customer order SKU quantity per carton. Your operation must assure that 1) total SKU number per carton is clearly printed on a packing slip/invoice; 2) SKU weight, cube, and shipping carton internal cube dimensions are accurate; 3) shipping carton weight and utilization factors are accurate in the WMS computer; and 4) with a SKU quantity check activity, potential SKU quality or miss pick errors could occur because check employees only count picked SKUs in a shipping carton that is compared to a SKU total quantity that is printed on a customer order pack slip/invoice. The design requires few employees, handles a high volume, it is easy to train employees, requires no reading, needs less building space than other designs, and for high checker productivity, additional cost for a conveyor travel path queue prior to a check station.

Computer-Controlled Check Design

A computer-controlled check design uses a warehouse scale to determine the actual carton weight compared to the warehouse/WMS computer-projected carton weight. Each projected SKU and suggested carton/tote weight is sent to the warehouse scale computer. The warehouse/WMS computer-controlled check designs are:

1. Manual weight check, which are a) stationary scale design and b) dynamic scale design
2. "Check-on-the-fly" design

Pack Activity

Picked and sorted pack/fill station activity occurs in any small-item pick design, whether it services retail, catalog, e-mail, direct mail, wholesale, or a commercial customer (see Figure 10.3). Pack/fill station activity occurs in any pick operation, whether it is a manual, mechanized, or automated single pick/pack design; a batched-order picked, sorted, transported, and pack operation; or a batched-order picked, transported, sorted, and pack design. Master carton unitize onto a pallet, slip sheet, or four-wheel carrier, and plastic wrap/secure a master carton onto pallet, slip sheet, or four-wheel that are pack activities in a master-carton or pallet operation.

In a pick operation, the shipping options are a) small items in carton, corrugated, or chipboard box; b) small items in a corrugated, treated, or plastic bag; c) master cartons stacked on a delivery truck floor, pallet, slip sheet, or BMC; or pallets.

If at a customer delivery location (retail store), the customer has the ability to return empty plastic containers to a warehouse, then a pack activity is to seal/lock a lid to a plastic container. A shipping carton, bag or plastic container pack activity ensures that a picked, checked, and packed SKU is protected against damage or from being lost during delivery, and that delivery address and company return address are visible on the package's exterior.

Centralized and Decentralized Pack Activity

Pack activity includes:

1. Select and form a warehouse-, WMS-computer-, or packer-suggested shipping carton/tote
2. Perform a check quantity/quality activity
3. Place picked SKUs and bottom filler material into a carton/tote
4. Add sales literature, print a packing slip and place in shipping carton/tote and add top filler material to carton/tote empty spaces
5. Seal a shipping carton/tote
6. Print and apply delivery address label to carton/tote exterior and transfer a completed package to a take-away conveyor

The pack sequence varies depending on a) pack station type; b) whether it is a manual, mechanized, or automated pick operation; and c) the carton/tote.

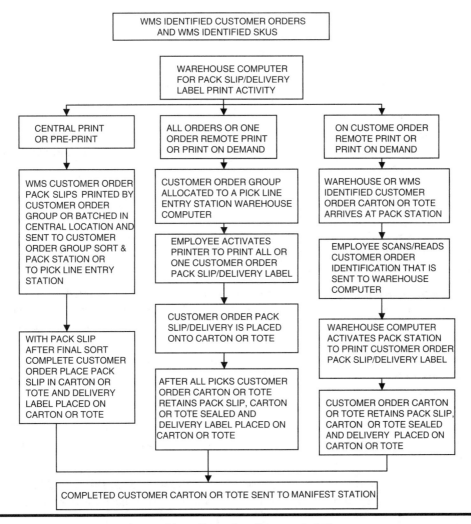

Figure 10.3 Customer-Order Packing Slip and Delivery Label Flow

A pick/pass or pick/pack design in which SKUs are picked directly into a shipping carton/tote, a pack activity is a decentralized pack activity. In a decentralized pack activity, the pack activity is separated into several activities along a pick line. In a design that picks/packs into a shipping carton/tote, pack activities are at different locations on a pick line.

After the shipping carton/tote is formed and transferred to a pick line, a shipping label is placed onto a shipping carton/tote by an employee or label applicator machine at a start station and prior to a first pick position. At a pick-line start station, an employee or insert machine transfers a preprinted or print-on-demand packing slip into a carton/tote or clips a packing slip to a carton/tote side, after which the SKUs are picked or transferred from pick positions directly into a shipping carton/tote. After the last pick position, check activity is performed by an employee or a "weight check on the fly" design is used. After check activity, the next pick-line activity is carton/tote pack/fill activity. At a pack/fill station, an employee or machine transfers filler material into a shipping carton/tote to fill empty spaces. The penultimate pick/pass design activity is to seal the shipping carton/tote: An employee or machine places a tape strip(s) over the carton top flaps or a plastic band around the carton/tote. After the carton is sealed, a delivery address label is applied to the shipping carton/tote and the completed carton/tote is transferred to the in-house transport.

Other centralized pack activity designs are pick operations in which:

- A WMS identified customer order SKU picks by an employee or automatic pick machine are made directly into a warehouse identified captive tote that is associated to a WMS identified customer order, and then at a pack station, an additional packer activity is to WMS zero scan a warehouse tote identification. The warehouse tote identification zero scan disconnects the customer order WMS identification to the warehouse tote identification that allows a tote to be used for another WMS identified customer order.
- SKUs are batched for an order pick, sort, transfer, and pack into a carton/tote
- SKUs are batched for an order pick, transfer, sort, and pack design

Pack activities are performed at several pack stations located in a single warehouse area in a variety of pick designs: centralized pick/pack into a captive tote; batched order pick, sort, transfer, and pack; or batched pick, transfer, sort, and pack. At a centralized pack station, a packer:

1. Scans the warehouse or order identification to have a packing slip printed, or to remove a preprinted packing slip from a carton/tote. If the design uses a warehouse tote identification that is associated with an order identification, an additional activity at a pack station is to zero scan the warehouse tote identification.
2. Reads a packing slip to obtain a computer suggested shipping carton
3. Completes the check quantity/quality activity and transfers picked SKUs and the packing slip into a shipping carton
4. Adds filler material to fill empty spaces in a shipping carton/tote
5. Seals carton top flaps and applies a shipping label to the carton's exterior
6. Transfers a completed carton/tote to a take-away transport and sends an empty captive pick tote back on the in-house transport

In some operations, orders are sent out in captive totes with a secured lid. There are additional steps necessary to have the tote returned to the warehouse and to verify that the tote is empty and clean.

Shipping Label and Packing Slip Printing: Warehouse Locations

In the catalog or direct mail pick industry a question is at what location or where in the pick and pack process to print a customer order shipping label and packing slip/invoice. Print location options are at a central print location, at a remote location, or at the pack station.

Shipping Label and Packing Slip Printing: Central Location

A central print location has one or several printers in a central location inside the pick facility. Prior to a pick/pass activity, the WMS computer downloads to the central print location all the shipping labels, packing slip information, and other delivery documents (e.g., COD, bank transfer, hazardous SKU, or day-to-deliver labels) for an order wave. Packing slips and delivery labels are a) printed *en masse,* and matched to order identifications or b) packing slips and delivery labels are printed on one sheet and sent to a location on a pick-line start, pick aisle, or pack station.

A shipping label is placed onto a shipping carton's exterior in a pick/pass operation at a pick-line start station. A packing slip is placed inside or clipped to a shipping carton or captive pick tote. The features are minimal network and wiring cost, pick-line/pack-station attachment activities, improved print paper and label stock inventory control, easy to implement and control, and per your print volume, potential for several printers or higher speed computer controlled printer.

Shipping Label and Packing Slip Printing: Pack Station

A shipping label and packing slip remote print location option is to have the printing done at each pack station. Prior to a pack activity, a packer scans a packing slip or carton/tote identification. The label information is sent to the WMS or warehouse computer. The WMS or warehouse computer sends a message to the pack station printer to print a packing slip and shipping label. After completing a pack activity, the pack employee scans the tote identification to ensure that the WMS computer cancels the order identification with a tote identification.

After preparing a shipping carton, a packer places picked and checked SKUs and a packing slip inside the carton, seals the carton top flaps and places a shipping label on the carton. The features are higher print machine number, network and wiring cost, to have a packer employee scan a customer order identification that creates slightly lower packer productivity, increased print paper and label stock inventory and stock outs at a print location, pack station employee training, and it is not necessary to correct delivery papers as a consequence of inventory problems.

Carton Make-Up and Introduction to a Pick-Line Start Station

In a pick/pass, single-order, or automatic pick operation, carton make-up/tote introduction is the first pick-line station or occurs before the first pick position. In a batched SKU pick design with a pick/sort and transport design or pick/transport and sort design, a shipping carton is introduced at the sort or pack station. A pick carton make-up or empty tote transferred onto a pick-line, pick vehicle, or automatic pick machine provides means to retain a customer order picked SKUs, ensure customer order picked SKU movement in a container past each pick position, and move a customer order picked SKU from a pick area last pick position to a next pick area activity or to a pack station. If a pick carton is a shipping carton, the carton moves from a conveyor pick line onto a completed take-away conveyor. A take-away conveyor transports a pick carton/tote to the next pick area or pack station.

Pick-Line Transport Designs

Pick area transport designs are:

1. A carton with flaps up, with flaps down, or a tote
2. In a tote
3. Loose on a belt conveyor

To ensure loose picked SKU separation on a belt conveyor, a conveyor belt surface has full-width cleats. Cleats are attached to a belt conveyor's surface and extend upward from the surface.

Customer Order and Picked SKU Queue Prior to a Pack Station

To have an efficient and cost effective centralized or decentralized pack activity, the pack station area or overhead conveyor, pallet, or cart design must have a sufficient carton, tote, basket, or loose SKU queue prior to a pack table. If the picked SKUs are manually delivered to a pack station, a pack station design factor is prior to a pack station to have sufficient completed customer order set-down or queue area:

- For in-feed carts or overhead baskets, which ensures a constant order flow to a pack station
- Easy packer access to cart or overhead basket in-feed travel path lane and queue
- Easy packer access to empty cart or overhead basket out-feed travel path lane and queue

Picked SKU queue designs are:

- Pallets set on a floor or delivered by a powered roller conveyor
- Four-wheel cart
- Overhead basket or trolley
- Tote/carton on a conveyor
- Slide or chute

Computer-Suggested Shipping Carton Picked with SKUs

When a pick operation uses a computer-suggested shipping carton picked with SKUs, the carton and SKUs are sent together in or on a carton/tote from a pick area to a pack station. (A shipping supply pick design can be used to handle shipping bags.) In a pick area, each shipping carton is allocated to a pick position. The tote associated with an order is sent to a pick position that has the shipping carton and filler material. At the pick position the computer suggested carton and filler material pick instructions for a customer order appears to a packer on a customer order pack slip/invoice, customer order delivery label or RF device display screen or pick to light display. With one shipping carton pick station for each carton size and with one customer order per carton philosophy, as a customer order tote arrives at a carton/filler material pick station, it is a simple one shipping carton/filler material transfer transaction into a tote. The simple task requires a tote to appear at the pick station and the tote serves as a pick instruction for a picker to transfer a carton/filler material into a tote.

After ordered and picked SKUs are transferred into a tote, the tote is transported to a shipping-carton pick position. At the pick position, a shipping carton is transferred from a pick position into a tote. The picked SKUs and shipping carton are transferred to a pack area. The features of this design are:

- Used for made-up or not made-up small size shipping cartons that fit into a tote
- Improved shipping carton inventory control
- Less employee time to replenish shipping cartons to each pack station
- Less crowded pack table
- Requires an employee picker
- Requires additional pick positions

Packing Slip and Shipping Label Preparation

Central Print Design

To print packing slips and shipping labels printing is done at a central location or office in the warehouse. After printing and combining documents, the documents are delivered to a pick-line start station or to a sort/pack station.

At a Warehouse Pick-Line Start Station

In this design, prior to the beginning of pick activity, a packing slip with a shipping label is pre-printed or printed on demand and is manually or mechanically applied onto a carton/tote. After a picker completes the pick transactions, the picker (or in-house transport) delivers a carton/tote with picked SKUs, a packing slip, and a shipping label to a pack station with a mechanized sort concept, the pack slips are separate and distributed to the appropriate pack station. Depending on the operation, a packer performs an SKU quantity/quality check. The features are:

- High-speed or several print machines at each pick line
- Minimal installation expense
- Supply central inventory and increased control
- Additional space at a pack station
- No additional pack station activity
- When a printer problem occurs without a back-up printer, this can shut down pick and pack activities
- Minimal preprinted document distribution errors
- Minimal difficulty and costs to relocate or remodel a pack area

Print at the Pack Station

An alternative print location is to have a printer at each pack station. At a pack station, a packer scans the customer-order identification and/or SKU identification. The customer-order or SKU identification is sent to a computer, which activates the pack station printer. The printer prints a packing slip and shipping label. The features of this design are:

- It requires a large number of print machines.
- There will be an expense of installing the wire run between a computer and each pack station printer.
- The manifest and shipping document supplies minimal control.
- It requires additional space at a pack station.
- It adds to the packers' activity.
- It requires back-up printers for pack station printer problems.
- There are no print document distribution errors.
- It is difficult and requires additional cost to relocate or remodel the pack area.
- Printers must deal with pack area environmental conditions.
- There will be license fees.

Shipping Label

The address label on a shipping container ensures that the order's shipping address is clearly visible on a carton/bag.

Shipping-Label Design Considerations

Shipping-label design factors are:

- Lines preprinted on the label face, e.g., company return address and bar code/RF tag, delivery company bar code/RF tag
- Customer order delivery code that is printed on a customer order delivery label is per the delivery company requirement
- Attached to any shipping carton or bag
- Manual or mechanical label application
- Preprinted or print on demand
- Easy to remove a label from its back
- Label stays on a shipping carton/bag

Self-Adhesive Label

A self-adhesive label is preprinted or printed on demand and has a pick-line start-station employee or packer remove the label from a roll, sheet, stack, or printer, remove the protective back, and place the label onto a carton or bag. (The backing is thrown in the trash.) With a self-adhesive label, prints maximum label number per minute, preprinted company lines or information can be preprinted on the label face by a label vendor.

Peel-Off Label

A peel-off label is a self-adhesive label that is preprinted or printed on demand onto another self-adhesive label. A peel-off label is used in a pick operation that:

1. Picks small cube customer orders into a standard carton that requires a customer-order identification on the side
2. Used when your delivery company obtains a package delivery receipt from a customer such as COD or carbon copy.

At a pick-line start station or pack station, a pick-line starter/packer removes a peel-off self-adhesive label from a label roll, stack, or printer, removes the protective back from the first label and places the label onto a carton/bag. If a peel-off label is used on a standard carton, a packer peels off a shipping label from a standard size carton and places a shipping label onto a small shipping carton. A label back is peeled off or remains on the carton and the backing is thrown in the trash. With a peel-off self-adhesive label, to have a high label print per minute, assure that the maximum non-customer order related or company information is preprinted on the label face by the label vendor. When a peel-off self-adhesive label is compared to a regular label, the features are a) it is slightly more expensive, b) it requires additional employee activity, c) the base label requires a larger carton area, and d) the warehouse needs to determine if a customer will accept a label back on a carton.

Envelope Label

A slapper envelope is used for high-volume pick/pack SKU activity on a vendor ready-to-ship carton. A slapper envelope has a transparent window or front side, and a preprinted packing slip with sales literature inside each envelope. The packing slip has the shipping address, SKU number, and pick-position number facing the window and all packing slip information facing a solid carton side. The slapper envelope is attached to the carton with self-adhesive backing, double-sided adhesive tape, glue pot, or glue sprayed on the carton. Envelope label features are:

- Company return address on the outside
- Transparent window or side that permits a packer or scanner/reader to read the customer-order identification and delivery address
- The capacity to hold a packing slip and company literature

A slapper envelope may also be used with low-volume SKUs. The envelope is used as a pick instruction; the picker applies the envelope to a carton in the pick area.

A manual option has an employee fold and place the packing slip and sale literature into an envelope with a clear window or front. After stuffing the envelope, the employee seals the envelope, queues the envelopes, and sends them to a pack station. The features are low volume, additional employee activity, no cost, and it is performed on a simple table top.

A mechanical option uses a machine that folds, stuffs, and seals envelopes. Stuffed envelopes are queued and sent to a pack station. Feature requires customer order high volume for vendor ready to ship cartons that are single line/single SKU customer orders, high employee productivity, requires only one employee and floor space for a machine with an electrical outlet and an air compressor.

Prior to using glue or double-sided adhesive tape, design tests will ensure that:

- Glue or tape holds an envelope as designed and specified to a carton
- When placed onto a carton, the glue or tape does not extend beyond the envelope, or pass through an envelope onto the window
- The warehouse and freight company scanners/readers can achieve a good read through the plastic window
- An envelope label remains on a carton as the carton flows through the supply chain to the delivery address
- The customer accepts a slapper envelope

As noted above, glue options are:

1. A glue pot, in which an employee feeds envelopes through a glue pot. Electric rollers drive the envelope through a glue pot and apply a thin layer of glue to the envelope. When the envelope passes through the glue pot, the employee places the envelope's glue side onto a carton's exterior surface. The features are a) low cost, b) it can be performed at any location, c) potential to over- or underapply glue applied onto an envelope that creates potential carton handling problems such when two cartons with over glued envelopes become glued together and when a carton with an under glued envelope falls from a carton that creates a lost

customer order, d) it handles low- to medium-volume, and e) it only requires one employee.

2. A mechanical sprayed glue design has a conveyor pull a gap between two cartons; the lead carton is sensed by a photo-eye. The photo-eye sends a message to the warehouse computer, which activates a glue-spray machine. As a carton arrives at the glue-spray machine, glue is sprayed onto the carton's exterior surface. An employee or mechanical envelope applicator places a slapper envelope onto the glue. The labeled carton travels on a conveyor for a predetermined length of time or an air blower ensures that glue is dry. The features are a) less glue waste, b) required maintenance, c) it handles a high volume, d) requires a powered conveyor, e) requires an employee or machine to place a label on glue surface, and f) with a machine design there is minimal setup labor.

3. A double-sided adhesive tape design uses two double-sided self-adhesive tape stripes, which are attached to the back of an envelope. In this design, envelopes are received at an envelope application station with the tape stuck against the envelope back; the outward-facing tape has a removable paper back. At an envelope application station an employee removes the back from the tape and places the envelope onto a carton.

Chapter 11

Customer Order Package Manifest, Ship, Sort, and Load Activities

Introduction

The last outbound warehouse activities are manifest, ship-sort, and load activities for a sealed and labeled shipping carton, package, or pallet. Manifest, ship-sort, and load activities ensure that a carton/pallet leaves a pick operation, and that the warehouse computer updates the WMS computer. The WMS computer in turn sends a customer-order identification to the host computer to update order-identification status in its files. The warehouse should have a direct connection to the delivery-company computer, and package numbers and routing information are sent at this time. This is an important interface because transmitting information about packages and routing allows a delivery company to pre-plan.

Carton/package manifest activity involves having an employee or fixed-position scanner/reader list each shipping carton, package, or pallet. After customer order activity, an order package sort activity sorts/transfers the package from an employee, conveyor, or travel path into a shipping location staging lane. The load activity ensures that each carton, package, or pallet is transferred from a shipping dock into a delivery vehicle.

Shipping Carton, Package or Pallet Manifest Activity

In manifest activity, the pallet, carton, or bag identification is scan/read by an employee or a fixed-position scanner/reader. An order-identification list is sent from the pick operation to the delivery-company office. The list may be a paper copy, diskette, on-line, or delayed communication network, depending on the delivery company. After the warehouse computer receives a manifest transaction, the computer sends the order-identification status to the WMS computer. The WMS computer sends each order identification as a completed order to the host computer.

Manifest, Ship, and Load Activity: Functional Description

In a manifest, ship, and load activity, a carton/tote/pallet is scanned/read, the information is sent to the WMS computer (on time or delayed), and the ordered SKU is moved from a shipping dock into a delivery vehicle. After each order identification is read/scanned, a scanner/reader verifies that the order has been transferred from a conveyor or shipping dock into a delivery truck. The warehouse computer sends the order identification to the WMS computer to update the order status. The WMS computer sends a "completed customer order" message to the host computer to update its files.

If the order identification cannot be read by a scanner/reader, or the order identification has not been downloaded from the WMS computer to the warehouse computer, the order is listed as "cannot read" or "nonexistent order," and is held in the warehouse. The warehouse and WMS computer team takes corrective action to resolve the order-identification status.

After the delivery company confirms that the order was delivered and received at the delivery address, the freight company notifies the warehouse. The warehouse computer notifies the WMS computer, which updates the order status and sends an update to the host computer.

Depending on the delivery company's procedures and practices, after packing an order but prior to package seal activity, the delivery company creates a customer order RF tag or symbology with the delivery address and human-/machine-readable information. The customer order code is sent to your freight delivery company to develop a customer order delivery routing and for customer order package sort onto a freight delivery company truck for final customer order delivery. The customer order delivery routing is achieved by a freight delivery company computer reading the customer order delivery address (or postal zip code). By using the bar code with RF tag or symbology, the delivery company is able to track each customer order package as it flows through the delivery company's spoke-and-wheel transport design.

Manifest, Ship, and Load Activity: Exception Handling

During manifest, ship, and load activities, there is a potential for an order exception or a handling problem. The design team should identify these potential problems or exceptions and prepare resolutions for them. For example:

1. Overflow in a delivery vehicle, bulk mail carrier (BMC), or truck. In a manual or mechanized load design when order packages' cube or volume exceed a BMC, truck, or delivery vehicle capacity this creates an overflow situation. If the warehouse and WMS computer prints/sends an order-identification manifest for an entire work day to the delivery company, overflow packages are placed into another BMC, delivery vehicle, or truck. If the warehouse and WMS computer creates an order manifest for each delivery vehicle, truck, or BMC, and if a package is considerd loaded after a scan/read, there is an exception. To handle the exception, a new BMC or truck is identified in the warehouse and WMS computer programs and overflow packages are moved from the old BMC, truck, or vehicle to a new BMC or truck and scanned. The scan transactions are sent to the computer to update the order status.

2. Removing an order identification from a BMC or truck. For an operational reason, several manifested and loaded packages are off-loaded from a BMC or truck, placed on your warehouse shipping dock, and are scheduled for manifest, ship, and load activity for the next work day (day 2). To handle this exception, an employee with scanner/reader collects off-loaded packages and scans/reads each order identification. Packages are placed and scanned/

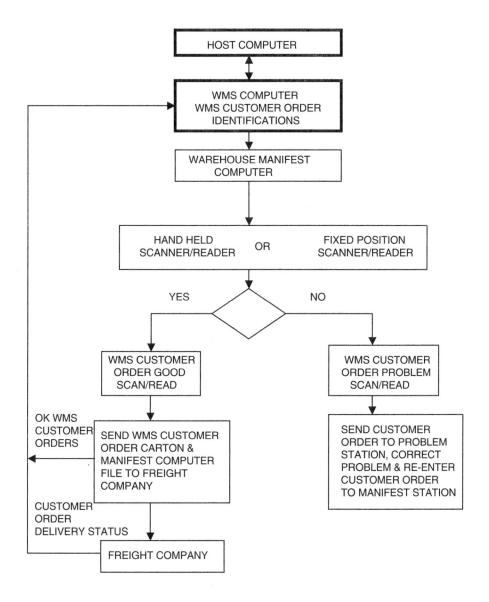

Figure 11.1 Order Manifest Flow

read into a temporary holding position; scan/read transactions are sent to the WMS computer for file update. The warehouse manifest and WMS computer considers these packages as being in the warehouse and not shipped orders, nor are they on the day 1 manifest list. The warehouse and WMS computer add these held orders to work day 2 as orders available for manifest, ship, and load activity. During day 2, the packages are removed from the hold position, manifested, shipped, and loaded onto a BMC or truck. They appear in the freight company manifest and WMS computer as completed and shipped orders.

3. Damaged manifested order package. As a package is transferred into a BMC or truck, an employee notices a damaged package; the employee does not transfer the package into a BMC or truck. Because the package was .anned/read at a manifest station and in the warehouse and WMS computers, the package is considered on a manifest list and shipped from the warehouse. A damaged package is handled the same as an off-loaded package from a truck or BMC.

4. A canceled order identification. The WMS computer receives a message from the host computer that an order has been canceled; the computer sends a cancel message to the warehouse computer. If an order is canceled and warehouse is a manual or mechanized sort/manifest design, as the canceled order identification is scanned/read a cancel message appears on a hand-held display or PC screen, or a mechanized sort design transfers the canceled order to a "do not ship" lane. All canceled orders are scanned/read and placed into a temporary hold position that is "on hold" or "not available for sale." Scan transactions are sent to the WMS computer to update the SKU status. As required, SKUs are moved from the temporary hold position to a pickable position; the WMS computer is updated. Cancel orders as early as possible or at least before your sort/manifest activity because it does not require a modification to a standard sorter/manifest computer program and requires minimal labor cost to phyiscally handle a canceled customer order.

5. An order is placed on wrong truck or BMC occurs when the shipping activity has an order package loaded onto the wrong truck such as when you are loading several freight trucks with one freight truck for regular delivery, one truck for express delivery, one truck for quarranted next day delivery and one truck for dangerous/hazardous goods.

6. A manifested package left on a sorter travel path. In this situation, the WMS computer has received an order identification from a warehouse manifest scanner/reader and considers an order identification to have been shipped and loaded onto a BMC or delivery truck. A full truck departed the warehouse and all order identifications are considered manifested and on a truck. At a freight terminal, a truck transfers order identifications (packages) into the freight company's manifest and sort design. To ensure that the warehouse manifest is accurate, the options are a) to make a special trip with packages to the freight company terminal or b) on your shipping dock transfer and scan WMS identified packages to the warehouse WMS identified temporary hold storage position; scan transactions are updated in the WMS computer; order identifications are deleted from the completed/manifested customer order status; a completed customer order manifest message is sent to the freight company. Retained orders are sent to the WMS computer, which updates the host computer.

7. A sorter travel path is broken. With a broken sorter travel path, orders cannot pass a fixed-position scanner/reader and travel into a delivery truck or to a BMC transfer location. To resolve the situation, the options are a) to hand scan/read and manually bulk load all order packages onto a delivery truck or BMC, which satisfies the warehouse and WMS computer scan transactions/load activities, or b) hold packages between a pack area and conveyor and load the next workday.

8. A broken sorter scanner/reader. Use a hand-held scanner/reader.

Shipping-Carton/Package Sort Activity

Shipping-carton/package sort activity are manual and mechanized design. Shipping-carton/package sort activity ensures that cartons/packages from a mixed order group of labeled cartons/packages are separated by delivery-company terminal location, postal zip code, or other delivery-company criteria. The sort activity permits a pick operation to freight delivery company zone skip that reduces delivery charges and results in a reduction in the customer order delivery day number. The results are due to a freight company delivery truck with customer order packages for one postal zone departs from your warehouse and by-passes your freight company local sort terminal and travels direct to a freight company sort terminal in your customer order delivery/postal zone area. For a work day customer order, if the warehouse has the host computer programmed to have different host computer customer order cut off times for different postal zones, this feature helps your pick/pack operation to guarantee a 24-hour delivery to all customer orders geographically close to your warehouse. A sort of customer order packages by postal zip codes example is customer order delivery postal zip codes within a 100 mile travel distance from a freight company terminal would have a host computer customer order cut off time of 2000 and all customer order delivery zip codes more than 100 mile travel distance from a freight company terminal would have a host computer customer order cut off time of 1900.

Ship-Sort Instruction

With manual and mechanized ship-sort designs, a ship-sort instruction is a human-/machine-readable code printed onto a label. A manual ship-sort activity has a large human-readable section of a human-/machine-readable label on each customer-order carton/package. In a ship sort activity, customer order labeled cartons/packages are mixed on a belt sort conveyor. Each carton/package has an order identification or sort label attached to the exterior. After a customer order carton/package delivery label is read by a scanner/reader, the customer order identification is sent to the sort computer. The sort computer and sort travel path has a labeled carton/package transferred from a sort conveyor to divert lane for travel to a pallet or BMC unitize station that is identified for a customer order delivery label. To complete an order identification manifest scan transaction, an unitize employee with a hand-held scanner/reader scans/reads a carton/package label. Order identification scan transactions are sent from the warehouse computer to the WMS computer (on-line or delayed), which sends an order identification to the host computer to update files.

With a mechanized design, the ship-sort activity has a human-/machine-readable identification on each carton/package. After the sort conveyor diverts a carton/package onto a conveyor lane that is assigned for customer order cartons for a frieght company delivery region, each carton/package identification is scanned/read by an unitize employee, or the delivery company accepts the warehouse scanner/reader order identification scan transactions, and a load conveyor employee transfers the cartons/packages to a freight company regional terminal, assigned pallet, or BMC or delivery truck.

Machine-Printed Self-Adhesive Ship-Sort Label

A self-adhesive machine-printed label is a human-/machine-readable label created by a warehouse computer-controlled printer. Each carton/package has a label with alpha characters and numeric digits plus a bar-code/RF tag that determines the delivery or sort location. The important items on the label face are: a) the customer name and address, b) alpha/numeric order identification or sort location, and c) black bars with white spaces or a bar code/RF tag.

In a manual design, in a ship sort area after a package is transferred from a sort conveyor to a divert conveyor that is assigned for a delivery-company terminal, a sort employee picks up a carton/package, reads a carton sort identification (delivery-company terminal), and matches the carton/package identification location to the sort location human-readable identification attached to a pallet or BMC. With a delivery-company terminal human-readable identification location and order sort identification match, the employee places an order package onto a pallet or BMC. If required, the employee completes a scan/read for each package label. Scan transactions are transferred (delayed or on-line) from the manifest computer to the WMS computer; the WMS computer then updates the host computer.

In a mechanized design, in a ship sort area after a sort conveyor order-identification scanner/reader and sort conveyor diverts a customer order package from a sort conveyor onto a conveyor lane that is assigned to company delivery terminal, the conveyor lane directs a customer order carton/package to a load/unitize station or into a delivery truck. At a load/unitize station conveyor lane end, an employee transfers a carton/package onto a pallet or BMC. When cartons travel from a sort conveyor onto a conveyor lane into a delivery truck approach, an employee transfers a carton/package from a conveyor lane onto a delivery truck floor. Customer order WMS identification scan transactions are delayed or on-line transferred from a manifest computer from a warehouse computer to the WMS computer for WMS computer transfer to a host computer for customer order file update.

Shipping-Carton Sort Designs

Ship-sort design ensures that cartons are diverted from a sort conveyor onto a divert conveyor lane for travel to a customer order or delivery-company terminal assigned ship dock staging area or directly into a customer order or delivery-company terminal delivery truck. Carton or delivery-company terminal sort designs may be manual or mechanized/mechanical designs. The latter include active and passive sort designs, or a combination of both.

In a customer-order or delivery-company-terminal manual or mechanized sort design, order or carton travel path options are to:

1. Travel on powered conveyor lanes and unitized onto pallets or BMCs and later loaded onto a delivery truck.
2. Travel direct to a delivery truck.

Mechanized Shipping-Carton Sort Designs

A mechanized sort operation has all customer-order cartons transferred from a pack area, travel over a sort conveyor through an induction station to a divert station, and from there to a sort station or shipping lane. From a shipping lane, cartons are either loaded directly onto a delivery truck or palletized onto a pallet, slip sheet, or BMC. At a later time, BMCs, slip sheets, or pallets are transferred from the ship dock staging area onto a delivery truck.

For a mechanized sort design to operate efficiently, it requires that each carton have human-/machine-readable identification label. The label contains an order or delivery-company terminal sort location. After an employee or scanner/reader inducts an order or delivery-company terminal carton into the warehouse computer, the computer and tracking device control the sort activity. The sort activity transfers a carton from a sort conveyor onto the order or delivery-company terminal staging lane for a) transfer onto a pallet, slip sheet, or BMC/cart or b) direct load into a delivery truck.

Shipping-Carton Sort Surfaces or Conveyor Travel Paths

A carton sort conveyor is a major component of a delivery-company terminal carton sort design. The types of conveyor are roller conveyor, smooth-top belt, slat tray, tilt tray, horizontal or vertical moving belt conveyor, and gull wing.

Single Straight-Line Sort Conveyor

In a straight-line sort conveyor design, the travel path is a straight line from an induction station to the last sort station. After the last sort station, the travel path ends and descends to the floor. Alternative straight-line designs are a) an "L" shaped or straight-line layout or b) a horseshoe or "U" shaped layout. A characteristic of the straight-line design is that there is no "did not sort" carton automatic recirculation to an induction station. In a straight-line design, a "did not sort" carton is created by a full sort lane or a divert device malfunction. The options for handling a "did not sort" carton are a) to manually return the carton to an induction station or b) to manually transfer the carton to an order unitize station. At an order unitize station, an employee with a hand-held scanner/reader verifies that the carton was loaded onto a delivery truck. After loading activity, the scan/read is downloaded to the warehouse computer to create a manifest. The computer transfers (on-line or delayed) all manifested order identifications to the delivery company and the WMS and host computers for order update.

The "did not sort" cartons are removed from the sort conveyor a) by diverting all cartons to the last divert location or b) an employee unitizes the cartons onto a cart/pallet at a divert lane or travel path end. The cartons are manually transported to an induction station or to a delivery-company unitize station. The disadvantages of this approach are a) the need for additional employees, b) employees move cartons, and it handles a low volume. The advantage is a lower conveyor cost.

Endless-Loop Ship-Sort Conveyor

An endless-loop sort conveyor starts at an induction station's discharge end and ends at the station's charge end. Possible designs are "L" shaped, "U" shaped, "O" or elliptically shaped, and rectangularly shaped. All "did not sort" cartons in an endless-loop design are automatically recirculated (via a recirculation conveyor) to an induction station. At the induction station, "did not sort" cartons are reintroduced to the sort travel path by an induction employee or scanner/reader. A dual induction sort concept has two customer order induction stations. There are customer order carton sort locations between each dual induction station. The dual induction feature means that induction station A inducts customer packages for sort to divert locations from induction station 1 to 2 and induction station B inducts customer packages for sort to divert locations from induction station 2 to induction station 1. Some sort conveyor travel path options are:

1. An over-and-under design to have sufficient clearance between two conveyor travel paths

2. A side-by-side design to have sufficient clearance between front and rear sort conveyor travel paths

3. Having two divert or shipping lanes merge into a single shipping lane with sufficient carton queue, merge control, and carton control travel

The disadvantages of an endless-loop design are a) the recirculation carton volume adds to a sort volume and b) increased carton induction and sort volume. The advantages are a) few employee are needed, b) minimal employee injuries, c) it handles high volume, and it provides automatic recirculation.

Mechanical Divert Components

A mechanical divert device transfers a carton from a sort conveyor onto a delivery-company terminal unitize station or shipping lane. A divert device is designed to pull, push, tip, slide, or pass a carton from a sort conveyor onto a divert lane. In a carton sort-conveyor divert-lane design, sort stations progress arithmetically from the induction station to the last sort station. Most sort stations are are numbered so that all numbers that end with all odd numbers are on the travel path's left side and all even numbers are on the travel path's right side.

Mechanical divert designs are:

1. An active sorter design, which has a powered induction station, conveyor surface, and mechanical divert device that pushes or pulls a carton from a sort travel path onto a sort lane.

2. An active-passive sorter design, which has a manual induction station and a powered conveyor surface that tips or plows a carton from a sort travel path onto a sort lane.

3. A passive sorter design, which has a manual induction station and a powered conveyor that uses gravity to remove a carton from a sort travel path to a sort station.

Divert Devices or Designs

Various divert devices are solid metal deflector, pusher diverter, powered belt diverter, plow diverter, cross-horizontal or vertical-moving belt, tilt tray, nova sort, tilt slat, gull wing, sliding shoe, pop-up diverts (which includes a pop-up wheel, pop-up chain, and pop-up chain with a blade), rotating paddle, and flap sorter.

Left-and-Right Tilts to Separate Shipping Lanes

A left-and-right tilt-tray sort travel path design is designed with top-sort cartons and bags to separate locations: a less complex tilt-tray design. The design has shipping lanes on either side of a tilt-tray travel path. The travel path leaves induction station 1, travels to shipping lanes, passes a clean-out sort location, leaves induction station 2, travels to shipping lanes, passes a clean-out sort location, and returns to induction station 1. The carton or bag is tilted from the travel path, and cartons flow directly to a unitize station or delivery truck. In addition, the travel path has an "O"—a rectangular or elliptical shape—with customer order sort lanes on each sort conveyor straight run side means maximum customer order sort locations and less cost.

Over-and-Under Tilts to Separate Shipping Lanes

An over-and-under tilt-tray is designed to sort cartons/bags, and is used when dock space is limited and the carton/bag packages require separate sort locations. The travel path leaves induction station 1, descends to ensure proper sort elevation above the floor, diverts cartons to shipping lanes, and passes a clean-out sort location. The tilt-tray travel follows the same procedure for induction station 2, then inclines to run above the lower path (i.e., tilt-tray travel path from induction station 1), and arrives back at induction station 1. An over-and-under design features:

- If the travel path is shaped like a figure-eight or bow-tie, there will be additional cost for curves and straight lengths for travel past induction stations.
- Separate sort locations.
- It sorts to docks on one side of the building.

Side-by-Side with Tilts to One Shipping Lane

A side-by-side conveyor design has front and rear sort conveyors that tilt cartons to single or combined shipping lanes and has the rear divert lane to travel under a tilt tray travel path. With a dual shipping-lane configuration, as a rear divert lane goes under a tilt tray travel path, the divert travel path has sufficient decline to permit the tallest carton to travel under the tilt tray travel path.

If a side-by-side tilt-tray divert or shipping lane service one unitizes station or direct load station, it assures controlled and constant carton flow to a shipping conveyor lane end. If a side-by-side tilt-tray front divert or shipping lane and a rear divert or shipping lane merge into a single shipping lane, the front and rear shipping lanes should have sufficient carton queue length, merge controls, and carton control to ensure a constant carton flow to the unitize or direct load stations. In a side-by-side design, the shipping lane uses belt conveyor sections to control carton flow.

Shipping-Carton Load Design

In a design in which order cartons are sorted at the end of a shipping lane, cartons may be placed onto BMC/cart, slip sheet, or pallet, or directly onto the delivery truck. In a ship-sort design, the labeled cartons are sorted for placement onto an appropriate BMC or pallet. As a carton leaves an induction area and travels to a sort design encode station, the carton's identification is entered into the WMS computer. The computer and a sort device activates a divert device at the required time to divert a carton from a sort conveyor into an assigned shipping lane.

Shipping-Carton Unitize or Direct-Load Activity

Shipping-carton stage, load, and shipping activity ensures that the shipping carton/bag is placed onto a delivery truck. Load activity design factors are:

1. Individually sort cartons by delivery address/region
2. Bulk load cartons onto a single delivery truck
3. Unitize cartons onto a pallet or four-wheel cart or BMC
4. Cartons travel directly into a delivery truck and are loaded onto the truck floor

Loading by Delivery Address or Region

To individually sort customer order cartons/bags by delivery address or region involves the following design factors:

- The warehouse uses a conveyor travel path and sort design.
- The warehouse has a large number of customer orders (and cartons) for a given region.
- The IT department programs a sort design or computer to accept or collect delivery addresses for the freight company's regional terminal.
- The bar codes/RF tags used on the cartons present delivery addresses as human-/machine-readable sort instructions.
- The freight company uses a "spoke-and-wheel" delivery design. In a spoke-and-wheel design, a freight company truck picks up cartons from the warehouse and other businesses and brings all shipping cartons to a freight company sort terminal. At each freight terminal, cartons are sorted for each region and transferred to a freight shuttle truck for delivery to the freight company terminal in the appropriate region. At the regional terminal, cartons are sorted by delivery address and loaded onto freight company trucks for delivery.

If a warehouse uses this design, the transport conveyor and sort design ensures that each carton/bag (with a WMS customer-order or freight terminal customer-order identification) is diverted from a main conveyor onto an assigned divert lane. For a warehouse to receive a lower customer order delivery rate, customer order cartons are sorted to consolidated customer order cartons as regional customer order cartons onto a freight company delivery truck for delivery to the freight company regional terminal. Freight company delivery travel is from the warehouse to the freight company's regional terminal, and by-pass the freight company local terminal. The features are sort concept, the need for the IT department to collect customer order delivery addresses for the freight company's local and regional terminals, lower freight rate due to "zone skip" (i.e., skipping a freight company local terminals) delivery that means a cost reduction due to the freight company does not double handle your customer order packages at both a local and regional frieght terminal and faster customer order carton delivery that means improved customer service.

Bulk Loading Cartons onto a Single Delivery Truck

In this design, cartons/bags are bulk loading cartons/bags onto single delivery truck for later sort at a freight termial. This design is best for a warehouse with small number of cartons/bags being shipped to man different delivery regions. To obtain the best customer order delivery rate, cartons/bags for mixed regions are sent to the local freight company terminal. At the local terminal, the cartons are sorted to various delivery regions and combined with other company packages. The disadvantages are higher delivery charges and slightly slower delivery. The advantages are low cost, only minimal buiilding space needed, and it may be used with any carton load design.

Unitizing Cartons onto a Pallet or Four-Wheel Cart (BMC)

Depending upon the warehouse's shipping volume and design, cartons/bags can be unitized onto a pallet or four-wheel cart (BMC) that are sent to a freight company local terminal. At the local freight conmpany terminal your customer orders are sorted onto trucks for transport from your warehouse to a freight company regional terminal. If the warehouse customer order volume has one or several pallets or BMCs for a specific freight company region/terminal at your warehouse your customer order cartons are sorted and unitized onto pallets or BMCs. Each pallet or BMC is identified for a freight company region/terminal. At the freight company local terminal the regional identified pallets/BMCs flow as a pallet or BMC through a delivery-company local sort terminal not as individual cartons over the freight company local terminal conveyor sort concept. When a warehouse unitizes shipping cartons/bags by region on a pallet or BMC, unitized pallets or BMCs reduce the freight company local terminal handling, because the freight company handles pallets/BMCs rather than individual cartons. The features are your IT department to collect delivery addresses for the freight company's regional terminals, lower freight rate due to "zone skip" (i.e., skipping local terminals) delivery that means a cost reduction, faster customer order carton delivery that means improved customer service and at your operation, the freight company ensures a supply of empty BMCs.

Nonconveyable items are jiffy bags, cartons whose dimensions exceed the warehouse or freight company conveyor/sort design parameters, cartons whose physical shape does not match the warehouse or freight company conveyor transport design parameters, cartons/bags for which the customer has requested special handling, or cartons/bags that require special handling in accordance with local government regulations. Nonconveyable cartons/bags are loaded onto a pallet, large container, or BMC. The features of handling nonconveyable items in this way are handling empty and full BMCs, potential employee injury, lower delivery truck utilization, improved delivery time, lower delivery charge.

Loading Cartons Directly onto a BMC or a Delivery Truck

When cartons are to be delivered to a large geographical area or are sorted at the freight company terminal, the warehouse should use a direct-load design. In a direct-load and ship design cartons travel from a sort conveyor over a divert conveyor shipping lane directly into a BMC or delivery truck. In the delivery vehicle, an employee transfers cartons onto the floor or into another carton. This approach features no double handling cartons, few shipping docks, a smaller dock staging area, it handles high volume, and reduces load errors. With a BMC design, employees on a load dock transfer cartons onto a BMC; full BMCs are loaded onto a freight truck. This design features double handling of cartons, additional shipping docks and dock staging area, it handles a medium to high volume, and there is the potential for loading errors.

Shipping Carton Unitize Designs

In a carton unitize design, the customer-order or freight company cartons travel on a shipping-lane conveyor. Each conveyor has a path from a sort conveyor to a unitize station. At the unitize station, cartons are placed onto a cart, slip sheet, or pallet. After the cart, slip sheet, or pallet is unitized to a predetermined height, a full cart, slip sheet, or pallet is identified with a customer order or delivery-company terminal carton code and is either transferred to an assigned outbound staging area or placed onto a delivery truck. The disadvantages of this design are the need for a cart, slip-sheet, or pallet unitizing area, some double handling, the need for additional ship dock space, and the need for a pallet/slip-sheet handling device. The advantages are that it permits easy loading, it increases nonconveyable delivery load, and it allows cartons to be handled without a delivery truck at a shipping dock. It is preferred for a cart delivery design.

After the warehouse IT or WMS computer group customer-order WMS identifications for a shipping lane or freight company regional terminal, the sort design groups customer orders for a sort conveyor shipping lane. The BMC/pallet unitize station layout options are:

- One divert lane to service unitize cart stations on both sides of a shipping lane or conveyor travel path. With sufficient conveyor length there are 4 to 5 unitize stations on a conveyor lane side. The features are: provides per shipping conveyor lane a maximum unitize station number, requires top labeled customer order carton, and requires accurate and fast shipping lane employee transfer activity.
- Side-by-side divert or shipping lines, in which each line service unitize cart stations on one side of a shipping conveyor lane. The option is used when your operation has your sort conveyor complete an intial sort that minimizes your shipping lane transfer employee effort and reading requirement, you require a medium sort station number, customer order cartons are top label and require fast shipping lane employee transfer activity.
- One angled divert lane with load stations on one side. After a sort conveyor divert location, the shipping conveyor lane is parallel to the sort conveyor. The option is used when your operation has few divert locations because it provides 4 to 5 unitize station numbers, used when there is limited floor space between a sort conveyor and shipping door because the shipping conveyor lane requires less floor space and customer order cartons are top or side label and require fast shipping lane employee transfer activity.

Customer Order Ship Nonconveyable Carton Sort

Many companies have implemented mechanized carton sort designs to reduce operating expenses, increase through-put volume, improve sort accuracy, and enhance customer service but non-conveyable cartons account for 5 to 25% of warehouse carton volume.

Nonconveyable Shipping-Carton Sort Designs

A nonconveyable carton handling design is used when a warehouse needs to sort a) picked cartons from warehouse pallets/load carrying surface to an assigned ship staging location (i.e., BMC or pallet), or b) onto a sort vehicle/pallet/cart with cartons in rack positions.

Carton/Pallet Delivery Vehicle Loading Activity

At a warehouse, the carton load and ship operation ensures that a carton is transferred from a staging area or sort travel path to a delivery truck. The load and ship function can be a direct-load activity or it can temporarily hold cartons in a staging area for later loading time onto a delivery truck. The load activity handles conveyable cartons/pallets, slip sheets, BMCs, containers that have conveyable/nonconveyable orders, or freight-company cartons, bags, or pallets.

In a manually controlled pallet load vehicle design, a pallet from a storage/pick position or ship dock area is transferred onto a delivery vehicle. Manually controlled vehicles are separated into a) the powered vehicle group and b) the battery/internal combusiton engine powered vehicle group. The manually powered vehicle group includes:

- Two-wheel hand truck
- Platform truck and four-wheel cart
- Roller pallet or dolly
- Manual pallet truck

The battery/internal combustion engine group includes:

- Powered forklift truck with a set of forks
- Counterbalanced fork lift truck with a slip-sheet attachment
- Electric pallet truck with a set of forks or slip-sheet attachment

Mechanized or Automatic Pallet Load Designs

Mechanized or automatic pallet load designs ensure that a pallet is transferred from a shipping dock onto a delivery truck. Mechanized or automatic pallet load designs are a) pallet handling device or PHD, b) pallet flow device, and c) Strad-O-Lift.

Off-Loading Cartons/Pallets from a Delivery Truck

During a manifested customer order delivery truck load activity or unitize onto a pallet or BMC activity, a load employee could receive manifested cartons or pallets that cannot fit onto an assigned BMC or delivery truck. The situation requires an employee to off-load manifested cartons or pallets from a BMC or delivery truck. A second situation is that the BMC or truck is full, but the warehouse has special or high-priority packages, cartons, or pallets that must be loaded onto a BMC or delivery truck that requires an employee to off-load manifested cartons or pallets from a BMC or delivery truck.

To ensure that packages are properly manifested and scanned on a BMC or delivery truck or to add special or high priority cartons or pallets onto a BMC or delivery truck, a load employee is required to remove manifested, scanned, and loaded cartons or pallets from a BMC or delivery truck onto the shipping dock WMS identified temporary hold position. As a load employee removes a manifested, scanned, and loaded carton, or pallet from a BMC or delivery truck, an employee scans/reads each customer order identification. Scan transactions are sent to the warehouse computer to update or delete the removed and scanned/read customer order identifications from the manifested customer-order identification list. The warehouse computer notifies the WMS computer that the identifications are held in the warehouse and are not completed orders. The WMS computer sends the identifications to the host computer, which updates order status.

At a later time or on the next BMC or delivery truck, a load employee completes a scan transaction for each package, carton, or pallet, and transfers the cartons onto the BMC or delivery truck. The scan/read transactions are sent to the warehouse manifest computer as shipped and loaded customer orders.

Chapter 12

Returns Process, Customer Return, and Vendor Rework Warehouse Activities

Introduction

In addition to receiving, shipping, storage, and pick and pack activities, other important warehouse activities are the customer-returns process, vendor and customer-returns rework, and trash removal. In a warehouse with a WMS program, the last two warehouse activities that interface with the WMS program are 1) the customer-returns process, with its return-to-stock (RTS) and return-to-vendor (RTV) activity and 2) vendor rework activity. Trash removal is not related to a WMS program but it is important for a warehouse to have an on-time, cost-effective, and efficient returns operation.

The objectives of this chapter are to a) develop, identify, and evaluate warehouse design parameters and operational characteristics for the customer-returns process, vendor rework, and trash removal activities. Understanding design parameters and operational characteristics are key factors in making a warehouse more cost effective and efficient with the warehouse's company customer-service standard. In this chapter, we shall 1) review manual and mechanical customer return process designs and SKU procedures; 2) RTS manual sort and WMS interface and routing patterns; 3) sort area equipment layouts and types; 4) activities that ensure an efficient and on-time returned, processed, and disposed SKU flow; and 5) vendor rework locations and flows.

Customer-Returns Process or Activity Functional Description

The customer-returns process or activity is the warehouse activity that ensures a SKU returned by a customer is valid per a customer order that is obtained from a computer file (see Figure 12.1). After a SKU quality is determined to be valid, a SKU is disposed per the warehouse standard as a return to stock or return to vendor SKU. Per a SKU disposition, a SKU flows from the returns

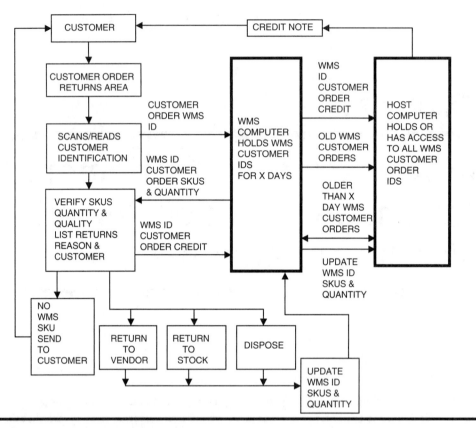

Figure 12.1   Returns Flow

process station to a temporary SKU hold position. At the temporary hold position, a SKU is WMS scanned and physically placed into an appropriate WMS identified position. SKU and position scan transaction is sent to the WMS computer for updated SKU status

Customer-Returns Process or Activity Exception Handling

In a customer-returns process, there is the potential that a returned order will have an exception or problem. The design team will identify these potential exceptions and the associated resolutions. Some of these are:

1. The return bag/carton does not have the customer-order identification, but only the customer's name and address or a customer-returns slip. An employee accesses the warehouse or WMS computer customer-order file to establish a customer-order identification that is associated with the order-return information. With the information, the returns process identifies the original customer-order identification and completes the returns process activity.
2. The SKU in the customer-returns package is not on the order because the customer used an incorrect return label.
3. The customer received the wrong SKU. Customer returned a SKU and per the customer order packing slip/invoice, a SKU does not appear on the customer returned document. The correct SKU is picked and shipped to the customer or the customer receives a credit.

The wrong SKU is scanned and placed back into a position. The scan is sent to the WMS computer for update. The inventory control department is requested to complete a count for both SKU WMS identifications. Counts are updated in the WMS computer.

4. A damaged SKU at a returns process station. The SKU receives a damage, rework, or RTV disposition label, depending on company policy. The SKU is placed into a position and the scan transaction is updated in the WMS computer. If a returned SKU leaks or has sharp edges, the SKU is placed into a solid wall/bottom trash container at a returns-process station. The disposition label is placed onto the disposition document with a scan transaction sent to a WMS computer, which the inventory control department uses to ensure an accurate inventory.

5. If a warehouse has two customer-returns process activity locations, and each location is for a specific SKU, and a SKU is returned to the incorrect location. At the receiving location, the options are a) the customer-returns identification is registered as received by the company and the receiving location sends the SKU to the correct location. A normal customer-returns process is completed at the correct returns location; or b) an employee from the correct returns location is sent to the receiving location and completes the customer-returns process. After the customer has received credit, the employee with the SKU returns to the correct location and ensures that the SKU is accurately disposed and placed into a position.

6. An incorrectly disposed SKU is detected at a rework station or put-away position. An employee notifies a supervisor, who completes a correct disposition label and throws away the incorrect label. Because a SKU is part of warehouse inventory, there are required adjustments to SKU quantities, or counts are completed for SKUs. The SKU quantity and position is updated in the WMS computer.

7. A returned SKU is a substitute for what was originally shipped, such as a jewelry chain and cross with a different chain, which has a different value. An employee notifies a supervisor, who places a hold on the returns activity. The host computer is notified of the customer's action and the corrective action taken. The options are a) notify the customer via telephone/e-mail and send the SKU back to the customer or b) accept the SKU as a new SKU and scan/place the SKU into a charity or damage position and update the WMS computer.

8. A very old or aged order is returned. In such a case, the customer-order identification is not in the immediate warehouse, WMS, or host computer files. The situation requires research time; the options are a) a supervisor creates a new identification for each SKU and scans/places the SKU with the customer documentation into a position. The SKU and position status in a "nonpickable" position are updated in the WMS computer. After the correct order is obtained, the returns process is completed; or b) the SKUs are accepted as new SKUs, each with a WMS identification; the SKUs are scanned/placed into a charity or damaged hold position and the WMS computer is updated.

Rework Activities

Warehouse rework activities are created from a) returned SKUs and warehouse quality control or b) vendor delivered SKUs rejected by QA. Rework groups have similarities and differences. The similarities are that SKUs have an inventory status of "not available for sale or customer orders" and to meet company standards some SKUs will require rework labor and material expense. The differences are that vendor rework inventory is not entered into the company "inventory for sale," vendor rework labor and material expenses are reimbursed by the vendor, and customer-order returned SKUs are in the "not saleable" inventory status until a good quality and disposed SKU is transferred to a pick position and updated in the WMS computer and host computer files.

Customer-Order Return and Rework Activity

In any industry (e.g., catalog, direct market, industrial or retail distribution), customer-order SKU return and rework are warehouse activities. Return and rework volume ranges from 5% to 38% of the SKU volume that was shipped to customers. Return and rework activities are labor intensive, require a large area, handle surges, handle a wide SKU mix, and with WMS customer-order returns, there is a time delay from receipt of a returned SKU and final disposition. To have an efficient and cost-effective return process, quality SKUs are returned to a pick position and updated in the WMS and host computer files as "available for sale;" poor quality SKUs are properly disposed and updated in WMS and host computer files as "not available for sale" but in a position.

When we compare customer-order outbound operational requirements to customer-return operational requirements, the differences are that a return activity is a more complex and time-consuming activity and customer order SKU return package queues have more frequent occurrences. The features make returns and rework activities candidates for improvement.

Customer SKU Returns

A customer-order SKU return is a picked, packed, manifested, and shipped package that was returned by a customer or delivery company (i.e., was undeliverable) to a warehouse. A return package contains at least one SKU; the industry average is two to four SKUs per package. At the warehouse, the major return groups are a) unopened packages, which can be either undeliverable customer-order packages or packages for which the customer refused delivery and b) opened and returned package group.

An undeliverable or unopened return package is important. An undeliverable package means that the customer did not break the seal on the package. Unless there is shipping damage, the SKU(s) inside a package will be of good quality. In most cases, an undeliverable package will not require an employee to complete a detailed inspection. After the SKU is placed into a pick position, the WMS inventory file is updated and the SKU is designated "available for sale" in both the WMS and host computers. If the warehouse's return activity has a high SKU volume, it must be decided where to place a disposed SKU: in a normal pick position or a "fast mover" pickable position. If a SKU has been listed as "out of stock" in the WMS inventory for a short period of time, the SKU is considered "out of stock." A SKU "out of inventory" situation, however, means that an undeliverable, returned, processed, and disposed SKU reduces "out of stock" SKUs by one. With an employee spending less time processing undeliverable returned SKUs, the employee has higher productivity and the customer-returns operation needs fewer returns process stations, and additional SKUs can be scanned and transferred to pick positions and made "available for sale."

The second type of customer return is a package that was opened, resealed, and returned in a package by a customer to the warehouse. A resealed package indicates that a customer has opened or broken the package's seal. When the resealed package arrives at the warehouse, the company assumes that the customer has removed the SKU from the delivery carton, and completed a SKU test, fit, or application.

An employee determines the SKU quality of each opened, resealed, and returned package. The decision factors are:

- If a SKU is in a vendor carton, if the seal been broken or unbroken.
- If the customer has a) used a SKU, b) received a poor quality SKU, c) received a damaged SKU, d) received the SKU, or received the wrong color or size SKU.
- If a SKU was damaged during the return transport to the warehouse.
- If the SKU is a type that comes in contact with human skin or is edible, the SKU is disposed of according to warehouse policy.

The reasons customers return SKUs are:

- The wrong SKU was received because of a warehouse pick or order error.
- The order package was received late.
- The SKU was received damaged.
- The customer ordered several colors or sizes.
- The SKU does not match the catalog or television picture or stated dimensions.
- The SKU is out-of-date.
- The SKU is recalled by a vendor.
- There is an overstock situation at the company retail store.
- With a catalog/direct market warehouse a) the customer was not home, b) the package was not accepted by a customer, or c) the package was delivered to the wrong address.
- The customer did not like the SKU.

The main objective of return activity is to ensure that the returned package is received at the warehouse. After opening the returned package, the return process verifies:

- That the returned SKU agrees with the original order's packing slip.
- That the customer receives appropriate credit.
- That the returned SKU follows a route: a) quality SKUs are transferred from the returns area and scanned to a pick position, each scan transactions is sent to the WMS and host computers, and the SKU is listed as "available and saleable" in the inventory files. Depending on the warehouse layout, the pick position is either the present SKU pick position or another pick position that receives quality returned and disposed SKUs. This depends on the SKU type. For example, electrical products must be checked before they are placed into a pickable position; other SKUs require a verification of the manufacturer lot and expiry date; b) poor quality SKUs are returned to a "not available and saleable" inventory location. The returned SKU can be reworked to become a SKU available for sale. Depending on the warehouse layout, the rework area will be adjacent to the returns process area or is connected to it by in-house transport concept; c) nonquality or nonsaleable SKUs are entered into a "nonsaleable" inventory and are transferred to a temporary storage position. Scans of the SKU, quantity, and storage position identifications are sent to the WMS computer for file update; the WMS computer notifies the host computer to update inventory files. "Nonsaleable" SKUs in temporary storage positions will be sent to the vendor, outlet stores, jobbers, or employee stores; rework locations; donated to charity; thrown away because of damage, are out-of-date, or because of company policy concerning human consumable or cosmetic SKUs; are returned to the vendor; or are used for repair parts for another SKU.

SKU Rework

A rework SKU requires modification or repair to have a returned SKU become a saleable SKU that meets company standards. Rework SKU types are vendor rework and customer-order return rework.

Vendor Rework SKU

A vendor rework SKU is a SKU that, after it is unloaded at the warehouse, does not meet company standards. After the QA department has notified the receiving and purchasing departments that a SKU delivery does meet company standards, the purchasing department confirms that the vendor has given permission for the company to rework the SKU. The warehouse then performs the necessary rework activity (modification or repair) to bring the SKU up to company standards, or the SKU is held for vendor pick-up. A vendor will compensate the warehouse for the rework activity. To asssure inventory control, a vendor rework SKU is received and entered into the "nonsaleable" inventory status and deposited into a storage position. After the rework process is completed, the SKU is transferred from the rework area through the receiving and QA processes to confirm that quantity and quality are acceptable. After the QA and receiving department's approval, each SKU receivies a WMS identifier and is entered into the "saleable" inventory status and is transferred to a storage position.

Vendor Rework Activity Locations

Vendor SKU rework locations are a) on a receiving dock, b) in a predetermined area, or c) sent off-site to a vendor or a third party.

Vendor Rework on the Receiving Dock

A receiving dock rework design is used to handle small SKU quantities. If vendor rework SKUs are not entered in the inventory files (i.e., the company purchase order is not closed and the SKUs are not identified in the WMS computer) or located on the receiving dock, the SKUs are reworked on the dock. If the SKUs have been transferred to a storage position and entered in the WMS inventory as "not availabe for sale," the SKUs are removed from the storage position and transferred to an assigned receiving dock location. At the receiving dock, the SKUs are scanned from inventory. If the warehouse uses a disposable WMS identification, the SKU identification is removed and thrown in the trash. If a permanent identification is used, the identification is zero scanned and sent to the WMS computer for update. After employees receives rework instructions, the rework activity is performed in the dock area. An employee uses vendor cartons as a rework table (or a mobile table) to support rework SKUs and tools. When the rework is completed, the SKUs are handled as new vendor-delivered SKUs with an existing company purchase, and the SKUs flow through the standard receiving and QA activities. The QA activitiy assures that a SKU quality matches your company purchase order specifications. The company receiving activity assures that a vendor delivered quantity matches a company purchase order quantity, attaches a WMS identification to each master carton or pallets and closes the purchase order.

Specific Rework Area

Work activity in a specific area can be located on a receiving dock or near the return/storage area. SKUs to be reworked are transferred from the receiving dock, storage area, or return area to a specific rework area. If the SKUs have been transferred to a storage position and entered in the WMS inventory as "not availabe for sale," the SKUs are removed from a storage position and transferred to the assigned rework location. The activities that follow are the same described above.

Off-Site or Third Party Rework

In some cases, the company sends SKUs to be reworked to a vendor facility or to a third-party facility (assigned by the vendor). If the SKUs have been transferred to a storage position and entered in the WMS inventory as "not availabe for sale," the procedures for scanning and transferring the SKUs are the same as those described above. A vendor or third party completes the rework activity. When reworked SKUs are returned to the warehouse, the SKUs are received under a new purchase order and the receiving/QA departments repeat their activities. Using a third-party approach means no cost, it does not require warehouse space, and does not require warehouse labor.

Rework on Returned SKUs

A returned SKU is received and entered into "nonsaleable" inventory status and transferred to a rework area in a storage position. After the required rework (i.e., modification or repair) is completed, the SKU is entered "available and saleable" inventory status and placed into a position.

Return Considerations

The factors in improving customer-return process activity are:

1. outbound or customer-order delivery factors
2. handling return package(s) at a warehouse
3. customer-order look-up table location

Return Process

A customer return process activity is the physical activity involved in moving a returned package and SKU through the returns process area as a return to stock, return to vendor, charity or re-work SKU is placed into a WMS identified position that is updated in the WMS and host computer files.

Separate Returns Label Delivery Address for SKU Groups

If the warehouse has multiple SKU classifications in one facility and customer orders are for single line, multi-line, and combined SKU classifications, a returned package could have SKUs from several classifications or a single SKU from one classification. If an order was a combination order for several SKUs, each with a different classification, the returns label's address should be for the highest value SKU in the order. To improve the return process in a mail-order or catalog business, a warehouse should have a pre-addressed return label attached to each packing slip. To improve the return process and provide security for high value SKUs, the design options for pre-addressed return labels are one return address for all SKUs or a separate address for each SKU classification.

One Address for All SKUs

One address for all SKUs uses a single return address that is printed on each packing slip. With this design, a preprinted return address label is on each packing slip, which minimizes packing print time. All returned packages arrive at a single returns process dock location. In a high-volume warehouse with returned SKUs from all SKU classifications, this approach features:

■ High-value SKUs are handled in a general return area, which means low security, good space utilization, high return unload and open productivity, and fewer returns delivery locations.

Separate Address for Each SKU Classification

In a design in which there is a separate warehouse return address for each major SKU classification, the warehouse return address printed on each packing slip is based on the SKU classification. If the warehouse uses separate address labels, the delivery company presorts return packages by SKU classification, and delivers returned packages to separate warehouse addresses (i.e., returns docks) or in separate containers. In a high-volume warehouse in which returned packages are separated by SKU classification, high-value SKUs are handled in a separate returns area, which means higher security; there is good space utilization; high return unload and open productivity; additional returns delivery locations; and quick transport from a returns process area to a RTS or vendor position.

Returns Presorted or Not Sorted by the Delivery Company

The return process starts when the delivery company presorts returned packages by the return address label. In this design, there is a human/machine-readable preprinted return package label on each package. The label is printed on each packing slip, and the customer need only apply the label to a package being returned. When we state that the delivery company presorts the returned packages by SKU classification, this means that the company sorts the packages by using the preprinted return address label. After the delivery company completes the presort, separated, and unitized packages are delivered to the designated returns process area dock.

If there are multiple SKUs on a customer order, a printed customer return code identifies the highest value SKU in the order, size, or another criteria that was established by the warehouse. With a multiple SKU order (i.e., a mix from different SKU classes), the return code is a criteria established by the warehouse and the WMS computer. Examples of return label address criteria are:

■ An order with multiple SKUs that contained jewelry and hard goods has a jewelry return address code printed on the return label.
■ An order with multiple SKUs that contained flatwear (shirt) and GOH (garment on hanger) has a GOH return address code printed on a return label.

Returns Delivery Activity

Returns delivery activity is the process by which returned packages are transported by the delivery company terminal to the returns dock at the warehouse. The route to the warehouse dock (or to a separate customer return facility) is determined by:

1. Company practice to have returns arrive at the returns dock. The returns activity is directed by the return address label and delivery company procedure.
2. The delivery company's ability to drop a returns truck in the truckyard staging area. Late in the workday, the delivery company (or the company's truck yard) moves a truck from the staging area to a returns dock position. With most operations, FIFO truck rotation is important because customer returns is a time-critical business.
3. The return address code for SKU type and package characteristics, such as large size, small to medium size, or high value.
4. The return package device, such as BMC; four-wheel cart; cages with fork openings; returned packages floor loaded (freight company places customer return packages) on a delivery truck floor; or palletized and secured on a pallet.
5. The package shipping method and the deliver company's ability to drop empty delivery and full return trucks in the truckyard.

Returned Package and SKU Processing

The returns process activity station is where an employee removes a returned and opened package from the in-house transport. At the station, the steps are:

1. Scan the return label into a computer. A computer display screen shows the order's original SKU and quantity so that an employee can verify that the return is based on an associated customer order. If there is no label, the employee completes a manual transaction or places the return package in a problem order position.
2. Remove the returned SKU from the returned and opened package or captive tote.
3. Review the return reason and enter the reason into the warehouse computer.
4. Determine the returned SKU quality and disposition.
5. If a SKU does not have an identification, the WMS computer-controlled printer prints a disposition label, and the employee applies the label to the SKU.
6. Determine if a SKU is an "out of stock" or "back ordered" (BO) SKU.
7. Transfer the return package to the trash, into a captive tote on transport travel path, or onto a device.
8. Transfer the labeled SKU to a disposition or temporary holding design.
9. Issue credit to the customer.

Returns Carton Presliced and Opened

At a returns process station, as a returned and opened carton arrives at the station, an employee removes the carton from the in-house transport and scans the packing slip and label. After the order is displayed on a PC screen, the empty return carton is transferred into the trash. The employee completes the returns process activity as previously described above.

Returned SKU Disposed Label Identifications

In a return process design in which disposed and labeled SKUs go through presort or final sort process, the disposition on the SKU serves as an instruction for the presort or final sort. The options for the disposition of a returned SKU are:

■ "Out of stock" and "back order" SKU that has "BO" or QA inspection.
■ Return-to-stock with "RTS" blank label face or QA inspection label that is applied next to an existing SKU identification. If a label is blank, it is easily identified by a returns process employee; if a SKU with a blank label or a QA inspection label is sent to a customer, there is less customer concern.
■ Marked for "RTV."
■ Damaged, and marked with a "D."
■ Marked for outlet store ("OS") or company store ("CS").
■ Marked for retail or jobber with a "J."
■ Marked for charity with a "C."
■ Marked for rework with "RW."
■ Marked for spare parts with "SP."

From a return large, medium, or small SKU disposition classification group, the most important groups are the RTS or BO dispositions. An RTS or BO SKU disposition means that a) a SKU is in good or resale quality, and may be used to complete future customer orders, and b) the SKU is "out of stock," on "back order," or is temporarily unavailable, and the company has an existing order for the SKU. A BO SKU is transferred from a returns process area to a pick position or pick area. In the pick area, the SKU is placed into a pick position, entered into the WMS inventory, and is available to satisfy an existing order.

Packing Slip Look-Up Table Location

To ensure proper credit and to minimize invalid customer refunds, each return process station matches each returned SKU and order number to an order number and packing slip in the company's historical records. To complete the return process activity, the returns process employee is required to verify the order details. A look-up table (i.e., order detail historical records) may be located in the host or WMS computer. The factors governing the location of the look-up table are:

■ Computer capacity and ability to handle addtional activity transactions that are on-time transactions. An on-time transaction has no waiting time for a computer response and permits a returns process employee to complete a customer order return reseach that verifies a SKU is on a customer order
■ The projected peak number of return transactions.
■ The number of transactions per hour.
■ Computer security.
■ The number of returns and SKUs/lines per customer order.
■ The number of days (e.g., 30, 60, or 90) in which the warehouse will receive a given percentage (e.g., 60%, 70%, 80%, or 90%) of returns from a delivery date.
■ The average/maximum host or WMS computer minutes required to look-up order details.

- The average/maximum required time for a returns process employee to complete return transaction.
- The need to have a credit issued and returned SKU disposition as an on-line or delayed return transaction.
- Past performance of existing design.
- Computer hardware and communication cost and expense.

The selected option should be designed for the company's capabilities, and the warehouse and WMS program's features and policies. The company business, product classification, and characteristics determine the return policy, such as a) do not return medical SKUs, b) do not return SKUs with an expired date, and c) do not return perishable food SKUs.

RTS Put-Away Transaction and Inventory Tracking Considerations

A warehouse uses different criteria to ensure that the RTS activity complies with proper SKU rotation or tracking. The criteria are:

1. If a LIFO rotation is used, there is no specific requirement to track a specific SKU; the SKU is placed into a separate pick position or the pick position with mixed SKUs.
2. If a FIFO rotation is used, a) the SKU is placed into separate pick position, and the first SKU that is placed into a pick position is the first SKU picked for an order. FIFO rotation is maintained by the WMS computer, which recognizes the first RTS put-away transaction as the oldest SKU, the next put-away transaction as the next oldest SKU, and so on. To ensure maximum pick position utilization, SKUs with different WMS identifications are placed into a single pick position. With this option, a picker will need additional time to locate an ordered SKU; or b) The put-away transaction is to a pick position that contains the same SKUs. The WMS computer recognizes all SKUs with the same age. When a picker is directed to pick a SKU from a mixed pick position, the actual SKU pick is random.
3. If a SKU has a manufacturer lot number requirement, to ensure accurate SKU tracking, the put-away process is to separate pick positions (see the description of the FIFO rotation, above).

RTS Position or Identification Label Designs

At a returns process station, an employee completes the returns process and determines if a returned SKU meets company quality standards and can be returned to stock and made "available for sale." An "available for sale" SKU is moved to a pick position, entered into inventory, and is designed as "available for sale." Each SKU requires an identification to instruct an employee, who physically transfers the SKU to a pick position and send the scan transaction and SKU quantity to the WMS computer inventory files. The SKU identification or put-away instruction options are:

- Use an RTS label (with or without a pick position), return date, and other company information. An additional RTS label, which is placed onto a SKU exterior package, has human/machine readable code. The design issues are a) possible put-away employee confusion with a second code, b) customer concern with a second label on a picked SKU, c) the need to remove the RTS label after an employee places a SKU into a pick position, d) additional computer time to look up each SKU pick position and print the second lable, and c) the cost of the label print machine and labels.

▪ Use the existing SKU code with a QA inspection label. This approach uses preprinted QA inspection labels at each process station, which are placed on to each RTS SKU after SKU disposition. A QA inspection label has a human/machine readable code, with QA inspection information printed on the face, and has a colored label not the standard white label face. The design features a) minimal put-away employee confusion, b) minimal customer concern with a QA inspection label, c) minimal computer time to look-up each SKU pick position, d) no label print machine or label expense.

At a Process Returns No-Sort or Presort Activity

For a returned, disposed, and labeled SKUs, the return process station activity options are a) not to sort or have mixed SKUs in a tote or on an in-house transport or b) presort SKUs by a warehouse criteria into a tote.

SKUs with Broken Sharp Edges and a Container with a Leak

At a returns process station, an employee transfers all SKUs with broken sharp edges or containers with leaks (e.g., cracks in the side of the container) into a proper trash container (see Figure 12.2). During returns process, an employee applies a disposition label onto a paper document. At the end of the workday, or at predetermined times, a document with labels are sent to a returns process office for inventory update. The feature of this design is that when an employee completes the SKU disposition, it removes a poor quality SKU that could damage other SKUs or injure an employee and it ensures the warehouse is able to account for all SKUs.

```
RETURNS EMPLOYEE NAME          _____
RETURNS EMPLOYEE ID NUMBER     _____
DATE                           _____
```

SKU WMS IDENTIFICATION	SKU QUANTITY	CUSTOMER ORDER IDENTIFICATION	DATE

Figure 12.2   Broken or Sharp SKU Form

No Presort of Returned SKUs

If there is no presort of disposed and labeled returned SKUs, SKUs for any disposition classification are randomly transferred to a chute, carton, tote, or onto a belt conveyor. At the end of the conveyor, mixed SKUs are transferred into a tote. (Depending on warehouse policy and the WMS computer, one option is to have a SKU allocated to a license plate carton/tote.) After the tote is full, it is sent to a storage/pick area, and then transferred to a storage/pick position. At this time an individual SKU in the mixed SKU tote is updated in the inventory files, and the mixed SKUs are allocated to a storage/pick position. The mixed SKUs are now ready to complete an order.

The design features of a not-to-sort or mixed SKU are:

- No sort labor and it minimizes an employee activity
- Constant SKU flow
- Mixed SKUs in totes are randomly located in any storage/pick position
- High put-away employee productivity
- Low storage/picker productivity
- Low RTV or SKU consolidation activity
- Minimal returns process station space needed

Presort Designs

The objective of presorting returned, disposed, and labeled SKUs at a returns process station or at the end of a belt conveyor is to have an employee separate the SKUs into predetermined disposition groups. A presort increases the possibility of placing multiple SKUs in a single tote. (In a pick area, multiple SKUs in one tote minimizes employee nonproductive time to complete a final sort to a pick position.) The options for presorting are a) at a returns process station, and b) transferring loose SKUs onto a smooth-top powered belt conveyor for transport to a remote presort area.

Presort at a Return Process Station

If presorting is done at a return process station, an employee transfers a returned, disposed, and labeled SKU from a returns process table into an assigned tote. All full totes are transferred from the sort location to a final sort area or a pick area.

Mixed SKUs Transferred onto a Powered Belt Conveyor for Remote Presort

- In this design, RTS, RTV, and disposed and labeled SKUs are mixed on the conveyor and moved to a remote presort location, which can be manual or mechanical.

"Out of Stock" or "CO Back Order" Disposed SKUs

In a returns operation, "out of stock" or "back ordered" (BO) individual SKUs are placed into a presort location or tote. If a disposition label is printed at the returns process station, an employee completes the "out of stock" or BO presort activity. An employee removes the "out of stock" or BO SKU from the returns process table and transfers it into a license plate or color-coded tote/carton onto a four-wheel cart shelf. A belt conveyor or transport device moves the "out of stock" or BO SKU to a) presort area to a pick area or b) directly to a pick area. After the tote/carton arrives in a pick area, the SKU is transferred to a temporary holding pick position, and the SKU inventory is changed to "available for sale."

SKU Presort Instruction Designs

At a returns process station or at a remote presort location (other than a returns process station), SKU presort process instruction is used to identify a SKU disposition and each presort design opening, chute, carton, tote, or cart shelf. Each particular presort disposition is based on the information that appears on the disposition label. The presort options are:

- Return to stock by a) SKU inventory number first digit or alpha character, b) SKU inventory number last digit or alpha character, or c) SKU pick aisle
- Return to vendor by a) SKU inventory number first digit or alpha character, b) SKU inventory number last digit or alpha character, or c) SKU pick aisle

Mechanical Disposed Presort Design

In a mechanical presort design, an employee removes a disposed and labeled SKU from a returns process tote, carton, four-wheel cart, pallet cage, or conveyor, and inducts the SKU onto a mechanical travel path. If the SKU is not manually inducted onto the travel path, a presort travel path directs the SKU with its disposition label face up under a scanner/reader. The scanner/reader sends SKU information to the warehouse computer. The computer directs a mechanical divert device to transfer the SKU to an assigned sort location. At the end of the sort location, sorted SKUs are queued or directed into a tote. If the chute is full, an employee transfers SKUs from the chute into a tote or replaces a full tote with an empty tote. In a mechanical sort application, a tote has mixed SKUs and totes are transferred via in-house transport from the presort area to a carton AS/RS, or carousel concept for final transfer to a WMS identified storage/pick location. This design features:

- SKU double handling or sorting but minimal labor to add a SKU to an existing container
- The need for additional investment because a pick concept could not have time to complete return put-away
- Additional area
- The use of human/machine readable labels

Mechanical returned SKU sort designs are the same sort designs that are used to sort picked and labeled SKUs for a pack station. Mechanical sort designs include tilt trays, flap sorters, Bombay drops, ring sorters, and brush sorters. When compared to manual sort designs, mechanical sort designs require more space, more utilities, high volume, human/machine readable labels, and cost more.

Various Presort Locations

Presort locations provide queues for presorted SKUs and ensure that the SKUs are collected in a carton/tote for transport to the final sort activity. Presort location types are a chute; a carton/tote on a shelf on a cart, fixed shelf, or a flow rack; and a pallet or pallet cage.

Separate Returns Label Delivery Address for Product Groups

If a warehouse has multiple SKU classifications in a single facility and customer orders are for single-line, multi-line, or combined SKU classifications, there is potential that a returned package could have SKUs from several classifications or a single SKU from a single classification. To improve the return process, a company should attach a pre-addressed return shipping label to each packing slip. The warehouse could use one return address for all SKUs or a separate return address for each SKU classification. A combination order would use the return address for the highest value SKU's classification.

One Address for All SKUs

In a design in which one address is used for SKU classifications, with one address design, a pre-printed rerturn address label is attached to packing slips. Returns arrive at one dock location. In a high-volume warehouse with returns from all classifications, this design features:

- High-value SKUs are handled in a general returns area, which means low security
- Maximum space utilization
- High return package unloading productivity
- Few return delivery locations

Separate Address for Each SKU/Product Classification

In a design that uses separate return addresses for each major SKU classification, a return address is printed on each packing slip based on each SKU. The options are:

- A preprinted return address on each packing slip; orders are separated on the WMS computer by SKU classification for a print activity, which requires increased controls. One printer for a paper packing slip/delivery label means separate printers for packing slips and delivery labels to minimize print time.
- A delivery company separates or presorts returns by warehouse return address (i.e., SKU classification) and delivers packages to separate returns docks or in separate containers.

In a high-volume warehouse with returns separated by SKU classifications, the features are:

- High-value SKUs are handled in a separate returns area
- Good space utilization
- Good return unload and open productivity
- Additional warehouse returns delivery locations

Very Small Items Presort Designs

To handle returns of very small SKUs, each SKU has an inventory number and is part of a classification group. For example, in a jewelry operation, the groups are watches, earrings, finger and foot rings, chains, bracelets, pins, brochettes, packages or sets, damaged and RTV, and rework. In a returns process for very small items, the options at a disposition station are to:

- Mix SKUs in a tote and have SKUs presorted at a remote location that has SKUs pre-sorted by pick aisle/zone and transferred to a pick aisle for final sort to a pick position;
- Mix SKUs in a tote and have SKUs presorted at a remote location by pick position and then transferred to each pick position;
- Presort SKUs into separate totes by SKU groups, first inventory number, or last inventory number. Each tote is for a specific pick aisle/zone;
- Presort SKUs by group into separate totes and have the SKUs sorted into temporary pick positions, then transfer sorted SKUs to a pick position;
- Use inventory procedures that handle SKUs with a FIFO rotation, expiration date, or manufacturer lot number.

In a Remote Location Mixed SKUs in a Tote are Presorted by Pick Aisle

If a disposition station mixes SKUs in a tote, the tote is sent to a presort area for a SKU presort by pick aisle/zone. In the pick aisle, SKUs are final sorted to a pick position. At a disposition station, very small items are disposed, placed in a plastic bag, and mixed into a tote. Full totes are transferred to a remote area for mixed SKU tote presort activity in separate totes with one tote for each pick aisle/zone. In the remote presort area, there is a sort location for each pick aisle/zone.

In a design in which SKUs are presorted by pick aisle/zone design, presort employees will require presort instructions.

- At a presort area, the disposition label is scanned/read and a display screen indicates the pick aisle/zone.

After an employee removes the SKU from a carton/tote, the employee reads/scans the disposition label. The disposition label instructs the employee to transfer the SKU into a specific tote. Each tote is identified for a pick aisle/zone. The sort activity is repeated for each SKU in the carton/tote. When the pick aisle/zone tote is full, the tote is transferred to a pick aisle/zone for final sort to a pick position. This approach features:

- Increased SKU hit density and concentration per trip (SKUs in a tote are assigned to one pick aisle/zone and for a return employee stop or SKU transfer to a position, increases potential for multiple SKUs in a tote for one position within an aisle/zone) in a final sort activity;
- Minimized employee walking distance and time between pick positions;
- Minimized transport costs;
- Reduced confusion.

In a Remote Area Mix SKUs in a Tote are Presorted by Pick Position

If a disposition station mixes SKUs in a tote, the tote is sent to a presort area. When the presort activity is complete, each SKU is transferred to pick position. At each returns process station, an employee places disposed SKUs as mixed jewelry SKUs into one tote. Full totes are transferred to a remote area. SKUs are presorted by SKU and transferred to a tote that is identified with a pick position. Presort instruction options are:

- At a disposition station, the disposition system interfaces with the WMS computer, and the SKU pick position is printed onto each disposition label;
- At a presort area, disposition labels are scanned/read and a display screen indicates the pick position.

The remainder of the activity is the same as described above.

Depending on company practice and the WMS computer, the SKU presort position is a pickable position. This means that SKUs are scanned (and updated in the WMS computer), transferred to a presort position, and are available for customer orders. The features of this design are:

- It requires a large number of presort locations and a large area (in square feet).
- It increases SKU hit density and hit concentration per trip.
- It minimizes employee walking distance and time between two pick locations.
- It minimizes transport costs.
- Presorted SKUs are in a pick location.
- It reduces confusion.

Disposition Station to Presort Small SKUs by Pick Aisle/Zone

In this design, each disposition station has a tote for each pick aisle/zone. Partial or full totes with SKUs are sent to each pick aisle/zone. Presort instruction options are: a) to have the returns disposition system interface with the WMS computer at a disposition station and to have a pick aisle/zone printed on each SKU disposition label; or b) to have the SKU disposition label scanned/read, a display screen at the presort area indicates the pick aisle/zone, and an employee transfers the SKU to the proper tote.

In this design, a final sort employee removes a SKU from a tote. The employee reads/scans the disposition label, which instructs the employee to transfer the SKU to a specific pick position. The sort activity is repeated for each SKU in a tote. This presort activity has a tote warehouse identifier for each SKU in the tote as part of the final sort instruction. This allows the employee to remain in one aisle. The features of this approach are:

- It increases SKU hit density and hit concentration in final sort activity because all the SKUs in a tote are assigned to a pick position in one aisle.
- Presorting by pick aisle minimizes employee walking distance and time between two pick locations; presorting by pick zone reduces employee walking distance and time between two pick locations.
- SKUs are final sorted to a pick position.
- It reduces confusion.

Presorting by Very Small Item Groups into Totes

If a disposition station presorts very small SKUs by group into totes, full totes are sent to a remote sort area. In the sort area, an employee presorts SKUs from the tote temporary pick positions and transfers the SKUs into final sort totes or pick positions.

Full totes are transferred from a disposition station to a specific warehouse location in a pick aisle or specific pick aisle. In an aisle, and after a presort employee removes a SKU from a tote, the employee scans/reads the disposition label. If the SKU (scanned to a pickable position) has been presorted to a temporary pick position, an employee scans/reads the disposition label (a display screen instructs the employee) and transfers the SKU into a temporary pick position. If the SKU is new, or has not been presorted to a temporary pick position, and after an employee scans/reads the disposition label, a display screen instructs the employee to transfer the SKU into a vacant temporary pick position. The sort activity is repeated for each SKU in a disposition tote. If the temporary pick position tote is full and the presorted SKU quantity will not fit into the position, the tote is transferred to a permanent pick position in a pick aisle. At a predetermined time, the tote is transferred to the permament pick position; if the SKU quantity does not fit into the permanent pick position, the tote is transferred to another pick position in the pick aisle/zone. Tote transfer to a permament pick position or transfer to an overflow (i.e., ready reserve position) is the final sort to a pick position. In a remote area (or temporary pick position) during a presort activity, the presort position is recorded in the WMS computer as the pick position for a SKU. Depending on company policy, the temporary presort position can be a pick location. During presort, and depending on the order and the WMS computer, this means that the SKU is available for an order.

The features of this design are:

- There is a tote for each SKU group at each disposition station.
- There will be some additional returns disposition employee activity.
- This design increases SKU hit density and hit concentration per final SKU sort trip.
- The design minimizes employee walking distance and time between two pick positions.
- The design minimizes transport costs.
- Presorted SKUs are in a pick position.
- The design reduces confusion.

Return to Stock Presort Locations

After the presort process, RTS SKU sort options are to transfer a) a SKU final sort to a SKU present pick location, b) a SKU sort to a temporary sort location that has pickable status, or c) a tote of mixed SKUs that are scanned and transferred to a pick position.

Return Stock Final Sort to a Pick Position

In this design, returned, disposed, and labeled RTS SKUs are sorted to a pick position. SKUs in presort totes, cartons, carts, or pallets are moved from a presort area to a specific pick aisle. In the pick aisle, RTS SKUs are transferred to a pick position. The inventory quantity is updated in the WMS computer inventory file; the SKU is available for sale or ready for a customer order. The final SKU sort activity, direct from a carrier to the pick position design requires:

- Sufficient mobile equipment and totes, cartons, carts, or pallets to handle the number of (i.e., volume) returned SKUs
- A sufficient SKU or carton, tote, cart, or pallet queue area in a returns process area or pick area
- Transport to move SKUs and totes
- An RTS SKU sort instruction format, which can be paper document or RF device
- The ability to handle mixed SKUs *en masse* for one aisle in a tote, carton, cart, or pallet
- That a picker remove the disposition labels during order pick activity

After an employee fills a presort tote, the tote is transferred to a pick area. In the pick area, an employee places the tote onto a four-wheel cart shelf, removes a SKU from the tote, or dumps the tote's SKUs onto a cart shelf. After reading the SKU RTS label or scanning the SKU bar code label/RF tag, the employee is directed to an assigned pick position. Arriving at the pick position, the employee transfers the SKU to the position and completes a scan transaction to update the WMS inventory. At an aisle position, the employee makes a visual check to determine other same SKUs in a tote and repeats the put-away activity. If the next SKU is a new SKU, the location is random but is in the same aisle. Features are additional time needed to complete a SKU RTS transaction, interfaces with a document or paperless RTS instruction, and requires less building area and equipment.

RTS Presort to a Temporary Pickable Position

RTS SKU sort to a separate area or to a temporary holding position is performed for medium, small, or very small SKUs. A temporary holding position is a pick position within a pick area or specific aisles in a pick area. In a temporary pick aisle, RTS SKUs are transferred from a presort tote, carton, or cart shelf to a temporary pick position. After the SKU is transferred to a pick position, the inventory quantity is communicated to the WMS computer and updated in the inventory file. The SKU is now available for a customer order. After a predetermined time period or when a temporary holding position is full, sorted SKUs are transferred to a pick position or new pick aisle position. The features of this design are:

- Separate temporary SKU sort locations and aisles
- During sort activity, the WMS computer or an employee assigns a new SKU to a position in a temporary sort area/aisle
- Sufficient SKU position number to handle the RTS SKU quantity
- After a temporary sort position is full, at predetermined times, or as customer orders deplete a pick position, SKUs are transferred from a temporary SKU sort position to the pick position
- Mobile equipment and totes to handle RTS SKU number and volume
- Bar code/RF tag identification on each SKU and position and a RF device with a communication network

Features are employee SKU double handling, additional building space for a sort area, additional SKU sort equipment needed, WMS computer bar code/RF tag identification for each SKU, final sort location and RF device, less congestion in pick aisles, SKU queue area, improved inventory control by minimizing SKU number or inventory quantity, and when compared to other RTS designs, faster SKU sort process due to fewer aisles.

RTV and Other Disposed, Presorted SKU Locations

After the presort process, RTV and other disposed SKU are transferred to a storage location. Rework or spare part SKUs are sent to a storage or rework area. Returned SKUs, classified as damaged or charity, are handled according to company policy, and transferred to a storage location.

Transfer Mixed RTV SKUs in Tote to a Storage or Pick Position

Tote transfer with mixed SKUs to a storage/pick position is used for medium or small SKUs. When a mixed tote design is used for RTS SKUs, the tote is transferred to a pick position. When this design is used for RTV SKUs, the tote is transferred to a storage position. During the presort process, as SKUs are transferred into a tote, each tote identification and SKU bar code label/RF tag is scanned/read and sent to the WMS computer for inventory update. In this design, the WMS computer knows each SKU in a mixed SKU identified tote. As an employee transports a mixed SKU tote through a pick/storage area aisle, the employee:

1. Locates an open pick position or WMS computer-assigned SKU pick/storage position
2. Reads the pick/storage position number
3. Scans the pick/storage position label with an RF device
4. RF scans the tote warehouse label
5. Transfers the tote into the pick/storage position

Depending on how the WMS program is configured, the inventory file update transaction is an on-line or delayed communication to the WMS computer. The design features are:

■ SKU quick return a pickable location
■ Minimizes aisle congestion
■ High put-away employee productivity
■ Minimal double handling
■ Low picker productivity when looking for a particular SKU in a tote

In the RTV SKU final sort design, an employee transfers an RTV SKU from a presort tote to a storage location. RTV final sort options are a) each vendor SKU is returned to a fixed storage position or b) vendor SKUs are mixed in a tote in a fixed position.

Presorted RTV SKUs to a Single Final Sort Position

A RTV SKU returned or transferred to a fixed SKU storage position means that there is one position for each RTV SKU. A RTV SKU sort to a fixed SKU position has one tote for one vendor. Presorted and mixed SKUs tote, an employee removes a SKU from a tote in a vendor return aisle, and scans a SKU bar code/RF tag. The RF device shows a SKU position or a first RTV SKU to enter a storage area has a computer suggest or an employee select a position for a first RTV SKU. At a position, the vendor SKU is transferred to a fixed storage position and the SKU bar code/RF tag and position bar code are scanned/read into the WMS computer files. For future RTV SKUs, the position becomes the position for additional RTV SKUs. An employee travels through the aisle and completes all SKU sorts. The design features are:

- Each SKU has a position
- Large final sort area
- Low put-away employee productivity
- Vendor return SKU consolidation is easier and quicker
- Accurate inventory

Vendor Mixed SKUs in a Tote Final Sorted to a Position

In this design, an employee transfers a tote with return vendor mixed SKUs to a fixed storage position. The employee travels through an aisle with presorted return vendor mixed SKUs in a tote. As the employee transfers the tote to a storage position, and per a WMS program, a final sort employee completes position and tote scan transactions, travels through an aisle, and completes other warehouse tote transfer transactions to positions. Scan transactions are communicated to the WMS computer. The design features are:

- Minimal number of positions
- Smaller final sort area
- Improved put-away employee productivity
- Slower and more difficult SKU consolidation for a vendor shipment
- Potential SKU inventory control problems

Manual Final RTS SKU Sort Design to a SKU Fixed Position

In this design, an employee transports a mixed SKU tote through pick aisles. As the employee travels in the aisle, the employee picks up a SKU, reads/scans the RTS label, travels to a pick position, transfers the SKU into a pick position, and scans the pick position label. The scan transactions are sent to the WMS computer to update the inventory files. This design is used for a RTS SKU activity in a manual pick operation.

Mechanical Final RTS SKU Sort Design and SKU in a Fixed Position

In a mechanical carousel or carton AS/RS design, a presorted SKU is placed into a fixed position. An RTS SKU transfer to a pick position is completed at a mechanical transfer station. At the transfer station, a picker/sorter has a mixed SKU tote. As the employee removes an RTS SKU from the tote, the employee scans the SKU number into a control panel. The pick computer directs the mechanical pick to withdraw an assigned tote from a storage position and transport it to a transfer station. After the tote arrives at the transfer station (P/D), an employee transfers a SKU into a tote/carton and completes scan transactions. The scan transactions are sent to the WMS computer inventory files. With an AS/RS or automated carousel design, the storage position is communicated by the warehouse computer to the WMS computer. Depending on the WMS computer, file updating is completed on-line or is a delayed communication. The warehouse computer directs the mechanical design to return the warehouse tote/carton to an assigned storage location.

Manual Pick Design and Mixed SKU Tote in a Pick Position

In a manual pick design in which a mixed SKU tote is transferred to a pick position, an employee transports a mixed SKU tote through pick aisles. As the employee travels in a pick aisle, the employee:

1. Locates an open tote position or a position assigned by the warehouse or WMS computer
2. Reads/scans the pick position number
3. Scans the tote label
4. Transfers a mixed SKU tote into the pick position

The WMS computer file update is on-line or is delayed communication. The design features are:

- Slower SKU return to a pick position
- Medium picker productivity because of mixed SKUs in a tote
- Slow to consolidate SKUs for RTV or transfer to an outlet store
- Easier to complete a fiscal inventory

Mechanical Pick Design Mixed SKU Tote in a Pick Position

In a carton AS/RS or carousel (mechanical) pick design with a mixed SKU tote transfer to a pick position design has a pick employee at a (P/D) transfer station, to transfer mixed SKUs in a warehouse tote. During a RTS activity, an employee scans a tote bar code and storage design tray identification. A mechanical pick design warehouse computer directs a mechanical design to transport an empty tray to a transfer position. After a mechanical design tray stops at a transfer station, an employee transfers a mixed SKU tote on a warehouse design tray. A mechanical pick design returns a mixed SKU tote on a tray to a warehouse computer assigned storage location. With a carousel design, an employee completes a storage position WMS scan transaction. Per the WMS program, a warehouse design storage position communication to a WMS program file update is on-line or delayed communication to a WMS program. The design features are:

1. Faster SKU return to a pick position
2. To pick SKUs, low picker productivity
3. Difficult and time consuming to consolidate SKUs for RTV or transfer to an outlet store
4. Difficult to complete a fiscal inventory.

Presort/Final Sort Position Instruction Designs

Presort or final sort instruction directs an employee to remove a SKU from a tote, conveyor surface, or cart shelf and transfer a SKU into predetermined presort or final sort position. To have a complete instruction, an employee sort instruction appears on a returns disposition SKU label and on a sort position. Presort or final sort instruction designs are a) human readable digits, alpha characters, or a combination with a machine readable section on a SKU disposition label and sort position, or b) machine readable or RF device and a bar code label/RF tag with a human readable section on a SKU and sort position that is shown on a RF display screen.

Manual Design with a RF Device for Final Sort

A manual design that uses a RF device in a returns final sort design has a final sort employee transfer a return tote for a particular pick aisle to cart shelves. Each tote has a human readable aisle number or pick area on a tote face. A tote with a pick aisle lowest number is dumped onto a cart top shelf. A tote has mixed presorted SKUs that have pick positions in an aisle. Tote dumping activity spreads mixed presorted SKUs over a shelf and has SKUs easily seen by a final sort employee. After a tote is empty, a final sort employee returns an empty tote to a cart shelf. After a final employee picks up a SKU, an employee reads or scans a SKU WMS bar code label/RF tag. A RF device shows a SKU pick position in a pick aisle. An employee pushes a cart to an assigned pick location, an employee scans a pick position and final sorts a SKU into a pick position or RTV location. A final sort activity is repeated for each presorted SKU on a cart shelf. Per the WMS program, a WMS program file update is on-line or delayed communication to the WMS program.

Mechanical Design that Uses a RF Device for Final Sort

In a mechanical design that uses a RF device, an employee transfers a presort SKU tote onto a mechanical transfer (P/D) location. At the transfer location, the tote's SKUs are dumped onto a shelf. The SKUs are spread over a shelf and each identified SKU easily seen by a final sort employee. An employee scans the SKU bar-code label and the warehouse computer activates a carton AS/RS or carousel design to move the tote/carton/tray to a transfer location. As the tote/carton/tray arrives at the transfer station, a scanner/reader reads the tote bar code and sends the data to the warehouse computer. The computer activates the transfer station display screen. The screen shows the SKU number, and a final sort employee checks to make sure that the display screen number matches the SKU number. With a proper match, the employee final sorts the SKU to the tote/carton/tray by scanning/reading the SKU bar code/RF tag and the tote bar code/RF label. The display screen shows the accurate SKU transfer completion and the scanner/reader transfers data (delayed or on-line) to the WMS computer. If the SKU is not the correct SKU, the display screen shows a problem and the employee picks the correct SKU.

Age RTS and RTV Temporary Hold Positions

An age RTS and RTV temporary hold position design is designed to ensure that active SKUs have positions in the warehouse RTS/RTV temporary hold area. It is common that the majority of returned packages are received 90 to 120 days after delivery. The company historical identified SKU sale/delivery date and customer-return date allows for a more precise determination of when the company (or each major SKU group) will receive the majority of returned SKUs.

Age RTS and RTV temporary hold position options are:

- A manual approach, which has a temporary location sort employee write a sort date onto a document on a tote or carton side
- A RTS or RTV label on each SKU; an employee removes the label from the SKU and places a label onto the tote/carton side

The design features are:

- It ages an RTS and RTV inventory
- It ensures that only active SKUs are in tempoary sort and hold positions
- It improves space utilization
- It improves SKU put-away concentration and density, and it improves employee put-away productivity

Temporary Hold Position Full RTS or RTV Tote/Carton Handling

The objective of a temporary hold position full SKU RTS/RTV tote/carton handling is to have an employee transfer each full RTS/RTV tote/carton from a temporary sort/hold position to a storage position. The handling activity involves having an employee determine if a SKU RTS/RTV tote/carton is full, and to identify the SKU quantity per tote/carton. After the employee scans the tote/carton identification and SKU quantity per tote/carton, the tote/carton is transferred to a storage position. The tote/carton identification, SKU quantity, and new position is updated in the WMS computer files. The design features are: a) it improves space utilization, b) it creates a small temporary hold area, c) it minimizes consolidation pick activity, and d) it improves put-away employee productivity.

Return-to-Vendor (RTV) Consolidation Activity

RTV activity is a vendor SKU consolidation pick, pack, and ship activity for a vendor-approved SKU shipment from the facility to the vendor's facility. After the vendor has given permission to return a SKU, the employees consolidate the loose SKUs into one carton on a warehouse device. After the consolidation activity, an employee lists the SKU quantity in each carton and seals the cartons. When the sealed cartons are ready for shipment to the vendor, the carton identifications are scanned. The scan transactions and SKU quantities are sent to the WMS computer for update. A RTV consolidation activity is determined by a) how SKUs are inventoried in a storage position and b) whether a SKU position is a manual or mechanical design. RTV consolidation designs are:

- In a manual storage design that uses a human-readable consolidation instruction format, an employee travels through aisles and consolidates SKUs into a tote/carton.
- A mixed vendor SKU tote delivered to a sort station. SKUs are sorted into separate cartons.

Consolidation/Reverse SKU Pick from a Fixed Position

In a consolidation or reverse SKU pick from a fixed pick/storage position, an employee or machine travels to each pick/storage position that has a SKU assigned to it. At each appropriate pick/storage position, an employee transfers a tote, carton, or SKU quantity from the position to a carton on a vehicle or on-board carrying device. All cartons are transferred onto a warehouse device for vendor shipment preparation. An employee scans the SKU and carton and enters the SKU quantity into a scanner/reader. The data is sent to the WMS computer (on-line or delayed), which updates inventory files and position status. The features are:

- During an RTS process, an employee has increased walking distance and time
- It minimizes pick position space or cube utilization
- It improves inventory control and slow-moving SKU allocation in a pick area
- In RTV or final disposition activity, it requires minimal employee walking distance and time because SKUs are in a fixed pick/storage position

Consolidation/Reverse SKU Pick from a Mixed SKU Tote

In a reverse consolidation or reverse SKU pick from a mixed SKU tote in randomly located pick/storage positions, an employee or machine travels to every pick/storage position that has a SKU assigned to it. In this design, a SKU and its quantity in a mixed SKU tote is assigned to each position. At each appropriate pick/storage position, the employee locates a vendor-approved SKU from the mix, and transfers a SKU quantity from the position to a vehicle or on-board carrying device. After transferring the assigned SKU from a mixed SKU tote, the tote is returned to the pick/storage position. Depending on the WMS computer, the inventory transfer transaction is an on-line or delayed transaction. The features are:

- During a RTS process, an employee has a short walking distance and time because a mixed SKU tote was placed in the pick/storage position
- The potential to maximize a pick position space or cube utilization
- Potential pick errors
- In RTV or final disposition activity, it requires maximum employee walking distance and time because SKUs are in more pick or storage positions.

Chapter 13

Across-the-Dock, Prepack, Value-Added, Noncustomer Bonded Storage/Pick, Advance Customer Orders, and Inventory Control Activities

Introduction

This chapter looks at several activities that company management could consider for implementation into a supply chain's logistics strategy or in a warehouse operation. These strategies or activities are across-the-dock operation, prepack SKU activity, value-added activity, advance customer orders, noncustomer-order activity, bonded SKU activity, and inventory control. Each section below defines the activity and looks at what is required from a material handing design and WMS program.

Across-the-Dock Operation

An across-the-dock warehouse is a supply chain logistics strategy design that requires minimal SKU storage or customer-order pick activities. An across-the-dock warehouse moves individual customer orders or SKUs directly from a receiving dock, via a warehouse transport concept and sort area, and into an order shipping staging area or directly onto a delivery vehicle. In a manual across-the-dock design, there is a WMS identification on the exterior of each SKU. An employee scans/reads each identification and transfers the SKU to a staging area or delivery truck. Because a manual across-the-dock design is not conveyor supported to assure an efficient and cost effective operation, a SKU flow from a receiving area to a pack/ship area, scan, sort and unitize/direct load activities are well organized and occur in the proper sequence. In a mechanical across-the-dock warehouse, the preferred characteristics are a powered conveyor sort design, human-/machine-readable codes on the exteriors of SKUs surface (which permits an employee to scan/read the delivery address), and computer-controlled divert devices on the sort travel path. In an across-the-dock operation, SKUs flow through a value-added activity prior to a sort activity, in which an employee or a machine enhances the SKU value to the customer (e.g., a retail price ticket on each retail SKU).

Across-the-Dock Warehouse Operation Objectives

The objectives of an across-the-dock operation are to a) reduce the number of days required for SKUs to flow from a vendor, to a warehouse as SKUs, and through a warehouse onto the company or customer retail sales floor and b) lower warehouse costs by reducing inventory carrying costs and SKUs handling costs.

Drop Point

At the receiving dock staging area, the SKU identification is scanned, and the SKU is transferred to a transport and sort concept. After vendor-delivered SKUs are unloaded/received at across-the-dock operation, each SKU receives (or already received from the vendor) a WMS identification before being transferred to a customer order shipping staging location. In most across-the-dock operations, a master carton/pallet is either handled by a manually controlled powered transport vehicle or a forklift truck, or is transferred to a powered conveyor, powered pallet AGV (automatic guided vehicle), tow-line, or overhead tow-veyor (powered chain with pendant to pull a 4-wheel vehicle) for a transport/transfer to the sort design.

In a transport design that uses a forklift truck, the SKU/customer-order drop point/staging area is indicated on the truck's scanner/tag reader. Each drop point has a WMS identification. As the truck arrives at each drop point, the driver scans/reads the SKU and drop-point identifications. The scan transactions are sent to the WMS computer to update the inventory files. The SKU is then placed into a delivery vehicle or a dock staging area.

If a SKU is placed onto a powered transport and sort design, again a scanner/reader reads the drop point, and the scan is sent to the warehouse computer. As the SKU moves within transport and sort design, the warehouse computer (in conjunction with the warehouse's tracking design) ensures that the SKU is diverted from the transport to the drop point. The WMS computer accepts the divert transaction as completed transfer transaction, or an employee (or a fixed-position scanner/reader) completes the SKU identification scan transaction at the drop point.

Warehouse Operation Across-the-Dock Formats and SKU Flow Design

When an across-the-dock SKU flow design is being considered for a warehouse, there are three possible across-the-dock SKU flow patterns: manufacturing, distribution center, and terminal.*

---

* See according J. Eric Peters article in the WERC Sheet Sept. 1995.

SKU Identification Characteristics and Classifications

SKU identifications' characteristics are:

- Unsorted, which means that a pallet contains SKUs for several customer orders.
- Sorted, which means that a pallet contains SKUs for a single order.
- Unlabeled, which means that the SKU has no order identification/code. This means that the SKU is sent to any customer.
- Labeled, which means that the SKU has an order identification code. This means that the SKU is assigned to a specific order.

Across-the-dock classifications are:

1. Unsorted and unlabeled SKUs are considered vendor SKUs that have been ordered by several customers. The SKUs do not have order identification labels on the exterior of the master carton. Unsorted and unlabeled SKUs are unloaded from the vendor's delivery truck; the quantity is verified; company labor is required to label each SKU, depending on the order requirement; they are separated/sorted by customer name; and mixed with other ordered SKUs. The SKUs are held in an assigned holding area or are loaded directly onto a delivery truck.
2. Unsorted and labeled SKUs have been ordered by several customers; each SKU has an order address label on its exterior. SKUs are sorted by order number. After sorting, the SKUs are palletized with other SKUs that are going to the same customer or loaded onto a delivery truck.
3. Sorted and labeled SKUs are preferred for an across-the-dock operation. Per a customer order SKU quantity, SKUs are presorted by the vendor by customer order identification. The order identification is on each SKU's exterior. Sorted and labeled SKUs are secured onto a pallet/slip sheet; each pallet is identified with an order code, name, number, or address. At the warehouse, SKUs are unloaded from the delivery truck, verified, and placed onto a ship staging area or are loaded directly onto a delivery truck. An option for unloading is to off-load ordered SKUs or master cartons from the vendor's delivery truck onto a powered conveyor for transport to a ship staging area or delivery truck.

Requirements

To maximize the WMS program's return on investment, and provide the best customer service, the company develops several elements for a across-the-dock strategy. These ensure:

- Company vendors meet strict SKU quality and quantity standards and have a WMS identification
- Good information paper or data flow system
- Excellent SKU flow pattern through the facility
- Good warehouse layout at receiving and ship docks
- Required customer order delivery vehicle at a ship dock
- Accurate and on-time customer orders

When a company develops an across-the-dock operation with a WMS program, most applications are combined with a conventional (i.e., store-and-hold) distribution operation. A store-and-hold inventory flow pattern, combined with an across-the-dock SKU flow design, provides a) an increased return on investment, b) maximum service to customers, c) requires vendors and customers to increase their involvement, and d) have a WMS program in the logistics strategy. The areas of vendor and customer involvement are:

- Vendors provide the correct SKUs, and ensure high quality and exact quantities
- Smaller SKU quantity per individual customer order
- Vendors ensure that the SKU has proper order identification (used by all segments in the logistics strategy) and proper price tickets
- Vendors ensure that SKUs are conveyable

Who Is Involved

As the company becomes involved in an across-the-dock program, the distribution operation establishes a good communication network and becomes a communications center coordinating the purchasing department; material handling equipment vendors; accounting, inventory control, and quality control departments; IT department; transportation department; warehouse and WMS program team members; and customers. After the distribution company decides to undertake an across-the-dock operation, the options are a) a pass-through strategy, which handles pallets or master cartons, or b) to handle large quantities of small-item SKUs, which are broken down into single items or master cartons at an across-the-dock facility. These individual items are price ticketed and distributed into smaller quantities to complete customer orders.

In a master-carton/pallet across-the-dock design, the purchasing department is required to send a vendor the total SKU quantity required for the company sales program. If the operation has multiple facilities, a purchase order can be used for the entire sales program, but the purchase order is separated into required SKU quantities (i.e., subtotals) for each facility. Each regional distribution or across-the-dock facility becomes a terminal segment in the company's logistics strategy. Each regional facility is responsible for receiving, separating, or sorting SKUs by a quantity that accommodates each region's customer orders.

Vendor Responsibility

In an across-the-dock operation, the vendor's responsibilities are to provide quality pieces that a) are in accord with the purchase order, b) are in the correct quantities, and c) have an order or SKU identification on the exterior (in an appropriate location) of each SKU. The last factor minimizes the SKU flow time through the operation and company distribution expenses, but slightly increases the cost of goods sold. One option would be to have the vendor provide SKUs with a description on the exterior of each SKU but without a SKU or order identification. This option requires a company employee at the receiving dock to apply a SKU or order identification to each SKU. The option slightly increases SKU flow time through the operation; label cost would be a distribution expense, and would be reflected in the cost of goods.

SKU/Order Identification

The SKU/order identification is a key component in an efficient and cost-effective across-the-dock operation. SKU/order identification activity uses a human-/machine-readable code on the exterior of each SKU. To obtain optimum results from the transport and sort design, the factors governing SKU or customer order identifications are that they:

1. Are placed in each appropriate location on each SKU. The location allows each reader, bar code, RF tag, or employee in the company to read each identification.
2. Unique for each customer, number, or address.
3. Can be read at each segment, i.e., vendors, company facilities, freight company terminals, and customer locations. The preferred code is machine printed and human/machine readable.

As an ordered SKU travels through a conveyor sort and transport design, the master carton/pallet is transported past an automatic scanner/reader. The scanner/reader scans/reads the bar code label/RF tag signal and sends the information about the order identification to the warehouse computer for receiving department recording keeping and receipt preparation. A conveyor computer and conveyor (sort) tracking device requires an order identification for proper carton sort. As the SKU travels on the travel path, the warehouse computer (or a tracking device) tracks the master carton. When the carton arrives at an assigned divert location, a divert device transfers the carton onto an order load conveyor travel path. It is understood that a hand-held scanner/reader and a nonconveyable transport and sort design will handle nonconveyable master cartons.

Receiving and Ship Dock Areas

In an across-the-dock operation, receiving and ship functions and dock areas are more important than storage/pick functions and areas. Receiving and ship functions and areas include the truck yard and vendor/customer order delivery truck control. The emphasis on SKU flow through the facility, a) increases the number of necessary receiving and ship docks/doors; b) requires larger receiving and ship dock staging areas; and c) a sufficient number of well-designed SKU travel paths (from a receiving dock area, through the sort design, to a ship dock area).

Across-the-Dock Ordered SKU Unload and Load Activities

The flow pattern for ordered SKUs involves a direct load of SKUs onto a delivery truck. This requires the largest number of docks but a smaller building due to minimal receiving and ship dock staging areas. The flow pattern for temporary hold-and-stage SKUs concept requires fewest docks but a large building, because the receiving and ship dock staging areas are large. The warehouse transports ordered SKUs from a receiving dock area, sorts the SKUs in a correct customer order location, and moves the SKUs to a staging area or directly onto a truck.

If the receiving department handles master cartons or pallets, the objective is to unload a vendor delivery vehicle on schedule and verify that a) the delivered SKU matches the purchase order quantity, b) the SKU quantity for each master-carton/pallet is correct and c) the SKUs meet company order identification standards.

Warehouse Mechanical Unload/Load Designs

Mechanical unload/load designs use gravity, electric- or fuel-powered warehouse vehicles, or conveyor surfaces to move SKUs to a delivery truck or staging area. Mechanical designs include an electric pallet truck/forklift truck with a set of forks or a slip sheet attachment and nonpowered and powered SKU conveyor transport and sort designs.

SKU Change

Some companies that use an across-the-dock operation realize a SKU, as a SKU flows through the operation, per a customer order SKU quantity that does not match a carton or pallet SKU quantity a SKU may change its physical characteristics. If a master carton/pallet is used, the SKU identification options are:

- No change, SKU handled as a full master carton or pallet.
- Have SKUs removed from a WMS identified master carton and sent as individual SKUs to customers that require a pick, sort, and pack operation.
- Have individual or multiple master cartons removed/WMS moved from a WMS identified pallet and sent as WMS identified master cartons to customer's SKU.

In most single-item across-the-dock operations, items are received at the warehouse in master cartons or as a large SKU quantity on a pallet, and are sent as individual or multiple SKUs to customers, which ensures proper accounting.

Small-Item Across-the-Dock Operation: Customer Order and Shipping

As small SKUs flow through an across-the-dock sort area that is based on a customer order quantity, per a customer order the SKU quantity changes from a full master carton to small SKUs quantity (less than a master carton) that is sorted (collected) per each customer order. With a customer order sort and pack small SKU across-the-dock operation, the operation a) provides a secure container for the wide SKU mix (e.g., a cardboard carton that could be disposed of by a customer or a reusable plastic-ship container that requires a customer return concept); b) has a low cost container; and c) provides a container that is handled by the across-the-dock facility and customer facility employees.

Small-Item Across-the-Dock Operation

Small item designs for an across-the-dock operation can be manual, mechanical, or automated. If the operation handles single-items SKUs that are received in master cartons or pallets, the options are to have the SKUs separated by customer order location or per customer order. Each SKU receives a price ticket and re-pack with other SKUs by an employee and sent to a customer order location. A price ticket operation has open, ticket sort, and pack activities and area. The price ticket process is considered an across-the-dock valued process with activities that are sequentially located between receiving and ship areas.

Small-Item Sort Designs

Small-item across-the-dock sort design ensures from a SKU mix group for several customer orders that per a customer order, a SKU quantity is allocated to a customer pack station or lane. At a pack station/lane, mixed SKUs for one customer order are consolidated and packed in a delivery carton for transfer to a transport and sort design. The transport and sort design moves the customer order carton to an order staging area or directly into a delivery truck.

Manual Small-Item Sort Designs

In a manual sort design, an employee performs a variety of activities, including sorting from storage positions, bulk-picked SKU movement through a sort area, and completed order transfer to a take-away travel path. Manual small-item across-the-dock sort designs are:

- SKUs occupy a shelf or rack position.
- The order sort location is a shelf or rack position.

These designs have similar design parameters and operational characteristics.

Warehouse Operation Mechanical Small-Item Sort Designs

The features of mechanical small-item sort designs are:

- Each ordered small-item SKU is delivered *en masse* to an encoding device/station.
- A human-/machine-readable identification must be placed on the exterior of each SKU.
- Along a sort conveyor travel path, the sort stations have an arithmetic progression from a low number to a high number. Each order sort location is a slide, captive container, or shipping container.
- The design uses completed order shipping container take-away transport system.
- An empty ship container replacement and discreet identification label print system is required.

Mechanical across-the-dock small-item sort designs are Bombay drop, flap sorter, and tilt tray. In a mechanical sort design ordered SKUs, which have been labeled, are delivered *en masse* to an induction (encode) station. At the induction station, an employee or mechanical belt conveyor places a SKU onto a carrying surface, which transfers the SKU to a divert location. A divert location is a slide, captive container, or shipping carton. Prior to the carrying surface's return to the induction station, the sort design prepares the carrying surface to accept another SKU.

Master-Carton Sort Designs

Master-carton carton sort designs can be manual or mechanical. Mechanical designs include active sort designs, passive sort designs, and a combination of active and passive designs. When the carton sort activity is a batch mode, customer cartons are considered mixed customer order cartons. Each carton with a SKU or customer order identification is unloaded from a vendor delivery truck onto a transport/sort conveyor. The SKU or customer order identified cartons travel past or under an employee or scanner/reader. With a manual sort design, an employee reads the order code/tag and transfers the carton from the conveyor to a pallet or cart. In a mechanical sort design, scanner/reader scans/reads the order identification and sends the identification to the warehouse computer. The warehouse computer and tracking device ensure that the carton arrives on a sort conveyor at the assigned divert or sort location. At the divert or sort location, a divert device transfers the carton onto a divert spur. A divert spur is a conveyor for transporting cartons to an assigned dock staging area, unitize station, or directly into a delivery truck.

On-line or delayed order identifications are sent from a hand-held or mechanical scanner to the warehouse computer. The computer prepares an order manifest list, and sends the order identification to the WMS computer, which verifies that the order was shipped from the facility.

Manual across-the-dock carton sort designs use one of our conveyor designs: a single conveyor, double-stacked conveyors, a recirculation conveyor, or an apron conveyor.

Sort Surfaces or Conveyor Travel Paths

An across-the-dock sort design can use different travel path options: roller conveyor, smooth-top belt, slat tray, tilt tray, and moving belt conveyor. The conveyor surface/travel path ensures that cartons are moved at a constant travel speed and there is a travel path from the induction station to all sort locations. Sort conveyor travels path can be a single straight-line or an endless-loop conveyor.

Nonconveyable Carton Sort

This section reviews nonconveyable carton sort designs, along with their operational characteristics and disadvantages and advantages. A nonconveyable sort design is considered a manual sort design. In the past years, many companies have implemented mechanical conveyable master-carton across-the-dock sort designs to reduce operating expenses, increase through-put volume, improve sort accuracy, and enhance customer service. One segment of an across-the-dock operation that is not handled by these designs are nonconveyable SKUs. A nonconveyable SKU is characterized as oversized, odd (irregular) shaped, high cube, or heavy weight, and that accounts for 5 to 25% of an operation's carton volume.

Vehicles or Transport Surfaces

Nonconveyable carton sort designs can use a variety of vehicles:

- Manual designs can use a manual push-or-pull four-wheel cart, pallet truck, or platform truck; an electric pallet truck/tugger with a train cart; an unpowered pallet roller conveyor, or a forklift truck.
- Mechanical designs can use a powered roller conveyor, an in-floor or overhead tow-veyor, or an AVG (automatic guided vehicle).

Pallet or Unit Load Designs

Pallet or unit load activities involve unloading pallets/loads from a vendor truck and transporting pallets to a ship staging dock area or delivery truck. The most common pallet load support devices are a wood pallet or a corrugated slip-sheet.

Pallet In-House Transport Designs

In a pallet across-the-dock operation, an important consideration is a design to transport a pallet from a vendor truck to a receiving dock area to an assigned ship dock staging area or directly into a delivery truck. The objectives of a transport design or link between a receiving dock area and ship docks are to a) enter and exit a vendor or delivery truck, b) lift and lower a pallet or unit load, and c) transport, sort, and deposit a pallet at an assigned ship dock staging location or to place a pallet into a delivery truck. Transport designs for pallets are:

1. A powered fork lift truck with a set of forks;
2. A counterbalanced fork lift truck with a slip-sheet attachment;
3. A manual or electric pallet truck with a set of forks or slip-sheet attachment;
4. An electric tugger with a cart train;
5. An in-floor tow line;
6. An overhead tow-veyor;
7. An AGV.

SKU Prepack Activity

In prepack activity, a SKU is placed into a shipping carton/bag without a packing slip/invoice or delivery label. Prepack activity can include a single SKU, two or three SKUs placed together, or gift wrapped, or special literature such as a rebate or promotion. An option to improve customer service in a conventional warehouse is to complete prepack activity for a SKU from a master carton/pallet that management considers to have extremely high sales. After prepack activity, the prepacked SKUs are placed onto a pallet and placed into a temporary storage position. Scan transactions are sent to the WMS computer for file update.

Why Prepack SKUs

An increasing number of small-item pick operations are attempting to operate more efficient and cost-effective operations, to minimize the customer order/delivery cycle, to handle a greater number of customer orders, and to promote 24-hour customer service. Prepack SKU activity can optimize SKU flow through a warehouse that has customer orders for a high-volume single-line single-piece and/or single-line multiple pieces (i.e., pairs).

Reducing Pick/Pack Spikes

A small-item pick operation minimizes the number of customer order spikes and their magnitude. With a demand pull or pre-entered customer order number for each SKU, SKU mix, and company customer service standard (customer order/delivery cycle time), a small-item pick design develops a prepack plan to reduce customer-order spikes. For an efficient prepack concept, the design factors are:

- The sales program or merchandise department identifies promotional SKUs;
- The past sales program or historical SKU volume for similar SKUs as single customer orders The exact identified SKU inventory quantity;

■ The suggested SKU single or SKU pairs customer order ship carton size.

The manager's prepack options are a) to complete a pre-pack SKU in a sealed shipping container. To complete a future customer order, a sealed pre-pack SKU requires a slapper envelope (envelope with a packing slip and delivery label) or b) semi-complete pre-pack a carton with a SKU, bottom fill, and no top fill, without a packing slip, tape, or delivery label. To complete a future customer order, a semi-completed pre-pack carton requires regular pick activitiy but a regular pack activity with no carton make-up and bottom fill activities.

Sales Program Identifies Promotion SKU

The company sales program and merchandise department identifies SKUs that are expected to have high sales or are promotional SKUs. The forecasted SKU sales volume allows a warehouse to determine each work day which SKUs are candidates for prepacking. Using the receiving dock schedule, ASN, PO, or WMS inventory files, an operations manager determines if candidate SKUs are in stock in the WMS inventory, or which day the SKUs are scheduled for delivery from the vendor. The sales program determines each SKU classification.

Using Past SKU Sales Volume to Plan Prepack Activity

Historical sales program records will indicate SKU volume that was sold as single-line or multi-line customer orders as a percentage of inventory quantity and classification. From the sales data, a manager has a PC or staff member forecast each candidate SKU's single-line and multi-line order volume. Using the projected prepack SKU volumes, the manager estimates labor hours required to prepack a candidate SKU quantity. Prepack labor hours are based on budgeted productivity rates.

Suggested SKU Single-Line Customer-Order Shipping Carton Size

To prepare for prepack activity, a manager verifies the WMS computer suggested shipping carton size for each candidate SKU. Using the projected prepack volume, the manager reviews the inventory quantity. After verifying carton size and inventory, the operations manager is ready to set up a fast-pack line. A fast-pack line is a pre-pack process that has a series of activity stations to assure high productivity and large completed pre-pack carton number. A fast-pack line starts with a ship carton make-up/entry station, next station has an employee transfer a SKU into a carton and next station has an employee place a top fill onto a SKU. With a completed pre-pack carton, the pre-pack carton is sealed and placed onto a pallet/cart. With a partial complete pre-pack carton, the pre-pack is open and placed onto a pallet/cart.

Prepacking a Promotional SKU

After a warehouse manager has finalized the SKU and shipping carton inventory quantities, the operations manager's prepack options are a) prepack a SKU with a slapper label or b) semi-complete an order that requires top fill, a packing slip, tape, and delivery label.

Prepack Activity

With the decision to prepack a promotional SKU with a slapper label, an operations manager actions are:

1. Select a pack line
2. Schedule a SKU quantity to be transferred from a fixed storage position and suggest shipping carton quantity to an assigned fast-pack line
3. Decide if a new WMS identification will be applied to each prepack pallet
4. Decide on SKU identification procedures
5. Transfer prepacked SKUs to a storage position

SKU Identification Designs

Prior to a prepack activity, a manager's SKU identification options are:

■ Complete a transfer transaction and SKU quantity depletion for an existing SKU identification. This option has an employee deplete zero scan and throw a SKU identification into the trash. An employee completes a SKU count, applies a new SKU disposable identification (or reuses a permament identification) to a pallet and enters the new SKU identification into the WMS inventory. The option ensures an accurate SKU inventory transaction and that employee transfer transaction instructions are simple.
■ Reuse an existing SKU identification, which is applied to a prepacked SKU pallet. In this option, an employee transfers a disposable SKU identification from a pallet to a prepack pallet or reuses a permament identification and an employee verifies that the SKU quantity on a pallet is equal to the old SKU identification quantity. This approach has the potential for low employee productivity, additional employee work, potential SKU inventory imbalance, and, if a permament identified label is used, a zero scan will be necessary.

SKU Identification Designs

A manager's SKU identification options are a) retain the same identification for the prepack. This option is a simple employee activity, but it requires the WMS program to allocate prepack SKUs for single-line customer orders and nonprepack SKUs to multi-line orders; or b) change the SKU identification, which requires complete SKU flow activity.

Prepacking a SKU as a Slapper Label SKU

Prepacking a promotional SKU as a slapper label package involves having a fast-pack line prepack a SKU with required filler material in a shipping carton. Each carton is sealed and stacked onto a pallet. Each full pallet receives a new SKU identification and an employee counts the SKU quantity. The scan transactions are sent to the WMS computer, which associates a SKU identification with a SKU quantity. This permits the SKU prepack pallet to be placed into a storage position specifically for single-line customer orders. To complete a single-line customer order, the WMS computer allocates a SKU from that storage position. The features of this approach are:

- It requires one day or prepack day of additional labor cost to prepack SKUs, which increases a day cost per unit.
- It increases management discipline, procedures, and controls.
- The WMS program tracks and allocates SKUs.
- It requires some additional SKU handli.
- The cost per unit is lower due to fewer activities to complete an order.
- It has high through-put volume.
- It spreads the operation's pick and pack volume over a two-day period.

Semi-Completed or Packed Prepack SKU

Prepacking a promotional SKU as a semi-packed or semi-completed SKU involves having a fast-pack line pack a SKU with required bottom filler material in a shipping carton. Each carton is stacked onto a pallet. Given the potential of unstable cartons on a pallet, each pallet is wrapped in plastic and receives a new SKU identification and quantity per pallet. The scan transactions are sent to the WMS computer. The WMS computer associates the SKU identification with a quantity, which permits the prepack pallet to be placed into a storage position. Prepacked SKUs are allocated to single-line orders.

Prepack Singles

If a warehouse handles small items and SKUs are considered "A" moving SKUs, the warehouse has a potential to prepack a SKU quantity into a shipping carton. Depending on labor cost, labor availability, and slapper label use, prepack activity either seals the shipping carton or the carton remains open. Using the historical (or estimated) SKU sales and the WMS computer's ability to prioritize a prepacked SKU quantity (e.g., FIFO SKU rotation), the warehouse determines the number of SKUs that are prepacked and not prepacked. During receiving activity, each SKU receives a WMS identification. Each identification and its associated SKU quantity are entered into the WMS inventory files. A design team prepack SKU options (1) pre-pack prior to a pallet/cart receiving a WMS identification and (2) remove a WMS identified pallet from a storage position. Prepack SKUs from a WMS identified pallet options are (a) prepacked SKU retains the same SKU number, (b) re-packed SKUs on a pallet retain the same WMS pallet and SKU identifications, (c) re-packed SKUs on a pallet receive a new pallet WMS identification and new SKU number and (d) re-packed SKUs on a pallet receive a new WMS pallet identification.

Prepack Prior to Receiving a WMS Identification

After a vendor delivered SKU is unloaded on a dock, an employee receives a completed purchase order and the delivered SKUs, updates the WMS computer and closes the vendor purchase order. After receiving QA approval, the warehouse notifies the WMS computer, which updates the host computer (see Figure 13.1). In an area adjacent to the receiving area, employees complete SKU prepack activity, and prepacked SKUs are placed into a shipping carton; cartons with a SKU are placed onto a pallet. Each pallet with prepacked shipping cartons receives a SKU identification. The identification and associated SKU quantity and first (FIFO) SKUs are scanned into the WMS

PRE-PACK ACTIVITY WMS IDENTIFICATION AND SKU IDENTIFICATION OPTIONS

WMS IDENTIFIED PALLET HAS 100 PIECES, 10 MASTER CARTONS ON A PALLET
AND EACH MASTER CARTON HAS 10 PIECES

	SAME SKU ID & SAME WMS ID	NEW SKU ID & SAME WMS ID	SAME SKU ID & NEW WMS ID	NEW SKU ID & NEW WMS ID
BEFORE PRE-PACK PALLET WMS ID SKU ID	1900 AD57	1900 AD57	1900 AD57	1900 AD57
AFTER PRE-PACK PALLET WMS ID SKU ID	1900 AD57	1900 PP99	2222 AD57	2222 PP99

Figure 13.1   Prepack Activity SKU and WMS Identification Flows

computer inventory file. The SKU is ready for transport to a storage position. After scan transactions are sent to the WMS computer, the prepacked SKUs are available for sale.

Prepacked SKU Retains Number; Receives a New Identification

After SKUs are sent to a storage position, and in accordance with a plan to sell a certain quantity of SKUs on a specific date, the WMS program requests that the warehouse move a SKU from the storage position to a prepack work station. At the work station, an employee completes a scan transaction, which updates WMS computer inventory files, removes the disposable identification from the pallet disposal, and starts the prepack activity. The prepacked SKU is placed in a shipping carton and onto a pallet. Each pallet receives a new SKU identification and associated quantity. The warehouse moves the prepacked SKUs to predetermined storage positions and completes scan transactions to update the WMS computer. In a WMS computer file, to complete a customer order wave for a single-line/single piece SKU, a WMS computer recognizes a prepack SKU in the pallet position to have SKUs that are first available to a WMS computer for allocation to a customer order wave. SKUs that have not been repacked remain in a storage position and retain their SKU identification and associated quantity. These SKUs are the last SKUs in the WMS computer inventory file and are the last SKUs made available for customer orders.

Prepacked SKU Retains the Number and Identification

At a prepack station, an employee completes scan transactions, and either leaves the WMS identification remains on the pallet or zero scans the (disposable or permanent) label, and starts the prepack activity. A prepacked SKU is placed into a shipping carton and onto a pallet. Each prepacked SKU retains the same SKU number. At a prepack station, each prepack SKU has the same SKU number and retains the pallet WMS identification as is required for a ship carton quantity on a pallet. The employee scans the pallet WMS identification and quantity into the WMS computer, which updates the SKU quantity. The warehouse moves the prepacked SKUs to predetermined storage positions and completes scan transactions to update the WMS computer. In WMS computer files, for a customer order wave single-line/single SKU orders, a WMS computer recognizes prepack WMS identified pallet in the pallet position to have SKUs that are first available for WMS computer to allocate for a customer order wave single-line/single SKU orders. SKUs that have not been repacked remain in a storage position and retain their SKU identification and associated quantity. These SKUs are the last SKUs in the WMS computer inventory file and are the last SKUs made available for customer orders.

Prepacked SKU Receives a New Number; Retains SKU Identification

At a prepack station, an employee completes scan transactions, and either leaves the WMS identification remains on the pallet or zero scans the (disposable or permanent) label, and starts the prepack activity. A prepacked SKU is placed into a shipping carton and onto a pallet. Each prepacked SKU receives a new number. At the prepack station, the new SKU number and a retains the pallet WMS identification is required adjusted for the shipping carton quantity on a pallet. The employee scans the pallet WMS identification and quantity into the WMS computer, which updates the SKU quantity. The warehouse moves the prepacked SKUs to predetermined storage positions and completes scan transactions. In WMS computer files, for a customer order wave single-line/single SKU orders, a WMS computer recognizes prepack WMS identified pallet in the pallet position to have SKUs that are first available for WMS computer to be allocated for customer order wave single-line/single SKU orders. SKUs that have not been repacked remain in a storage position and retain their SKU identification and associated quantity. These SKUs are the last SKUs in the WMS computer inventory file and are the last SKUs made available for customer orders.

Prepacked SKU Receives a New Number and Identification

After a vendor-delivered SKU is unloaded, received on the warehouse dock, and receives a WMS identification, the WMS computer records the identification and associated quantity. After QA approval, the warehouse closes the purchase order and updates the WMS computer, which updates the host computer. SKUs are sent to a storage position and made available for sale. In accordance with a predetermined sales plan, the WMS program requests that the warehouse move a SKU from a storage position to a prepack work station. At the work station, an employee completes a scan transaction to update the WMS computer inventory files, removes the disposable WMS identification from the pallet, and starts the prepack activity. The prepacked SKU is placed into a shipping carton and onto a pallet. Each prepacked pallet receives a new pallet WMS identification and associated SKU quantity. The warehouse moves the prepacked SKUs to predetermined storage positions and completes a scan transaction to update the WMS computer. In the WMS computer files, for a customer order wave single-line/single SKU orders, the WMS computer recognizes prepack WMS identified pallet in the pallet position to have SKUs that are first available for WMS computer to allocate for a customer order wave single-line/single SKU orders. SKUs that have not been repacked remain in a storage position and retain their SKU identification and associated quantity. These SKUs are the last SKUs in the WMS computer inventory file and are the last SKUs made available for customer orders.

Value-Added Activity

A value-added service involves adding something of value-added to an ordered SKU. The change in value and physical appearance makes a value-added SKU different from the previous SKU or non-value-added SKUs. In a warehouse, value-added SKU activity occurs after customer-order pick activity and before pack activity. In value-added activity, the warehouse can either change the SKU inventory number or retain the same inventory number.

Changing the SKU Inventory Number

All SKUs are assigned to a position. With a predetermined SKU quantity allocated to a value-added activity, the WMS program creates a move SKU transaction to move a SKU quantity from a storage position to a position in a value-added area. In the value-added area, an employee completes a SKU identification scan and entry transaction to change the existing SKU inventory quantity to a new SKU number with the same SKU quantity. As the WMS computer receives a customer order for a value-added SKU, in accordance with the warehouse's order wave plan, the WMS computer allocates a SKU quantity in a value-added area to the customer order. After completion of the value-added process, the value-added SKU has a different WMS identification, which ensures proper handling for customer returns.

Retaining the Same SKU Inventory Number

A value-added SKU that has the same SKU inventory number as a non-value-added SKU means that each SKU has the same inventory number. With a customer order for a value-added SKU, the warehouse creates a customer order wave plan, in which the WMS computer allocates a SKU quantity for a value-added activity. The WMS computer has the warehouse pick a value-added SKU quantity and send the quantity to a value-added area. In the value-added area, a SKU is physically changed to complete the customer order but retains the same SKU number. For customer returns, having the same SKU inventory number for value-added or non-value-added SKU creates a problem and the SKU is disposed as "not available for sale."

SKU Inventory Counts

Inventory counts are made to obtain a SKU inventory quantity. Inventory counts are entered into WMS inventory files at a storage/pick position with a hand-held scanner/reader. The options for inventory counts are:

- A cycle count, which includes a regular count or special (problem) SKU count
- A fiscal inventory count, which includes counting all storage or pick positions or counting specific positions
- A pick position zero count

Cycle Count

A cycle count activity ensures that the SKU quantity at each position is accurate. Cycle count options are either a regular cycle count or a special (or problem) SKU cycle count, which is created by an over, shortage, or damage situation in a pick position.

Regular Cycle Count

In a regular cycle count, an employee completes a predetermined number of SKU counts for each time period. An employee counts the SKU quantity in each position with a hand-held scanner. After completion of the cycle count, the cycle count quantity for each SKU storage or pick position and associated SKU quantity is updated in the WMS inventory files. A design team suggests a SKU for a count activity. SKU selection factors are SKU value, SKU age, most recent SKU pick or deposit activity, length of time from last SKU count, and random.

Special or Problem SKU Cycle Count

A special (or problem) SKU cycle count has an employee complete a SKU count activity. During storage or pick activity, If an employee realizes that a storage/pick position has an over (O), shortage (S), or damage (D) SKU situation, then the situation indicates that a position actual SKU quantity has potential not to match the WMS computer files storage or pick position's SKU quantity. When an over, shortage, or damage situation occurs, or to prepare for a sales promotion in a warehouse, an employee completes a cycle count for each SKU or each storage or pick position. The cycle count quantity for each position is entered into the WMS computer inventory files.

Pick Position Zero Count

After a pick line has completed all customer order SKU picks, a pick position will be depleted of SKUs. To ensure accurate WMS computer inventory status of the pick positions, an employee with a hand-held scanner completes a pick position zero count. Each pick position zero count is sent to the WMS computer, which updates the pick position inventory status.

Warehouse Operation Fiscal Inventory Count

A fiscal physical inventory count in a warehouse occurs once a year. A fiscal inventory count becomes the SKU inventory quantity for each position in the company WMS files and in a company balance sheet (financial statement). The fiscal inventory count options are count all storage/pick positions or count specific storage/pick positions.

Fiscal Count All Storage/Pick Positions

A fiscal physical inventory count is completed once per year and includes a count of all positions and SKUs. Warehouse staff and employees count each position and associated SKU quantity.

Fiscal Count Specific Storage/Pick Positions

A fiscal inventory count is completed for a specific storage or pick position. Each position has a SKU inventory quantity that recorded in the WMS computer files. After an employee counts a specific SKU from a position, if the counted SKU quantity and actual SKU position number match the position file SKU quantity, the company accepts the position inventory count.

Obsolete or Scrap Inventory Control

A warehouse will have damaged SKUs and obsolete physical inventory. An inventory scrap design allows a warehouse to:

- Remove damaged and obsolete inventory from a storage position
- Create vacant storage positions and improve storage utilization
- Improve housekeeping
- Improve employee productivity
- Reduce SKU damage

Scrap inventory are damaged SKUs that do not meet company quality standards for customer orders; obsolete SKUs are SKUs that have not been ordered by customers. In a warehouse, SKU scrap inventory is generally created from:

- SKUs damaged from warehouse handling
- Buy-ins that have low sales and whose inventory exceeds a reasonable volume
- Customer order returns
- SKUs whose expiry date has passed
- SKUs stored in wrong temperature
- SKUs not in favor with customers

How to Identify Scrap Inventory

SKUs in inventory that are candidates for scrap are determined by:

- A SKU with accumulated dust on the master carton;
- A SKU with an old receiving date tag;
- A SKU shows no volume from a year to date in the WMS computer movement report.

SKU physical scrap options are book inventory, random selection, age, and SILO.

Advanced Customer Order Sales

In a warehouse that allows a customer to pre-order a SKU or request a late delivery date, the warehouse must ensure customer satisfaction and the WMS program must ensure accurate SKU and customer order flow. In a catalog or telemarketing warehouse with a customer order pre-order design, after a vendor SKU delivery and completion of the warehouse acceptance process, a SKU life cycle starts or is offered for sale to customers in 6 to 13 weeks.

As the company host computer receives pre-orders, late delivery orders, or orders with special delivery times or days, the computer sends the ordered SKU to the WMS computer. The WMS computer assigns a flag that indicates that the SKU is a pre-order or late order delivery. The options are:

1. To hold the order in the WMS computer and have the computer restrict (e.g., "not available for sale" but in inventory status) the SKU quantity. On the order delivery date, the WMS computer releases the order to the warehouse for an order wave plan. Based on the order wave plan, the WMS computer allocates the SKU for a WMS move from a storage position to a pick position. This minimizes the possibility of withdrawing the SKU for another customer order and ensures that the warehouse completes the order per the customer indicated time.

2. To send the order to the warehouse computer for an order wave plan. Using the order wave plan, the WMS computer allocates SKUs from a storage position and the warehouse completes a SKU transfer from a storage position to a pick position. All orders are picked and sent from a pack station.

During a work day, the WMS computer transfers all order identifications in the order wave plan to the warehouse computer, which transfers both regular and late customer order deliveries. As a late order delivery carton travels through an automatic symbology reader/scanner station, the reader/scanner scans/reads and sends all order identifications to a ship sorter computer. Using the previous order identification transfer, a sorter computer has the carton mechanically sorted onto a late delivery sort lane. The diverted order is treated as a "did not sort" carton in warehouse computer. This means that the warehouse ship sorter computer has a sorter complete a carton divert transaction but the warehouse ship computer does not register a customer order as manifested. At the carton spur end, an employee transfers and scans the order identification to a temporary hold position. The scan transactions are sent to the WMS computer, which updates the order status and location. Following the update, the WMS computer schedules a time for the carton to become an active customer order. This means that the WMS computer sends the order identification to the warehouse computer. With this information, the warehouse sorter computer expects that the order identification will be read/scanned at the automatic induction station and that the ship staff will transfer or complete a move transaction of the carton from the temporary hold position to a warehouse sorter in-feed conveyor.

Noncustomer Orders

Noncustomer orders are return to vendor, vendor recall, charity or donation, employee award program, jobber or discount outside company sales store, company outlet store, and other nonpaid demand for a SKU quantity.

After a warehouse receives a noncustomer order, an employee completes the SKU pick activity and transfers a picked SKU quantity to a special pack station. At the pack station, a packer verifies the picked quantity, matches the quantity and description to the order request and scans the quantity. The scan transaction and quantity are sent to the WMS computer to update the inventory files. The WMS computer updates the host computer as to the SKU quantity.

If a vendor recall or stop sales occurs, a vendor or government office will advise the warehouse to stop selling a SKU and to prepare the SKUs for return to the vendor. With a vendor recall, the host computer and WMS program place the SKU on "not available for sale" status. The status applies to both storage and pick positions. The WMS computer reviews the pick positions and if there are vendor recall SKUs in a pick position, the WMS computer suggests to the warehouse that it move a SKU from a pick position to a storage position. All SKUs are withdrawn from storage positions and transferred to a special pack station or ship dock.

Customs Bonded or Duty Free Positions

If a warehouse receives vendor delivered SKUs from foreign countries, the warehouse is required to pay customs duty to the U.S. government. In a bonded warehouse, SKUs from foreign countries are stored in a specific area (for bonded SKUs only) and the customs duty is paid as each SKU is sold to a customer.

As the warehouse merchandise department communicates a vendor purchase order to the host computer, the merchandiser/buyer indicates that a foreign vendor is delivering SKUs that are manufactured in another country; the QA approved SKUs are assigned to the warehouse's bonded storage section. The WMS computer notices the bonded requirement from a purchase order. The bonded requirement becomes a flag in the WMS program, which in turn suggests a storage position in the bonded storage section. The WMS computer directs a warehouse printer to print bonded storage requirements on the receiving documents and tally sheet. After the foreign manufactured SKUs are unloaded and purchase order closed, a receiving clerk attaches a WMS identification to each SKU. Each identification and quantity is entered into the WMS computer. In the WMS computer, the SKU number has a flag that indicates that the SKU is to be moved from the receiving department to the bonded storage position. The SKU is transported to a drop point for entry into the bonded warehouse section. After the SKU arrives at the bonded storage section, the SKU is placed and scanned to a storage position. The scan transaction and quantity are sent to the WMS computer to update inventory files.

Using the host computer, the company finance departments determine the actual time for the bonded sale to a customer and duty payment to the government. Host computer bond payment options are (a) at the customer order entry or (b) after the customer order is manifested at the ship dock. The WMS computer then updates the host computer that the customer order (bonded SKU) has departed the warehouse.

As the host computer receives orders for a SKU in a warehouse bonded position, the options for completing an order are a) using pick positions in a warehouse bonded section or b) transferring a SKU to a conventional warehouse pick position. The host computer transfers orders to the WMS computer, which transfers the order pool to the warehouse staff for completion as part of an order wave plan. Based on the order wave plan, the WMS computer allocates SKUs in storage positions to orders. To handle a SKU for a customer order, the design considerations are customer order SKU volume, available space in the bonded section, and a pick position in a bonded section for slow movers and pick line for fast movers. If the warehouse uses the bonded storage or pick position option, the warehouse must ensure an accurate inventory for all SKUs placed in the bonded section.

Customs Duty Draw Back

If a warehouse does not have a bonded or duty-free section, but receives foreign manufactured SKUs, the company will pay the U.S. customs duty as the SKUs are entered into the WMS inventory. Because the warehouse was required to pay customs duty on foreign SKU a) as the SKU was sold or b) on receipt of the entire delivery, when unsold or returned SKUs are returned to the vendor, the warehouse receives a duty drawback. To ensure an accurate inventory, the WMS computer identifies each SKU. Employees at pack stations count SKUs in storage positions for duty drawback.

Chapter 14

Project Management, Interface, and Integration in an Existing Operation or New Facility

Introduction

As people from outside the company join the design team (e.g., architect, building construction company, warehouse equipment vendor, WMS program company and warehouse integrator), the prior team members ensure that the new team members have a comprehensive understanding of both the existing and the proposed warehouse. After the design team has a clear understanding of all aspects of warehouse business, as well as the proposed activities for the new warehouse, project design events are scheduled and completed. These project events are:

1. Warehouse and WMS program integration and interface, which includes hardware and software, PCs, printers, server, network and hierarchy for a host computer, WMS computer, and warehouse computer
2. Project team organization and responsibilities
3. Master project schedule
4. Building design parameters
5. Warehouse design and drawing development
6. Project management and contract administration
7. Local government building design and drawing approval
8. Project brain-storming sessions
9. Project conference room pilot study
10. WMS business narrative that is based on a warehouse operation
11. PCs, printers, bar codes, and scanners/readers, which includes wireless and wire devices
12. WMS program development

13. Description of operations and employee training program
14. WMS program supported and nonsupported transaction projections
15. WMS program equipment or transaction locations on warehouse drawings
16. Warehouse equipment specification and location drawing
17. WMS program business narrative and equipment changes
18. WMS program equipment bid and purchase
19. Building roof, walls, floor, utilities, and warehouse, and WMS program start-up and test
20. Testing and implement of a) the building, b) the WMS program, c) the warehouse, and d) WMS program integration
21. With vendor delivered SKUs and actual customer orders, warehouse operation start-up, acceptance and turn-over
22. Review and audit

As the project progresses from the initial design and development phase, the project team will revise the project event schedule or activity sequence as necesssary, as the design and implementation, start-up, or scope of work changes.

Design Parameters and Operational Aspects

A key step in the project is to develop warehouse operation design year parameters and operational aspects that include projected warehouse vendor SKUs, customer order SKUs, lines, volume, WMS-supported and nonsupported transactions.

The key components of a WMS program are:

- Company host computer
- Warehouse management system
- Warehouse computers

Warehouse activities that interact and interface with a WMS program for a SKU or customer order are:

- Receiving
- Storage
- Replenishment
- Pick
- Pack
- Manifest and load activity
- Customer-order returns
- Inventory adjustments

Warehouse Control or Operation Design

Design year parameters are developed for average and peak volumes (minimum of five-year forecast) by vendor delivered SKUs and customer-order groups. Each table shows:

- Vender delivery SKU volumes, including a) purchase order numbers and lines, b) ASN numbers and lines by delivery method, c) receiving tally sheet number and lines, d) WMS identification label number and lines, and e) company SKU identification label number and lines
- SKU class and QA rejected volumes
- Customer-order number, pack slip number and lines, label number and lines, pick and pack SKUs by customer-order type, e.g., a) single pieces, b) single SKU multiple pieces, c) multiple SKUs from same SKU group, d) multiple pieces from different SKU groups, and d) customer-order ship carton volumes
- Customer-order shipping cartons (conveyable and nonconveyable)
- Inventory volumes and SKU storage/pick position numbers
- Customer returns cartons and SKUs as RTV, RTS, rework, outlet store, jobber, charity, and damaged
- In-house vendor SKU rework
- SKU and customer-order transport: a) for put-away between receiving and storage area, b) for QA department inspection between receiving and QA department, c) for put-away between a QA department and storage area, d) for replenishment or pick line setup between storage area and pick area, e) for transport between pick area and pack area, f) for transport between pack and ship areas, g) between customer returns unload area to returns process area, h) by customer returns disposition, i) by SKU customer returns from returns process area to a sort station, j) for vendor return from storage area to a ship dock area, and k) non-customer order and non-WMS program supported SKUs and carton volumes

To have effective design year parameters, each warehouse and WMS program activity is tabulated for each year's projected growth or by the percentage increase from a base year, each year between a base and start-up year, and each year between start-up and operational year. Design year operational aspects include the activity list for each warehouse activity/area. These include:

1. Vendor delivery date after purchase order receipt
2. Receiving dock appointment scheduling procedure and receiving hours per day and days per week
3. Allowable vendor delivery vehicle unloading and receiving hours and palletizing methods; based on vendor master-carton data, each pallet ti and hi appears on a receiving tally sheet
4. QA sample size and procedure
5. SKU WMS identification print method, which can be preprinted or print-on-demand
6. SKU WMS identification procedure
7. SKU put-away strategy, e.g., a) rejected SKUs held on dock or placed into a position, b) SKUs placed in a storage position as QA hold and "not available for sale," c) select a QA sample size with a WMS identification that is transfer to a QA position, or d) handle SKUs as pallets, master cartons and single items in totes
8. Transport concept design for SKUs per hour as master cartons, totes, and pallets
9. And storage concept put-away of a SKU to a storage position for a) forklift truck and AS/RS crane transactions as pallets or cartons per hour and as single or dual commands per hour, b) conveyor or cart handling speeds, and c) for an AS/RS storage concept size, weight, and scan/read station transactions per hour as pallets or cartons
10. Host computer customer-order entry, processing, and release time to the WMS program
11. Warehouse staff time for customer-order wave creation and transfer to the WMS program by SKU group

12. Based on a customer-order wave, WMS program WMS identified SKU allocation and warehouse WMS identified SKUs move transactions sent to a warehouse for WMS identified SKUs withdraw, setup, and replenish SKUs to a pick position

13. For each customer-order wave, warehouse WMS identified SKU transfer to a pick position and SKU and pick position WMS identifications and SKU quantity communicated to a WMS program computer

14. WMS program customer-order release to a pick area

15. WMS program and warehouse customer-order identification

16. Pick area SKU pick activity

17. Completed customer-order transport from a pick area, to another pick area (manual, mechanized, or automatic), through a pick check area to a pack area, or through a sort design (manual or mechanized) to a pack area

18. Transfer to a customer-order pack station; pack station employee completes a WMS identified customer order or zero scans a warehouse tote identification to disconnect a customer order WMS identification to a warehouse tote identification that allows a warehouse tote used for another WMS identified customer order

19. Pack station employee transfers completed customer orders to a manifest/ship area or transfers problem orders to a problem order station for correction and pack-out for transport to manifest station

20. Manifest station that has a customer-order WMS identification sent to WMS program and a warehouse transport/sort conveyor that moves a manifested WMS identified customer order to a ship dock and onto a customer-order delivery truck. If required have a warehouse employee off-load WMS identified customer orders and transfer each WMS identified customer order to a WMS identified position and send each customer order and position WMS identifications to a WMS computer as a non-manifested and non-shipped WMS identified customer order

21. Returns transported from unload/open station a) to a process station for host computer customer credit, b) WMS SKU disposition and WMS label print, or c) warehouse SKU transport to a sort station for sort of return-to-stock SKU to a WMS identified position and for return-to-vendor SKU sort to WMS identification position

22. Removing return-to-vendor SKUs from an "available for sale" storage position for transport to a pack area or dock

23. WMS noncustomer order or non-WMS program supported SKUs (shipping supplies) and warehouse withdrawal of SKU from a storage/pick position and transport to a special pack station

A table is created for each SKU quantity, and is based on regular and overtime work hours for average and peak volumes. Each table shows:

1. Receiving hours

2. Number of delivery trucks, receiving docks, and dock unload forklift/pallet trucks for unloading at docks

3. Forklift trucks and conveyor travel speeds on in-house transport from a receiving dock to the next station

4. For an AS/RS storage concept size, weigh and bar code scanner/reader station number

5. Number of conventional pallets that determines forklift truck number needed to complete SKU put-away transactions

6. Number of AS/RS cranes needed that are based on single command and dual command transactions per hour

7. Number of conventional pallets that determines forklift truck number needed to complete SKU withdrawal transactions

8. Number of master cartons or single items that determines number of HROS vehicles or AS/RS cranes needed to complete SKU withdrawal transactions

9. Number of forklift trucks and transport vehicles per hour (or conveyor travel path speed) necessary to setup/replenish a pick line

10. Number of pickers and pick vehicles needed (depending on the pick design chosen) to transport picked customer orders from a main pick area to another pick area, a pack area, or through a sort design to a pack station

11. Number of pack stations

12. Number of problem customer-order stations

13. Number of manifest stations

14. Sort conveyor travel speeds and number of sort locations

15. Number of shipping dock staging areas or door numbers

16. Number of truck unloading doors needed for returns

17. Conveyor speed (or number of vehicles) needed for returns

18. Number of processing/disposition stations needed for customer-order returns

19. Projected number of returned SKUs, sorted by RTV, RTS, charity, jobber, company store, or rework

20. Number of return-to-vendor pack stations

21. Number noncustomer-order pack stations

The design team completes design year tables for warehouse- and WMS-program-supported and non-WMS supported transactions for each warehouse activity and each WMS scan activity per hour. For the average, frequent, and peak SKU and customer-order volumes.

WMS Program SKU Storage and Pick Positions

A WMS identification is used for and on each WMS SKU storage, pick, customer returns sort, QA sample and problem customer-order position, or every physical SKU location within a facility. To complete a SKU physical and WMS program put-away, pick-line set, replenishment, or move transaction, an employee or warehouse computer directs a SKU to a position. After the employee completes all scan transactions or the warehouse (AS/RS crane) communicates the SKU transaction completion and SKU quantity to the WMS program computer, the WMS computer updates the SKU inventory and position status in its files.

WMS Program SKU Pick Position Projection

To implement a WMS program in a storage/pick operation, a warehouse team must make an accurate projection of all storage, pick, customer-order returns sort, QA sample, and problem customer-order positions. To project a design year SKU pick positions, the options are a) apply a historical annual SKU growth rate to a base year SKU number or b) using a base year SKU number, have the merchandise department estimate a new SKU growth. A WMS SKU pick position projection determines:

- Pick design, which can be manual, mechanized, or automated
- Pick area size
- Type of pick, sort, pack, and in-house transport design
- Cost
- Location in a facility and number of floors in a facility
- WMS program design considerations

In a warehouse design, each warehouse pick position faces a pick aisle:

- In a single-item operation, a tote, box/carton in a shelf, hand stack or pallet rack, flow rack, carousel, S.I. Cartrac, or AS/RS mini-load identified pick position faces a pick aisle.
- In a master-carton operation, a floor stack, shelf, hand stack or pallet rack, flow rack, carousel, S.I. Cartrac, or AS/RS mini-load pick position faces a pick aisle.
- In a pallet operation, a floor stack, pallet rack, flow rack, S. I. Cartrac or AS/RS pick position faces a pick aisle.

WMS Program Identified SKU Storage Position Projection

To project the warehouse SKU inventory volume and associated storage position number that is housed in a facility, projection methods are similar for small items, master cartons, or pallets. In each storage/pick operation type, the storage position number is based on:

- SKU inventory volume
- SKU storage position physical characteristics, which can be a) tall or short pallet positions, b) special conditions (e.g., low temperature controlled storage area, hazardous SKU, human consumable, toxic, temperature sensitive, or high value)
- Storage position utilization factor

Storage utilization factors are a) dense storage designs that are floor stack, drive-in or drive through rack (66%), b) single deep standard, flow rack, or AS/RS rack (85%), and c) two-deep racks have an interior utilization of 85% and an exterior utilization of 66%.

The options for a SKU inventory volume projection are a) for a complete year to develop an average volume or b) develop a moving average inventory volume projections for a predetermined month period (such as 3 month moving average inventory volume). For storage area size, a 3 month moving average with the highest inventory volume is preferred. In most operations, the highest predetermined period is the last three months of the fiscal year. After a projection method is selected, the base year data is multiplied by the company's growth factor to obtain the design inventory volume.

After the inventory volume is projected for the design year, the inventory volume is divided by the number of SKUs in each storage device with a WMS identification. In a single-item operation, that would be the number of SKUs per tote, box/carton with one tote, box/carton on a shelf, rack carousel basket, or AS/RS tray/device. In a master-carton operation, it is the number of SKUs per master carton with one master carton per shelf, hand stack or pallet rack, carousel basket, AS/RS tray or device, or pallet in a rack position. In a pallet operation, it is number of SKUs per master carton and the number of master cartons per pallet, slip sheet, or container in a floor stack, pallet rack, or AS/RS pallet position.

An important storage position projection is of non-WMS program (non-SKU) supported storage positions. A nonWMS program SKU requires labor or a forklift truck/AS/RS crane to complete a non-WMS supported storage transaction. An example of a non-WMS program SKU is a shipping supply item. A warehouse operation staff estimates the SKUs inventory quantities in the area, based on the design's peak quantity requirement (which includes vendor lead time and safety stock). A ship supply pallet with overhang or convex bowed top restricts its allocation to a pallet storage rack storage but is placed into a floor stack design that is two or three high with a pyramid floor stack. For minimum shipping supply inventory, the vendor supply is on a "just-in-time" basis.

A warehouse SKU storage position projection determines storage/pick operations:

- Storage design, which can be wide aisle (WA), narrow aisle (NA), very narrow aisle (VNA) fork lift truck, or automatic storage and retrieval system (AS/RS) crane
- Storage area size
- Storage design, which can be floor stack, stacking frame, conventional racks, or dense storage racks, AS/RS or rack supported building
- Location in a facility
- WMS program design considerations

Predetermined Monthly Average Warehouse and SKU Inventory

To project a storage operation design monthly average unit inventory with a WMS program, design parameters are:

- Additional new SKU number
- SKUs that require regular storage conditions, special storage conditions, or FIFO SKU rotation
- Storage inventory number of units such as pallets, master cartons, or single pieces
- The following is an example of a predetermined monthly average storage operation with a WMS program inventory: annual SKU inventory is 15,000 and to have three months as an average inventory in an operation. The annual SKU inventory is divided by 12 months, which is a monthly inventory of 1,250 SKUs. A three-month SKU inventory is 1,250 SKU multiplied by 3, which equals 3,750 SKUs: the operation design year inventory SKU volume. With a standard rack 85% utilization factor, the design year storage positions are 4,411.

Three-Month Moving Average SKU Inventory

To project the three-month moving average inventory, the design parameters are:

- For the design year, determine the highest three month number of units in inventory such as pallets, master cartons, or single pieces
- For each SKU number that requires normal storage conditions, special storage conditions, or FIFO SKU rotation
- Storage inventory number of months

An example of a three-month moving average SKU inventory follows. The total annual inventory is 15,700 SKUs. The monthly SKU inventory is:

January = 1,000
February = 1,000
March = 1,000
April = 1,100
May = 900
June = 1,100
July = 1,400
August = 1,400
September = 1,400
October = 1,700
November = 1,700
December = 2,000

A three-month moving average SKU inventory projection design has the following groupings:

January, February, and March = 3,000
February, March, and May = 3,100
March, May, and April = 3,000
May, April, and June = 3,100
April, June, and July = 3,400
June, July, and August = 3,900
July, August, and September = 4,200
August, September, and October = 4,500
September, October, and November = 4,800
October, November, and December = 5,400
November, December, and January = 4,700
December, January, and February = 4,000

From the above example, the three-month moving average peak SKU inventory is 5,400 in the October, November, and December group. With a standard rack 85% utilization factor, design year storage positions are 6,352.

Warehouse Layout Drawings

Warehouse layout (plan view) drawings show all dimensions and notes necessary to show a completed warehouse. A warehouse layout drawing shows each piece of warehouse equipment, identifies SKU or customer travel paths, and leaves no questions for the warehouse and WMS program design team, WMS program vendor, warehouse equipment vendor, local/building code authority, or insurance company. To have an effective warehouse drawing, each warehouse functional area is identified, each work station has a standard identification (e.g., symbol or number). Warehouse layout and detail drawings are based on the objectives:

■ Control operational costs and earn a profit

- Satisfy customers, improve customer service standard, increase number of customers
- Maximize space utilization
- Improve employee productivity
- Enhance vendor SKU, customer order, and information flows
- Ensure operation expansion, SKU transaction accuracy, and on-line communication between the warehouse and WMS program

A warehouse layout and site shape determines a building shape and size.

Organization, Responsibilities, and Integrator

After the architect, building construction company, and WMS program and warehouse equipment vendors become members of the design team, a project team develops and releases a revised and updated organization chart and specifies team member responsibilities. The organization chart is dated and identifies each team member and project position. It indicates to whom each team member reports. The organization chart is given to each design team member and a copy is placed in company files.

Project Team Organization

After the executive management group creates a project management team, the team is assigned the responsibility of completing the project. With an approved capital expenditure for the project, the design project team is given the authority to purchase and implement the project, execute contracts, and make payments to the architect, construction company, local building authorities/tax payments, warehouse equipment vendors, WMS program vendor, and consultants.

The warehouse management team levels are:

1. The executive management team or steering committee level, which has senior executives from the company's key departments that are affected by the WMS program. The management level is the top project organization level, and are the project sponsors who define the scope of work.
2. A venture manager—a senior manager who reports to the executive management team. The venture manager is responsible for seeing the project completed on-budget and on-schedule, provides project visibility, determines responsibilities, establishes priorities, and oversees the project.
3. A project manager who reports to a venture manager, develops a warehouse design and writes WMS program functional specifications, reviews plan view and detailed view drawings, selects a warehouse and WMS program vendor, schedules warehouse operation and WMS program installation, oversees warehouse and WMS program implementation and integration, oversees warehouse and WMS program start-up, reviews warehouse and WMS program performance, and ensure that payments are made to the architect, building construction company, and warehouse and WMS program vendor.
4. Specialists on a warehouse and WMS program project team are managers and employees from company departments that are involved or affected by the warehouse project. Managers and employees are specialists who know each department activities, vendor SKU or customer-order flow, and information flow, have experience with IT program installation, and

know past warehouse operation. A company department list includes warehouse, inventory control, IT, purchase and traffic, finance and accounting, engineering, and construction.

5. Warehouse and WMS program vendors, equipment vendors, consultants, integrator, and local/building authority—noncompany representatives on the project team who contribute equipment knowledge, and project installation and start-up experience.

Drawing Group

In a proposed warehouse project, it will be important to have drawings that show how the warehouse will look and operate and where the warehouse and WMS program will interact and interface. Warehouse drawings are:

- Plan-view drawings that show a) each storage and pick position and SKU depth or number per position or b) a site drawing that shows the facility located on a proposed site
- A side-view detail drawing with an entire elevation, including the number of positions. Positions start at an aisle entrance and end at an aisle exit. Positions are pallet, master carton, single SKU storage positions; master-carton or single SKU pick positions; customer-order returns temporary sort positions, grouped by customer-order return SKU group (RTV, RTS, jobber, charity, rework, damage, and store); QA sample department storage positions; and problem customer-order storage positions.
- Detail drawings that show storage or pick position SKU depth or in cross section. With a single deep storage design, a cross section drawing shows single storage and pick position depth and rack positions high, aisle width, back to back storage and pick positions, aisle width, and next storage and pick position depth. With a dense storage design a cross section shows the rack depth.

Working with drawings permits the warehouse and WMS design team to identify each storage and pick position, how to complete a customer-order pick line setup or replenishment transaction, and how to determine the number of SKUs that will fit into a pick position. Based on a warehouse forklift truck, AS/RS crane or picker routing pattern, a project team member ensures that each SKU position has a WMS identification.

WMS Program and Warehouse Operation Design: Integration and Interface

It is important that the warehouse, WMS program vendor, company IT, and integration team members develop communication between team members to ensure data and information communication exchange between team members. Moreover, it enhances each team member's understanding of warehouse interaction, integration, and interface factors. The factors require a WMS program computer communication between a company host computer and WMS program computer between warehouse computers. The communications ensure a) accurate and timely WMS identification SKU and position status, b) WMS program supported and non-WMS program SKU transaction updates, c) accurate and timely warehouse activity to satisfy a customer order, and d) customer-order completion communicated to the WMS program computer and WMS computer to the host computer.

Project Management, Master Project Schedule, and Contract Administration Meeting

At the beginning of a warehouse design and WMS program project, the project manager calls a project team meeting. During the meeting, the project manager:

1. Sets management meeting dates and project review ;
2. Updates the project master schedule;
3. Restates the company's contract administration procedures for warehouse equipmentr and WMS program vendors to submit a modification (based on your company's request to add a feature to a standard WMS program) of the a job, scope of work, or contract. To ensure good communication between a company and warehouse equipment vendors, WMS program vendor and between project team members, the project manager sets dates, locations, and times for major team member group meetings;
4. Establishes a project progress report, which is circulated to warehouse and WMS program team members

Building Construction, Warehouse Operation, and WMS Program Project Progress Report

Other project management responsibilities are building construction and warehouse equipment installation progress reports, daily building construction and warehouse vendor record keeping, and WMS program development progress report. A complete project progress report is sent to top management, the architect, the building construction company, warehouse equipment and WMS program vendors, and project files. To keep management up to date on a building/job site status, warehouse equipment progress, and WMS program development progress, the project manager prepares and distributes a weekly progress report to top management, the architect, the builder, and the design vendor. To be an effective tool, a report should be simple, precise, and to the point. A weekly project progress report measures building construction and warehouse equipment vendor performance against vendor schedules and the master project schedule. During an on-site project meeting with the architect, building contractor, warehouse equipment vendor, and the WMS program vendor, the project leader and the building construction, warehouse equipment, and WMS program vendors review equipment installation progress and identify, evaluate, and approve solutions to improve an off-schedule project event. If necessary, they discuss a construction, warehouse equipment, or WMS program installation/development problem. Because the problem is known and is associated with building construction, warehouse equipment, or WMS program development installation/development, this shows the problems were reviewed and resolved by team members at on-site project meetings. This shows project control and shows top management that the project manager is in control of the building construction, warehouse equipment, and WMS program installation/development.

Various Project Progress Reports

Project progress report forms can be:

- Preprinted forms that are a specially prepared for the building construction and warehouse equipment installation project. With a preprinted form, the manager fills in the date and, for the building construction and warehouse equipment vendors and WMS program development, the figures specifying the percent of the project completed. A preprinted form is easily understood, and when it is required to go back and trace the weekly project progress, it is easily obtained from the files. If the project is on schedule, a preprinted form is a good progress report.

■ Letter progress reports are preferred if a qualitative, rather than quantitative, statement is desired. A letter can be attached to a preprinted progress report form or layout copy project progress report form (see below). If the project is off-schedule with numerous delays, changes of scope, or job extras, the letter form is preferred to provide an explanation.

■ A combined building design and design layout plan view drawing. A layout drawing copy is an excellent means of communicating progress about building construction and warehouse equipment vendor installation. As building construction and warehouse equipment installation are completed on site, it is identified in the plan view layout drawing copy. When top management or key vendor management personnel visit a site, the project progress report format is quickly and easily understood. A plan view layout drawing report provides a building and warehouse picture with sufficient space to write any explanatory notes, shows most building design and warehouse operation key areas, and shows the flow to building construction or warehouse equipment installation from a receiving area through storage, pick and pack/check, manifest, and shipping areas. A layout drawing project progress form copy, when attached to a preprinted form or letter report, allows the layout progress report to be used for an on-schedule or off-scheduled project.

Project Schedule

At the first project team meeting, the project manager and the attendees review the project schedule. The project manager and each team member reviews, revises, and circulates the company master project schedule and team-member and associated subcontractors' project schedules. During this first meeting, the project manager and key company design team members review contract administration project requirements. The project manager and company team members:

1. Ensure that each warehouse equipment and WMS program vendor or noncompany team member invoice cost break out by your company finance department requirements such as subtotal for labor, equipment, and taxes that is per contract and includes a partial and final waiver of liens for a vendor payment to their labor and suppliers
2. For your company management vendor payment release an up-to-date major component cost statement. The statement shows actual, incurred, or invoiced costs; vendor payments; and warehouse equipment, WMS program or noncompany vendor project estimated cost and project life
3. Confirm budgeted cost estimate for warehouse equipment or WMS program vendor(s), and sample of how to prepare an extra or change of scope contract
4. A method to dispose of existing equipment.

Reviewing Drawings and Reports; Local Authority Approval

The design team receives the building construction plan, detail view drawings, and WMS program development report. To maintain the project schedule, the design team periodically reviews and revises the drawings and WMS program development report, and promptly returns the revised drawings and report. During the review process, the design team responds with "approved," "approved as noted," or "not approved." The design team makes corrections, revisions, or adjustments on the drawing or notes (letter) that accompany the returned drawing and WMS program development report. The notes should summarize items of concern. Communication to an architect/building construction company, and vendors for each drawing or report will be in a form of a transmittal form or letter. A copy of the transmittal form or letter is sent to assigned design team members and placed in company files. After the design team approves the warehouse equipment, the WMS program report, building plan view, and detail drawings, the team prepares drawings and documents for submission to local authorities. Local authority approval (or denial) determines the progress of the project from the design phase to construction/installation and start up.

If the local authority does not approve the building/warehouse design, the design team goes "back to the drawing board" and implements the local code authority's suggested revision. It is understood that local code authority nonapproval means a revised project start date, which requires a revised master schedule, which needs to be sent to all team members. Local code authority approval means that the project goes forward as designed. It is understood that local code authority approval means the project start date remains as shown on the master schedule, which is sent to all team members.

SKU/Customer-Order Flows; Developing a Phase Strategy

It is important to know what is needed for SKUs and customer-order flows to provide on-time and accurate customer service. The design team outlines (in the business narrative) WMS program supported activities and warehouse activities needed to complete customer orders. All WMS program supported activities or transactions are individually outlined in detail. The design team reviews and ranks each WMS program supported activity. This review and ranking identifies:

- What determines which phase a WMS program supported activity is implemented in the new or remodeled warehouse.
- Which warehouse activity is to continue or operate parallel in the existing facility or with the existing system as the new warehouse is started up.

The ranking approach has four phases:

- Phase I: start-up, which is critical
- Phase II: within six months, and is very important
- Phase III: within one year, and is important
- Phase IV: within two years, and somewhat important

What Can Be Moved from the Existing Warehouse to the New/Remodeled Warehouse

After a design team has reviewed the existing warehouse, completed the business narrative and project schedule, and determined start-up date, the team identifies the WMS supported activities, the symbology types, the symbology reader or scanner, the WMS identification scan transaction numbers, and the material handling equipment. With this information, the design team determines what warehouse equipment, procedures, and practices can be implemented in the existing warehouse and transferred to the new warehouse. Having the proposed new warehouse equipment, symbology, procedures, and practices in an existing warehouse will shorten the learning curve of the warehouse managers, staff and employees when a new warehouse is started up. Some items are:

- Identified each master carton/pallet with a symbology
- Symbology type for pallet/master carton
- Storage and pick position symbology
- Totes
- Forklift truck, hand-held, and fixed position scanners
- Customer packing slip/delivery label with symbology
- Customer return label and process activity
- Pallet type
- Symbology printers

Brain-Storming Sessions

After company management has determined the warehouse and WMS program type (e.g., basic, basic with some modifications, and basic with major modifications) or a WMS program design direction, the design team holds brain-storming sessions. The attendees are design team members, including the project manager, company warehouse specialists, and company IT or WMS program specialists. The specialists know all processes and flows in the existing operation and for the proposed operation. If the decision has already been made to go with a particular material handling equipment vendor or WMS program vendor, the design team will invite those vendors and the WMS program vendor project managers. If the WMS program or warehouse equipment vendors have not been selected, the design team will have all warehouse equipment mechanical and computer literature, WMS program basic literature, outline, description of operation. In brain-storming sessions, the design team will bring the following to the meeting:

- Available warehouse drawings with potential WMS program equipment locations
- Design warehouse volumes
- Warehouse, IT, and WMS equipment capabilities
- IT, WMS program, and material handling equipment operational data
- Warehouse activity list; number of WMS transactions; WMS program outline; SKU and customer-order flows
- Customer-order flow from the company host computer through the customer-order wave planning phase, through the WMS computer's SKU allocation and warehouse SKU transfer, pick line setup, IT/WMS customer-order release, and pick instruction print and warehouse customer-order completion
- WMS and host computer SKU inventory, position, and customer-order status update

The results of WMS brain storming sessions are put into a report that is circulated to the warehouse and WMS program design team members. The data becomes a) the basis for a WMS conference pilot study, b) the basis for WMS program modifications and warehouse design, and c) the total projected WMS program and warehouse costs, which should match the WMS program and warehouse budgeted costs.

Warehouse Operation Block Drawing

A useful tool in a brain storming session is a "not to scale" warehouse block drawing that shows a facility inside four walls. A block layout drawing is a schematic building representation developed quickly at low cost. A block drawing shows possible building column locations, fire walls, load-bearing walls, receiving and shipping dock areas, where each warehouse activity/process is located in a facility, and SKU and customer-order flow travel path. The drawing does not show any warehouse equipment. Each facility floor level is identified as the ground floor or an elevated floor. If there are multiple elevated floors in a facility, each elevated floor is identified and shown in sequence adjacent or above the ground floor. The floor arrangement permits a design team member to understand the relationship between elevated floors, potential vertical SKU or customer-order in-house transport concept travel paths, and employee stairways. A block drawing permits lines drawn between two warehouse operations and WMS program supported or non-WMS program supported activities/processes, which helps ensure proper SKU/customer-order flow. Additional lines represent communication lines between various warehouse activity locations.

From the brain storming sessions, the design team develops a list of WMS program supported activities/transactions and non-WMS program supported activities. From this, the team develops charts that show SKU and customer-order flow paths for vendor-delivered SKUs or customer orders sent from the host computer to the WMS program computer. In a WMS computer the warehouse staff has access to a WMS identified customer order pool for customer-order wave creation. Other charts show SKU data flow between the WMS computer and the warehouse computer; between the WMS computer and the host computer; and between the warehouse computer and a WMS program scan transaction station; and WMS data communication flow paths for vendor-delivered SKUs or host computer customer orders. This information is used to write an initial description of operations and to develop warehouse activity flow charts. Warehouse/SKU flow charts show the process that begins at a receiving dock, flows through storage positions to a pick position to a customer-order pack station, to a customer-order manifest station, and ends at a delivery vehicle. Directional arrows on the flow charts show SKU or customer-order flow direction, activity/operation descriptions, SKU classification change, warehouse and WMS program equipment, WMS program supported transactions, and non-WMS program supported transactions.

Typical brain-storming session results are listed below.

Proposed Warehouse Operation Design Activities that Have a WMS Scan Transaction

The design team reviews the existing and a proposed warehouse activity that is considered a WMS program supported transaction and non-WMS program supported transaction. The supported transactions are:

1. A receiving clerk with a hand-held scanner scans a SKU WMS identification master carton/pallet on a receiving dock, a receiver enters an associated WMS identification SKU quantity
2. A rejected vendor-delivered SKU placed into a position
3. A fork lift truck driver with a hand-held scanner scans a SKU WMS identification label on a receiving dock

4. A fork lift truck driver with a hand-held scanner scans a WMS SKU identification label and QA hold position label at a QA area and sends the scan transactions to the WMS computer

5. A QA staff member with a hand-held scanner scans a WMS SKU identification label and QA SKU transfer position label in a QA area

6. In a QA area, all disposed or damaged QA samples are a non-WMS transaction on WMS transaction sheet. The WMS program supported transaction is later entered into a WMS program as a SKU depletion transaction.

7. In a pallet/carton AS/RS crane operation at a size, weigh, and scan/read station storage design, a fixed-position scanner (e.g., fixed beam, moving beam, or waving beam) reads a pallet/master-carton WMS identification label

8. In a carton or pallet AS/RS crane storage operation, an AS/RS crane computer sends a SKU put-away transaction or deposit completion and a WMS identified position message to a WMS computer

9. In a WA, NA, or VNA forklift driver operation or manual storage put-away operation, a forklift truck driver or employee with a hand-held scanner/reader scans a WMS identified master-carton/pallet i label and storage/pick position label and sends transactions and SKU quantity to WMS computer

10. SKU moves from one position to another

11. WMS computer suggests a SKU withdrawal from a position

12. The warehouse completes a SKU pick line setup and replenishments to a pick position and completes scan transactions and SKU quantity are sent to the WMS computer

13. As a WMS identified customer order container enters a pick line to create and assure a customer order pack slip/delivery label is placed with a customer order container

14. Customer-order picks from a pick position into a warehouse or customer-order tote/carton. If a tote/carton becomes full and to complete a customer order, a picker completes a scan transaction that is sent to a WMS computer for a new carton or tote entry to a pick line to complete a WMS identified customer order. If damaged SKUs occur at a pick position, each damaged SKU is removed from the pick position and transferred to a damaged SKU container. A picker reduces the SKU quantity from the inventory with a SKU move transaction.

15. Zero scan transactions/counts for a depleted pick position, warehouse identified stacking frame or trolley, or zero scan a warehouse identified tote/carton at a pack station.

16. Add warehouse-identified container in a pick/pass design to scan a new warehouse carton/tote to complete a customer order

17. On a warehouse scale at customer-order check station, scan a customer-order identification and have the projected WMS customer-order weight displayed on a display screen. Have an employee or machine transfer out-of-weight (variance between a computer estimated and customer order container actual weight) customer order cartons/totes to a problem customer-order position at a customer order pack station with a remote printing customer order pack slip/ship label concept. Have an employee scan a warehouse tote identification for a pack station printer to print a WMS identified customer order pack slip/ship and label with central print customer order pack slips/ship labels concept sent to a pick line entry or sort station. At a pick line entry or sort station, an employee places a customer order WMS identification onto a customer order carton and transfers a customer order pack slip into a WMS identified customer order pick carton.

18. At a customer-order problem (O, S, and D) station, scan a customer order for SKU quantity and correct a customer-order problem
19. SKU reorganized or moved from one pick position to another pick position; vacant zero scan completed. All WMS move transactions, SKU quantity, and zero scan transactions are sent to the WMS computer.
20. At a customer-order pack station, zero scan a warehouse permanent identified captive tote
21. At a warehouse manifest station to automatic scan WMS identified customer order conveyable packages or to have an employee hand scan WMS identified nonconveyable packages
22. Off-load customer-order identified packages from a delivery truck and send to the warehouse computer
23. Customer returns unloaded onto customer returns process station in-feed concept
24. At a customer-returns process station, WMS scan a customer-order identification and issue customer credit
25. At a customer-returns process station, print a disposition slip for each SKU
26. Customer return-to-stock or return-to-vendor SKUs are warehouse employee sorted to initial SKU sort location
27. Customer return-to-stock or return-to-vendor SKU is sorted and scanned to a temporary holding WMS identified position; WMS scan transactions and SKU quantity are sent to a WMS computer for update
28. From a return-to-stock or return-to-vendor holding position, reverse or consolidate SKU pick into a container
29. A full WMS identified return-to-stock and return-to-vendor consolidated carton put-away to a WMS identified storage position that is sent to a WMS computer for WMS identified SKU and position update
30. Noncustomer order SKUs are picked, packed, manifested, and loaded
31. Cycle count or scan a SKU at a position and, per accounting procedures, update the SKU quantity in the WMS computer
32. Fiscal physical count or scan a SKU at a position and, per accounting procedures, update the SKU quantity in the WMS computer.

Define Terms, Develop Abbreviations

During the brain-storming session, the design team lists and defines terms and activities, and develops abbreviations used in the existing operation and will be used in the proposed operation, used by the WMS program, and used by the warehouse equipment vendor.

Conference Room Pilot Study

After a brain-storming session, the warehouse and WMS program team members attend a WMS program and warehouse conference room pilot study. Brain-storming sessions created the initial outline process for the WMS program and description of warehouse operations, list of WMS program supported/involved and non-WMS program supported/involved activities, SKU and customer-order flow paths for vendor-delivered SKUs or customer orders, WMS program data communication flow paths for vendor-delivered SKUs and customer orders, and activity flow charts. A pilot study follows a logical vendor-SKU and customer-order flow through the warehouse. The WMS program and warehouse pilot study team arrange warehouse activities in a sequence that has the first activity completed prior to the next activity. A pilot study starts with a high level (i.e., macro) view of the warehouse. It shows that warehouse activities or transactions start at a receiving dock and end at a shipping dock. For an effective pilot study, meetings should include key design team members: company team members from the brain-storming session, a representative of WMS program vendor, warehouse representatives (per an organization chart), and the WMS program integrator.

The pilot meeting team members use:

- Brain-storming session results, including a) the initial description of operations, b) the reviewed and revised list of WMS program supported/involved and non-WMS program supported/involved warehouse activities, c) SKU flow paths for vendor-delivered SKUs, d) WMS data communication flow paths for vendor-delivered SKUs and customer orders, and a flow chart for each warehouse activity
- Warehouse block, plan-view, and detail-view drawings
- Warehouse activity list
- Projected average and peak SKU vendor-delivery and customer-order volumes
- Projected SKU inventory volumes
- SKU change locations
- SKU scan transactions projection, SKU drop points or locations as shown on the WMS program and warehouse plan view drawing
- Work hours per day
- Existing warehouse or IT operational manuals and procedures, inventory control procedures, and the revised list of brain-storming session terms and abbreviations

The pilot study macro view starts at the receiving process, and shows that SKU/customer-order and data flow options are a) through the warehouse receiving process for a WMS identified SKU that is supported by a WMS program and ends at a warehouse shipping process or b) bypass a WMS program that is for a nonWMS identified SKU and ends at a warehouse shipping process.

The pilot study has a section for each WMS program supported or nonWMS program supported process or activity. A pilot study WMS program process macro view and micro (detailed) flow charts results are:

1. A macro view for each WMS program and warehouse process with a description of operations and charts that track the flow through the warehouse from when a SKU or customer order enters the WMS program supported activity or non-WMS program supported activity and end as a customer order leaves a facility.
2. A micro view for each WMS program and warehouse process, which includes a) each warehouse activity, b) WMS program data and physical SKU description, b) definitions of terms and words, d) a list of exceptions to WMS program supported activity, and e) SKU and WMS program date flow charts that trace sequential events to complete all activities.

The pilot study process sections are

- SKU vendor delivery, unloading, receiving, and WMS identification process
- QA SKU sample process
- SKU put-away and WMS program file update
- Customer-order wave plan activity that your warehouse staff completes in a WMS computer; a customer order wave that is released to a WMS computer.

- Based on a customer order wave, a WMS computer allocates SKUs for a warehouse to complete SKU move transactions; and based on a SKU transfer to a pick position (pick line setup) WMS identified SKU and positions and SKU quantity, scan transactions are sent to a WMS computer that releases customer orders to a pick line/activity,
- Pick
- Pack
- Customer-order pick error handling station
- Pick line SKU replenishment
- Customer-order manifest and shipping
- Customer returns process, disposition, and SKU put-away
- Return-to-vendor and other noncustomer order and WMS program supported activities
- Cycle and specific SKU counts

Conference Room Pilot Study Flow Charts

Each warehouse and WMS program conference room pilot activity section has macro and micro flow charts. A macro flow chart starts as a SKU or customer order enters a warehouse activity area. A flow chart has one line that shows a WMS program information transfer and a second line that shows a SKU flow that ends as the SKU or customer order leaves one warehouse activity station/area and enters another warehouse activity station/area. A warehouse and WMS program conference room pilot study micro flow group contains several flow charts.

Business Narrative

The business narrative contains written text, sketches, and flow charts. It is written by the WMS program and design team. The business narrative is derived from brain-storming sessions, conference room pilot study reports, warehouse drawings, and description of operations and the WMS program. An effective business narrative is separated in sections that focus on each warehouse activity. The business narrative operational section or process:

- Traces SKU or customer-order and information flows through each warehouse activity section.
- Describes communication between a) the host computer and WMS computer, b) the WMS program and warehouse computer
- Indicates each warehouse activity that is a WMS program-supported transaction and describes the SKU and information flows.
- Indicates the warehouse location of each SKU or customer-order transaction and indicates the WMS equipment type.
- Defines terms and abbreviations.
- Explains and shows the relationship, interface, and interaction between various warehouse activities as shown on the WMS program and warehouse plan view drawing.

The business narrative is the basis for all future WMS program or warehouse documentation, WMS transaction equipment type and number, WMS program and warehouse drawing revisions, descriptions of warehouse operations, staff/employee training manuals, and WMS program development and design. The warehouse operation layout drawings are complete and detailed. For the

WMS program and warehouse project, the business narrative is considered the heart of an efficient and cost effective design, development, installation, implementation, start-up, and turn-over.

A well-written business narrative provides:

- A warehouse manager, department process manager, or staff with an understanding of how to complete a WMS program supported transaction to achieve a warehouse objective.
- WMS program writers or code employees an understanding of a warehouse process and the purpose of a WMS program supported transaction, and enables them to write a computer program that achieves warehouse and WMS objectives.
- Warehouse equipment vendors and computer staff an understanding of the interface, relationship, and interaction between WMS program transactions and warehouse computer and the WMS computer and company host computer
- The WMS program and warehouse integrator the ability to visualize a macro view of warehouse and WMS program systems and to understand each warehouse activity. It further allows an integrator to understand the interface, relationship, and interaction between the WMS program supported transactions and warehouse equipment and the WMS computer and company host computer.
- The company and IT staff an understanding of the interface, relationship, and interaction between the WMS program supported or non-WMS supported transactions, warehouse computer, and WMS computer and company host computer.

The completed business narrative will be made up of a cover page with a revision number and names of the development team; a table of contents; building, warehouse, and general information on the WMS program; and sections on the WMS program and warehouse. The WMS program and warehouse sections are:

- Receiving dock appointment schedule
- Receiving and purchase order closure, WMS identification of SKU with quantity entry to the WMS computer, and SKU transport
- QA process on a SKU
- SKU put-away or deposit and scanning/reading the size/weight/bar code/RF tag read
- Customer-returns unloading, customer-order credit process with the host or WMS computer, and SKU disposition and transfer to a position
- Host computer customer-order receipt and process, customer-order wave plan and SKU allocation, warehouse SKU withdrawal or replenishment, and pick line setup and reorganization of SKU from one pick position to another
- Customer-order release to pick activity that transfers SKUs into a warehouse identified tote that is associated to a customer order WMS identification or into a customer order WMS identified carton, and, if required, a warehouse (pick to light or automatic pick machine) computer sends a SKU pick transaction completion message to a WMS program for a picked SKU depletion from inventory
- Warehouse customer-order packing and, if required, an employee WMS scans each SKU and a message is sent to a WMS program for a picked/packed SKU depletion from inventory
- Warehouse customer-order SKU pick error handling
- Customer-order manifest, loading, and shipping, customer-order update to the WMS computer, and WMS computer update to the host computer
- Inventory control and SKU adjustments

- Noncustomer orders and SKU pick
- Vendor and customer order return rework and value added activities.

Finally, the business narrative should include appendices with pictures, sketches, forms, and charts.

Revision History

The revision history section states the completion date for the first draft and location of the business narrative. Each business narrative revision or rewrite has a draft number, revision date, change location, and is circulated to all team members.

Business Narrative Circulation List

The business narrative circulation list identifies recipients of the business narrative. The list indicates team members and ensures that all key design team members received the latest business narrative copy. Design team members are responsible for ensuring that key internal company staff assigned to the project (e.g., WMS program vendor, warehouse equipment vendor, integrator), company IT department, and warehouse staff receive a copy.

Business Narrative Management Overview

The business narrative overview provides a reader with an understanding of a busniess narrative, warehouse operation design, and WMS program development, and is separated into three parts. First, is the history of the existing warehouse and its characteristics. Second, proposed WMS program features. Finally, a proposed macro-view description of the warehouse.

The section on the features of the proposed WMS program states that the objective is to develop a cost effective and efficient vendor-delivered SKU and customer-order flow through the warehouse, accurate and on-time information or data communications, and the best customer service at the lowest possible cost. The description of operations offers a brief description of each warehouse activity supported—or not—by the WMS program. Each brief description indicates how the warehouse and WMS program will interface/interact with employee activity to successfully complete an accurate and on-time SKU, customer-order SKU, or information/WMS transaction flow.

Each overview section is a detailed explanation or outline for each warehouse activity. A warehouse activity is defined as a WMS program supported or non-WMS program supported transaction. A design team member or reader has to have a complete understanding of a WMS identified SKU or customer-order flow, information flow through a warehouse as a WMS program supported transaction or a nonWMS program supported transaction. To provide this picture, each business narrative section has 1) overflow SKU or customer flow chart, 2) warehouse activity description overview, 3) warehouse functional description that includes sketches, pictures, document samples or other material and 4) exception or problem to a warehouse activity and corrective action to have a warehouse activity completed is a WMS program supported or nonWMS program supported transaction.

Business Narrative General Information

The general information sections of the business narrative are:

- Each warehouse building feature and as required a building number
- Warehouse design features
- Warehouse activities
- SKU and customer-order characteristics
- Terms and abbreviations

Each warehouse building section is assigned to a major warehouse activity and the identification for each activity. Each description outlines important warehouse characteristics, such as:

- Pallet, master-carton, and single-item storage or pick positions
- Storage transaction vehicles, e.g., WA, NA, or VNA employee-controlled forklift truck or AS/RS crane number and type
- Customer-order pick design, e.g., pick/pass, pick and sort, cart, powered vehicle, or automatic pick machine
- In-house transport design
- Customer-order pack design
- Warehouse storage/pick rows and aisle number with the height and aisle width
- Warehouse functional overview description with SKU and customer-order characteristics
- Warehouse activities that are completed in the building

Business Narrative Flow Chart Section

The business narrative process/activity overview flow chart is developed from the brain-storming session and conference room pilot process flow charts, block drawings, plan-view drawings, description of operations, and other warehouse or WMS program material. Each flow chart is a macro view of an entire warehouse process, starting from when a SKU or customer order enters the warehouse process station/area, identifies all subactivities or WMS or non-WMS transactions involved in completing a SKU/customer-order transaction, and indicates a SKU or customer-order exit to the next warehouse activity or facility.

The business narrative overview flow chart uses the same components as the conference room pilot study flow charts. The flow chart components are:

1. The title (a brief statement that identifies the warehouse process).
2. A square, rectangle, circle, or four-sided or elliptical image for each warehouse/WMS program segment/section (which represents an employee, conventional forklift truck, or automatic process activity as a WMS program supported/non-WMS program supported transaction or communication). Each warehouse employee, automatic pick machine. or AS/RS crane process activity is arranged sequentially.
3. A brief written statement within each warehouse activity/communication square, rectangle, circle, four-sided, or elliptical image. The statement describes a warehouse activity as a WMS program supported/non-WMS program supported transaction or communication event.
4. Lines that connect shapes/images. Each line has a directional arrow for SKU or customer-order information and flow between actitivies and locations.

A warehouse employee activity moves a WMS identified SKU or customer order as a WMS program supported transaction.

Business Narrative Process Description Overview

The business narrative process description overview is a text that is used to develop your standard warehouse procedures. A process description overview is used with an overview flow chart to provide a macro view of the warehouse's physical SKU flow. It permits the design team (or reader) to understand that flow and how a warehouse operation benefits from a warehouse operation that has WMS program supported transactions (processes, events, or activities). A process description includes:

- SKU or customer order physical characteristics, documentation (e.g., receiving tally sheet, WMS SKU identification label, customer-order pick instructions, WMS identification for a storage/pick position, customer-order packing slip/delivery label, delivery drop point)
- A description of the flow between two warehouse locations or to and from locations
- Employee job titles and equipment responsibility

Business Narrative Functional Description Section

The business narrative functional description is a summary document based on the overview flow chart and process description overview. Using these business narrative sections and other WMS program and warehouse design material, the design team prepares a document that includes a description of the interface between the WMS program and the warehouse and can be used to develop each warehouse operation (employee) activity job description. A functional description describes the first warehouse activity, each subsequent warehouse activity, and what is required from warehouse employee, automatic pick machine, or AS/RS crane to complete a WMS identified SKU activity. A warehouse activity is a WMS program supported activity that moves a WMS identified SKU from one warehouse activity/position to another warehouse activity/position that complete a WMS identified SKU move transaction or has a WMS identified customer order exits (manifest) a warehouse.

Business Narrative Exception Handling Section

The business narrative exceptional handling activity section outlines each potential SKU or customer-order handling problem, documents the impact of a problem on the WMS program, and provides information on problem resolution.

Business Narrative and Warehouse Design Issues and Options

The business narrative WMS program and warehouse issues involve how a SKU or customer order transaction is completed and outlines an impact on a WMS program or warehouse computer/ operations. In the business narrative, the design team defines:

- How a SKU or customer-order transaction is completed.
- When a SKU or customer-order transaction is completed or sent to the WMS computer.

- What is required to complete a SKU or customer-order transaction.
- How a warehouse employee, automatic pick machine, or AS/RS crane completes a SKU or customer-order transaction.
- Where a SKU or customer-order transaction is completed.

After the design team defines issues of a WMS program operating with a warehouse and identifies alternative options, the team selects a preferred option for implementation or installation in the WMS program or warehouse. Some WMS program and warehouse issues are:

- Warehouse type
- SKU classification
- WMS program supported or non-WMS program supported transactions
- Storage or pick location number sequence
- Electrical back-up
- Purchase order or advance shipping notice
- Dock schedule
- Type of across-the-dock operation
- Warehouse customer-order wave plan
- WMS computer SKU allocation
- Customer-order pack/delivery label print location
- Customer-order pick line or warehouse tote identification associated with a WMS identification

Warehouse Operation Options

The type operation has a major impact on the planned warehouse and WMS program. Drawing on information from top management and the business plan, the design team indicates whether a warehouse is:

1. A store-and-hold (i.e., conventional) warehouse. This is basically a demand-pull business model in which customers place orders for SKUs. SKUs are held in a warehouse storage area or pick position and, per the customer-order wave plan, customer-order SKU quantities are withdrawn from inventory, packed into a shipping carton, the customer-order WMS identification is manifested, and and the carton is delivered to a customer. A store-and-hold business model is more common in catalog, telemarketing, e-mail, wholesale, pharmaceutical businesses, and some retail business industries (e.g., food industry). A store-and-hold design has a greater number of WMS program supported and non-WMS program supported transactions than other types of operations. WMS transactions occur within a short time period and customer orders may have one or several SKU classifications. SKU classifications are single items, master cartons, or pallets.
2. An across-the-dock operation is a push (i.e., predetermined demand) business model in which SKUs are pre-allocated to each customer. As SKUs are unloaded from a vendor delivery truck, each SKU is sent to a customer-order staging/drop point. As the SKU is placed onto a delivery truck, the order is scanned (manifest activity). This business model is common in the retail hard goods industry, in which there are fewer WMS supported transactions. Transactions occur at receiving, manifest, and shipping docks.

The WMS business narrative for a store-and-hold warehouse with a WMS program is more complex and comprehensive for a store-and-hold operation than an across-the-dock operation. A standard across-the-dock operation has only move transactions, no SKU storage or change activities and no customer return activities. A store and hold warehouse WMS program is more complex due to additional activities, higher move transactions, customer return activities and potential SKU change such as pre-pack.

SKU Classifications

When the design team develops the business narrative, SKU classification and SKU number in a warehouse has an impact on a business narrative magnitude. Each SKU subgroup is described in the business narrative and provides a WMS program writer with the information to ensure that proper flags are in a WMS program. WMS program flag examples are SKU special handling appears on a receiving tally sheet or to have a WMS identification that identifies a storage area or to have a warehouse complete a suggested SKU transaction.

Pallet Warehouse Operation: Business Narrative

A pallet warehouse receives pallets from vendors. The WMS program identifies pallets and sends pallets to customers. A pallet operation has fewer SKUs, fewer WMS transactions, and fewer warehouse activity stations. A pallet operation has a less complex business narrative.

Master-Carton Warehouse Operation Business Narrative

A master-carton warehouse receives pallets/master-cartons from vendors and sends master cartons/pallets to customers. A master-carton operation has a business narrative of medium complexity.

Single-Item Warehouse Operation: Business Narrative

A single-item operation receives pallets or master-cartons from vendors. each SKU receives a WMS identification and sends pallets, master cartons, or single items to customers. A single-item warehouse business narrative is most complex to write.

WMS Program SKU/Customer-Order Transaction/Activity

A warehouse has a warehouse employee, automatic pick machine, or AS/RS crane to complete a transaction or activity. A transaction/activity moves a vendor-delivered SKU from a receiving dock to a storage position, or moves a customer-order SKU from a storage/pick position to a pack station, drop point, or delivery vehicle. Warehouse transaction activity can be:

1. A WMS program supported transaction. In a WMS supported activity/transaction, a warehouse moves or handles a SKU from a vendor delivery (or for a customer order) between two positions. As a warehouse employee, pick machine, or AS/RS crane completes the transaction, the SKU and storage/pick position status is sent to the WMS computer for update in WMS inventory files. An SKU involved in a WMS program supported transaction is available for sale (customer order) or is a SKU on QA hold, which is placed into a storage/pick position, completed at a pack station, or manifested at a shipping dock.
2. A non-WMS program supported transaction. A WMS program nonsupported transaction/activity moves a non-SKU (e.g., shipping supplies) from a vendor delivery truck (or for a customer order) between two identified positions. As an employee completes the transaction, the employee completes a document to indicate the SKU and associated position. In an office, a clerk updates files.

Using WMS program supported transaction definitions, the design team lists each warehouse transaction as a WMS program supported or non-WMS program supported transaction.

Where Are Supported Activities Connected

A key to the successful design, implementation, and start-up of a warehouse operation is to identify the "where, when, how, who, and what" questions. The design team identifies the warehouse activities that are or are not WMS program supported. The design team focuses their attention first on WMS program supported activities: receiving, QA, storage deposit and withdrawal, moves, relocation, withdrawal and picks, pack, manifest, customer returns, and inventory counts. Non-WMS program supported activities are noncustomer orders and office and shipping supplies.

Warehouse Operation and WMS/Warehouse Computers: Electrical Considerations

A modern warehouse will have computer-controlled equipment and WMS program computer or scanner/reader components that require electrical power. Electrical design considerations are:

■ Have sufficient KVA in-feed based on warehouse and WMS program transaction demands operating all building, IT, and warehouse operation equipment at one time.
■ A spike-free electric power supply.
■ A back-up electric power supply or an uninterruptible power supply.

To ensure there is a sufficient KVA electrical power supply, the design team should have the warehouse vendor, architect, building contractor, WMS/IT vendor, and local power company estimate a design year required KVA and facility-provided KVA. If there is a power supply short fall, the design team develops a cost estimate and time schedule for having a proper KVA electric power supply provided at a preferred location at a facility. The design team and local power company evaluate the quality of the electric power supply. If there are spikes, the design team develops a cost estimate and time schedule for equipment to filter/level-off the power flow. It is noted that a spike filter can be a component on back-up electric power supply equipment. The design team has the warehouse, IT group, WMS program vendor, architect, and power company determine the specification of the back-up electric power supply equipment. Specifications include:

- KVA requirement
- What warehouse operation, WMS and IT equipment, and building components will be operating and what the operation duration will be.
- The back-up electric power supply provider type, which can be a battery, a manually activated generator, or an automatically activated generator. The issues include whether to include a spike filter, time schedule, and cost.

Drop, Divert, or In-House Transport Design Delivery or Drop Location

To complete an across-the-dock move or a conventional storage/pick operation customer-order SKU pick transaction, the WMS program communicates with the warehouse to complete the required physical warehouse storage withdrawal transaction, move, divert, and pick transaction. To ensure an efficient, cost-effective, and on-time warehouse SKU or customer-order transaction, the WMS computer has each warehouse drop point, transaction point, or storage/pick position identified in the WMS program. To ensure that the warehouse design has a clear and precise road map for each SKU transaction, the design team identifies each drop point, transaction point, or storage/pick position in the warehouse. On the warehouse plan-view drawing, the design team identifies each SKU or customer order drop point, transaction point, warehouse storage and pick aisle, divert location, and pick point. An elevated view drawing shows storage/pick positions with relevant elevations. There is a legend on each warehouse drawing to show an abbreviation use.

WMS Customer-Order Identifications

The design team's options for WMS customer-order identification and associated SKU transfer to a pick design are to use total customer-order allocation or specific SKU or customer order.

Specific SKU or Customer-Order Allocation

A specific SKU or customer-order allocation design has the WMS program complete a specific SKU or customer-order separation prior to the order (and associated SKU quantity) is transferred to the pick design. In a warehouse, the customer-order type, customer-order SKUs, and associated pieces are constantly changing variables. In most WMS programs, a special written program or program section is required to allocate a specific SKU or customer order. A special written customer-order WMS program adds to the WMS program cost, WMS program development and implementation time, extends the WMS computer's time period for customer-order release to a pick design, and potentially adds pick line SKU setup or replenishment transactions.

SKU/Customer Order WMS Program and Non-WMS Program Supported Transaction Projection

The design team projects SKU/customer order transactions (WMS program or non-WMS program supported). The transaction projection provides the design team with insight into:

- What the WMS program computer has to work with.
- Where a given transaction starts.

- What device creates a transaction.
- What computer a) warehouse computer for later transfer to a WMS computer or b) direct transfer to a WMS computer
- How long it takes to complete a transfer transaction.

Using SKU/customer-order and volume design parameter tables, the design team uses projections (e.g., average, most frequent, or peak) of vendor-delivered SKUs, customer orders, or non-SKU transactions as basis for projecting WMS program supported and nonsupported transactions. Tables are completed for each WMS program supported warehouse activity. To determine a transaction volume for design year, the design team:

- Identifies each warehouse activity and location
- Defines a warehouse activity as a WMS program supported transaction or non-WMS program supported transaction.
- Determines the number of transactions per hour
- Decides if a transaction will be delayed, batched, or put on-line from the warehouse to the WMS computer
- Determines transaction equipment type

To answer these questions, the design team uses a WMS program and warehouse activity spreadsheet (see Figure 14.1). The spread sheet sections are a) warehouse activity list, b) warehouse work hours per day, c) projected peak transactions per hour, d) delayed, batched, or on-line transaction communication between the warehouse and the WMS computer, e) transaction equipment.

The spreadsheet's first column has a line for each warehouse process/activity. To be more easily understood, the activity list is arranged in a warehouse activity sequence:

WAREHOUSE ACTIVITY	WMS DEVICE HAND HELD	FIXED SIDE	FIXED TOP	TOTAL NUMBER DEVICES	WMS SCAN TRANSACTIONS HOURS OF WORK 1 2 3 4 5 6 7 8 9 TOT	ACT DELAY	TRANSMISSION ON-LINE	TO	FROM
RECEIVING									
QA									
TRANSPORT									
PUT-AWAY									
REPLENISH									
PICK									
PICK CHECK									
PACK									
MANIFEST									
ON/OFFLOAD									
RETURNS									
INVENTORY									
OTHERS									

Figure 14.1 WMS Program Supported Transaction Projection Form

1. Vendor SKU delivery, beginning with vendor dock appointment schedule activity, which includes unloading, SKU WMS identification, and transport to a storage position for warehouse SKU storage put-away or deposit activity

2. After a warehouse customer-order wave plan, a WMS computer completes SKU allocations and sends SKU move transactions to a warehouse. A warehouse completes SKU move transactions to pick positions and sends SKU and position WMS identifications and quantity message to a WMS computer for update and customer order release to a warehouse pick concept

3. Customer-order SKU flow through a warehouse, starting from a storage position, to a pick area, customer-order pack station, customer-order manifest, load area, SKU depletion, and customer-order status updated in the WMS computer

With this format, the spreadsheet activity or process sequence is as follows:

1. Vendor dock appointment schedule with purchase order release

2. Unloading/receiving process with WMS label print, SKU WMS identification scan transaction, and WMS identification SKU entry

3. QA sample transfer to QA with WMS SKU identification and WMS holding position WMS scan transactions and SKU entry

4. QA sample transfer from QA with WMS SKU identification and holding position WMS scan transactions and SKU entry

5. SKU WMS scan/read for transport from receiving/QA to a storage area

6. For a pallet AS/RS concept, equipment to a) verify a pallet quality or pallet bottom deck board warehouse, b) to assure a pallet size/weigh is acceptable, c) to assure a pallet wrap activity permits bar code scanner to read a bar code, and d) if a SKU (pallet) is rejected, to show the SKU WMS identification and associated reject reason that is displayed on a work station PC screen or printed on a paper document

7. SKU bar code/RF tag read for in-house transport

8. In a manual forklift truck operation, SKU and storage position WMS scan transaction for a SKU deposit or put-away; with an AS/RS design, warehouse SKU transaction completion communication to the WMS computer

9. SKU move transaction in which a SKU is moved from a storage position to a new position,

10. SKU withdrawal scan transaction and entry from a storage position

11. SKU bar code, code/RF tag read for in-house transport

12. SKU transfer, setup, or replenishment to a pick position with SKU WMS identification and SKU entry WMS scan transactions

13. Company host customer order entry to the WMS computer

14. Warehouse customer-order wave creation and transfer to the WMS to allocate SKUs for a warehouse move and WMS scan transaction

15. Warehouse transfers a SKU from a storage to a pick area, customer-order WMS identification associated with a pick-to-light warehouse tote identification, or print a customer order pick, pack, and delivery label document

16. WMS SKU pick transaction completion and pick position zero scan transaction

17. Warehouse pick-clean or re-organization WMS SKU identification scan and SKU entry transaction and warehouse transport

18. WMS SKU identification scan to a new WMS pick position identification and SKU entry transaction

19. Customer-order SKU pick transaction complete and transfer to conveyor for warehouse transaction
20. Completed customer-order in-house transport to a customer-order pack station
21. Customer-order SKU pick check activity, warehouse customer-order identification scan, and computer weight check
22. Pack activity warehouse divert, customer-order identification scan, print pack slip and delivery label, and zero WMS scan warehouse tote label
23. Customer-order transport to a problem customer-order station
24. WMS problem customer-order scan
25. Customer-order in-house transport to a customer-order manifest station
26. Customer-order WMS identification scan and customer-order WMS identification transfer to the WMS computer and warehouse sort computer
27. Warehouse did not read and sort to problem station with WMS scan customer-order identification and label print
28. Nonconveyable SKU customer-order WMS identification and customer-order WMS identification WMS scan transfer to the WMS computer
29. Warehouse off-load customer-order WMS identification from delivery truck and WMS customer-order identification WMS scan transfer to the WMS computer
30. Customer returns unload, open, transport, and warehouse divert
31. Customer-return WMS identification scan and communication to host computer/WMS computer
32. Warehouse issue customer credit to host computer
33. Customer returns processed and disposed SKU WMS identification and print WMS SKU label
34. Warehouse WMS SKU identification scan and transfer to sort area
35. WMS SKU identification scan and WMS scan to a storage position and SKU entry
36. WMS computer reverse pick customer order returns SKUs in a position
37. Disposed customer returns warehouse transport
38. WMS customer-order returns SKU identification scan, WMS storage position scan, and SKU entry to complete deposit
39. Cycle or fiscal count WMS scan transaction and SKU entry
40. Noncustomer order WMS pick instruction print or label creation
41. Noncustomer order WMS pick activity and SKU entry and pick position scan
42. Customer-order pack transactions and label creation
43. Noncustomer order WMS manifest transaction

The spreadsheet has a column for each work day hour. Under each column are seven rows:

1. Hand-held scanner (HH)
2. Fixed position scanner (F)
3. WMS supported transaction (W)
4. Non-WMS supported transaction (N)
5. Held communication (H)
6. Delayed communication (D)
7. On-line communication (O)

For each warehouse activity line intersection with a work-hour column, the design team enters the number of transactions calculated in operational design tables. Example: An 8-hour operation runs from 0800 to 1800, with 15-minute break in the morning, a 1-hour lunch, and and 15-minute break in the afternoon. For a split shift or 24-hour operation, the table would include additional hour columns.

After the design team has completed the spreadsheet, by totaling each column the design team determines number of scan transactions that are:

- Completed by hand-held scanners/readers
- Completed by fixed position scanner/readers
- WMS program supported
- Non-WMS program supported
- WMS scan transactions held by a scanner/reader and delayed before being communicated to the WMS computer
- WMS scan transactions are sent to a PC that communicates with the WMS computer
- WMS scan transactions are communicated on-line to the WMS computer

WMS Program Equipment Location Drawing

After the building plan-view drawing is approved by the design team and the local building authority, the members of the design team responsible for the WMS program and warehouse operation use the warehouse plan-view drawing to develop a WMS equipment drawing. On the WMS program drawing, the WMS program vendor and design team use symbols (with a legend) to identify each warehouse location that has a WMS program supported transaction that uses WMS communication equipment. Examples of these locations are: WMS SKU or customer-order label printer, WMS hand-held scanner/reader, WMS fixed-position scanner, size/weigh/bar code scanners/RF tag readers, WMS computer room, and warehouse computer room.

Drop Point Location Drawing

On a drop-point or location drawing, the design team uses symbols to identify each warehouse location that has a drop point. Examples of drop point locations: receiving dock lane, AS/RS crane or storage P/D station, pick position or replenishment aisle, size/weigh/bar code/RF tag station, pack stations, and ship dock staging area or door.

WMS Equipment Specification

The design team determines the necessary WMS equipment and its specification by the business narrative, WMS transaction tables, plan-view drawings, and description of operations. The number of transactions per hour (on-line, delayed, or held; WMS supported or non-WMS supported) affects the WMS program computer capacity to receive all transactions, the number of scanners (hand held or fixed position), and required cable or RF antennas.

WMS Program Development

Using the business narrative, WMS transaction number, description of operations, WMS program and warehouse layout drawing, and warehouse manuals, the WMS program vendor starts to develop code or WMS program for a warehouse. The design team and WMS program vendor project schedule establishes "milestone" dates for:

1. Initial WMS program review meeting
2. Mid-project WMS program review meeting
3. Final project WMS program review meeting
4. Initial test
5. Pre-test prior to installation
6. Each installation milestone event

The design team meets to ensure that the WMS program development and WMS program and warehouse interface phases are progressing on schedule and as designed. During the meetings, the design team and WMS program coders or writers set integration or interface dates.

WMS Business Narrative: Equipment Changes and Revisions

After the business narrative is completed, and the scope of the work is reviewed by the WMS vendor program development team and warehouse vendor, WMS program and warehouse integrator, IT department, and design team, who also confirm that the narrative provides a realistic time line for each WMS program and warehouse operation component. If a WMS vendor program vendor wishes to change the scope of the work, the design team prioritizes the scope of work objectives for the WMS program and separates the scope of work into phases I and II. Phase I items are WMS program items required to operate a basic warehouse and are included in the start-up and turn-over phases. After phase I items are accepted by the warehouse and IT operations, phase II items are included for the WMS program and warehouse project.

The design team updates and revises the company master project schedule, WMS program vendor project schedule, warehouse vendor project schedule, WMS program and warehouse integrator schedule, and building construction schedule. The design team holds a meeting to review, explain, and confirm an understanding of the company master and each vendor project schedule. The WMS program vendor, warehouse equipment vendor, WMS program and warehouse integrator, architect, and building construction company receive an updated schedule and a copy is placed in the company files.

The project design team develops new WMS program and warehouse equipment vendor payment estimates, and works with the WMS program vendor, warehouse equipment vendor, and WMS program and warehouse integrator to adjust equipment purchase and installation plans. Letters are sent to each project team member and copies are placed in the company files. On a weekly or monthly basis, the project team prepares a progress report on building construction, WMS program development, and warehouse equipment installation. The project progress reports are sent to each team member, top company management team, and copies are placed in the files.

Bid and Purchase of WMS Program Equipment

After the WMS program vendor's completed bids are returned to the design team, the team completes a bid review. The bid review results determines which WMS program vendor will be recommended to top management and establishes a basis for vendor negations. The WMS program bid review includes major factors and subgroups:

- WMS program economics, with separate lines for a) standard WMS program, b) specialized WMS program, and c) proposed revision or change costs
- Bar code scanner/RF tag reader costs (e.g., hand held, fixed position, associated communication network)
- IT or computer equipment
- Back-up electrical supply and spike or surge protector
- Time line that has all major events and work day number, including development, code, test, on-site, install and start-up, turn-over, and revisions or modifications
- Guarantee time period from a WMS program and warehouse equipment turn-over to a warehouse operation to handle actual vendor delivered SKUs and customer orders
- Taxes included
- Required KVA, including air conditioning requirement
- Integration cost as an option
- License cost

Description of Operations and Employee Training Manuals

The description of operations and training manual is based on the business narrative, WMS program and warehouse operation drawings, and vendor literature. The description of operations and training manuals are used to educate company managers, employees, and vendors about SKU/customer-order flows and physical characteristics, proper methods for completing a WMS scan transaction

Description of Operations

The descriptions of operations is a written description that presents macro- and micro-pictures of each warehouse activity. The description of operations includes:

- Warehouse business total facility description, with subsections including site, buildings, warehouse equipment and layout, WMS program, warehouse and WMS program interfaces and interaction locations, WMS data or information flow, vendor and non-SKU flows, customer-order flow and customer-returns SKU flow, characteristics, and volumes.
- Each warehouse SKU or customer order activity as a WMS program supported and non-WMS program supported activity/transaction.

Each section is sequenced to match as closely as possible to the vendor SKU, customer-order, and customer-order returns SKU flow through the warehouse.

The micro view shows the host computer, WMS program computer, and warehouse computer interaction and interface locations, data, WMS program supported transactions or non-WMS program supported transactions, customer-order flow, customer-order wave plan (and WMS program SKU allocation to match a customer-order wave), and customer-order returns flow to a return-to-stock or return-to-vendor position. A micro view includes drawings, explanations, exceptions, and problem situations with resolutions.

Training Manuals

The training manual is produced by the company and the warehouse and WMS program vendor, which looks at each employee, machine, or warehouse computer controlled machine/crane activity, transaction, or process. Detailed statements trace vendor-delivered SKUs, customer orders, and customer-order returns SKU as they flow through the warehouse, along with information and data flows to satisfy a customer order or noncustomer order for a SKU. After reading a training manual or attending a training session, there should be no unanswered questions.

WMS Program and Operation Integration: Test, Implementation, and Turn-Over

After the warehouse equipment vendor, the WMS program vendor, and the warehouse WMS program integrator have completed the manufacturing, code development, installation, and implementation, the vendors notify the company that they are ready to complete an on-site warehouse and WMS program debugging activities. The company provides vendors with sample vendor delivered SKUs, customer orders, and customer-order returns to test and debug the warehouse. During a test, a company completes a punch list and performance test. Based on a warehouse and WMS program contracts, the punch list and acceptance tests are completed with warehouse and WMS program vendors. Most acceptance tests are based on a certain number of continuous hours of operation that moves SKUs, customer orders, and customer-order returns through a warehouse, all as WMS supported transactions. If there is a shut down or major problem, the acceptance test hour clock returns to zero. After a successful acceptance test, a warehouse or WMS program is turned-over to the operations department for use.

Audit, Review, and Operation Reports

After a successful start-up and on-going operation without negative events, the design team completes an audit and review and implements operation reports. The operation design team has meetings that focus on a) the design parameters in comparison to actual SKU and customer-order volumes and practices, b) actual warehouse and WMS program performance, c) SKU and customer-order mix and volume changes, and d) suggested warehouse and WMS program enhancements, modifications, and operation reports.

The operation reports are added to use WMS program data to:

- Measure employee productivity in each warehouse major activity (e.g., receiving, pick, pack)
- Check the completeness of picked, packed, and shipped customer orders
- Take care of customer orders with a fixed or special pick-up time (e.g., FX or international customers)
- Review the handling of customer orders with a critical SKU (e.g., a SKU with a potential backorder situation) and informing the customer about the situation
- Synchronize the data between WMS and the freight company/transporter IT system
- Provide an operation with reports to improve labor control and on-time monitor an operation performance

A short interval schedule is used in a warehouse operation to track a storage/pick, employee's, or transport vehicle's performance for on-time or delayed completion of a task. A short interval schedule is used in a manually controlled storage vehicle design, manual walk/ride to a pick position pick, or transport design to provide an operation manager with accurate design or picker productivity data. Because each SKU has a WMS identification and the warehouse computer determines the deposit/pick-up location or storage position, to track a SKU flow, each employee or vehicle receives an identification. When the identifications are scanned into a computer, then the computer determines the projected time for an employee- or computer-controlled vehicle to complete a transaction. After an employee- or computer-controlled vehicle returns to home base, the actual return time is scanned into the computer, which compares the actual time to the projected time. The comparison identifies employee or vehicle on-time performance.

Monitoring the Pick and Pack Activity

Being able to monitor pick and pack activity provides an order fulfillment manager with accurate and real-time pick and pack productivity and the number of completed customer orders per hour. A WMS customer order wave or work day customer orders are sent in a warehouse manifest computer and after each ship carton WMS customer order identification is scanned/read and a message sent to a manifest computer, a warehouse or WMS computer has an opportunity to show the total completed customer order number on a display screen and at a specific time the number of completed customer orders. With this information, a warehouse manager can allocate the correct amount of labor to ensure customer order wave completion.

The monitor design uses customer-order classification group numbers. The classifications are the single line/single SKU, single line/multiple SKU, multi-line, and a combination order, which are sent to a warehouse manifest computer. The computer maintains the classification and the total number of customer orders. As a customer order is scanned/read by a manifest device and sent to the manifest computer, the warehouse computer reduces the customer order quantity by one from the appropriate classification, and reduces the total number of customer orders by one. Customer-order classification is a micro-view; total customer-order completion is a macro-view, which shows a pick/pack operation productivity.

The second component of a monitor design is the order fulfillment productivity standard (i.e., the expected number of completed customer orders for each work hour in a work day), which is entered into the warehouse computer. The standard/expected number of completed customer orders is a) an average for the work day hour, b) the historically completed number of customer orders per hour, or c) the budgeted number of customer orders per hour. For each work day hour, as a completed/manifest customer order is registered, the number of completed customer orders within the hour is increased by one. The warehouse computer compares the standard/expected number of completed customer orders to the actual completed/manifest number of customer orders; the variance is shown on a display screen. The analysis provides a manager with insight into the pick and pack labor allocation effectiveness and shows real-time productivity.

Index

R